EIGHTBALL

EIGHTBALL

EIGHTBALL

EIGHTBALL

eightball

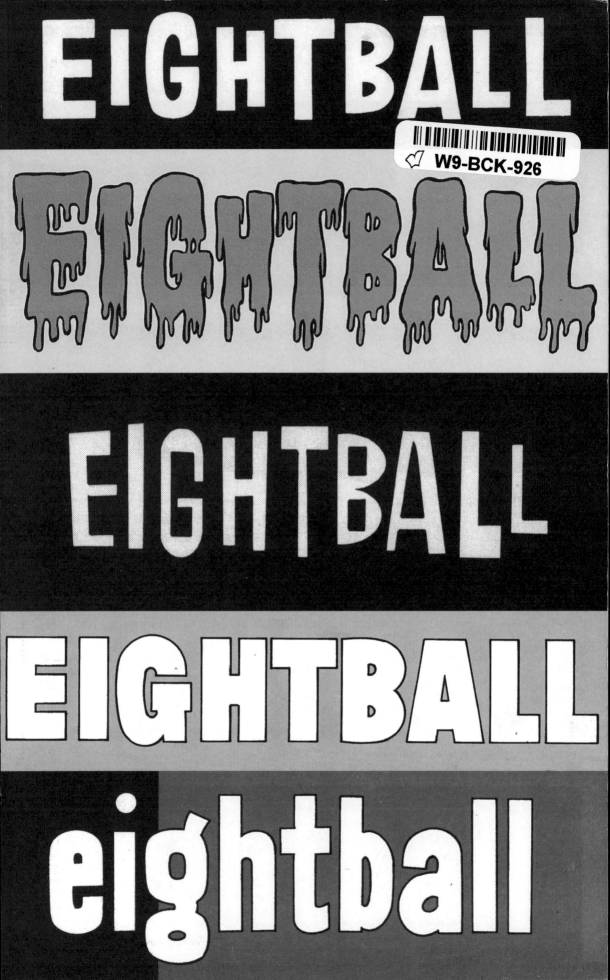

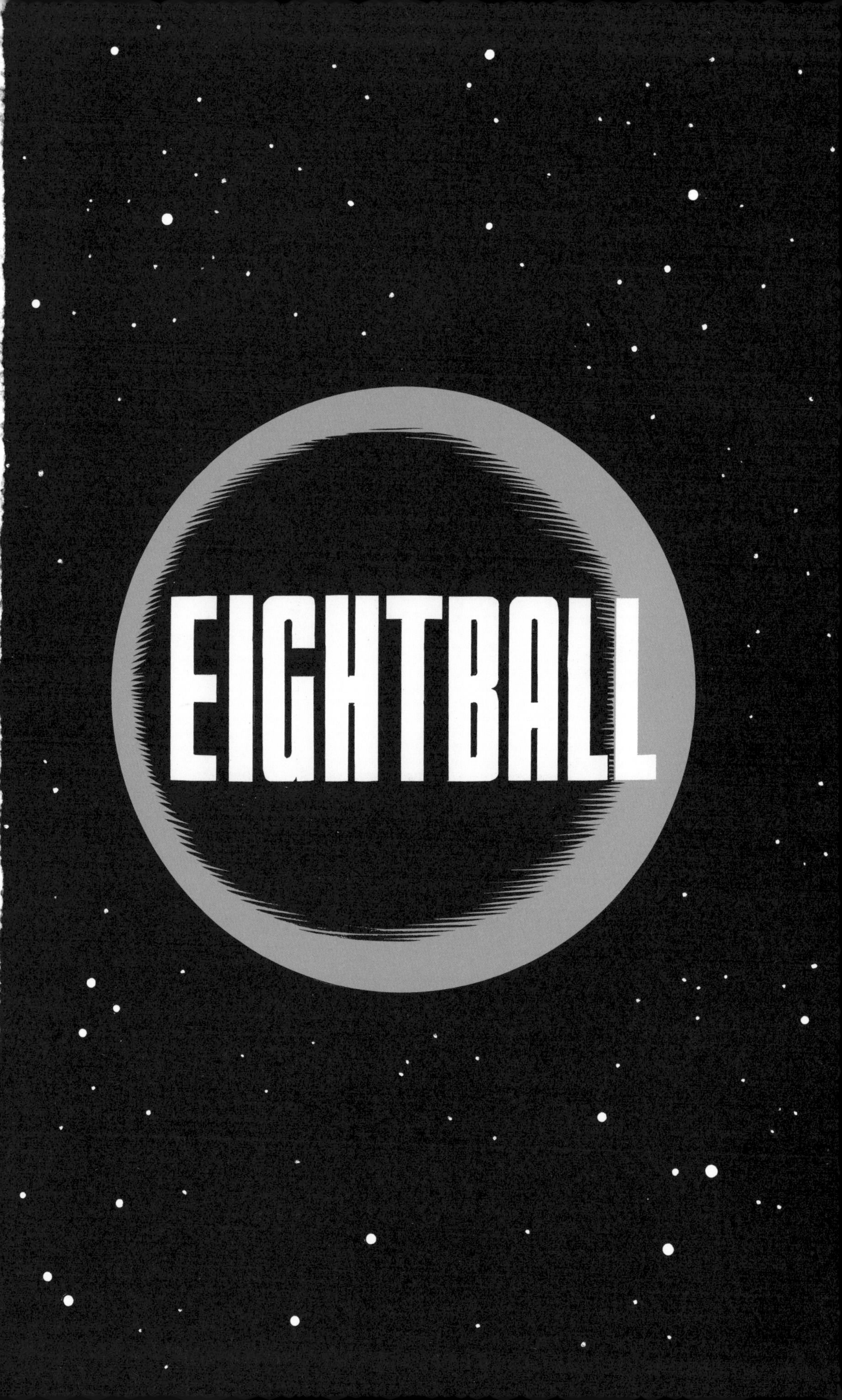
EIGHTBALL

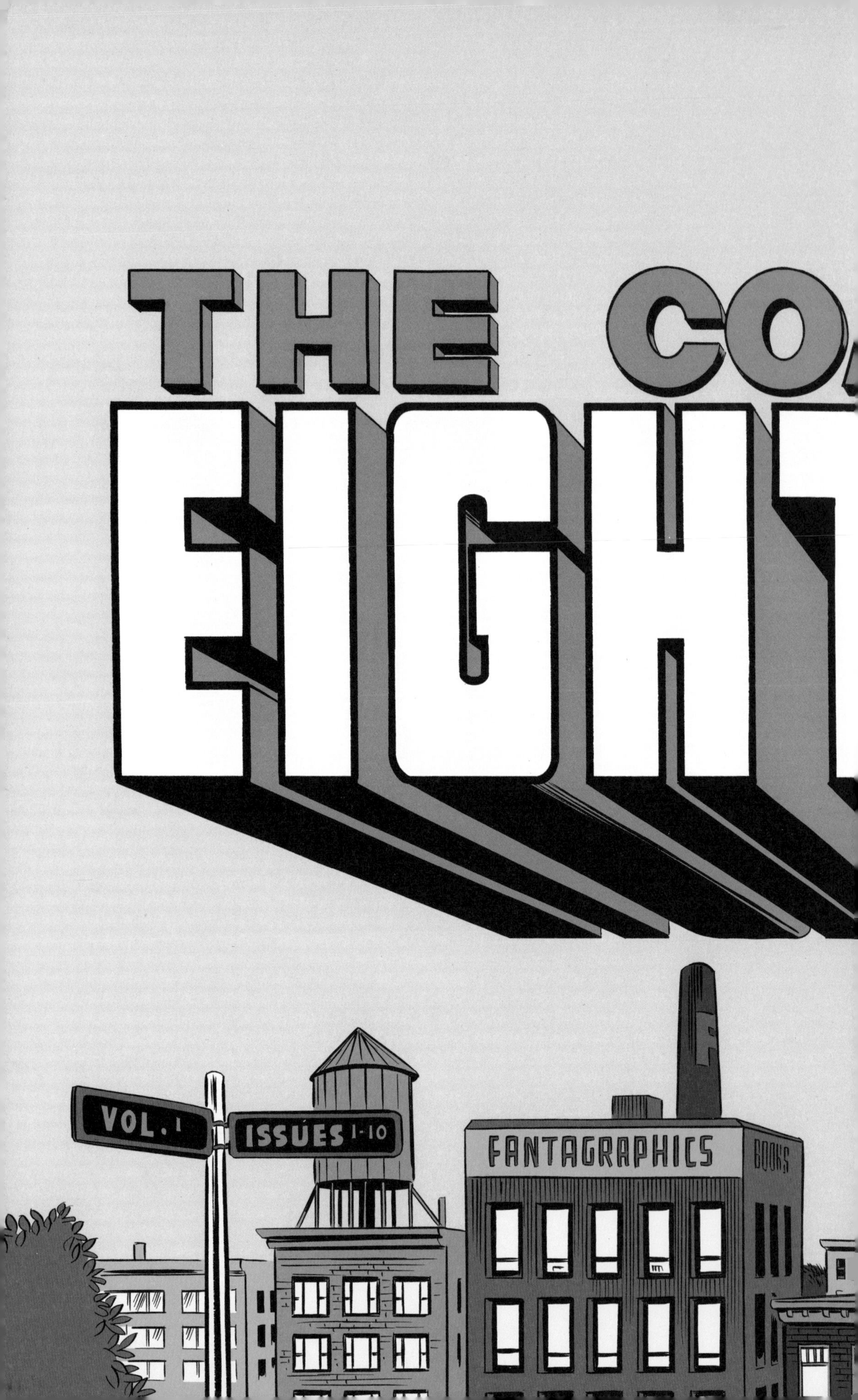
THE
VOL. 1
ISSUES 1-10
FANTAGRAPHICS
BOOKS

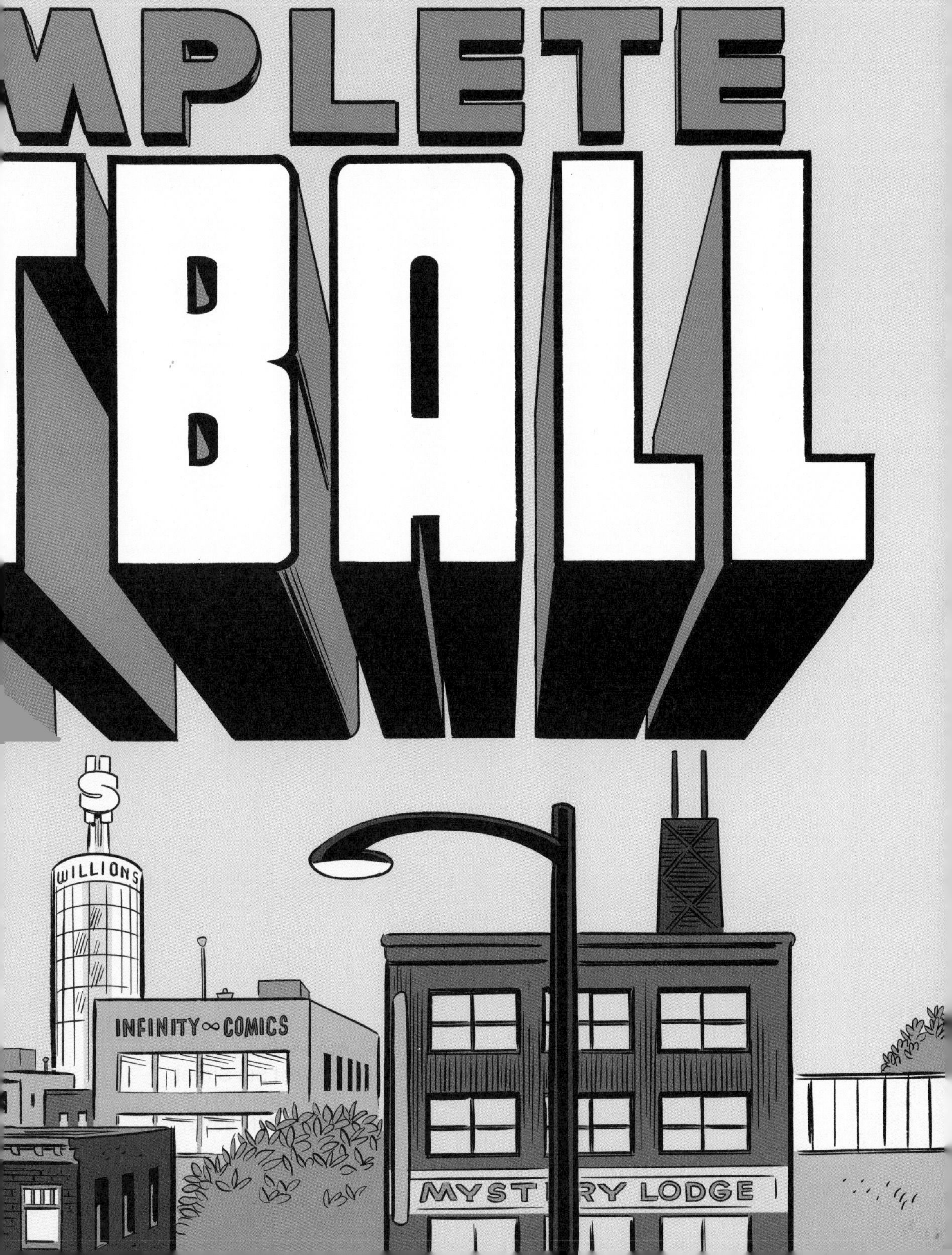
MPLETE
BALL
WILLIONS
INFINITY∞COMICS

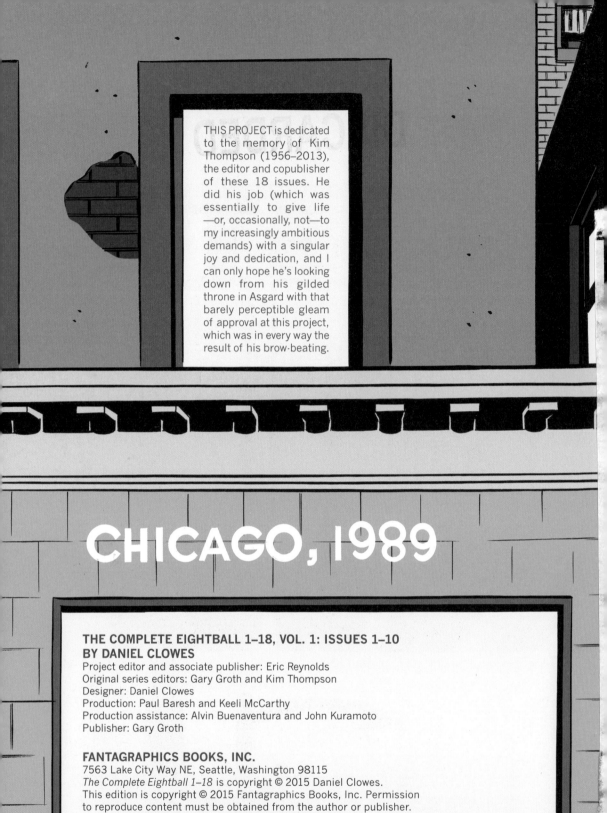

THIS PROJECT is dedicated to the memory of Kim Thompson (1956–2013), the editor and copublisher of these 18 issues. He did his job (which was essentially to give life —or, occasionally, not—to my increasingly ambitious demands) with a singular joy and dedication, and I can only hope he's looking down from his gilded throne in Asgard with that barely perceptible gleam of approval at this project, which was in every way the result of his brow-beating.

CHICAGO, 1989

THE COMPLETE EIGHTBALL 1–18, VOL. 1: ISSUES 1–10
BY DANIEL CLOWES
Project editor and associate publisher: Eric Reynolds
Original series editors: Gary Groth and Kim Thompson
Designer: Daniel Clowes
Production: Paul Baresh and Keeli McCarthy
Production assistance: Alvin Buenaventura and John Kuramoto
Publisher: Gary Groth

FANTAGRAPHICS BOOKS, INC.
7563 Lake City Way NE, Seattle, Washington 98115
The Complete Eightball 1–18 is copyright © 2015 Daniel Clowes.
This edition is copyright © 2015 Fantagraphics Books, Inc. Permission
to reproduce content must be obtained from the author or publisher.
www.danielclowes.com • www.fantagraphics.com
ISBN 978-1-60699-757-4
First printing: March 2015
Printed in Korea

Library of Congress Control Number: 2014951638

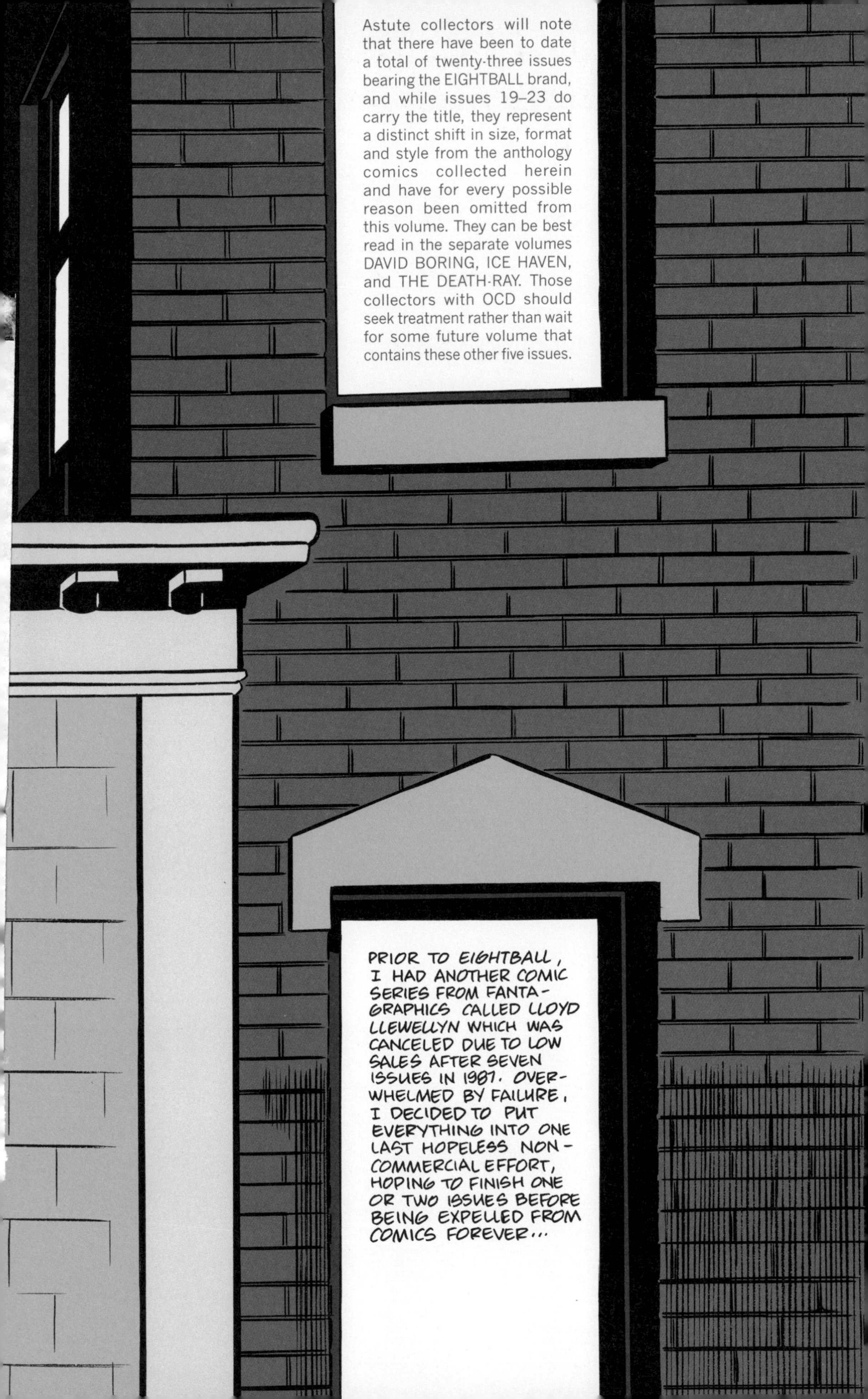
Astute collectors will note that there have been to date a total of twenty-three issues bearing the EIGHTBALL brand, and while issues 19–23 do carry the title, they represent a distinct shift in size, format and style from the anthology comics collected herein and have for every possible reason been omitted from this volume. They can be best read in the separate volumes DAVID BORING, ICE HAVEN, and THE DEATH-RAY. Those collectors with OCD should seek treatment rather than wait for some future volume that contains these other five issues.
PRIOR TO EIGHTBALL, I HAD ANOTHER COMIC SERIES FROM FANTAGRAPHICS CALLED LLOYD LLEWELLYN WHICH WAS CANCELED DUE TO LOW SALES AFTER SEVEN ISSUES IN 1987. OVERWHELMED BY FAILURE, I DECIDED TO PUT EVERYTHING INTO ONE LAST HOPELESS NON-COMMERCIAL EFFORT, HOPING TO FINISH ONE OR TWO ISSUES BEFORE BEING EXPELLED FROM COMICS FOREVER...

CONT

ENTS

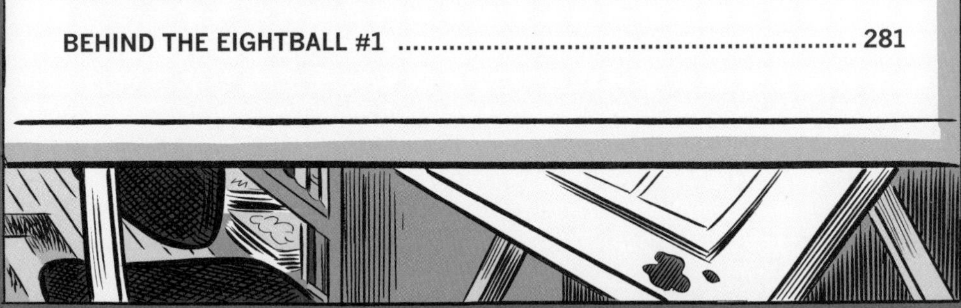

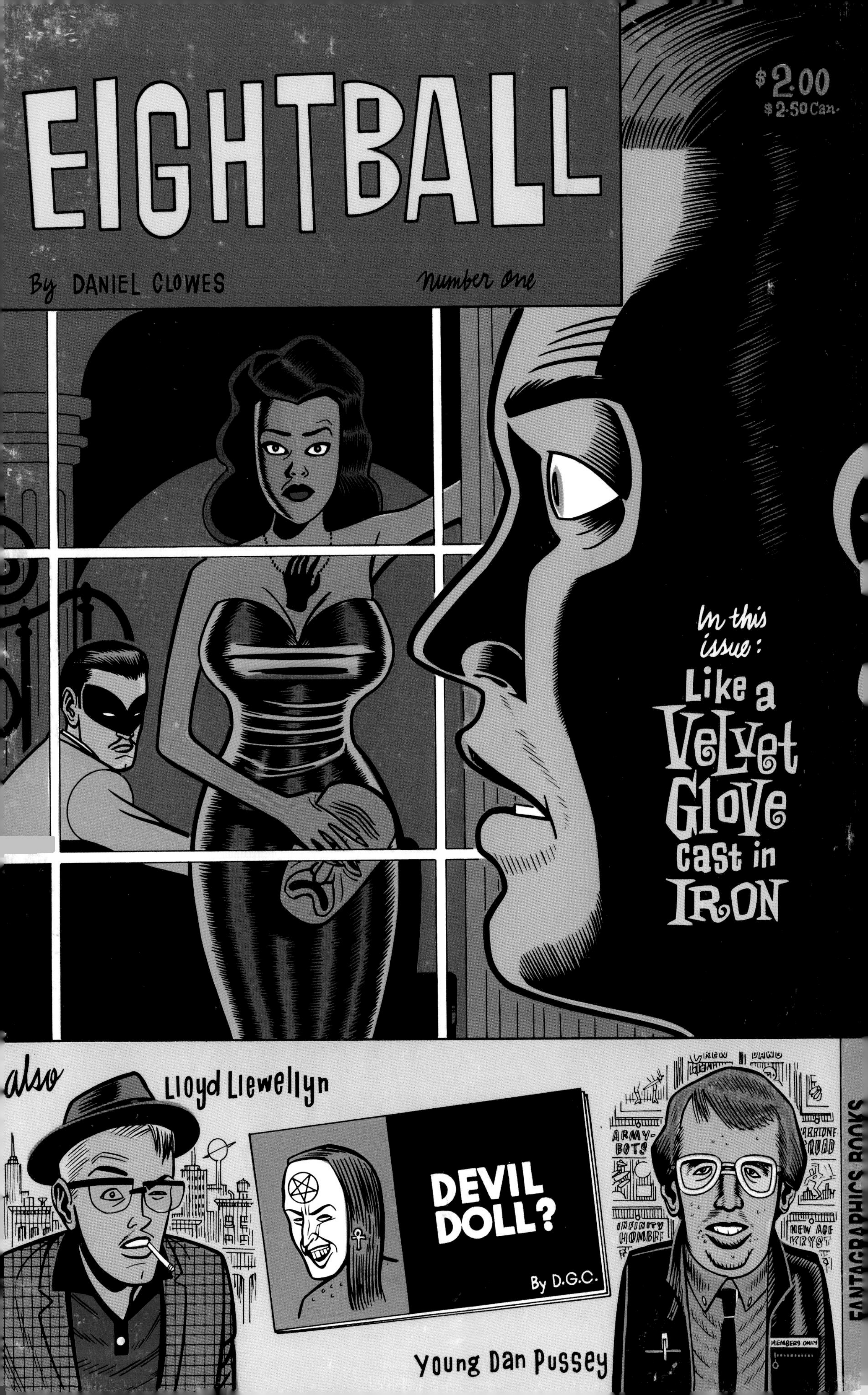
EIGHTBALL
$2.00
$2.50 Can.
By DANIEL CLOWES
number one
In this issue:
Like a Velvet Glove cast in IRON
also
Lloyd Llewellyn
DEVIL DOLL?
By D.G.C.
ARMY-BOTS
INFINITY HOMBRE
NEW AGE KRYST
MEMBERS ONLY
Young Dan Pussey
FANTAGRAPHICS BOOKS

DANIEL CLOWES *presents*

Eightball

An Orgy of Spite, Vengeance, Hopelessness, Despair and Sexual Perversion

Contents

Special Thanks, Important Facts and Embarrassing Admissions:

A ten-gallon tip of the hat to my pal Fred Altergott for his help with "Young Dan Pussey" and "Devil Doll." He must be given full credit for such things as "Infinity Hombre," Dan Pussey's ring zipper and "Delta Tau Omega." Further thanks goes to gag-meister Charlie Schneider, the real-life Laffin' Spittin' Man and to the lonely Mrs. Clowes for her help with the first chapter of "Like a Velvet Etc." The back cover is the first of a series of back covers featuring material gleaned from David Greenberger's incredible mag, DUPLEX PLANET (subscriptions: $12 from PO BOX 1230, Saratoga Springs, NY, 12866) which features surreal, non-sequitur interviews with nursing-home patients. Read it or die!

WRITE TO: EIGHTBALL c/o DAN'L CLOWES. 5545 WOODLAWN AVENUE CHICAGO, IL. 60637 (LETTERS PAGE DEBUTS NEXT ISSUE)

Eightball #1, August, 1989. **Eightball** is published three times a year by Fantagraphics Books, Inc., and is copyright © 1989 Fantagraphics Books, Inc. All stories and all characters therein are © 1989 Daniel Clowes "Eightball" and Lloyd Llewellyn are registered Trademarks of Daniel Clowes. No part of this magazine may be reproduced without written permission from Fantagraphics Books and the author. No similarity between any of the names, characters, persons, and institutions in *Eightball* and those of any living or dead persons is intended except for satirical purposes, and any such similarity that may exist is purely coincidental. Letters to *Eightball* become the property of the magazine and are assumed intended for publication in whole or in part, and may therefore be used for those purposes. First printing, June, 1989. Available from the publisher for $2.00 + 50¢ postage and handling: Fantagraphics Books, 7563 Lake City Way, Seattle, WA 98115. Write us for a complete catalogue of fine comics, including *The Lloyd Llewellyn Collection*.

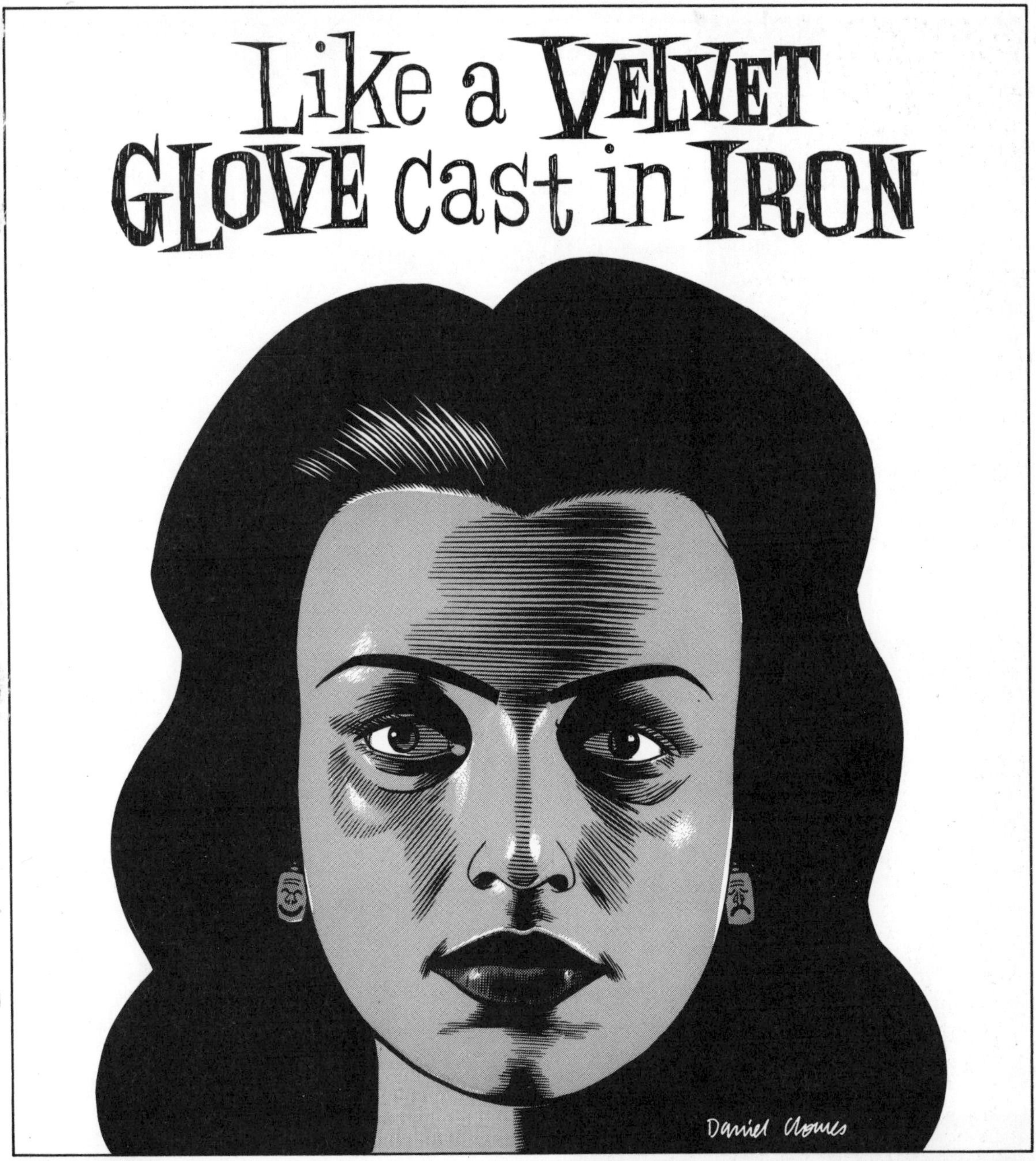
Like a VELVET GLOVE cast in IRON
Daniel Clowes

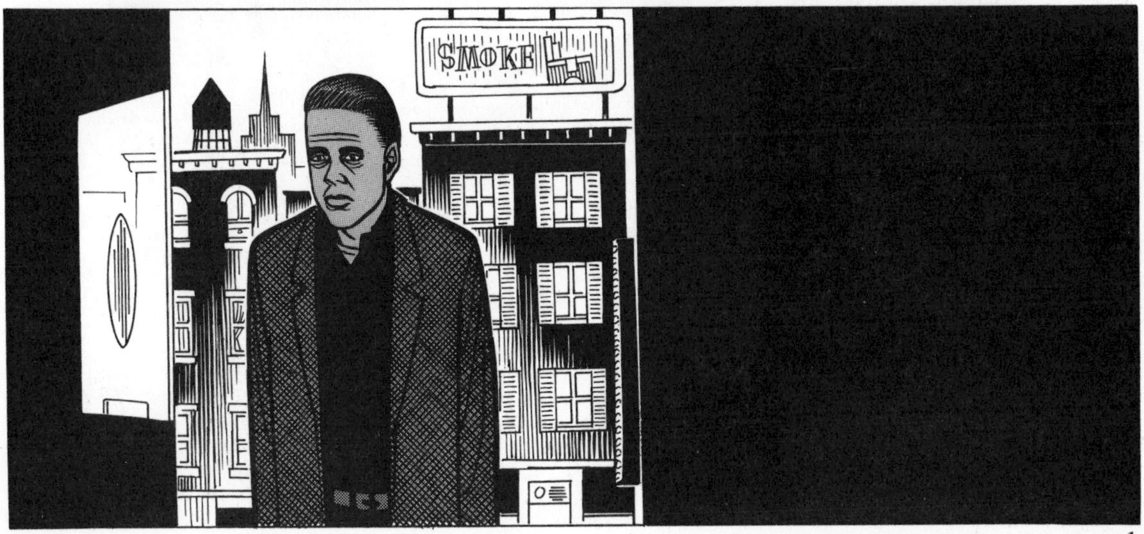
SMOKE

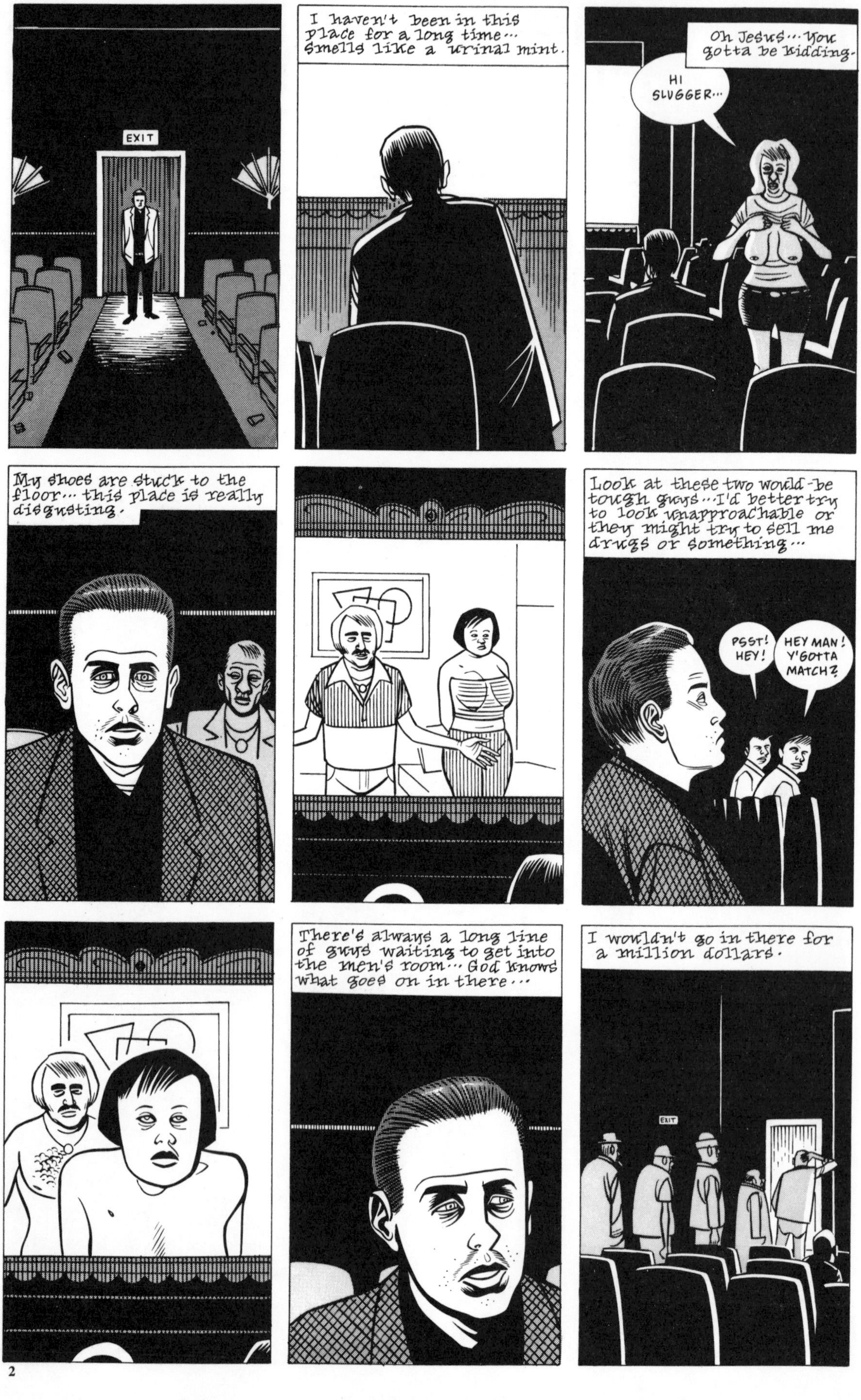
EXIT
I haven't been in this place for a long time... Smells like a urinal mint.
Oh Jesus... You gotta be kidding-
HI SLUGGER...
My shoes are stuck to the floor... this place is really disgusting.
Look at these two would-be tough guys... I'd better try to look unapproachable or they might try to sell me drugs or something...
PSST! HEY!
HEY MAN! Y'GOTTA MATCH?
There's always a long line of guys waiting to get into the men's room... God knows what goes on in there...
I wouldn't go in there for a million dollars.
EXIT

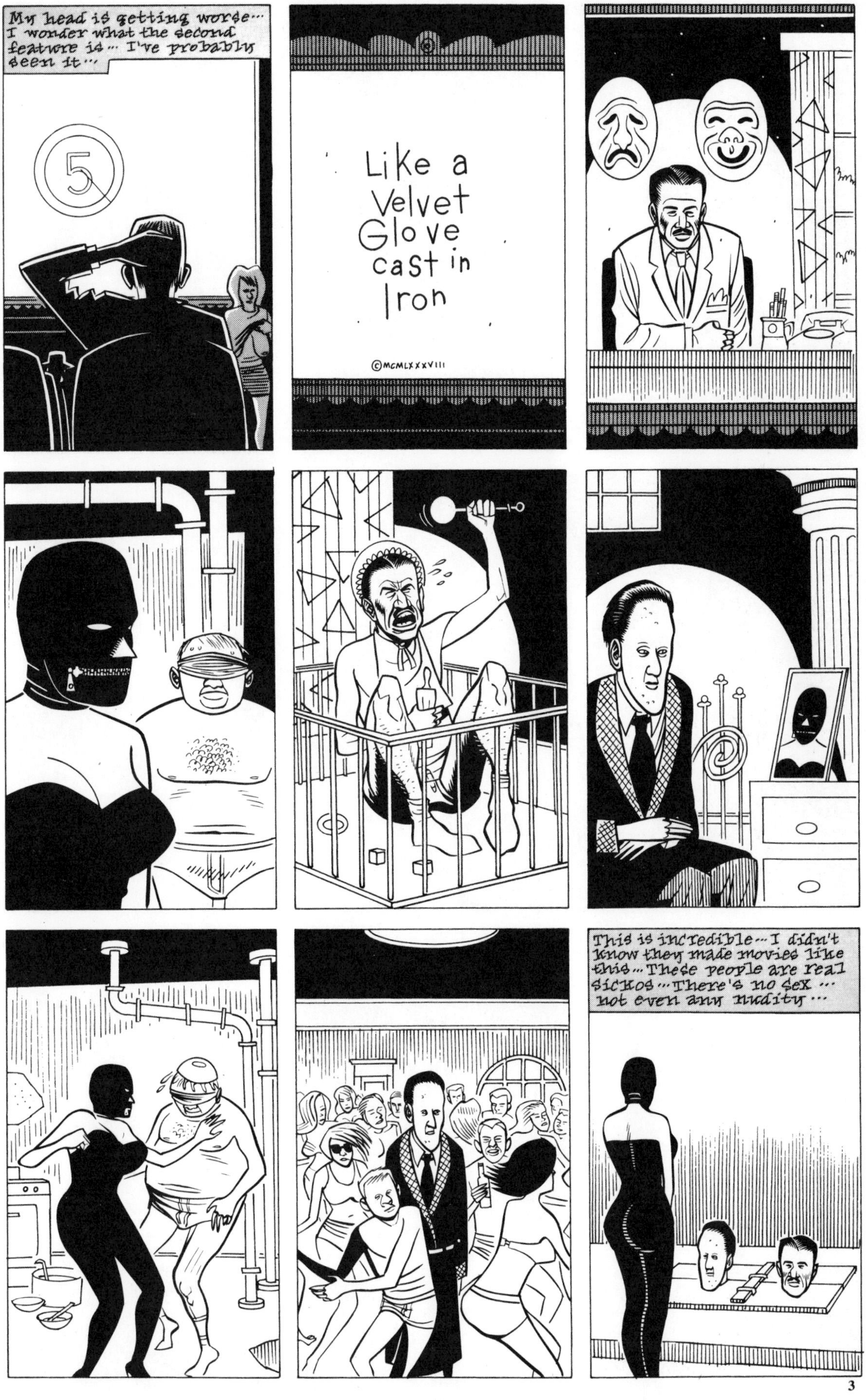

My head is getting worse... I wonder what the second feature is... I've probably seen it...
5
Like a Velvet Glove cast in Iron
©MCMLXXXVIII
This is incredible... I didn't know they made movies like this... These people are real sickos... There's no sex... not even any nudity...

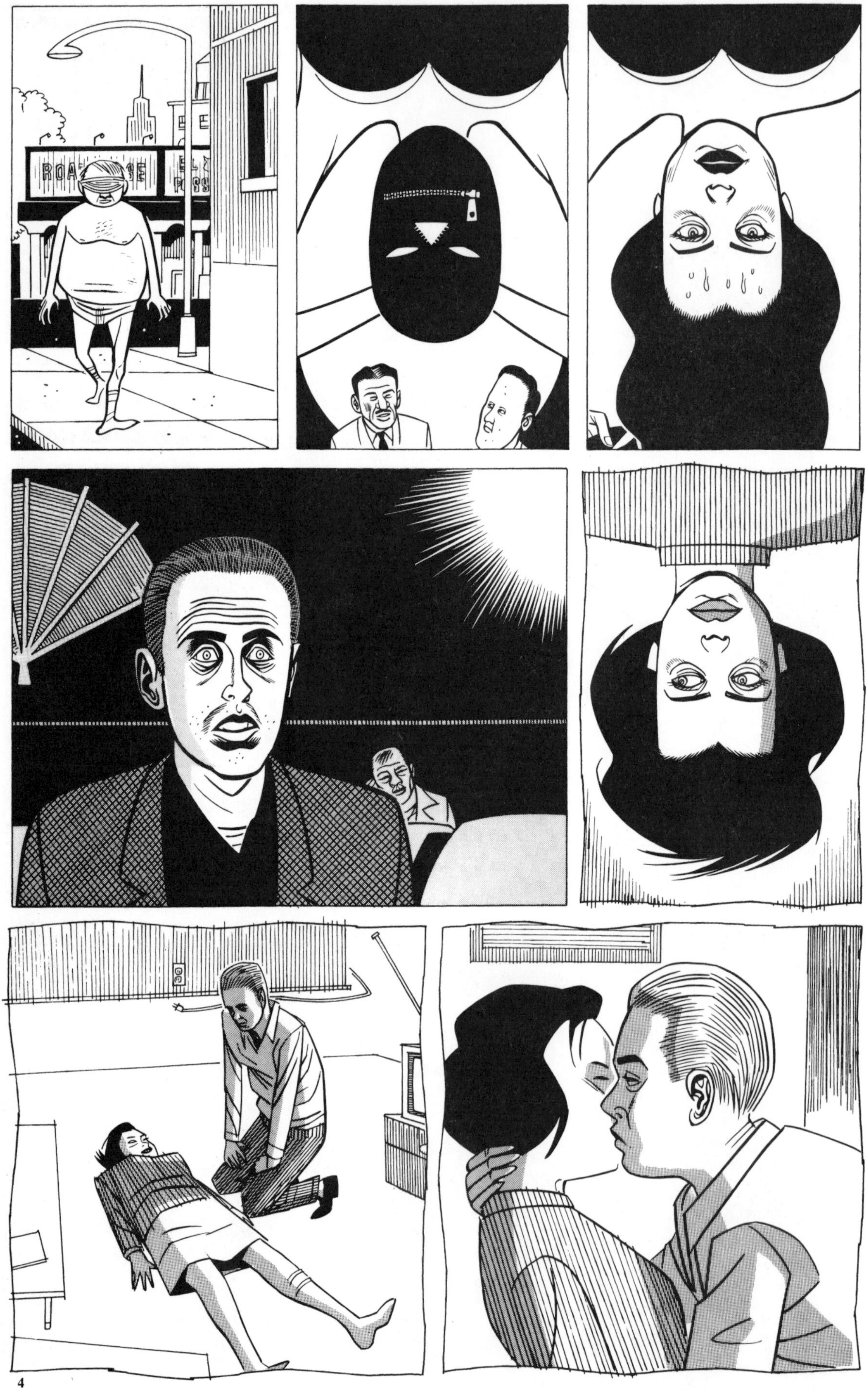

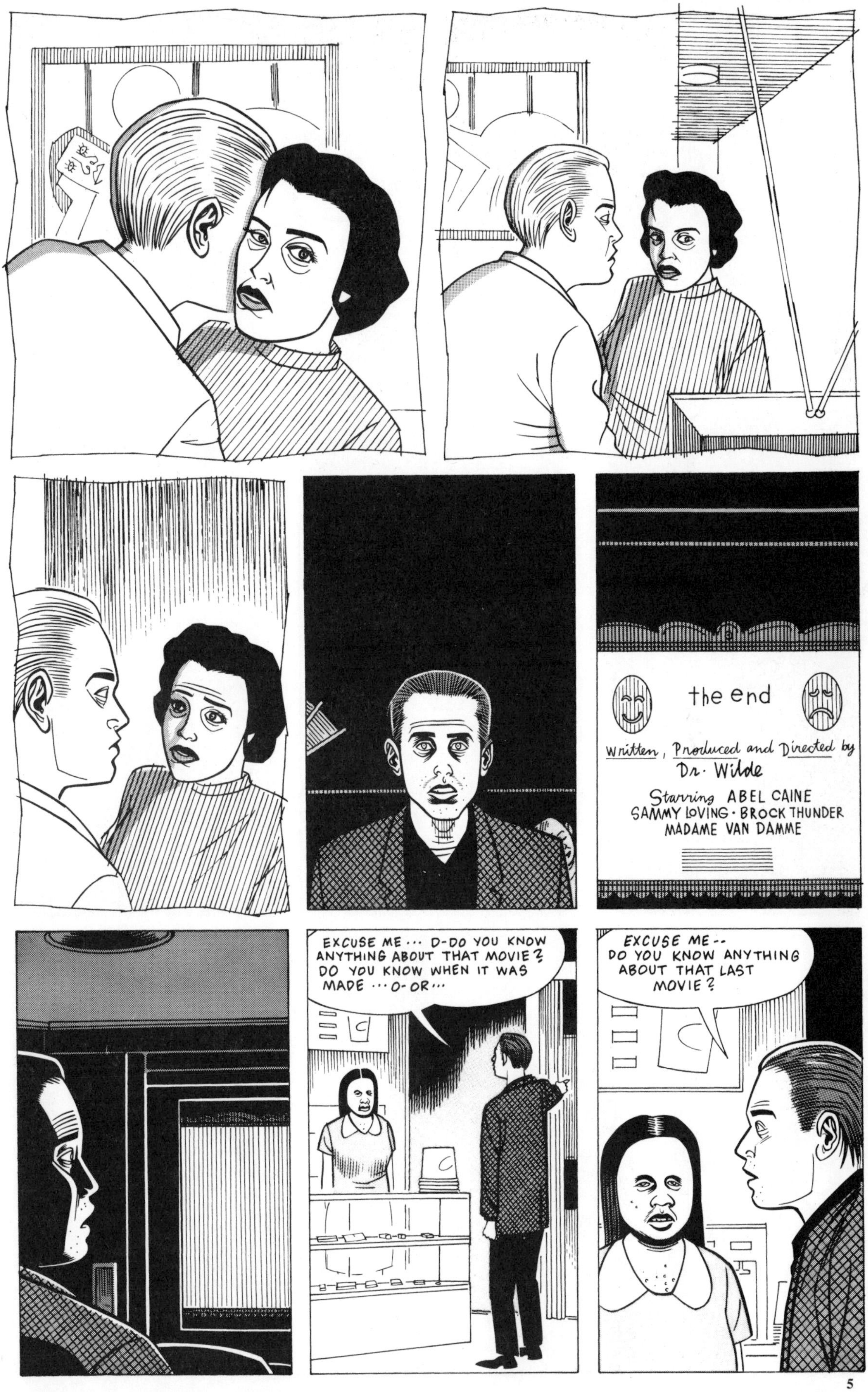
the end
Written, Produced and Directed by
Dr. Wilde
Starring ABEL CAINE
SAMMY LOVING · BROCK THUNDER
MADAME VAN DAMME
EXCUSE ME ··· D-DO YOU KNOW ANYTHING ABOUT THAT MOVIE? DO YOU KNOW WHEN IT WAS MADE ··· O-OR ···
EXCUSE ME -- DO YOU KNOW ANYTHING ABOUT THAT LAST MOVIE?

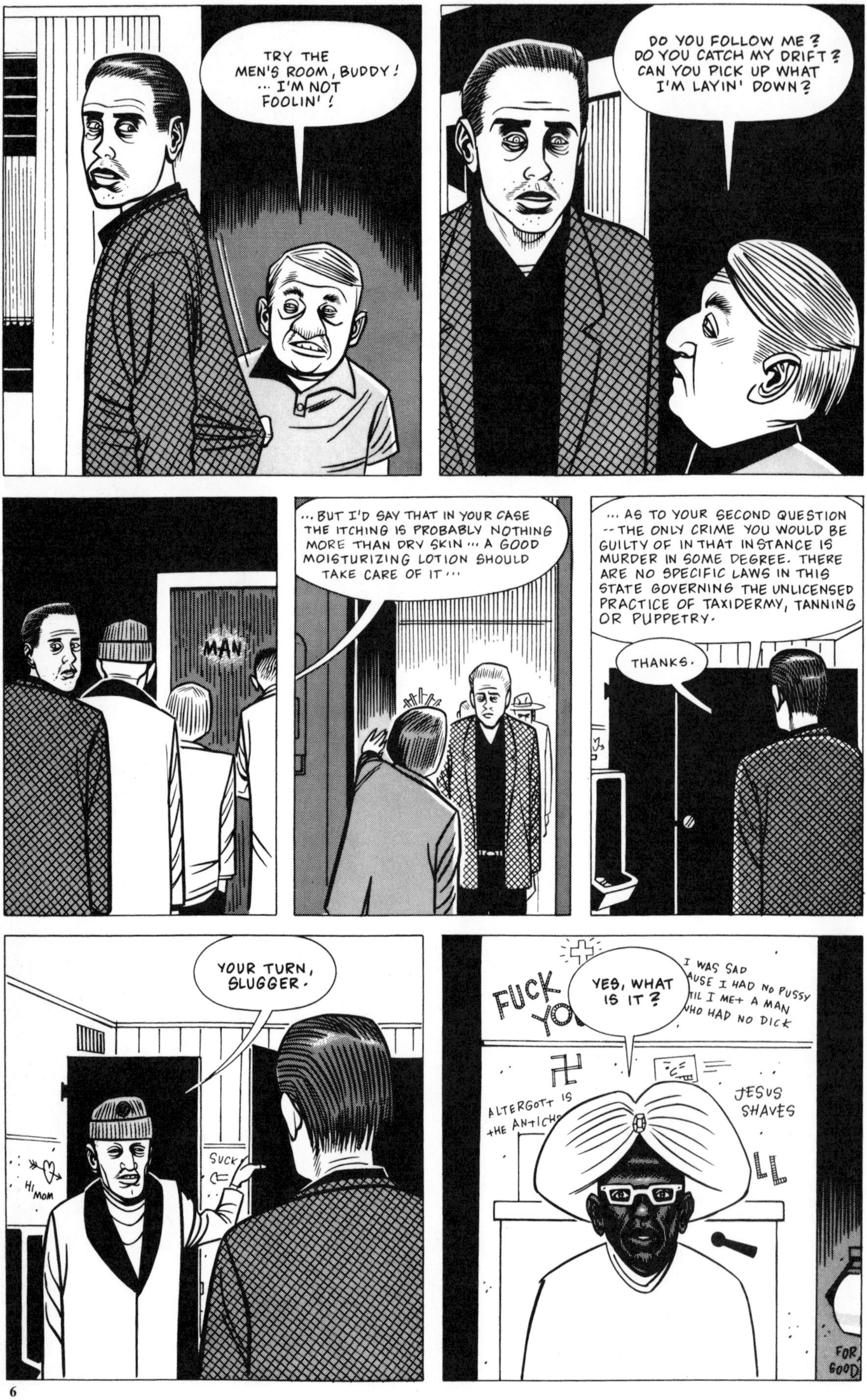
TRY THE MEN'S ROOM, BUDDY! ... I'M NOT FOOLIN'!
DO YOU FOLLOW ME? DO YOU CATCH MY DRIFT? CAN YOU PICK UP WHAT I'M LAYIN' DOWN?
MAN
...BUT I'D SAY THAT IN YOUR CASE THE ITCHING IS PROBABLY NOTHING MORE THAN DRY SKIN... A GOOD MOISTURIZING LOTION SHOULD TAKE CARE OF IT...
...AS TO YOUR SECOND QUESTION -- THE ONLY CRIME YOU WOULD BE GUILTY OF IN THAT INSTANCE IS MURDER IN SOME DEGREE. THERE ARE NO SPECIFIC LAWS IN THIS STATE GOVERNING THE UNLICENSED PRACTICE OF TAXIDERMY, TANNING OR PUPPETRY.
THANKS.
YOUR TURN, SLUGGER.
HI MOM
SUCK
YES, WHAT IS IT?
FUCK
I WAS SAD
AUSE I HAD NO PUSSY
TIL I MET A MAN
WHO HAD NO DICK
ALTERGOTT IS
THE ANTICH
JESUS SHAVES
FOR GOOD

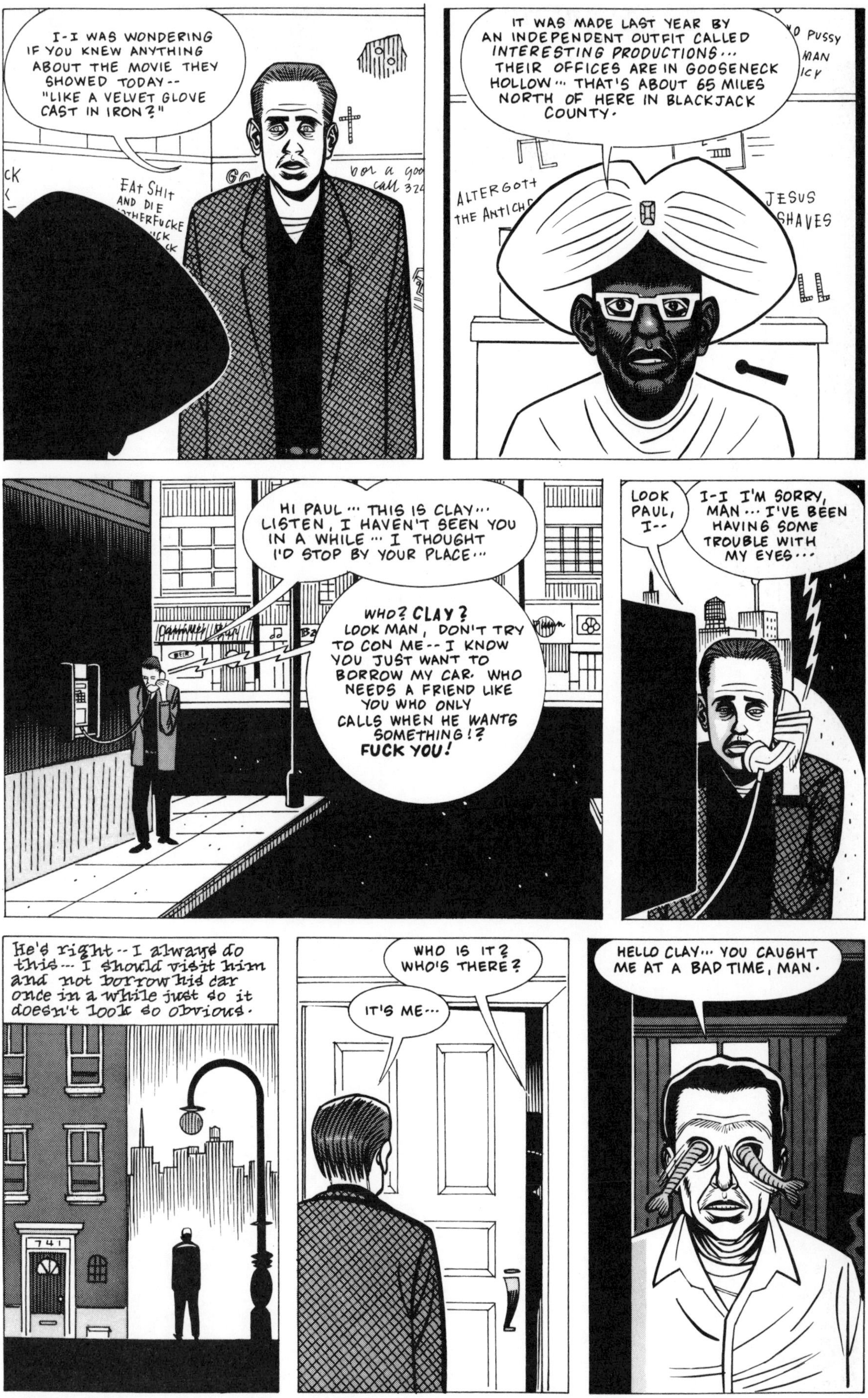
I-I WAS WONDERING IF YOU KNEW ANYTHING ABOUT THE MOVIE THEY SHOWED TODAY -- "LIKE A VELVET GLOVE CAST IN IRON?"
EAt SHit AND DIE
IT WAS MADE LAST YEAR BY AN INDEPENDENT OUTFIT CALLED INTERESTING PRODUCTIONS... THEIR OFFICES ARE IN GOOSENECK HOLLOW... THAT'S ABOUT 65 MILES NORTH OF HERE IN BLACKJACK COUNTY.
JESUS SHAVES
HI PAUL... THIS IS CLAY... LISTEN, I HAVEN'T SEEN YOU IN A WHILE... I THOUGHT I'D STOP BY YOUR PLACE...
WHO? CLAY? LOOK MAN, DON'T TRY TO CON ME -- I KNOW YOU JUST WANT TO BORROW MY CAR. WHO NEEDS A FRIEND LIKE YOU WHO ONLY CALLS WHEN HE WANTS SOMETHING!? FUCK YOU!
LOOK PAUL, I--
I-I I'M SORRY, MAN... I'VE BEEN HAVING SOME TROUBLE WITH MY EYES...
He's right -- I always do this... I should visit him and not borrow his car once in a while just so it doesn't look so obvious.
741
WHO IS IT? WHO'S THERE?
IT'S ME...
HELLO CLAY... YOU CAUGHT ME AT A BAD TIME, MAN.

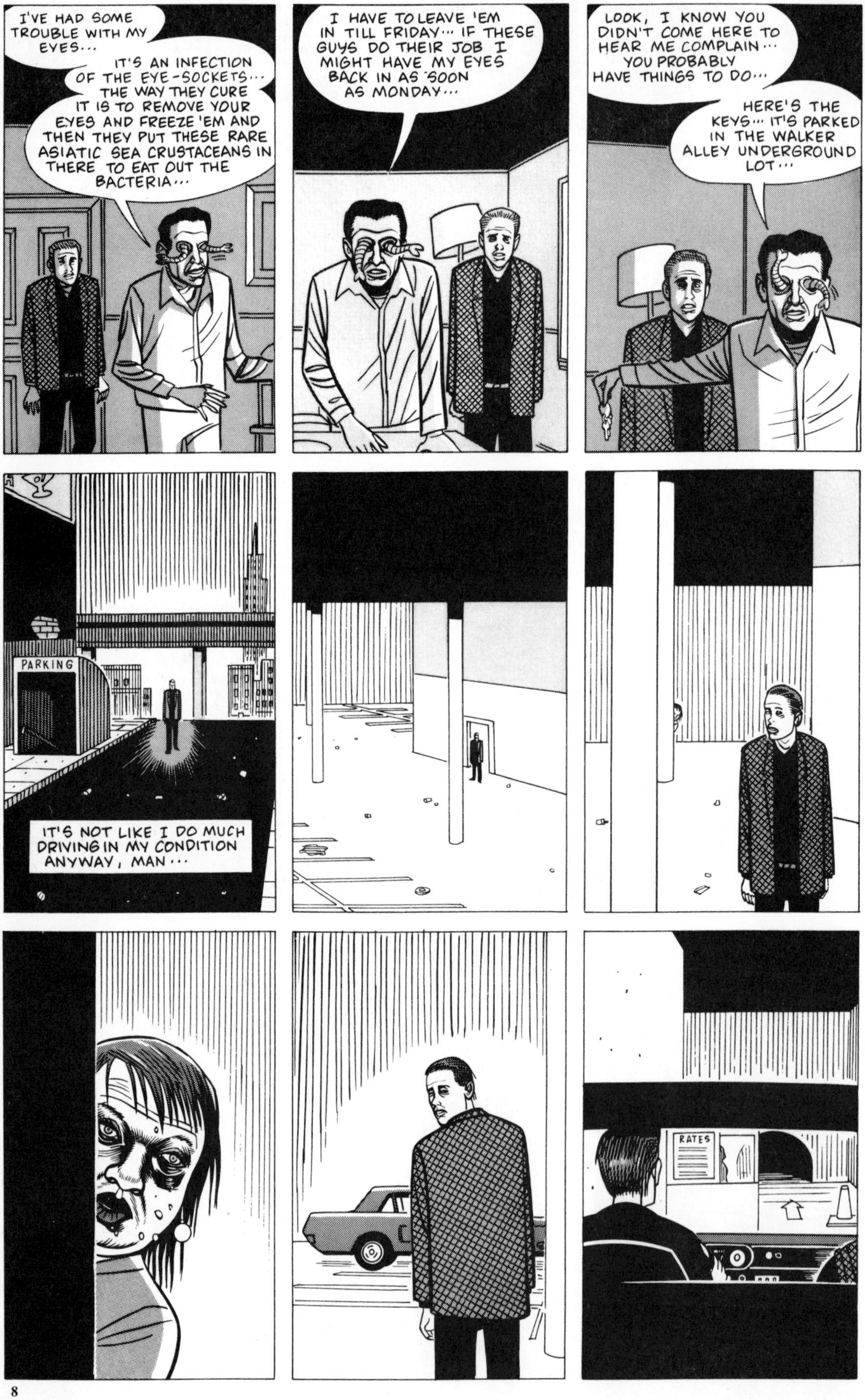
I'VE HAD SOME TROUBLE WITH MY EYES...
IT'S AN INFECTION OF THE EYE-SOCKETS... THE WAY THEY CURE IT IS TO REMOVE YOUR EYES AND FREEZE 'EM AND THEN THEY PUT THESE RARE ASIATIC SEA CRUSTACEANS IN THERE TO EAT OUT THE BACTERIA...
I HAVE TO LEAVE 'EM IN TILL FRIDAY... IF THESE GUYS DO THEIR JOB I MIGHT HAVE MY EYES BACK IN AS SOON AS MONDAY...
LOOK, I KNOW YOU DIDN'T COME HERE TO HEAR ME COMPLAIN... YOU PROBABLY HAVE THINGS TO DO...
HERE'S THE KEYS... IT'S PARKED IN THE WALKER ALLEY UNDERGROUND LOT...
PARKING
IT'S NOT LIKE I DO MUCH DRIVING IN MY CONDITION ANYWAY, MAN...
RATES

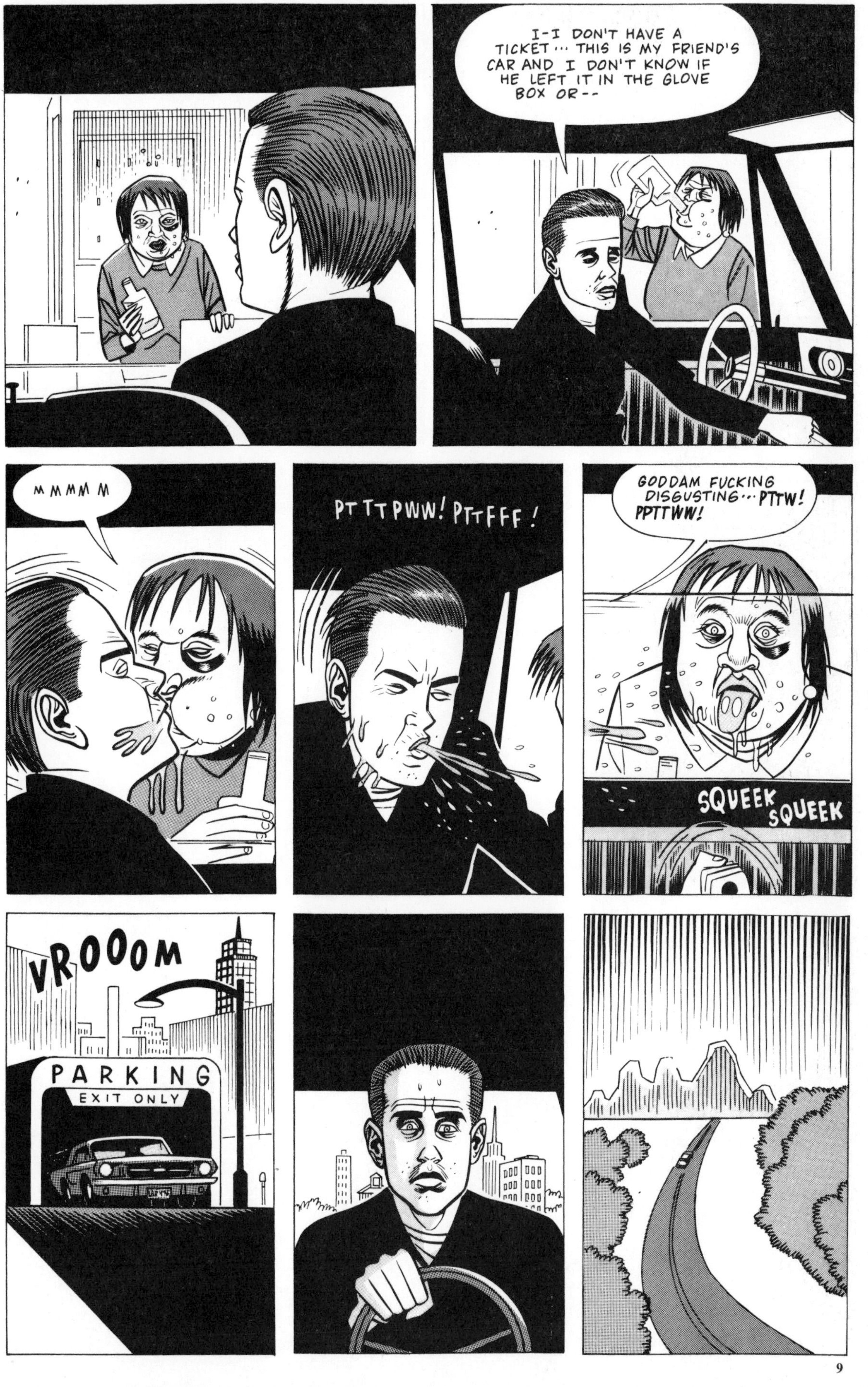
I-I DON'T HAVE A TICKET... THIS IS MY FRIEND'S CAR AND I DON'T KNOW IF HE LEFT IT IN THE GLOVE BOX OR--
MMMMM
PTTTPWW! PTTFFF!
GODDAM FUCKING DISGUSTING... PTTW! PPTTWW!
SQUEEK SQUEEK
VROOOM
PARKING
EXIT ONLY

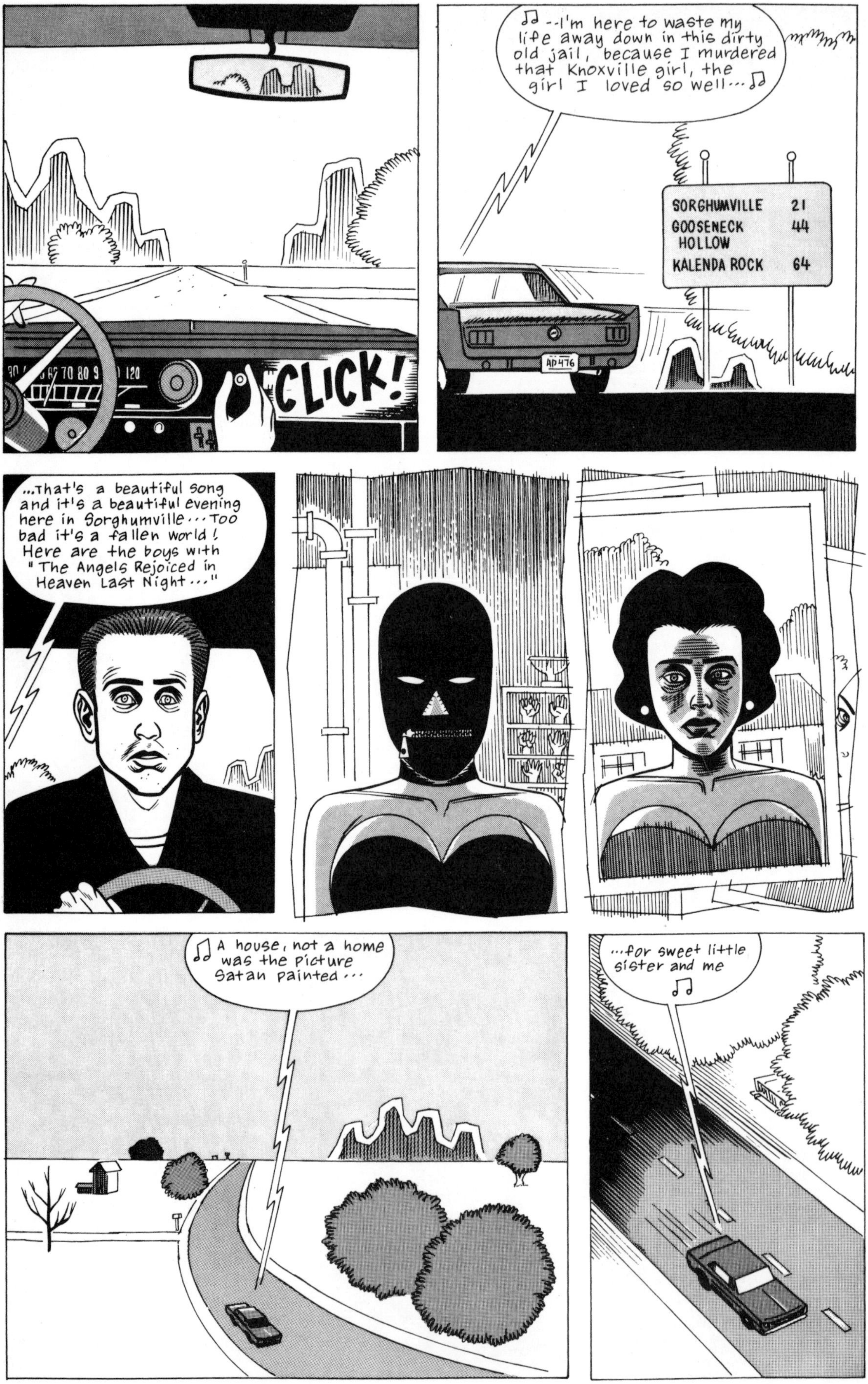
CLICK!
♫ --I'm here to waste my life away down in this dirty old jail, because I murdered that Knoxville girl, the girl I loved so well... ♫
SORGHUMVILLE 21
GOOSENECK HOLLOW 44
KALENDA ROCK 64
AP476
...That's a beautiful song and it's a beautiful evening here in Sorghumville... Too bad it's a fallen world! Here are the boys with "The Angels Rejoiced in Heaven Last Night..."
♫ A house, not a home was the picture Satan painted...
...for sweet little sister and me ♫

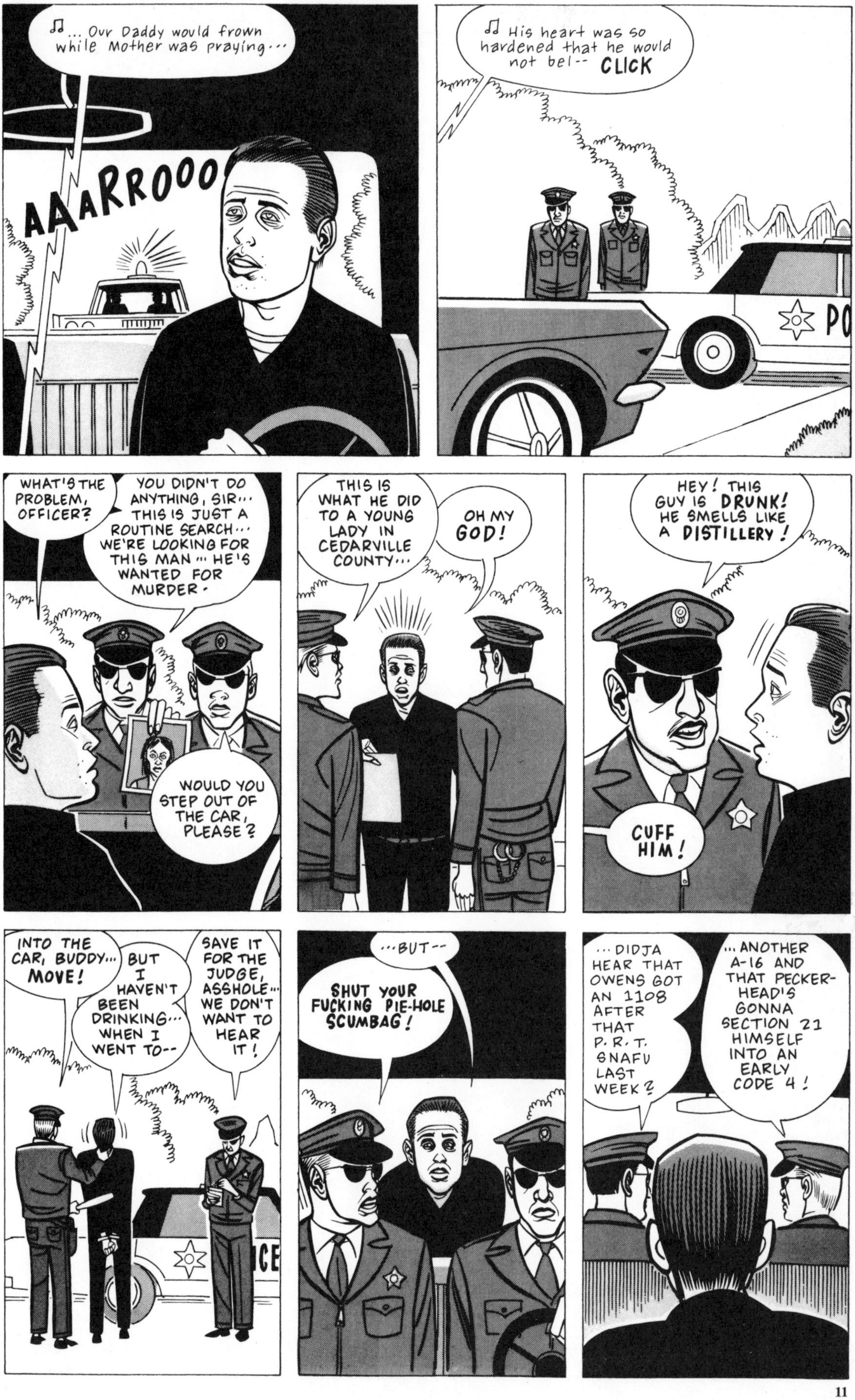
♫ ... Our Daddy would frown while Mother was praying ...
AAARROOO
♫ His heart was so hardened that he would not bel-- CLICK
PO
WHAT'S THE PROBLEM, OFFICER?
YOU DIDN'T DO ANYTHING, SIR... THIS IS JUST A ROUTINE SEARCH... WE'RE LOOKING FOR THIS MAN ... HE'S WANTED FOR MURDER.
WOULD YOU STEP OUT OF THE CAR, PLEASE?
THIS IS WHAT HE DID TO A YOUNG LADY IN CEDARVILLE COUNTY...
OH MY GOD!
HEY! THIS GUY IS DRUNK! HE SMELLS LIKE A DISTILLERY!
CUFF HIM!
INTO THE CAR, BUDDY... MOVE!
BUT I HAVEN'T BEEN DRINKING... WHEN I WENT TO--
SAVE IT FOR THE JUDGE, ASSHOLE... WE DON'T WANT TO HEAR IT!
ICE
...BUT--
SHUT YOUR FUCKING PIE-HOLE SCUMBAG!
...DIDJA HEAR THAT OWENS GOT AN 1108 AFTER THAT P.R.T. SNAFU LAST WEEK?
...ANOTHER A-16 AND THAT PECKER-HEAD'S GONNA SECTION 21 HIMSELF INTO AN EARLY CODE 4!

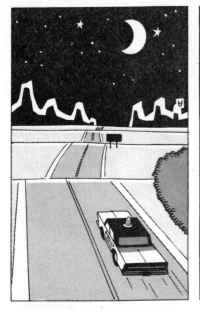

HEY JOEY··· WHAT'S THAT UP AHEAD?···

···Hmm?

A PROSTITUTE!

YOU'RE UNDER ARREST! YOU HAVE THE RIGHT TO REMAIN SILENT ≥UGN≥ YOU HAVE THE ≥UGN≥ ···THE RIGHT TO ·· ≥UGN≥

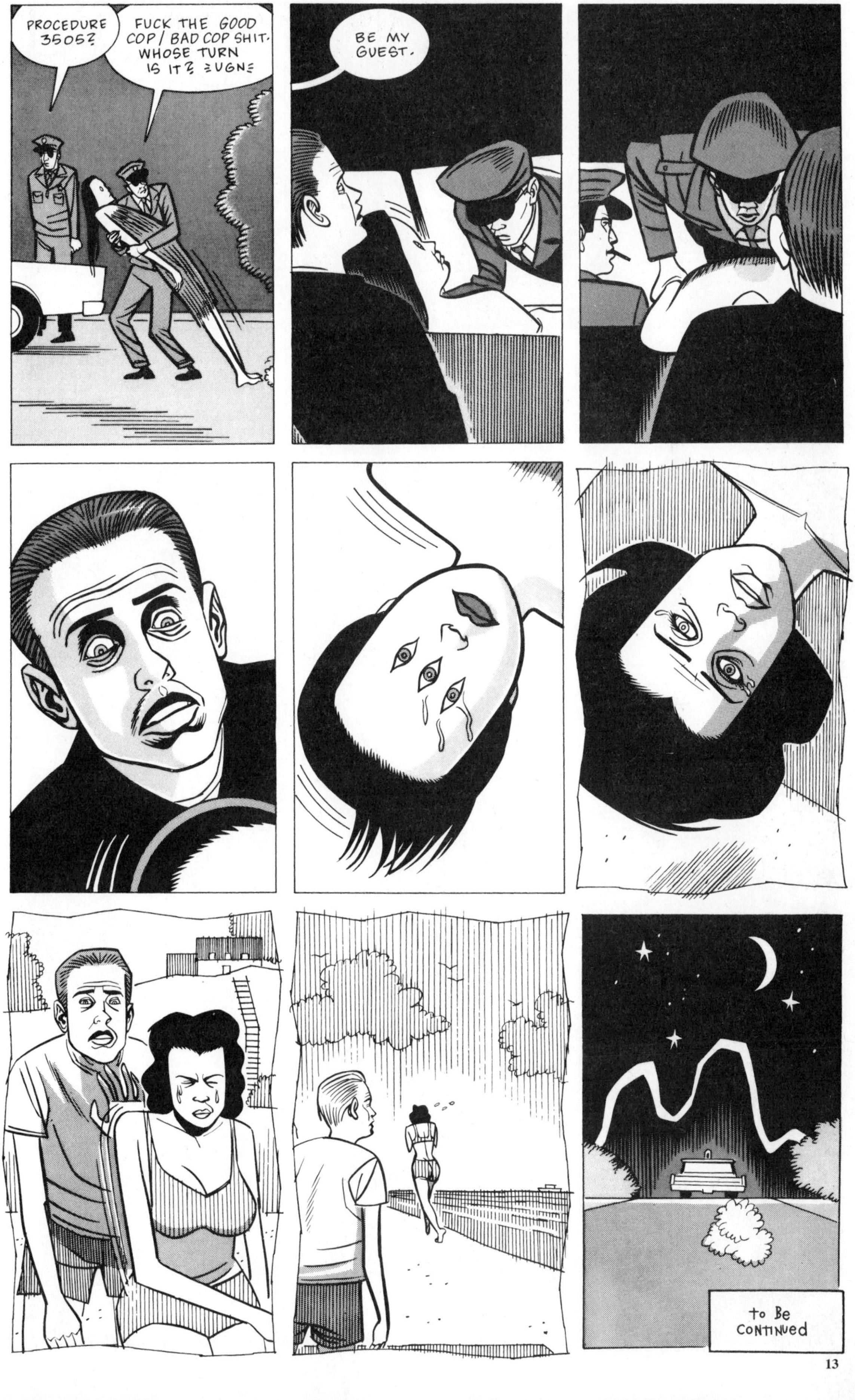
PROCEDURE 3505?
FUCK THE GOOD COP / BAD COP SHIT. WHOSE TURN IS IT? =UGN=
BE MY GUEST.
to Be Continued

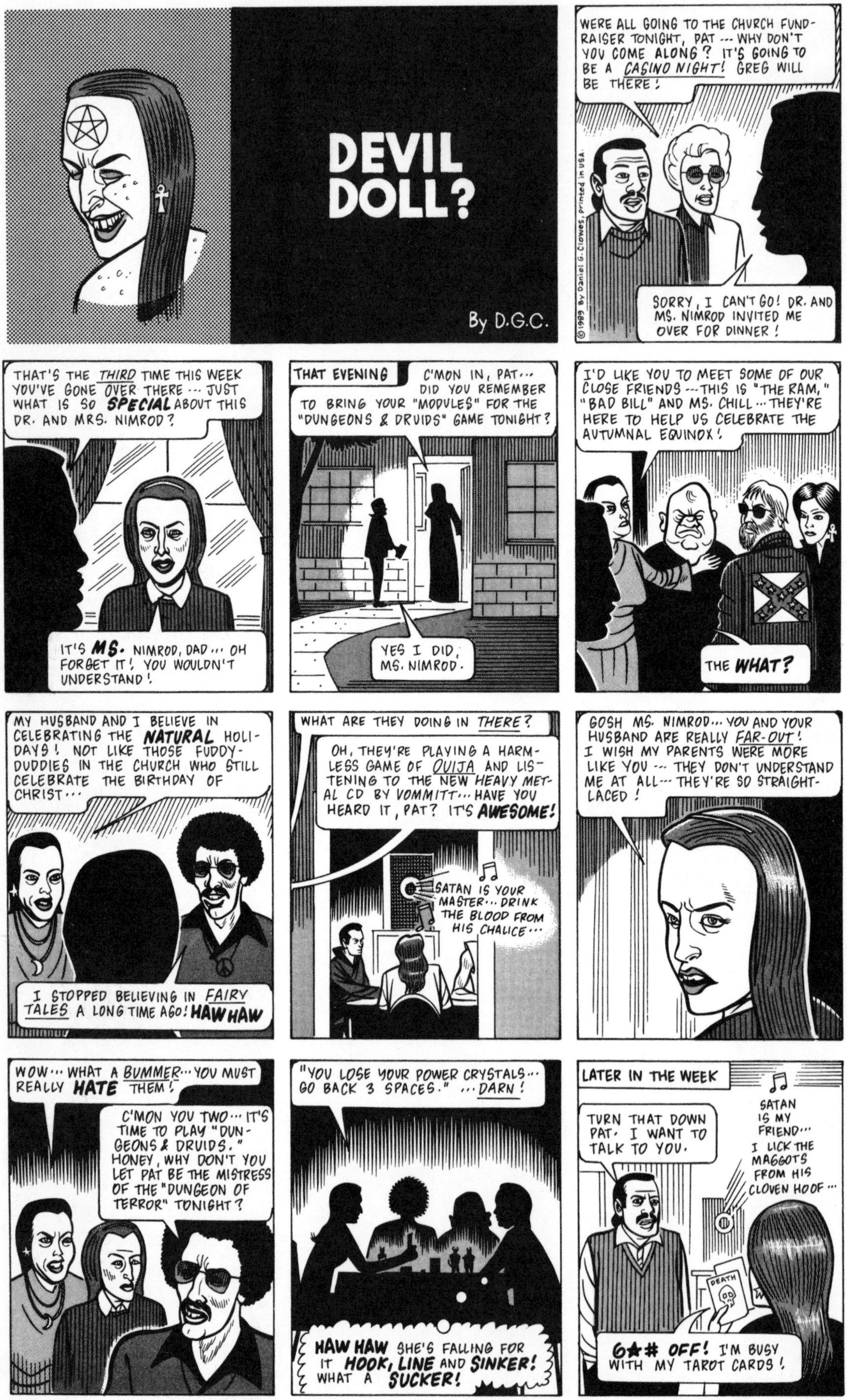
DEVIL DOLL?
By D.G.C.
WERE ALL GOING TO THE CHURCH FUND-RAISER TONIGHT, PAT --- WHY DON'T YOU COME ALONG? IT'S GOING TO BE A CASINO NIGHT! GREG WILL BE THERE!
SORRY, I CAN'T GO! DR. AND MS. NIMROD INVITED ME OVER FOR DINNER!
©1989 By Daniel G. Clowes. printed in USA.
THAT'S THE THIRD TIME THIS WEEK YOU'VE GONE OVER THERE --- JUST WHAT IS SO SPECIAL ABOUT THIS DR. AND MRS. NIMROD?
IT'S MS. NIMROD, DAD... OH FORGET IT! YOU WOULDN'T UNDERSTAND!
THAT EVENING
C'MON IN, PAT... DID YOU REMEMBER TO BRING YOUR "MODULES" FOR THE "DUNGEONS & DRUIDS" GAME TONIGHT?
YES I DID, MS. NIMROD.
I'D LIKE YOU TO MEET SOME OF OUR CLOSE FRIENDS --- THIS IS "THE RAM," "BAD BILL" AND MS. CHILL... THEY'RE HERE TO HELP US CELEBRATE THE AUTUMNAL EQUINOX!
THE WHAT?
MY HUSBAND AND I BELIEVE IN CELEBRATING THE NATURAL HOLIDAYS! NOT LIKE THOSE FUDDY-DUDDIES IN THE CHURCH WHO STILL CELEBRATE THE BIRTHDAY OF CHRIST...
I STOPPED BELIEVING IN FAIRY TALES A LONG TIME AGO! HAW HAW
WHAT ARE THEY DOING IN THERE?
OH, THEY'RE PLAYING A HARMLESS GAME OF OUIJA AND LISTENING TO THE NEW HEAVY METAL CD BY VOMMITT... HAVE YOU HEARD IT, PAT? IT'S AWESOME!
SATAN IS YOUR MASTER... DRINK THE BLOOD FROM HIS CHALICE...
GOSH MS. NIMROD... YOU AND YOUR HUSBAND ARE REALLY FAR-OUT! I WISH MY PARENTS WERE MORE LIKE YOU --- THEY DON'T UNDERSTAND ME AT ALL --- THEY'RE SO STRAIGHT-LACED!
WOW... WHAT A BUMMER... YOU MUST REALLY HATE THEM!
C'MON YOU TWO... IT'S TIME TO PLAY "DUNGEONS & DRUIDS." HONEY, WHY DON'T YOU LET PAT BE THE MISTRESS OF THE "DUNGEON OF TERROR" TONIGHT?
"YOU LOSE YOUR POWER CRYSTALS... GO BACK 3 SPACES." ...DARN!
HAW HAW SHE'S FALLING FOR IT HOOK, LINE AND SINKER! WHAT A SUCKER!
LATER IN THE WEEK
TURN THAT DOWN PAT. I WANT TO TALK TO YOU.
SATAN IS MY FRIEND... I LICK THE MAGGOTS FROM HIS CLOVEN HOOF...
DEATH
G☆# OFF! I'M BUSY WITH MY TAROT CARDS!

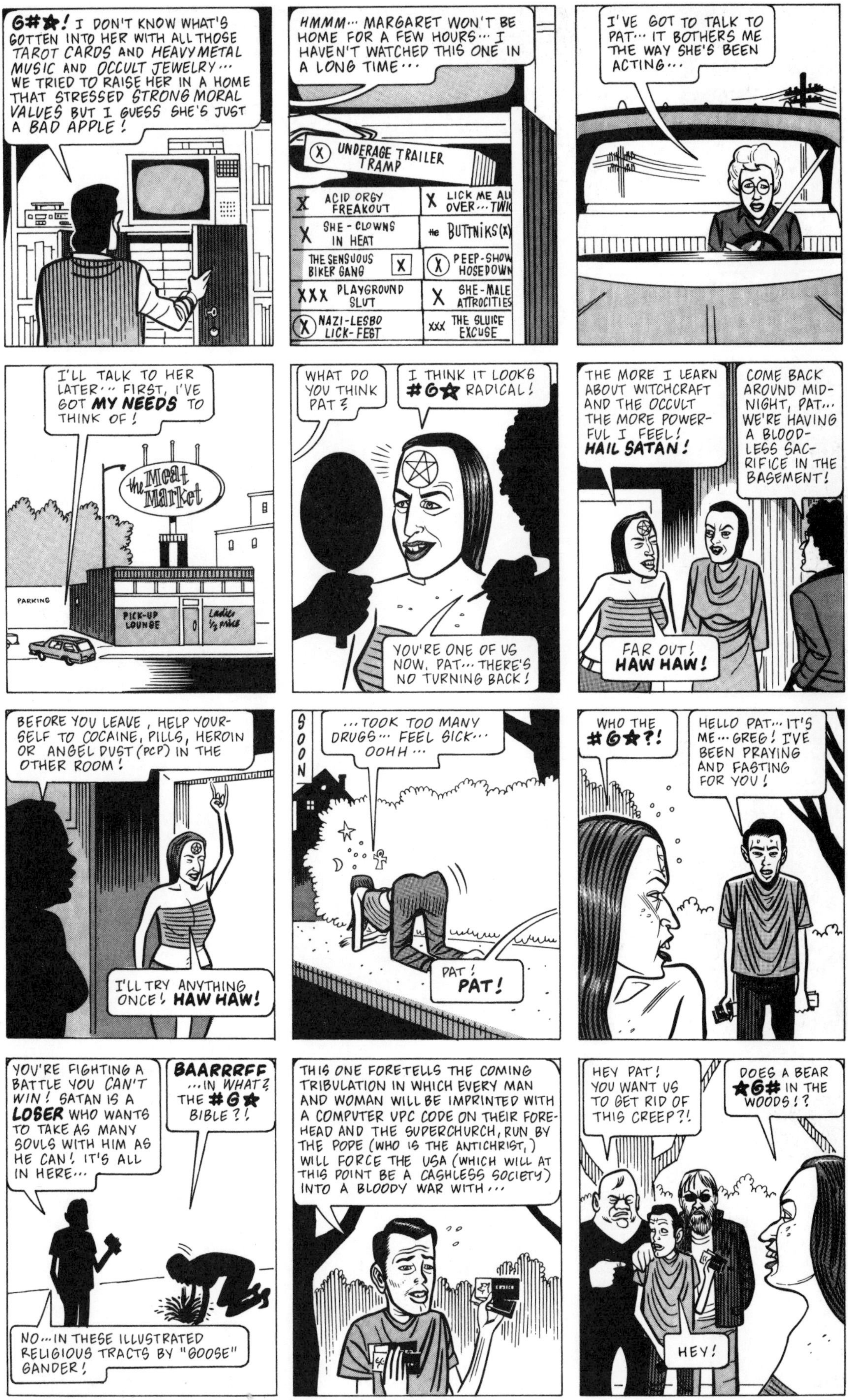

G#✪! I DON'T KNOW WHAT'S GOTTEN INTO HER WITH ALL THOSE TAROT CARDS AND HEAVY METAL MUSIC AND OCCULT JEWELRY… WE TRIED TO RAISE HER IN A HOME THAT STRESSED STRONG MORAL VALUES BUT I GUESS SHE'S JUST A BAD APPLE!
HMMM… MARGARET WON'T BE HOME FOR A FEW HOURS… I HAVEN'T WATCHED THIS ONE IN A LONG TIME…
X UNDERAGE TRAILER TRAMP
X ACID ORGY FREAKOUT
X LICK ME ALL OVER…TWIC
X SHE-CLOWNS IN HEAT
THE BUTTNIKS (X)
THE SENSUOUS BIKER GANG X
X PEEP-SHOW HOSEDOWN
XXX PLAYGROUND SLUT
X SHE-MALE ATTROCITIES
X NAZI-LESBO LICK-FEST
XXX THE SLUICE EXCUSE
I'VE GOT TO TALK TO PAT… IT BOTHERS ME THE WAY SHE'S BEEN ACTING…
I'LL TALK TO HER LATER… FIRST, I'VE GOT MY NEEDS TO THINK OF!
the Meat Market
PARKING
PICK-UP LOUNGE
Ladies ½ price
WHAT DO YOU THINK PAT?
I THINK IT LOOKS #G✪ RADICAL!
YOU'RE ONE OF US NOW, PAT… THERE'S NO TURNING BACK!
THE MORE I LEARN ABOUT WITCHCRAFT AND THE OCCULT THE MORE POWERFUL I FEEL! HAIL SATAN!
COME BACK AROUND MIDNIGHT, PAT… WE'RE HAVING A BLOODLESS SACRIFICE IN THE BASEMENT!
FAR OUT! HAW HAW!
BEFORE YOU LEAVE, HELP YOURSELF TO COCAINE, PILLS, HEROIN OR ANGEL DUST (PCP) IN THE OTHER ROOM!
I'LL TRY ANYTHING ONCE! HAW HAW!
SOON
…TOOK TOO MANY DRUGS… FEEL SICK… OOHH…
PAT! PAT!
WHO THE #G✪?!
HELLO PAT… IT'S ME… GREG! I'VE BEEN PRAYING AND FASTING FOR YOU!
YOU'RE FIGHTING A BATTLE YOU CAN'T WIN! SATAN IS A LOSER WHO WANTS TO TAKE AS MANY SOULS WITH HIM AS HE CAN! IT'S ALL IN HERE…
BAARRRFF …IN WHAT? THE #G✪ BIBLE?!
NO… IN THESE ILLUSTRATED RELIGIOUS TRACTS BY "GOOSE" GANDER!
THIS ONE FORETELLS THE COMING TRIBULATION IN WHICH EVERY MAN AND WOMAN WILL BE IMPRINTED WITH A COMPUTER UPC CODE ON THEIR FOREHEAD AND THE SUPERCHURCH, RUN BY THE POPE (WHO IS THE ANTICHRIST,) WILL FORCE THE USA (WHICH WILL AT THIS POINT BE A CASHLESS SOCIETY) INTO A BLOODY WAR WITH…
HEY PAT! YOU WANT US TO GET RID OF THIS CREEP?!
DOES A BEAR ✪G# IN THE WOODS!?
HEY!

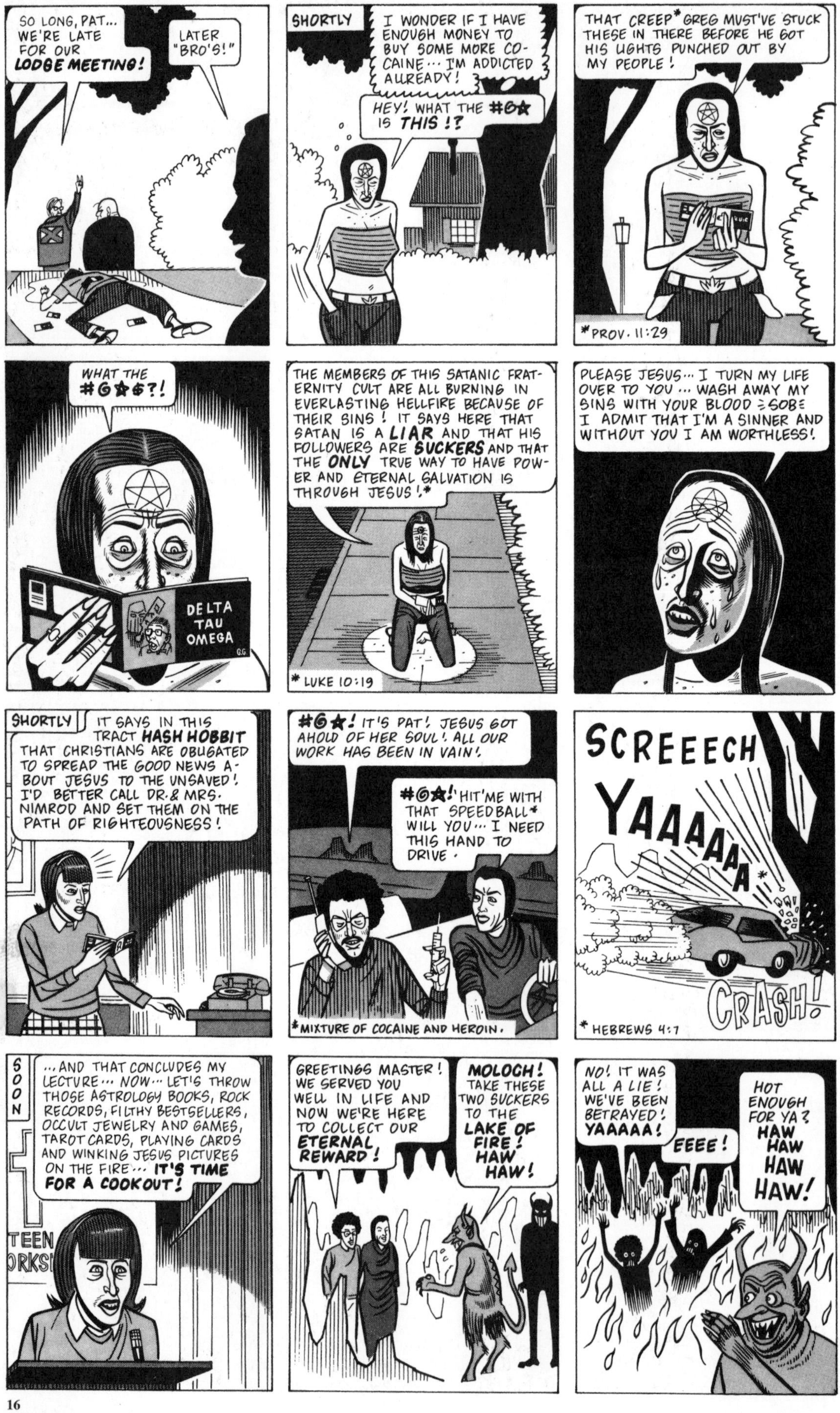

SO LONG, PAT... WE'RE LATE FOR OUR LODGE MEETING!
LATER "BRO'S!"
SHORTLY
I WONDER IF I HAVE ENOUGH MONEY TO BUY SOME MORE CO-CAINE... I'M ADDICTED ALLREADY!
HEY! WHAT THE #G★ IS THIS!?
THAT CREEP* GREG MUST'VE STUCK THESE IN THERE BEFORE HE GOT HIS LIGHTS PUNCHED OUT BY MY PEOPLE!
*PROV. 11:29
WHAT THE #G★$?!
DELTA TAU OMEGA
THE MEMBERS OF THIS SATANIC FRAT-ERNITY CULT ARE ALL BURNING IN EVERLASTING HELLFIRE BECAUSE OF THEIR SINS! IT SAYS HERE THAT SATAN IS A LIAR AND THAT HIS FOLLOWERS ARE SUCKERS AND THAT THE ONLY TRUE WAY TO HAVE POW-ER AND ETERNAL SALVATION IS THROUGH JESUS!*
*LUKE 10:19
PLEASE JESUS... I TURN MY LIFE OVER TO YOU... WASH AWAY MY SINS WITH YOUR BLOOD =SOB= I ADMIT THAT I'M A SINNER AND WITHOUT YOU I AM WORTHLESS!
SHORTLY
IT SAYS IN THIS TRACT HASH HOBBIT THAT CHRISTIANS ARE OBLIGATED TO SPREAD THE GOOD NEWS A-BOUT JESUS TO THE UNSAVED! I'D BETTER CALL DR. & MRS. NIMROD AND SET THEM ON THE PATH OF RIGHTEOUSNESS!
#G★! IT'S PAT! JESUS GOT AHOLD OF HER SOUL! ALL OUR WORK HAS BEEN IN VAIN!
#G★! HIT ME WITH THAT SPEEDBALL* WILL YOU... I NEED THIS HAND TO DRIVE.
*MIXTURE OF COCAINE AND HEROIN.
SCREEECH
YAAAAAA*
CRASH!
*HEBREWS 4:7
SOON
...AND THAT CONCLUDES MY LECTURE... NOW... LET'S THROW THOSE ASTROLOGY BOOKS, ROCK RECORDS, FILTHY BESTSELLERS, OCCULT JEWELRY AND GAMES, TAROT CARDS, PLAYING CARDS AND WINKING JESUS PICTURES ON THE FIRE... IT'S TIME FOR A COOKOUT!
TEEN
GREETINGS MASTER! WE SERVED YOU WELL IN LIFE AND NOW WE'RE HERE TO COLLECT OUR ETERNAL REWARD!
MOLOCH! TAKE THESE TWO SUCKERS TO THE LAKE OF FIRE! HAW HAW!
NO! IT WAS ALL A LIE! WE'VE BEEN BETRAYED! YAAAAA!
EEEE!
HOT ENOUGH FOR YA? HAW HAW HAW HAW!

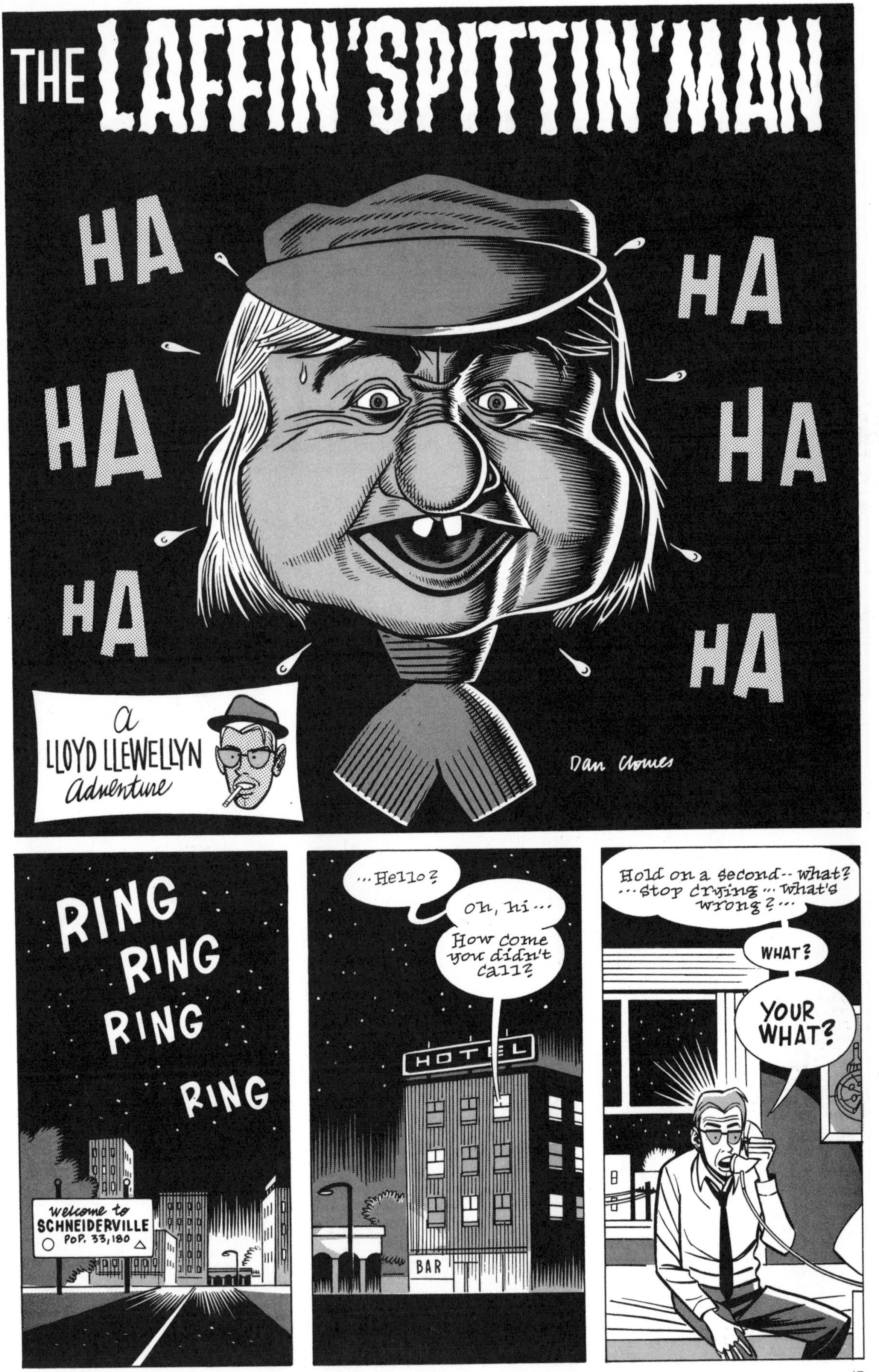
THE LAFFIN' SPITTIN' MAN
HA
HA
HA
HA
HA
HA
a LLOYD LLEWELLYN adventure
Dan Clowes
RING
RING
RING
RING
welcome to SCHNEIDERVILLE POP. 33,180
...Hello?
Oh, hi...
How come you didn't call?
HOTEL
BAR
Hold on a second -- what? ... stop crying ... what's wrong? ...
WHAT?
YOUR WHAT?

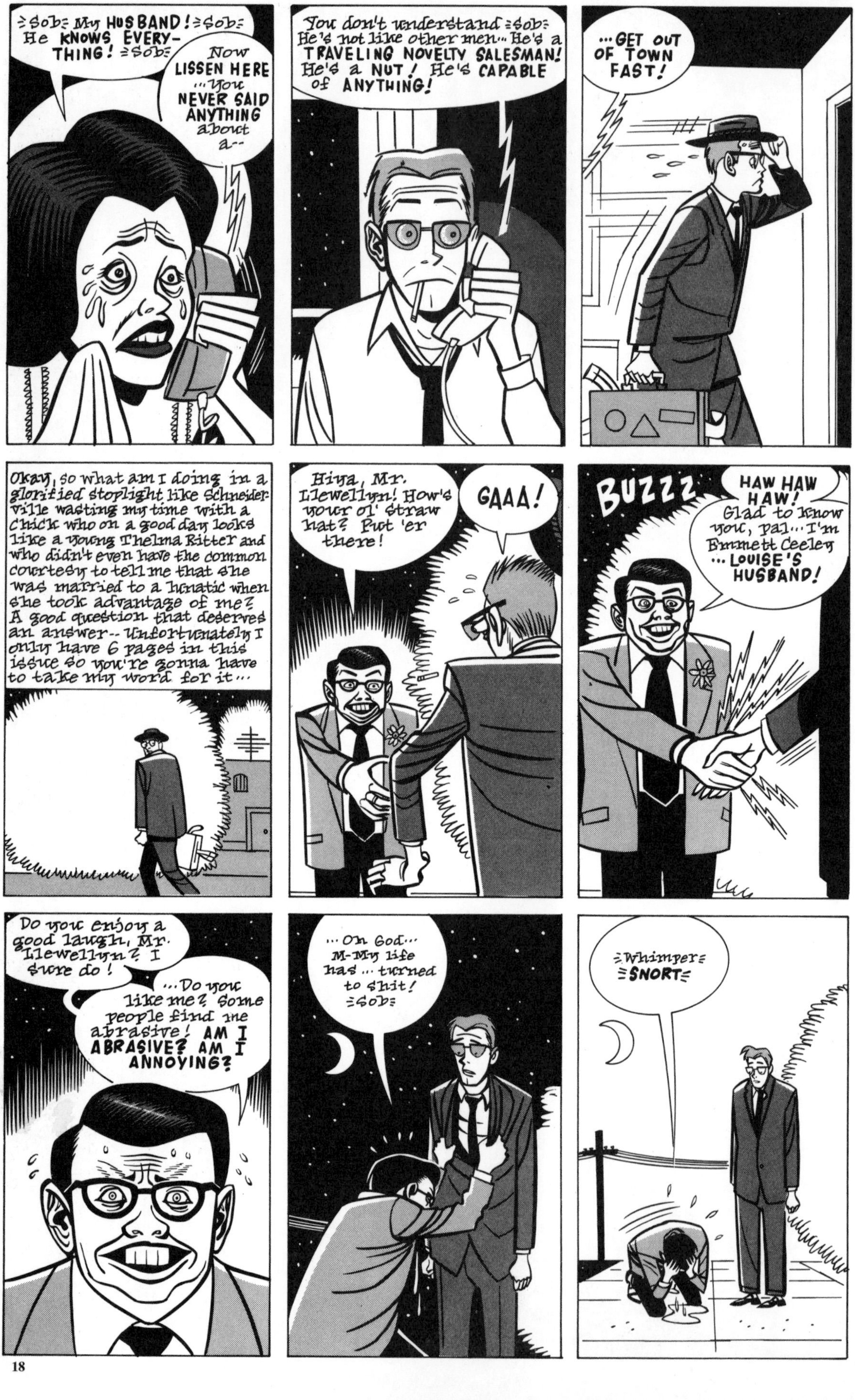

=Sob= My HUSBAND! =Sob= He KNOWS EVERY-THING! =Sob=
Now LISSEN HERE ...You NEVER SAID ANYTHING about a--
You don't understand =Sob= He's not like other men... He's a TRAVELING NOVELTY SALESMAN! He's a NUT! He's CAPABLE of ANYTHING!
...GET OUT OF TOWN FAST!
Okay, so what am I doing in a glorified stoplight like Schneider-ville wasting my time with a chick who on a good day looks like a young Thelma Ritter and who didn't even have the common courtesy to tell me that she was married to a lunatic when she took advantage of me? A good question that deserves an answer-- Unfortunately I only have 6 pages in this issue so you're gonna have to take my word for it...
Hiya, Mr. Llewellyn! How's your ol' straw hat? Put 'er there!
GAAA!
BUZZZ
HAW HAW HAW! Glad to know you, pal... I'm Emmett Ceeley ...LOUISE'S HUSBAND!
Do you enjoy a good laugh, Mr. Llewellyn? I sure do!
...Do you like me? Some people find me abrasive! AM I ABRASIVE? AM I ANNOYING?
...Oh God... M-My life has... turned to shit! =Sob=
=Whimper= =SNORT=

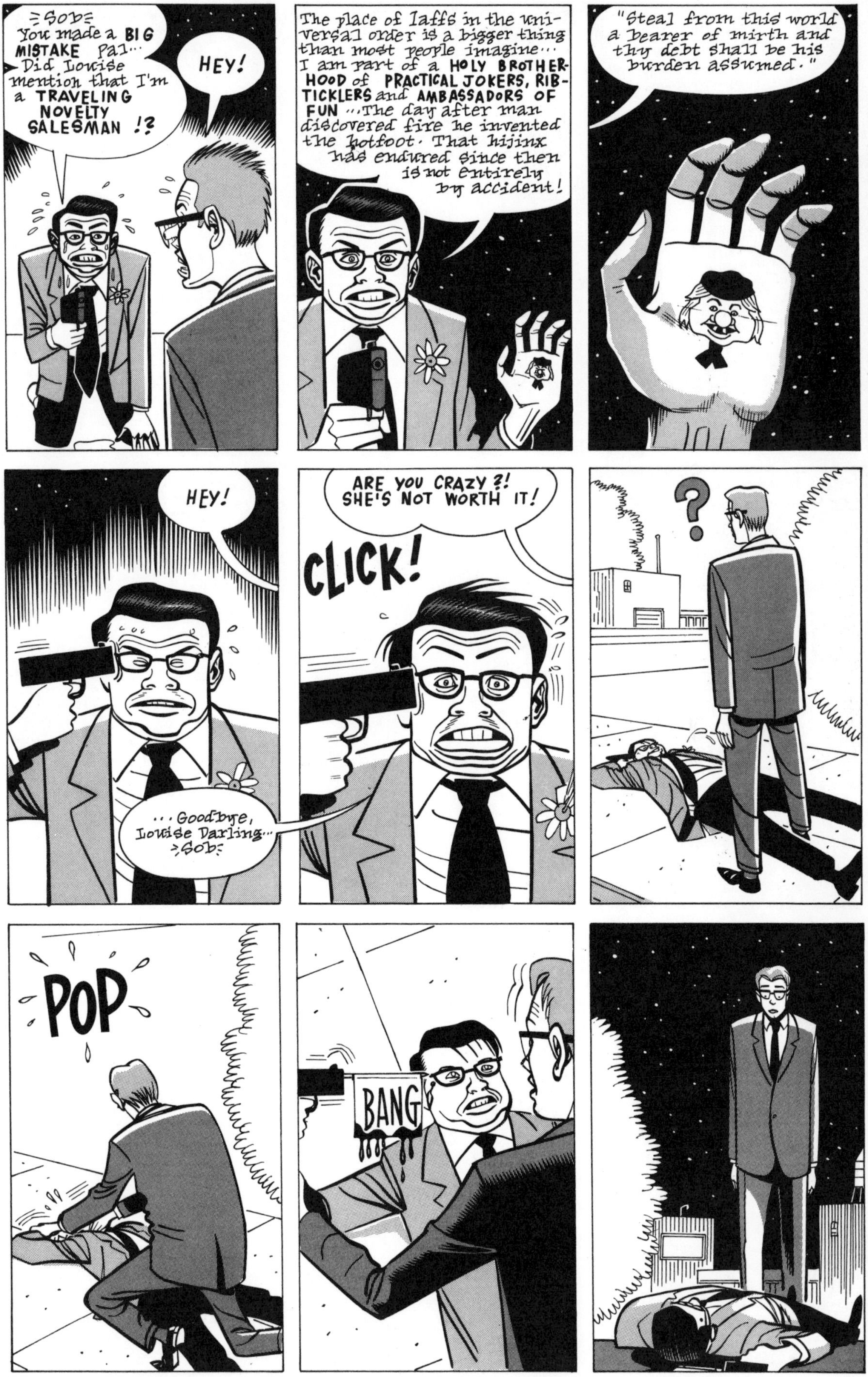

=Sob= You made a BIG MISTAKE Pal... Did Louise mention that I'm a TRAVELING NOVELTY SALESMAN !?
HEY!
The place of laffs in the universal order is a bigger thing than most people imagine... I am part of a HOLY BROTHERHOOD of PRACTICAL JOKERS, RIB-TICKLERS and AMBASSADORS OF FUN ...The day after man discovered fire he invented the hotfoot. That hijinx has endured since then is not entirely by accident!
"Steal from this world a bearer of mirth and thy debt shall be his burden assumed."
HEY!
ARE YOU CRAZY ?! SHE'S NOT WORTH IT!
CLICK!
...Goodbye, Louise Darling... =Sob=
?
POP
BANG

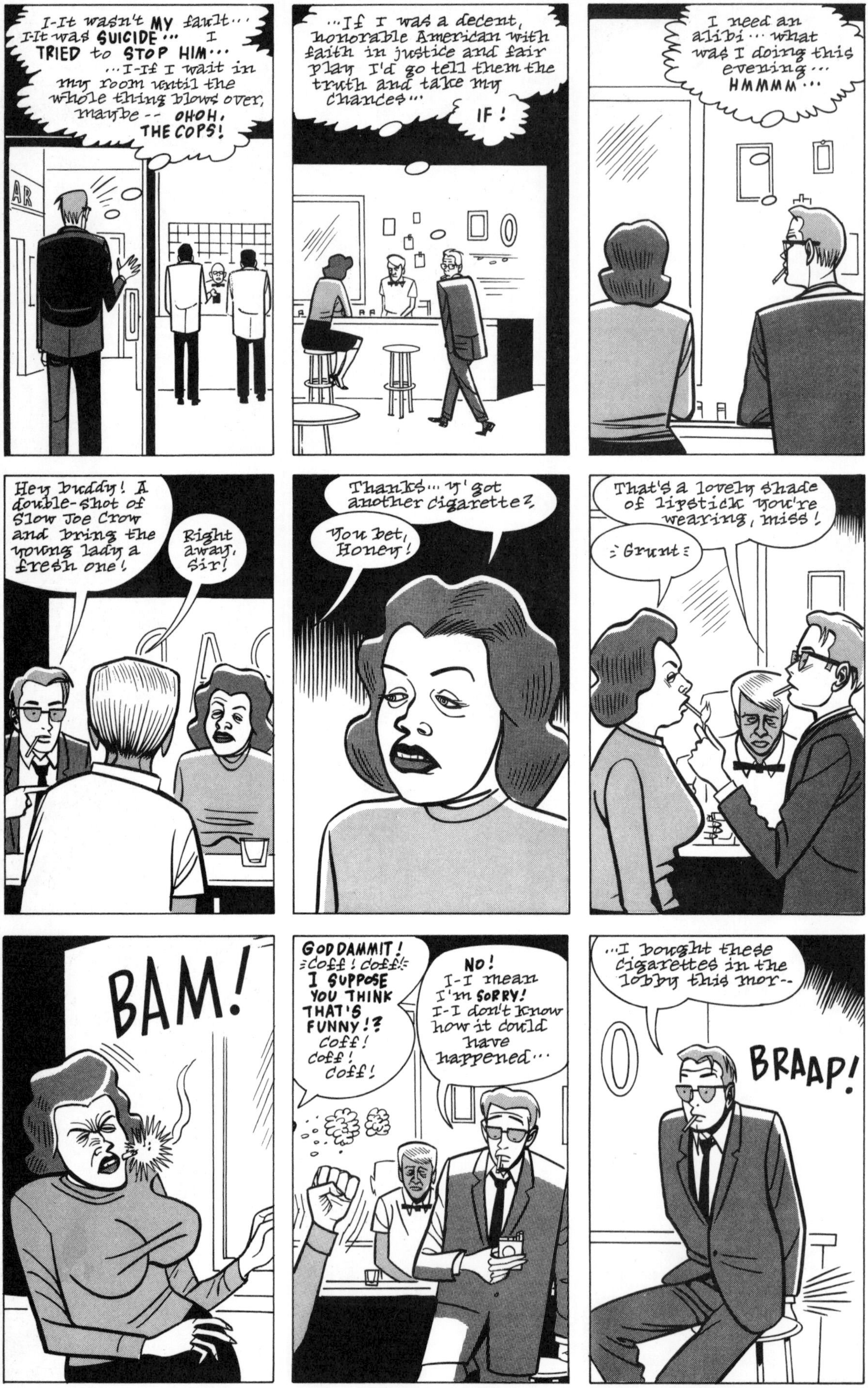
I-It wasn't MY fault... I-It was SUICIDE... I TRIED to STOP HIM... ...I-If I wait in my room until the whole thing blows over, maybe -- OHOH, THE COPS!
AR
...If I was a decent, honorable American with faith in justice and fair play I'd go tell them the truth and take my chances...
IF!
I need an alibi... what was I doing this evening... HMMMM...
Hey buddy! A double-shot of Slow Joe Crow and bring the young lady a fresh one!
Right away, Sir!
Thanks... y' got another cigarette?
You bet, Honey!
That's a lovely shade of lipstick you're wearing, miss!
Grunt
BAM!
GODDAMMIT! Coff! Coff! I SUPPOSE YOU THINK THAT'S FUNNY!? Coff! Coff! Coff!
NO! I-I mean I'm SORRY! I-I don't know how it could have happened...
...I bought these cigarettes in the lobby this mor--
BRAAP!

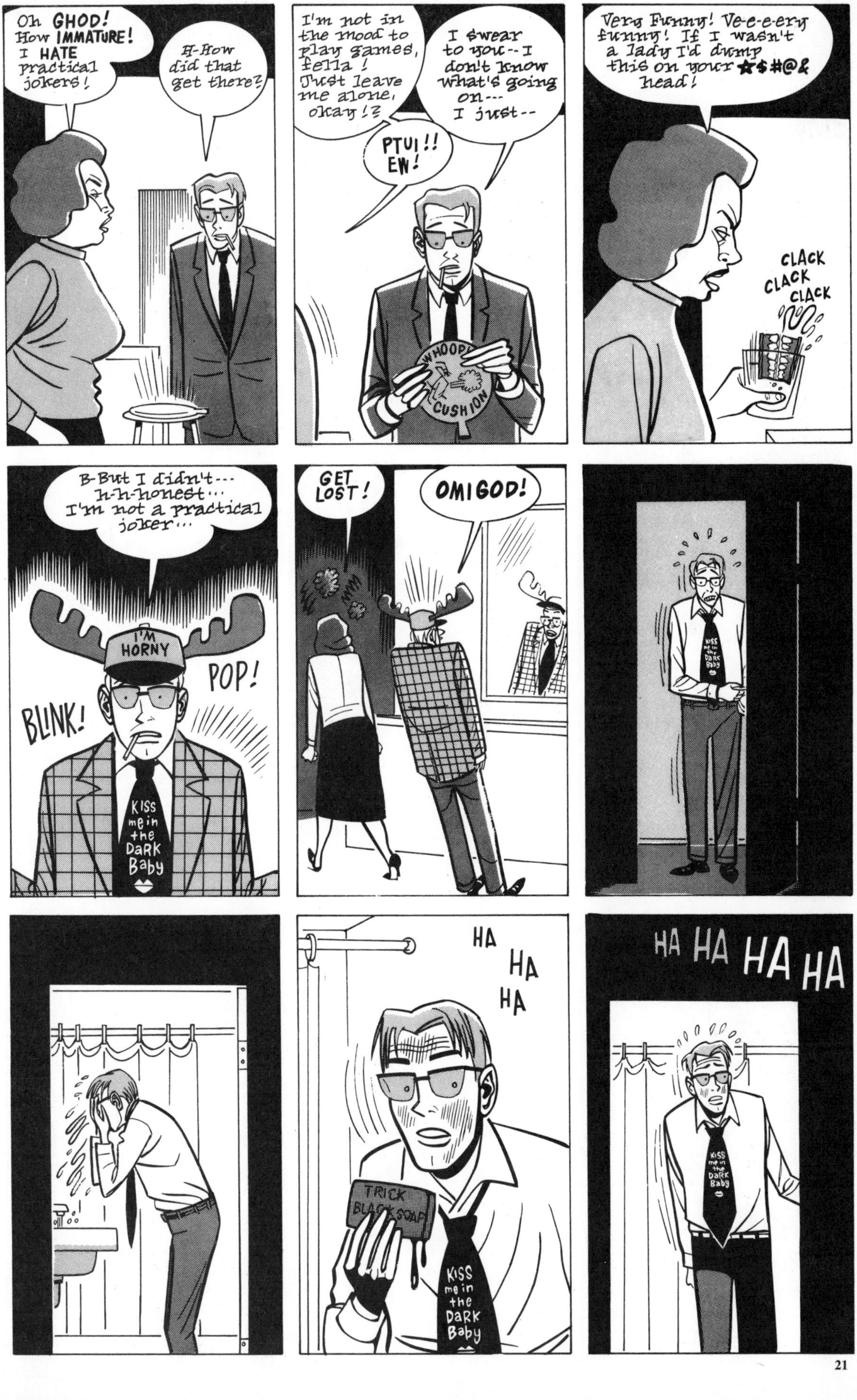
Oh GHOD! How IMMATURE! I HATE practical jokers!
H-How did that get there?
I'm not in the mood to play games, fella! Just leave me alone, okay!?
I swear to you--I don't know what's going on--- I just--
PTUI!! EW!
WHOOPI CUSHION
Very Funny! Ve-e-e-ery funny! If I wasn't a lady I'd dump this on your ✩$#@& head!
CLACK CLACK CLACK
B-But I didn't--- h-h-honest--- I'm not a practical joker---
I'M HORNY
POP!
BLINK!
KISS me in the DARK Baby
GET LOST!
OMIGOD!
KISS me in the DARK Baby
HA HA HA
TRICK BLACK SOAP
KISS me in the DARK Baby
HA HA HA HA
KISS me in the DARK Baby

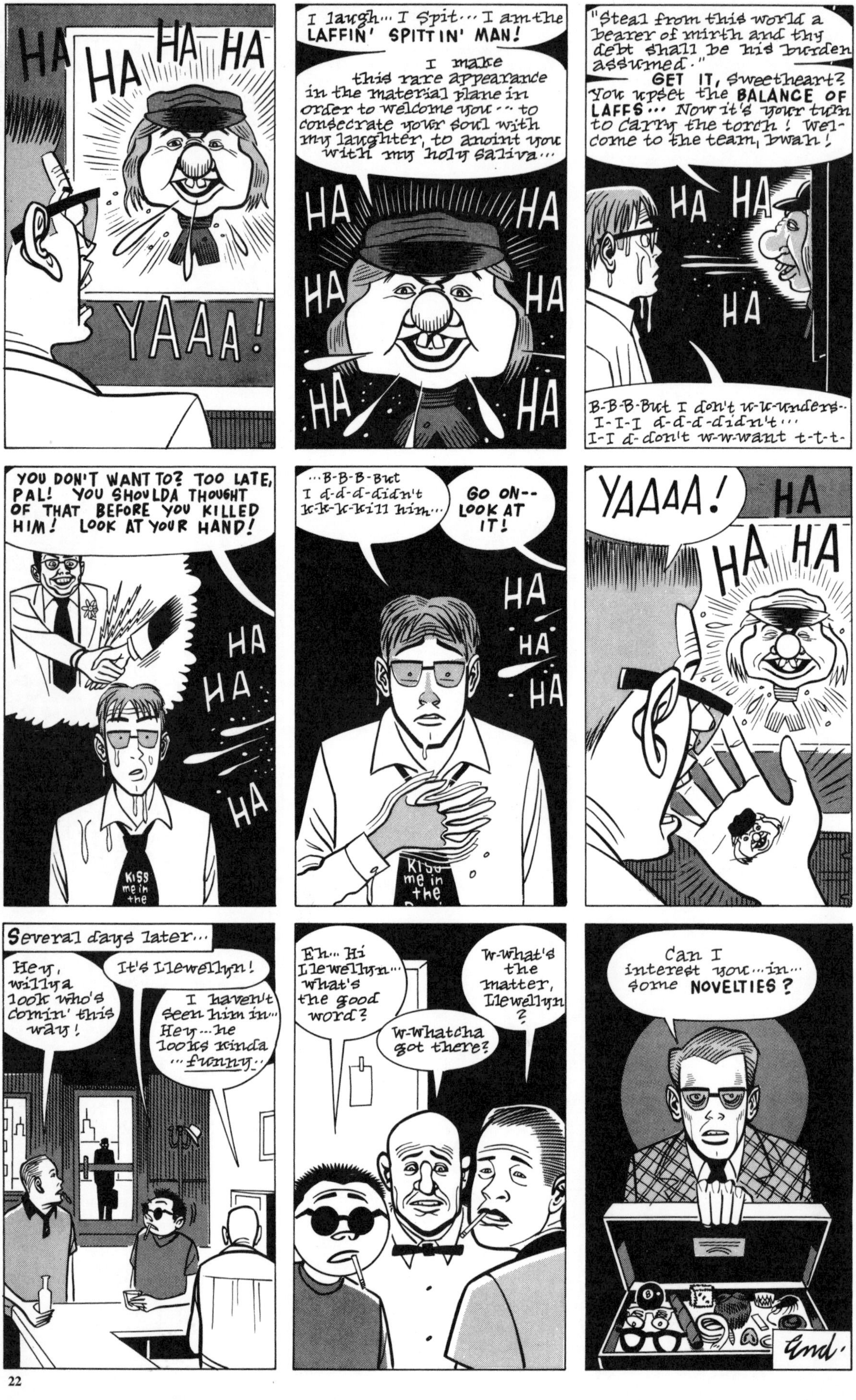
HA HA HA HA
YAAAA!
I laugh... I spit... I am the LAFFIN' SPITTIN' MAN!
I make this rare appearance in the material plane in order to welcome you... to consecrate your soul with my laughter, to anoint you with my holy saliva...
HA HA HA HA HA HA
"Steal from this world a bearer of mirth and thy debt shall be his burden assumed." GET IT, sweetheart? You upset the BALANCE OF LAFFS... Now it's your turn to carry the torch! Welcome to the team, bwah!
HA HA HA
B-B-B-But I don't u-u-unders-- I-I-I d-d-d-didn't... I-I d-don't w-w-want t-t-t-
YOU DON'T WANT TO? TOO LATE, PAL! YOU SHOULDA THOUGHT OF THAT BEFORE YOU KILLED HIM! LOOK AT YOUR HAND!
HA HA HA
KISS me in the
...B-B-B-But I d-d-d-didn't k-k-k-kill him...
GO ON-- LOOK AT IT!
HA HA HA
YAAAA!
HA HA HA
Several days later...
Hey, willya look who's comin' this way!
It's Llewellyn!
I haven't seen him in... Hey... he looks kinda ...funny...
Eh... Hi Llewellyn... what's the good word?
W-whatcha got there?
W-what's the matter, Llewellyn?
Can I interest you... in... some NOVELTIES?
End.

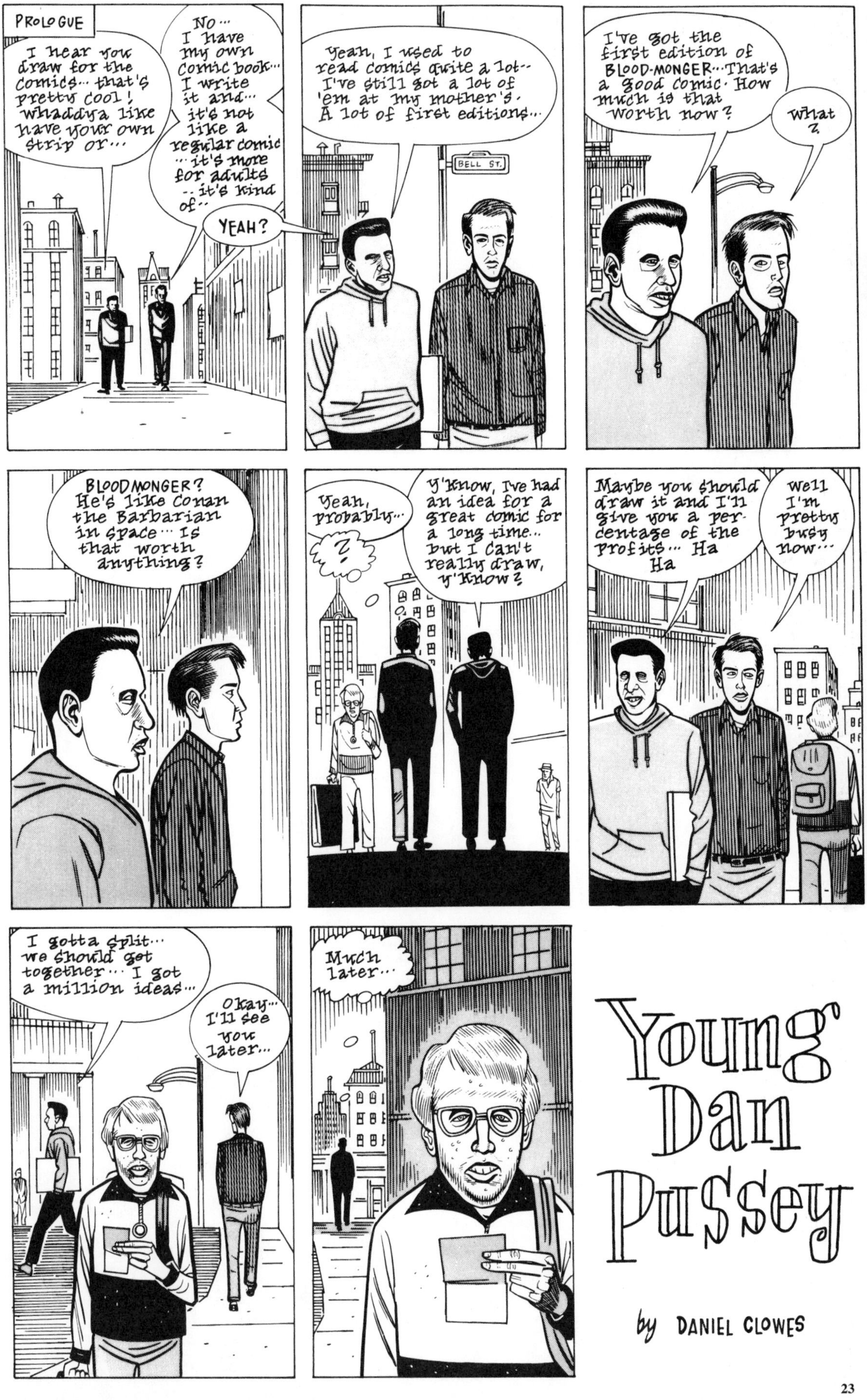
PROLOGUE
I hear you draw for the comics... that's pretty cool! whaddya like have your own strip or...
No... I have my own comic book... I write it and... it's not like a regular comic ... it's more for adults -- it's kind of...
YEAH?
Yeah, I used to read comics quite a lot-- I've still got a lot of 'em at my mother's. A lot of first editions...
BELL ST.
I've got the first edition of BLOOD-MONGER... That's a good comic. How much is that worth now?
What?
BLOODMONGER? He's like Conan the Barbarian in space... Is that worth anything?
Yeah, probably...
?
Y'know, I've had an idea for a great comic for a long time... but I can't really draw, y'know?
Maybe you should draw it and I'll give you a percentage of the profits... Ha Ha
Well I'm pretty busy now...
I gotta split... we should get together... I got a million ideas...
Okay... I'll see you later...
Much later...
Young Dan Pussey
by DANIEL CLOWES

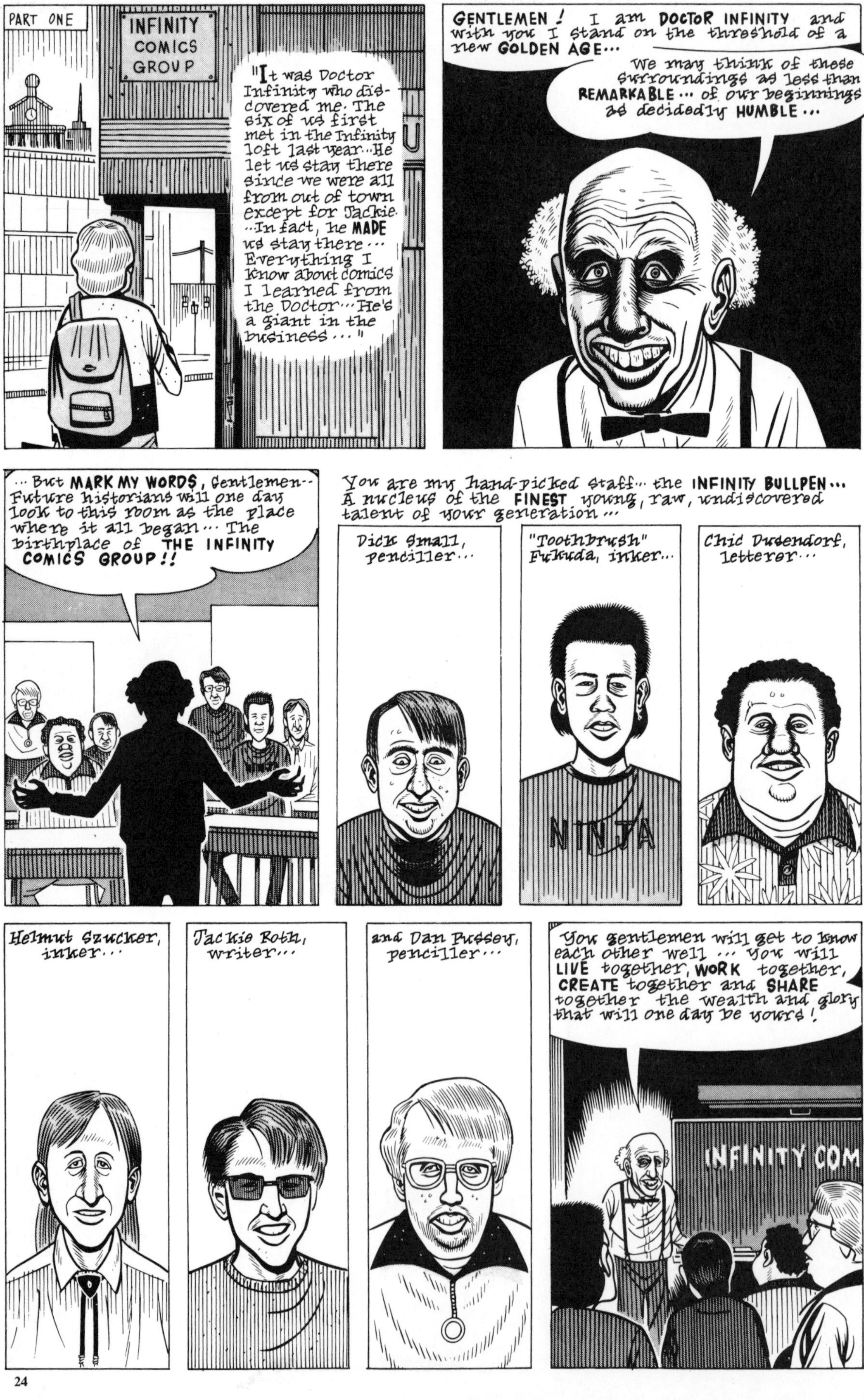
PART ONE
INFINITY COMICS GROUP
"It was Doctor Infinity who discovered me. The six of us first met in the Infinity loft last year... He let us stay there since we were all from out of town except for Jackie. ...In fact, he MADE us stay there... Everything I know about comics I learned from the Doctor... He's a giant in the business..."
GENTLEMEN! I am DOCTOR INFINITY and with you I stand on the threshold of a new GOLDEN AGE...
We may think of these surroundings as less than REMARKABLE... of our beginnings as decidedly HUMBLE...
...But MARK MY WORDS, Gentlemen-- Future historians will one day look to this room as the place where it all began... The birthplace of THE INFINITY COMICS GROUP!!
You are my hand-picked staff... the INFINITY BULLPEN... A nucleus of the FINEST young, raw, undiscovered talent of your generation...
Dick Small, penciller...
"Toothbrush" Fukuda, inker...
NINJA
Chic Dusendorf, letterer...
Helmut Szucker, inker...
Jackie Roth, writer...
and Dan Pussey, penciller...
You gentlemen will get to know each other well... You will LIVE together, WORK together, CREATE together and SHARE together the wealth and glory that will one day be yours!
INFINITY COM

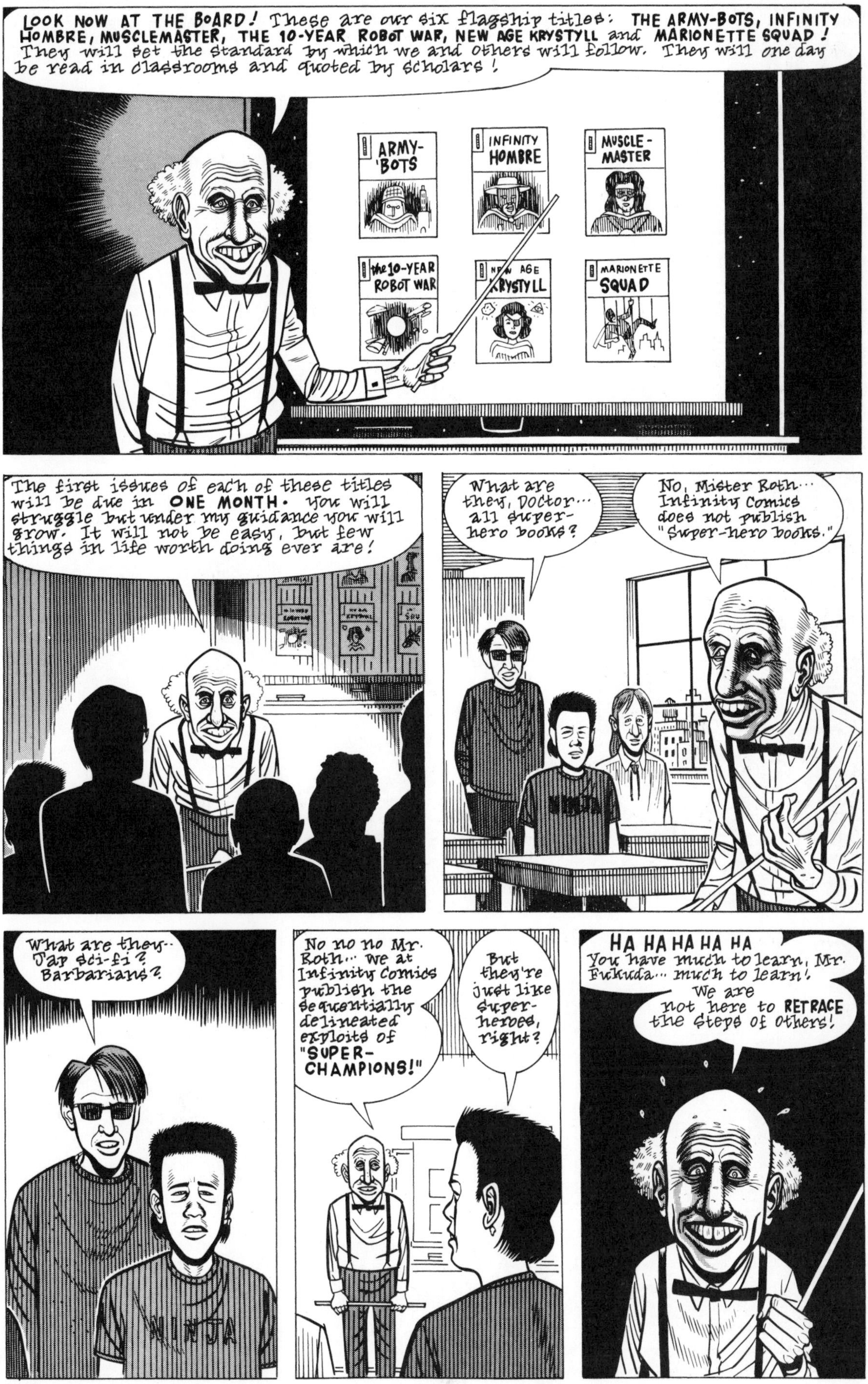
LOOK NOW AT THE BOARD! These are our six flagship titles: THE ARMY-BOTS, INFINITY HOMBRE, MUSCLEMASTER, THE 10-YEAR ROBOT WAR, NEW AGE KRYSTYLL and MARIONETTE SQUAD! They will set the standard by which we and others will follow. They will one day be read in classrooms and quoted by scholars!
ARMY-'BOTS
INFINITY HOMBRE
MUSCLE-MASTER
the 10-YEAR ROBOT WAR
NEW AGE KRYSTYLL
MARIONETTE SQUAD
The first issues of each of these titles will be due in ONE MONTH. You will struggle but under my guidance you will grow. It will not be easy, but few things in life worth doing ever are!
What are they, Doctor... all super-hero books?
No, Mister Roth... Infinity Comics does not publish "Super-hero books."
NINJA
What are they.. Jap sci-fi? Barbarians?
NINJA
No no no Mr. Roth... We at Infinity Comics publish the sequentially delineated exploits of "SUPER-CHAMPIONS!"
But they're just like super-heroes, right?
HA HA HA HA HA HA
You have much to learn, Mr. Fukuda... much to learn! We are not here to RETRACE the steps of others!

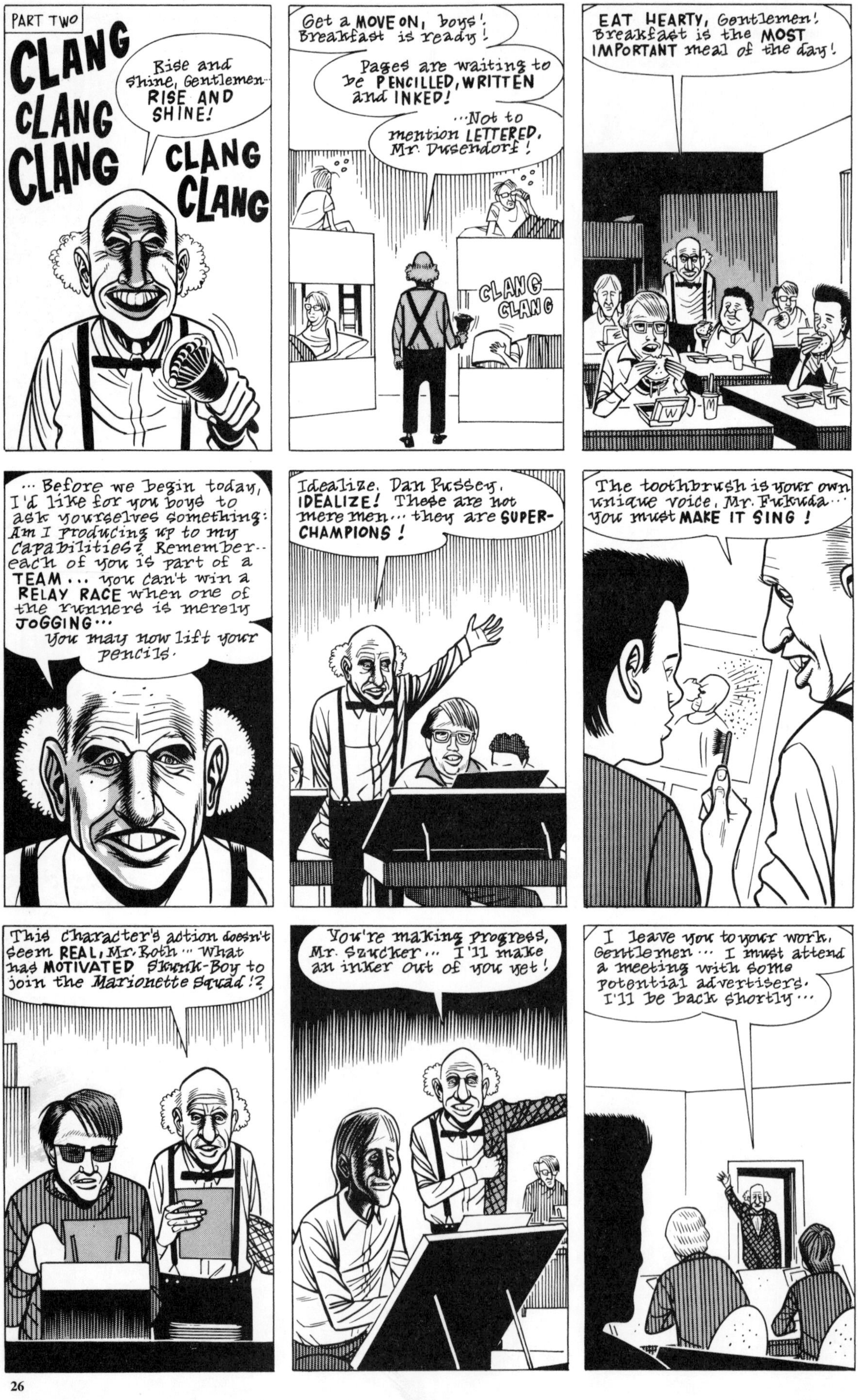
PART TWO
CLANG CLANG CLANG
Rise and Shine, Gentlemen... RISE AND SHINE!
CLANG CLANG
Get a MOVE ON, boys! Breakfast is ready!
Pages are waiting to be PENCILLED, WRITTEN and INKED!
...Not to mention LETTERED, Mr. Dusendorf!
CLANG CLANG
EAT HEARTY, Gentlemen! Breakfast is the MOST IMPORTANT meal of the day!
... Before we begin today, I'd like for you boys to ask yourselves something: Am I producing up to my capabilities? Remember... each of you is part of a TEAM... you can't win a RELAY RACE when one of the runners is merely JOGGING...
You may now lift your pencils.
Idealize, Dan Pussey. IDEALIZE! These are not mere men... they are SUPER-CHAMPIONS!
The toothbrush is your own unique voice, Mr. Fukuda... You must MAKE IT SING!
This character's action doesn't seem REAL, Mr. Roth... What has MOTIVATED Skunk-Boy to join the Marionette Squad!?
You're making progress, Mr. Szucker... I'll make an inker out of you yet!
I leave you to your work, Gentlemen... I must attend a meeting with some potential advertisers. I'll be back shortly...

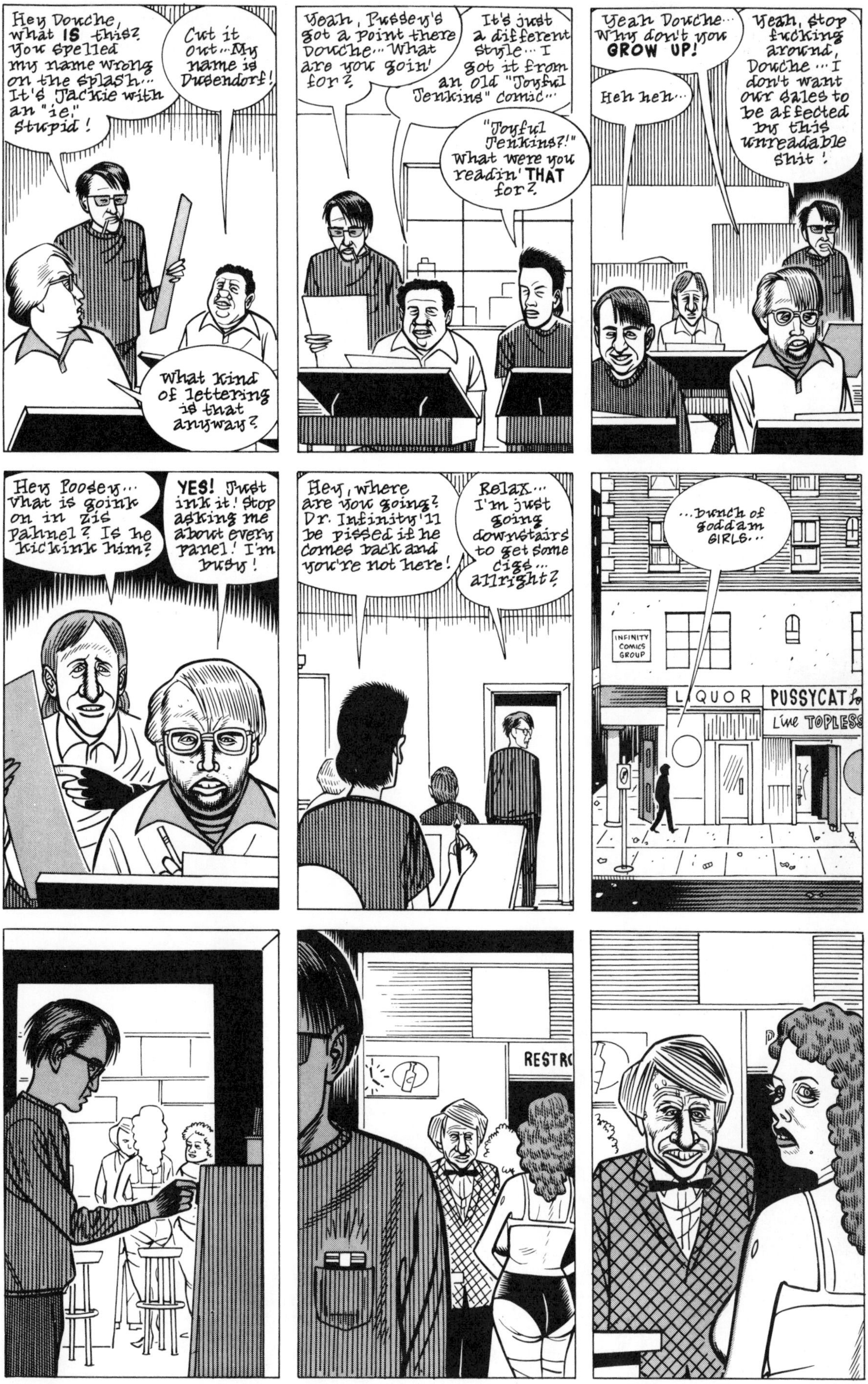
Hey Douche, what IS this? You spelled my name wrong on the splash... It's Jackie with an "ie," stupid!
Cut it out... My name is Dusendorf!
What kind of lettering is that anyway?
Yeah, Pussey's got a point there Douche... What are you goin' for?
It's just a different style... I got it from an old "Joyful Jenkins" comic...
"Joyful Jenkins?!" What were you readin' THAT for?
Yeah Douche... Why don't you GROW UP!
Heh heh...
Yeah, stop fucking around, Douche... I don't want our sales to be affected by this unreadable shit!
Hey Poosey... what is goink on in zis pahnel? Is he kickink him?
YES! Just ink it! Stop asking me about every panel! I'm busy!
Hey, where are you going? Dr. Infinity'll be pissed if he comes back and you're not here!
Relax... I'm just going downstairs to get some cigs... allright?
...bunch of goddam GIRLS...
INFINITY COMICS GROUP
LIQUOR
PUSSYCAT
Live TOPLESS
RESTRO

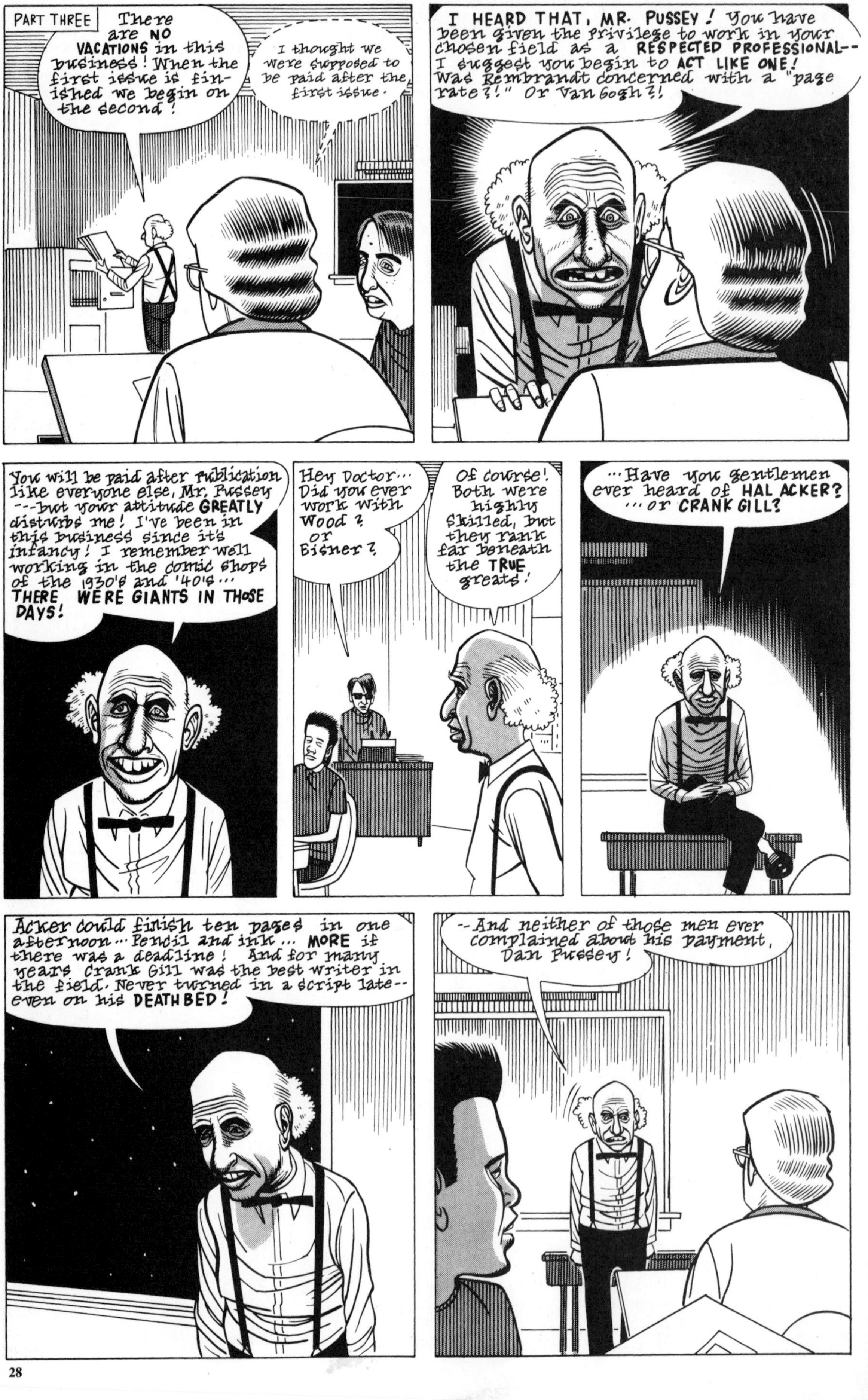
PART THREE
There are NO VACATIONS in this business! When the first issue is finished we begin on the second!
I thought we were supposed to be paid after the first issue.
I HEARD THAT, MR. PUSSEY! You have been given the privilege to work in your chosen field as a RESPECTED PROFESSIONAL-- I suggest you begin to ACT LIKE ONE! Was Rembrandt concerned with a "page rate?!" Or Van Gogh?!
You will be paid after publication like everyone else, Mr. Pussey ---but your attitude GREATLY disturbs me! I've been in this business since it's infancy! I remember well working in the comic shops of the 1930's and '40's... THERE WERE GIANTS IN THOSE DAYS!
Hey Doctor... Did you ever work with Wood? or Eisner?
Of course! Both were highly skilled, but they rank far beneath the TRUE greats!
...Have you gentlemen ever heard of HAL ACKER? ...or CRANK GILL?
Acker could finish ten pages in one afternoon... Pencil and ink... MORE if there was a deadline! And for many years Crank Gill was the best writer in the field. Never turned in a script late-- even on his DEATHBED!
--And neither of those men ever complained about his payment, Dan Pussey!

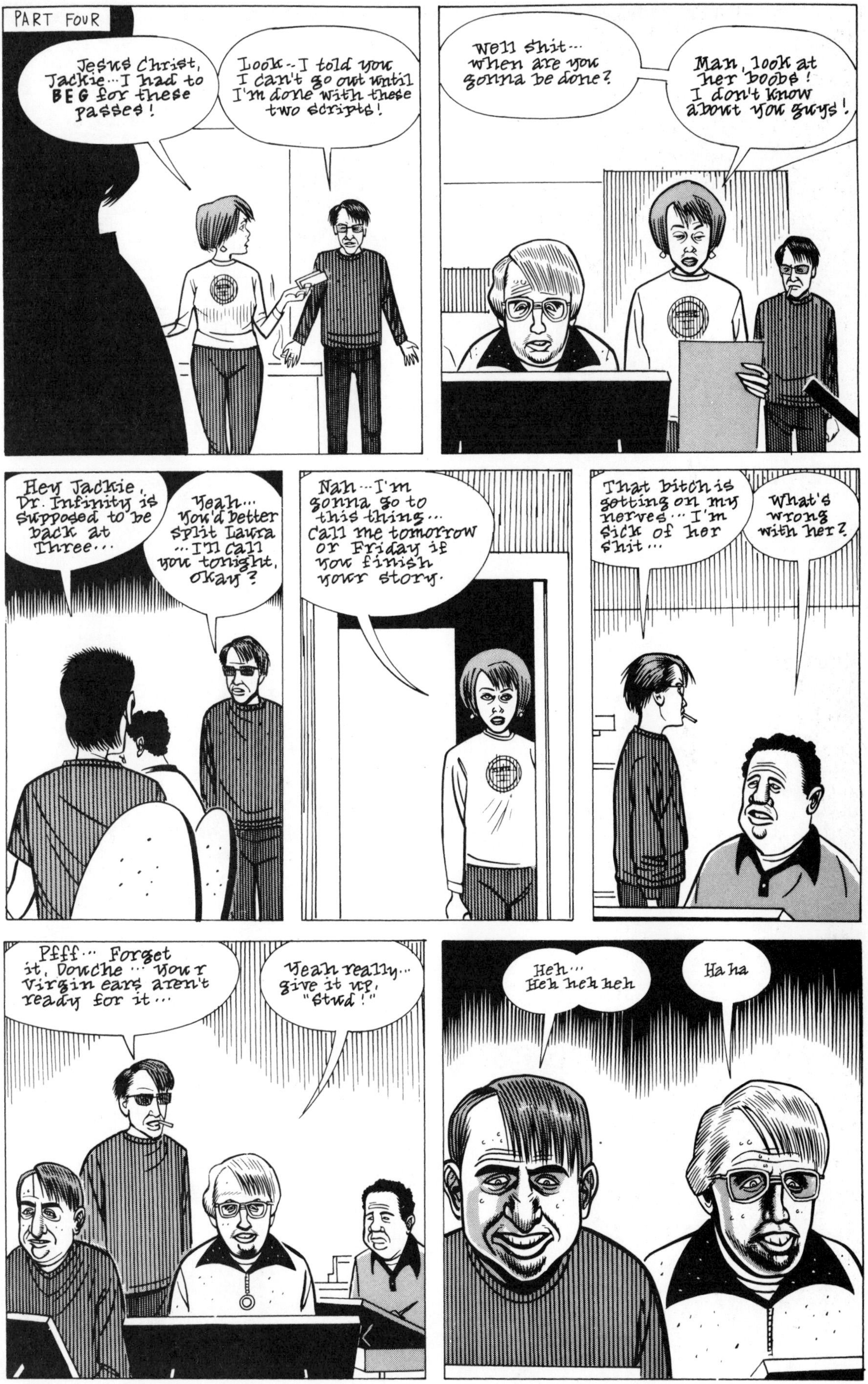
PART FOUR
Jesus Christ, Jackie... I had to BEG for these passes!
Look-- I told you I can't go out until I'm done with these two scripts!
Well shit... when are you gonna be done?
Man, look at her boobs! I don't know about you guys!
Hey Jackie, Dr. Infinity is supposed to be back at Three...
Yeah... You'd better split Laura ...I'll call you tonight, okay?
Nah... I'm gonna go to this thing... Call me tomorrow or Friday if you finish your story.
That bitch is getting on my nerves... I'm sick of her shit...
What's wrong with her?
Pfff... Forget it, Douche... Your virgin ears aren't ready for it...
Yeah really... give it up, "Stud!"
Heh... Heh heh heh
Ha ha

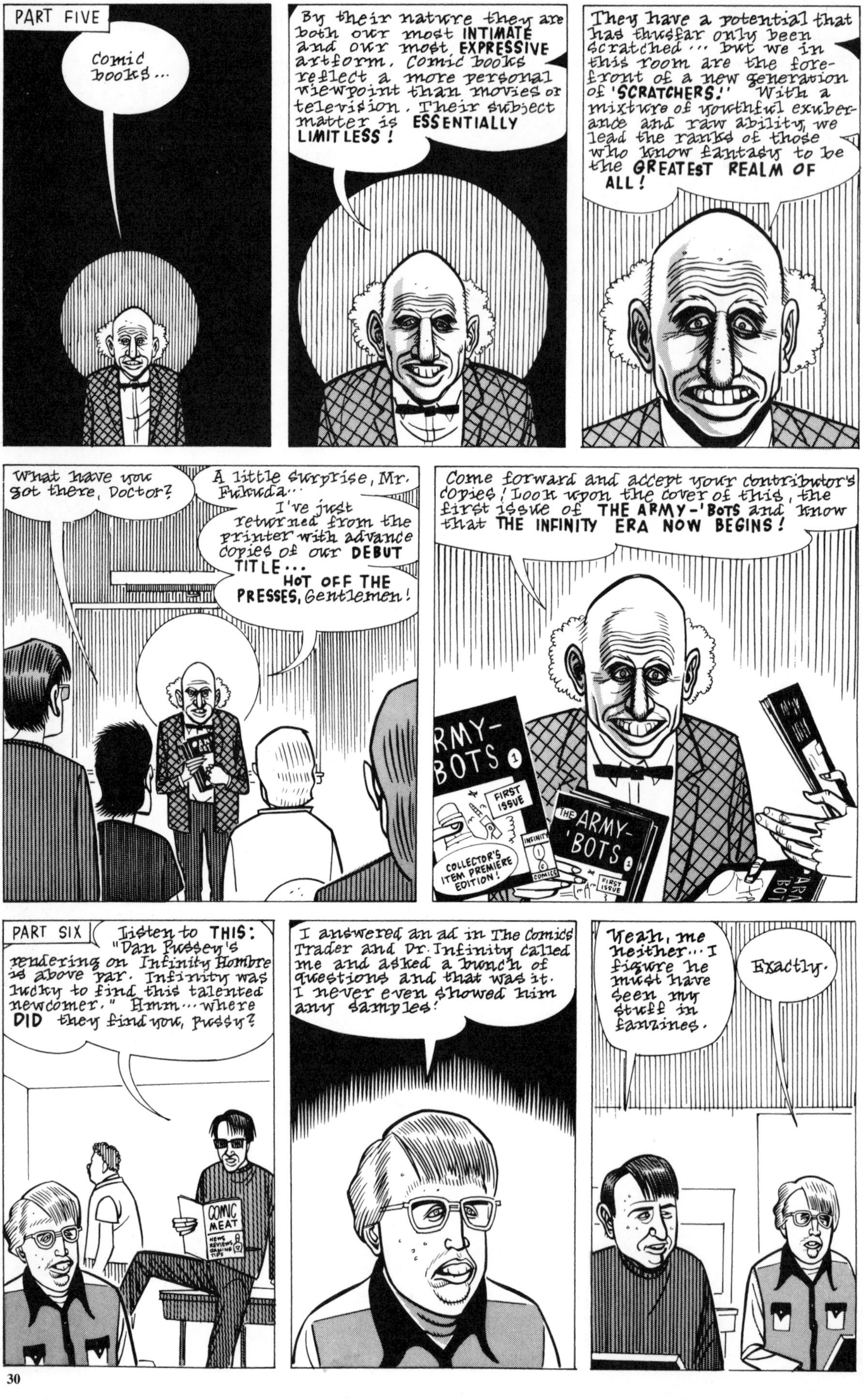
PART FIVE
Comic books...
By their nature they are both our most INTIMATE and our most EXPRESSIVE artform. Comic books reflect a more personal viewpoint than movies or television. Their subject matter is ESSENTIALLY LIMITLESS!
They have a potential that has thusfar only been scratched... but we in this room are the forefront of a new generation of 'SCRATCHERS!' With a mixture of youthful exuberance and raw ability, we lead the ranks of those who know fantasy to be the GREATEST REALM OF ALL!
What have you got there, Doctor?
A little surprise, Mr. Fukuda...
I've just returned from the printer with advance copies of our DEBUT TITLE...
HOT OFF THE PRESSES, Gentlemen!
Come forward and accept your contributor's copies! Look upon the cover of this, the first issue of THE ARMY-'BOTS and know that THE INFINITY ERA NOW BEGINS!
ARMY-BOTS 1
FIRST ISSUE
COLLECTOR'S ITEM PREMIERE EDITION!
INFINITY COMICS
THE ARMY-'BOTS 1
FIRST ISSUE
PART SIX
Listen to THIS: "Dan Pussey's rendering on Infinity Hombre is above par. Infinity was lucky to find this talented newcomer." Hmm... where DID they find you, Pussy?
COMIC MEAT
NEWS REVIEWS GAMING TIPS
I answered an ad in The Comics Trader and Dr. Infinity called me and asked a bunch of questions and that was it. I never even showed him any samples!
Yeah, me neither... I figure he must have seen my stuff in fanzines.
Exactly.

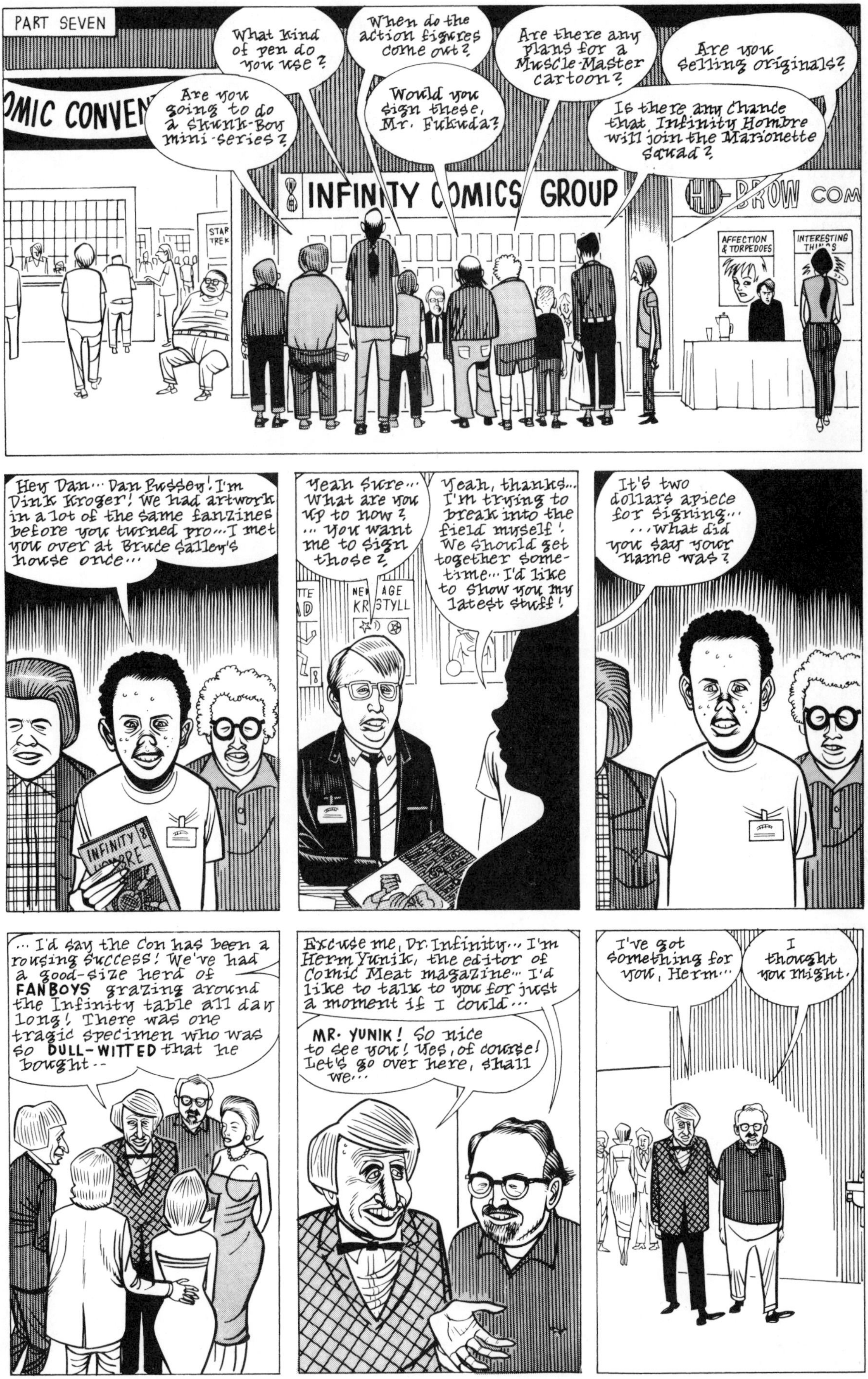
PART SEVEN
COMIC CONVEN
What kind of pen do you use?
When do the action figures come out?
Are there any plans for a Muscle-Master cartoon?
Are you selling originals?
Are you going to do a Skunk-Boy mini-series?
Would you sign these, Mr. Fukuda?
Is there any chance that Infinity Hombre will join the Marionette Squad?
INFINITY COMICS GROUP
HI-BROW COM
STAR TREK
AFFECTION & TORPEDOES
INTERESTING THINGS
Hey Dan... Dan Pussey! I'm Dink Kroger! We had artwork in a lot of the same fanzines before you turned pro... I met you over at Bruce Salley's house once...
INFINITY HOMBRE
Yeah sure... What are you up to now? ... You want me to sign those?
Yeah, thanks... I'm trying to break into the field myself! We should get together sometime... I'd like to show you my latest stuff!
NEW AGE KRYSTYLL
It's two dollars apiece for signing... ...what did you say your name was?
... I'd say the Con has been a rousing success! We've had a good-size herd of FANBOYS grazing around the Infinity table all day long! There was one tragic specimen who was so DULL-WITTED that he bought--
Excuse me, Dr. Infinity... I'm Herm Yunik, the editor of Comic Meat magazine... I'd like to talk to you for just a moment if I could...
MR. YUNIK! So nice to see you! Yes, of course! Let's go over here, shall we...
I've got something for you, Herm...
I thought you might.

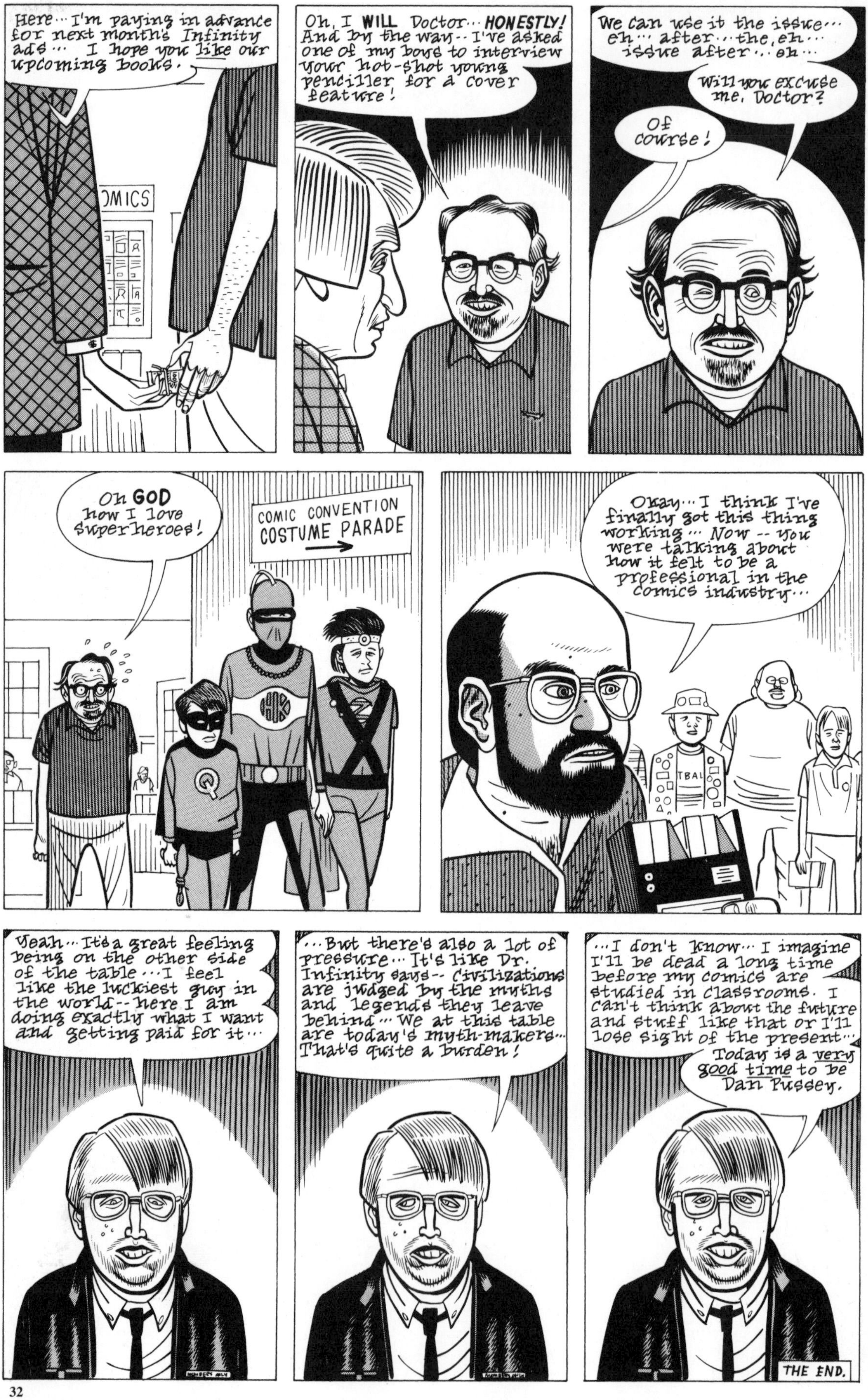
Here... I'm paying in advance for next month's Infinity ads... I hope you like our upcoming books.
OMICS
Oh, I WILL Doctor... HONESTLY! And by the way... I've asked one of my boys to interview your hot-shot young penciller for a cover feature!
We can use it the issue... eh... after... the, eh... issue after... eh...
Will you excuse me, Doctor?
Of course!
Oh GOD how I love superheroes!
COMIC CONVENTION COSTUME PARADE
Okay... I think I've finally got this thing working... Now -- you were talking about how it felt to be a professional in the comics industry...
TBAL
Yeah... It's a great feeling being on the other side of the table... I feel like the luckiest guy in the world -- here I am doing exactly what I want and getting paid for it...
...But there's also a lot of pressure... It's like Dr. Infinity says -- Civilizations are judged by the myths and legends they leave behind... We at this table are today's myth-makers... That's quite a burden!
...I don't know... I imagine I'll be dead a long time before my comics are studied in classrooms. I can't think about the future and stuff like that or I'll lose sight of the present...
Today is a very good time to be Dan Pussey.
THE END.

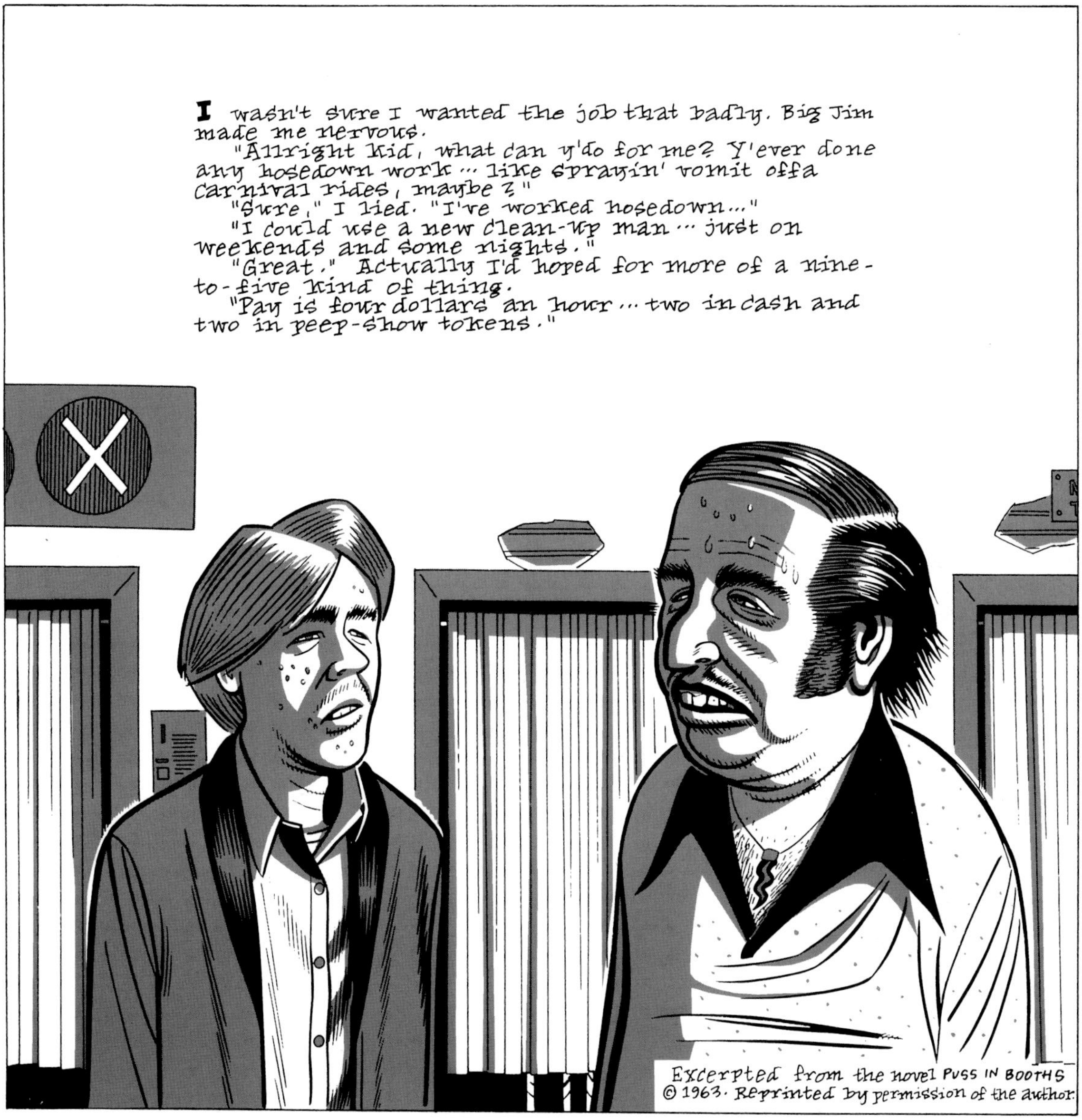
I wasn't sure I wanted the job that badly. Big Jim made me nervous.
"Allright kid, what can y'do for me? Y'ever done any hosedown work ... like sprayin' vomit offa carnival rides, maybe?"
"Sure," I lied. "I've worked hosedown..."
"I could use a new clean-up man ... just on weekends and some nights."
"Great." Actually I'd hoped for more of a nine-to-five kind of thing.
"Pay is four dollars an hour ... two in cash and two in peep-show tokens."
Excerpted from the novel PUSS IN BOOTHS © 1963. Reprinted by permission of the author.

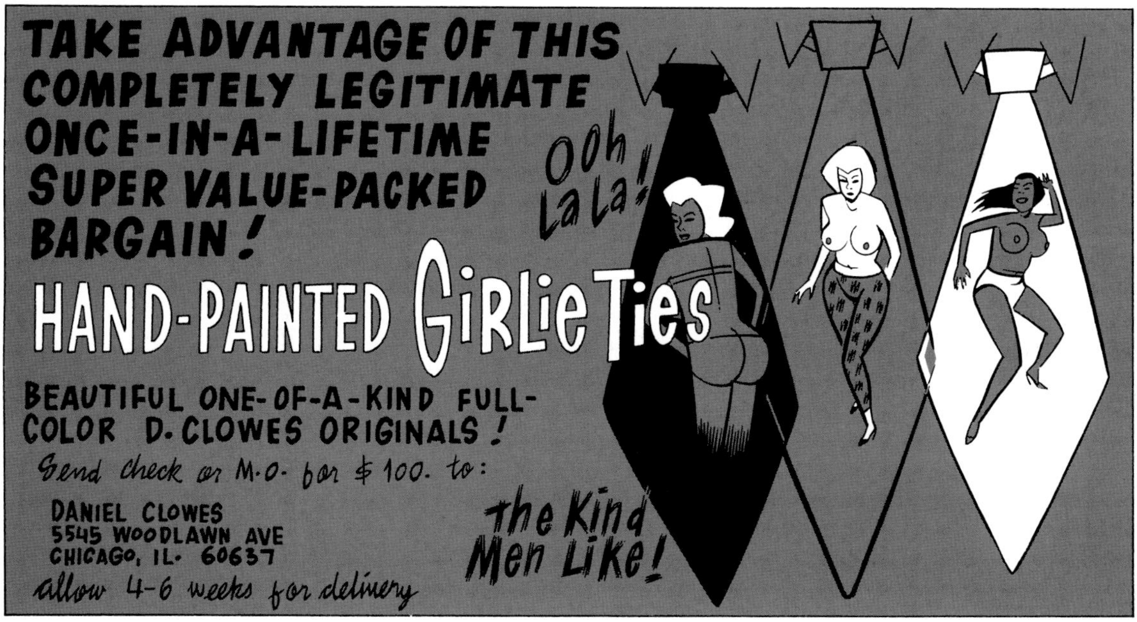
TAKE ADVANTAGE OF THIS COMPLETELY LEGITIMATE ONCE-IN-A-LIFETIME SUPER VALUE-PACKED BARGAIN!
Ooh La La!
HAND-PAINTED GirLie Ties
BEAUTIFUL ONE-OF-A-KIND FULL-COLOR D. CLOWES ORIGINALS!
Send check or M.O. for $100. to:
DANIEL CLOWES
5545 WOODLAWN AVE
CHICAGO, IL. 60637
allow 4-6 weeks for delivery
the Kind Men Like!

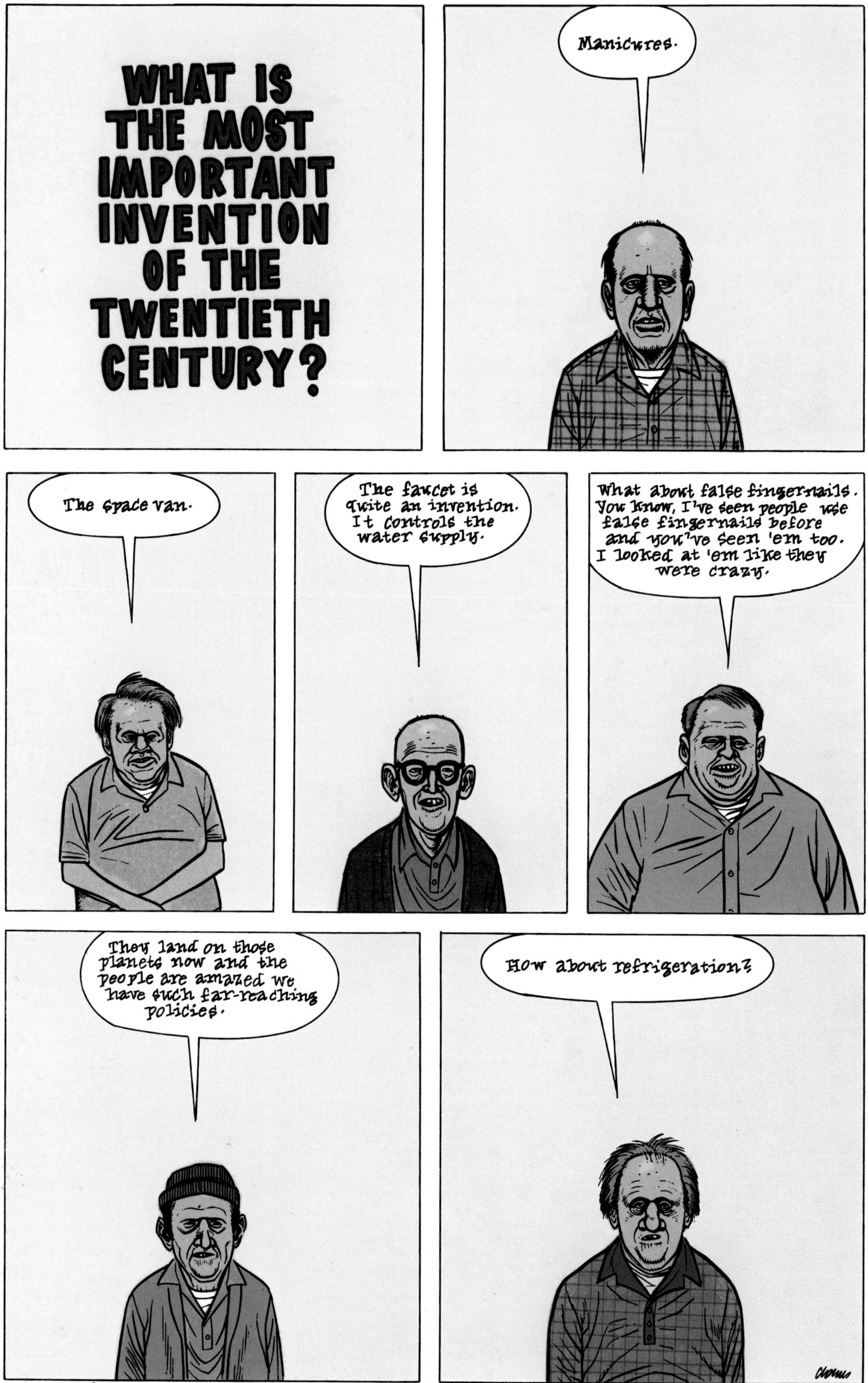
WHAT IS THE MOST IMPORTANT INVENTION OF THE TWENTIETH CENTURY?
Manicures.
The space van.
The faucet is quite an invention. It controls the water supply.
What about false fingernails. You know, I've seen people use false fingernails before and you've seen 'em too. I looked at 'em like they were crazy.
They land on those planets now and the people are amazed we have such far-reaching policies.
How about refrigeration?

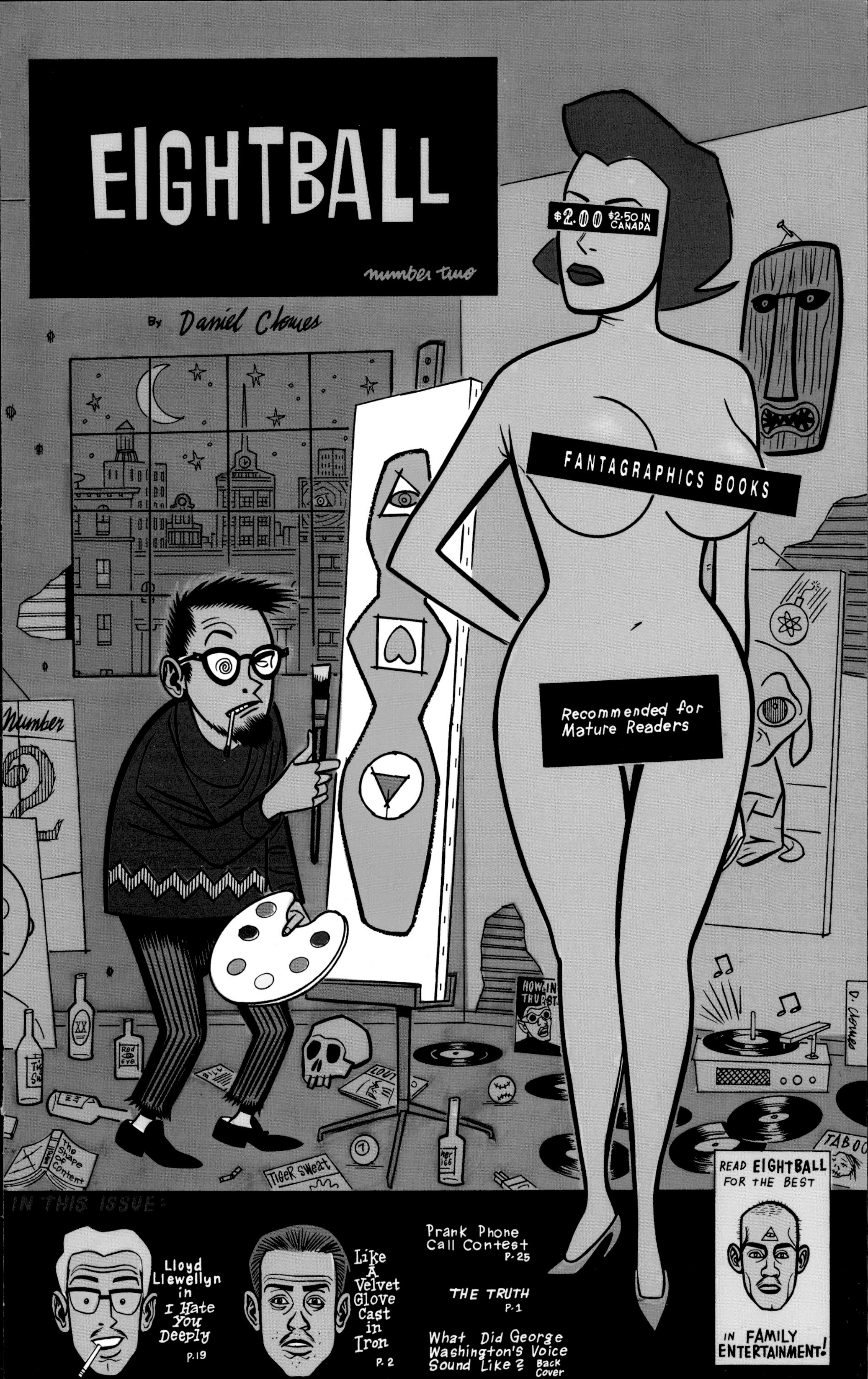
EIGHTBALL
number two
By Daniel Clowes
$2.00 $2.50 IN CANADA
FANTAGRAPHICS BOOKS
Recommended for Mature Readers
Number
The Shape of Content
TIGER SWEAT
HOWLIN THURST.
D. Clowes
TABOO
READ EIGHTBALL FOR THE BEST IN FAMILY ENTERTAINMENT!
IN THIS ISSUE:
Lloyd Llewellyn in I Hate You Deeply P.19
Like A Velvet Glove Cast in Iron P. 2
Prank Phone Call Contest P. 25
THE TRUTH P. 1
What Did George Washington's Voice Sound Like? Back Cover

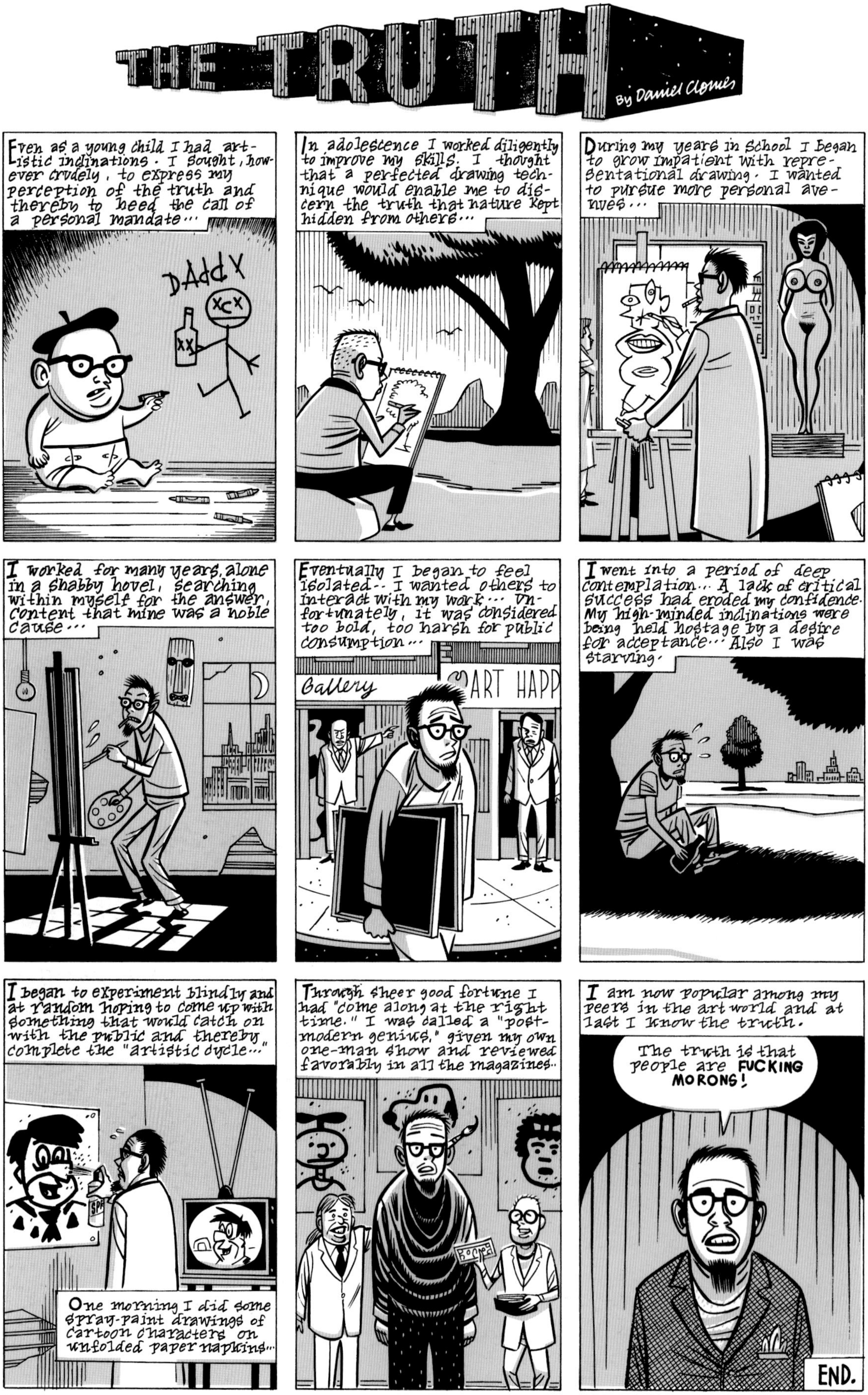
THE TRUTH
By Daniel Clowes
Even as a young child I had artistic inclinations. I sought, however crudely, to express my perception of the truth and thereby to heed the call of a personal mandate...
DADDY
XX
In adolescence I worked diligently to improve my skills. I thought that a perfected drawing technique would enable me to discern the truth that nature kept hidden from others...
During my years in school I began to grow impatient with representational drawing. I wanted to pursue more personal avenues...
I worked for many years, alone in a shabby hovel, searching within myself for the answer, content that mine was a noble cause...
Eventually I began to feel isolated -- I wanted others to interact with my work... Unfortunately, it was considered too bold, too harsh for public consumption...
Gallery
ART HAPP
I went into a period of deep contemplation... A lack of critical success had eroded my confidence. My high-minded inclinations were being held hostage by a desire for acceptance... Also I was starving.
I began to experiment blindly and at random hoping to come up with something that would catch on with the public and thereby complete the "artistic cycle..."
One morning I did some spray-paint drawings of cartoon characters on unfolded paper napkins...
Through sheer good fortune I had "come along at the right time." I was called a "post-modern genius," given my own one-man show and reviewed favorably in all the magazines...
I am now popular among my peers in the art world and at last I know the truth.
The truth is that people are FUCKING MORONS!
END.

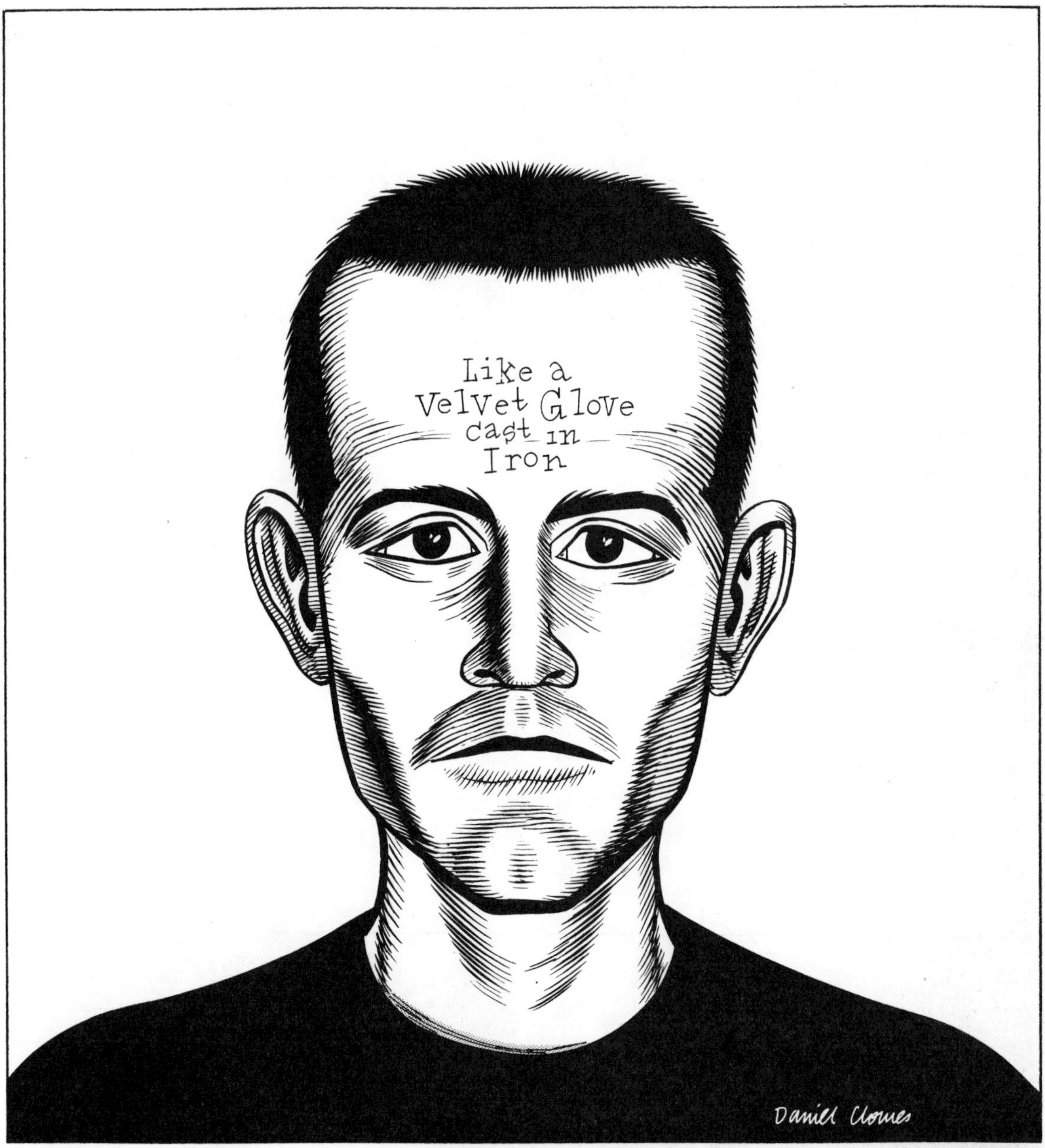
Like a
Velvet Glove
cast in
Iron
Daniel Clowes

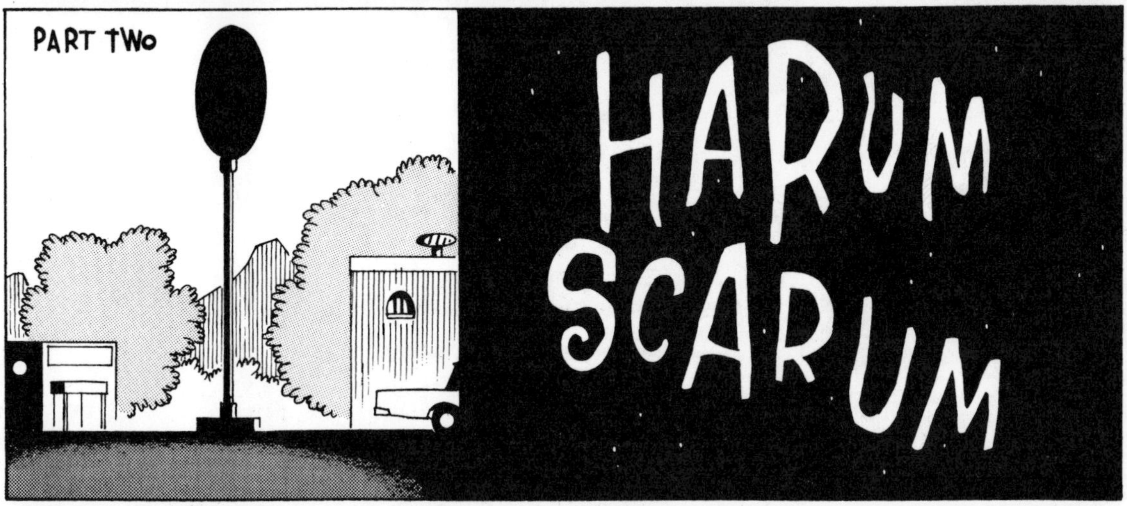
PART TWO
HARUM
SCARUM

Eightball #2, February, 1990. *Eightball* is published thrice yearly by Fantagraphics Books, Inc., and is copyright © 1989 Fantagraphics Books, Inc. All characters, stories, and art © 1989 Daniel Clowes. No part of this magazine may be reproduced without written permission from Fantagraphics Books or Daniel Clowes. No similarity between the any of the names, characters, persons, and institutions in *Eightball* and those of any living or dead persons is intended (except for satirical intent), and any such similarity that may exist is purely coincidental. Letters to *Eightball* become the property of the magazine and are assumed intended for publication in whole or in part, and may therefore be used for those purposes. First printing: November, 1990. This issue, as well as the previous issue, available from the publisher for $2.00 + 50¢ postage and handling: Fantagraphics Books, 7563 Lake City Way NE, Seattle WA 98115. **Send for our free catalogue**!

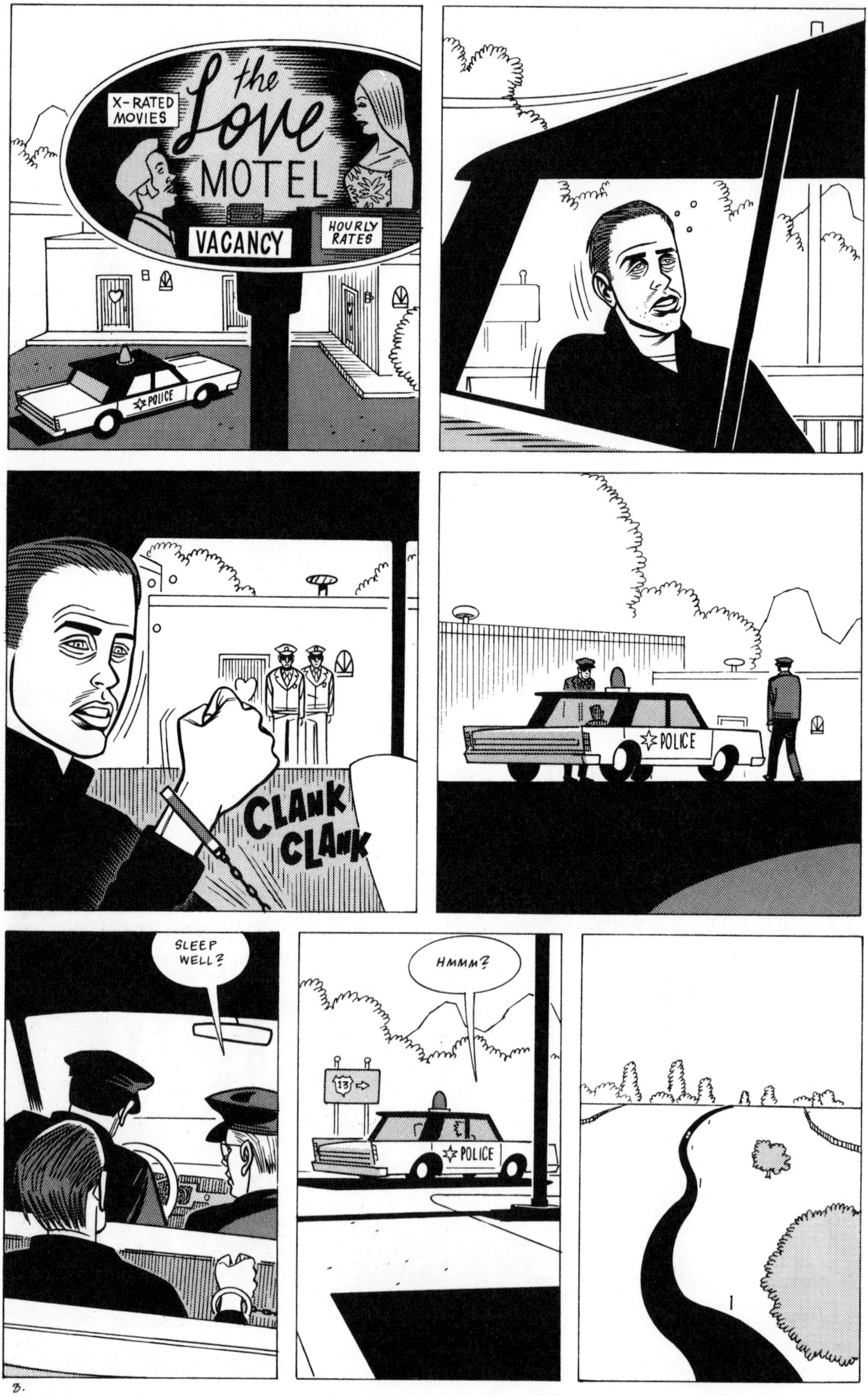
X-RATED MOVIES
the Love MOTEL
VACANCY
HOURLY RATES
POLICE
CLANK
CLANK
POLICE
SLEEP WELL?
HMMM?
13
POLICE

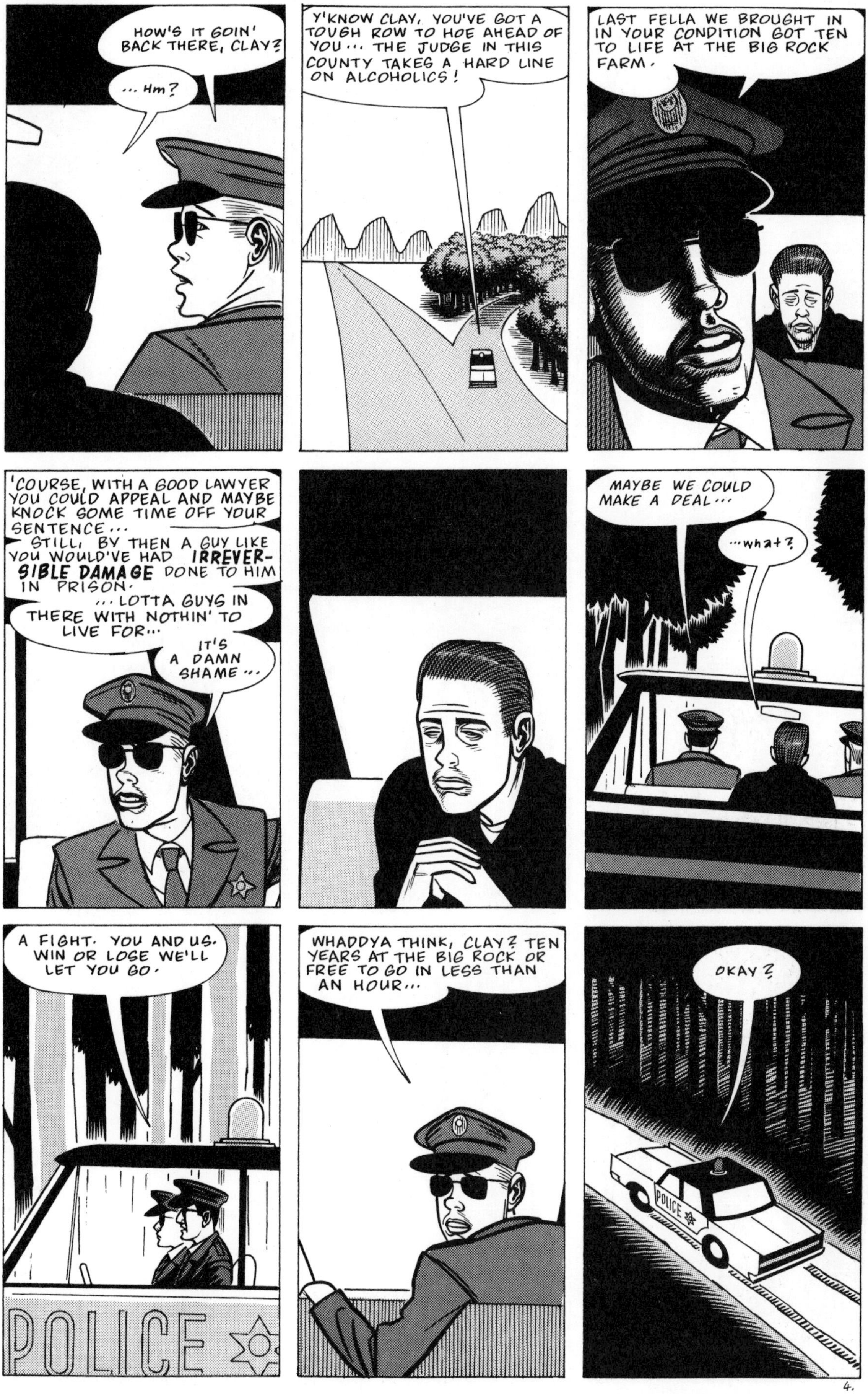
HOW'S IT GOIN' BACK THERE, CLAY?
... Hm?
Y'KNOW CLAY, YOU'VE GOT A TOUGH ROW TO HOE AHEAD OF YOU... THE JUDGE IN THIS COUNTY TAKES A HARD LINE ON ALCOHOLICS!
LAST FELLA WE BROUGHT IN IN YOUR CONDITION GOT TEN TO LIFE AT THE BIG ROCK FARM.
'COURSE, WITH A GOOD LAWYER YOU COULD APPEAL AND MAYBE KNOCK SOME TIME OFF YOUR SENTENCE...
STILL, BY THEN A GUY LIKE YOU WOULD'VE HAD IRREVERSIBLE DAMAGE DONE TO HIM IN PRISON.
... LOTTA GUYS IN THERE WITH NOTHIN' TO LIVE FOR...
IT'S A DAMN SHAME...
MAYBE WE COULD MAKE A DEAL...
...what?
A FIGHT. YOU AND US. WIN OR LOSE WE'LL LET YOU GO.
POLICE
WHADDYA THINK, CLAY? TEN YEARS AT THE BIG ROCK OR FREE TO GO IN LESS THAN AN HOUR...
OKAY?
POLICE

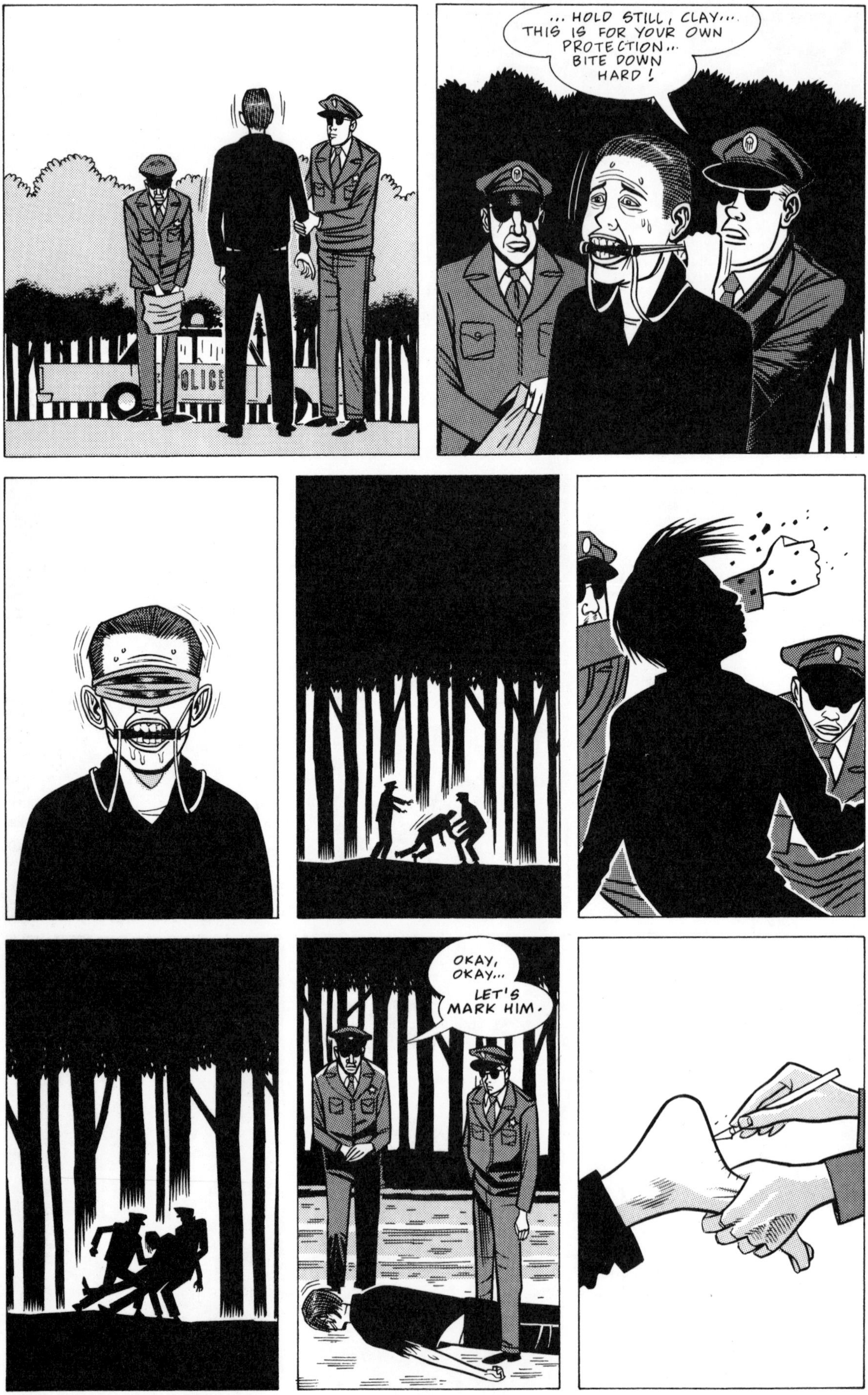
... HOLD STILL, CLAY...
THIS IS FOR YOUR OWN
PROTECTION...
BITE DOWN
HARD!
POLICE
OKAY,
OKAY...
LET'S
MARK HIM.

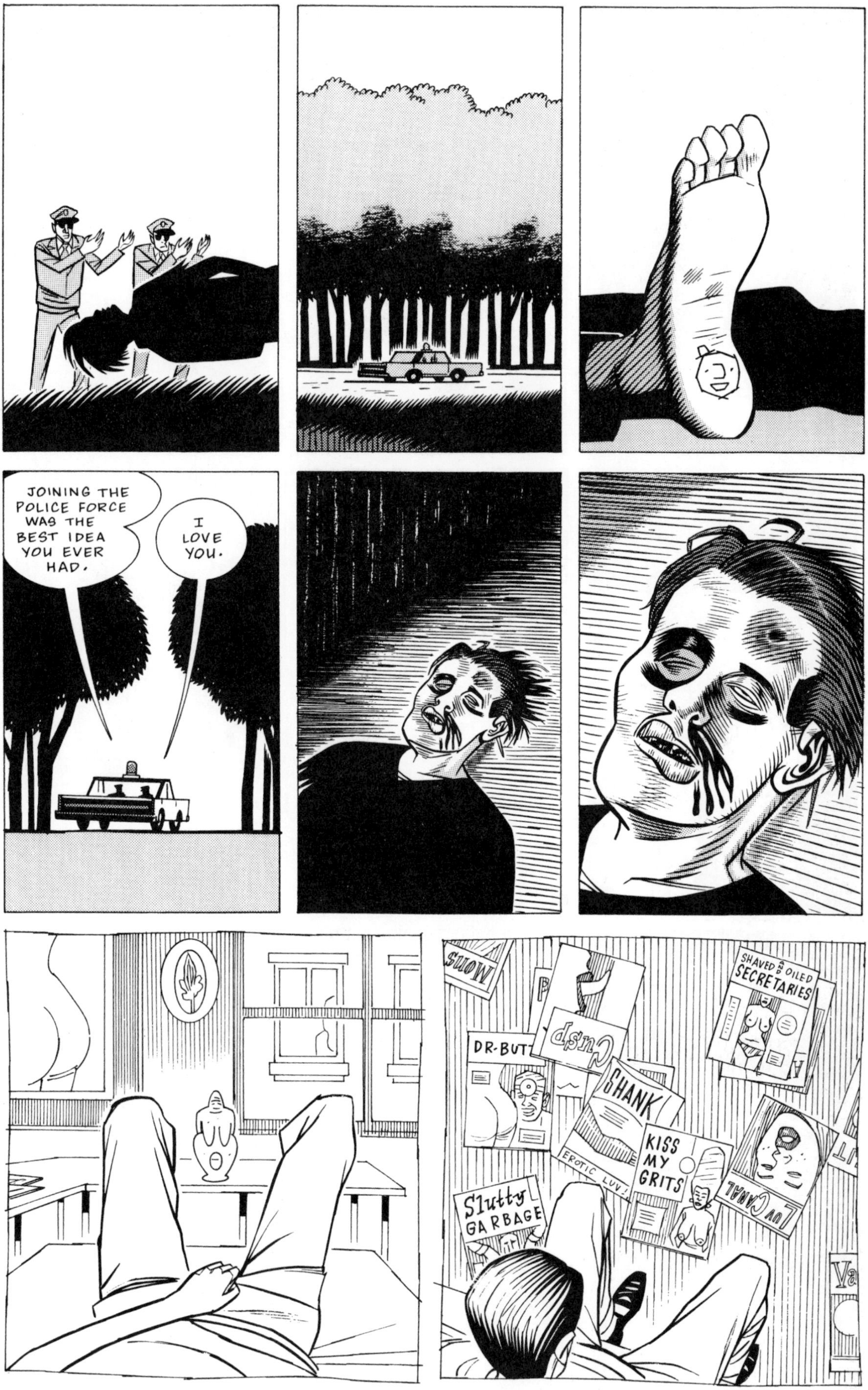
JOINING THE POLICE FORCE WAS THE BEST IDEA YOU EVER HAD.
I LOVE YOU.
SHAVED AND OILED SECRETARIES
DR-BUTT
SHANK
KISS MY GRITS
EROTIC LUV!
Slutty GARBAGE
LUV CANAL

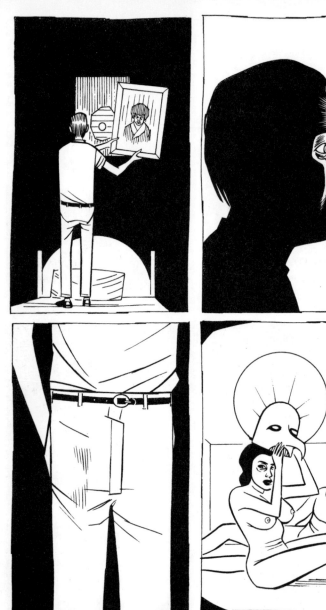

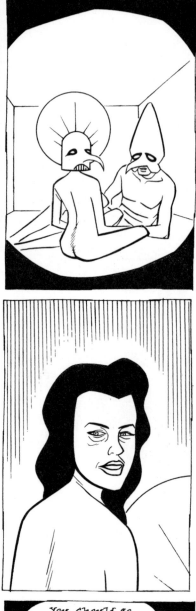

What do I do now? I-I... ohh God...

You should go outside the room... There's nothing out there. It's very interesting!

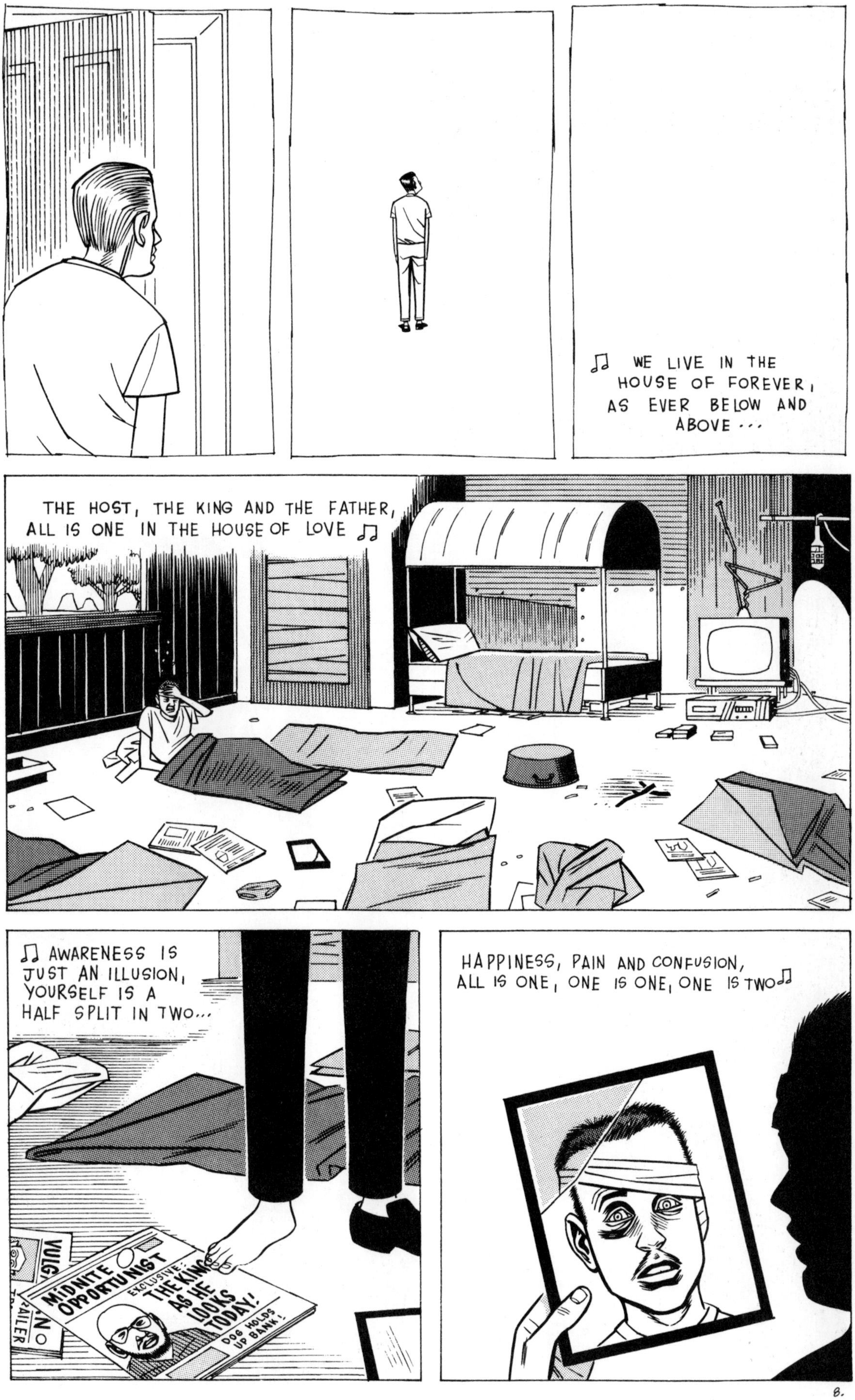
♫ WE LIVE IN THE HOUSE OF FOREVER, AS EVER BELOW AND ABOVE...
THE HOST, THE KING AND THE FATHER, ALL IS ONE IN THE HOUSE OF LOVE ♫
♫ AWARENESS IS JUST AN ILLUSION, YOURSELF IS A HALF SPLIT IN TWO...
MIDNITE OPPORTUNIST
EXCLUSIVE: THE KING AS HE LOOKS TODAY!
DOG HOLDS UP BANK!
HAPPINESS, PAIN AND CONFUSION, ALL IS ONE, ONE IS ONE, ONE IS TWO ♫

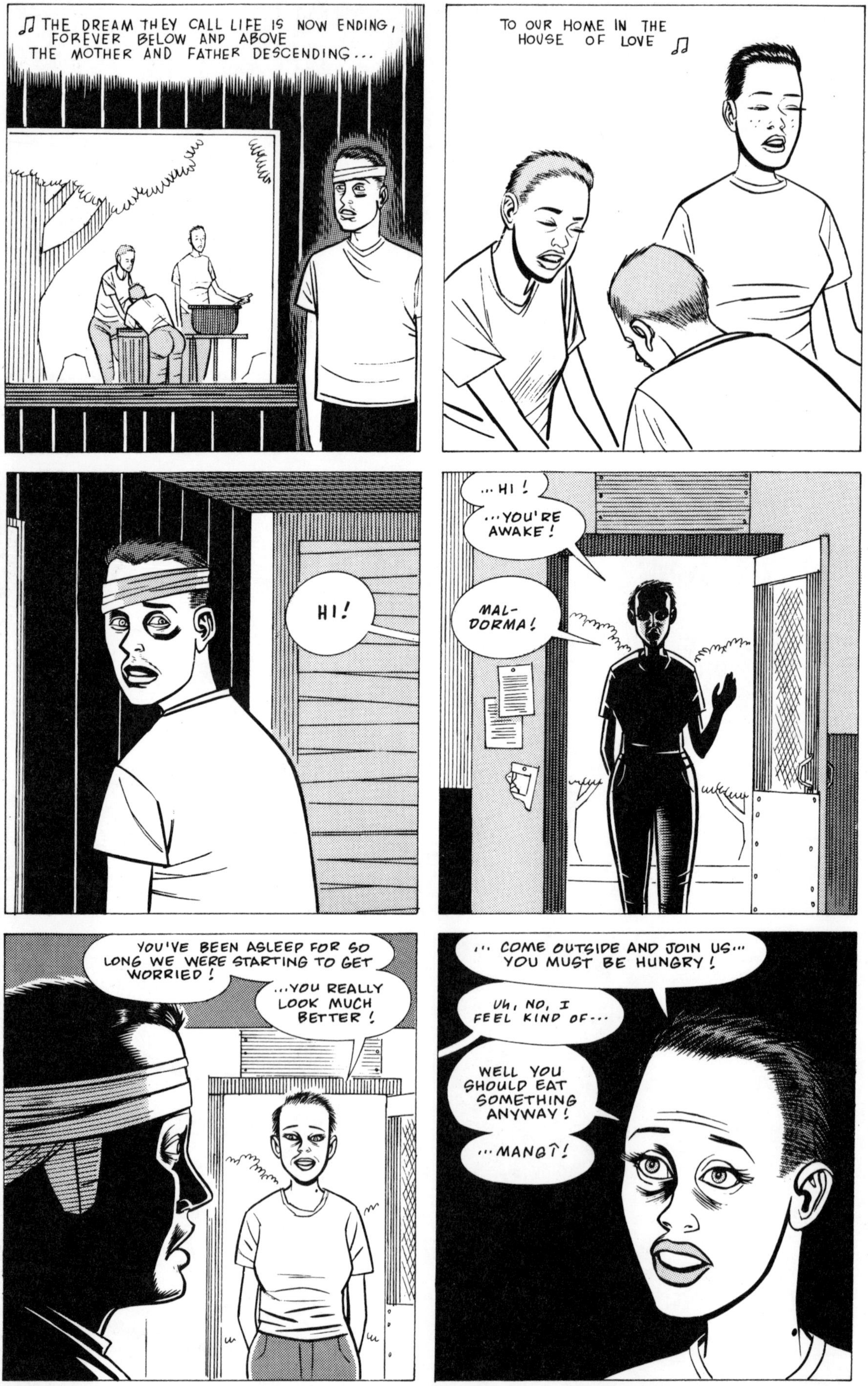

♫ THE DREAM THEY CALL LIFE IS NOW ENDING, FOREVER BELOW AND ABOVE THE MOTHER AND FATHER DESCENDING...
TO OUR HOME IN THE HOUSE OF LOVE ♫
HI!
...HI!
...YOU'RE AWAKE!
MAL-DORMA!
YOU'VE BEEN ASLEEP FOR SO LONG WE WERE STARTING TO GET WORRIED!
...YOU REALLY LOOK MUCH BETTER!
... COME OUTSIDE AND JOIN US... YOU MUST BE HUNGRY!
UH, NO, I FEEL KIND OF...
WELL YOU SHOULD EAT SOMETHING ANYWAY!
...MANGT!

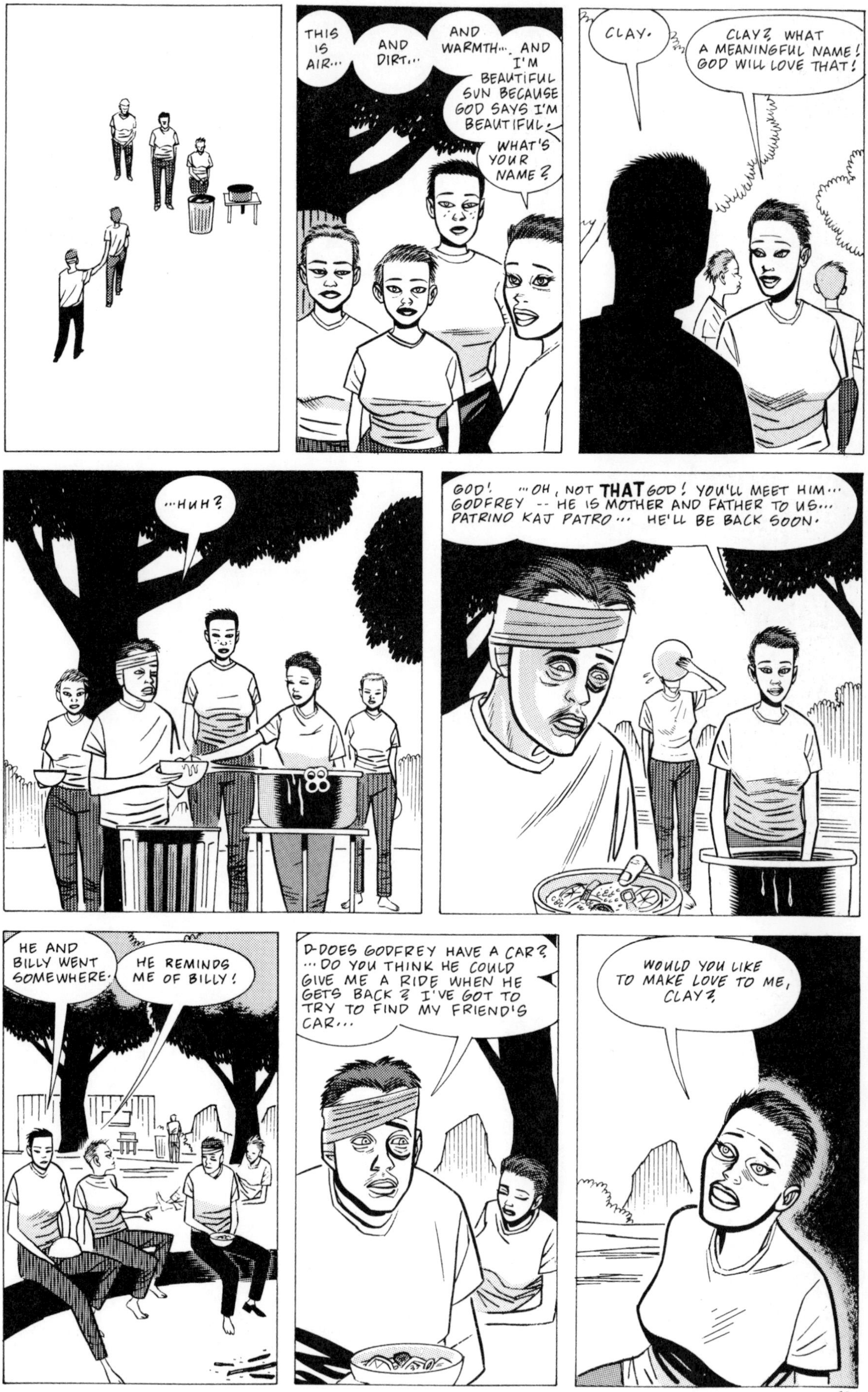

THIS IS AIR...
AND DIRT...
AND WARMTH... AND I'M BEAUTIFUL SUN BECAUSE GOD SAYS I'M BEAUTIFUL.
WHAT'S YOUR NAME?
CLAY.
CLAY? WHAT A MEANINGFUL NAME! GOD WILL LOVE THAT!
...HUH?
GOD! ...OH, NOT THAT GOD! YOU'LL MEET HIM... GODFREY -- HE IS MOTHER AND FATHER TO US... PATRINO KAJ PATRO... HE'LL BE BACK SOON.
HE AND BILLY WENT SOMEWHERE.
HE REMINDS ME OF BILLY!
D-DOES GODFREY HAVE A CAR? ...DO YOU THINK HE COULD GIVE ME A RIDE WHEN HE GETS BACK? I'VE GOT TO TRY TO FIND MY FRIEND'S CAR...
WOULD YOU LIKE TO MAKE LOVE TO ME, CLAY?

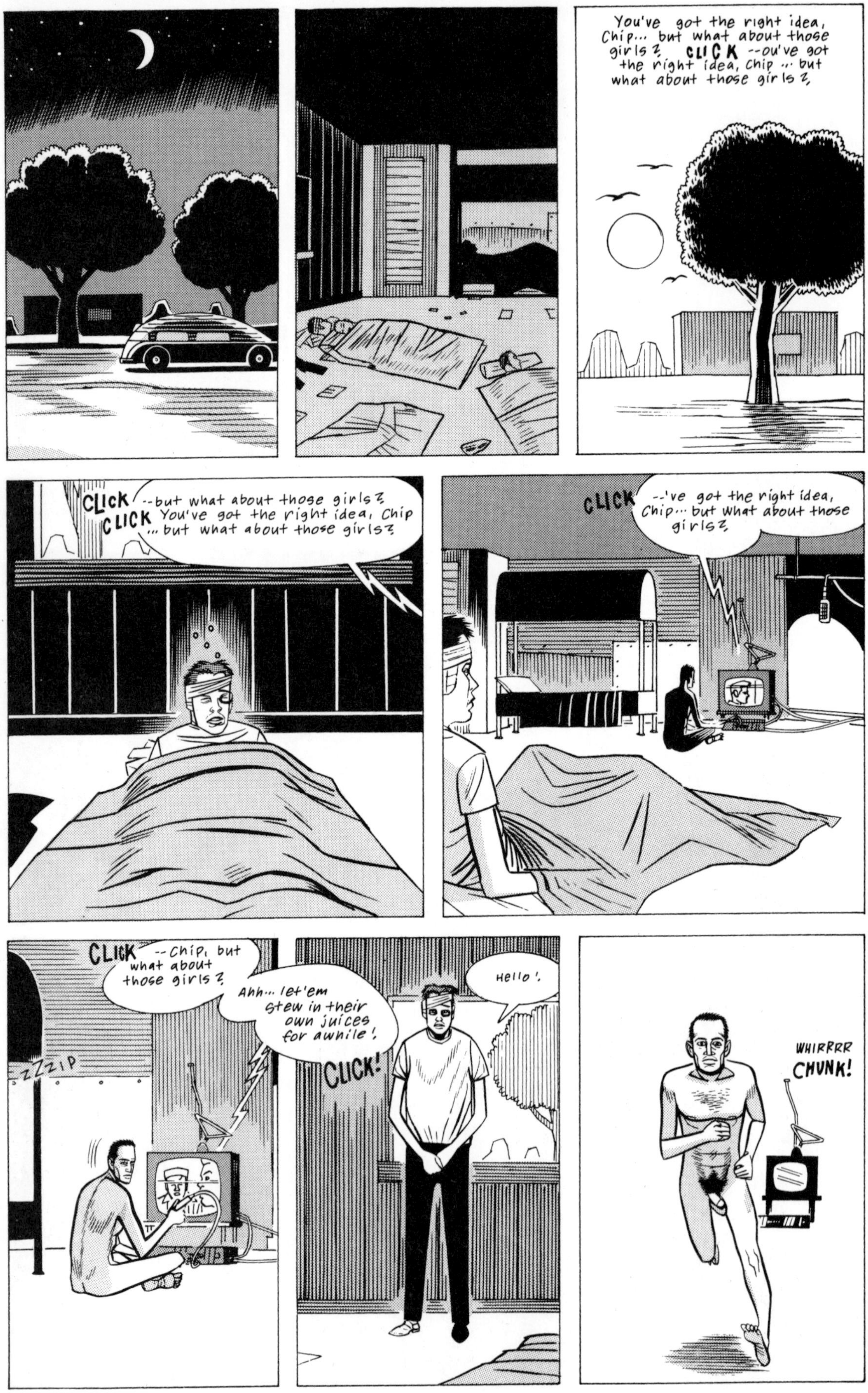

You've got the right idea, Chip... but what about those girls?,
CLICK
--ou've got the right idea, Chip... but what about those girls?,
CLICK
CLICK
--but what about those girls? You've got the right idea, Chip ... but what about those girls?
CLICK
--'ve got the right idea, Chip... but what about those girls?,
CLICK
--Chip, but what about those girls?
Ahh... let'em stew in their own juices for awhile!
ZZZIP
Hello!
CLICK!
WHIRRRR
CHUNK!

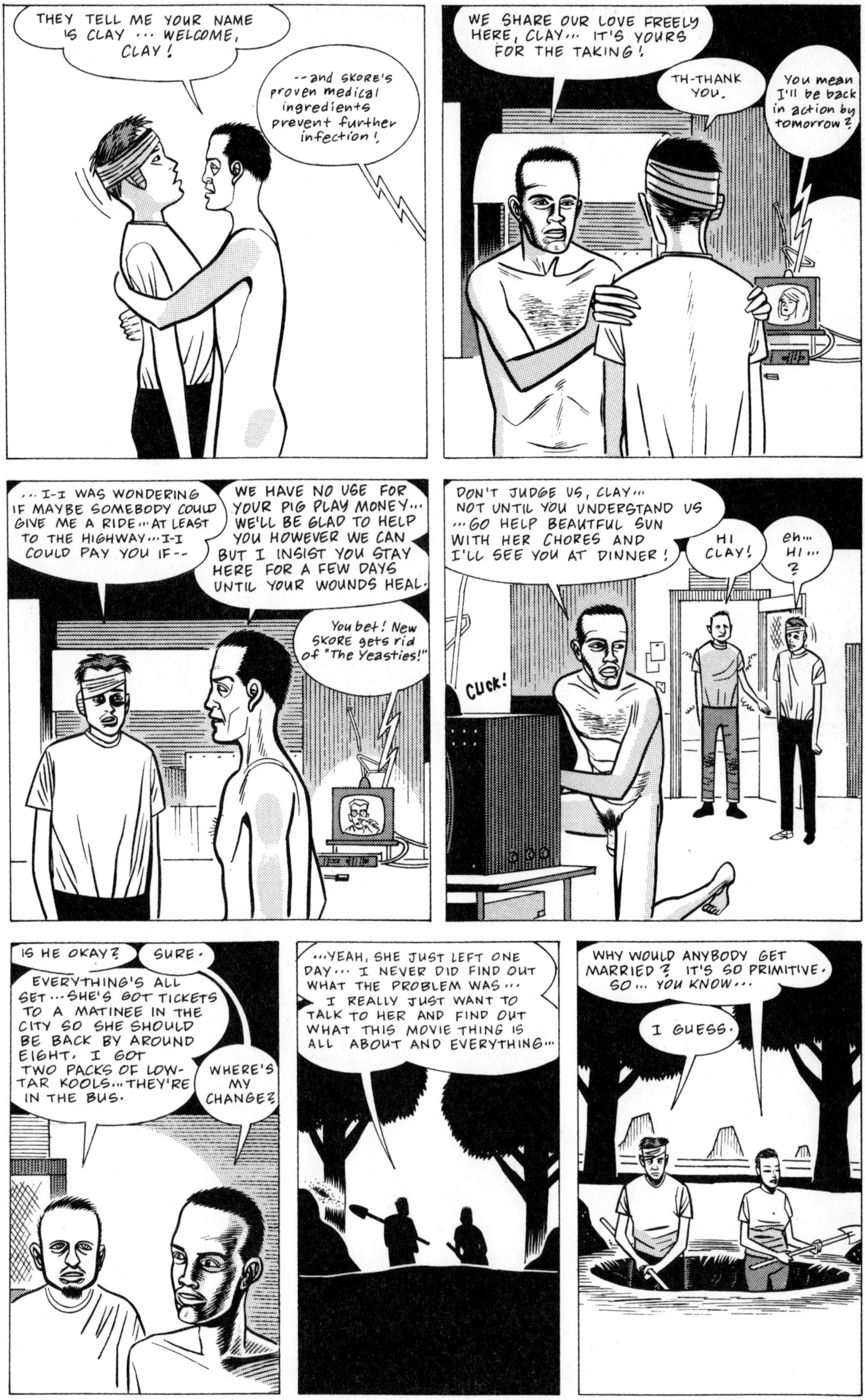
THEY TELL ME YOUR NAME IS CLAY ··· WELCOME, CLAY!
--and SKORE's proven medical ingredients prevent further infection!
WE SHARE OUR LOVE FREELY HERE, CLAY··· IT'S YOURS FOR THE TAKING!
TH-THANK YOU.
You mean I'll be back in action by tomorrow?
···I-I WAS WONDERING IF MAYBE SOMEBODY COULD GIVE ME A RIDE···AT LEAST TO THE HIGHWAY···I-I COULD PAY YOU IF--
WE HAVE NO USE FOR YOUR PIG PLAY MONEY··· WE'LL BE GLAD TO HELP YOU HOWEVER WE CAN BUT I INSIST YOU STAY HERE FOR A FEW DAYS UNTIL YOUR WOUNDS HEAL.
You bet! New SKORE gets rid of "The Yeasties!"
DON'T JUDGE US, CLAY··· NOT UNTIL YOU UNDERSTAND US ···GO HELP BEAUTIFUL SUN WITH HER CHORES AND I'LL SEE YOU AT DINNER!
HI CLAY!
eh··· HI··· ?
CLICK!
IS HE OKAY?
SURE.
EVERYTHING'S ALL SET···SHE'S GOT TICKETS TO A MATINEE IN THE CITY SO SHE SHOULD BE BACK BY AROUND EIGHT. I GOT TWO PACKS OF LOW-TAR KOOLS···THEY'RE IN THE BUS.
WHERE'S MY CHANGE?
···YEAH, SHE JUST LEFT ONE DAY··· I NEVER DID FIND OUT WHAT THE PROBLEM WAS··· I REALLY JUST WANT TO TALK TO HER AND FIND OUT WHAT THIS MOVIE THING IS ALL ABOUT AND EVERYTHING···
WHY WOULD ANYBODY GET MARRIED? IT'S SO PRIMITIVE. SO··· YOU KNOW···
I GUESS.

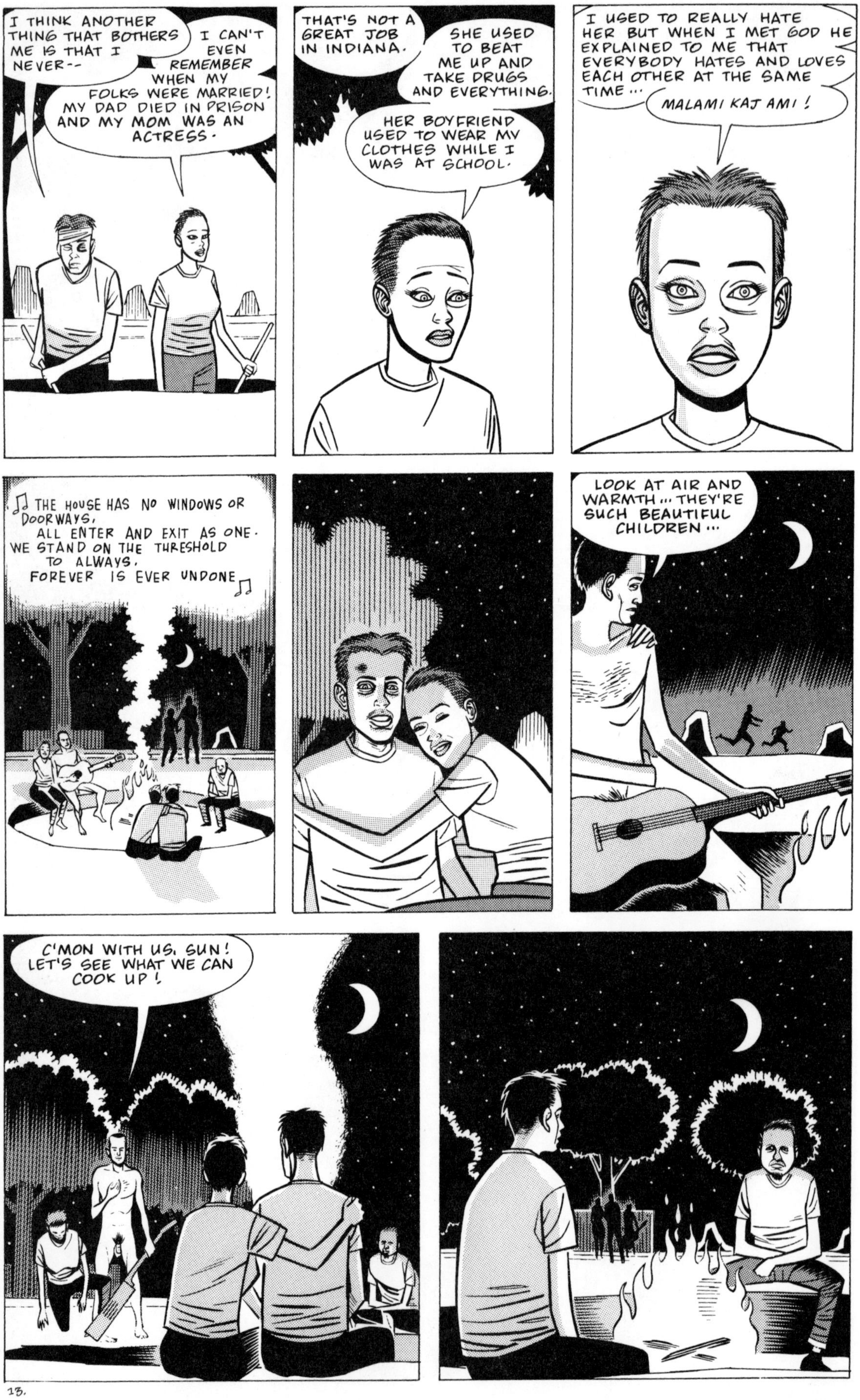

I THINK ANOTHER THING THAT BOTHERS ME IS THAT I NEVER--
I CAN'T EVEN REMEMBER WHEN MY FOLKS WERE MARRIED! MY DAD DIED IN PRISON AND MY MOM WAS AN ACTRESS.
THAT'S NOT A GREAT JOB IN INDIANA.
SHE USED TO BEAT ME UP AND TAKE DRUGS AND EVERYTHING.
HER BOYFRIEND USED TO WEAR MY CLOTHES WHILE I WAS AT SCHOOL.
I USED TO REALLY HATE HER BUT WHEN I MET GOD HE EXPLAINED TO ME THAT EVERYBODY HATES AND LOVES EACH OTHER AT THE SAME TIME...
MALAMI KAJ AMI!
♫ THE HOUSE HAS NO WINDOWS OR DOORWAYS, ALL ENTER AND EXIT AS ONE. WE STAND ON THE THRESHOLD TO ALWAYS, FOREVER IS EVER UNDONE ♫
LOOK AT AIR AND WARMTH... THEY'RE SUCH BEAUTIFUL CHILDREN...
C'MON WITH US, SUN! LET'S SEE WHAT WE CAN COOK UP!

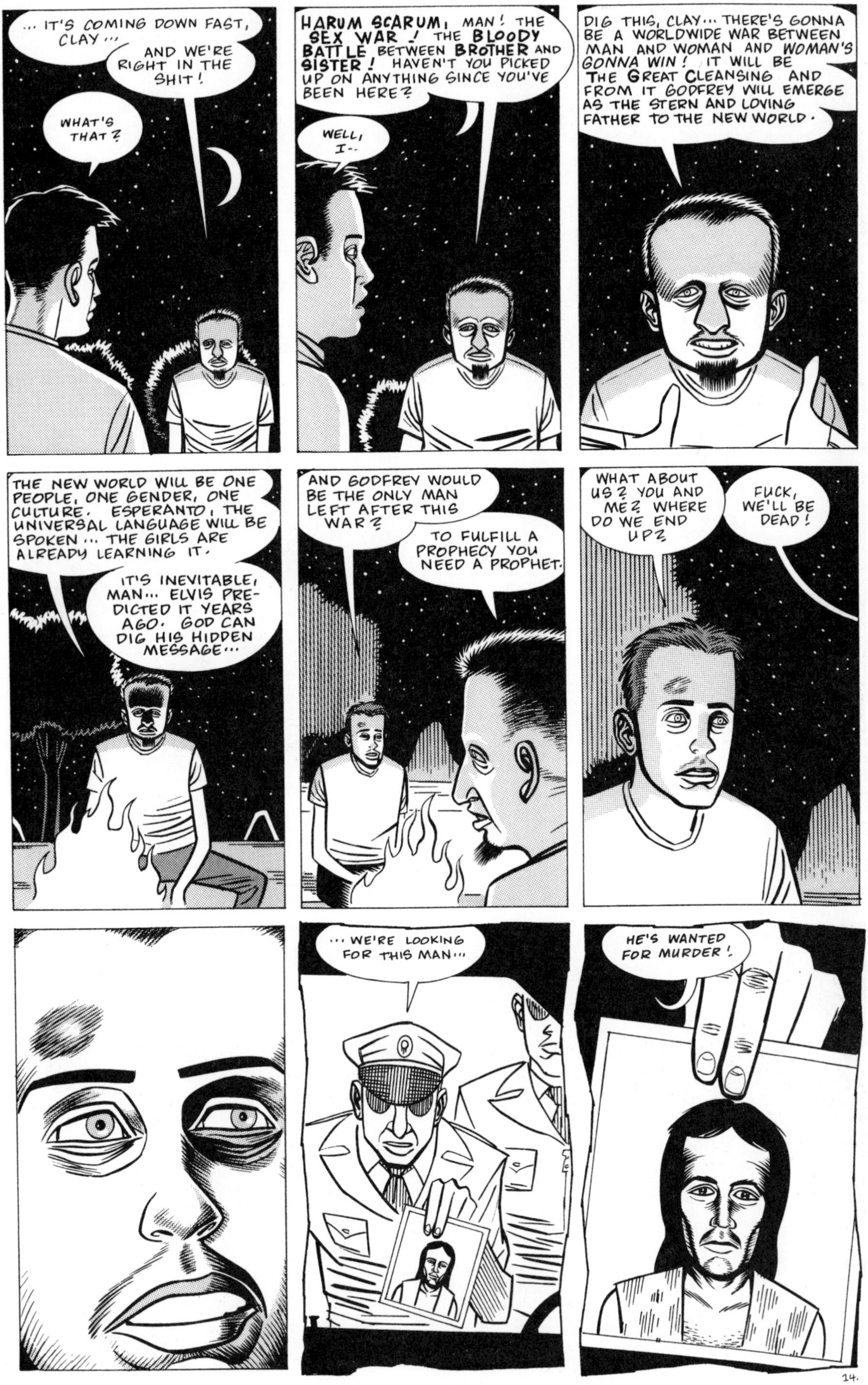
... IT'S COMING DOWN FAST, CLAY ...
AND WE'RE RIGHT IN THE SHIT!
WHAT'S THAT?
HARUM SCARUM, MAN! THE SEX WAR! THE BLOODY BATTLE BETWEEN BROTHER AND SISTER! HAVEN'T YOU PICKED UP ON ANYTHING SINCE YOU'VE BEEN HERE?
WELL, I--
DIG THIS, CLAY... THERE'S GONNA BE A WORLDWIDE WAR BETWEEN MAN AND WOMAN AND WOMAN'S GONNA WIN! IT WILL BE THE GREAT CLEANSING AND FROM IT GODFREY WILL EMERGE AS THE STERN AND LOVING FATHER TO THE NEW WORLD.
THE NEW WORLD WILL BE ONE PEOPLE, ONE GENDER, ONE CULTURE. ESPERANTO, THE UNIVERSAL LANGUAGE WILL BE SPOKEN ... THE GIRLS ARE ALREADY LEARNING IT.
IT'S INEVITABLE, MAN... ELVIS PREDICTED IT YEARS AGO. GOD CAN DIG HIS HIDDEN MESSAGE...
AND GODFREY WOULD BE THE ONLY MAN LEFT AFTER THIS WAR?
TO FULFILL A PROPHECY YOU NEED A PROPHET.
WHAT ABOUT US? YOU AND ME? WHERE DO WE END UP?
FUCK, WE'LL BE DEAD!
... WE'RE LOOKING FOR THIS MAN...
HE'S WANTED FOR MURDER!

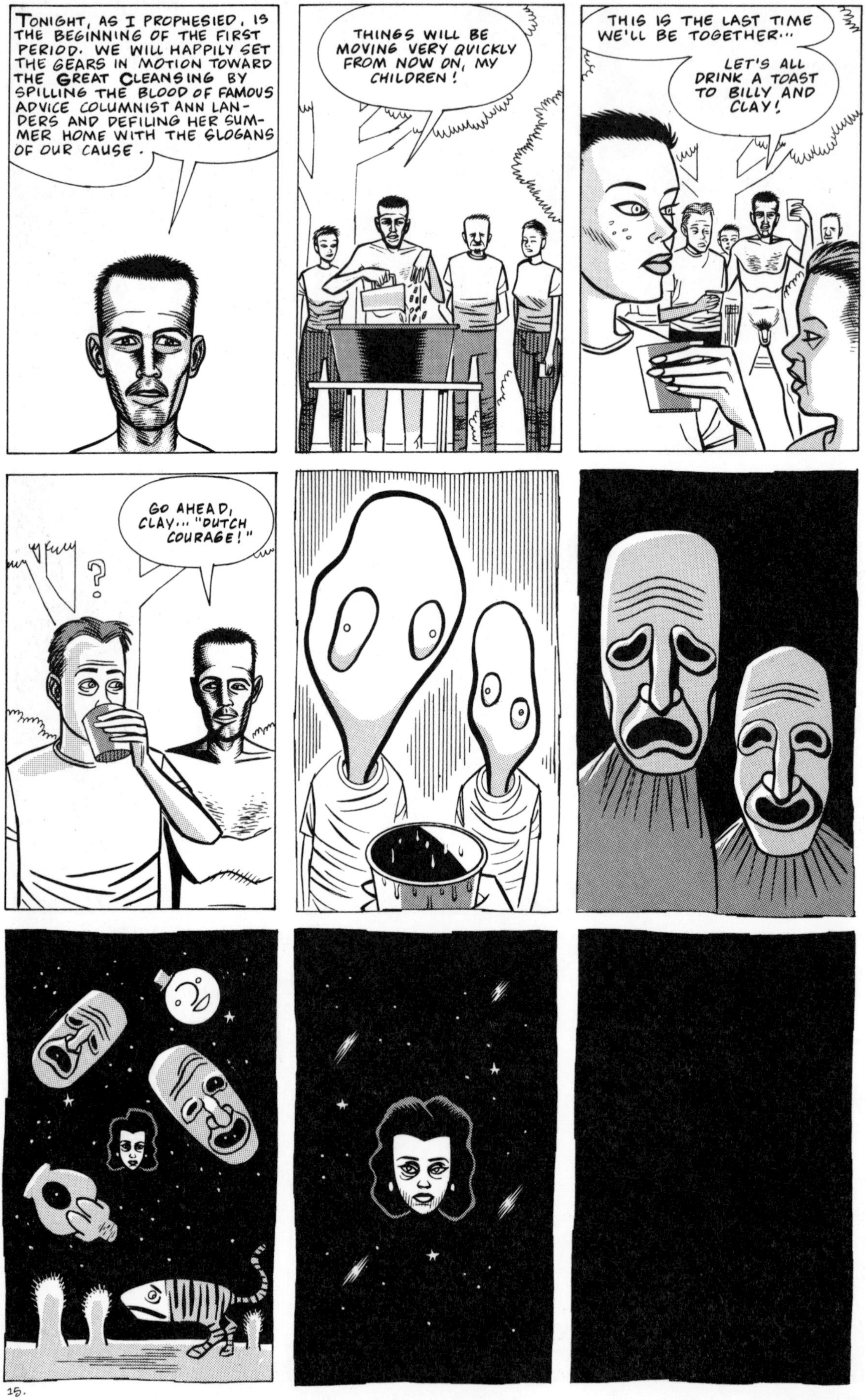
TONIGHT, AS I PROPHESIED, IS THE BEGINNING OF THE FIRST PERIOD. WE WILL HAPPILY SET THE GEARS IN MOTION TOWARD THE GREAT CLEANSING BY SPILLING THE BLOOD OF FAMOUS ADVICE COLUMNIST ANN LANDERS AND DEFILING HER SUMMER HOME WITH THE SLOGANS OF OUR CAUSE.
THINGS WILL BE MOVING VERY QUICKLY FROM NOW ON, MY CHILDREN!
THIS IS THE LAST TIME WE'LL BE TOGETHER...
LET'S ALL DRINK A TOAST TO BILLY AND CLAY!
?
GO AHEAD, CLAY... "DUTCH COURAGE!"

IT'S ABOUT TIME YOU WOKE UP, MAN!

THE BITCH ISN'T HOME YET.

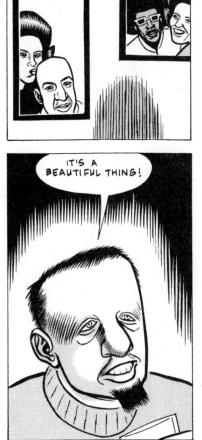

CLAY, AREN'T WE JUST ABOUT THE TWO LUCKIEST MOTHERFUCKERS IN THE WHOLE WORLD? I MEAN, MOST PEOPLE JUST DIE AND THAT'S IT... WHO CARES? BUT YOU AND ME, MAN...

HOW MANY PEOPLE ARE CALLED UPON TO LIVE AND KILL AND DIE FOR SOMETHING THEY REALLY BELIEVE IN?

IT'S A BEAUTIFUL THING!

SHIT! I LEFT MY CIGARETTES IN THE VAN!

... I-I'LL GET 'EM FOR YOU...

REALLY? THANKS A LOT, MAN!

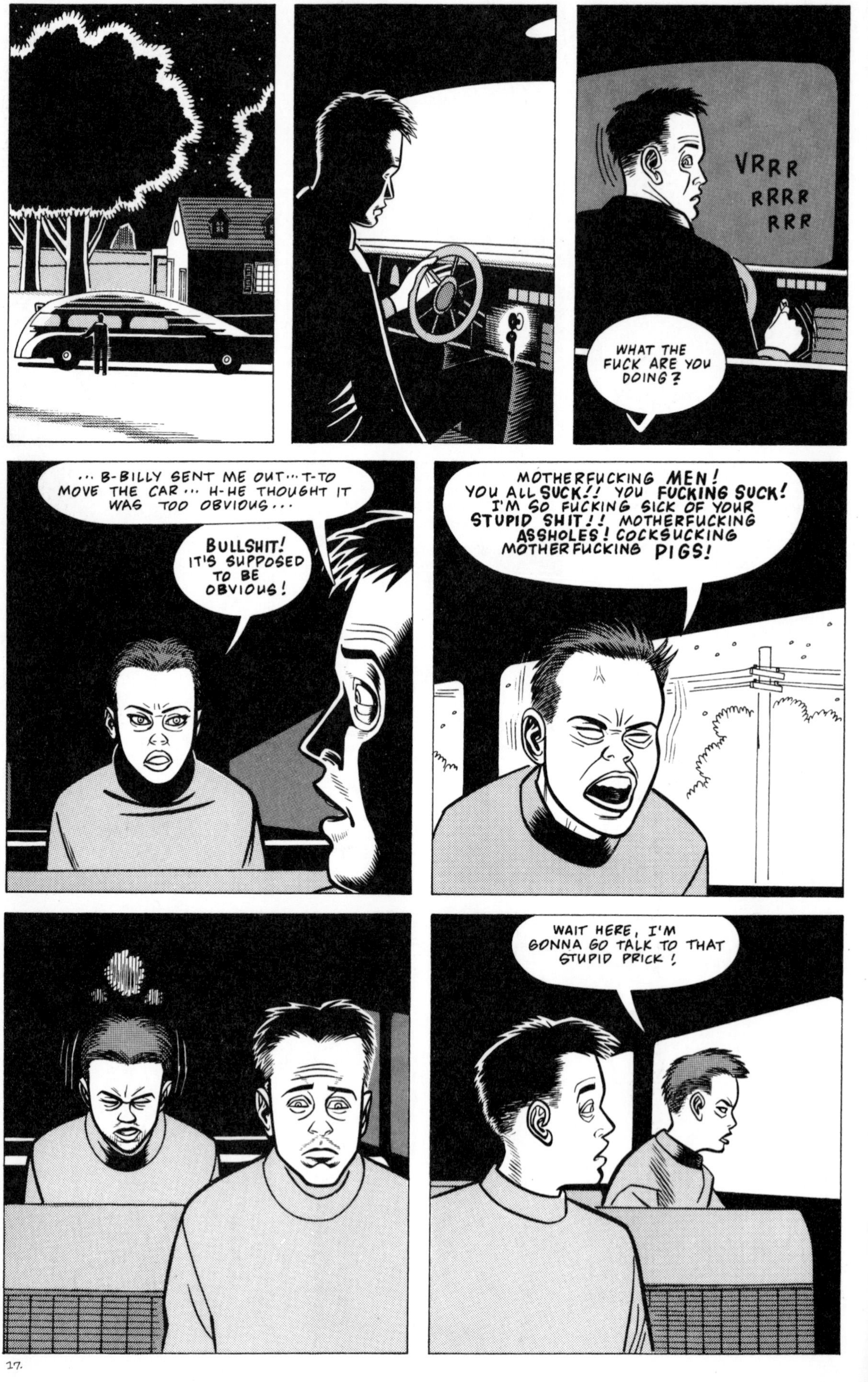
VRRR RRRR RRR
WHAT THE FUCK ARE YOU DOING?
... B-BILLY SENT ME OUT... T-TO MOVE THE CAR... H-HE THOUGHT IT WAS TOO OBVIOUS...
BULLSHIT! IT'S SUPPOSED TO BE OBVIOUS!
MOTHERFUCKING MEN! YOU ALL SUCK!! YOU FUCKING SUCK! I'M SO FUCKING SICK OF YOUR STUPID SHIT!! MOTHERFUCKING ASSHOLES! COCKSUCKING MOTHERFUCKING PIGS!
WAIT HERE, I'M GONNA GO TALK TO THAT STUPID PRICK!

The following night...

GRIMM'S Diner

READY TO ORDER?

e Octagon

WOMEN STO
CAPITOL
2 DEAD, 51 INJURED

PRESIDENT, FIRST
TO DIVORCE

R DELUXE 3.95
R PLATTER 3.50
CKLE LOAF . . 4.75

MERINGUE 1.95
KEY LIME . . . 1.95
HITE CAKE 2.60

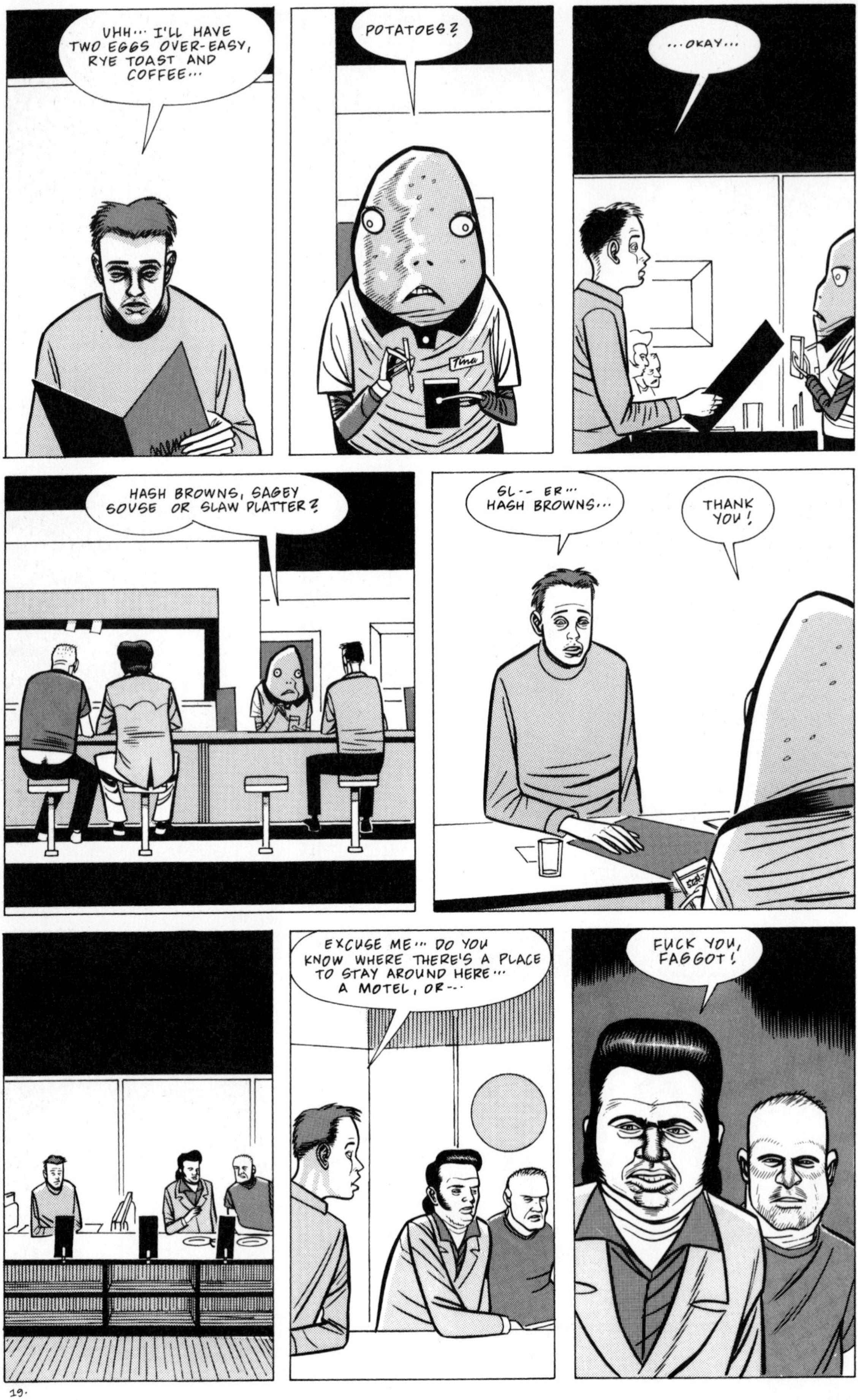
UHH... I'LL HAVE TWO EGGS OVER-EASY, RYE TOAST AND COFFEE...
POTATOES?
...OKAY...
HASH BROWNS, SAGEY SOUSE OR SLAW PLATTER?
SL-- ER... HASH BROWNS...
THANK YOU!
EXCUSE ME... DO YOU KNOW WHERE THERE'S A PLACE TO STAY AROUND HERE... A MOTEL, OR--
FUCK YOU, FAGGOT!

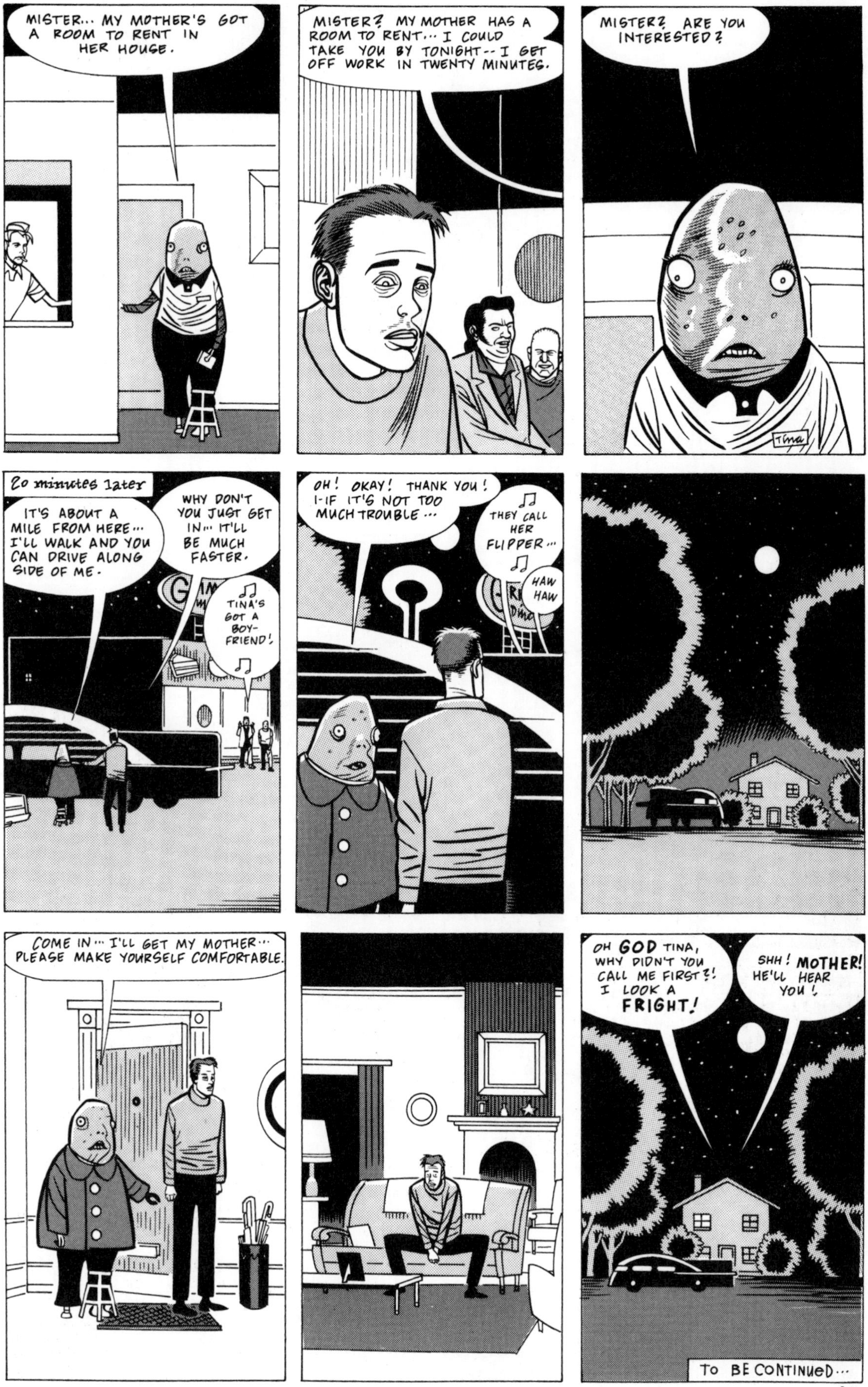
MISTER... MY MOTHER'S GOT A ROOM TO RENT IN HER HOUSE.
MISTER? MY MOTHER HAS A ROOM TO RENT... I COULD TAKE YOU BY TONIGHT -- I GET OFF WORK IN TWENTY MINUTES.
MISTER? ARE YOU INTERESTED?
TINA
20 minutes later
IT'S ABOUT A MILE FROM HERE... I'LL WALK AND YOU CAN DRIVE ALONG SIDE OF ME.
WHY DON'T YOU JUST GET IN... IT'LL BE MUCH FASTER.
♫ TINA'S GOT A BOY-FRIEND! ♫
OH! OKAY! THANK YOU! I-IF IT'S NOT TOO MUCH TROUBLE...
♫ THEY CALL HER FLIPPER... ♫
HAW HAW
COME IN... I'LL GET MY MOTHER... PLEASE MAKE YOURSELF COMFORTABLE.
OH GOD TINA, WHY DIDN'T YOU CALL ME FIRST?! I LOOK A FRIGHT!
SHH! MOTHER! HE'LL HEAR YOU!
TO BE CONTINUED...

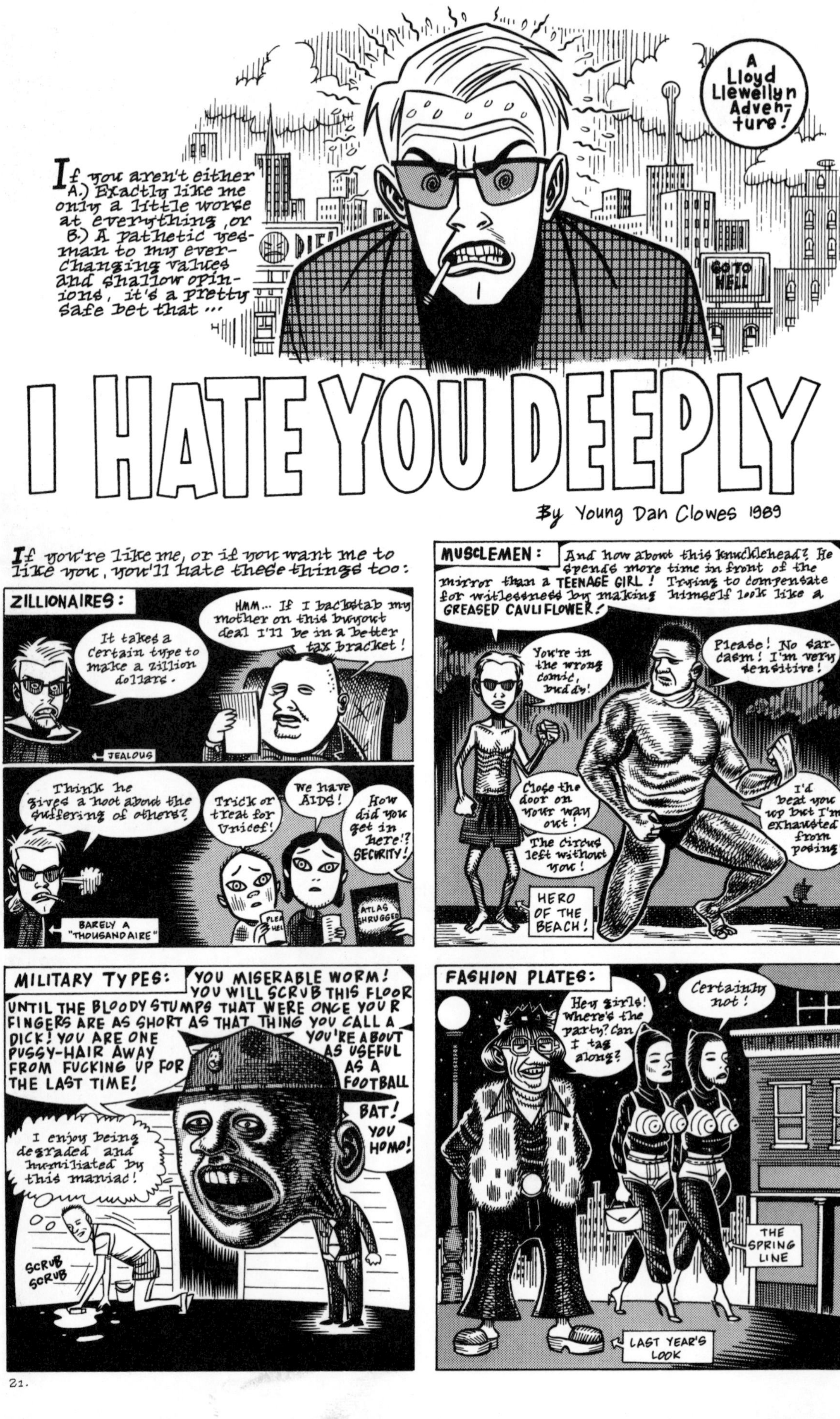

A Lloyd Llewellyn Adventure!
If you aren't either A.) Exactly like me only a little worse at everything, or B.) A pathetic yes-man to my ever-changing values and shallow opinions, it's a pretty safe bet that ...
GO TO HELL
I HATE YOU DEEPLY
By Young Dan Clowes 1989
If you're like me, or if you want me to like you, you'll hate these things too:
ZILLIONAIRES:
It takes a certain type to make a zillion dollars.
HMM... If I backstab my mother on this buyout deal I'll be in a better tax bracket!
JEALOUS
Think he gives a hoot about the suffering of others?
Trick or treat for Unicef!
We have AIDS!
How did you get in here!? SECURITY!
ATLAS SHRUGGED
BARELY A "THOUSANDAIRE"
MUSCLEMEN:
And how about this knucklehead? He spends more time in front of the mirror than a TEENAGE GIRL! Trying to compensate for witlessness by making himself look like a GREASED CAULIFLOWER!
You're in the wrong comic, buddy!
Please! No sarcasm! I'm very sensitive!
Close the door on your way out!
The circus left without you!
I'd beat you up but I'm exhausted from posing!
HERO OF THE BEACH!
MILITARY TYPES:
YOU MISERABLE WORM! YOU WILL SCRUB THIS FLOOR UNTIL THE BLOODY STUMPS THAT WERE ONCE YOUR FINGERS ARE AS SHORT AS THAT THING YOU CALL A DICK! YOU ARE ONE PUSSY-HAIR AWAY FROM FUCKING UP FOR THE LAST TIME! YOU'RE ABOUT AS USEFUL AS A FOOTBALL BAT! YOU HOMO!
I enjoy being degraded and humiliated by this maniac!
SCRUB SCRUB
FASHION PLATES:
Hey girls! Where's the party? Can I tag along?
Certainly not!
THE SPRING LINE
LAST YEAR'S LOOK

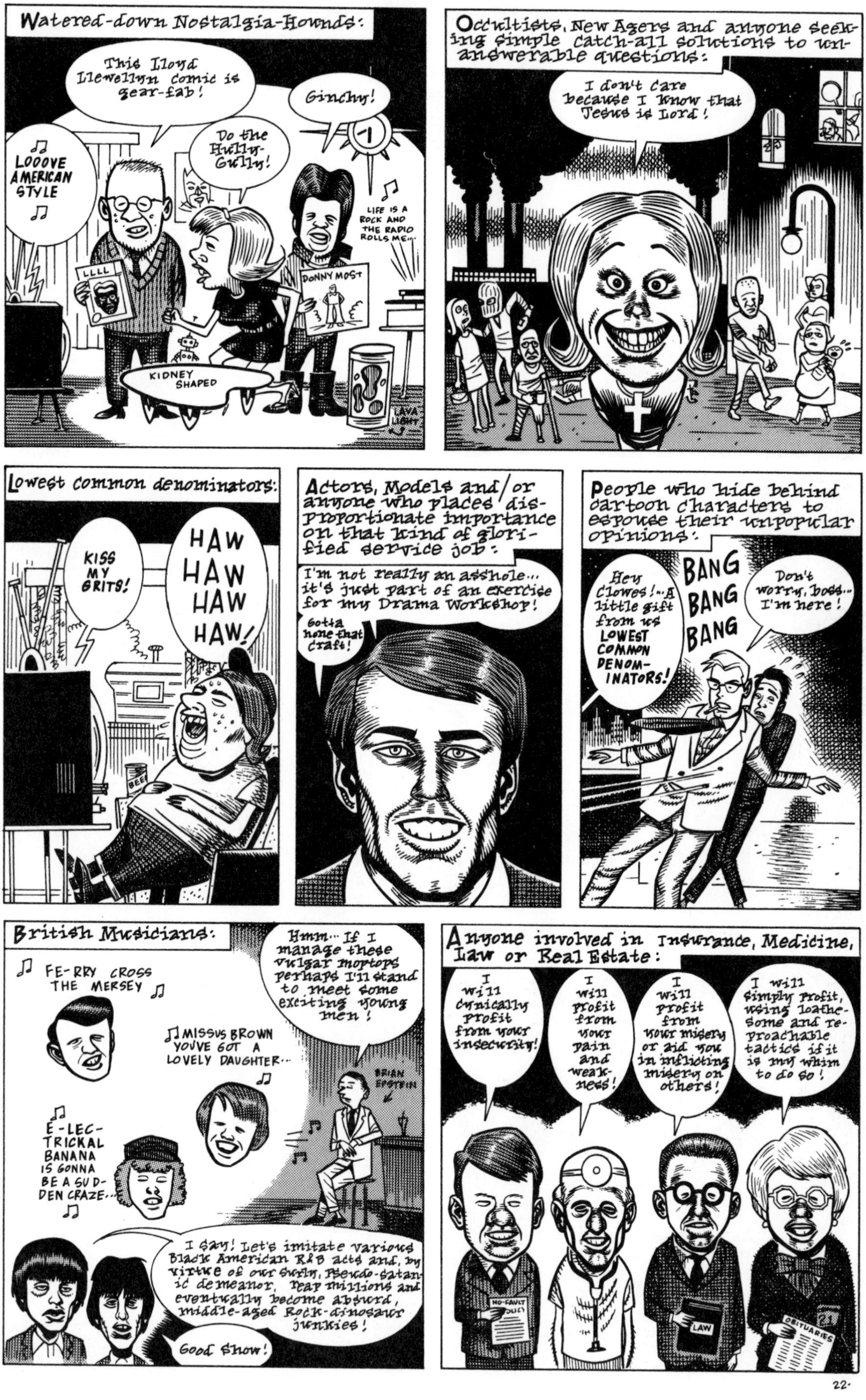
Watered-down Nostalgia-Hounds:
This Lloyd Llewellyn comic is gear-fab!
Ginchy!
Do the Hully-Gully!
LOOOVE AMERICAN STYLE
LIFE IS A ROCK AND THE RADIO ROLLS ME...
LLLL
DONNY MOST
KIDNEY SHAPED
LAVA LIGHT
Occultists, New Agers and anyone seeking simple catch-all solutions to unanswerable questions:
I don't care because I know that Jesus is Lord!
Lowest common denominators:
KISS MY GRITS!
HAW HAW HAW HAW!
BEER
Actors, Models and/or anyone who places disproportionate importance on that kind of glorified service job:
I'm not really an asshole... it's just part of an exercise for my Drama Workshop!
Gotta hone that craft!
People who hide behind cartoon characters to espouse their unpopular opinions:
Hey Clowes!... A little gift from us LOWEST COMMON DENOMINATORS!
BANG BANG BANG
Don't worry, boss... I'm here!
British Musicians:
FE-RRY CROSS THE MERSEY
Hmm... If I manage these vulgar moptops perhaps I'll stand to meet some exciting young men!
MISSUS BROWN YOU'VE GOT A LOVELY DAUGHTER...
BRIAN EPSTEIN
E-LEC-TRICKAL BANANA IS GONNA BE A SUD-DEN CRAZE...
I say! Let's imitate various Black American R&B acts and, by virtue of our surly, pseudo-satanic demeanor, reap millions and eventually become absurd, middle-aged Rock-dinosaur junkies!
Good show!
Anyone involved in Insurance, Medicine, Law or Real Estate:
I will cynically profit from your insecurity!
I will profit from your pain and weakness!
I will profit from your misery or aid you in inflicting misery on others!
I will simply profit, using loathesome and reproachable tactics if it is my whim to do so!
NO-FAULT POLICY
LAW
OBITUARIES

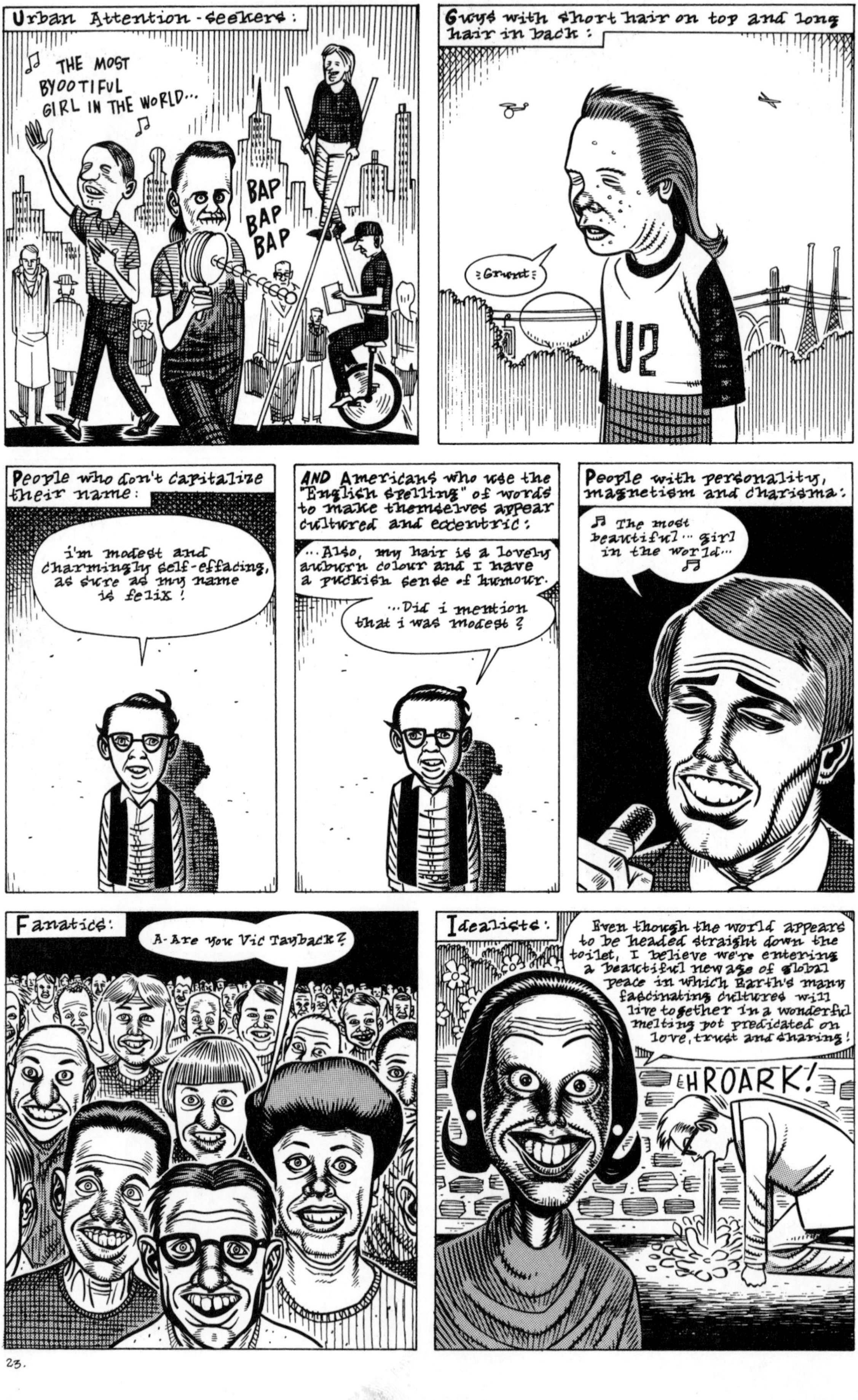
Urban Attention-seekers:
THE MOST BYOOTIFUL GIRL IN THE WORLD...
BAP BAP BAP
Guys with short hair on top and long hair in back:
Grunt
People who don't capitalize their name:
i'm modest and charmingly self-effacing, as sure as my name is felix!
AND Americans who use the "English spelling" of words to make themselves appear cultured and eccentric:
...Also, my hair is a lovely auburn colour and I have a puckish sense of humour.
...Did i mention that i was modest?
People with personality, magnetism and charisma:
The most beautiful... girl in the world...
Fanatics:
A-Are you Vic Tayback?
Idealists:
Even though the world appears to be headed straight down the toilet, I believe we're entering a beautiful new age of global peace in which Earth's many fascinating cultures will live together in a wonderful melting pot predicated on love, trust and sharing!
HROARK!

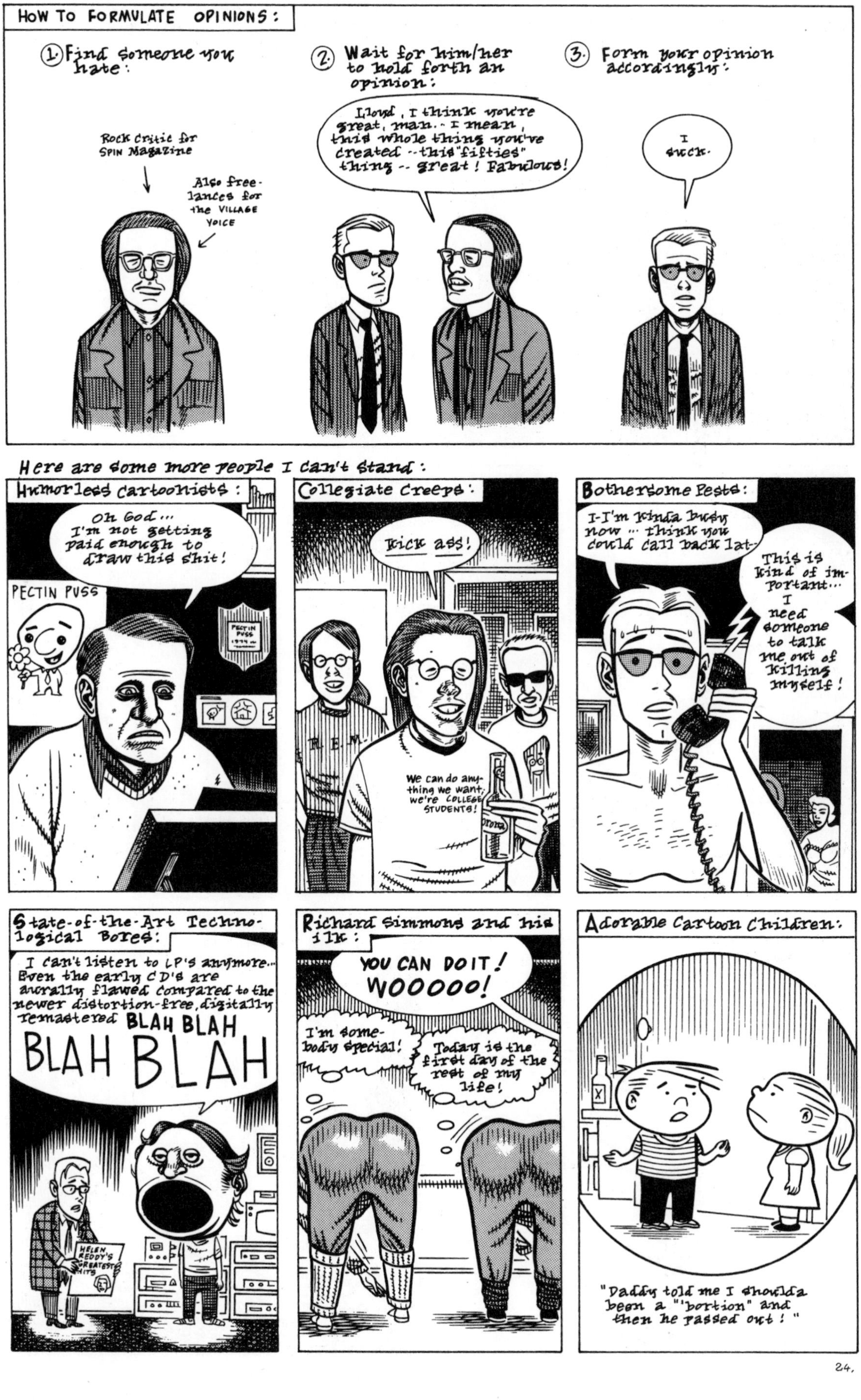
HOW TO FORMULATE OPINIONS:
1. Find someone you hate:
Rock critic for SPIN Magazine
Also free-lances for the VILLAGE VOICE
2. Wait for him/her to hold forth an opinion:
Lloyd, I think you're great, man. I mean, this whole thing you've created -- this "fifties" thing -- great! Fabulous!
3. Form your opinion accordingly:
I suck.
Here are some more people I can't stand:
Humorless cartoonists:
Oh God... I'm not getting paid enough to draw this shit!
PECTIN PUSS
Collegiate Creeps:
Kick ass!
R.E.M.
We can do anything we want, we're COLLEGE STUDENTS!
Bothersome Pests:
I-I'm kinda busy now ... think you could call back lat-
This is kind of important... I need someone to talk me out of killing myself!
State-of-the-Art Technological Bores:
I can't listen to LP's anymore... Even the early CD's are aurally flawed compared to the newer distortion-free, digitally remastered BLAH BLAH BLAH BLAH
HELEN REDDY'S GREATEST HITS
Richard Simmons and his ilk:
YOU CAN DO IT! WOOOOO!
I'm somebody special!
Today is the first day of the rest of my life!
Adorable Cartoon Children:
"Daddy told me I shoulda been a "bortion" and then he passed out!"

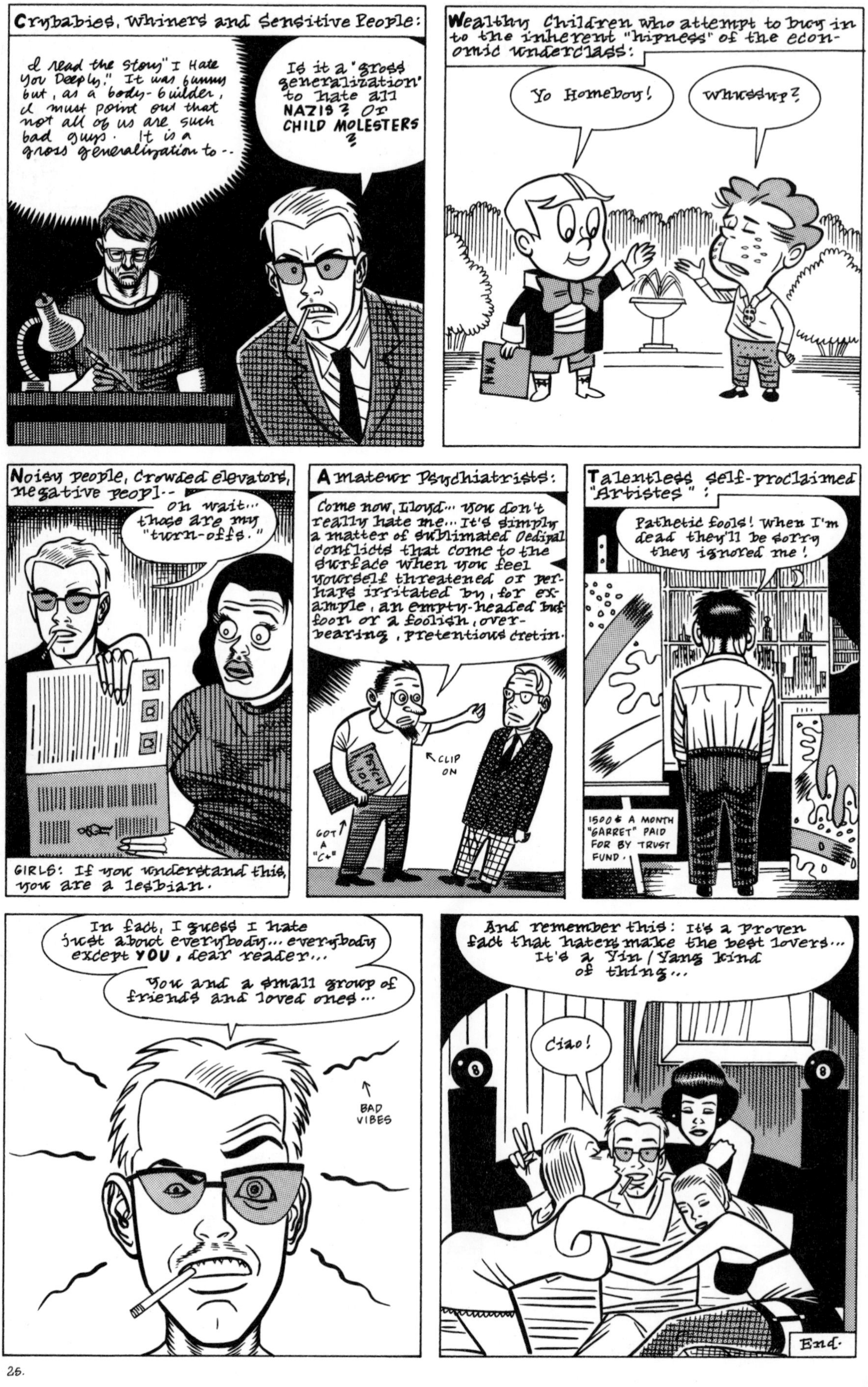

Crybabies, Whiners and Sensitive People:
I read the story "I Hate You Deeply." It was funny but, as a body-builder, I must point out that not all of us are such bad guys. It is a gross generalization to--
Is it a "gross generalization" to hate all NAZIS? Or CHILD MOLESTERS?
Wealthy Children who attempt to buy in to the inherent "hipness" of the economic underclass:
Yo Homeboy!
Whussup?
Noisy people, Crowded elevators, negative peopl--
Oh wait... those are my "turn-offs."
GIRLS: If you understand this, you are a lesbian.
Amateur Psychiatrists:
Come now, Lloyd... you don't really hate me... It's simply a matter of sublimated Oedipal conflicts that come to the surface when you feel yourself threatened or perhaps irritated by, for example, an empty-headed buffoon or a foolish, overbearing, pretentious cretin.
CLIP ON
GOT A "C+"
Talentless self-proclaimed "Artistes":
Pathetic fools! When I'm dead they'll be sorry they ignored me!
1500$ A MONTH "GARRET" PAID FOR BY TRUST FUND.
In fact, I guess I hate just about everybody... everybody except YOU, dear reader...
You and a small group of friends and loved ones...
BAD VIBES
And remember this: It's a proven fact that haters make the best lovers... It's a Yin/Yang kind of thing...
Ciao!
End.

PRANK PHONE CALL CONTEST

Have you been fuckin' around with my wife?!

Long denied it's rightful place as one of the great, indigenous American artforms, the Prank Phone Call appears ready to emerge triumphantly as a vital form of artistic expression for the communication era. In order to expedite the inevitable, we (me) here at EIGHTBALL are proud to announce the OFFICIAL EIGHTBALL™ PRANK PHONE CALL CONTEST! To become a contestant all you need is a tape recorder, a telephone and a healthy disrespect for the privacy of others!

INSTRUCTIONS: Send a tape (or several) (any length but the longer the better) of your prank phone calls. Be sure to write your name and address on the tape.

RULES: The best tape (as decided by me) wins.

TIP: Sound quality counts! Use a suction-cup phone mike (avail. at most Radio Shack-type stores.)

DEADLINE: The next 2 or 3 months.

GRAND PRIZE: An original page from EIGHTBALL #2, one deluxe hand-painted girlie tie, several meaningless trinkets and a gushing review (and/or transcript) of your tape on this page in the next issue of EIGHTBALL!

IS THIS LEGIT OR JUST A STUPID GAG?: Quite legit, I assure you.

Send those tapes to:

EIGHTBALL
BOX 3357
CHICAGO, IL.
60654

THE BULGING MAILSACK

...First ish was revolting, hypnotic, offensive, etc. "I didn't even like touching the pages"... Keep goin'...

Dave Stevenson
Altadena, Ca.

"...Velvet Glove" is the most terrifying love story I have ever read in any form...

Peter Hawkinson
Eau Claire, Wi.

...A fucking helluva damn good book...

David Leibow
Kent, Oh.

...A fine depressing opus of a comic...

Gilmore Tamny
Towson, Md.

...Brilliant...

Scott McCloud
Cambridge, Ma

...A masterpiece...

P. Bagge
Seattle, Wa.

...A masterpiece...

R. Crumb
Winters, Ca.

...Thank goodness there are still guys like you and Pete Bagge and ol' Bob Crumb quietly working producing comics with humor, heart and integrity...

Michael T. Gilbert
Eugene, Or.

I DON'T KNOW ABOUT ME BUT EVERYTHING THOSE GUYS DO IS A MASTERPIECE!

...Outstanding...

C.C. Cilia
Tucson, Az.

...Sad...

Jim Conatser
Dubuque, Ia.

...Some of the girls in your mag have big butts. Do you like chicks with big butts?

Michael Spadaccini
Darien, Ct.

NO. I'M MARRIED.

Dear Mr. Groth:
[NOTE: THIS ONE WAS SENT (FOR REASONS UNKNOWN) TO MEAN-SPIRITED FANTA-GRAPHICS PUBLISHER GARY GROTH]

So, you've seen fit to unleash Dan Clowes on the world again, this time with EIGHTBALL...

I keep noticing, with this book and Joe Sacco's Yahoo, how so many of Fantagraphics' titles are words that can also be used to describe people who are total jerks. Talk about targeting your audience...

I'm hoping that Dan is using these stories of his to poke fun, in a good-natured way, at various aspects of day-to-day life. On the surface, that's what it looks like he's doing, and I'm hoping that that's the case, because if it's not then I have-n't a clue as to what he's up to. Especially in this issue's lead-off tale, "Like a Velvet Glove Cast in Iron." The other stories in this book I can figure out (thank God) but this one I don't get at all.

In "Devil Doll" and "Young Dan Pussey," while I understand what Dan is saying and what he's making fun of, the fact is that at no point does he come out and say, "This wrong because of this," or "I don't like this and here's why." He never shares his own opinion of what he's parodying with us. The stories read like they're just reporting on a certain type of behavior and for me, that kills any sense of drama that Dan might be trying to inject into things. I can't work up any emotion about the characters or the things they're doing, because Dan hasn't provided us with the necessary guidelines to do so. It's sort of like watching TV with the sound off; you can pretty well guess what people are up to by how they act, but you're still missing something and knowing that you're missing it makes you more unsatisfied with the work as a whole.

I guess what I'm getting around to saying is that I didn't have a good time with this one. It is a safe bet that I won't be on hand for any future issues. I'd like to be able to see the same kind of magic in Dan's work that you do but right now it just isn't in the cards. C'est la vie.

David Beattie
Concord, Ca.

Address all correspondance to:
EIGHTBALL
BOX 3357
CHICAGO, IL.
60654

NOTE NEW ADDRESS

26.

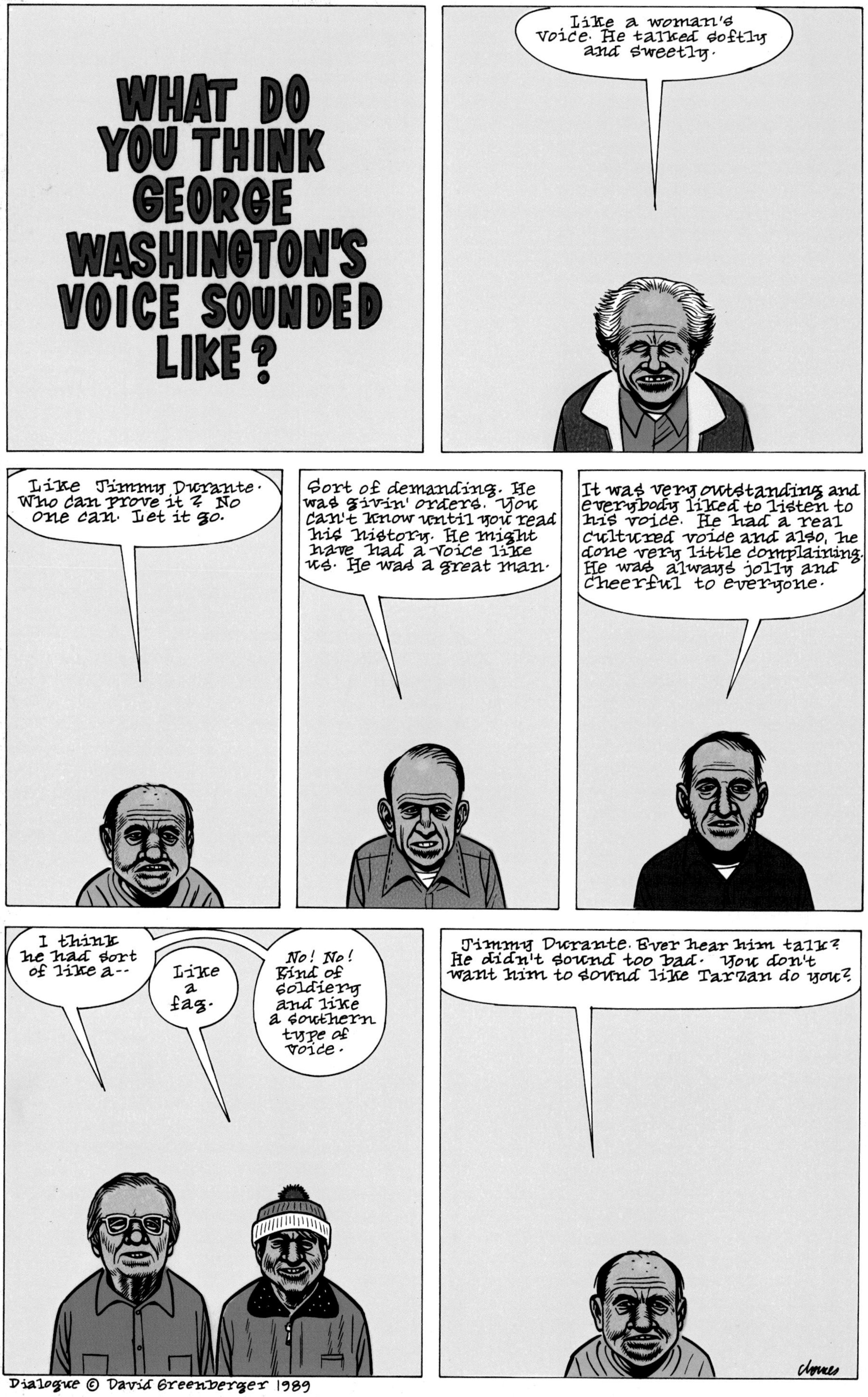
WHAT DO YOU THINK GEORGE WASHINGTON'S VOICE SOUNDED LIKE?
Like a woman's voice. He talked softly and sweetly.
Like Jimmy Durante. Who can prove it? No one can. Let it go.
Sort of demanding. He was givin' orders. You can't know until you read his history. He might have had a voice like us. He was a great man.
It was very outstanding and everybody liked to listen to his voice. He had a real cultured voice and also, he done very little complaining. He was always jolly and cheerful to everyone.
I think he had sort of like a--
Like a fag.
No! No! Kind of soldiery and like a southern type of voice.
Jimmy Durante. Ever hear him talk? He didn't sound too bad. You don't want him to sound like Tarzan do you?
clowes

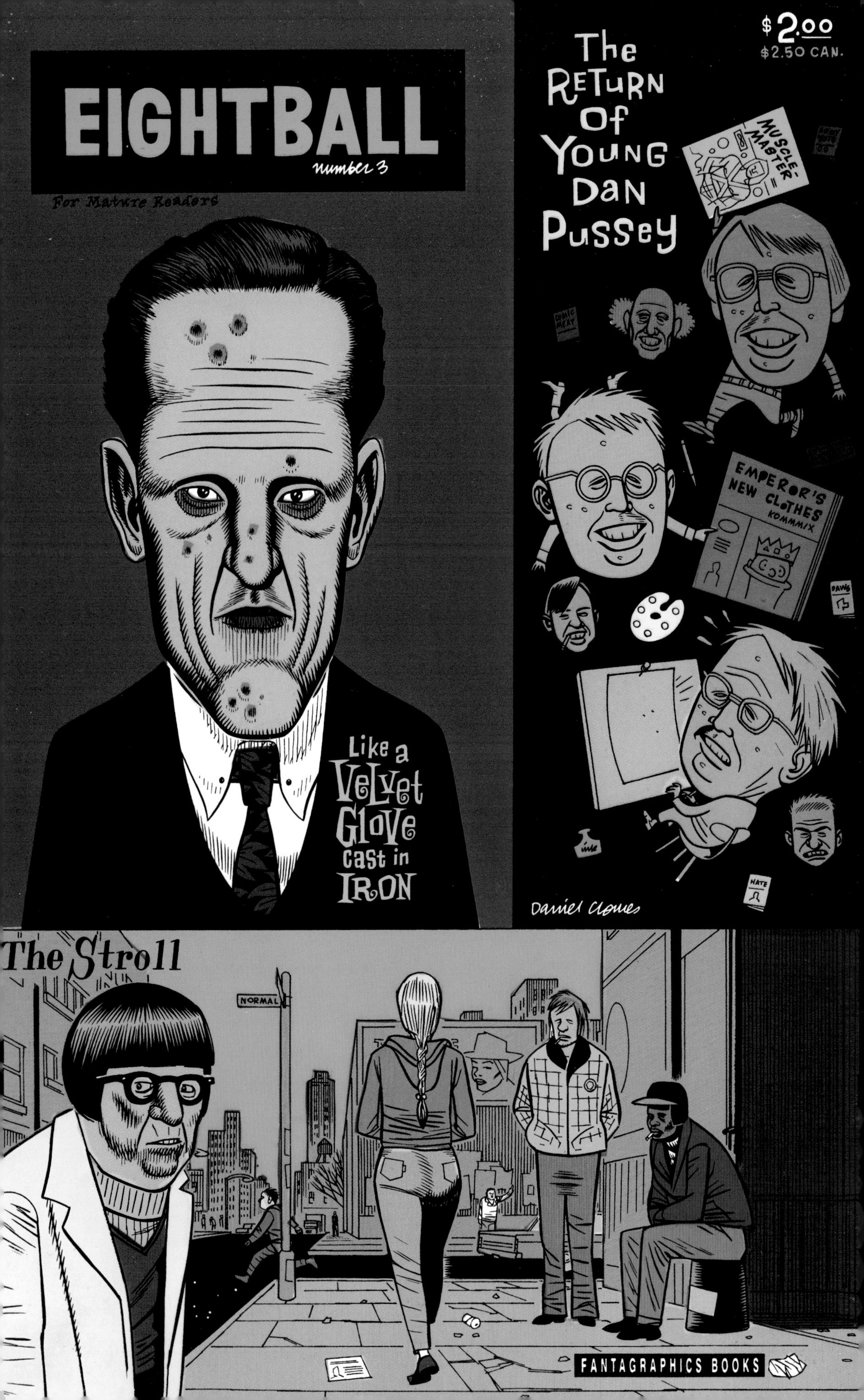

EIGHTBALL
number 3
For Mature Readers
$2.00
$2.50 CAN.
The Return of Young Dan Pussey
MUSCLE-MASTER
EMPEROR'S NEW CLOTHES KOMMMIX
Like a Velvet Glove cast in IRON
Daniel Clowes
The Stroll
NORMAL
HATE
FANTAGRAPHICS BOOKS

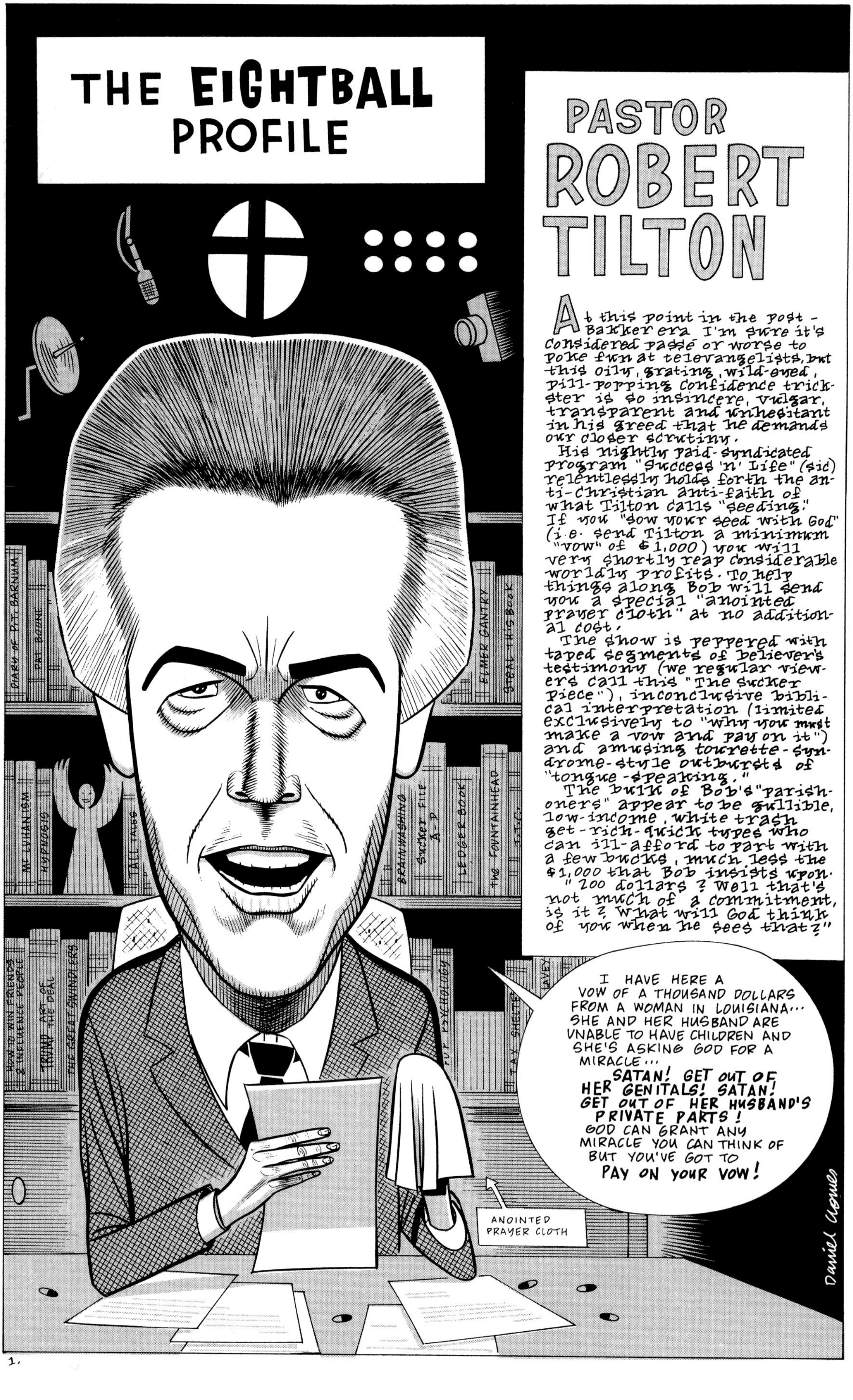
THE EIGHTBALL PROFILE
PASTOR ROBERT TILTON
At this point in the post-Bakker era I'm sure it's considered passé or worse to poke fun at televangelists, but this oily, grating, wild-eyed, pill-popping confidence trickster is so insincere, vulgar, transparent and unhesitant in his greed that he demands our closer scrutiny.
His nightly paid-syndicated program "Success 'n' Life" (sic) relentlessly holds forth the anti-Christian anti-faith of what Tilton calls "seeding." If you "sow your seed with God" (i.e. send Tilton a minimum "vow" of $1,000) you will very shortly reap considerable worldly profits. To help things along Bob will send you a special "anointed prayer cloth" at no additional cost.
The show is peppered with taped segments of believer's testimony (we regular viewers call this "The Sucker Piece"), inconclusive biblical interpretation (limited exclusively to "why you must make a vow and pay on it") and amusing tourette-syndrome-style outbursts of "tongue-speaking."
The bulk of Bob's "parishoners" appear to be gullible, low-income, white trash get-rich-quick types who can ill-afford to part with a few bucks, much less the $1,000 that Bob insists upon.
"200 dollars? Well that's not much of a commitment, is it? What will God think of you when he sees that?"
DIARY OF P.T. BARNUM
PAT BOONE
ELMER GANTRY
STEAL THIS BOOK
MC LUHANISM
HYPNOSIS
TALL TALES
BRAINWASHING
SUCKER FILE A-P
LEDGER BOOK
THE FOUNTAINHEAD
HOW TO WIN FRIENDS & INFLUENCE PEOPLE
TRUMP ART OF THE DEAL
THE GREAT SWINDLERS
POP PSYCHOLOGY
LAVEY
I HAVE HERE A VOW OF A THOUSAND DOLLARS FROM A WOMAN IN LOUISIANA... SHE AND HER HUSBAND ARE UNABLE TO HAVE CHILDREN AND SHE'S ASKING GOD FOR A MIRACLE... SATAN! GET OUT OF HER GENITALS! SATAN! GET OUT OF HER HUSBAND'S PRIVATE PARTS! GOD CAN GRANT ANY MIRACLE YOU CAN THINK OF BUT YOU'VE GOT TO PAY ON YOUR VOW!
ANOINTED PRAYER CLOTH
Daniel Clowes

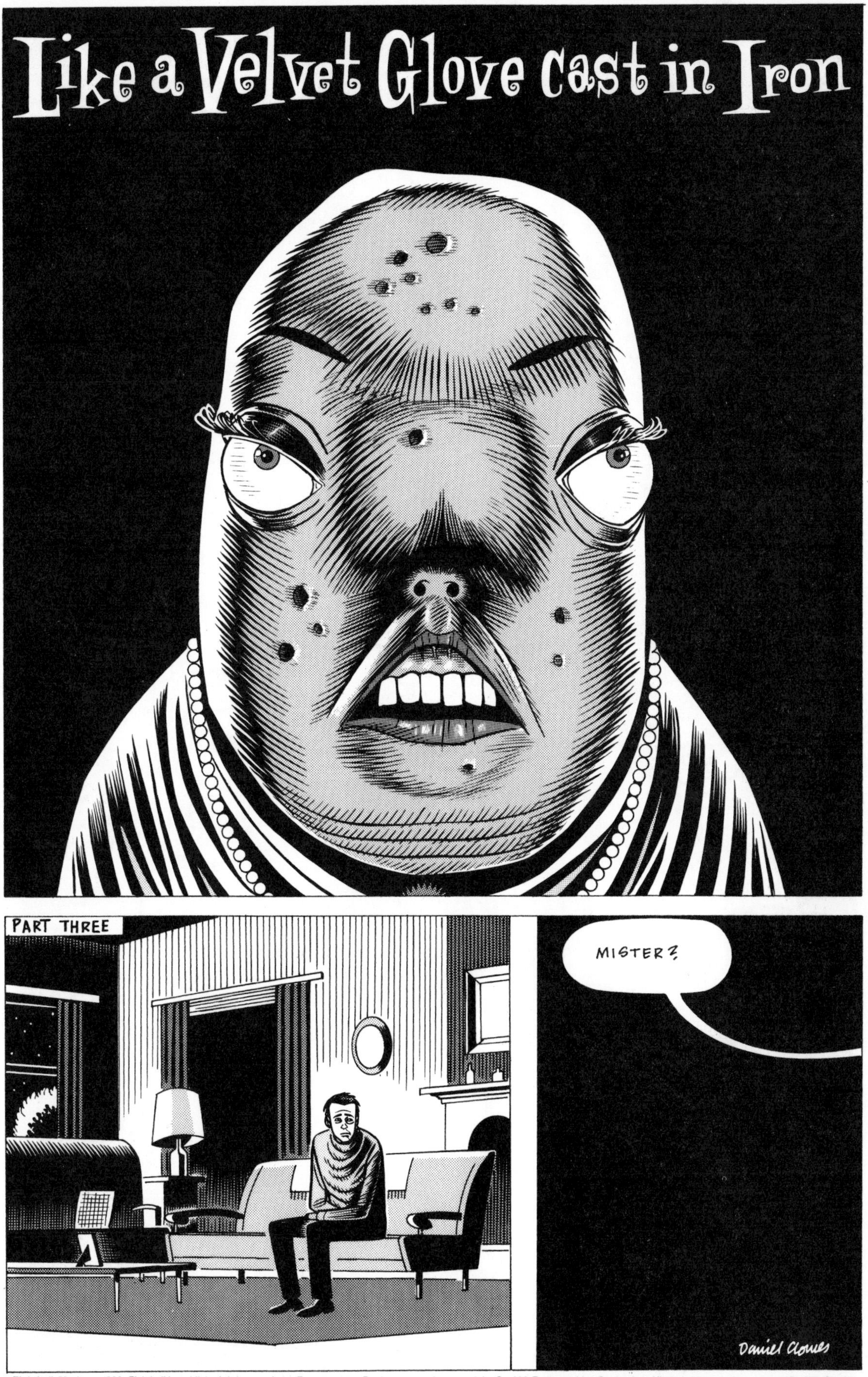

Like a Velvet Glove Cast in Iron
PART THREE
MISTER?
Daniel Clowes

Eightball #3, June, 1990. *Eightball* is published thrice yearly by Fantagraphics Books, Inc., and is copyright © 1990 Fantagraphics Books, Inc. All characters, stories, and art © 1989 Daniel Clowes. No part of this magazine may be reproduced without written permission from Fantagraphics Books or Daniel Clowes. No similarity between the any of the names, characters, persons, and institutions in *Eightball* and those of any living or dead persons is intended (except for satirical intent), and any such similarity that may exist is purely coincidental. Letters to *Eightball* become the property of the magazine and are assumed intended for publication in whole or in part, and may therefore be used for those purposes. First printing: March, 1990. This issue, as well as the previous issue, available from the publisher for $2.00 + 50¢ postage and handling: Fantagraphics Books, 7563 Lake City Way NE, Seattle WA 98115. **Send for our free catalogue!**

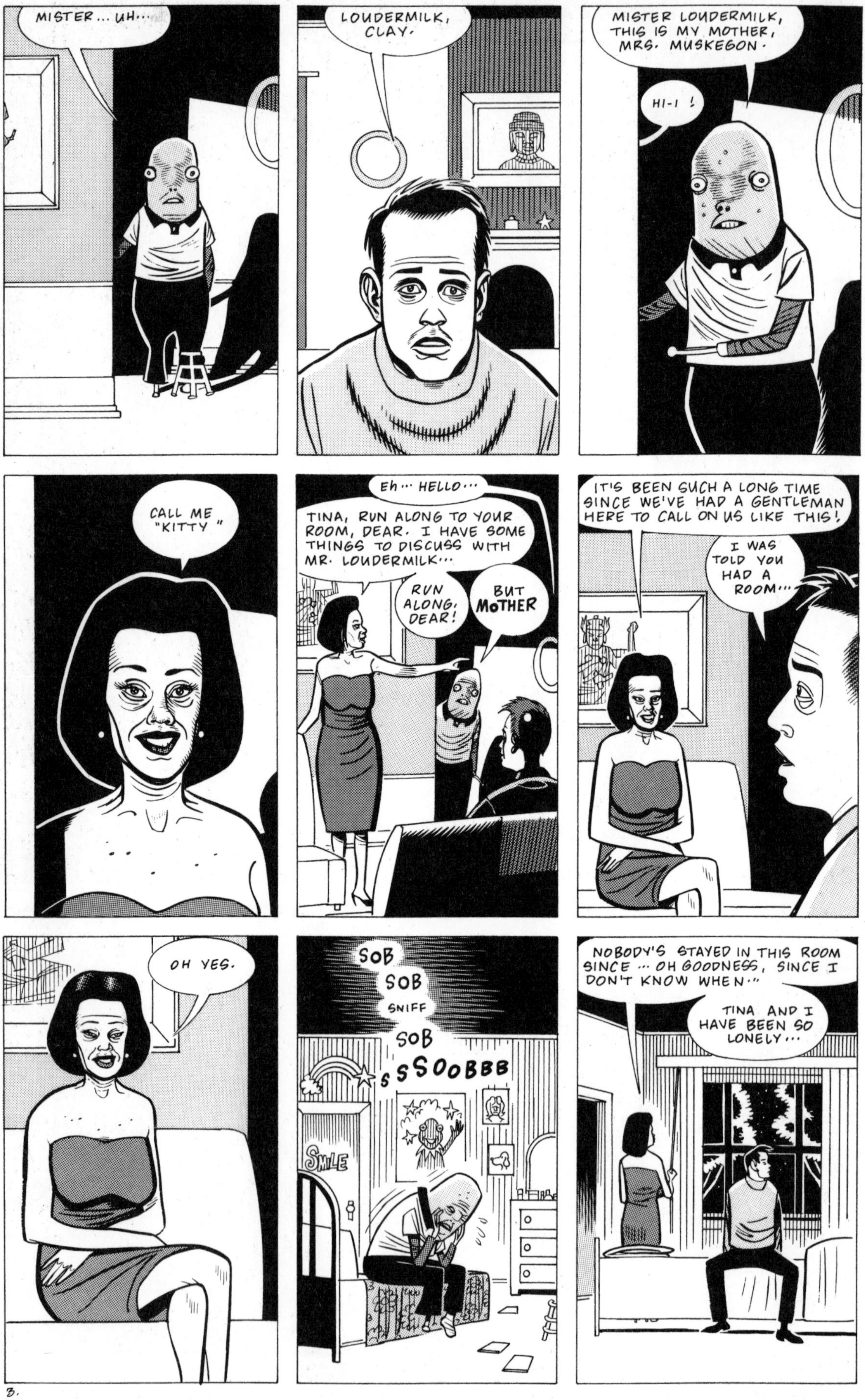
MISTER ... UH...
LOUDERMILK, CLAY.
MISTER LOUDERMILK, THIS IS MY MOTHER, MRS. MUSKEGON.
HI-I !
CALL ME "KITTY"
Eh... HELLO...
TINA, RUN ALONG TO YOUR ROOM, DEAR. I HAVE SOME THINGS TO DISCUSS WITH MR. LOUDERMILK...
RUN ALONG, DEAR!
BUT MOTHER
IT'S BEEN SUCH A LONG TIME SINCE WE'VE HAD A GENTLEMAN HERE TO CALL ON US LIKE THIS!
I WAS TOLD YOU HAD A ROOM...
OH YES.
SOB
SOB
SNIFF
SOB
sSSOOBBB
SMILE
NOBODY'S STAYED IN THIS ROOM SINCE ... OH GOODNESS, SINCE I DON'T KNOW WHEN..."
TINA AND I HAVE BEEN SO LONELY...

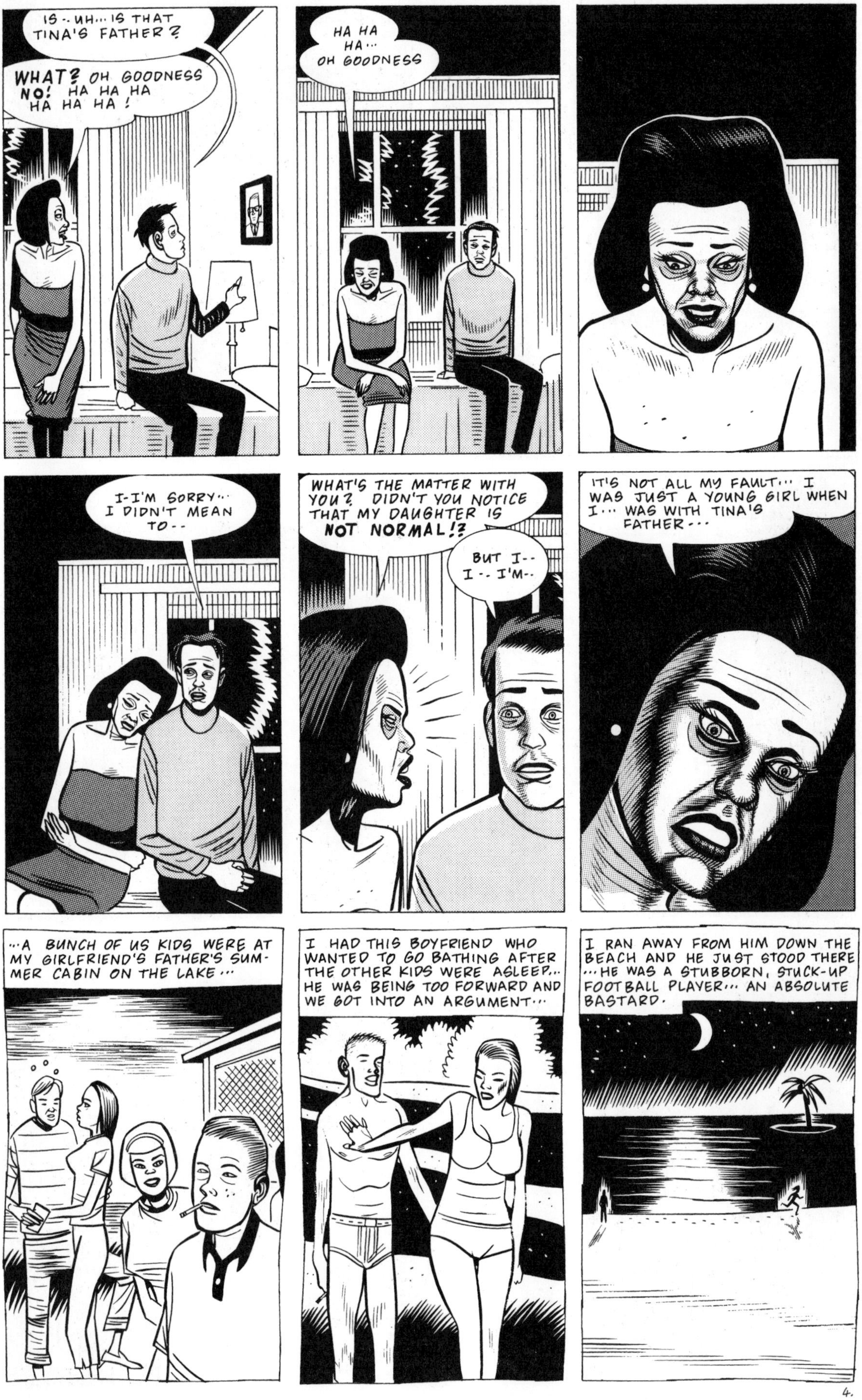
IS -. UH... IS THAT TINA'S FATHER?
WHAT? OH GOODNESS NO! HA HA HA HA HA HA!
HA HA HA... OH GOODNESS
I-I'M SORRY... I DIDN'T MEAN TO--
WHAT'S THE MATTER WITH YOU? DIDN'T YOU NOTICE THAT MY DAUGHTER IS NOT NORMAL!?
BUT I-- I -- I'M--
IT'S NOT ALL MY FAULT... I WAS JUST A YOUNG GIRL WHEN I... WAS WITH TINA'S FATHER...
...A BUNCH OF US KIDS WERE AT MY GIRLFRIEND'S FATHER'S SUMMER CABIN ON THE LAKE...
I HAD THIS BOYFRIEND WHO WANTED TO GO BATHING AFTER THE OTHER KIDS WERE ASLEEP... HE WAS BEING TOO FORWARD AND WE GOT INTO AN ARGUMENT...
I RAN AWAY FROM HIM DOWN THE BEACH AND HE JUST STOOD THERE ...HE WAS A STUBBORN, STUCK-UP FOOTBALL PLAYER... AN ABSOLUTE BASTARD.

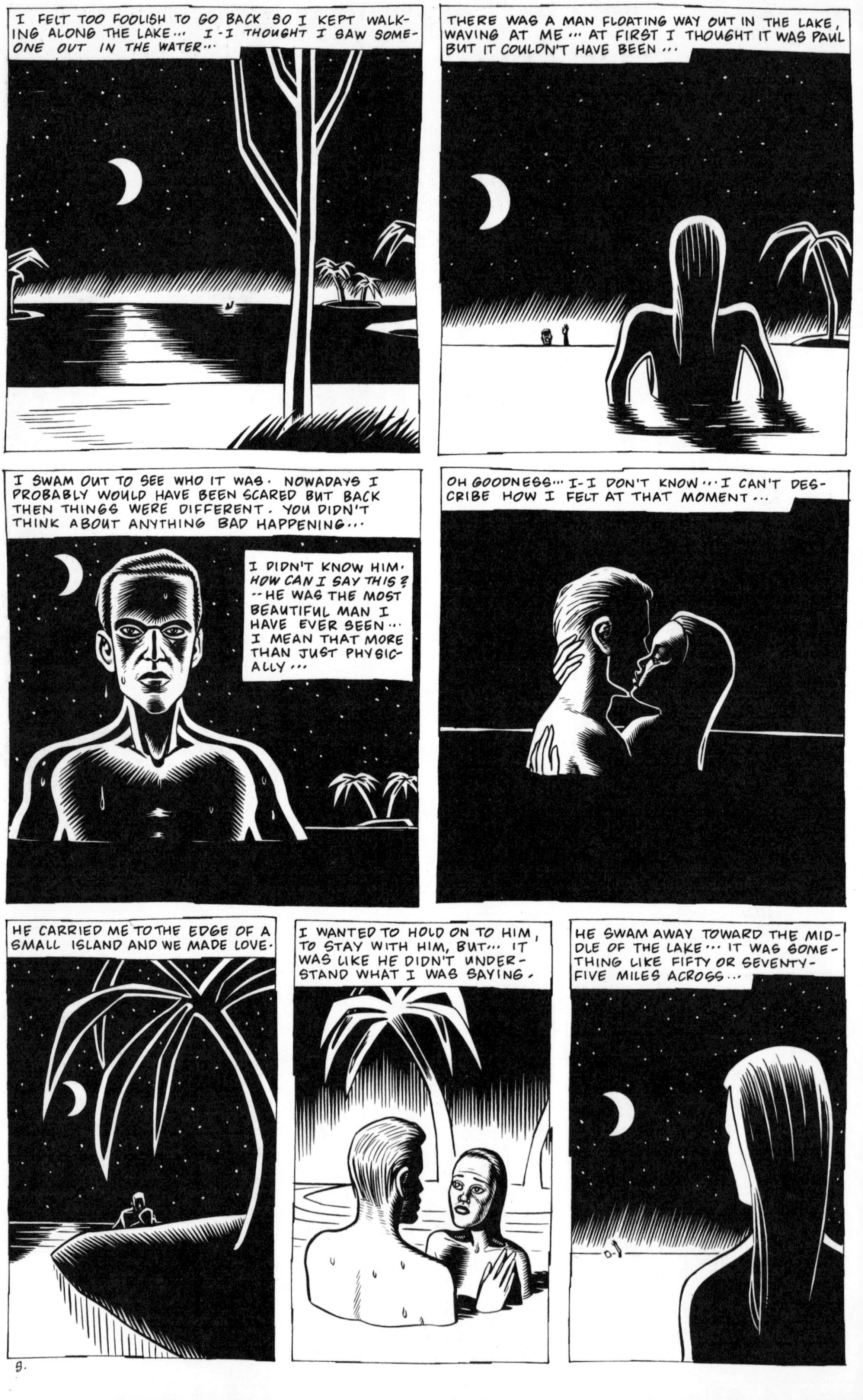
I FELT TOO FOOLISH TO GO BACK SO I KEPT WALKING ALONG THE LAKE... I-I THOUGHT I SAW SOMEONE OUT IN THE WATER...
THERE WAS A MAN FLOATING WAY OUT IN THE LAKE, WAVING AT ME... AT FIRST I THOUGHT IT WAS PAUL BUT IT COULDN'T HAVE BEEN...
I SWAM OUT TO SEE WHO IT WAS. NOWADAYS I PROBABLY WOULD HAVE BEEN SCARED BUT BACK THEN THINGS WERE DIFFERENT. YOU DIDN'T THINK ABOUT ANYTHING BAD HAPPENING...
I DIDN'T KNOW HIM. HOW CAN I SAY THIS? --HE WAS THE MOST BEAUTIFUL MAN I HAVE EVER SEEN... I MEAN THAT MORE THAN JUST PHYSICALLY...
OH GOODNESS... I-I DON'T KNOW... I CAN'T DESCRIBE HOW I FELT AT THAT MOMENT...
HE CARRIED ME TO THE EDGE OF A SMALL ISLAND AND WE MADE LOVE.
I WANTED TO HOLD ON TO HIM, TO STAY WITH HIM, BUT... IT WAS LIKE HE DIDN'T UNDERSTAND WHAT I WAS SAYING.
HE SWAM AWAY TOWARD THE MIDDLE OF THE LAKE... IT WAS SOMETHING LIKE FIFTY OR SEVENTY-FIVE MILES ACROSS...

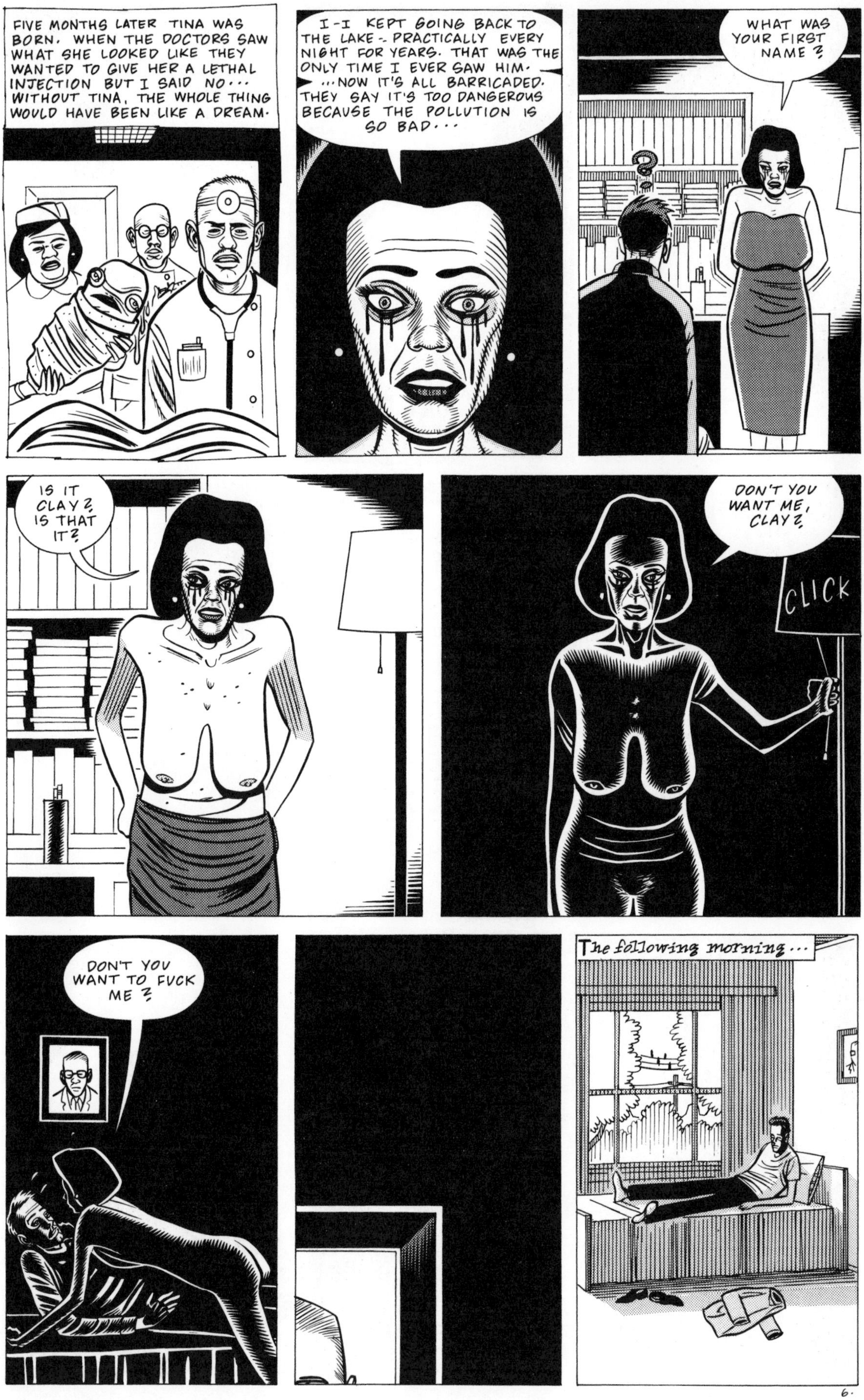
FIVE MONTHS LATER TINA WAS BORN. WHEN THE DOCTORS SAW WHAT SHE LOOKED LIKE THEY WANTED TO GIVE HER A LETHAL INJECTION BUT I SAID NO... WITHOUT TINA, THE WHOLE THING WOULD HAVE BEEN LIKE A DREAM.
I-I KEPT GOING BACK TO THE LAKE - PRACTICALLY EVERY NIGHT FOR YEARS. THAT WAS THE ONLY TIME I EVER SAW HIM. ...NOW IT'S ALL BARRICADED. THEY SAY IT'S TOO DANGEROUS BECAUSE THE POLLUTION IS SO BAD...
WHAT WAS YOUR FIRST NAME?
IS IT CLAY? IS THAT IT?
DON'T YOU WANT ME, CLAY?
CLICK
DON'T YOU WANT TO FUCK ME?
The following morning...

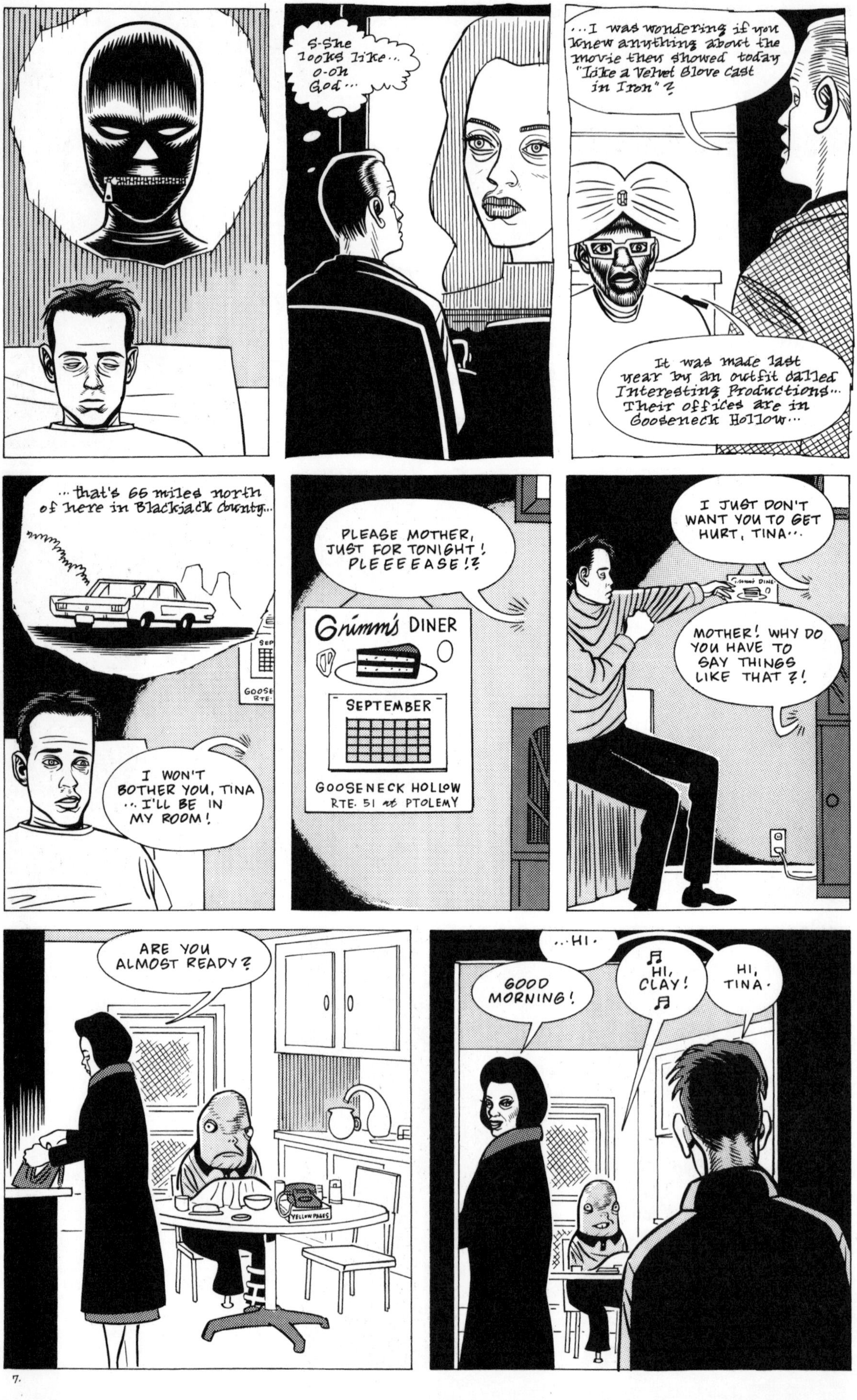
S-She looks like... o-oh God...
...I was wondering if you knew anything about the movie they showed today "Like a Velvet Glove Cast in Iron"?
It was made last year by an outfit called Interesting Productions... Their offices are in Gooseneck Hollow...
...that's 65 miles north of here in Blackjack County...
I WON'T BOTHER YOU, TINA ... I'LL BE IN MY ROOM!
PLEASE MOTHER, JUST FOR TONIGHT! PLEEEEEASE!?
Grimm's DINER
SEPTEMBER
GOOSENECK HOLLOW
RTE. 51 at PTOLEMY
I JUST DON'T WANT YOU TO GET HURT, TINA...
MOTHER! WHY DO YOU HAVE TO SAY THINGS LIKE THAT?!
ARE YOU ALMOST READY?
YELLOW PAGES
...HI.
GOOD MORNING!
HI, CLAY!
HI, TINA.

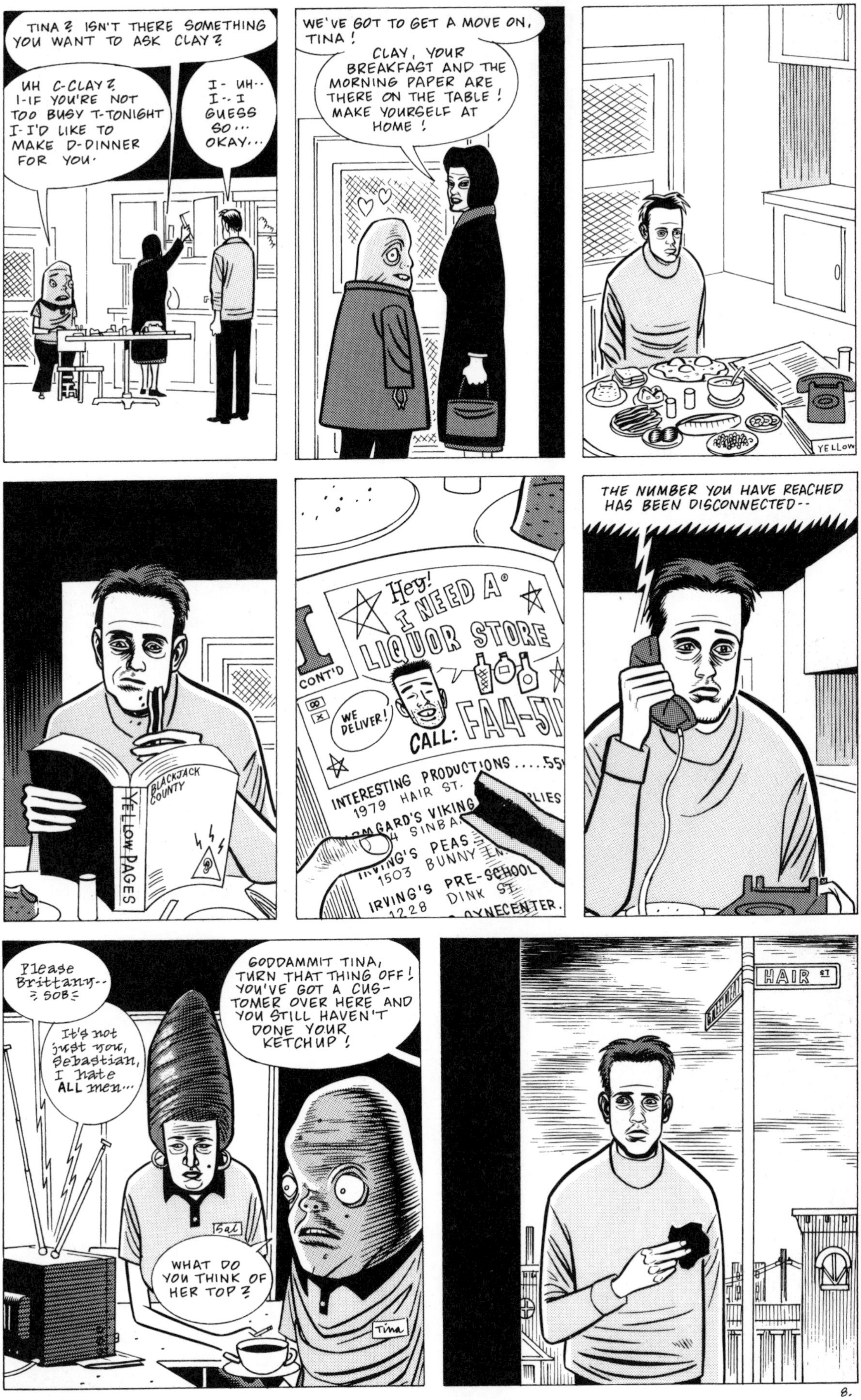
TINA? ISN'T THERE SOMETHING YOU WANT TO ASK CLAY?
UH C-CLAY? I-IF YOU'RE NOT TOO BUSY T-TONIGHT I-I'D LIKE TO MAKE D-DINNER FOR YOU.
I- UH-- I-- I GUESS SO... OKAY...
WE'VE GOT TO GET A MOVE ON, TINA!
CLAY, YOUR BREAKFAST AND THE MORNING PAPER ARE THERE ON THE TABLE! MAKE YOURSELF AT HOME!
YELLOW
BLACKJACK COUNTY
YELLOW PAGES
CONT'D
Hey! I NEED A LIQUOR STORE
WE DELIVER!
CALL: FA4-51
INTERESTING PRODUCTIONS.....55
1979 HAIR ST.
IRVING'S PEAS
1503 BUNNY LN.
IRVING'S PRE-SCHOOL
1228 DINK ST
THE NUMBER YOU HAVE REACHED HAS BEEN DISCONNECTED--
Please Brittany-- SOB
It's not just you, Sebastian, I hate ALL men...
GODDAMMIT TINA, TURN THAT THING OFF! YOU'VE GOT A CUSTOMER OVER HERE AND YOU STILL HAVEN'T DONE YOUR KETCHUP!
WHAT DO YOU THINK OF HER TOP?
Tina
HAIR ST

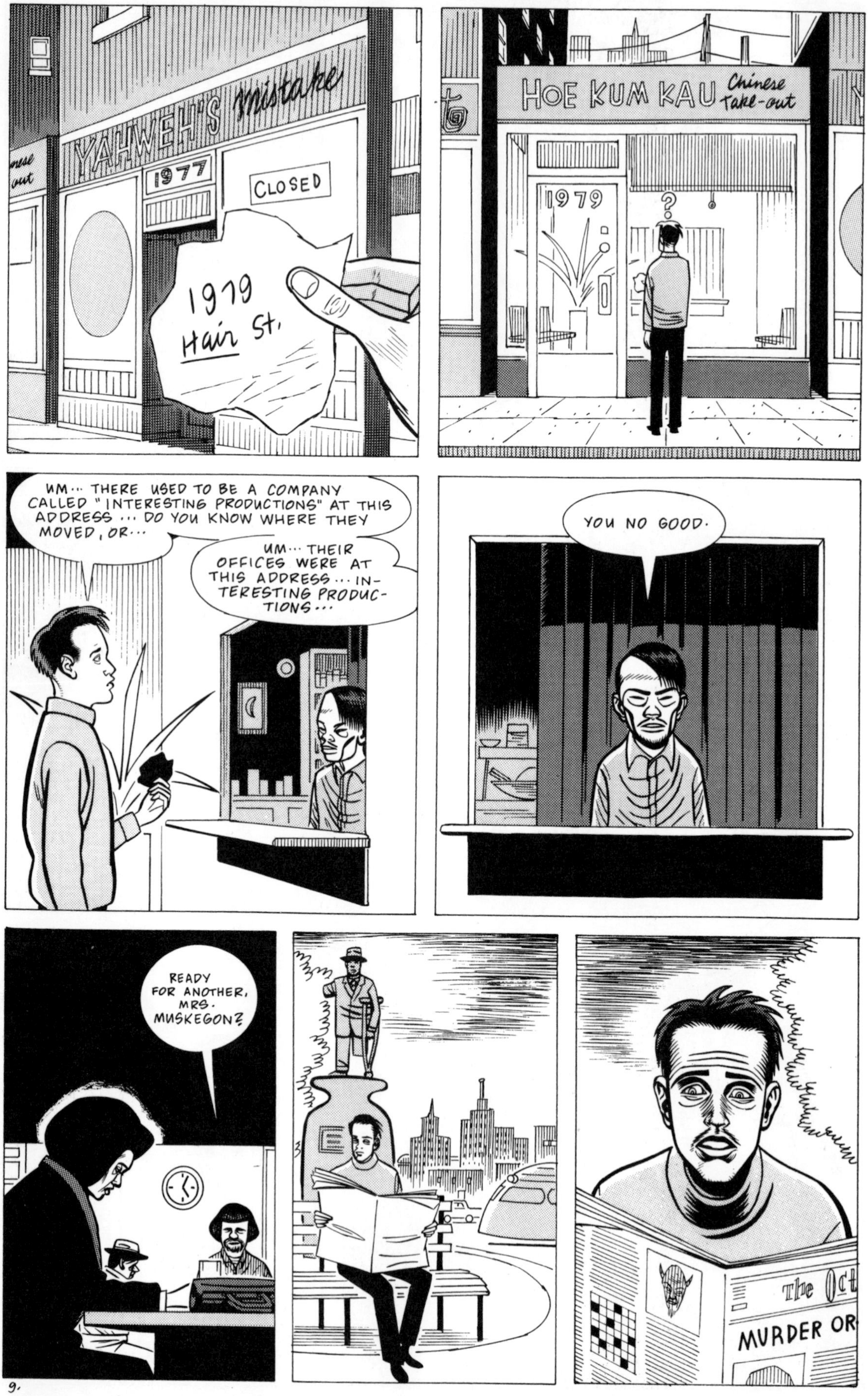
YAHWEH'S mistake
1977
CLOSED
1979
Hair St.
HOE KUM KAU
Chinese Take-out
1979
?
UM... THERE USED TO BE A COMPANY CALLED "INTERESTING PRODUCTIONS" AT THIS ADDRESS ... DO YOU KNOW WHERE THEY MOVED, OR...
UM... THEIR OFFICES WERE AT THIS ADDRESS ... INTERESTING PRODUCTIONS...
YOU NO GOOD.
READY FOR ANOTHER, MRS. MUSKEGON?
MURDER OR

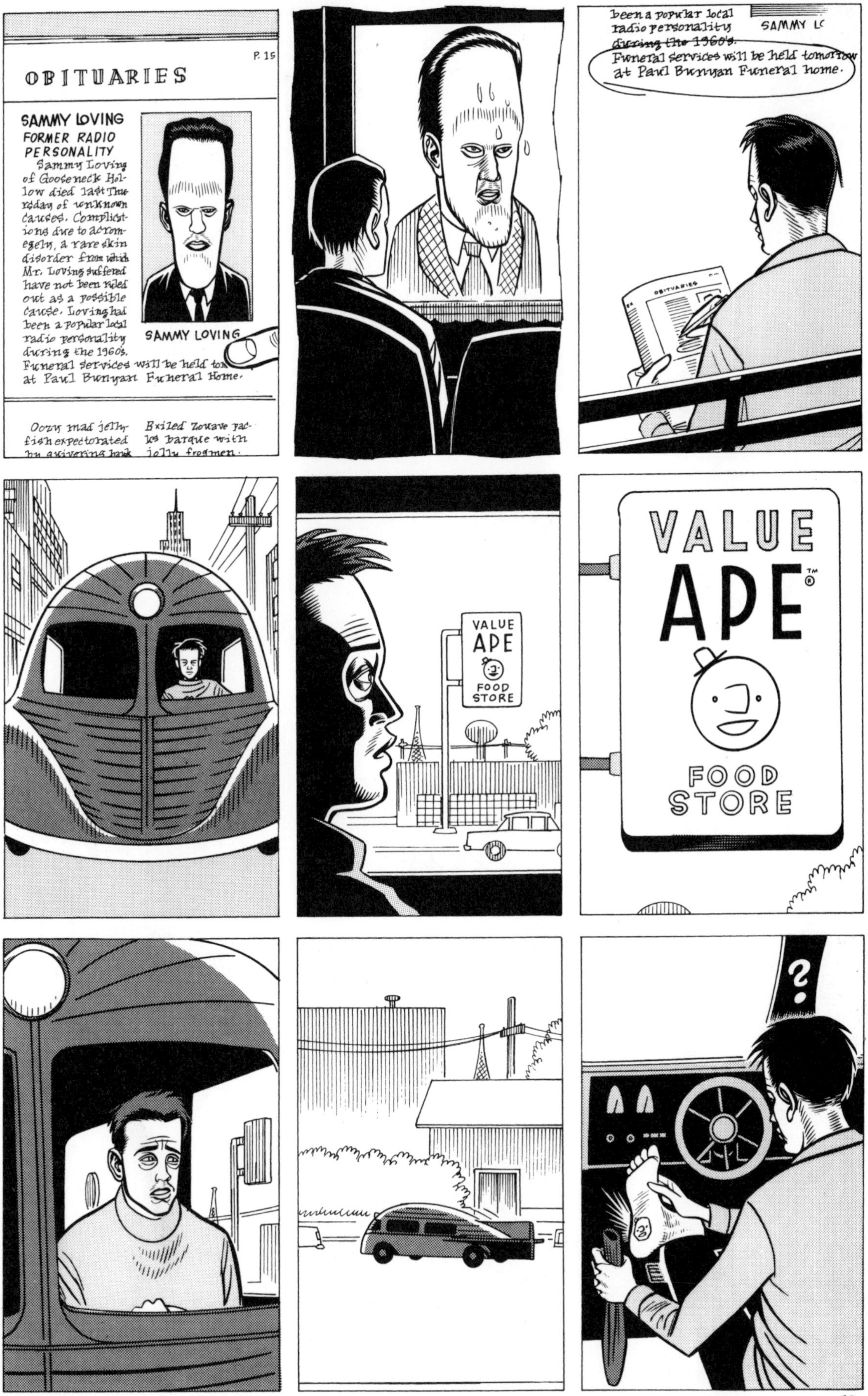

P. 15
OBITUARIES
SAMMY LOVING
FORMER RADIO PERSONALITY
Sammy Loving of Gooseneck Hollow died last Thursday of unknown causes. Complications due to acromegely, a rare skin disorder from which Mr. Loving suffered have not been ruled out as a possible cause. Loving had been a popular local radio personality during the 1960's.
Funeral services will be held tom
at Paul Bunyan Funeral Home.
SAMMY LOVING
Oozy mad jellyfish expectorated
Exiled Zouave packs barque with jolly frogmen.
been a popular local radio personality during the 1960's.
Funeral services will be held tomorrow at Paul Bunyan Funeral home.
SAMMY LC
OBITUARIES
VALUE APE FOOD STORE
VALUE APE™ ® FOOD STORE
?

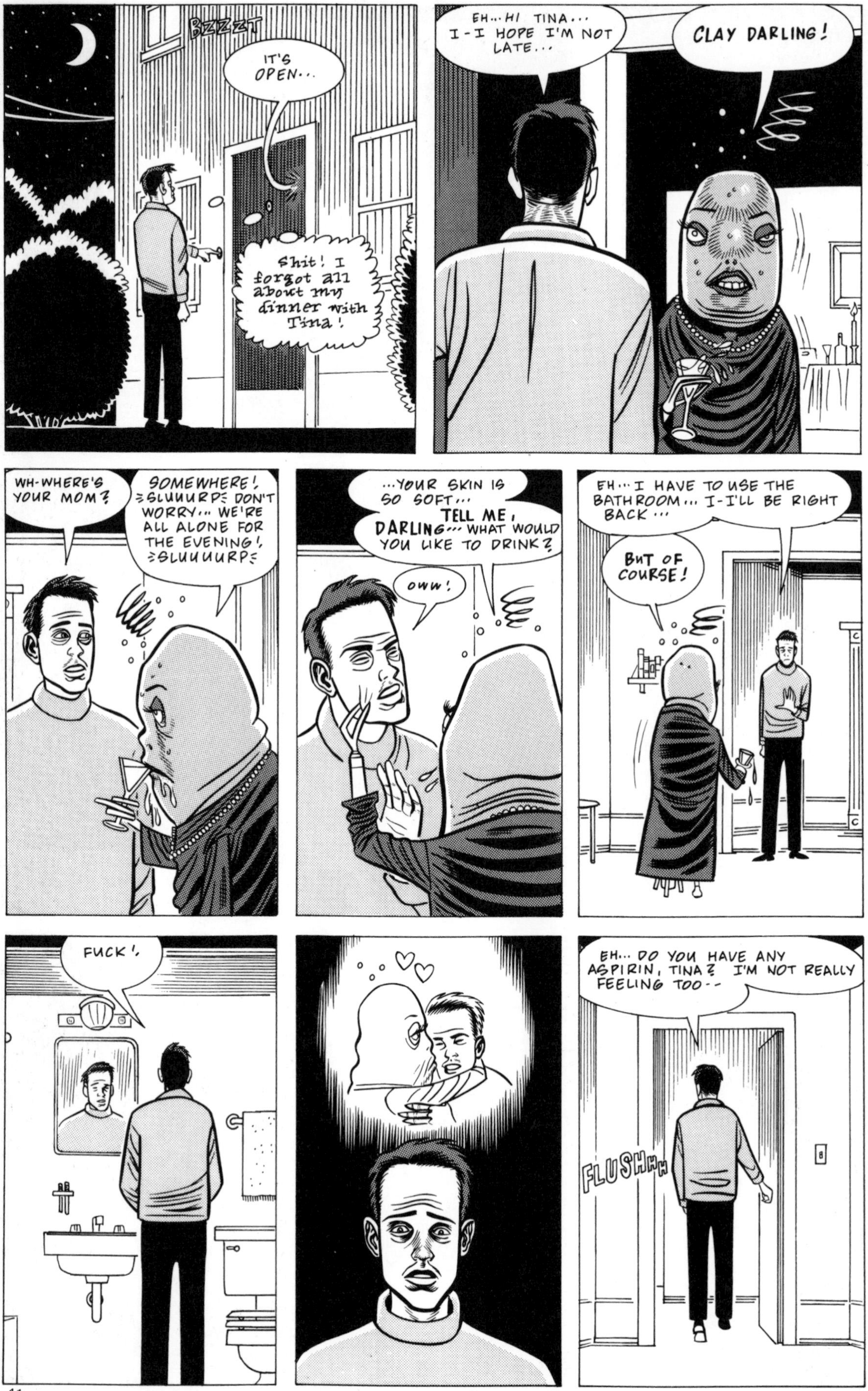
BZZZT
IT'S OPEN...
Shit! I forgot all about my dinner with Tina!
EH... HI TINA... I-I HOPE I'M NOT LATE...
CLAY DARLING!
WH-WHERE'S YOUR MOM?
SOMEWHERE! =SLUUURP= DON'T WORRY... WE'RE ALL ALONE FOR THE EVENING! =SLUUUURP=
...YOUR SKIN IS SO SOFT... TELL ME, DARLING... WHAT WOULD YOU LIKE TO DRINK?
OWW!
EH... I HAVE TO USE THE BATHROOM... I-I'LL BE RIGHT BACK...
BUT OF COURSE!
FUCK!
EH... DO YOU HAVE ANY ASPIRIN, TINA? I'M NOT REALLY FEELING TOO--
FLUSHHH

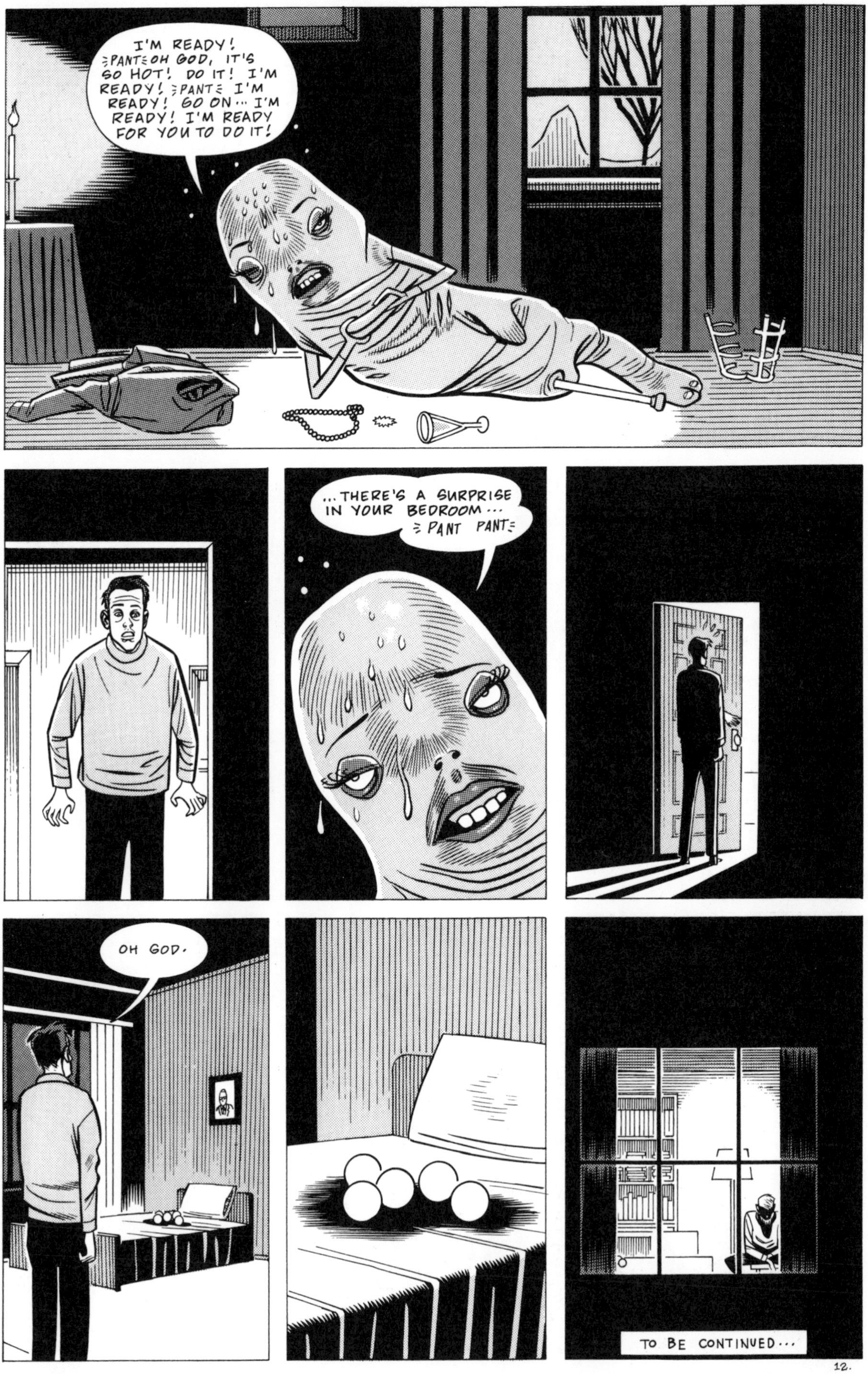
I'M READY! ≷PANT≶ OH GOD, IT'S SO HOT! DO IT! I'M READY! ≷PANT≶ I'M READY! GO ON... I'M READY! I'M READY FOR YOU TO DO IT!
...THERE'S A SURPRISE IN YOUR BEDROOM... ≷PANT PANT≶
OH GOD.
TO BE CONTINUED...

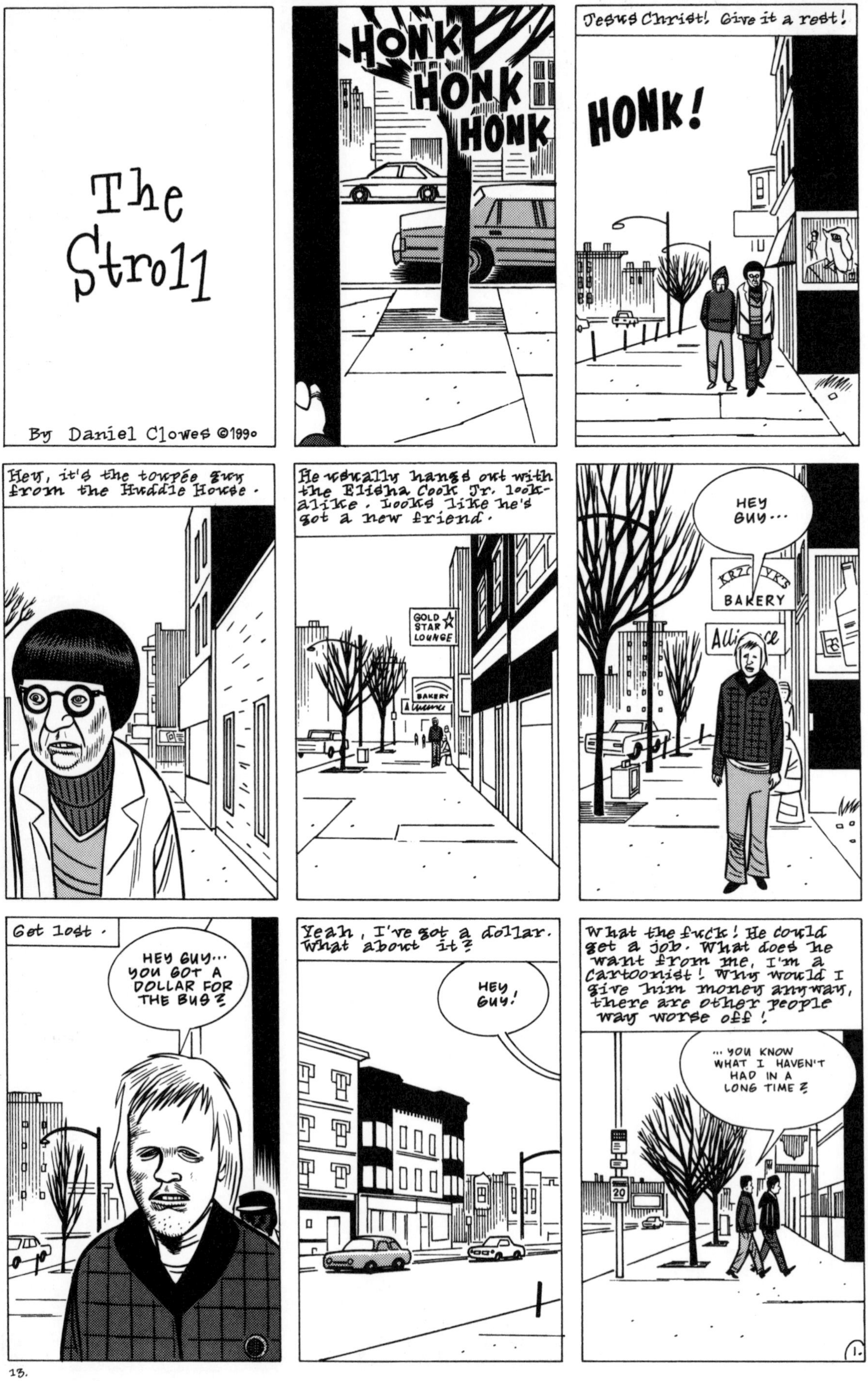

The Stroll
By Daniel Clowes ©1990
HONK
HONK
HONK
Jesus Christ! Give it a rest!
HONK!
Hey, it's the toupée guy from the Huddle House.
He usually hangs out with the Elisha Cook Jr. look-alike. Looks like he's got a new friend.
GOLD STAR LOUNGE
BAKERY
HEY GUY...
BAKERY
Get lost.
HEY GUY... YOU GOT A DOLLAR FOR THE BUS?
Yeah, I've got a dollar. What about it?
HEY, GUY!
What the fuck! He could get a job. What does he want from me, I'm a cartoonist! Why would I give him money anyway, there are other people way worse off!
...YOU KNOW WHAT I HAVEN'T HAD IN A LONG TIME?
20
1.

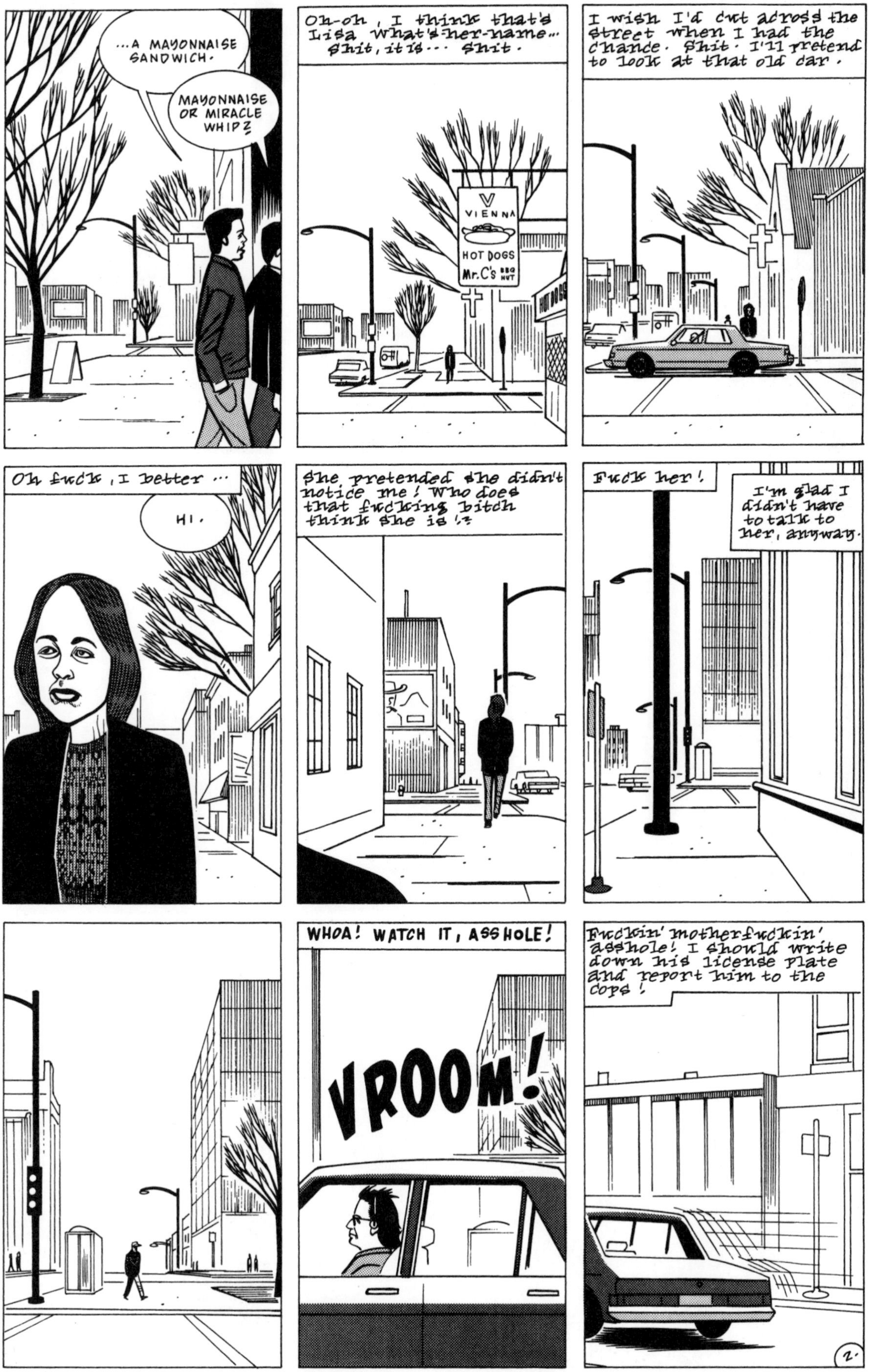
...A MAYONNAISE SANDWICH.
MAYONNAISE OR MIRACLE WHIP?
Oh-oh, I think that's Lisa what's-her-name... Shit, it is... Shit.
VIENNA
HOT DOGS
Mr. C's BBQ HUT
I wish I'd cut across the street when I had the chance. Shit. I'll pretend to look at that old car.
HOT DOGS
Oh fuck, I better ...
HI.
She pretended she didn't notice me! Who does that fucking bitch think she is!?
Fuck her!
I'm glad I didn't have to talk to her, anyway.
WHOA! WATCH IT, ASSHOLE!
VROOM!
Fuckin' motherfuckin' asshole! I should write down his license plate and report him to the cops!
2.

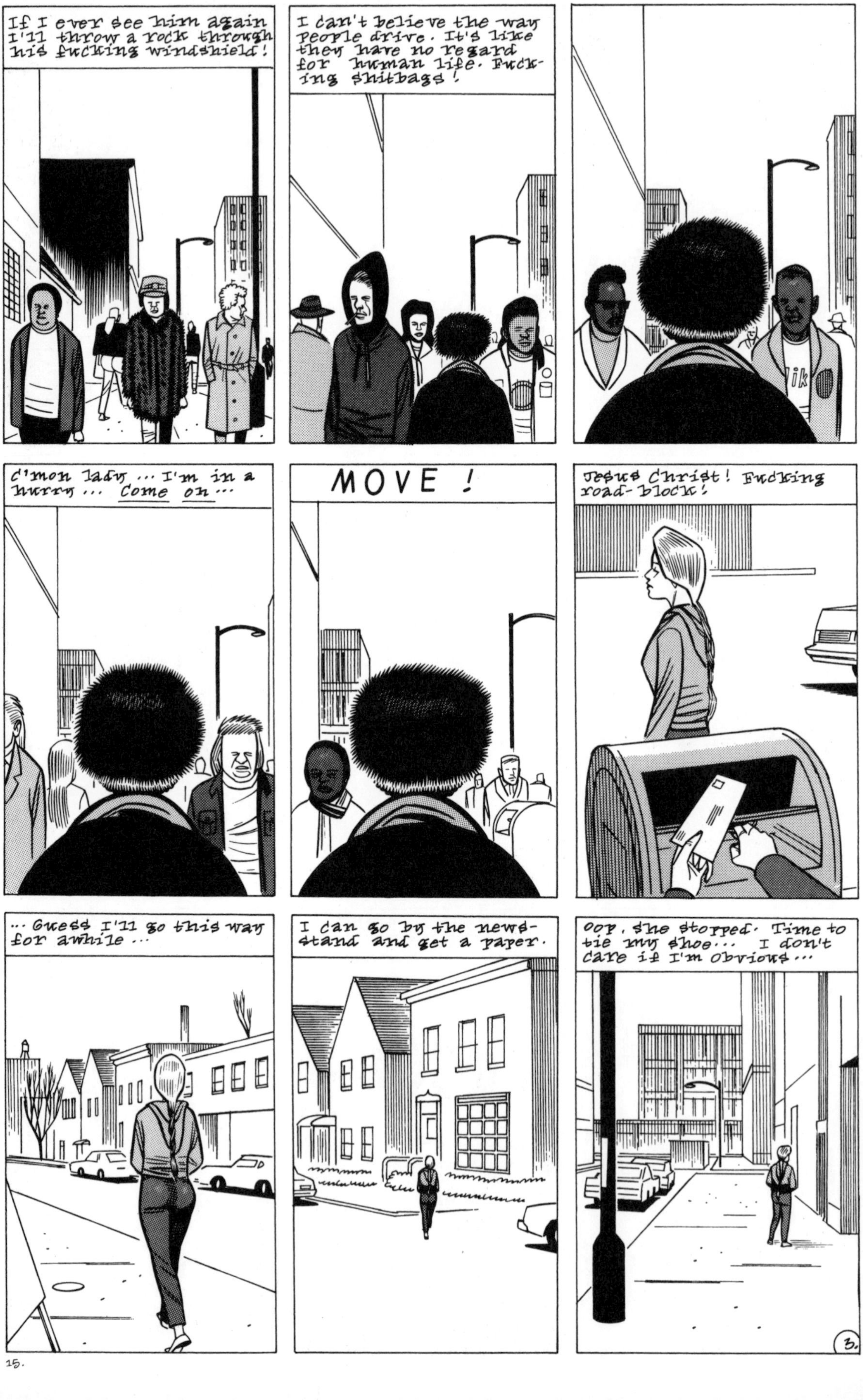
If I ever see him again I'll throw a rock through his fucking windshield!
I can't believe the way people drive. It's like they have no regard for human life. Fucking shitbags!
C'mon lady ... I'm in a hurry ... Come on ...
MOVE !
Jesus Christ! Fucking road-block!
... Guess I'll go this way for awhile ...
I can go by the news-stand and get a paper.
Oop, she stopped. Time to tie my shoe... I don't care if I'm obvious...
3.

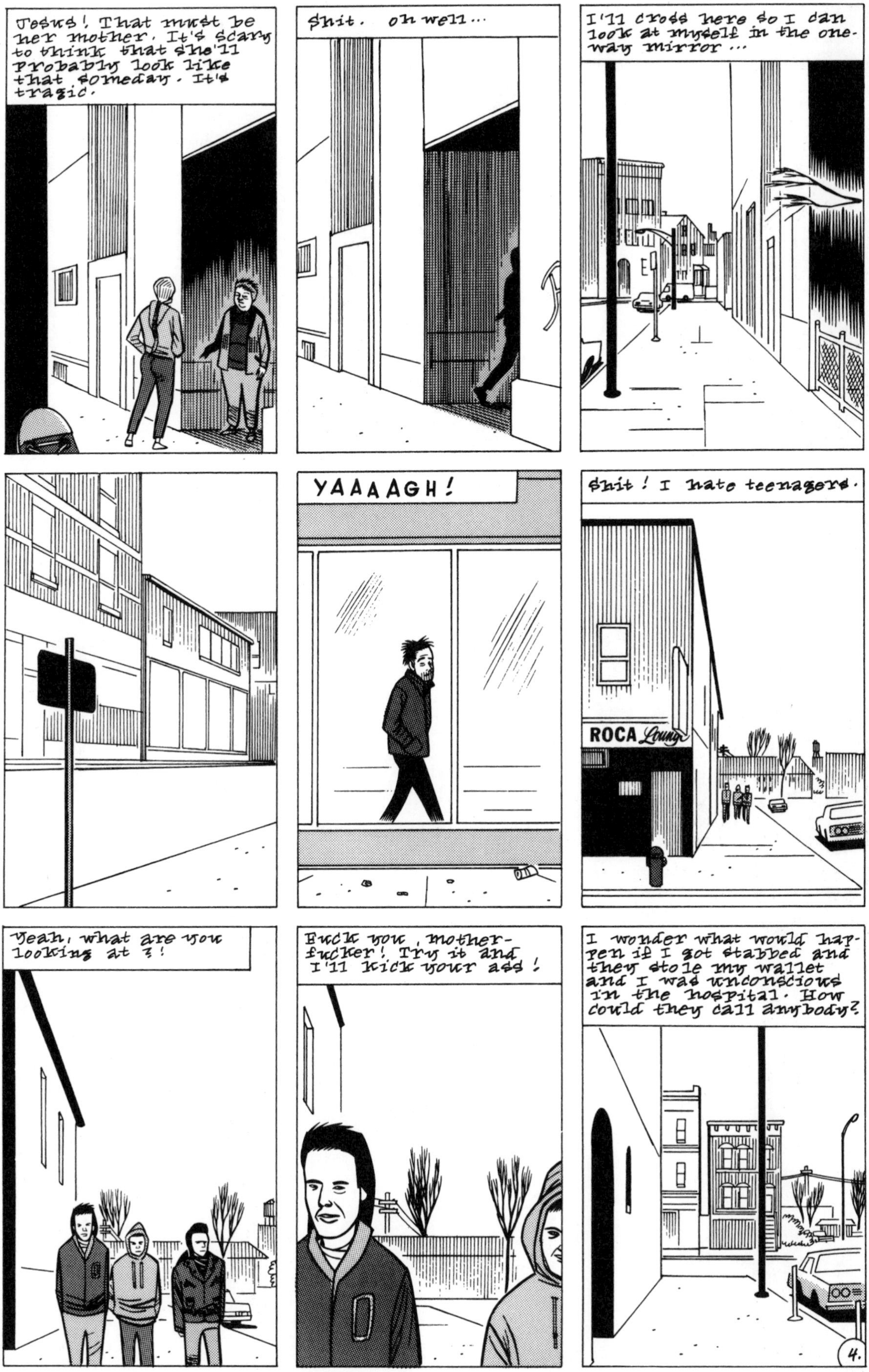
Jesus! That must be her mother. It's scary to think that she'll probably look like that someday. It's tragic.
Shit. Oh well...
I'll cross here so I can look at myself in the one-way mirror...
YAAAAGH!
Shit! I hate teenagers.
ROCA Lounge
Yeah, what are you looking at ?!
Fuck you, mother-fucker! Try it and I'll kick your ass!
I wonder what would happen if I got stabbed and they stole my wallet and I was unconscious in the hospital. How could they call anybody?
4.

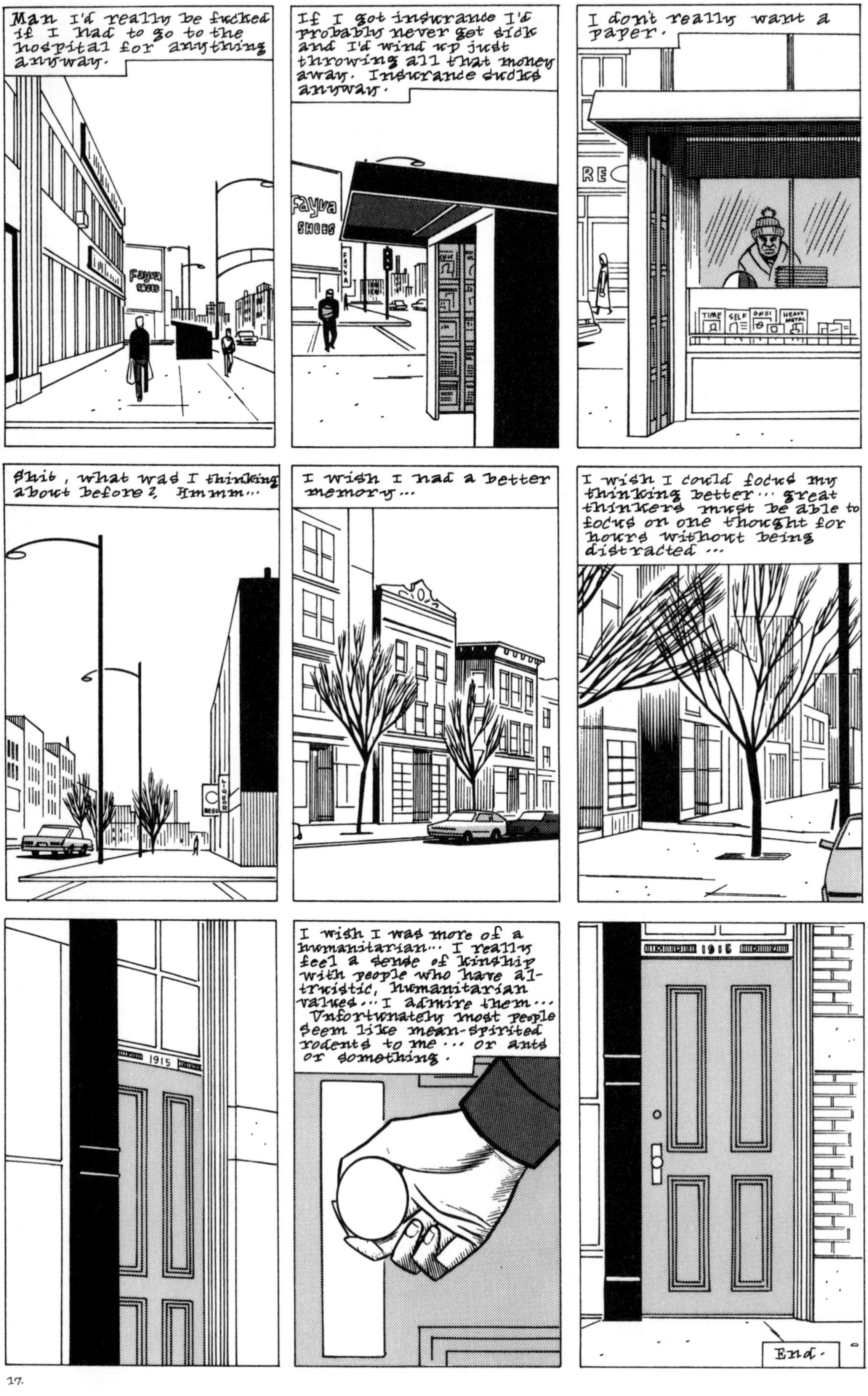
Man I'd really be fucked if I had to go to the hospital for anything anyway.
Fayva SHOES
If I got insurance I'd probably never get sick and I'd wind up just throwing all that money away. Insurance sucks anyway.
Fayva SHOES
I don't really want a paper.
RE
TIME
SELF
HEAVY METAL
Shit, what was I thinking about before? Hmmm...
I wish I had a better memory...
I wish I could focus my thinking better... great thinkers must be able to focus on one thought for hours without being distracted...
1915
I wish I was more of a humanitarian... I really feel a sense of kinship with people who have altruistic, humanitarian values... I admire them... Unfortunately most people seem like mean-spirited rodents to me... or ants or something.
1915
End.

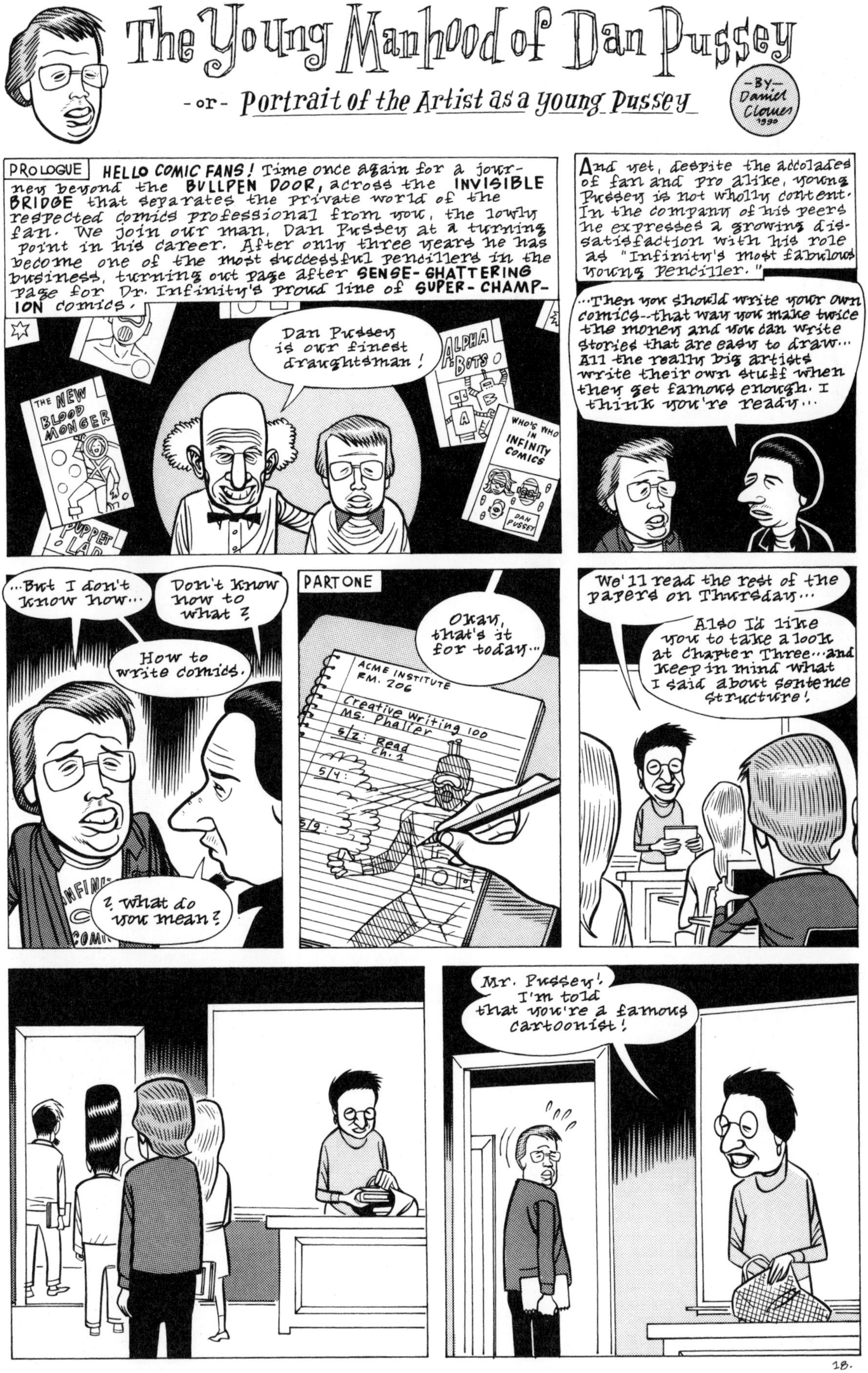
The Young Manhood of Dan Pussey
-or- Portrait of the Artist as a Young Pussey
-By- Daniel Clowes 1990
PROLOGUE
HELLO COMIC FANS! Time once again for a journey beyond the BULLPEN DOOR, across the INVISIBLE BRIDGE that separates the private world of the respected comics professional from you, the lowly fan. We join our man, Dan Pussey at a turning point in his career. After only three years he has become one of the most successful pencillers in the business, turning out page after SENSE-SHATTERING page for Dr. Infinity's proud line of SUPER-CHAMPION comics.
THE NEW BLOOD MONGER
PUPPET LAD
Dan Pussey is our finest draughtsman!
ALPHA BOTS
WHO'S WHO IN INFINITY COMICS
DAN PUSSEY
And yet, despite the accolades of fan and pro alike, young Pussey is not wholly content. In the company of his peers he expresses a growing dissatisfaction with his role as "Infinity's most fabulous young penciller."
...Then you should write your own comics--that way you make twice the money and you can write stories that are easy to draw... All the really big artists write their own stuff when they get famous enough. I think you're ready...
...But I don't know how...
Don't know how to what?
How to write comics.
?What do you mean?
INFINITY COMICS
PART ONE
Okay, that's it for today...
ACME INSTITUTE RM. 206
Creative Writing 100
Ms. Phaller
5/2: Read Ch. 1
5/4:
5/9:
We'll read the rest of the papers on Thursday...
Also I'd like you to take a look at Chapter Three...and keep in mind what I said about sentence structure!
Mr. Pussey! I'm told that you're a famous cartoonist!

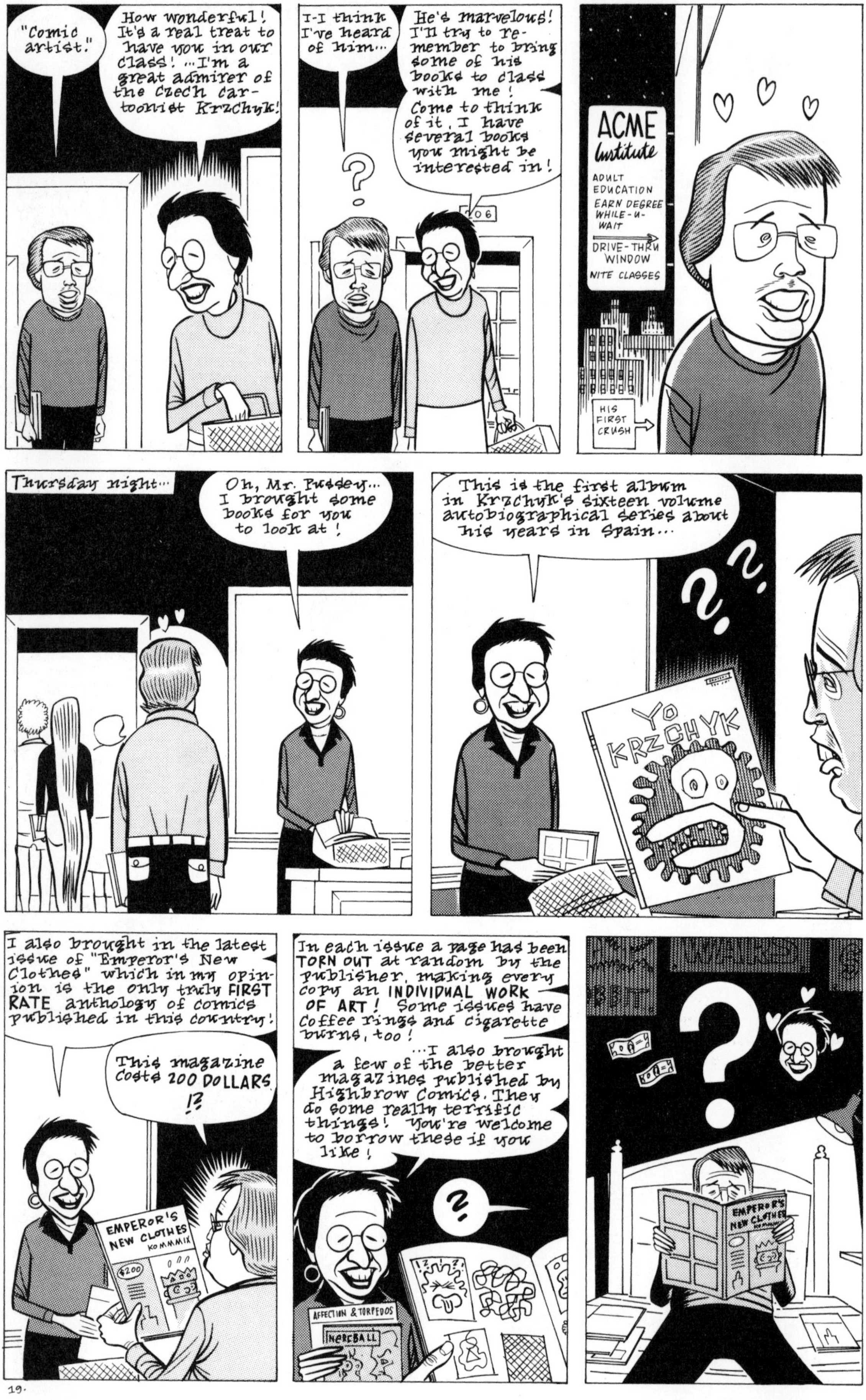
"Comic artist."
How wonderful! It's a real treat to have you in our class! ...I'm a great admirer of the Czech cartoonist Krzchyk!
I-I think I've heard of him...
He's marvelous! I'll try to remember to bring some of his books to class with me! Come to think of it, I have several books you might be interested in!
?
206
ACME Institute
ADULT EDUCATION
EARN DEGREE WHILE-U-WAIT
DRIVE-THRU WINDOW
NITE CLASSES
HIS FIRST CRUSH
Thursday night...
Oh, Mr. Pussey... I brought some books for you to look at!
This is the first album in Krzchyk's sixteen volume autobiographical series about his years in Spain...
??
YO KRZCHYK
I also brought in the latest issue of "Emperor's New Clothes" which in my opinion is the only truly FIRST RATE anthology of comics published in this country!
This magazine costs 200 DOLLARS!?
EMPEROR'S NEW CLOTHES KOMMIX
$200
In each issue a page has been TORN OUT at random by the publisher, making every copy an INDIVIDUAL WORK OF ART! Some issues have coffee rings and cigarette burns, too!
...I also brought a few of the better magazines published by Highbrow Comics. They do some really terrific things! You're welcome to borrow these if you like!
?
AFFECTION & TORPEDOS
INERBALL
?
EMPEROR'S NEW CLOTHES

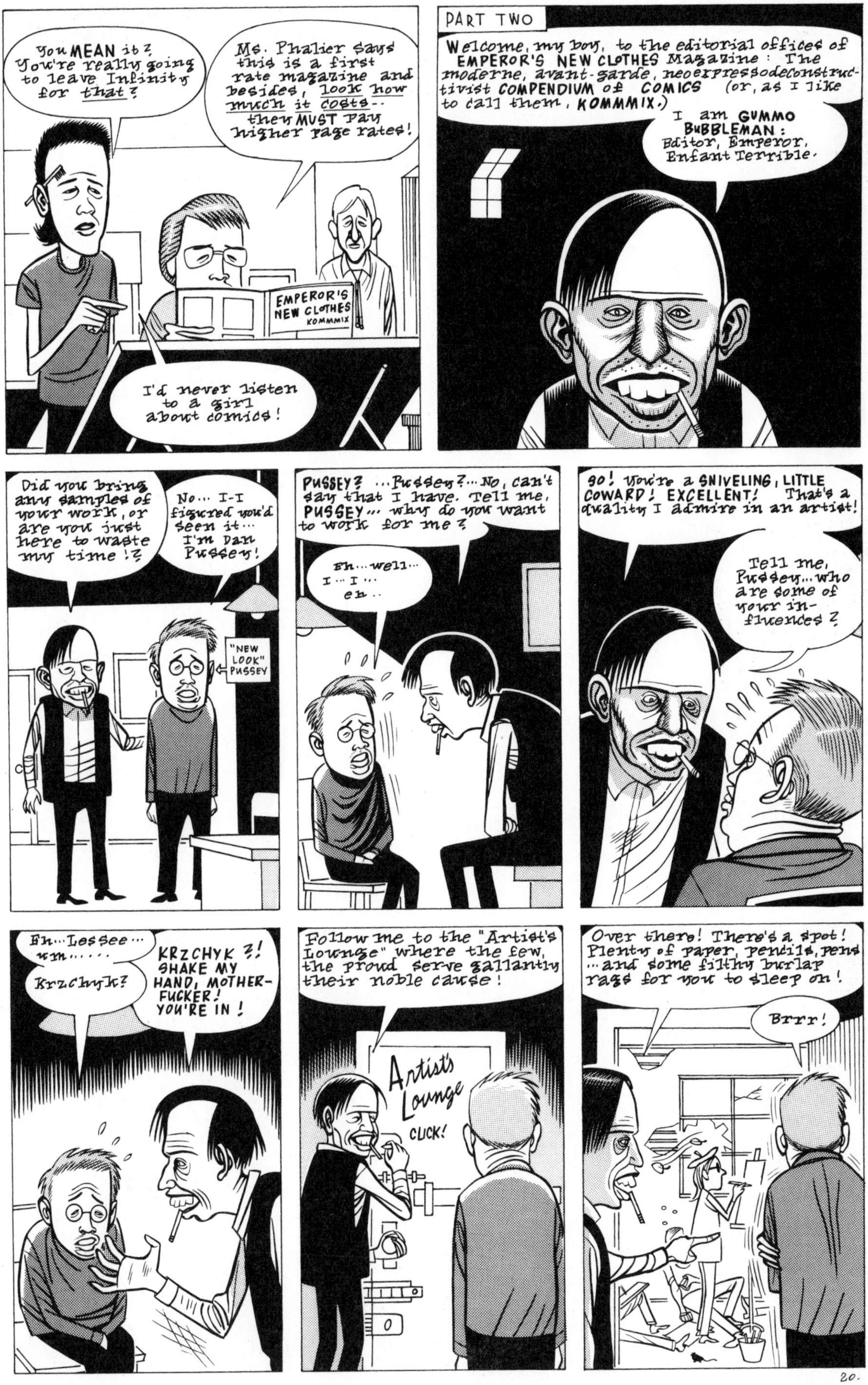
You MEAN it? You're really going to leave Infinity for that?
Ms. Phalier says this is a first rate magazine and besides, look how much it costs-- they MUST pay higher page rates!
EMPEROR'S NEW CLOTHES KOMMMIX
I'd never listen to a girl about comics!
PART TWO
Welcome, my boy, to the editorial offices of EMPEROR'S NEW CLOTHES Magazine: The moderne, avant-garde, neoexpressodeconstructivist COMPENDIUM of COMICS (or, as I like to call them, KOMMMIX.)
I am GUMMO BUBBLEMAN: Editor, Emperor, Enfant Terrible.
Did you bring any samples of your work, or are you just here to waste my time!?
No... I-I figured you'd seen it... I'm Dan Pussey!
"NEW LOOK" PUSSEY
PUSSEY? ...Pussey?... No, can't say that I have. Tell me, PUSSEY... why do you want to work for me?
Eh...well... I...I... eh..
So! You're a SNIVELING, LITTLE COWARD! EXCELLENT! That's a quality I admire in an artist!
Tell me, Pussey...who are some of your influences?
Eh...Lessee... um...... Krzchyk?
KRZCHYK?! SHAKE MY HAND, MOTHER-FUCKER! YOU'RE IN!
Follow me to the "Artist's Lounge" where the few, the proud serve gallantly their noble cause!
Artist's Lounge
CLICK!
Over there! There's a spot! Plenty of paper, pencils, pens ...and some filthy burlap rags for you to sleep on!
Brrr!

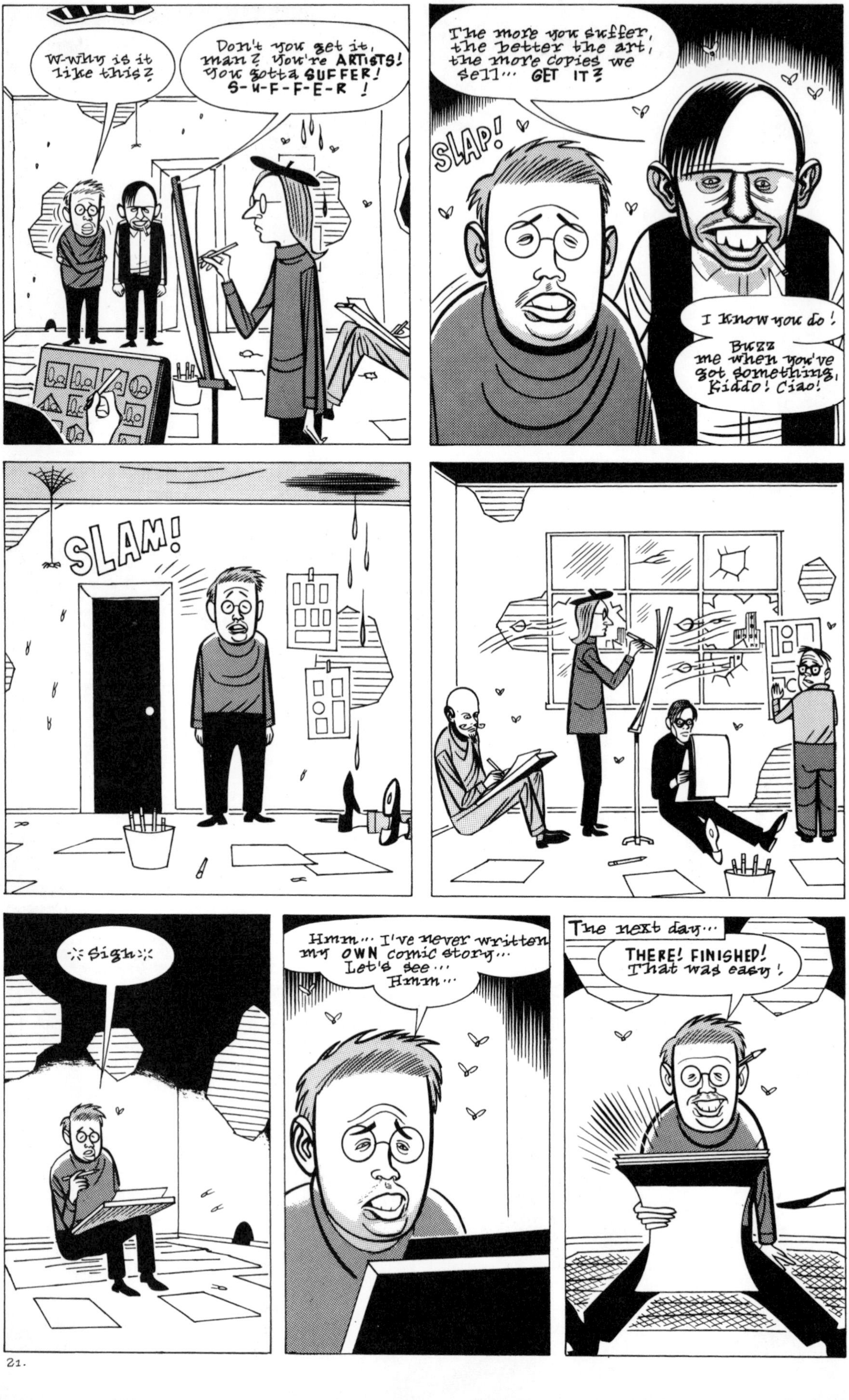
W-why is it like this?
Don't you get it, man? You're ARTISTS! You gotta SUFFER! S-U-F-F-E-R!
The more you suffer, the better the art, the more copies we sell... GET IT?
SLAP!
I know you do!
Buzz me when you've got something, Kiddo! Ciao!
SLAM!
Sigh
Hmm... I've never written my OWN comic story... Let's see... Hmm...
The next day...
THERE! FINISHED! That was easy!

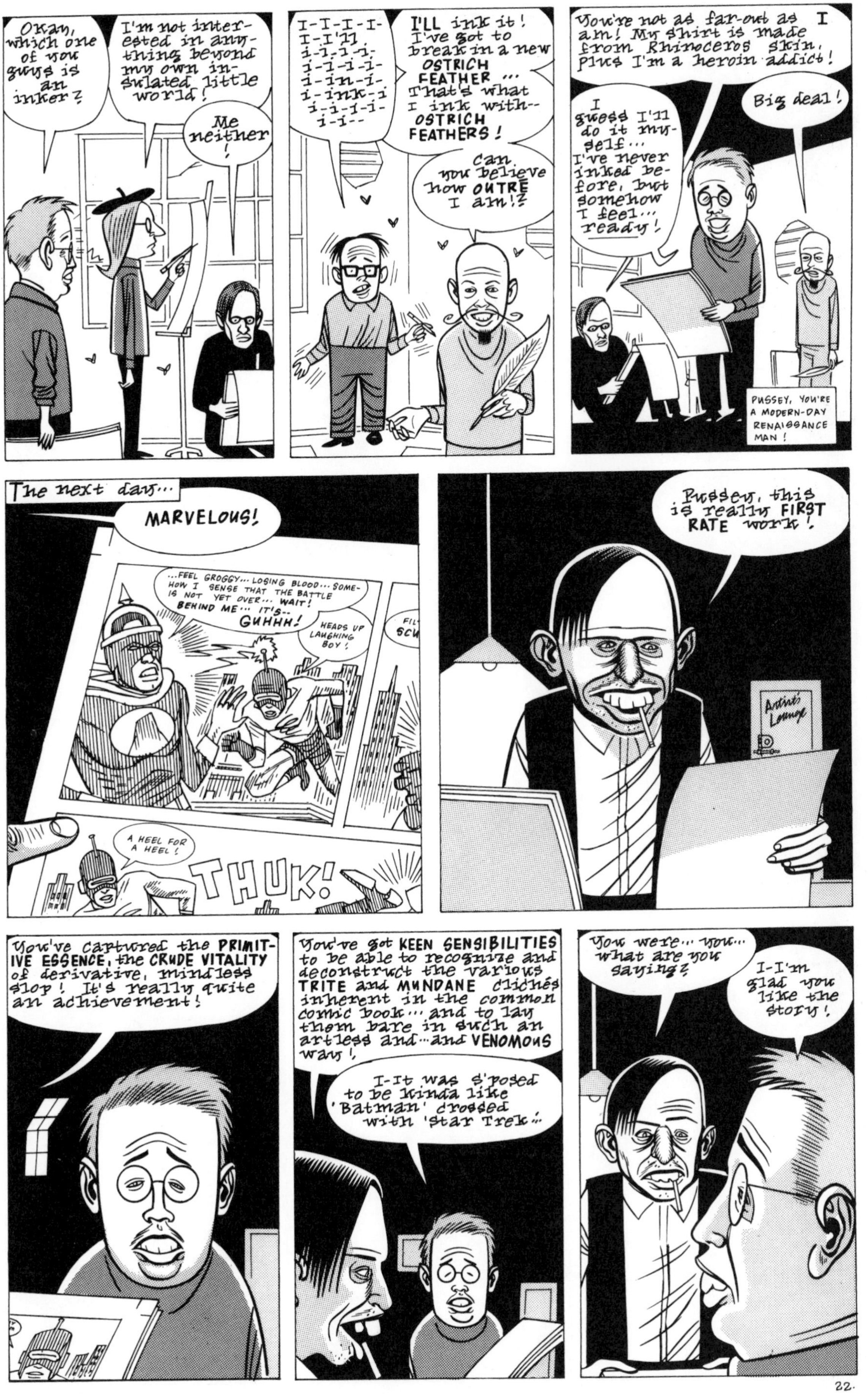
Okay, which one of you guys is an inker?
I'm not interested in anything beyond my own insulated little world!
Me neither!
I-I-I-I-I-I'll i-i-i-i-i-i-i-i-i-in-i-i-ink-i i-i-i-i-i-i-i--
I'LL ink it! I've got to break in a new OSTRICH FEATHER ... That's what I ink with-- OSTRICH FEATHERS!
Can you believe how OUTRE I am!?
You're not as far-out as I am! My shirt is made from Rhinoceros skin, plus I'm a heroin addict!
I guess I'll do it myself... I've never inked before, but somehow I feel... ready!
Big deal!
PUSSEY, YOU'RE A MODERN-DAY RENAISSANCE MAN!
The next day...
MARVELOUS!
...FEEL GROGGY... LOSING BLOOD... SOMEHOW I SENSE THAT THE BATTLE IS NOT YET OVER... WAIT! BEHIND ME... IT'S-- GUHHH!
HEADS UP LAUGHING BOY!
A HEEL FOR A HEEL!
THUK!
Pussey, this is really FIRST RATE work!
Artists Lounge
You've captured the PRIMITIVE ESSENCE, the CRUDE VITALITY of derivative, mindless slop! It's really quite an achievement!
You've got KEEN SENSIBILITIES to be able to recognize and deconstruct the various TRITE and MUNDANE clichés inherent in the common comic book... and to lay them bare in such an artless and... and VENOMOUS way!
I-It was s'posed to be kinda like 'Batman' crossed with 'Star Trek'...
You were... you... what are you saying?
I-I'm glad you like the story!

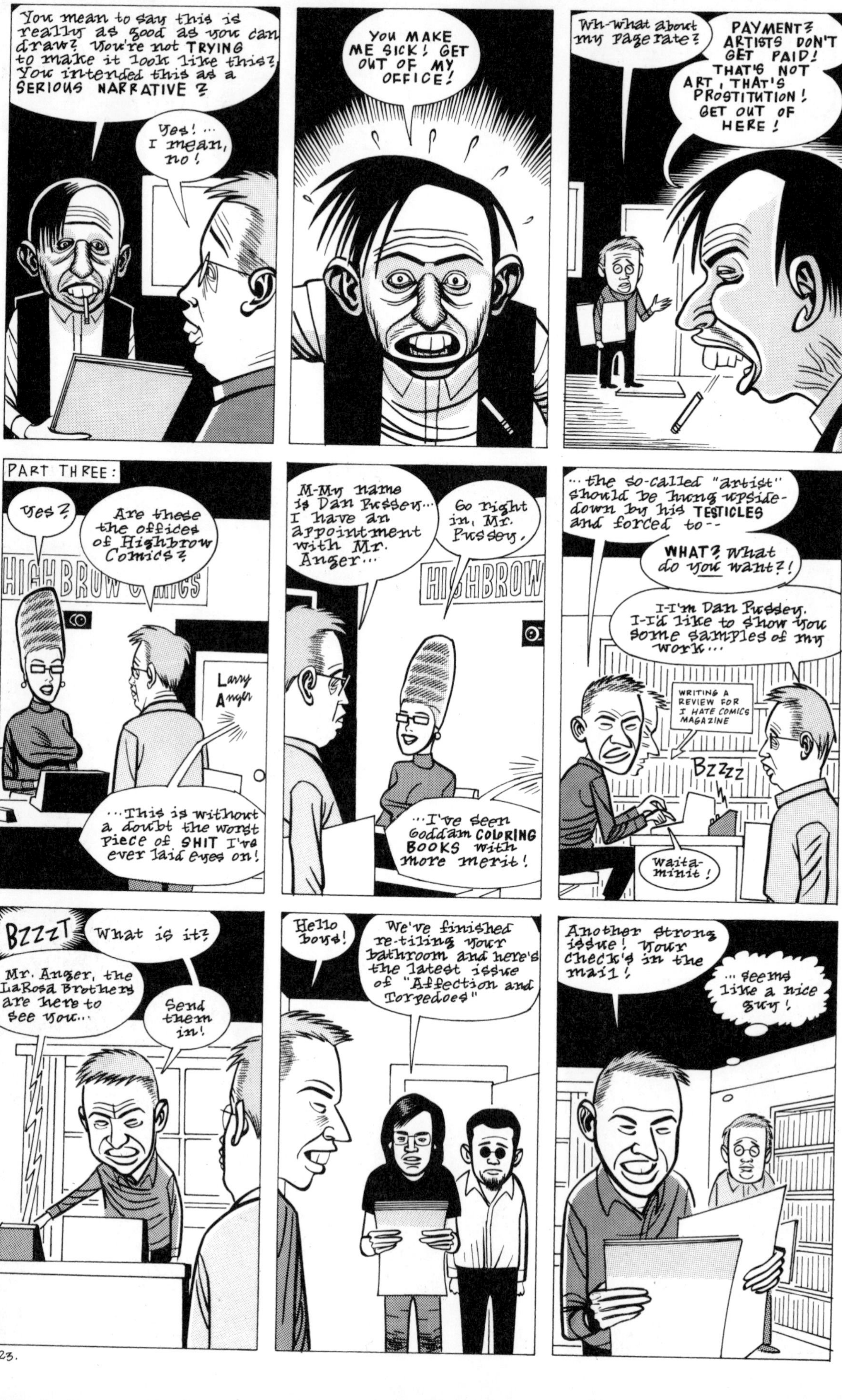

You mean to say this is really as good as you can draw? You're not TRYING to make it look like this? You intended this as a SERIOUS NARRATIVE?
Yes! ... I mean, no!
YOU MAKE ME SICK! GET OUT OF MY OFFICE!
Wh-what about my page rate?
PAYMENT? ARTISTS DON'T GET PAID! THAT'S NOT ART, THAT'S PROSTITUTION! GET OUT OF HERE!
PART THREE:
Yes?
Are these the offices of Highbrow Comics?
HIGHBROW COMICS
Larry Anger
...This is without a doubt the worst piece of SHIT I've ever laid eyes on!
M-My name is Dan Pussey... I have an appointment with Mr. Anger...
Go right in, Mr. Pussey.
HIGHBROW
...I've seen Goddam COLORING BOOKS with more merit!
...the so-called "artist" should be hung upside-down by his TESTICLES and forced to--
WHAT? What do you want?!
I-I'm Dan Pussey. I-I'd like to show you some samples of my work...
WRITING A REVIEW FOR I HATE COMICS MAGAZINE
BZZZZ
Waita-minit!
BZZZT
What is it?
Mr. Anger, the LaRosa Brothers are here to see you...
Send them in!
Hello boys!
We've finished re-tiling your bathroom and here's the latest issue of "Affection and Torpedoes"
Another strong issue! Your check's in the mail!
...seems like a nice guy!

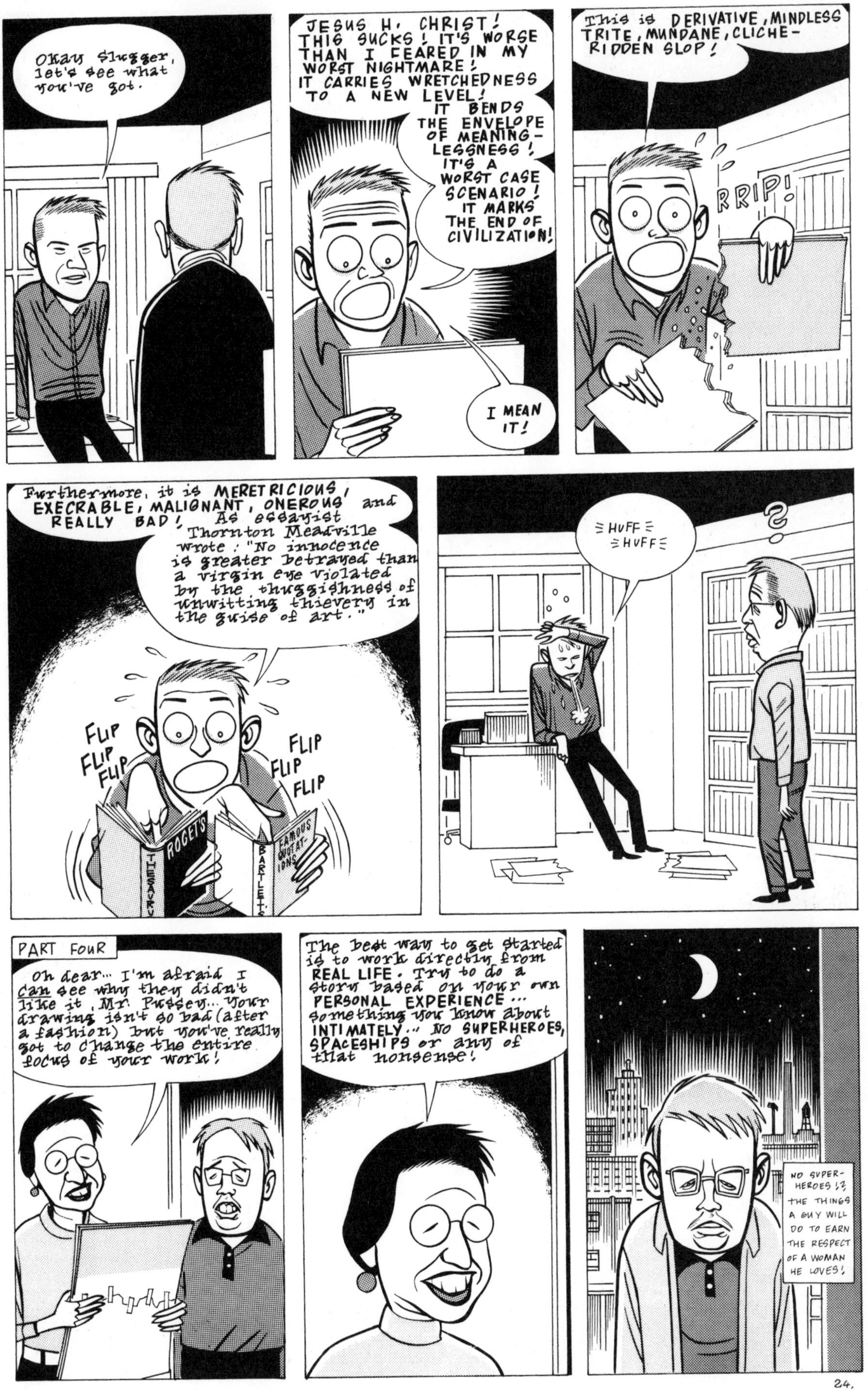
Okay Slugger, let's see what you've got.
JESUS H. CHRIST! THIS SUCKS! IT'S WORSE THAN I FEARED IN MY WORST NIGHTMARE! IT CARRIES WRETCHEDNESS TO A NEW LEVEL!
IT BENDS THE ENVELOPE OF MEANING-LESSNESS! IT'S A WORST CASE SCENARIO! IT MARKS THE END OF CIVILIZATION!
I MEAN IT!
This is DERIVATIVE, MINDLESS TRITE, MUNDANE, CLICHE-RIDDEN SLOP!
RRIP!
Furthermore, it is MERETRICIOUS, EXECRABLE, MALIGNANT, ONEROUS and REALLY BAD! As essayist Thornton Meadville wrote: "No innocence is greater betrayed than a virgin eye violated by the thuggishness of unwitting thievery in the guise of art."
FLIP FLIP FLIP
FLIP FLIP FLIP
ROGET'S THESAURUS
BARTLETT'S FAMOUS QUOTATIONS
HUFF HUFF
?
PART FOUR
Oh dear... I'm afraid I can see why they didn't like it, Mr. Pussey... Your drawing isn't so bad (after a fashion) but you've really got to change the entire focus of your work!
The best way to get started is to work directly from REAL LIFE. Try to do a story based on your own PERSONAL EXPERIENCE... something you know about INTIMATELY... No SUPERHEROES, SPACESHIPS or any of that nonsense!
NO SUPER-HEROES!? THE THINGS A GUY WILL DO TO EARN THE RESPECT OF A WOMAN HE LOVES!

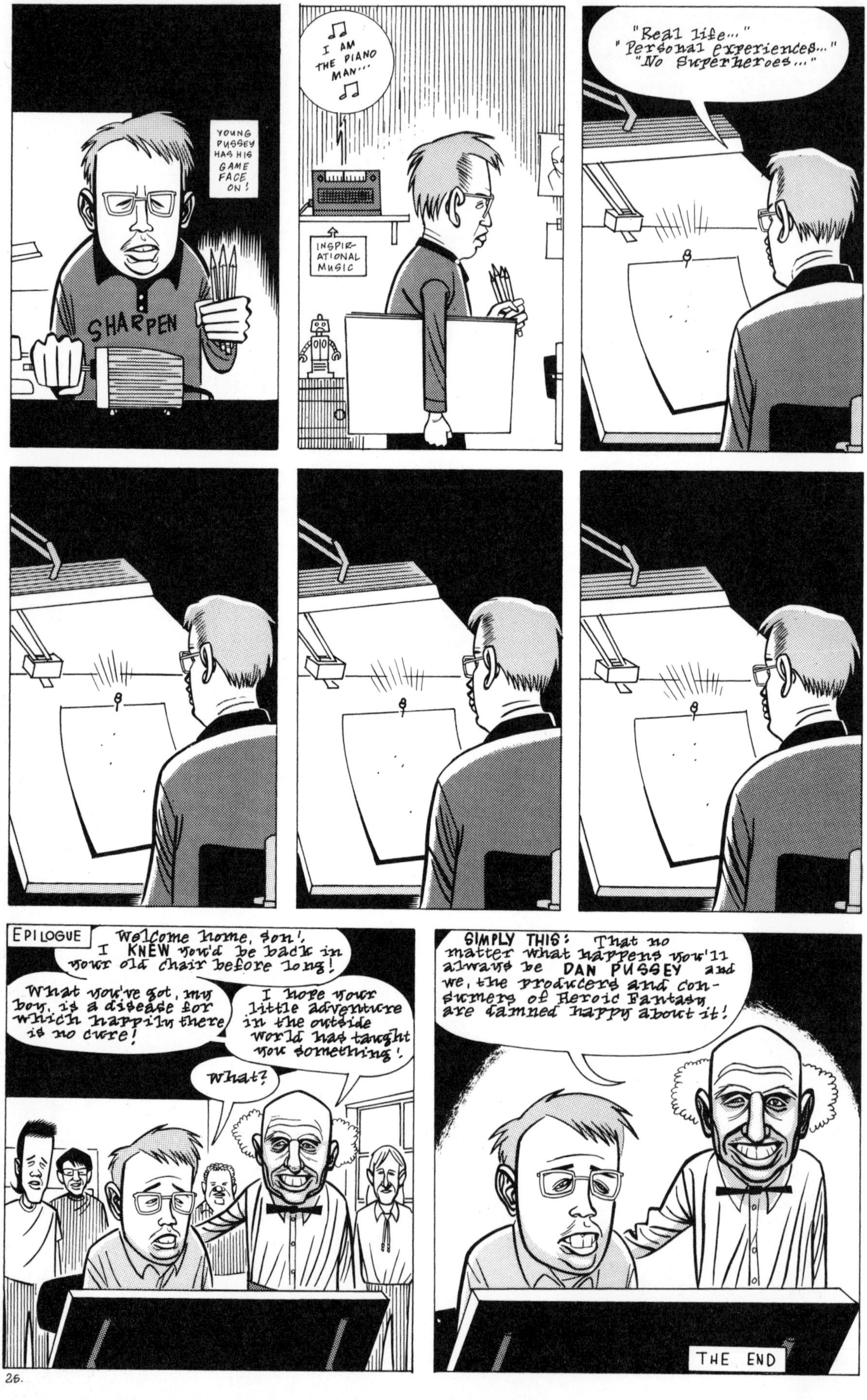
YOUNG PUSSEY HAS HIS GAME FACE ON!
SHARPEN
I AM THE PIANO MAN...
INSPIR-ATIONAL MUSIC
"Real life..." "Personal experiences..." "No Superheroes..."
EPILOGUE
Welcome home, son!, I KNEW you'd be back in your old chair before long!
What you've got, my boy, is a disease for which happily there is no cure!
I hope your little adventure in the outside world has taught you something!
What?
SIMPLY THIS: That no matter what happens you'll always be DAN PUSSEY and we, the producers and con-sumers of Heroic Fantasy are damned happy about it!
THE END

POSTAL INTERCOURSE

WRITE TO: EIGHTBALL
BOX 3357
CHICAGO, ILL.
60654

... Stop me if you've heard this one before, but EIGHTBALL #2 is unbelievably great...

Jim Woodring
Seattle, Wa.

..."I Hate you Deeply" was the funniest thing this side of Crumb. I feel this way even though I respect Richard Simmons, lift weights and love the Rolling Stones... [However] as an artist, you draw too much like Gilbert Hernandez... copying Gilbert's style only serves to prevent you from breaking into a style of your own!

Chris Speck
Durham, N.C.

...Except for "Foot-Foot" and LL on the TV there was nothing reassuring about "Velvet Glove" Pt. 2. Congrats!

Jim Donato
Orlando, Fl.

... So, you like practical jokes, eh? I figured I'd let you in on a little one me and my husband play on our friends during the holidays. It's a real pisser! ... We've been throwing a X-mas party over at our place for years - not much more than an excuse for everybody to get shit-faced - until the year my husband fills the ice-cube trays with water he scooped out of the toilet! Did we howl at our little joke! of course we made sure there was some trays of good cubes for ourselves.

Anyway, this last year he came up with an even funnier idea. Before our friends came over, he took the liberty of shooting a load of his cum into the Egg-Nog I always make. When we saw our guests drinking that shit my husband and I looked at each other for a second, and laughed our fucking heads off! Everyone looked at us but we just said, "oh nothing!" What do you think? Is this prank worth a free subscription to your magazine?

Mrs. Jane K. Lorenzen
Englishtown, N.J.

PRANK PHONE CALL CONTEST

FINAL RESULTS

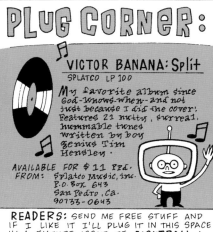

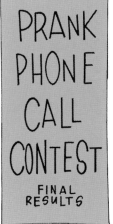

The Grand Prize goes to Jim Blanchard of Seattle for sending in a tape of calls made by his best friend in high school (a shy, anonymous Jehovah's Witness) during a long, hot summer in Oklahoma. This guy is the crown prince of telephone harassment, managing to come off as a bothersome menace without resorting cheap insults. For example: "Mildred, this is Mike Snyder, I live just a couple doors down from you and, well, I've got kind of a peculiar problem -- my plumbin's backed up and I was wondering, if you wouldn't object too strongly if I came over and took a bath." "I don't know you." "Well, y'know, this might be a good chance to get to know each other." Others include: "The Mail-order Dildo", obnoxious responses to want ads ("I'm not gonna drive all the way up there for a Goddamn canoe!"), The Homeowner's Neighborhood Association ("Get that lawn in shape or you'll never buy a house around here again!") and the classic opening line: "Clifford, what am I gonna do? I just shot furniture wax in my boy's eye!"

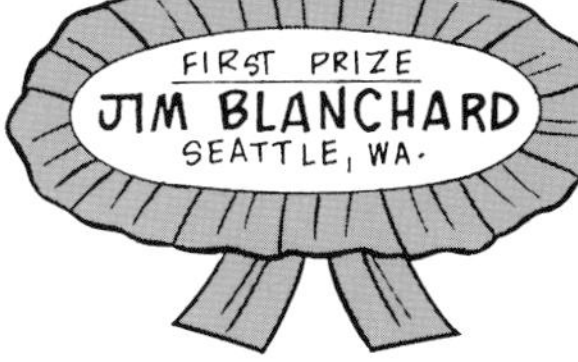

FIRST PRIZE
JIM BLANCHARD
SEATTLE, WA.

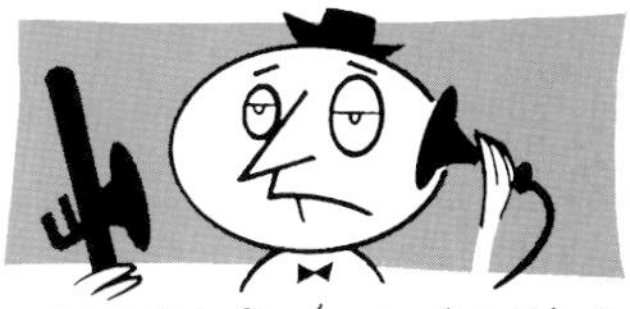

RUNNER-UP: PAUL COWEN of Pt. Pleasant, N.J. for impersonating a DJ and asking a non-English-speaking man if he thought the situation in Beijing was as bad as "that situation with Godzilla a few years back."

BACK ISSUES:

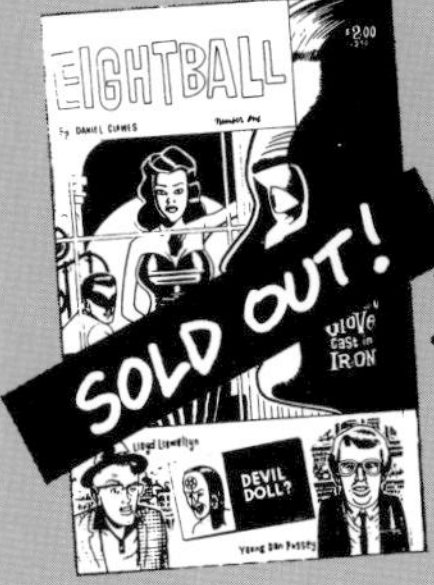

EIGHTBALL
SOLD OUT!

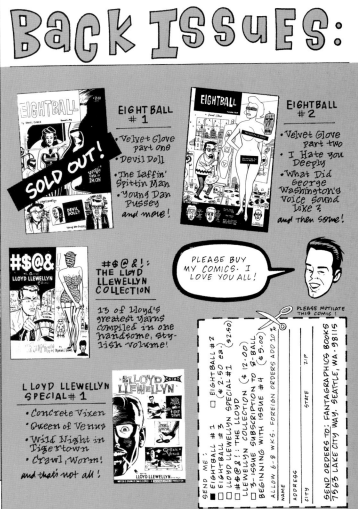

EIGHTBALL #1
- Velvet Glove part one
- Devil Doll
- The Laffin' Spittin Man
- Young Dan Pussey

and more!

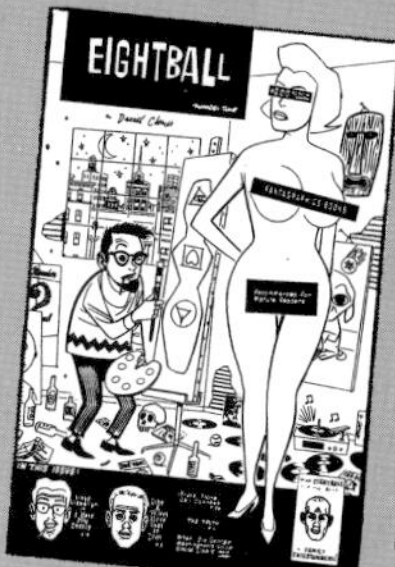

EIGHTBALL

EIGHTBALL #2
- Velvet Glove part two
- I Hate you Deeply
- What Did George Washington's Voice Sound Like?

and then some!

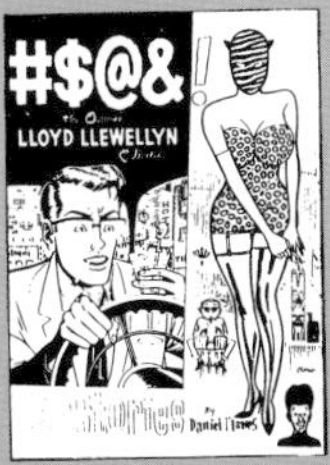

#$@&
LLOYD LLEWELLYN

#$@&!: THE LLOYD LLEWELLYN COLLECTION

13 of Lloyd's greatest yarns compiled in one handsome, stylish volume!

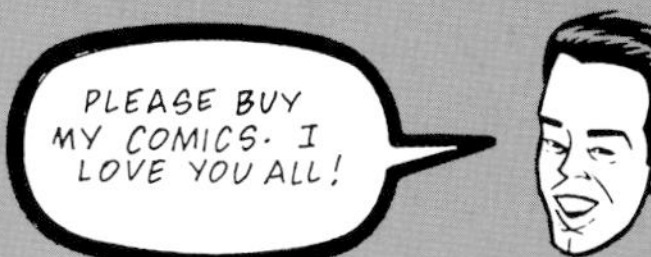

PLEASE BUY MY COMICS. I LOVE YOU ALL!

LLOYD LLEWELLYN SPECIAL #1
- Concrete Vixen
- Queen of Venus
- Wild Night in Tigertown
- Crawl, Worm!

and that's not all!

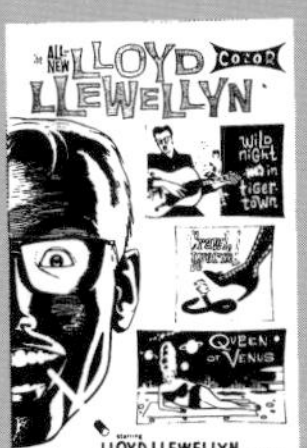

LLOYD LLEWELLYN

PLEASE MUTILATE THIS COMIC!

SEND ME:
- ■ EIGHTBALL #1 □ EIGHTBALL #2
- □ EIGHTBALL #3 ($2.50 ea.)
- □ LLOYD LLEWELLYN SPECIAL #1 ($2.50)
- □ #$@&!: THE LLOYD LLEWELLYN COLLECTION ($12.00)
- □ 3-ISSUE SUBSCRIPTION TO 8-BALL BEGINNING WITH ISSUE #4 ($5.00)

ALLOW 6-8 WKS. FOREIGN ORDERS ADD 10%

NAME
ADDRESS
CITY STATE ZIP

SEND ORDERS TO: FANTAGRAPHICS BOOKS
7563 LAKE CITY WAY. SEATTLE, WA. 98115

PLUG CORNER:

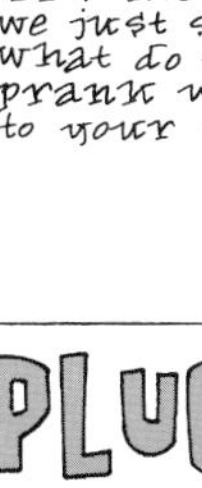

VICTOR BANANA: Split

SPLATCO LP 100

My favorite album since God-knows-when--and not just because I did the cover! Features 21 nutty, surreal, hummable tunes written by boy genius Tim Hensley.

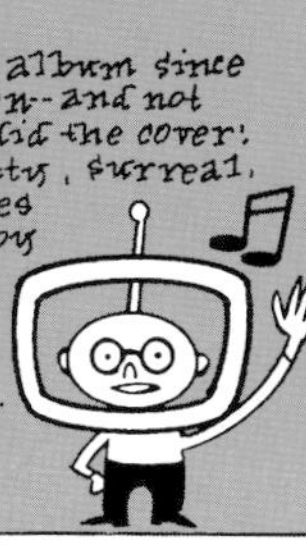

AVAILABLE FOR $11 Ppd. FROM: Splatco Music, inc.
P.O. Box 643
San Pedro, Ca.
90733-0643

READERS: SEND ME FREE STUFF AND IF I LIKE IT I'LL PLUG IT IN THIS SPACE IN A FUTURE ISSUE OF **EIGHTBALL!**

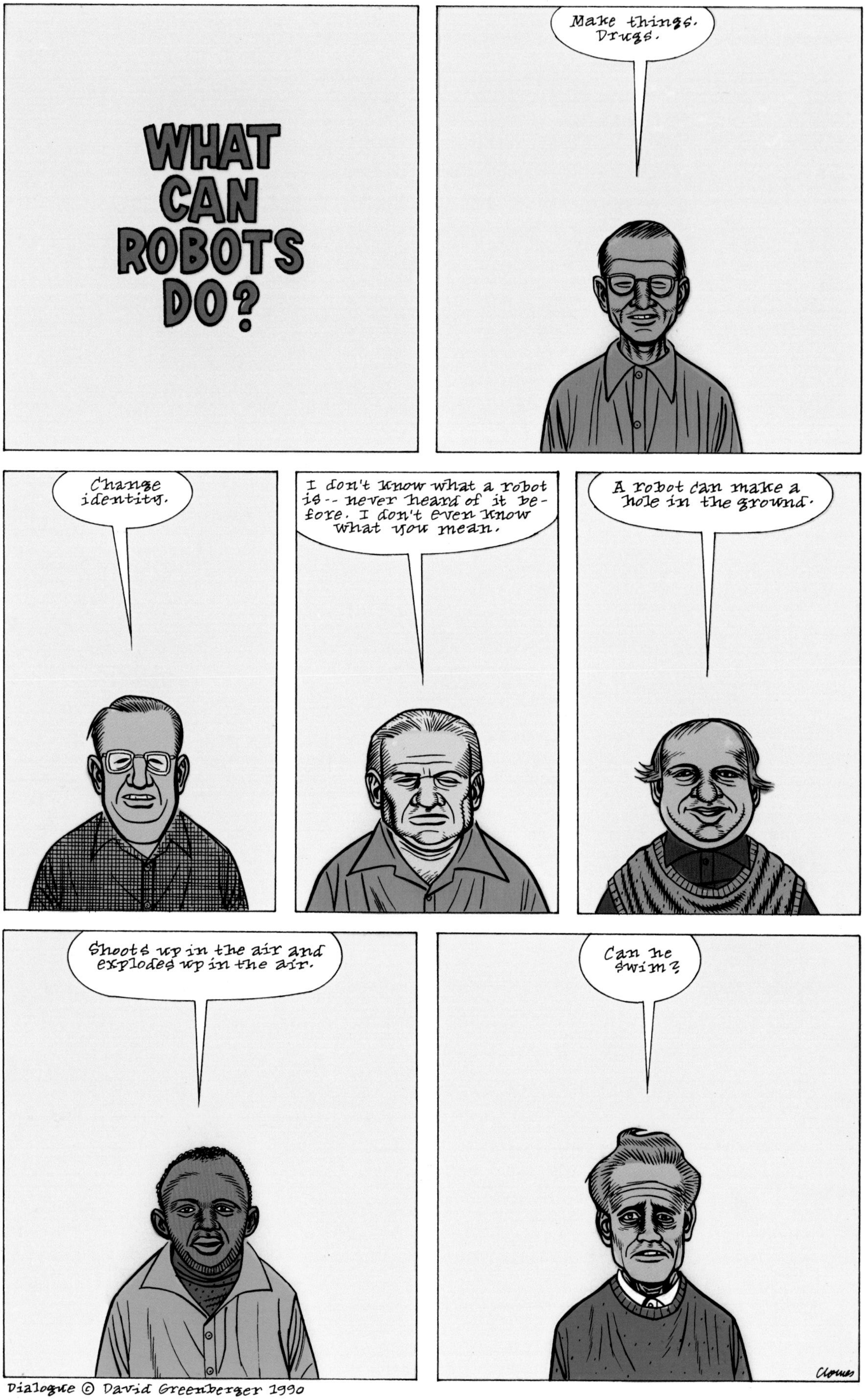
WHAT CAN ROBOTS DO?
Make things. Drugs.
Change identity.
I don't know what a robot is -- never heard of it before. I don't even know what you mean.
A robot can make a hole in the ground.
Shoots up in the air and explodes up in the air.
Can he swim?
Clowes
Dialogue © David Greenberger 1990

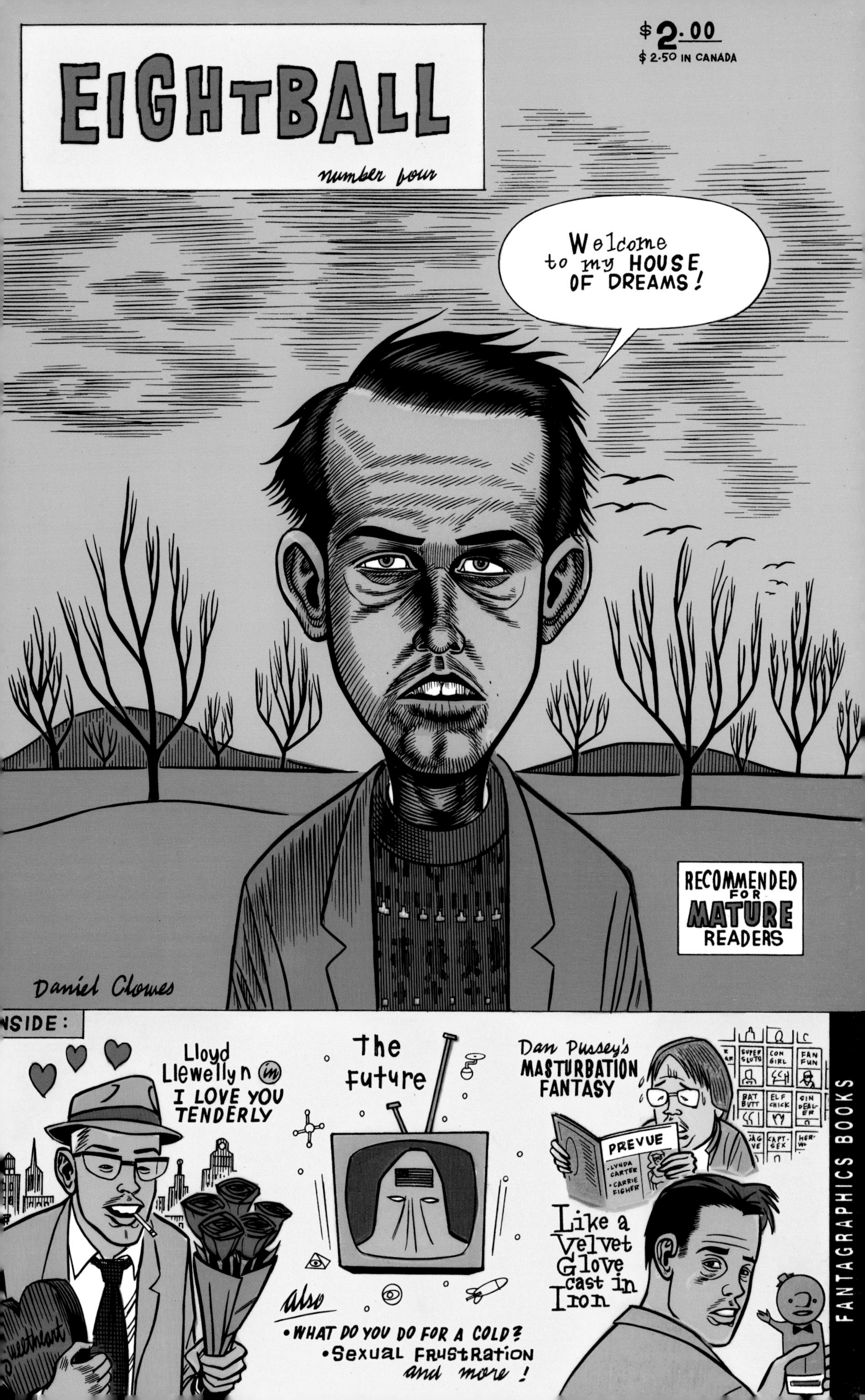
EIGHTBALL
number four
$2.00
$2.50 IN CANADA
Welcome to my HOUSE OF DREAMS!
RECOMMENDED FOR MATURE READERS
Daniel Clowes
INSIDE:
Lloyd Llewellyn in I LOVE YOU TENDERLY
the Future
Dan Pussey's MASTURBATION FANTASY
PREVUE
• LYNDA CARTER
• CARRIE FISHER
Like a Velvet Glove cast in Iron
also
• WHAT DO YOU DO FOR A COLD?
• Sexual Frustration
and more!
Sweetheart
FANTAGRAPHICS BOOKS

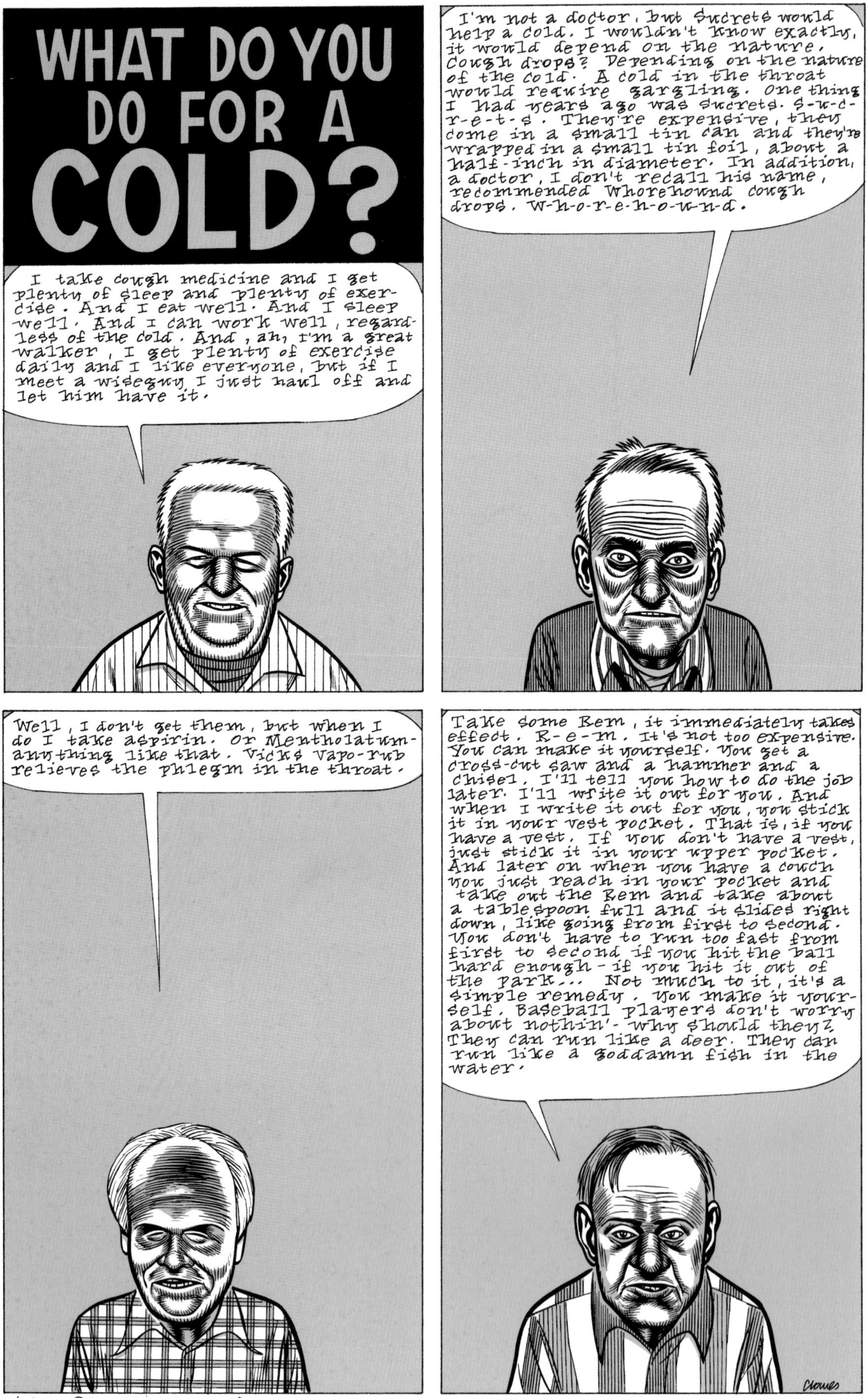
WHAT DO YOU DO FOR A COLD?
I take cough medicine and I get plenty of sleep and plenty of exercise. And I eat well. And I sleep well. And I can work well, regardless of the cold. And, ah, I'm a great walker, I get plenty of exercise daily and I like everyone, but if I meet a wiseguy I just haul off and let him have it.
I'm not a doctor, but Sucrets would help a cold. I wouldn't know exactly, it would depend on the nature. Cough drops? Depending on the nature of the cold. A cold in the throat would require gargling. One thing I had years ago was Sucrets. S-u-c-r-e-t-s. They're expensive, they come in a small tin can and they're wrapped in a small tin foil, about a half-inch in diameter. In addition, a doctor, I don't recall his name, recommended Whorehound cough drops. W-h-o-r-e-h-o-u-n-d.
Well, I don't get them, but when I do I take aspirin. Or Mentholatum-anything like that. Vicks Vapo-rub relieves the phlegm in the throat.
Take some Rem, it immediately takes effect. R-e-m. It's not too expensive. You can make it yourself. You get a cross-cut saw and a hammer and a chisel. I'll tell you how to do the job later. I'll write it out for you. And when I write it out for you, you stick it in your vest pocket. That is, if you have a vest. If you don't have a vest, just stick it in your upper pocket. And later on when you have a couch you just reach in your pocket and take out the Rem and take about a tablespoon full and it slides right down, like going from first to second. You don't have to run too fast from first to second if you hit the ball hard enough - if you hit it out of the park... Not much to it, it's a simple remedy. You make it yourself. Baseball players don't worry about nothin' - why should they? They can run like a deer. They can run like a goddamn fish in the water.
Clowes

Dialogue © Dave Greenberger from DUPLEX PLANET #33

LIKE A VELVET GLOVE CAST IN IRON

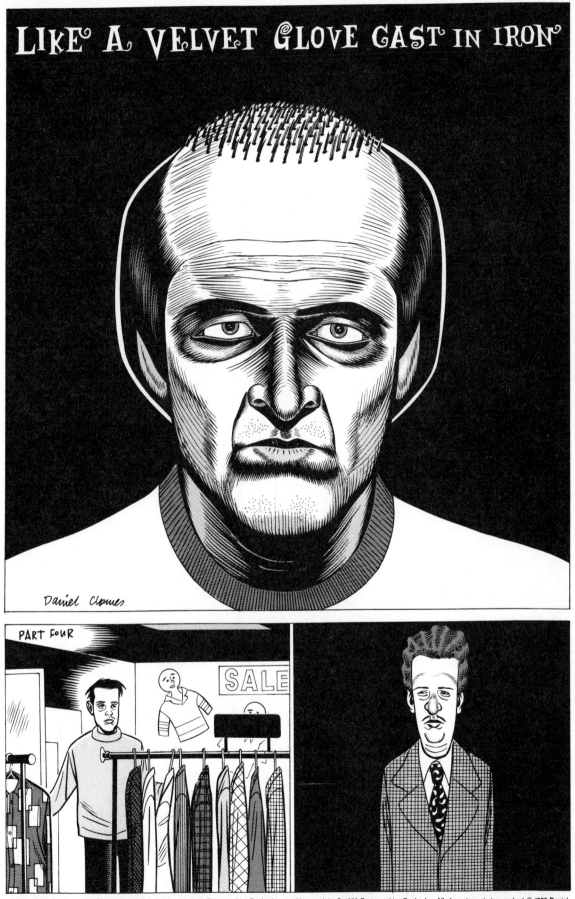

Daniel Clowes

PART FOUR

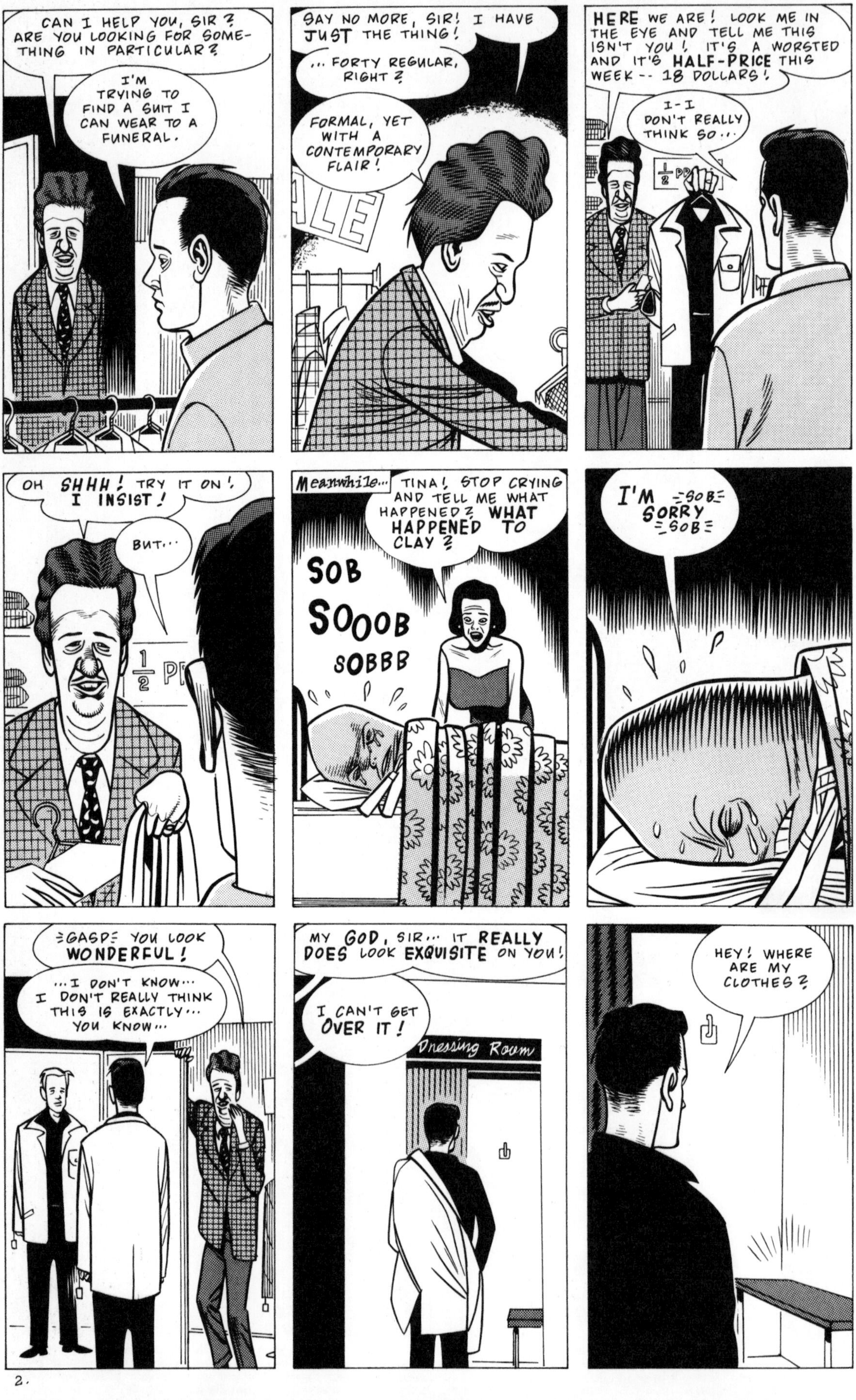
CAN I HELP YOU, SIR? ARE YOU LOOKING FOR SOMETHING IN PARTICULAR?
I'M TRYING TO FIND A SUIT I CAN WEAR TO A FUNERAL.
SAY NO MORE, SIR! I HAVE JUST THE THING!
... FORTY REGULAR, RIGHT?
FORMAL, YET WITH A CONTEMPORARY FLAIR!
HERE WE ARE! LOOK ME IN THE EYE AND TELL ME THIS ISN'T YOU! IT'S A WORSTED AND IT'S HALF-PRICE THIS WEEK -- 18 DOLLARS!
I-I DON'T REALLY THINK SO...
OH SHHH! TRY IT ON! I INSIST!
BUT...
Meanwhile...
TINA! STOP CRYING AND TELL ME WHAT HAPPENED? WHAT HAPPENED TO CLAY?
SOB
SOOOB
SOBBB
I'M =SOB= SORRY =SOB=
=GASP= YOU LOOK WONDERFUL!
...I DON'T KNOW... I DON'T REALLY THINK THIS IS EXACTLY... YOU KNOW...
MY GOD, SIR... IT REALLY DOES LOOK EXQUISITE ON YOU!
I CAN'T GET OVER IT!
Dressing Room
HEY! WHERE ARE MY CLOTHES?

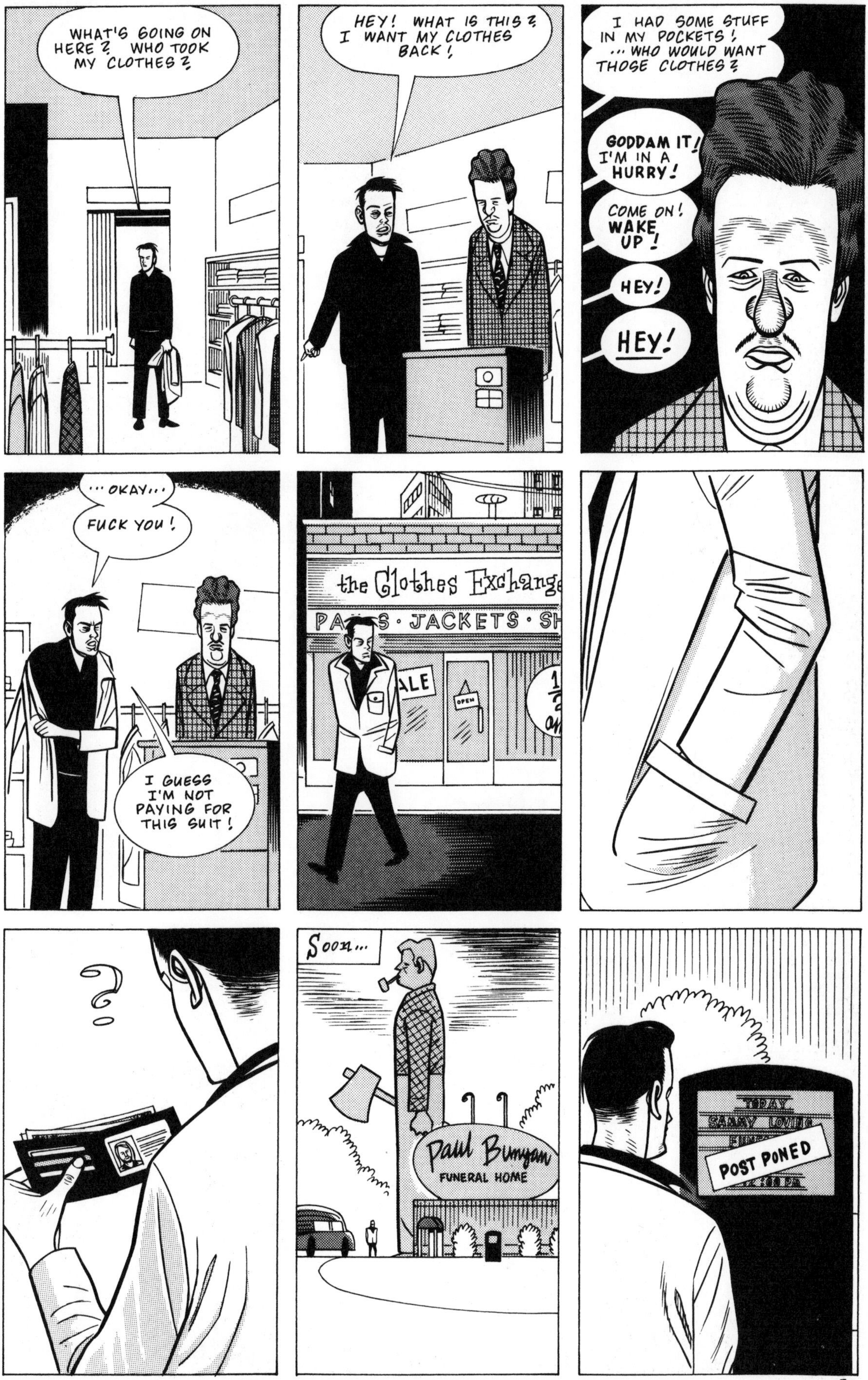
WHAT'S GOING ON HERE? WHO TOOK MY CLOTHES?
HEY! WHAT IS THIS? I WANT MY CLOTHES BACK!
I HAD SOME STUFF IN MY POCKETS! ... WHO WOULD WANT THOSE CLOTHES?
GODDAM IT! I'M IN A HURRY!
COME ON! WAKE UP!
HEY!
HEY!
... OKAY...
FUCK YOU!
I GUESS I'M NOT PAYING FOR THIS SUIT!
the Clothes Exchange
JACKETS
OPEN
Soon...
Paul Bunyan
FUNERAL HOME
TODAY
SAMMY LOVING
POST PONED

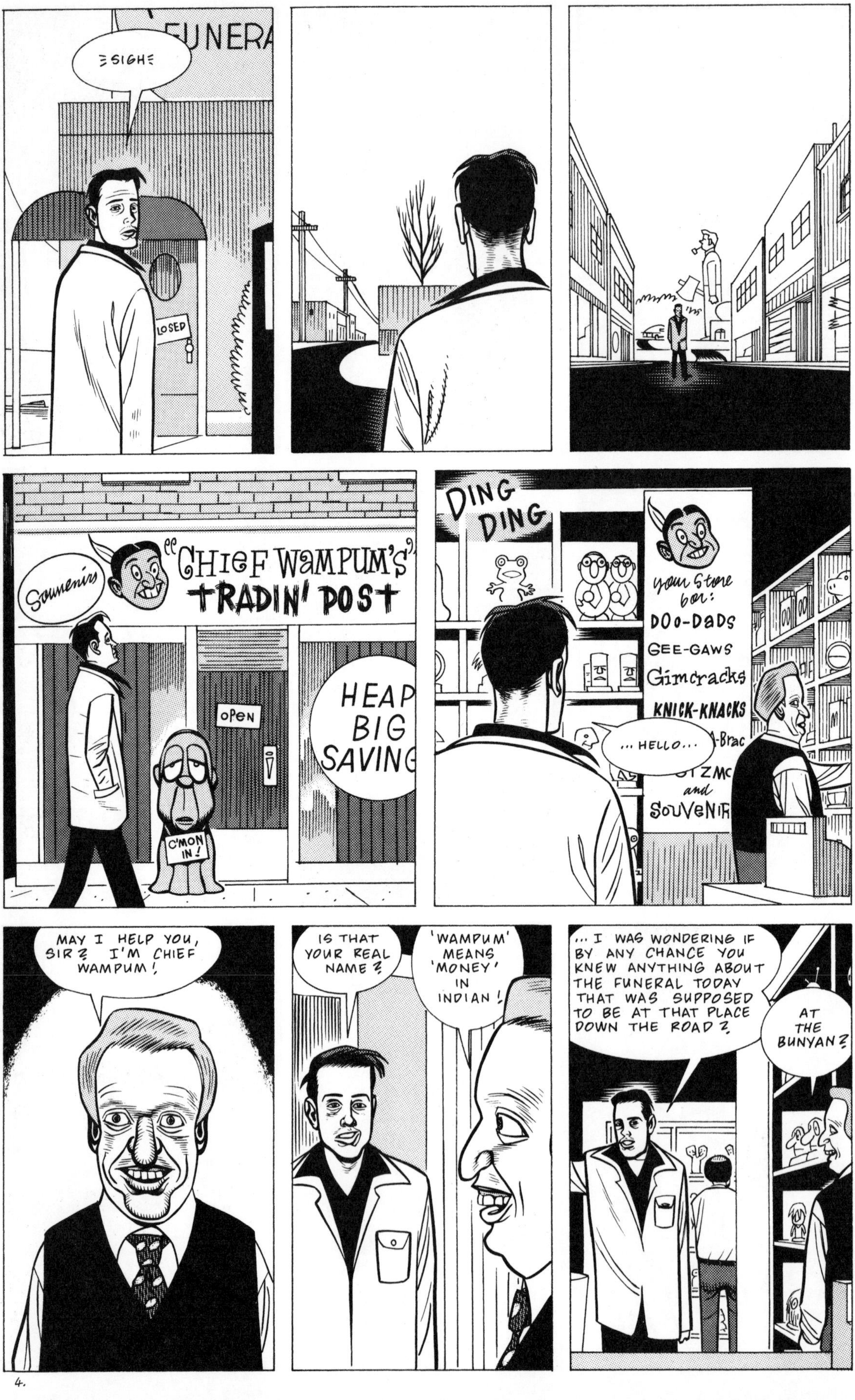

FUNERA
SIGH
LOSED
Souvenirs
"CHIEF WAMPUM'S"
TRADIN' POST
OPEN
C'MON IN!
HEAP BIG SAVING
DING DING
your Store for:
DOO-DADS
GEE-GAWS
Gimcracks
KNICK-KNACKS
-A-Brac
and
SOUVENIR
... HELLO ...
MAY I HELP YOU, SIR? I'M CHIEF WAMPUM!
IS THAT YOUR REAL NAME?
'WAMPUM' MEANS 'MONEY' IN INDIAN!
... I WAS WONDERING IF BY ANY CHANCE YOU KNEW ANYTHING ABOUT THE FUNERAL TODAY THAT WAS SUPPOSED TO BE AT THAT PLACE DOWN THE ROAD?
AT THE BUNYAN?

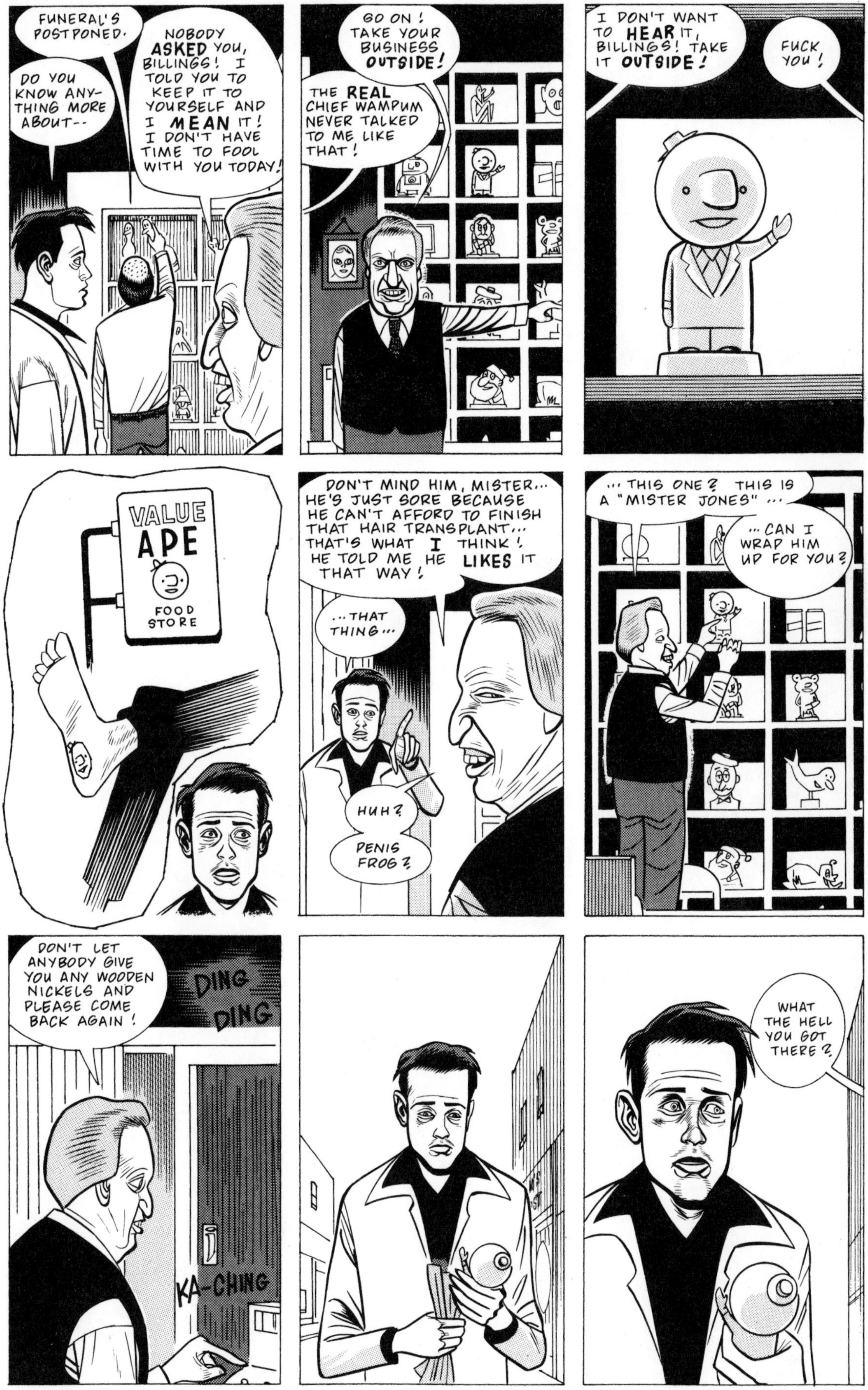
FUNERAL'S POSTPONED.
DO YOU KNOW ANYTHING MORE ABOUT--
NOBODY ASKED YOU, BILLINGS! I TOLD YOU TO KEEP IT TO YOURSELF AND I MEAN IT! I DON'T HAVE TIME TO FOOL WITH YOU TODAY!
GO ON! TAKE YOUR BUSINESS OUTSIDE!
THE REAL CHIEF WAMPUM NEVER TALKED TO ME LIKE THAT!
I DON'T WANT TO HEAR IT, BILLINGS! TAKE IT OUTSIDE!
FUCK YOU!
VALUE APE
FOOD STORE
DON'T MIND HIM, MISTER... HE'S JUST SORE BECAUSE HE CAN'T AFFORD TO FINISH THAT HAIR TRANSPLANT... THAT'S WHAT I THINK! HE TOLD ME HE LIKES IT THAT WAY!
...THAT THING...
HUH?
PENIS FROG?
...THIS ONE? THIS IS A "MISTER JONES"...
...CAN I WRAP HIM UP FOR YOU?
DON'T LET ANYBODY GIVE YOU ANY WOODEN NICKELS AND PLEASE COME BACK AGAIN!
DING DING
KA-CHING
WHAT THE HELL YOU GOT THERE?

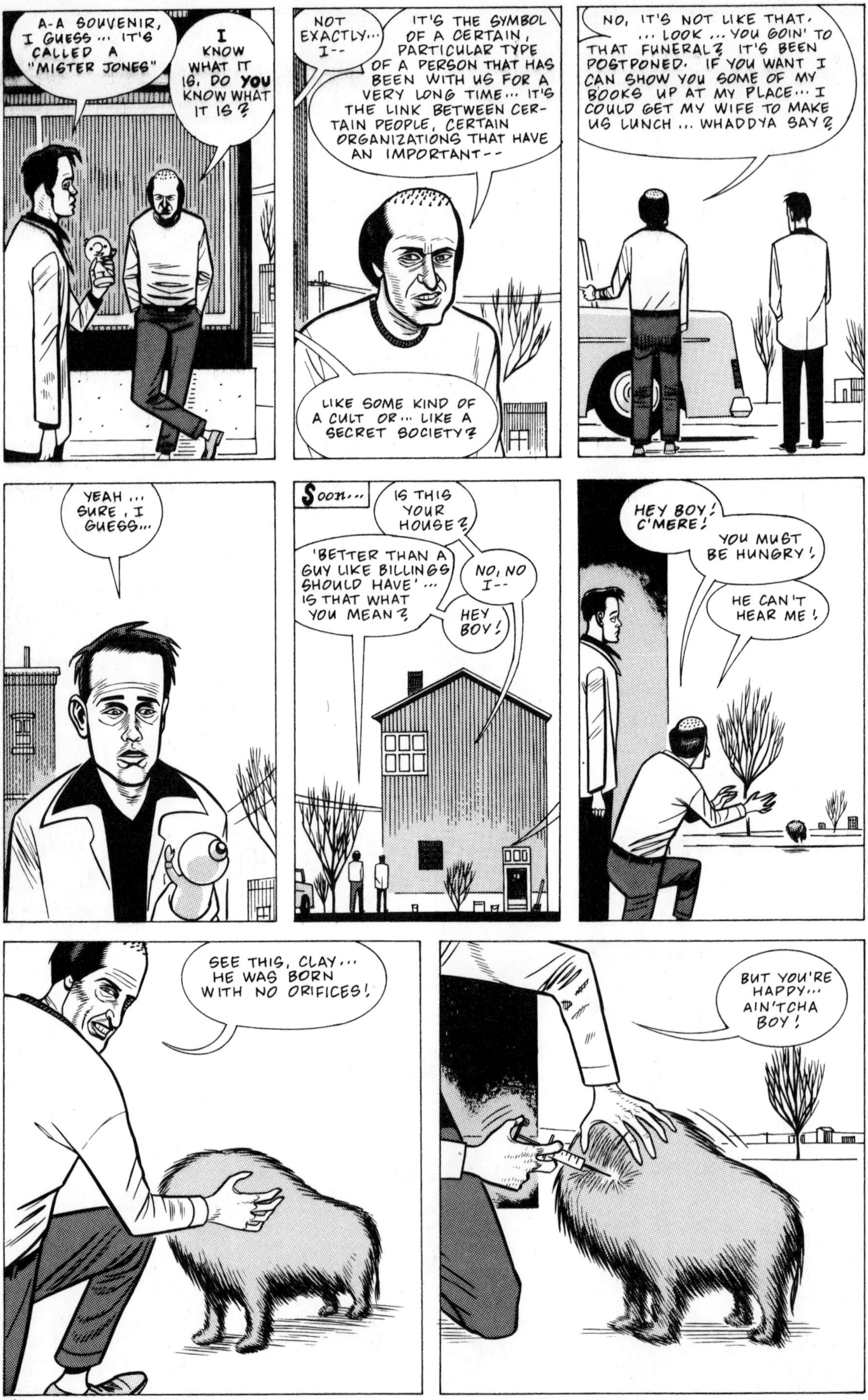
A-A SOUVENIR, I GUESS ... IT'S CALLED A "MISTER JONES"
I KNOW WHAT IT IS. DO YOU KNOW WHAT IT IS?
NOT EXACTLY... I--
IT'S THE SYMBOL OF A CERTAIN, PARTICULAR TYPE OF A PERSON THAT HAS BEEN WITH US FOR A VERY LONG TIME... IT'S THE LINK BETWEEN CERTAIN PEOPLE, CERTAIN ORGANIZATIONS THAT HAVE AN IMPORTANT--
LIKE SOME KIND OF A CULT OR... LIKE A SECRET SOCIETY?
NO, IT'S NOT LIKE THAT. ... LOOK ... YOU GOIN' TO THAT FUNERAL? IT'S BEEN POSTPONED. IF YOU WANT I CAN SHOW YOU SOME OF MY BOOKS UP AT MY PLACE... I COULD GET MY WIFE TO MAKE US LUNCH ... WHADDYA SAY?
YEAH ... SURE, I GUESS...
Soon...
IS THIS YOUR HOUSE?
'BETTER THAN A GUY LIKE BILLINGS SHOULD HAVE' ... IS THAT WHAT YOU MEAN?
NO, NO I--
HEY BOY!
HEY BOY! C'MERE!
YOU MUST BE HUNGRY!
HE CAN'T HEAR ME!
SEE THIS, CLAY... HE WAS BORN WITH NO ORIFICES!
BUT YOU'RE HAPPY... AIN'TCHA BOY!

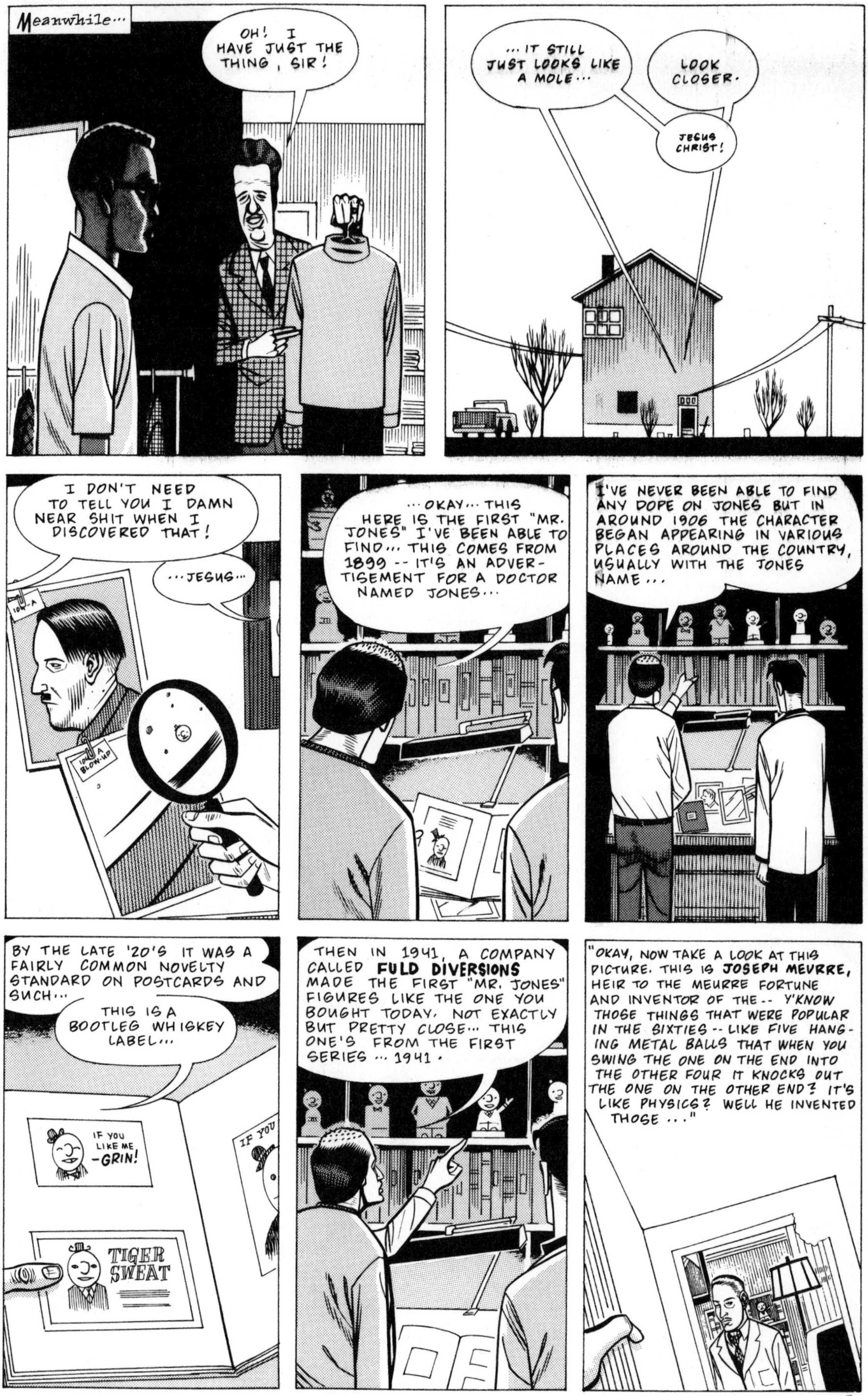
Meanwhile...
OH! I HAVE JUST THE THING, SIR!
... IT STILL JUST LOOKS LIKE A MOLE...
LOOK CLOSER.
JESUS CHRIST!
I DON'T NEED TO TELL YOU I DAMN NEAR SHIT WHEN I DISCOVERED THAT!
... JESUS...
BLOW-UP
... OKAY... THIS HERE IS THE FIRST "MR. JONES" I'VE BEEN ABLE TO FIND... THIS COMES FROM 1899 -- IT'S AN ADVERTISEMENT FOR A DOCTOR NAMED JONES...
I'VE NEVER BEEN ABLE TO FIND ANY DOPE ON JONES BUT IN AROUND 1906 THE CHARACTER BEGAN APPEARING IN VARIOUS PLACES AROUND THE COUNTRY, USUALLY WITH THE JONES NAME...
BY THE LATE '20'S IT WAS A FAIRLY COMMON NOVELTY STANDARD ON POSTCARDS AND SUCH...
THIS IS A BOOTLEG WHISKEY LABEL...
IF YOU LIKE ME, -GRIN!
IF YOU
TIGER SWEAT
THEN IN 1941, A COMPANY CALLED FULD DIVERSIONS MADE THE FIRST "MR. JONES" FIGURES LIKE THE ONE YOU BOUGHT TODAY. NOT EXACTLY BUT PRETTY CLOSE... THIS ONE'S FROM THE FIRST SERIES ... 1941.
"OKAY, NOW TAKE A LOOK AT THIS PICTURE. THIS IS JOSEPH MEURRE, HEIR TO THE MEURRE FORTUNE AND INVENTOR OF THE -- Y'KNOW THOSE THINGS THAT WERE POPULAR IN THE SIXTIES -- LIKE FIVE HANGING METAL BALLS THAT WHEN YOU SWING THE ONE ON THE END INTO THE OTHER FOUR IT KNOCKS OUT THE ONE ON THE OTHER END? IT'S LIKE PHYSICS? WELL HE INVENTED THOSE ..."

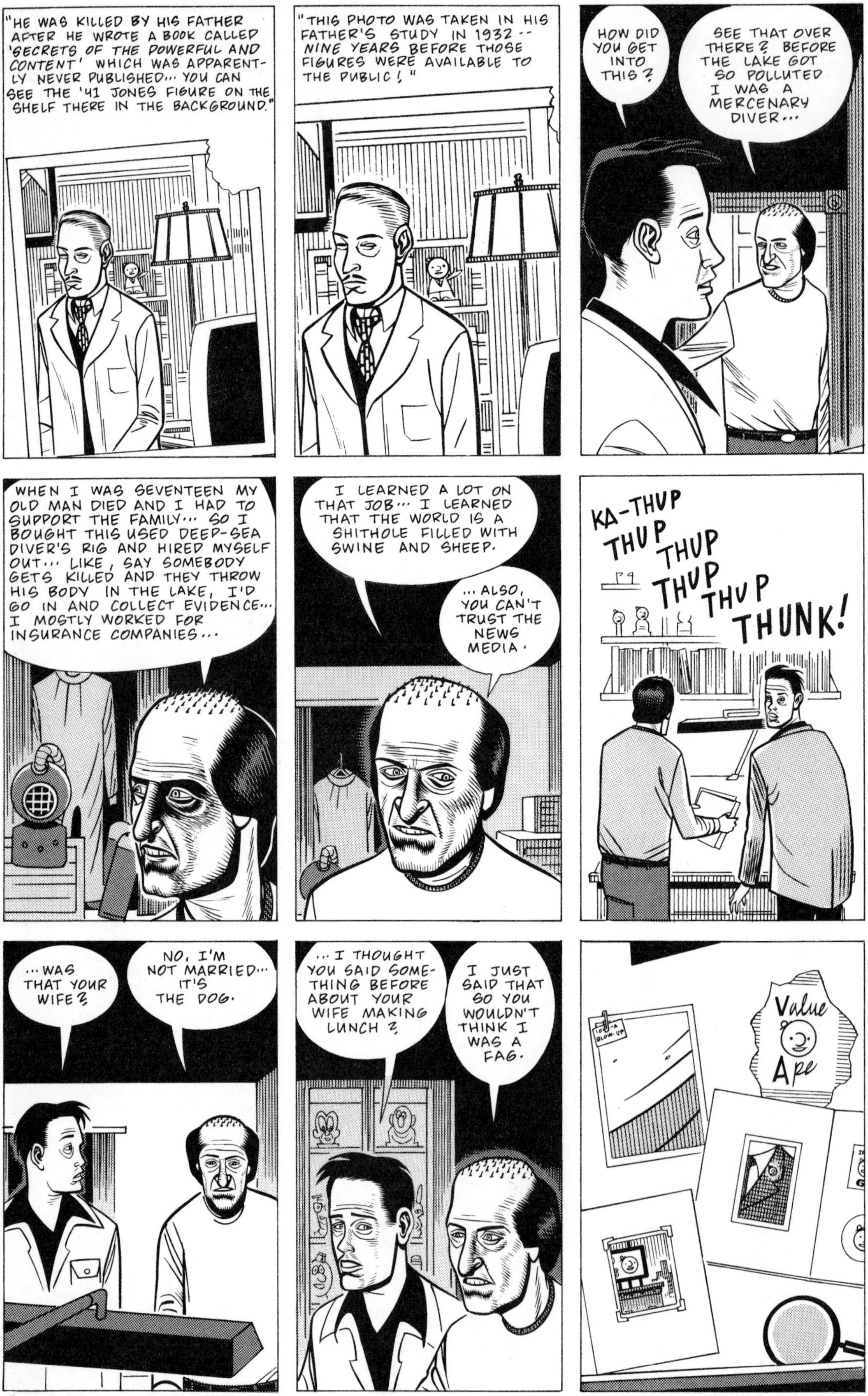
"HE WAS KILLED BY HIS FATHER AFTER HE WROTE A BOOK CALLED 'SECRETS OF THE POWERFUL AND CONTENT' WHICH WAS APPARENTLY NEVER PUBLISHED... YOU CAN SEE THE '41 JONES FIGURE ON THE SHELF THERE IN THE BACKGROUND."
"THIS PHOTO WAS TAKEN IN HIS FATHER'S STUDY IN 1932 -- NINE YEARS BEFORE THOSE FIGURES WERE AVAILABLE TO THE PUBLIC!"
HOW DID YOU GET INTO THIS?
SEE THAT OVER THERE? BEFORE THE LAKE GOT SO POLLUTED I WAS A MERCENARY DIVER...
WHEN I WAS SEVENTEEN MY OLD MAN DIED AND I HAD TO SUPPORT THE FAMILY... SO I BOUGHT THIS USED DEEP-SEA DIVER'S RIG AND HIRED MYSELF OUT... LIKE, SAY SOMEBODY GETS KILLED AND THEY THROW HIS BODY IN THE LAKE, I'D GO IN AND COLLECT EVIDENCE... I MOSTLY WORKED FOR INSURANCE COMPANIES...
I LEARNED A LOT ON THAT JOB... I LEARNED THAT THE WORLD IS A SHITHOLE FILLED WITH SWINE AND SHEEP.
...ALSO, YOU CAN'T TRUST THE NEWS MEDIA.
KA-THUP THUP THUP THUP THUP THUNK!
...WAS THAT YOUR WIFE?
NO, I'M NOT MARRIED... IT'S THE DOG.
...I THOUGHT YOU SAID SOMETHING BEFORE ABOUT YOUR WIFE MAKING LUNCH?
I JUST SAID THAT SO YOU WOULDN'T THINK I WAS A FAG.
Value Ape

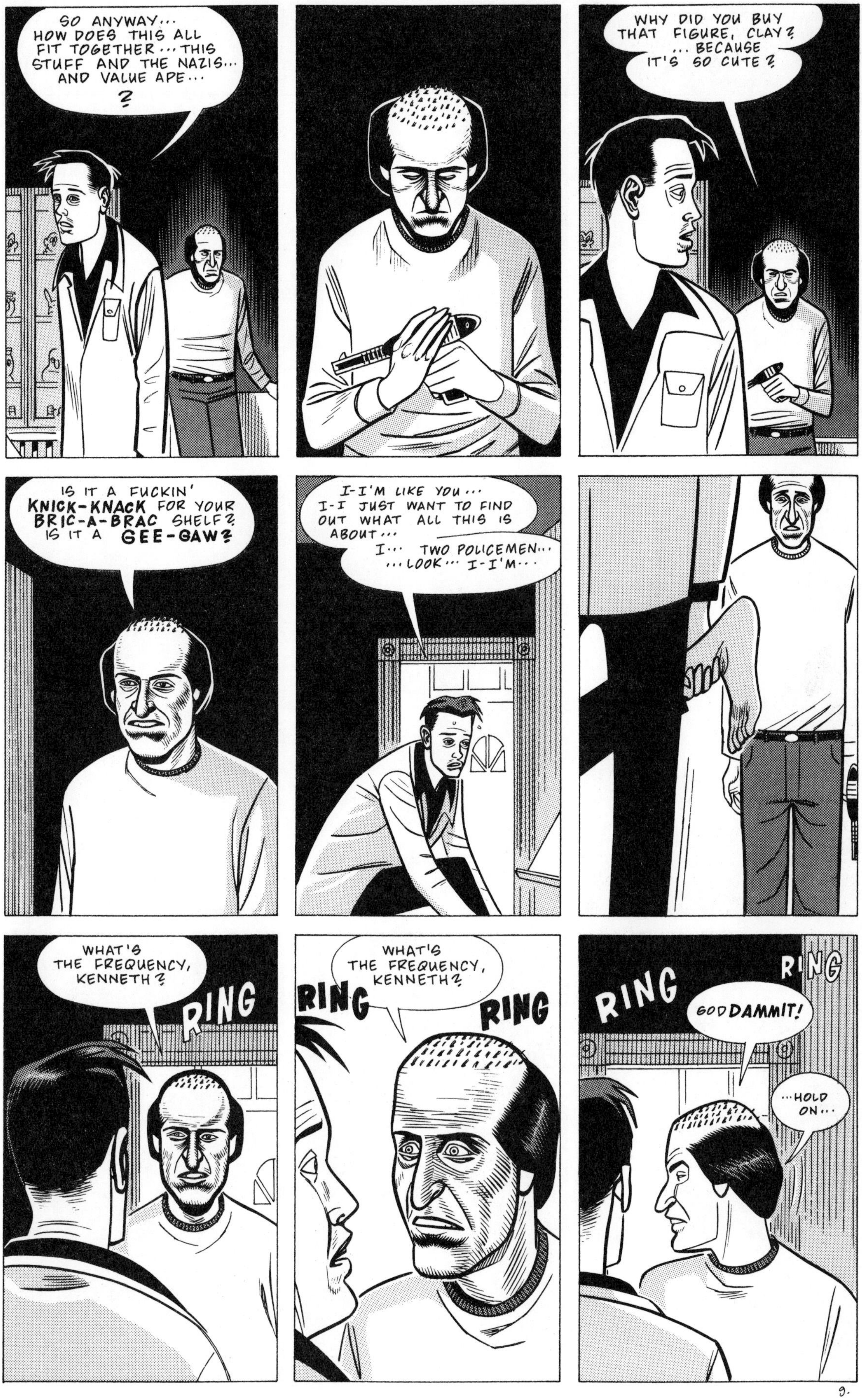
SO ANYWAY... HOW DOES THIS ALL FIT TOGETHER... THIS STUFF AND THE NAZIS... AND VALUE APE... ?
WHY DID YOU BUY THAT FIGURE, CLAY? ... BECAUSE IT'S SO CUTE?
IS IT A FUCKIN' KNICK-KNACK FOR YOUR BRIC-A-BRAC SHELF? IS IT A GEE-GAW?
I-I'M LIKE YOU... I-I JUST WANT TO FIND OUT WHAT ALL THIS IS ABOUT...
I... TWO POLICEMEN... ...LOOK... I-I'M...
WHAT'S THE FREQUENCY, KENNETH?
RING
RING
WHAT'S THE FREQUENCY, KENNETH?
RING
RING
RING
GOD DAMMIT!
...HOLD ON...

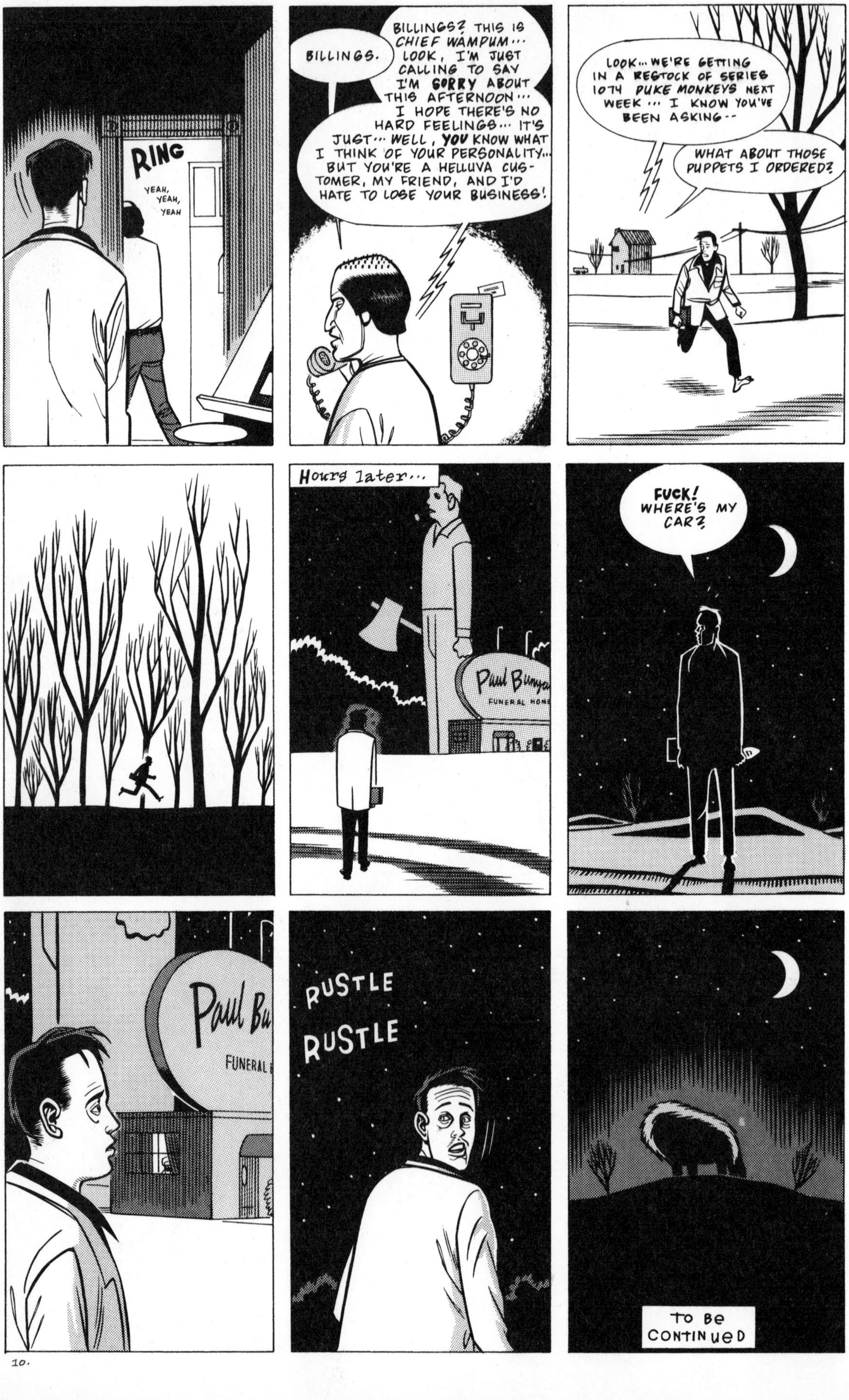
RING
YEAH, YEAH, YEAH
BILLINGS.
BILLINGS? THIS IS CHIEF WAMPUM... LOOK, I'M JUST CALLING TO SAY I'M SORRY ABOUT THIS AFTERNOON... I HOPE THERE'S NO HARD FEELINGS... IT'S JUST... WELL, YOU KNOW WHAT I THINK OF YOUR PERSONALITY... BUT YOU'RE A HELLUVA CUSTOMER, MY FRIEND, AND I'D HATE TO LOSE YOUR BUSINESS!
LOOK... WE'RE GETTING IN A RESTOCK OF SERIES 1074 DUKE MONKEYS NEXT WEEK... I KNOW YOU'VE BEEN ASKING--
WHAT ABOUT THOSE PUPPETS I ORDERED?
Hours later...
FUNERAL HOME
FUCK! WHERE'S MY CAR?
FUNERAL
RUSTLE
RUSTLE
TO BE CONTINUED

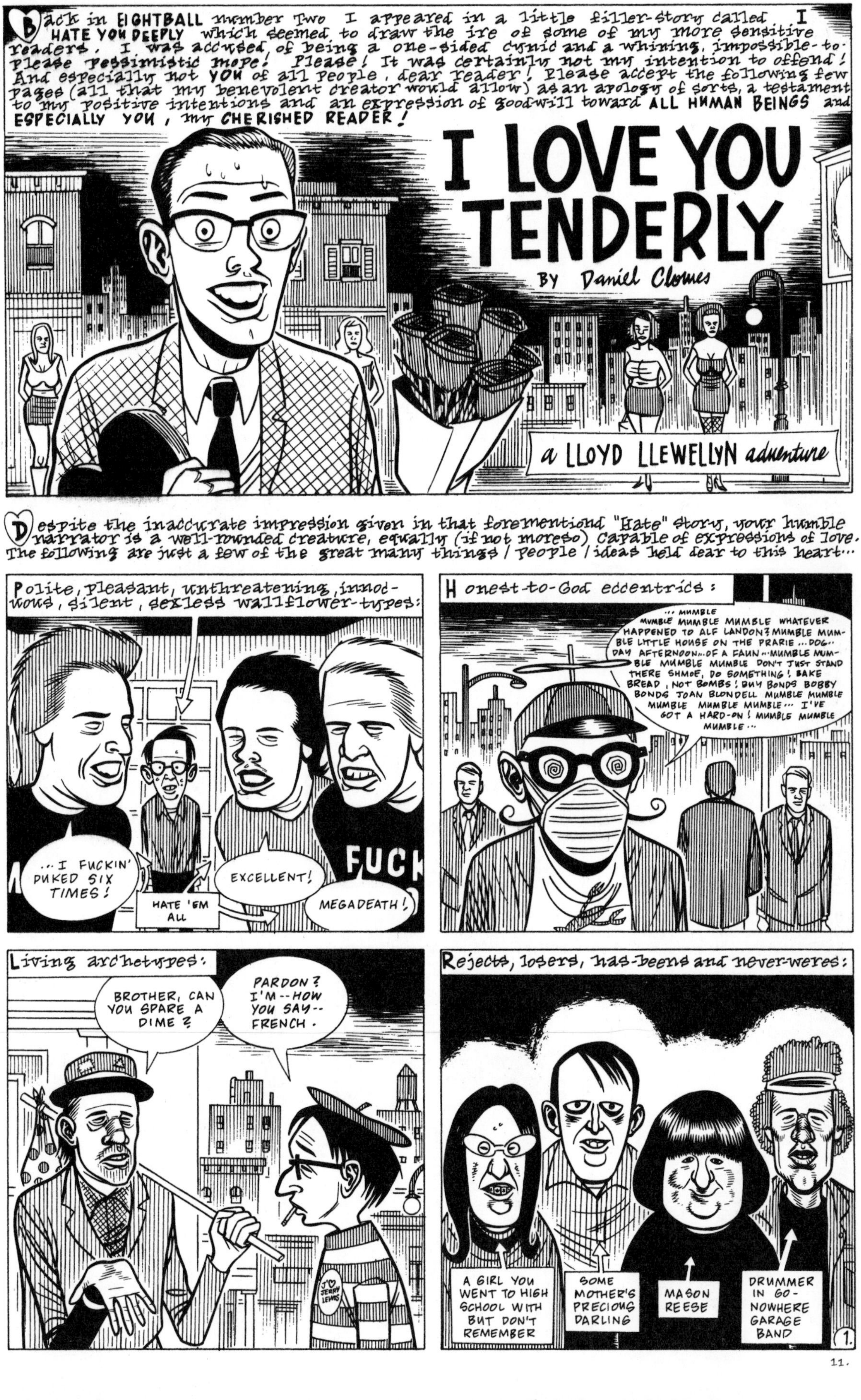
Back in EIGHTBALL number Two I appeared in a little filler-story called I HATE YOU DEEPLY which seemed to draw the ire of some of my more sensitive readers. I was accused of being a one-sided cynic and a whining, impossible-to-please pessimistic mope! Please! It was certainly not my intention to offend! And especially not YOU of all people, dear reader! Please accept the following few pages (all that my benevolent creator would allow) as an apology of sorts, a testament to my positive intentions and an expression of goodwill toward ALL HUMAN BEINGS and ESPECIALLY YOU, my CHERISHED READER!
I LOVE YOU TENDERLY
BY Daniel Clowes
a LLOYD LLEWELLYN adventure
Despite the inaccurate impression given in that forementiond "Hate" story, your humble narrator is a well-rounded creature, equally (if not moreso) capable of expressions of love. The following are just a few of the great many things / people / ideas held dear to this heart...
Polite, pleasant, unthreatening, innocuous, silent, sexless wallflower-types:
...I FUCKIN' PUKED SIX TIMES!
HATE 'EM ALL
EXCELLENT!
MEGADEATH!
FUCK
Honest-to-God eccentrics:
...MUMBLE MUMBLE MUMBLE MUMBLE WHATEVER HAPPENED TO ALF LANDON? MUMBLE MUMBLE LITTLE HOUSE ON THE PRARIE...DOG... DAY AFTERNOON...OF A FAUN...MUMBLE MUMBLE MUMBLE MUMBLE DON'T JUST STAND THERE SHMOE, DO SOMETHING! BAKE BREAD, NOT BOMBS! BUY BONDS BOBBY BONDS JOAN BLONDELL MUMBLE MUMBLE MUMBLE MUMBLE MUMBLE... I'VE GOT A HARD-ON! MUMBLE MUMBLE MUMBLE...
Living archetypes:
BROTHER, CAN YOU SPARE A DIME?
PARDON? I'M--HOW YOU SAY--FRENCH.
J'♡ JERRY LEWIS
Rejects, losers, has-beens and never-weres:
A GIRL YOU WENT TO HIGH SCHOOL WITH BUT DON'T REMEMBER
SOME MOTHER'S PRECIOUS DARLING
MASON REESE
DRUMMER IN GO-NOWHERE GARAGE BAND
1.

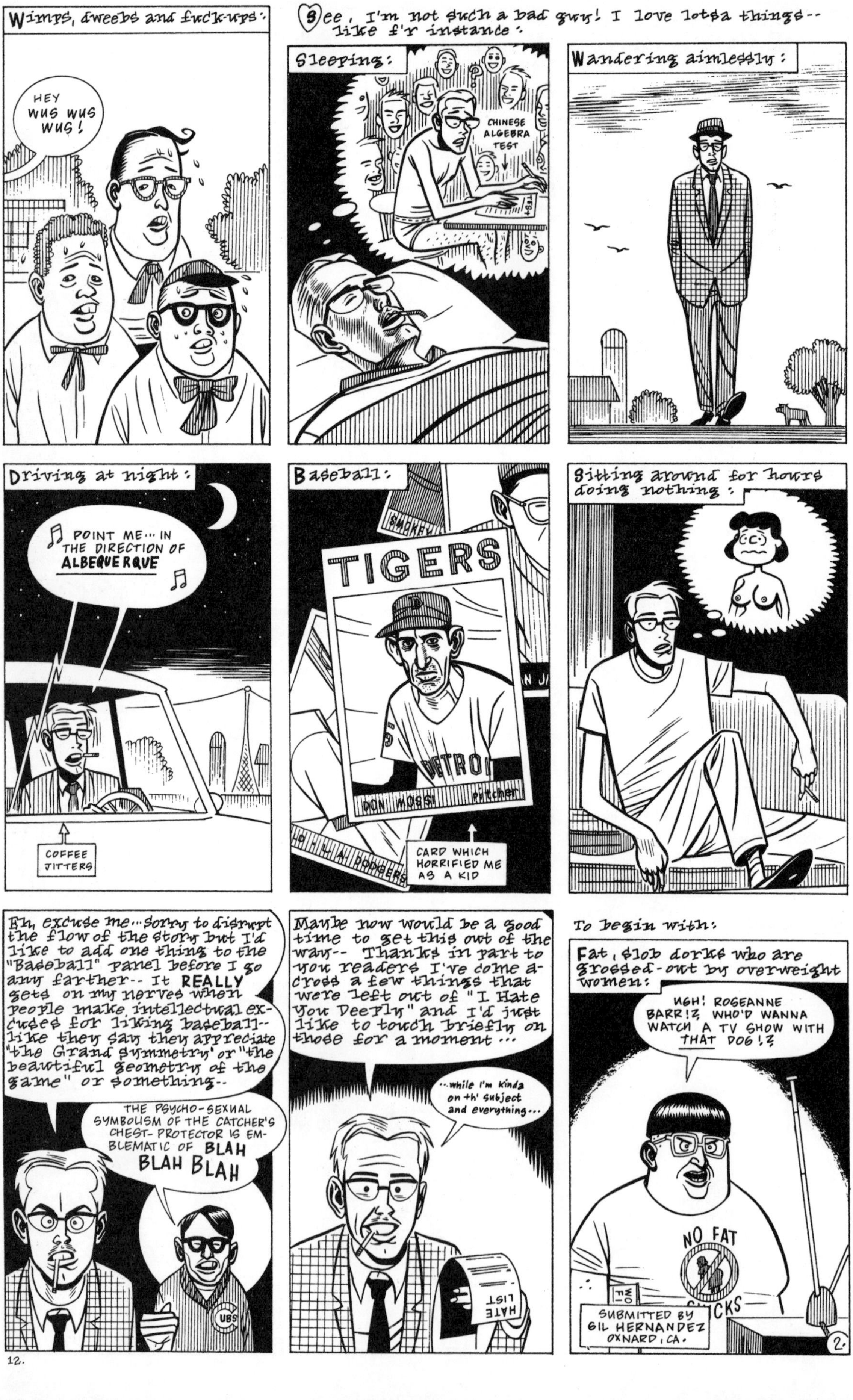
Wimps, dweebs and fuck-ups:
HEY WUS WUS WUS!
See, I'm not such a bad guy! I love lotsa things-- like f'r instance:
Sleeping:
CHINESE ALGEBRA TEST
TEST
Wandering aimlessly:
Driving at night:
POINT ME... IN THE DIRECTION OF ALBEQUERQUE
COFFEE JITTERS
Baseball:
TIGERS
DETROIT
DON MOSSI pitcher
L.A. DODGERS
CARD WHICH HORRIFIED ME AS A KID
Sitting around for hours doing nothing:
Eh, excuse me... sorry to disrupt the flow of the story but I'd like to add one thing to the "Baseball" panel before I go any farther-- It REALLY gets on my nerves when people make intellectual excuses for liking baseball-- like they say they appreciate "the Grand symmetry" or "the beautiful geometry of the game" or something--
THE PSYCHO-SEXUAL SYMBOLISM OF THE CATCHER'S CHEST-PROTECTOR IS EMBLEMATIC OF BLAH BLAH BLAH
CUBS
Maybe now would be a good time to get this out of the way-- Thanks in part to you readers I've come across a few things that were left out of "I Hate You Deeply" and I'd just like to touch briefly on those for a moment...
...while I'm kinda on th' subject and everything...
HATE LIST
To begin with:
Fat, slob dorks who are grossed-out by overweight women:
UGH! ROSEANNE BARR!? WHO'D WANNA WATCH A TV SHOW WITH THAT DOG!?
NO FAT CHICKS
SUBMITTED BY GIL HERNANDEZ OXNARD, CA.
2.

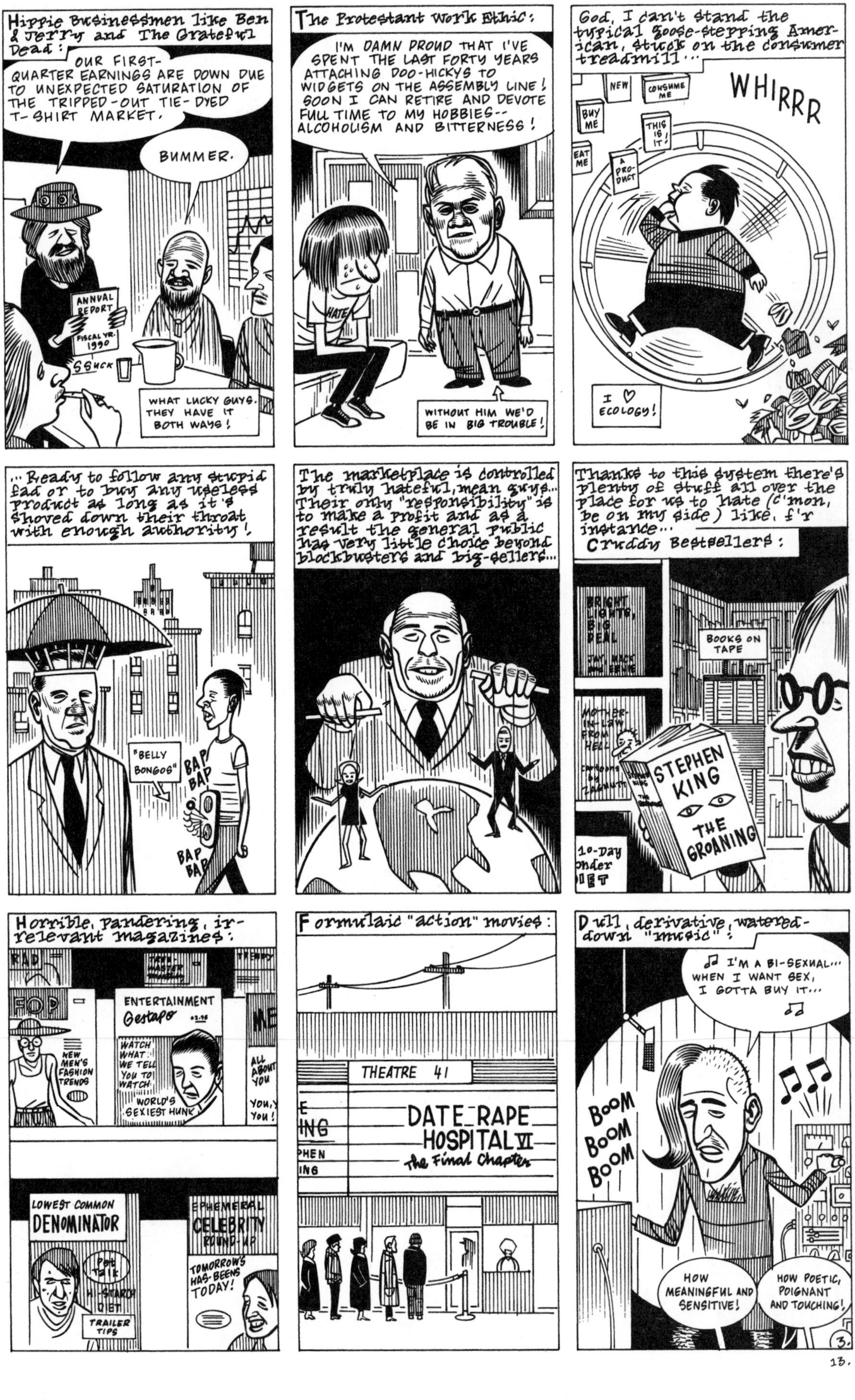

Hippie Businessmen like Ben & Jerry and The Grateful Dead:
OUR FIRST-QUARTER EARNINGS ARE DOWN DUE TO UNEXPECTED SATURATION OF THE TRIPPED-OUT TIE-DYED T-SHIRT MARKET.
BUMMER.
ANNUAL REPORT
FISCAL YR. 1990
SSUCK
WHAT LUCKY GUYS. THEY HAVE IT BOTH WAYS!
The Protestant Work Ethic:
I'M DAMN PROUD THAT I'VE SPENT THE LAST FORTY YEARS ATTACHING DOO-HICKYS TO WIDGETS ON THE ASSEMBLY LINE! SOON I CAN RETIRE AND DEVOTE FULL TIME TO MY HOBBIES-- ALCOHOLISM AND BITTERNESS!
HATE
WITHOUT HIM WE'D BE IN BIG TROUBLE!
God, I can't stand the typical goose-stepping American, stuck on the consumer treadmill...
NEW
CONSUME ME
BUY ME
THIS IS IT!
EAT ME
A PRODUCT
WHIRRR
I ♡ ECOLOGY!
...Ready to follow any stupid fad or to buy any useless product as long as it's shoved down their throat with enough authority!
"BELLY BONGOS"
BAP BAP
BAP BAP
The marketplace is controlled by truly hateful, mean guys... Their only "responsibility" is to make a profit and as a result the general public has very little choice beyond blockbusters and big-sellers...
Thanks to this system there's plenty of stuff all over the place for us to hate (C'mon, be on my side) like, f'r instance...
Cruddy Bestsellers:
BRIGHT LIGHTS, BIG DEAL
JAY, MACK AND ERNIE
BOOKS ON TAPE
MOTHER-IN-LAW FROM HELL
CARTOONS BY ZAGNUTT
STEPHEN KING
THE GROANING
10-Day onder IET
Horrible, pandering, irrelevant magazines:
RAD
TRENDY
FOP
ENTERTAINMENT Gestapo
WATCH WHAT WE TELL YOU TO WATCH
WORLD'S SEXIEST HUNK
NEW MEN'S FASHION TRENDS
ALL ABOUT YOU
YOU, YOU!
LOWEST COMMON DENOMINATOR
POT TALK
HI-STARCH DIET
TRAILER TIPS
EPHEMERAL CELEBRITY ROUND-UP
TOMORROW'S HAS-BEENS TODAY!
Formulaic "action" movies:
THEATRE 41
DATE RAPE HOSPITAL VI
The Final Chapter
Dull, derivative, watered-down "music":
♫ I'M A BI-SEXUAL... WHEN I WANT SEX, I GOTTA BUY IT... ♫
BOOM BOOM BOOM
HOW MEANINGFUL AND SENSITIVE!
HOW POETIC, POIGNANT AND TOUCHING!
3.

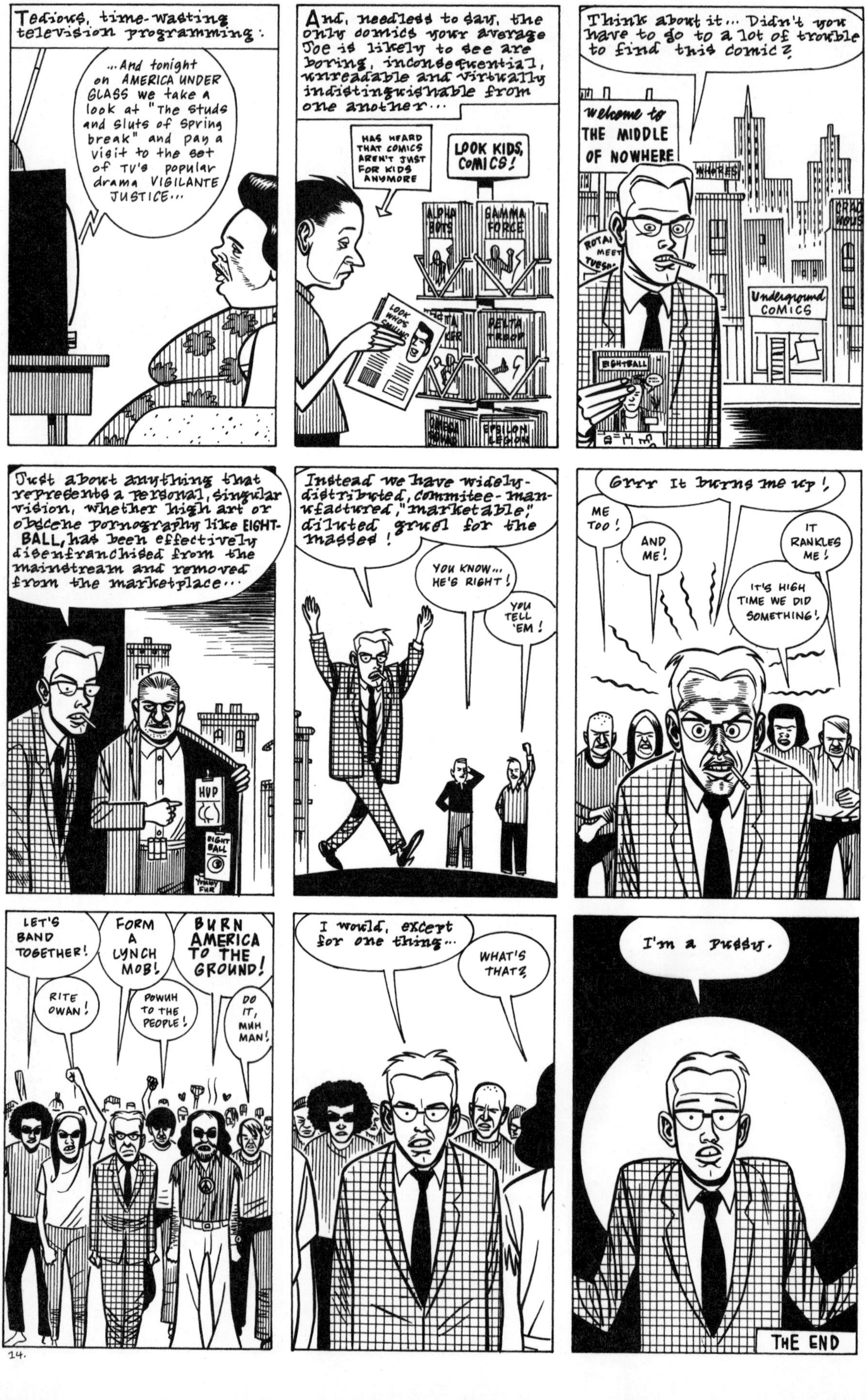

Tedious, time-wasting television programming.
...And tonight on AMERICA UNDER GLASS we take a look at "The studs and sluts of Spring break" and pay a visit to the set of TV's popular drama VIGILANTE JUSTICE...
And, needless to say, the only comics your average Joe is likely to see are boring, inconsequential, unreadable and virtually indistinguishable from one another...
HAS HEARD THAT COMICS AREN'T JUST FOR KIDS ANYMORE
LOOK KIDS, COMICS!
ALPHA BOTS
GAMMA FORCE
DELTA TROOP
OMEGA SQUAD
EPSILON LEGION
Think about it... Didn't you have to go to a lot of trouble to find this comic?
welcome to THE MIDDLE OF NOWHERE
WHORES
Underground COMICS
EIGHTBALL
Just about anything that represents a personal, singular vision, whether high art or obscene pornography like EIGHTBALL, has been effectively disenfranchised from the mainstream and removed from the marketplace...
HUD
EIGHT BALL
YUMMY FUR
Instead we have widely-distributed, commitee-manufactured, "marketable," diluted gruel for the masses!
YOU KNOW... HE'S RIGHT!
YOU TELL 'EM!
Grrr It burns me up!
ME TOO!
AND ME!
IT RANKLES ME!
IT'S HIGH TIME WE DID SOMETHING!
LET'S BAND TOGETHER!
FORM A LYNCH MOB!
BURN AMERICA TO THE GROUND!
RITE OWAN!
POWUH TO THE PEOPLE!
DO IT, MUH MAN!
I would, except for one thing...
WHAT'S THAT?
I'm a pussy.
THE END

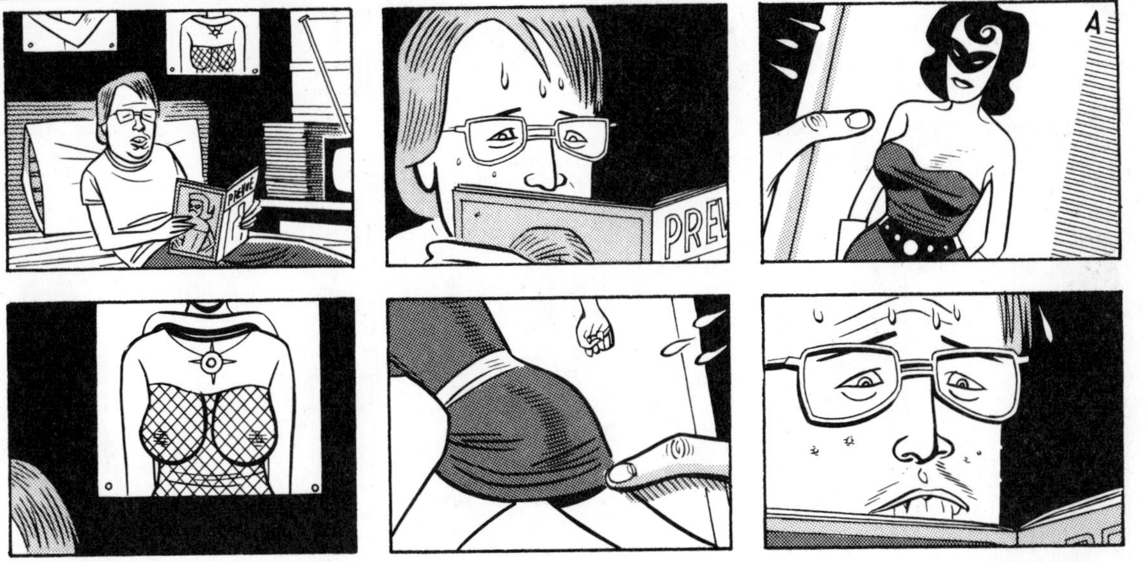
PREV

Dan Pussey's MASTURBATION FANTASY

by: D. Clowes

IF YOU THRILL-SEEKING VOYEURS THOUGHT YOU WERE GOING TO SEE DISTURBINGLY GRAPHIC PANELS OF YOUNG PUSSEY HANDLING HIS "JOHNSON" IN THIS STORY YOU'RE JUST SHIT OUTTA LUCK! NO, WHAT FOLLOWS IS SOMETHING FAR MORE UNSETTLING-- A BOLD, UNCENSORED LOOK INSIDE THE VAUNTED PUSSEY IMAGINATION DURING WHAT SOME CALL "SELF ABUSE," A STREAM-OF-CONSCIOUSNESS FANTASY EXACTLY AS SEEN BY OUR MAN DAN IN HIS MIND'S EYE! PROCEED WITH CAUTION!

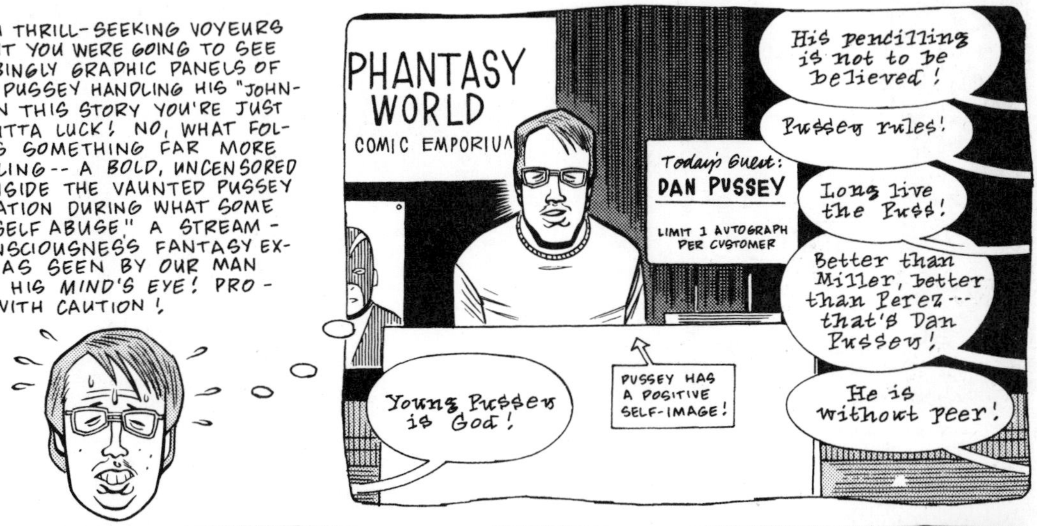
PHANTASY WORLD
COMIC EMPORIU
Today's Guest: DAN PUSSEY
LIMIT 1 AUTOGRAPH PER CUSTOMER
His pencilling is not to be believed!
Pussey rules!
Long live the Puss!
Better than Miller, better than Perez--- that's Dan Pussey!
Young Pussey is God!
PUSSEY HAS A POSITIVE SELF-IMAGE!
He is without peer!

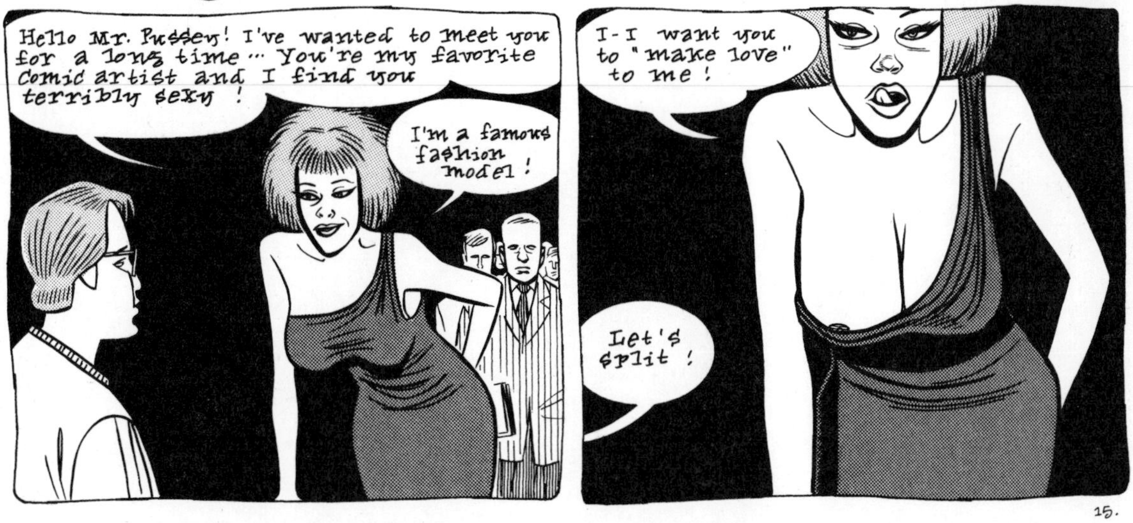
Hello Mr. Pussey! I've wanted to meet you for a long time... You're my favorite comic artist and I find you terribly sexy!
I'm a famous fashion model!
I-I want you to "make love" to me!
Let's split!

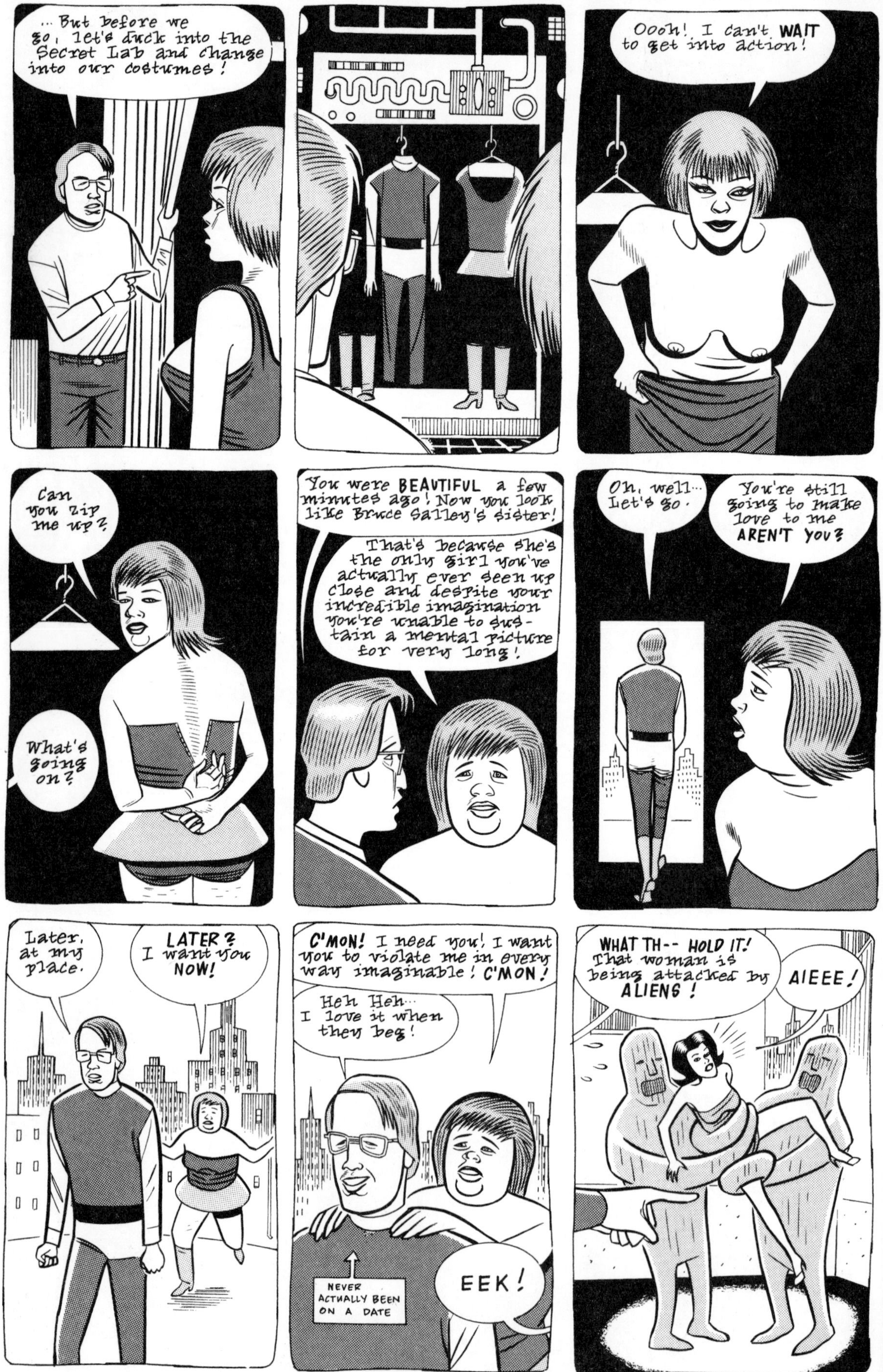
... But before we go, let's duck into the Secret Lab and change into our costumes!
Oooh! I can't WAIT to get into action!
Can you zip me up?
What's going on?
You were BEAUTIFUL a few minutes ago! Now you look like Bruce Salley's sister!
That's because she's the only girl you've actually ever seen up close and despite your incredible imagination you're unable to sustain a mental picture for very long!
Oh, well... Let's go.
You're still going to make love to me AREN'T YOU?
Later, at my place.
LATER? I want you NOW!
C'MON! I need you! I want you to violate me in every way imaginable! C'MON!
Heh Heh... I love it when they beg!
NEVER ACTUALLY BEEN ON A DATE
EEK!
WHAT TH-- HOLD IT! That woman is being attacked by ALIENS!
AIEEE!

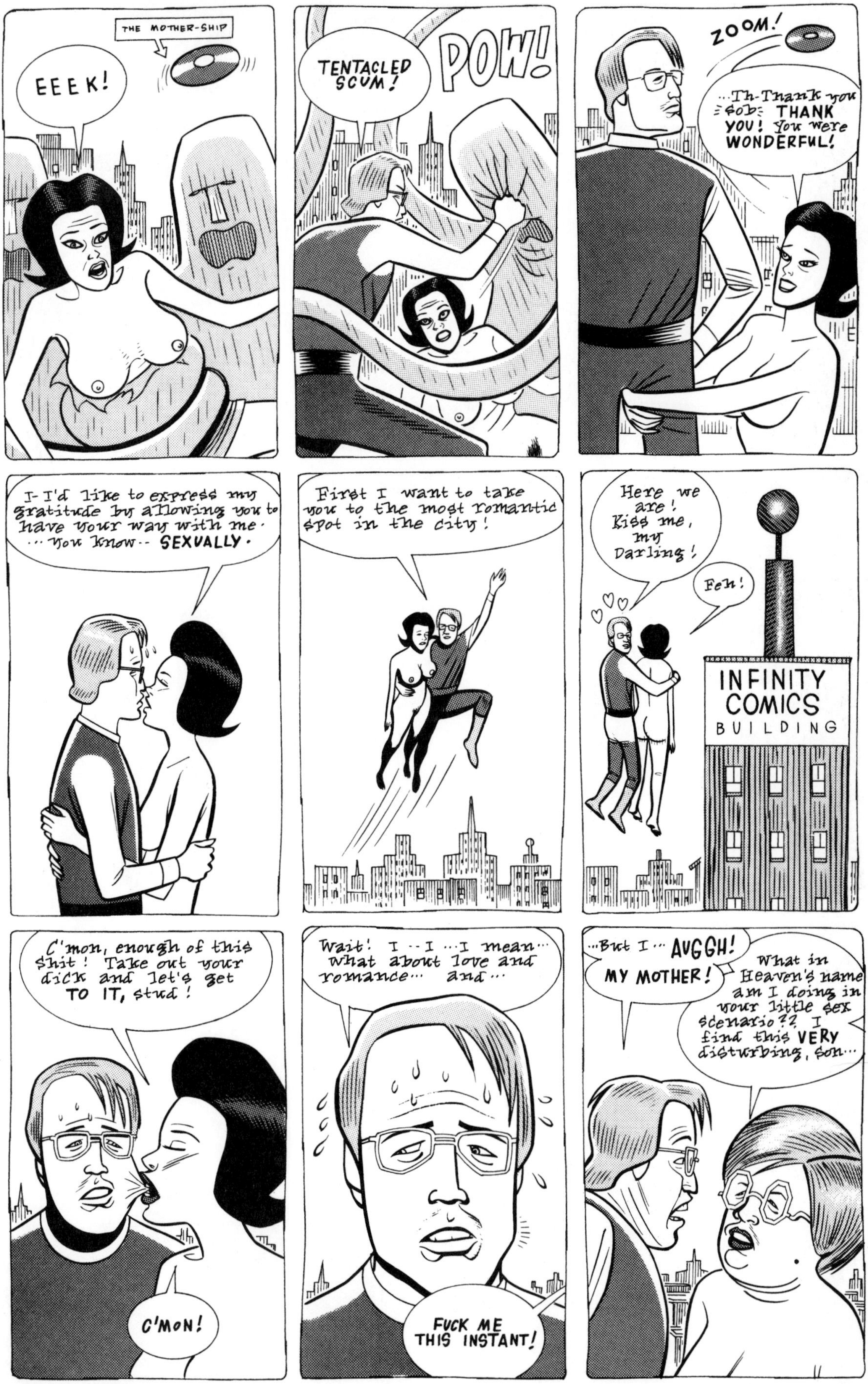
THE MOTHER-SHIP
EEEK!
TENTACLED SCUM!
POW!
ZOOM!
...Th-Thank you =sob= THANK YOU! You were WONDERFUL!
I-I'd like to express my gratitude by allowing you to have your way with me. ...You know-- SEXUALLY.
First I want to take you to the most romantic spot in the city!
Here we are! Kiss me, my Darling!
Feh!
INFINITY COMICS BUILDING
C'mon, enough of this shit! Take out your dick and let's get TO IT, stud!
C'MON!
Wait! I--I...I mean... what about love and romance... and...
FUCK ME THIS INSTANT!
...But I... AUGGH!
MY MOTHER!
What in Heaven's name am I doing in your little sex scenario?? I find this VERY disturbing, son...

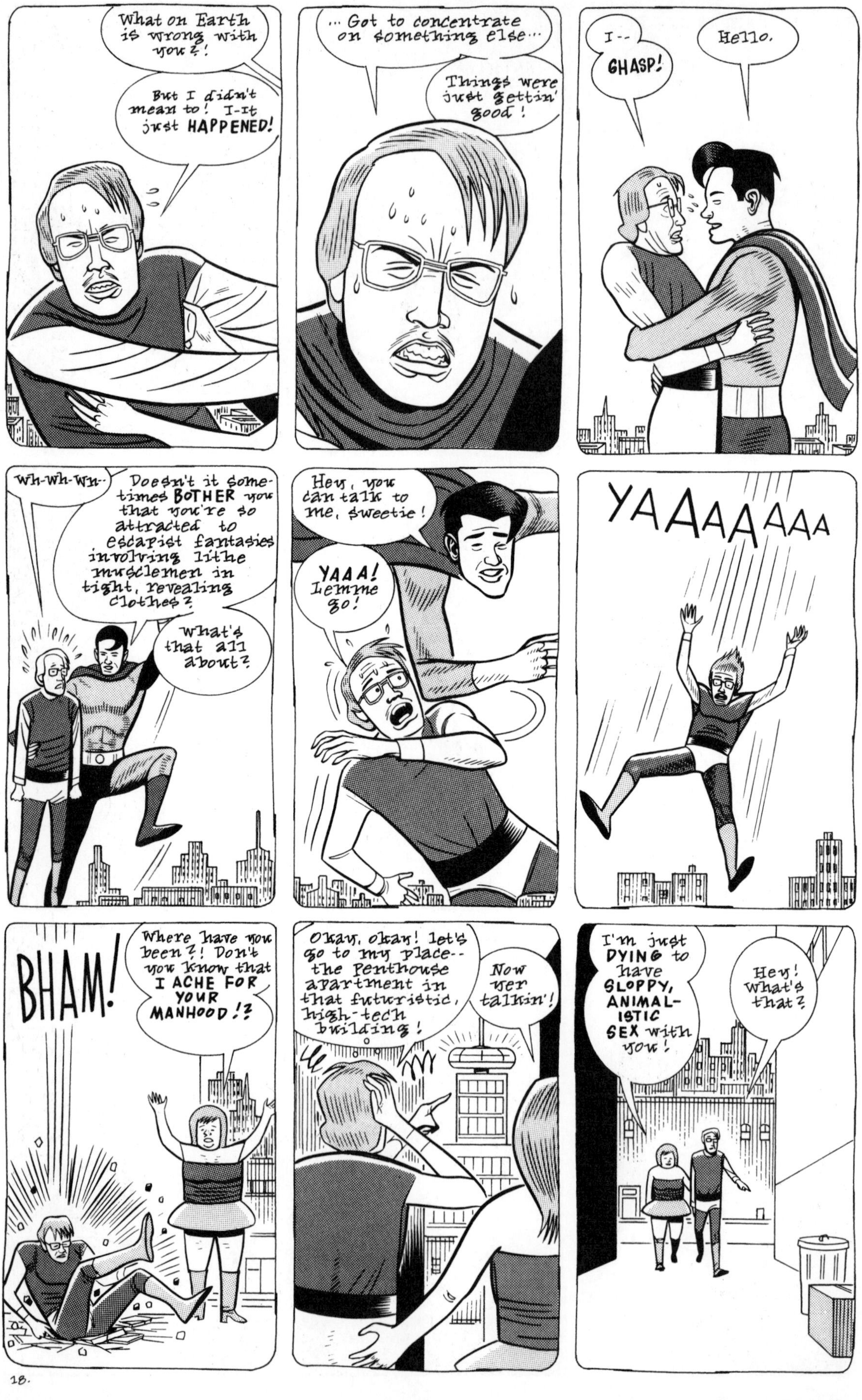
What on Earth is wrong with you?!
But I didn't mean to! I-It just HAPPENED!
... Got to concentrate on something else...
Things were just gettin' good!
I-- GHASP!
Hello.
Wh-Wh-Wh--
Doesn't it sometimes BOTHER you that you're so attracted to escapist fantasies involving lithe musclemen in tight, revealing clothes?
What's that all about?
Hey, you can talk to me, sweetie!
YAAA! Lemme go!
YAAAAAAA
BHAM!
Where have you been?! Don't you know that I ACHE FOR YOUR MANHOOD!?
Okay, okay! let's go to my place-- the Penthouse apartment in that futuristic, high-tech building!
Now yer talkin'!
I'm just DYING to have SLOPPY, ANIMALISTIC SEX with you!
Hey! What's that?

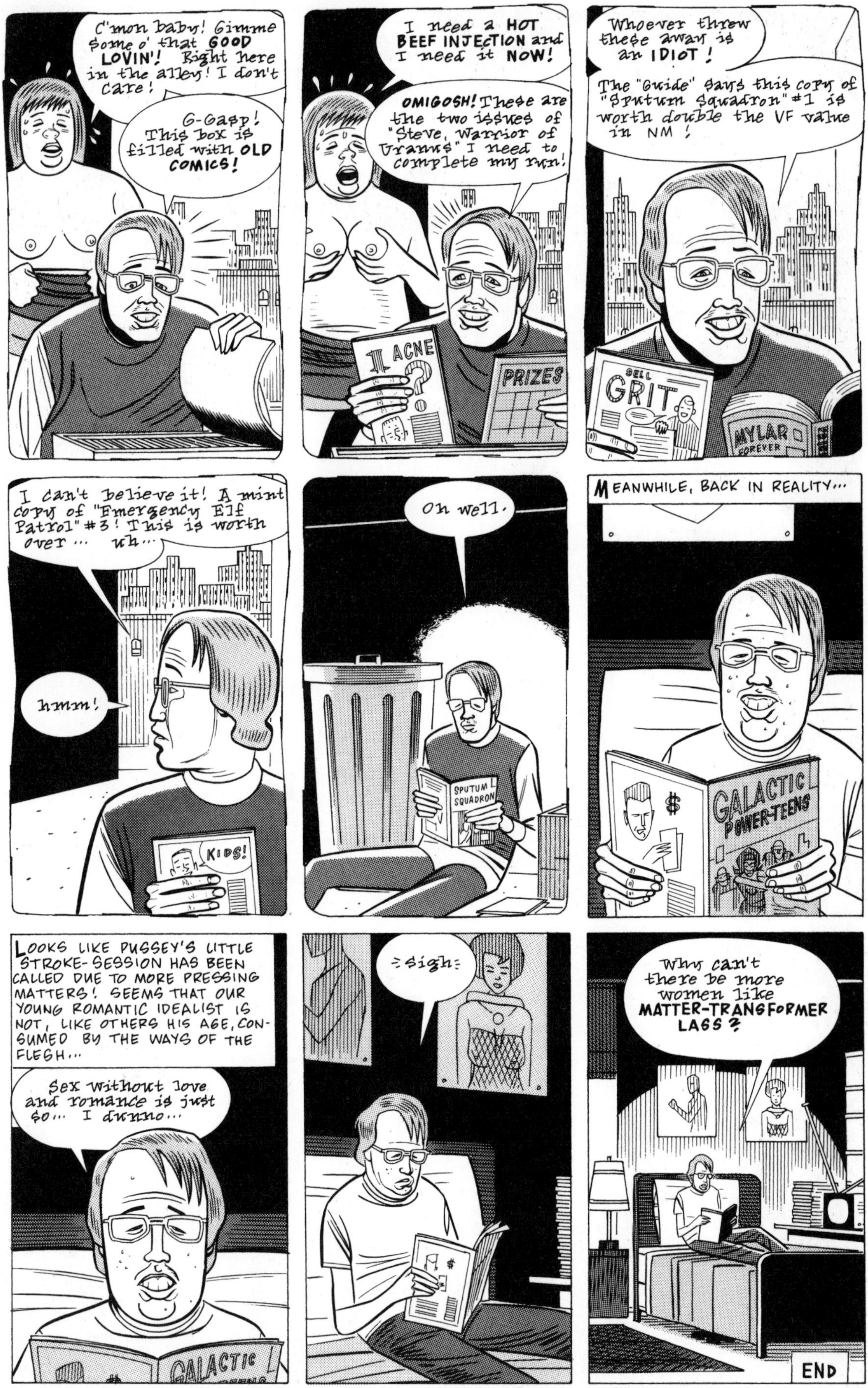
C'mon baby! Gimme some o' that GOOD LOVIN'! Right here in the alley! I don't care!
G-Gasp! This box is filled with OLD COMICS!
I need a HOT BEEF INJECTION and I need it NOW!
OMIGOSH! These are the two issues of "Steve, Warrior of Uranus" I need to complete my run!
ACNE
PRIZES
Whoever threw these away is an IDIOT!
The "Guide" says this copy of "Sputum Squadron" #1 is worth double the VF value in NM!
SELL GRIT
MYLAR FOREVER
I can't believe it! A mint copy of "Emergency Elf Patrol" #3! This is worth over... uh...
hmm!
KIDS!
Oh well.
SPUTUM SQUADRON
MEANWHILE, BACK IN REALITY...
GALACTIC POWER-TEENS
LOOKS LIKE PUSSEY'S LITTLE STROKE-SESSION HAS BEEN CALLED DUE TO MORE PRESSING MATTERS! SEEMS THAT OUR YOUNG ROMANTIC IDEALIST IS NOT, LIKE OTHERS HIS AGE, CONSUMED BY THE WAYS OF THE FLESH...
Sex without love and romance is just so... I dunno...
GALACTIC
=sigh=
Why can't there be more women like MATTER-TRANSFORMER LASS?
END

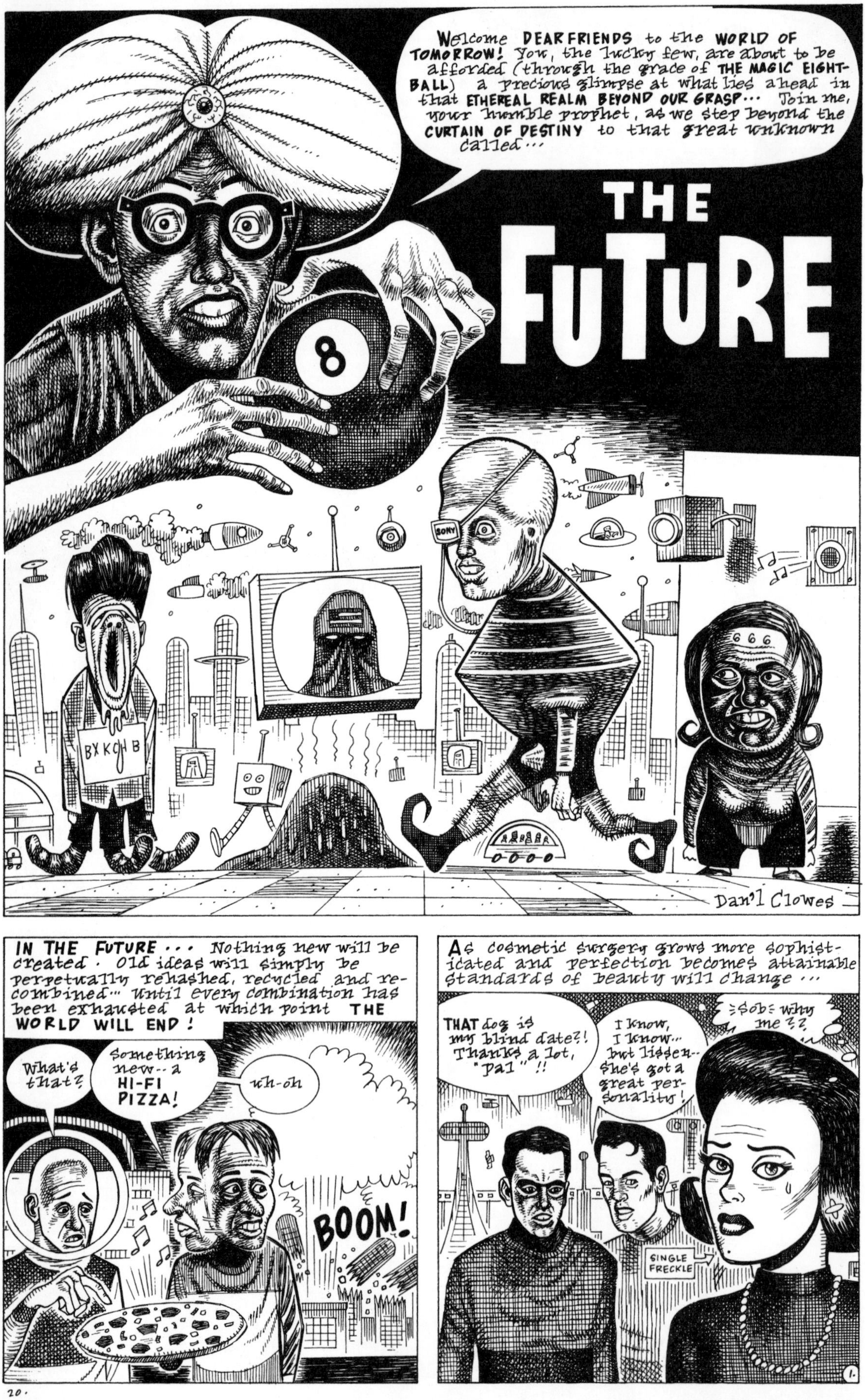

Welcome DEARFRIENDS to the WORLD OF TOMORROW! You, the lucky few, are about to be afforded (through the grace of THE MAGIC EIGHT-BALL) a precious glimpse at what lies ahead in that ETHEREAL REALM BEYOND OUR GRASP... Join me, your humble prophet, as we step beyond the CURTAIN OF DESTINY to that great unknown called...
THE FUTURE
8
SONY
666
Dan'l Clowes
IN THE FUTURE... Nothing new will be created. Old ideas will simply be perpetually rehashed, recycled and recombined... Until every combination has been exhausted at which point THE WORLD WILL END!
What's that?
Something new-- a HI-FI PIZZA!
uh-oh
BOOM!
As cosmetic surgery grows more sophisticated and perfection becomes attainable standards of beauty will change...
THAT dog is my blind date?! Thanks a lot, "pal"!!
I know, I know... but lissen-- she's got a great personality!
sob why me??
SINGLE FRECKLE
1.

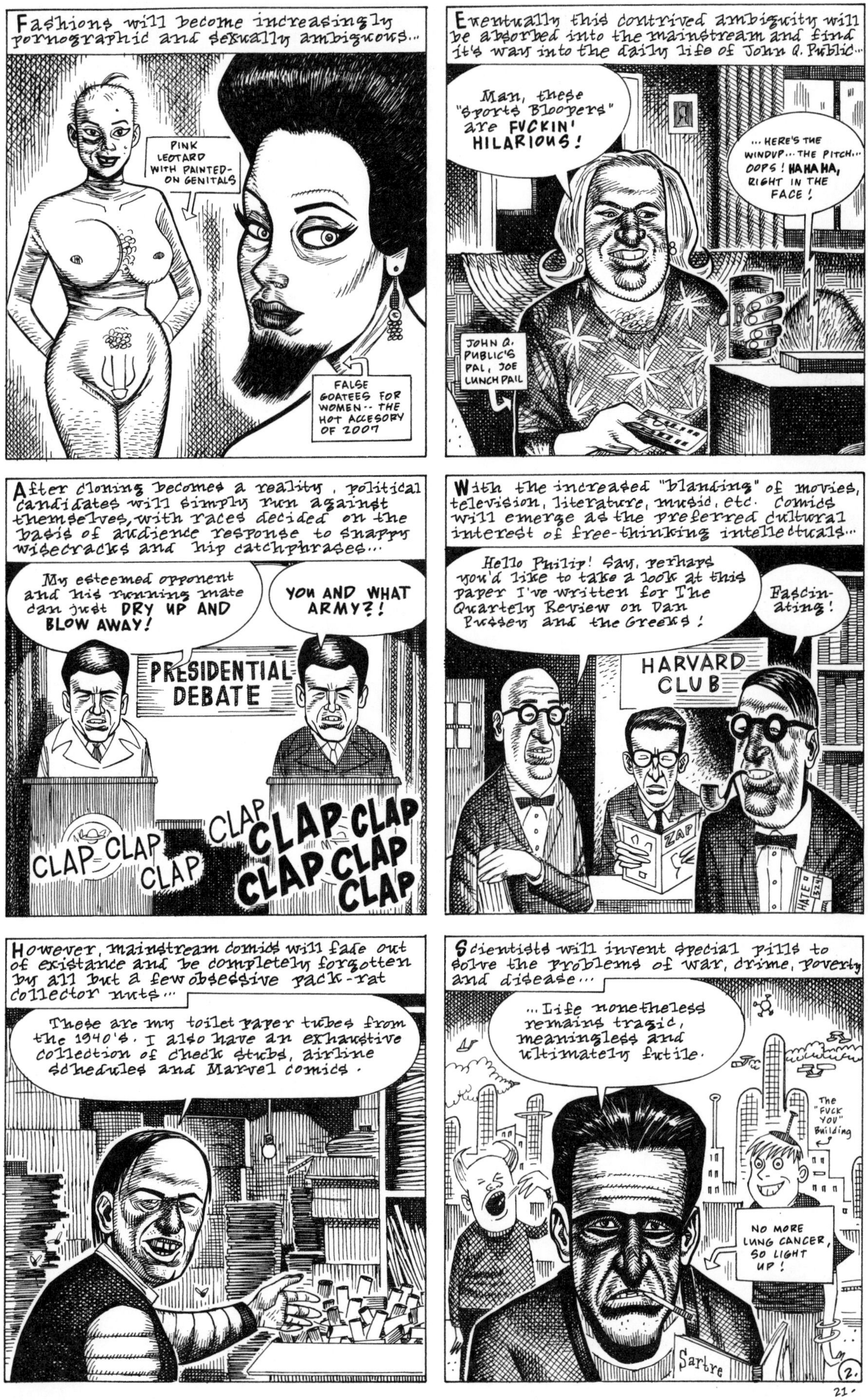

Fashions will become increasingly pornographic and sexually ambiguous...
PINK LEOTARD WITH PAINTED-ON GENITALS
FALSE GOATEES FOR WOMEN -- THE HOT ACCESORY OF 2007
Eventually this contrived ambiguity will be absorbed into the mainstream and find it's way into the daily life of John Q. Public...
Man, these "Sports Bloopers" are FUCKIN' HILARIOUS!
... HERE'S THE WINDUP... THE PITCH... OOPS! HA HA HA, RIGHT IN THE FACE!
JOHN Q. PUBLIC'S PAL, JOE LUNCHPAIL
After cloning becomes a reality, political candidates will simply run against themselves, with races decided on the basis of audience response to snappy wisecracks and hip catchphrases...
My esteemed opponent and his running mate can just DRY UP AND BLOW AWAY!
YOU AND WHAT ARMY?!
PRESIDENTIAL DEBATE
CLAP CLAP CLAP
CLAP CLAP CLAP CLAP CLAP CLAP
With the increased "blanding" of movies, television, literature, music, etc. Comics will emerge as the preferred cultural interest of free-thinking intellectuals...
Hello Philip! Say, perhaps you'd like to take a look at this paper I've written for The Quarterly Review on Dan Pussey and the Greeks!
Fascinating!
HARVARD CLUB
ZAP
HATE
However, mainstream comics will fade out of existance and be completely forgotten by all but a few obsessive pack-rat collector nuts...
These are my toilet paper tubes from the 1940's. I also have an exhaustive collection of check stubs, airline schedules and Marvel comics.
Scientists will invent special pills to solve the problems of war, crime, poverty and disease...
...Life nonetheless remains tragic, meaningless and ultimately futile.
The "FUCK YOU" Building
NO MORE LUNG CANCER, SO LIGHT UP!
Sartre
2.

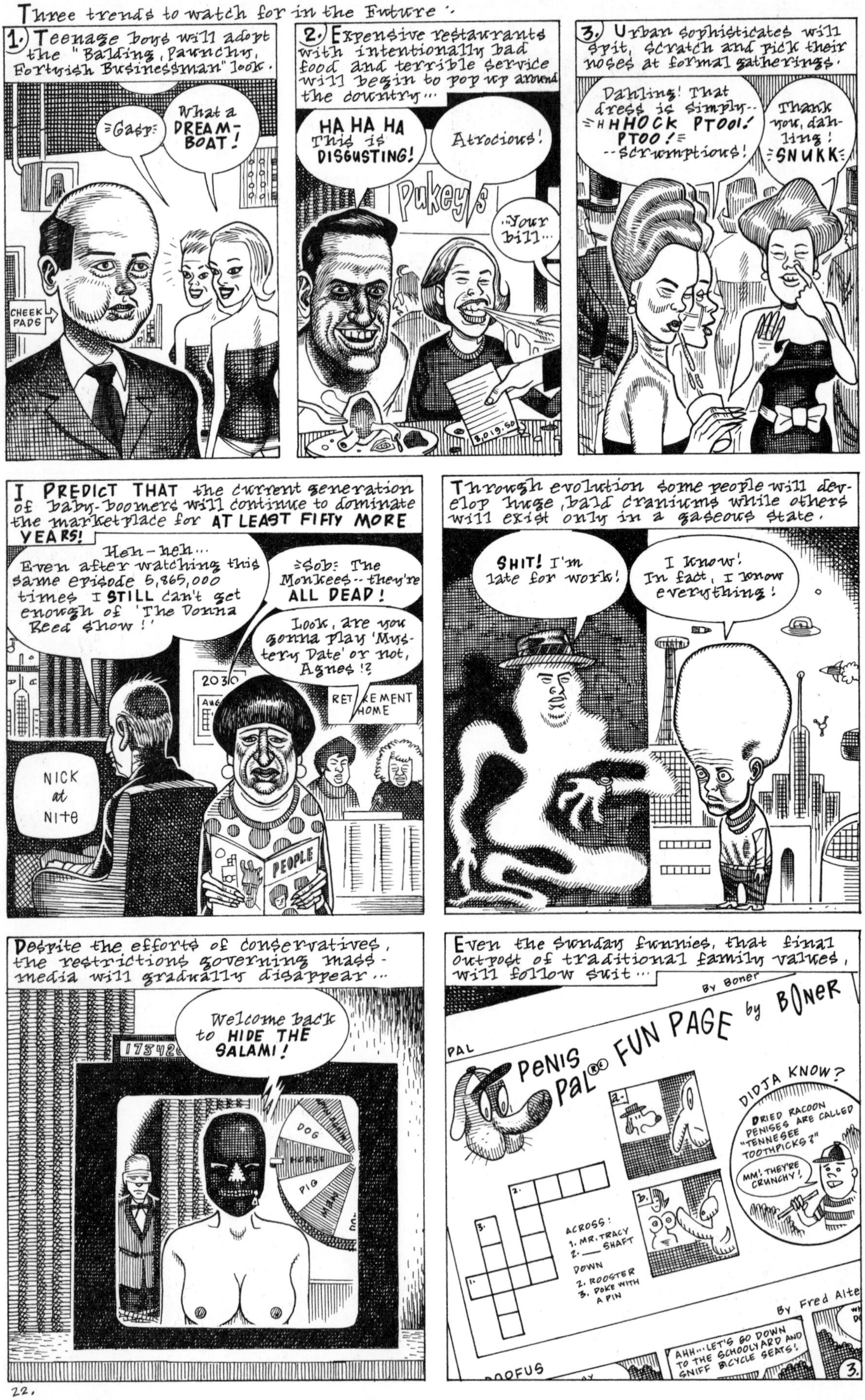
Three trends to watch for in the Future:
1. Teenage boys will adopt the "Balding, Paunchy, Fortyish Businessman" look.
=Gasp=
What a DREAM-BOAT!
CHEEK PADS
2. Expensive restaurants with intentionally bad food and terrible service will begin to pop up around the country...
HA HA HA This is DISGUSTING!
Atrocious!
Pukey's
"Your bill...
$,019.50
3. Urban sophisticates will spit, scratch and pick their noses at formal gatherings.
Dahling! That dress is simply-- =HHHOCK PTOO!! PTOO!= --Scrumptious!
Thank you, dahling! SNUKK
I PREDICT THAT the current generation of baby-boomers will continue to dominate the marketplace for AT LEAST FIFTY MORE YEARS!
Heh-heh... Even after watching this same episode 5,865,000 times I STILL can't get enough of 'The Donna Reed Show'!
=Sob= The Monkees--they're ALL DEAD!
Look, are you gonna play 'Mystery Date' or not, Agnes!?
2030
RETIREMENT HOME
NICK at Nite
PEOPLE
Through evolution some people will develop huge, bald craniums while others will exist only in a gaseous state.
SHIT! I'm late for work!
I know! In fact, I know everything!
Despite the efforts of conservatives, the restrictions governing mass-media will gradually disappear...
Welcome back to HIDE THE SALAMI!
17342
DOG
HORSE
PIG
Even the Sunday funnies, that final outpost of traditional family values, will follow suit...
By Boner
PENIS PAL® FUN PAGE by BONER
PAL
DIDJA KNOW?
DRIED RACOON PENISES ARE CALLED "TENNESEE TOOTHPICKS"?
MM! THEY'RE CRUNCHY!
ACROSS:
1. MR. TRACY
2. ___ SHAFT
DOWN
2. ROOSTER
3. POKE WITH A PIN
By Fred Alte
AHH... LET'S GO DOWN TO THE SCHOOLYARD AND SNIFF BICYCLE SEATS!
OOFUS

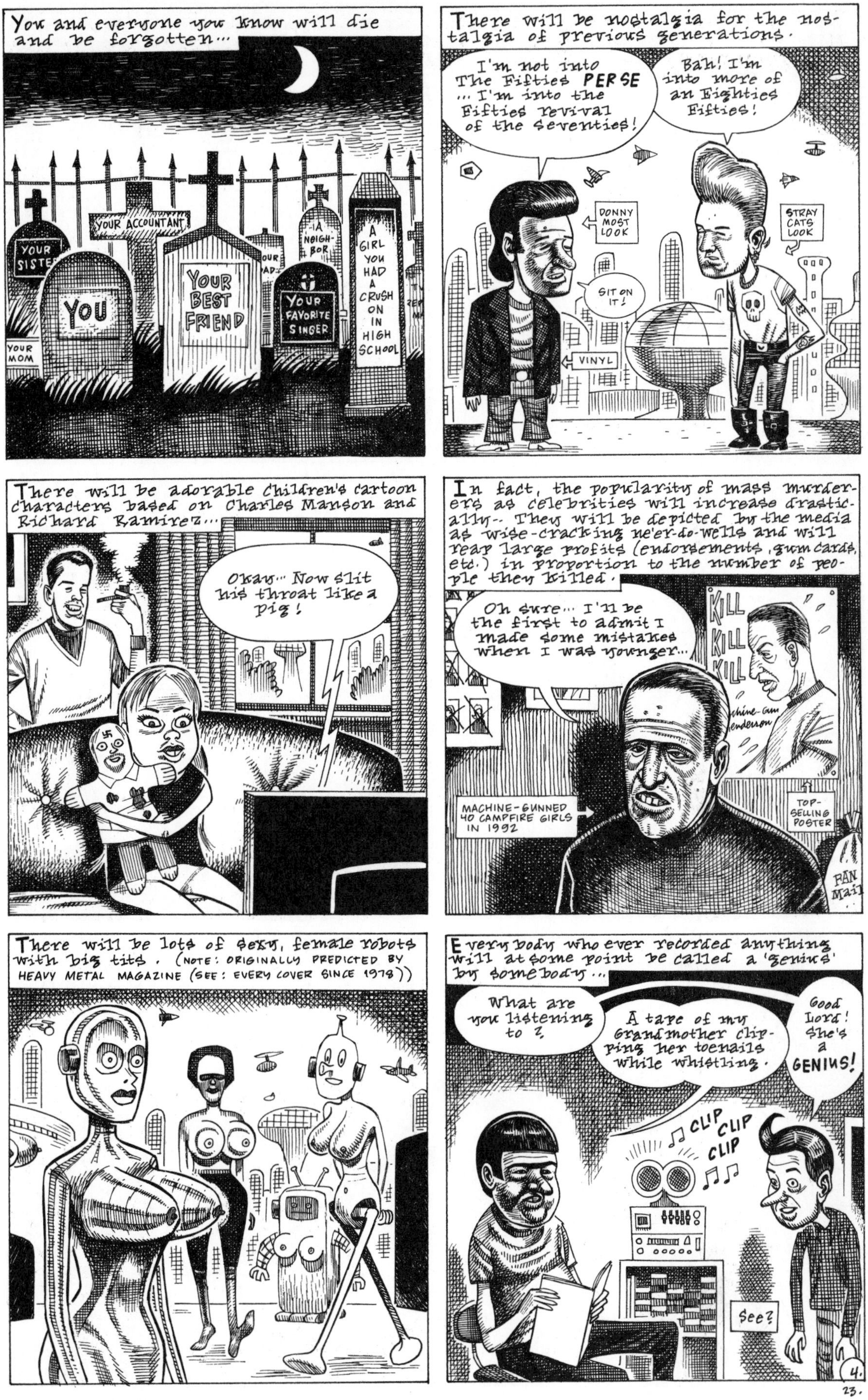
You and everyone you know will die and be forgotten...
YOUR SISTE
YOUR ACCOUNTANT
YOU
YOUR BEST FRIEND
A NEIGHBOR
YOUR FAVORITE SINGER
A GIRL YOU HAD A CRUSH ON IN HIGH SCHOOL
YOUR MOM
There will be nostalgia for the nostalgia of previous generations.
I'm not into The Fifties PERSE ... I'm into the Fifties revival of the Seventies!
Bah! I'm into more of an Eighties Fifties!
DONNY MOST LOOK
STRAY CATS LOOK
SIT ON IT!
VINYL
There will be adorable children's cartoon characters based on Charles Manson and Richard Ramirez...
Okay... Now slit his throat like a pig!
In fact, the popularity of mass murderers as celebrities will increase drastically.- They will be depicted by the media as wise-cracking ne'er-do-wells and will reap large profits (endorsements, gum cards, etc.) in proportion to the number of people they killed.
Oh sure... I'll be the first to admit I made some mistakes when I was younger...
KILL KILL KILL
MACHINE-GUNNED 40 CAMPFIRE GIRLS IN 1992
TOP-SELLING POSTER
FAN Mail
There will be lots of sexy, female robots with big tits. (NOTE: ORIGINALLY PREDICTED BY HEAVY METAL MAGAZINE (SEE: EVERY COVER SINCE 1978))
Everybody who ever recorded anything will at some point be called a 'genius' by somebody...
What are you listening to?
A tape of my Grandmother clipping her toenails while whistling.
Good Lord! She's a GENIUS!
CLIP CLIP CLIP
See?
4.

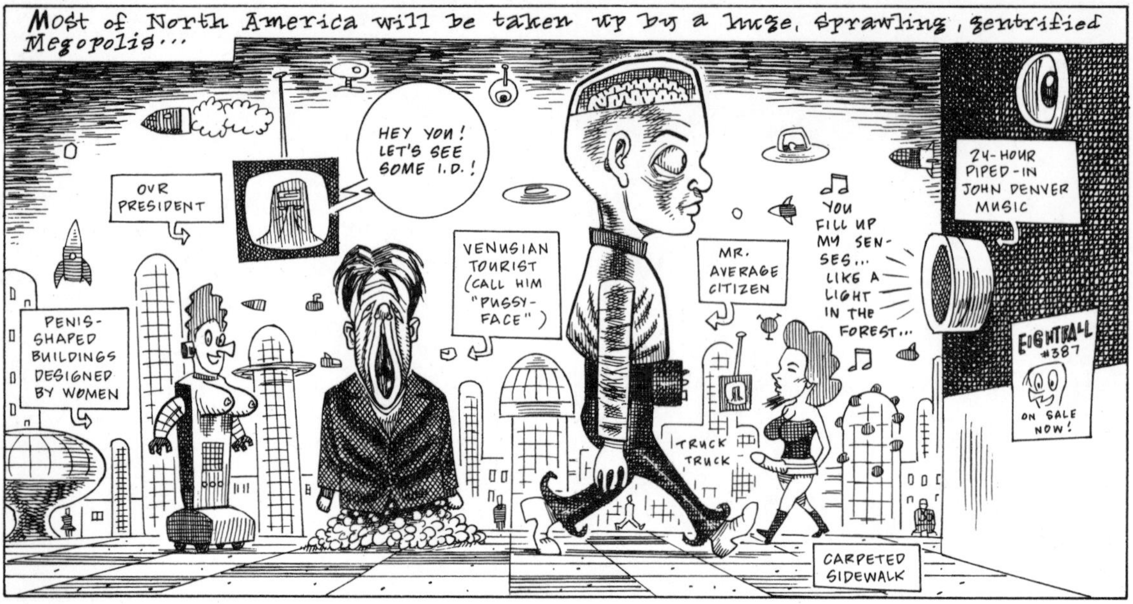
Most of North America will be taken up by a huge, sprawling, gentrified Megopolis...
HEY YOU! LET'S SEE SOME I.D.!
OUR PRESIDENT
VENUSIAN TOURIST (CALL HIM "PUSSY-FACE")
MR. AVERAGE CITIZEN
YOU FILL UP MY SEN-SES... LIKE A LIGHT IN THE FOREST...
24-HOUR PIPED-IN JOHN DENVER MUSIC
PENIS-SHAPED BUILDINGS DESIGNED BY WOMEN
EIGHTBALL #387 ON SALE NOW!
TRUCK TRUCK
CARPETED SIDEWALK

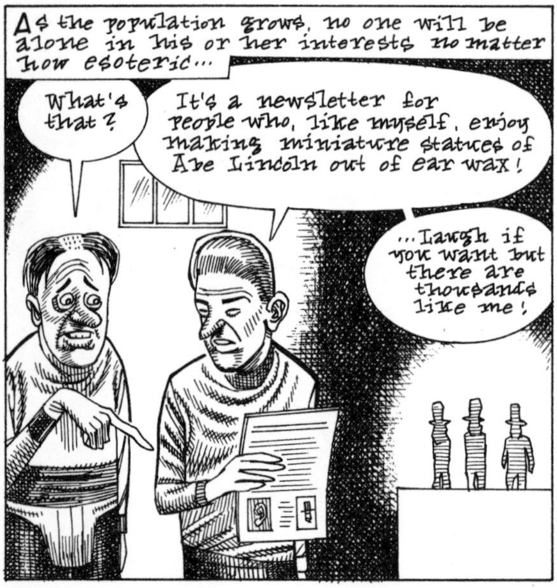
As the population grows, no one will be alone in his or her interests no matter how esoteric...
What's that?
It's a newsletter for people who, like myself, enjoy making miniature statues of Abe Lincoln out of ear wax!
...Laugh if you want but there are thousands like me!

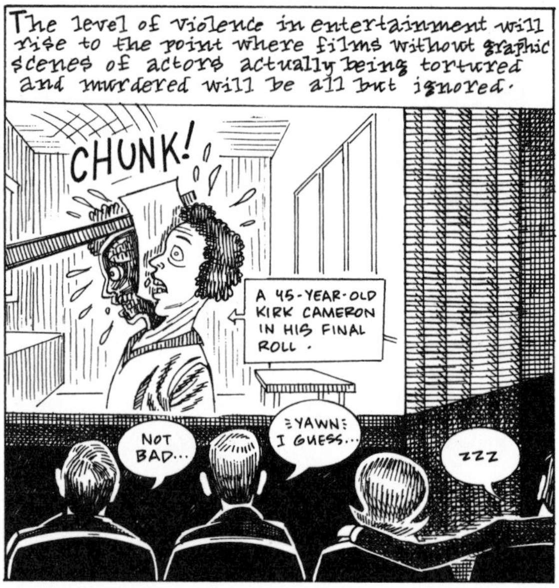
The level of violence in entertainment will rise to the point where films without graphic scenes of actors actually being tortured and murdered will be all but ignored.
CHUNK!
A 45-YEAR-OLD KIRK CAMERON IN HIS FINAL ROLL.
NOT BAD...
YAWN I GUESS...
ZZZ

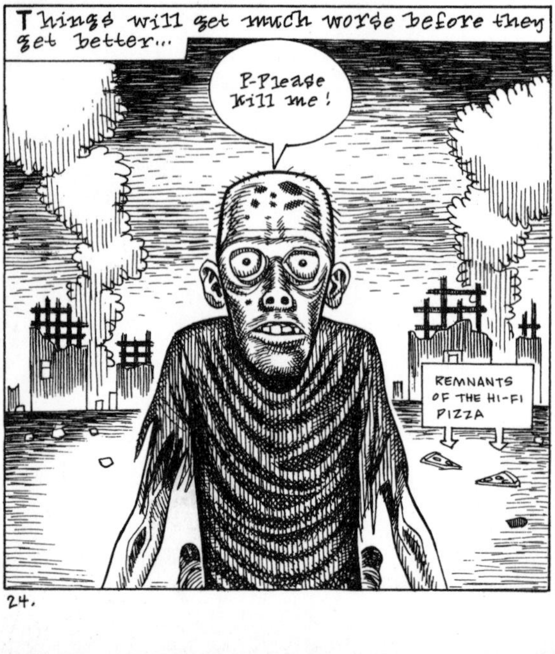
Things will get much worse before they get better...
P-Please kill me!
REMNANTS OF THE HI-FI PIZZA

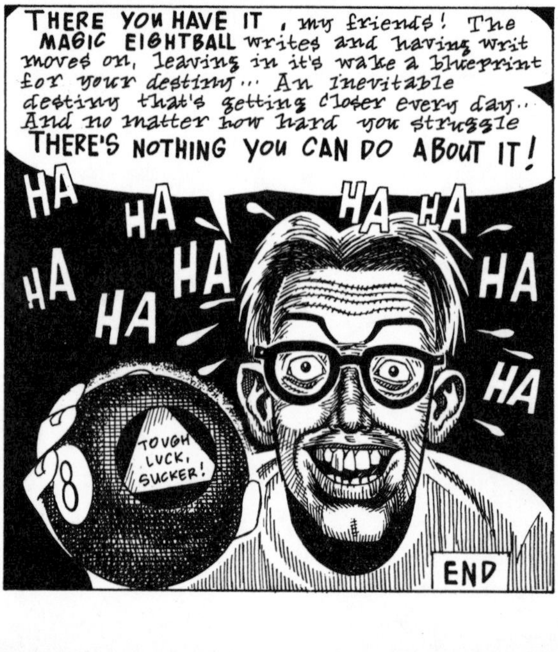
THERE YOU HAVE IT, my friends! The MAGIC EIGHTBALL writes and having writ moves on, leaving in it's wake a blueprint for your destiny... An inevitable destiny that's getting closer every day.. And no matter how hard you struggle THERE'S NOTHING YOU CAN DO ABOUT IT!
HA HA HA HA HA HA HA HA HA HA
TOUGH LUCK, SUCKER!
8
END

THE LOVE EXPLOSION

write to: EIGHTBALL
BOX 3357
CHICAGO, ILL.
60654

To Young Dan Clowes...
'The Simpsons' sucks.
'Twin Peaks' (except for the dancing midget) sucks.
Suck. Suck. Suck.
'Eightball' does not suck. It is better than very good. It's like sugar frosted flakes. "It's great!"
Great. Great. Great.

Gilberto Hernandez
Woodland Hills, CA.

P.S. Please print this so people will know I don't really hate everything.
P.P.S. Kitty Muskegon looks like how Harvey Pekar would like 'Luba' to look.

Daniel Clowes, whatsup!
I was in this 'Mystery Train' movie, I played the bellhop. Anyway, the thing is I'm not an actor, I'm a film-maker— an independant one at that, based in Brooklyn... Look, your 'Eightball' comic is amazing and I think "Like a Velvet Glove cast in Iron" would make an intense movie!

Cinqué Lee
Brooklyn, NY

Dear Daniel,
Yeah! 8#3!! Sheesh, best comic I've read in months!! Blast it— best one ever outta ya! D. Pussy hit harder-n-ever, V. Glove is getting more twisted— like it lots, etc. Sheeshola, I'd pay $5 for this book! Beautiful Job!

Roy Tompkins
Austin, TX

ALL YOU COMIC LOVERS OUT THERE MUST IMMEDIATELY SEND AWAY FOR ROY'S BRILLIANT MINI 'HARVEY THE HILLBILLY BASTARD' ($2 PPD. FROM ROY T., BOX 16022, AUSTIN, TX. 78761). FIND OUT WHAT "GUESS I'LL HONK ON BOBO JEST A LITTLE" MEANS!

Daniel,
Glad to see someone else appreciates the smarminess of Robt. Tilton. The only one I can think of that compares is "Dr." D. James Kennedy with his upper-class parishoners in Fla. Keep printing these vital bulletins!

Richard Evans Lee
Durham, NC

Dan,
Finally caught up with the first issue of 'Eightball' It's great stuff. All these clowns out there are trying so hard to do stories that are unsettling and perverse and you make it look so easy... Each story had its own feeling of dread and unease and tension. Especially 'Young Dan Pussey.' Too much truth in that one.
With all the 'stuff' that's out there these days yours is still among my favorites. It's like electro-shock! The rest is like oat meal.

Chuck Dixon
Lancaster, PA

Dear Daniel,
I really like the new 8-Ball ...In issue 2 (p.22, Pan.6) you show Donovan as a hated British musician. You're welcome to hate him, of course, but he's not British. He's... well, you can guess...

Charlie Harris
Tucson, AZ

WHAT??

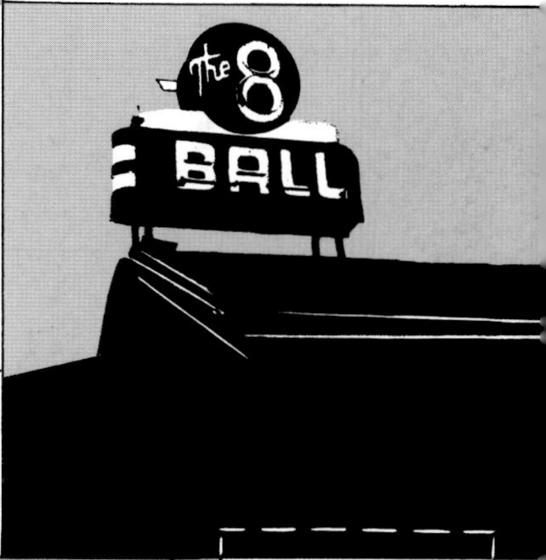
The 8
BALL

Plug Corner

"APOCALYPSE POOH"
VHS VIDEOCASSETTE
COLOR. 10 MIN.

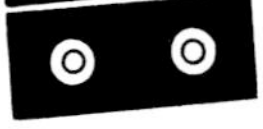

Simply a tape of Winnie the Pooh cartoon clips expertly overdubbed with dialogue from 'Apocalypse Now!' The results are hilarious and frightening. Also on the tape: 'Blue Peanuts' (Snoopy as Frank Booth) and a surprising clip of the Archies. A must-see!

AVAILABLE FOR: $24.95 (CANADIAN)
FROM: HOME FORMAT VIDEO
105 McCAUL #506
TORONTO, ONT.
M5T 2X4 CANADA

BACK ISSUES

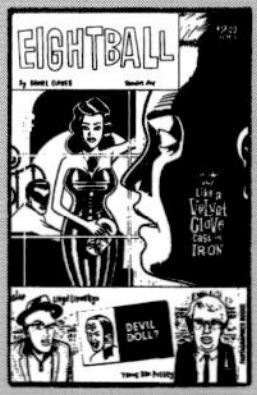
EIGHTBALL

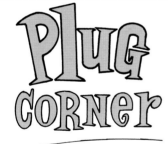

EIGHTBALL #1
This timeless classic is BACK IN PRINT!

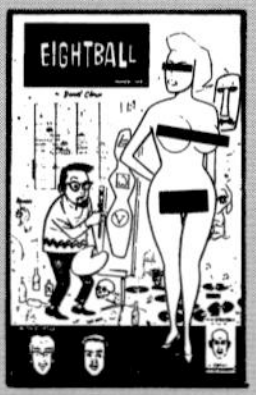
EIGHTBALL

EIGHTBALL #2
"I Hate You Deeply" and others!

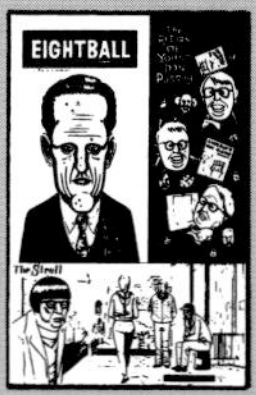
EIGHTBALL

EIGHTBALL #3
"The Stroll;" Gummo Bubbleman; More!

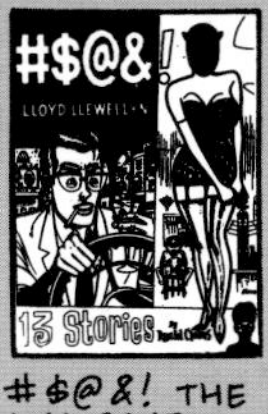
#$@&!
LLOYD LLEWELLYN
13 Stories

#$@&! THE LLLL COLLECTION
As seen in 'Entertainment Weekly' Wow.

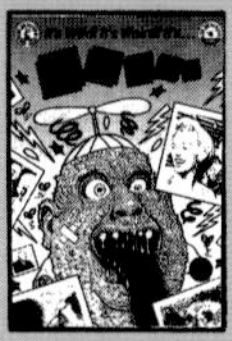

BLAB #4
Featured long, uninspired D. Clowes interview and other stuff!

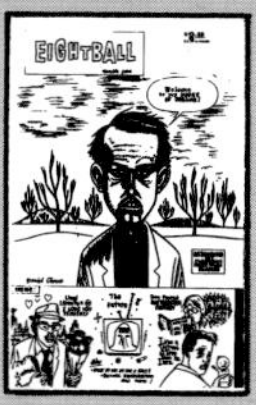
EIGHTBALL

3-ISSUE SUBSCRIPTION
A great gift idea!

Send me:
☐ EIGHTBALL #1 (2.50) ☐ EIGHTBALL #2 (2.50) ☐ #3 (2.50)
☐ #4 (2.50) ☐ #$@&!: LLLL COLLECTION (12.00)
☐ BLAB #4 (9.00) ☐ 3-ISSUE SUB. TO EIGHTBALL (5.00)
Foreign orders add 10% · Allow 6-8 weeks

Send orders to:
FANTAGRAPHICS BOOKS
7563 LAKE CITY WAY
SEATTLE, WA. 98115

Name
Address
City State Zip

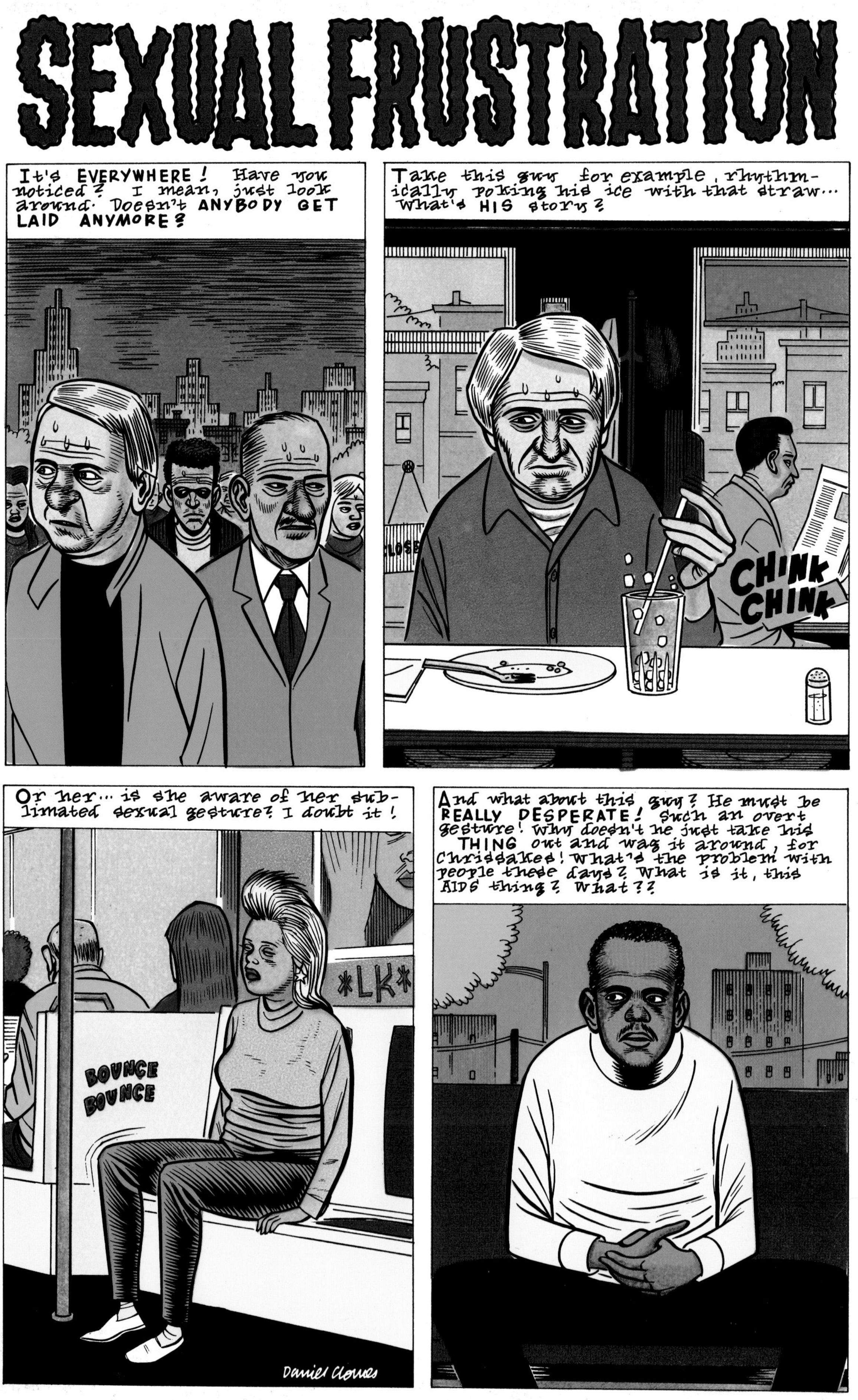
SEXUAL FRUSTRATION
It's EVERYWHERE! Have you noticed? I mean, just look around. Doesn't ANYBODY GET LAID ANYMORE?
Take this guy for example, rhythm-ically poking his ice with that straw... What's HIS story?
CHINK CHINK
Or her... is she aware of her sub-limated sexual gesture? I doubt it!
BOUNCE BOUNCE
Daniel Clowes
And what about this guy? He must be REALLY DESPERATE! Such an overt gesture! Why doesn't he just take his THING out and wag it around, for Chrissakes! What's the problem with people these days? What is it, this AIDS thing? What??

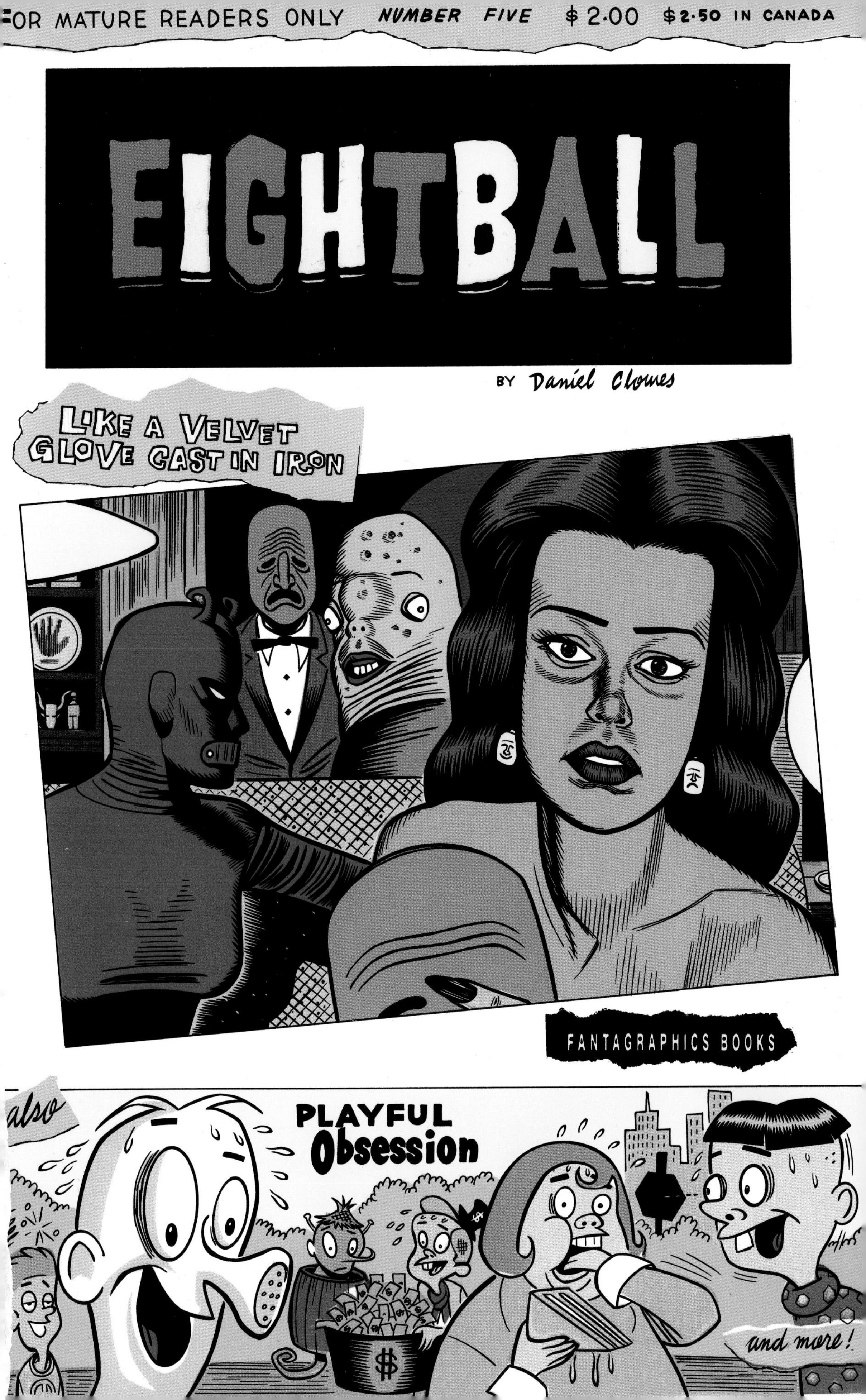
FOR MATURE READERS ONLY
NUMBER FIVE
$2.00
$2.50 IN CANADA
EIGHTBALL
BY Daniel Clowes
LIKE A VELVET GLOVE CAST IN IRON
FANTAGRAPHICS BOOKS
also
PLAYFUL Obsession
and more!

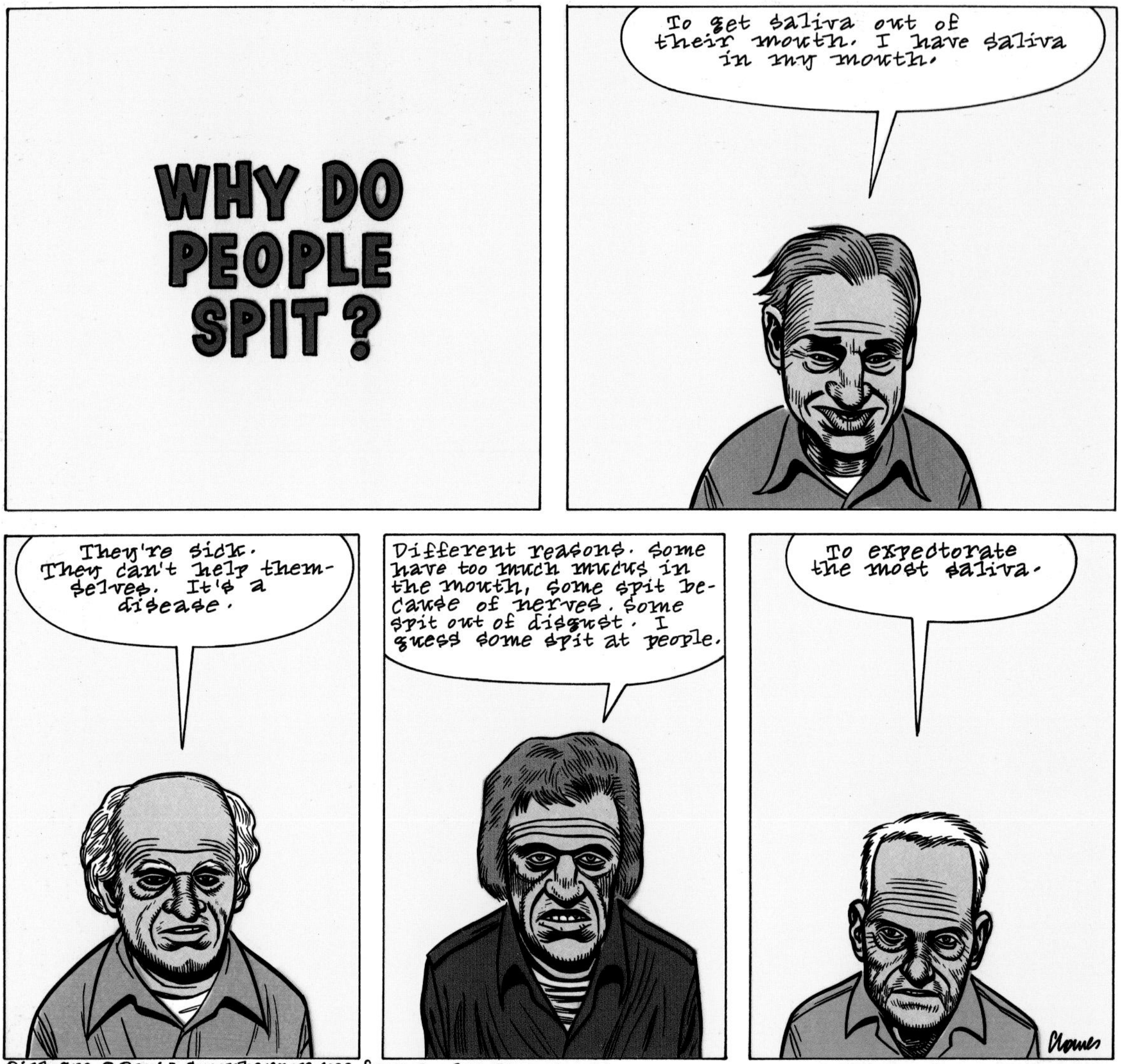
WHY DO PEOPLE SPIT?
To get saliva out of their mouth. I have saliva in my mouth.
They're sick. They can't help themselves. It's a disease.
Different reasons. Some have too much mucus in the mouth, some spit because of nerves. Some spit out of disgust. I guess some spit at people.
To expectorate the most saliva.
Clowes

Dialogue © David Greenberger 1990 from Duplex Planet # 99.

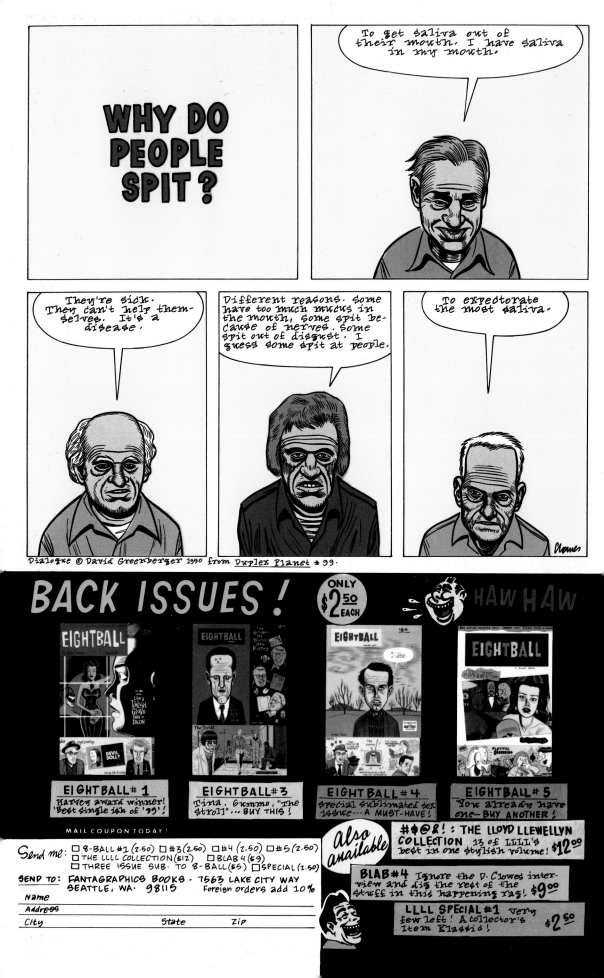

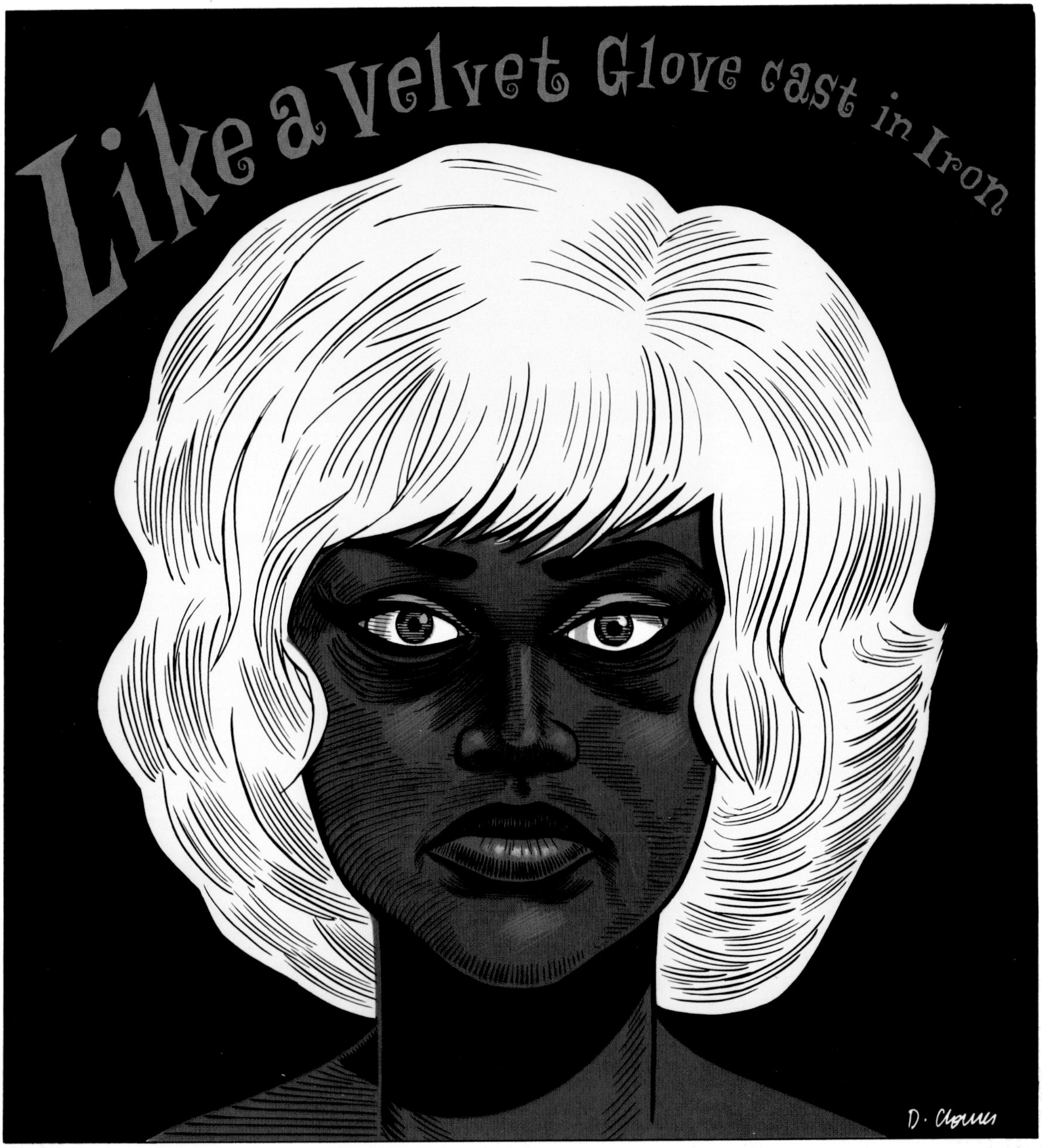
Like a velvet Glove cast in Iron
D. Clowes

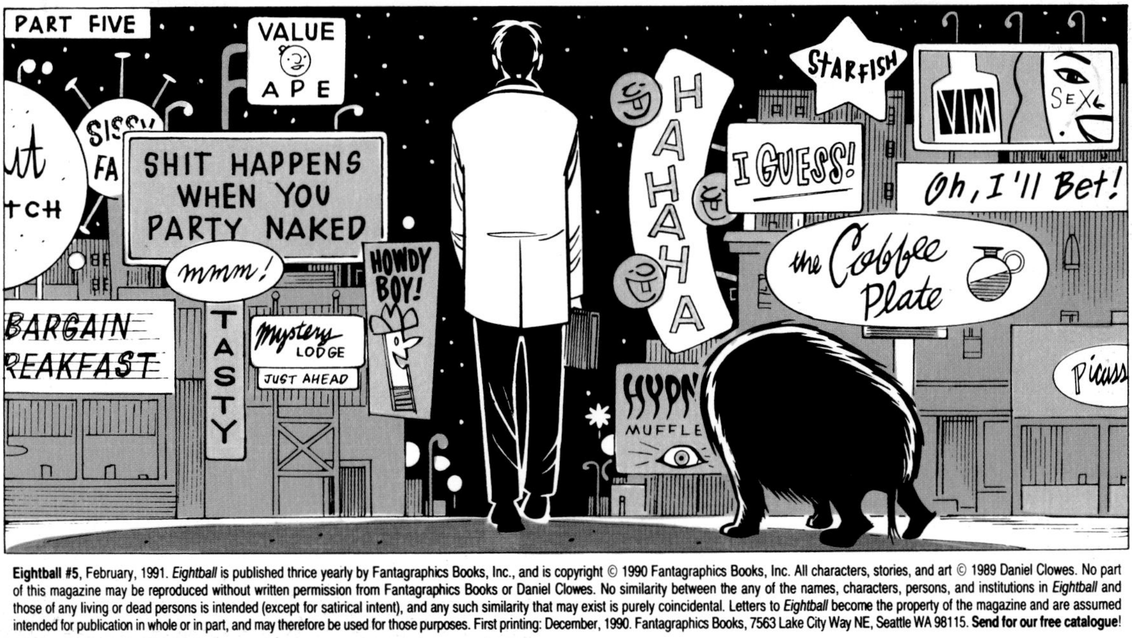
PART FIVE
VALUE APE
SHIT HAPPENS WHEN YOU PARTY NAKED
mmm!
BARGAIN
TASTY
Mystery LODGE
JUST AHEAD
HOWDY BOY!
HAHAHA
STARFISH
VIM
I GUESS!
Oh, I'll Bet!
the Coffee Plate
MUFFLE

Eightball #5, February, 1991. *Eightball* is published thrice yearly by Fantagraphics Books, Inc., and is copyright © 1990 Fantagraphics Books, Inc. All characters, stories, and art © 1989 Daniel Clowes. No part of this magazine may be reproduced without written permission from Fantagraphics Books or Daniel Clowes. No similarity between the any of the names, characters, persons, and institutions in *Eightball* and those of any living or dead persons is intended (except for satirical intent), and any such similarity that may exist is purely coincidental. Letters to *Eightball* become the property of the magazine and are assumed intended for publication in whole or in part, and may therefore be used for those purposes. First printing: December, 1990. Fantagraphics Books, 7563 Lake City Way NE, Seattle WA 98115. **Send for our free catalogue**!

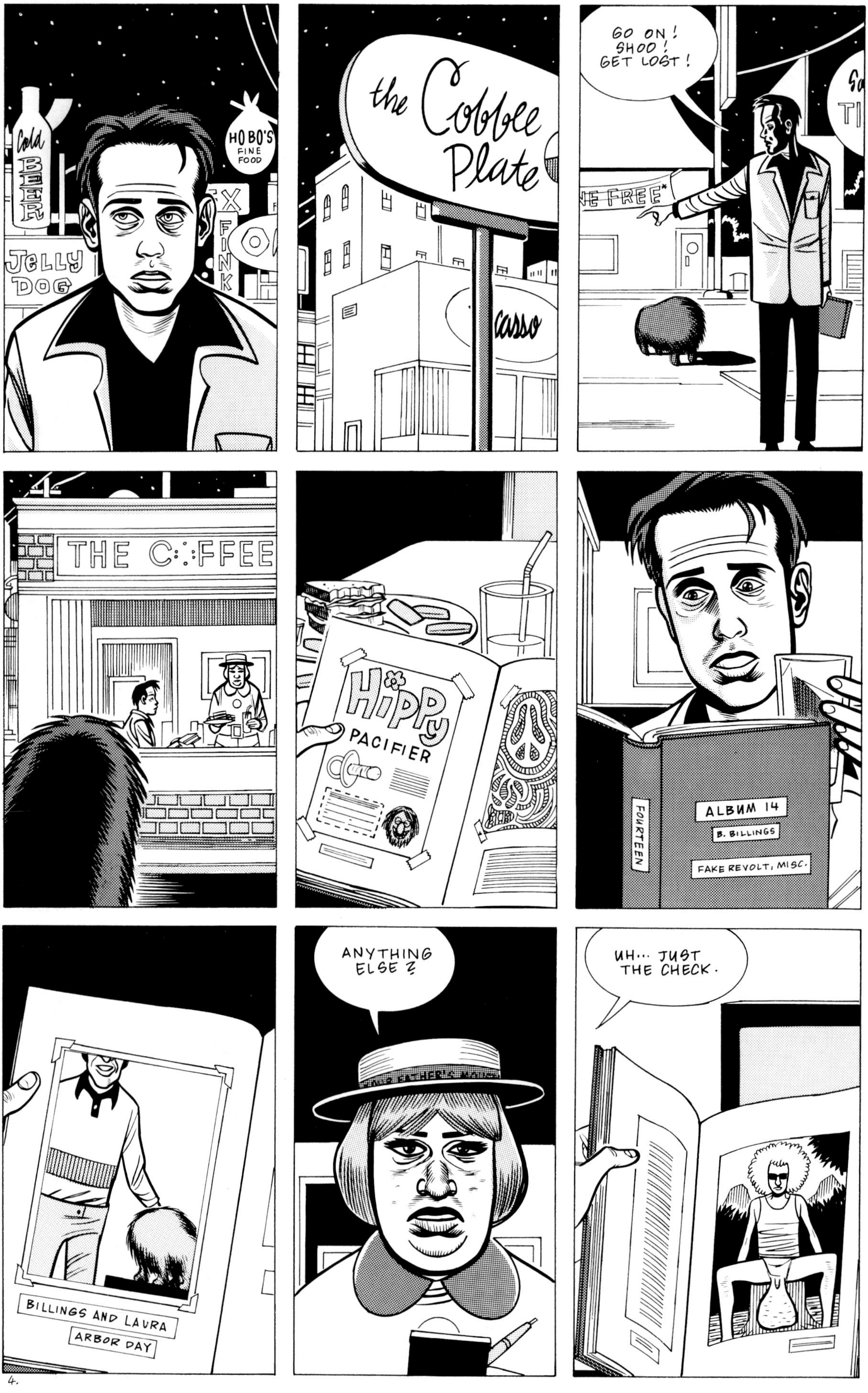
Cold BEER
HOBO'S FINE FOOD
Jelly DOG
FINK
the Cobble Plate
GO ON! SHOO! GET LOST!
HiPPy PACIFIER
FOURTEEN
ALBUM 14
B. BILLINGS
FAKE REVOLT, MISC.
BILLINGS AND LAURA
ARBOR DAY
ANYTHING ELSE?
UH... JUST THE CHECK.

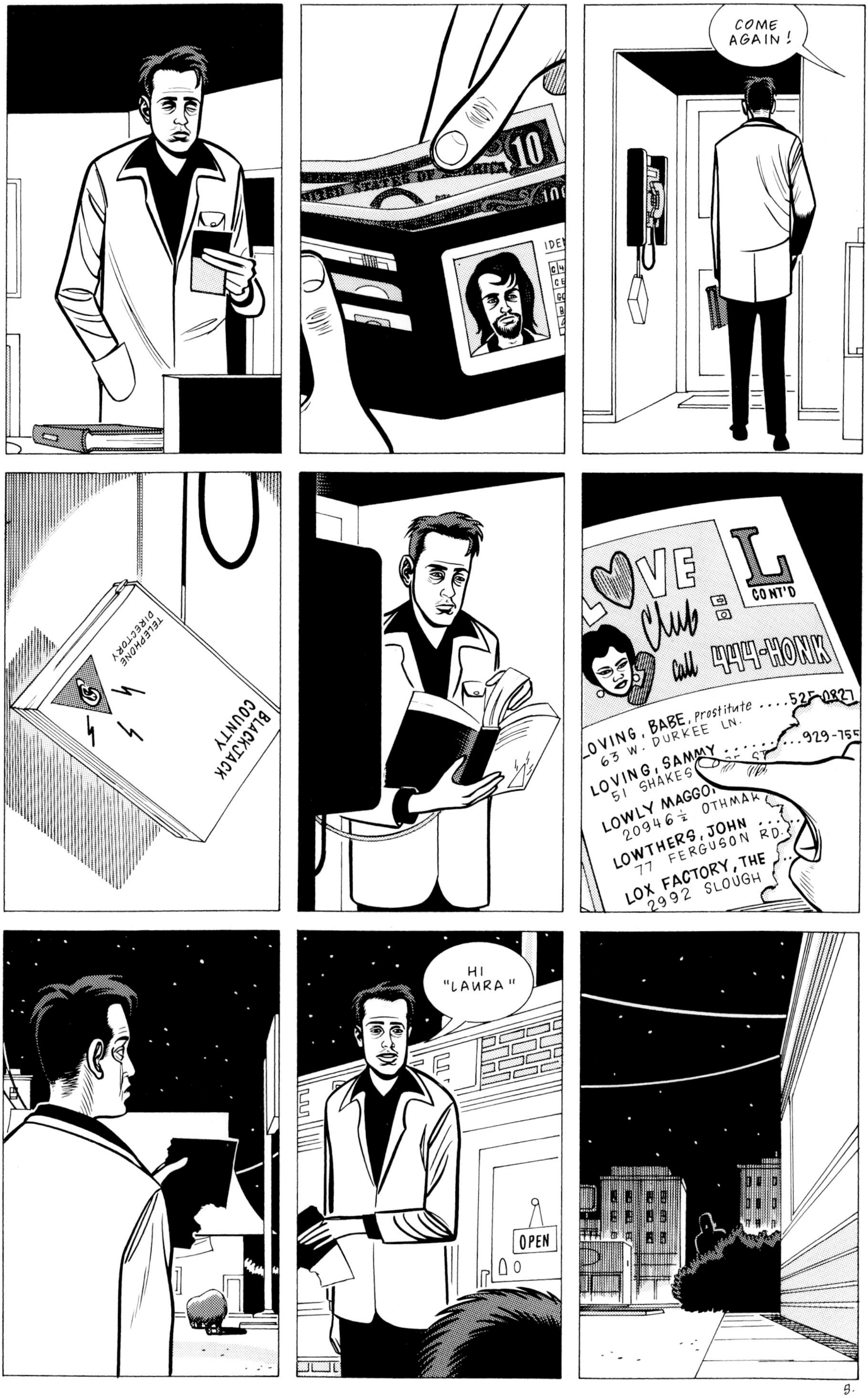
COME AGAIN!
BLACKJACK COUNTY
TELEPHONE DIRECTORY
LOVE Club call 444-HONK
L CONT'D
LOVING, BABE, Prostitute
63 W. DURKEE LN.
LOVING, SAMMY
51 SHAKES
LOWLY MAGGO
20946½ OTHMAK
LOWTHERS, JOHN
77 FERGUSON RD.
LOX FACTORY, THE
2992 SLOUGH
HI "LAURA"
OPEN

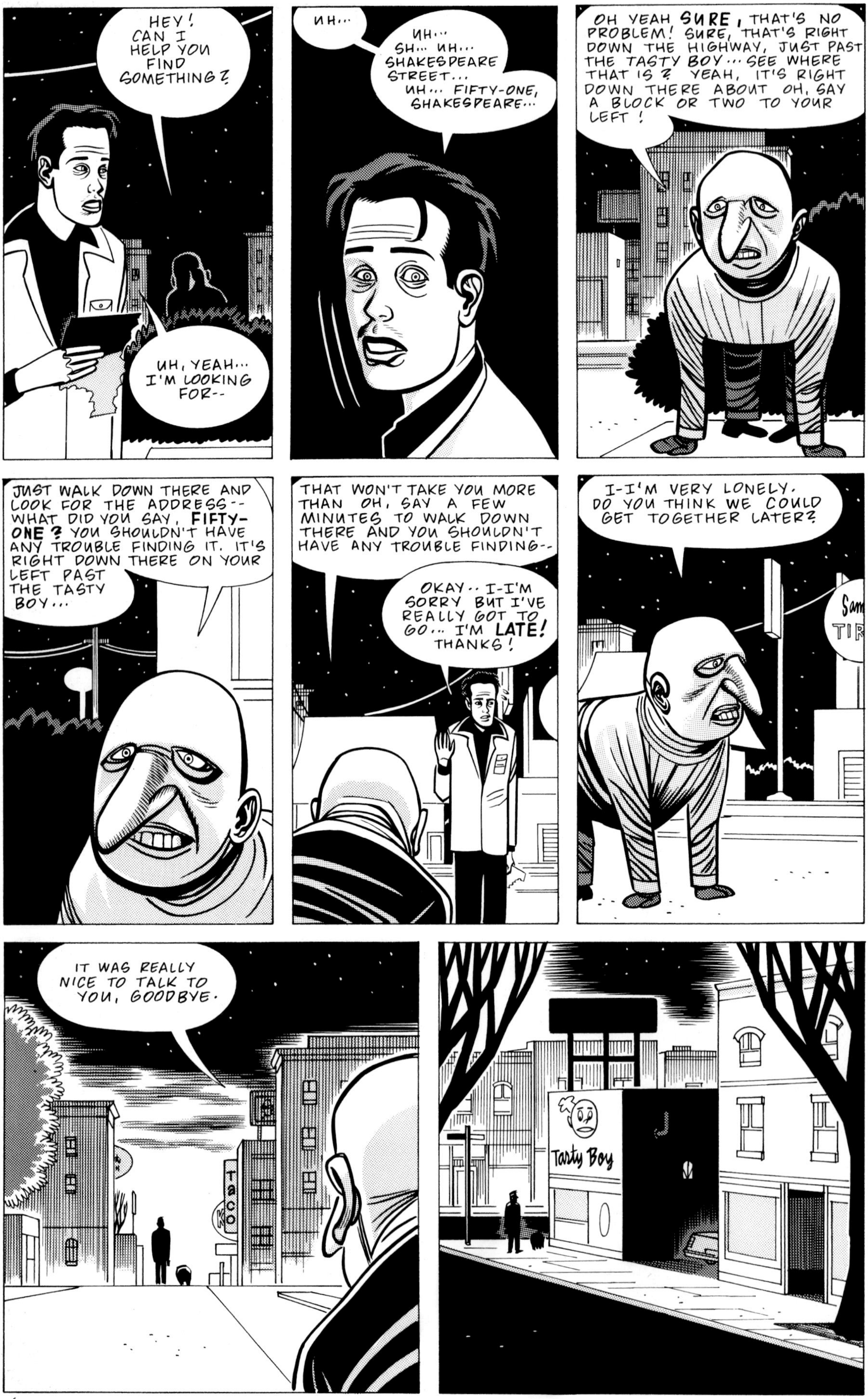
HEY! CAN I HELP YOU FIND SOMETHING?
UH, YEAH... I'M LOOKING FOR--
UH...
UH... SH... UH... SHAKESPEARE STREET... UH... FIFTY-ONE, SHAKESPEARE...
OH YEAH SURE, THAT'S NO PROBLEM! SURE, THAT'S RIGHT DOWN THE HIGHWAY, JUST PAST THE TASTY BOY... SEE WHERE THAT IS? YEAH, IT'S RIGHT DOWN THERE ABOUT OH, SAY A BLOCK OR TWO TO YOUR LEFT!
JUST WALK DOWN THERE AND LOOK FOR THE ADDRESS-- WHAT DID YOU SAY, FIFTY-ONE? YOU SHOULDN'T HAVE ANY TROUBLE FINDING IT. IT'S RIGHT DOWN THERE ON YOUR LEFT PAST THE TASTY BOY...
THAT WON'T TAKE YOU MORE THAN OH, SAY A FEW MINUTES TO WALK DOWN THERE AND YOU SHOULDN'T HAVE ANY TROUBLE FINDING--
OKAY.. I-I'M SORRY BUT I'VE REALLY GOT TO GO... I'M LATE! THANKS!
I-I'M VERY LONELY. DO YOU THINK WE COULD GET TOGETHER LATER?
IT WAS REALLY NICE TO TALK TO YOU, GOODBYE.
Taco
Tasty Boy

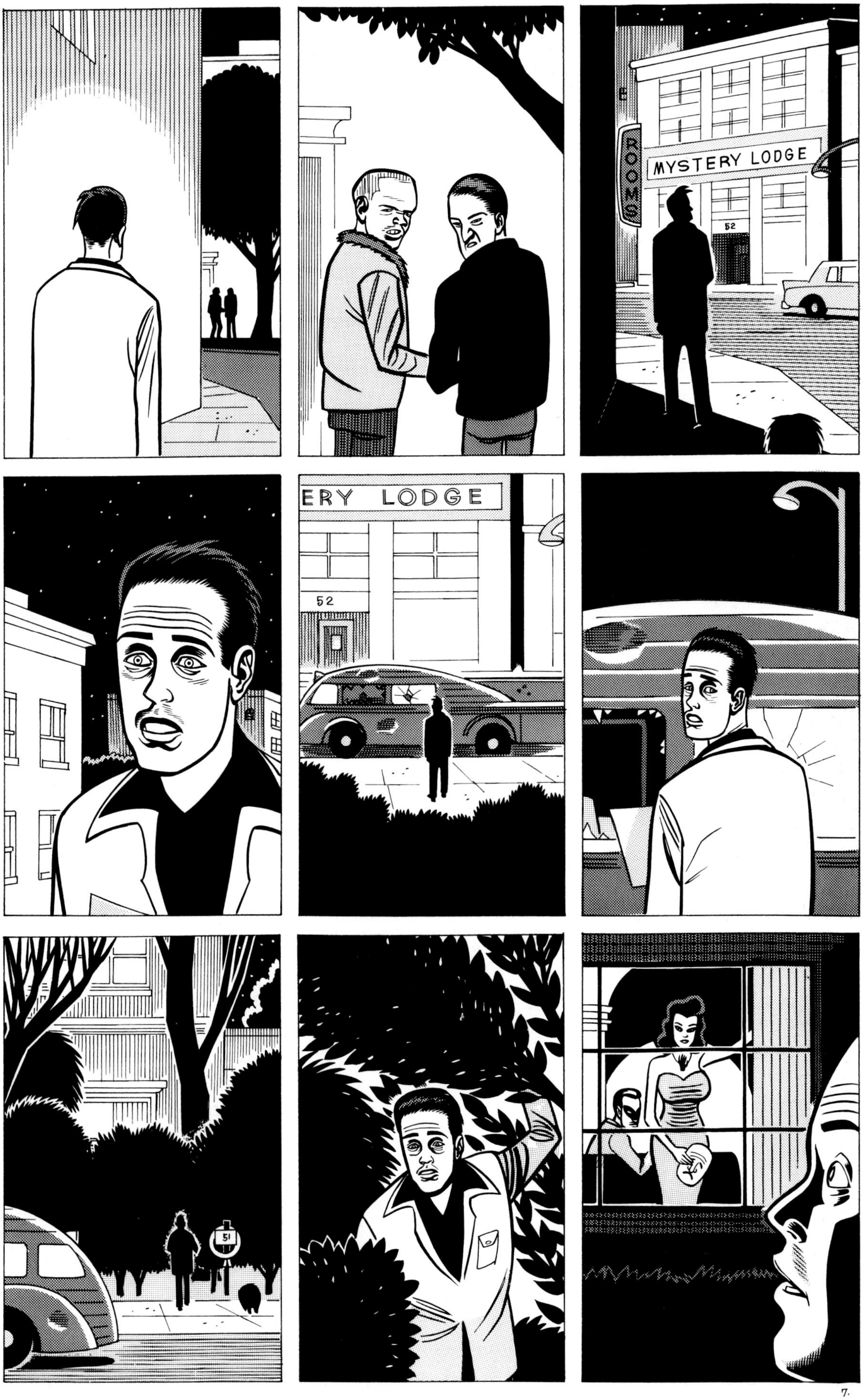
ROOMS
MYSTERY LODGE
52
ERY LODGE
52
51

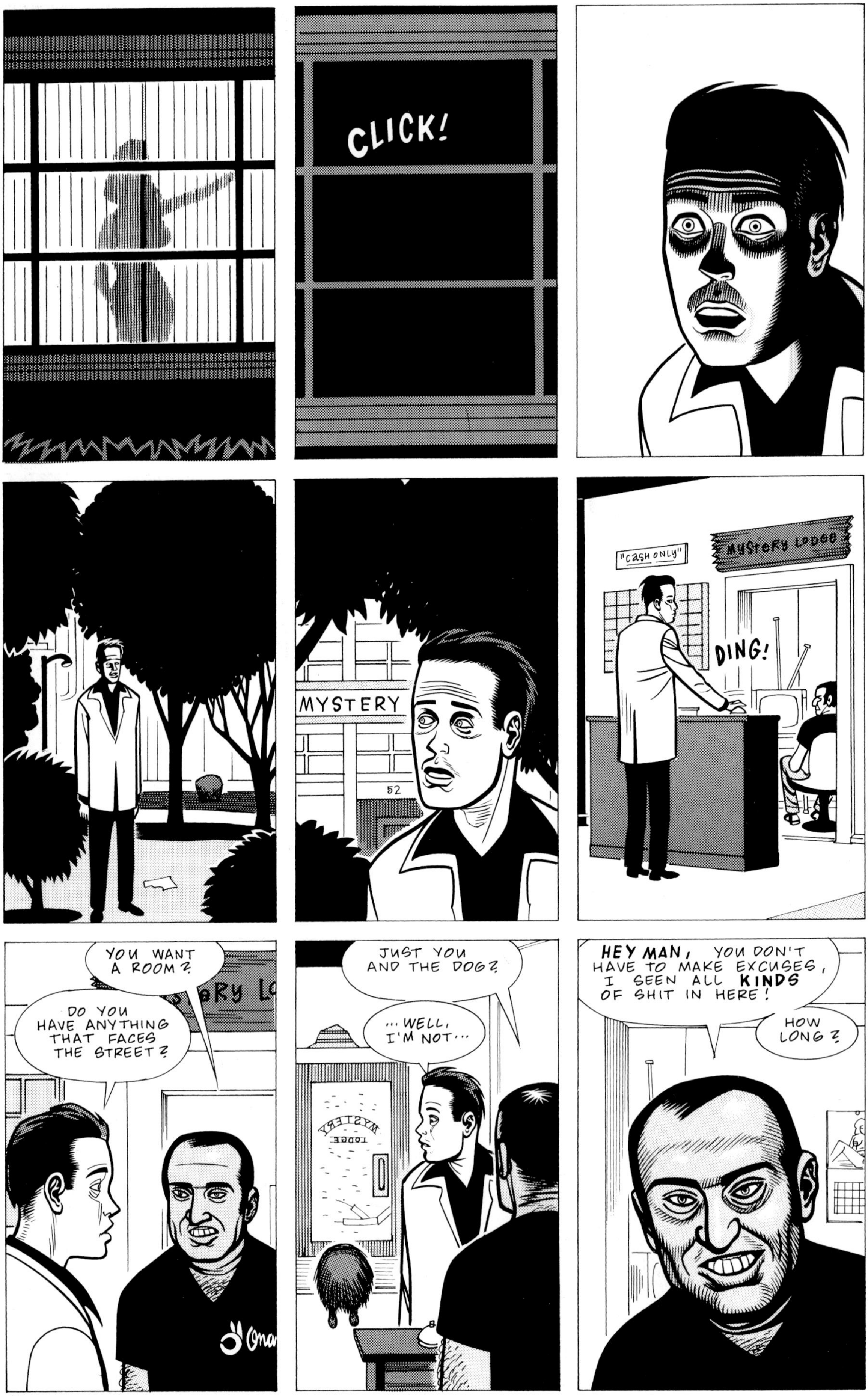
CLICK!
"CASH ONLY"
MYSTERY LODGE
MYSTERY
52
DING!
YOU WANT A ROOM?
DO YOU HAVE ANYTHING THAT FACES THE STREET?
JUST YOU AND THE DOG?
...WELL, I'M NOT...
HEY MAN, YOU DON'T HAVE TO MAKE EXCUSES, I SEEN ALL KINDS OF SHIT IN HERE!
HOW LONG?

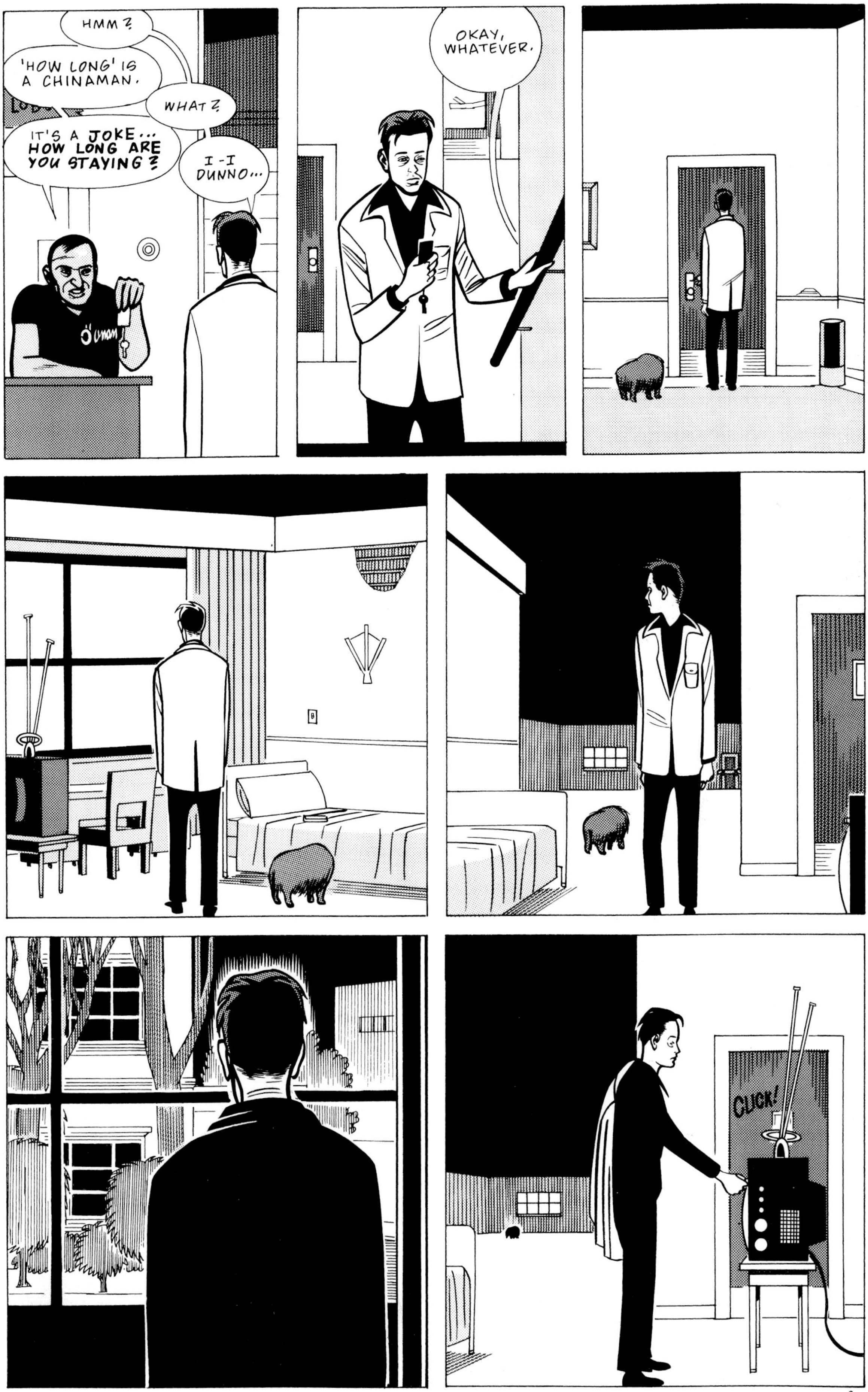

HMM?
'HOW LONG' IS A CHINAMAN.
WHAT?
IT'S A JOKE... HOW LONG ARE YOU STAYING?
I-I DUNNO...
OKAY, WHATEVER.
CLICK!

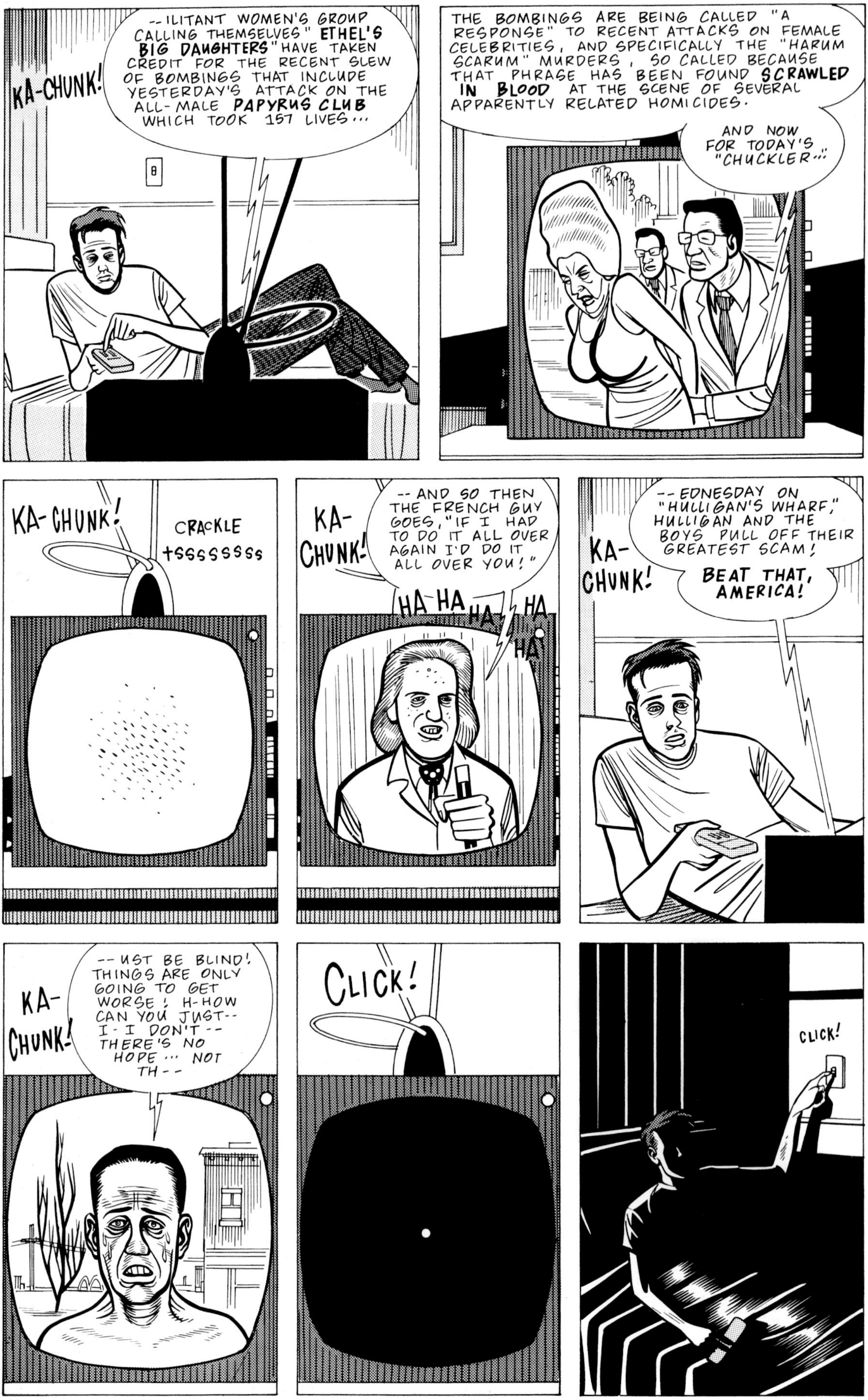
KA-CHUNK!
--ILITANT WOMEN'S GROUP CALLING THEMSELVES "ETHEL'S BIG DAUGHTERS" HAVE TAKEN CREDIT FOR THE RECENT SLEW OF BOMBINGS THAT INCLUDE YESTERDAY'S ATTACK ON THE ALL-MALE PAPYRUS CLUB WHICH TOOK 157 LIVES...
THE BOMBINGS ARE BEING CALLED "A RESPONSE" TO RECENT ATTACKS ON FEMALE CELEBRITIES, AND SPECIFICALLY THE "HARUM SCARUM" MURDERS, SO CALLED BECAUSE THAT PHRASE HAS BEEN FOUND SCRAWLED IN BLOOD AT THE SCENE OF SEVERAL APPARENTLY RELATED HOMICIDES.
AND NOW FOR TODAY'S "CHUCKLER..."
KA-CHUNK!
CRACKLE tssssssss
KA-CHUNK!
--AND SO THEN THE FRENCH GUY GOES, "IF I HAD TO DO IT ALL OVER AGAIN I'D DO IT ALL OVER YOU!"
HA HA HA HA HA HA
KA-CHUNK!
--EDNESDAY ON "HULLIGAN'S WHARF," HULLIGAN AND THE BOYS PULL OFF THEIR GREATEST SCAM!
BEAT THAT, AMERICA!
KA-CHUNK!
--UST BE BLIND! THINGS ARE ONLY GOING TO GET WORSE! H-HOW CAN YOU JUST-- I-I DON'T-- THERE'S NO HOPE... NOT TH--
CLICK!
CLICK!

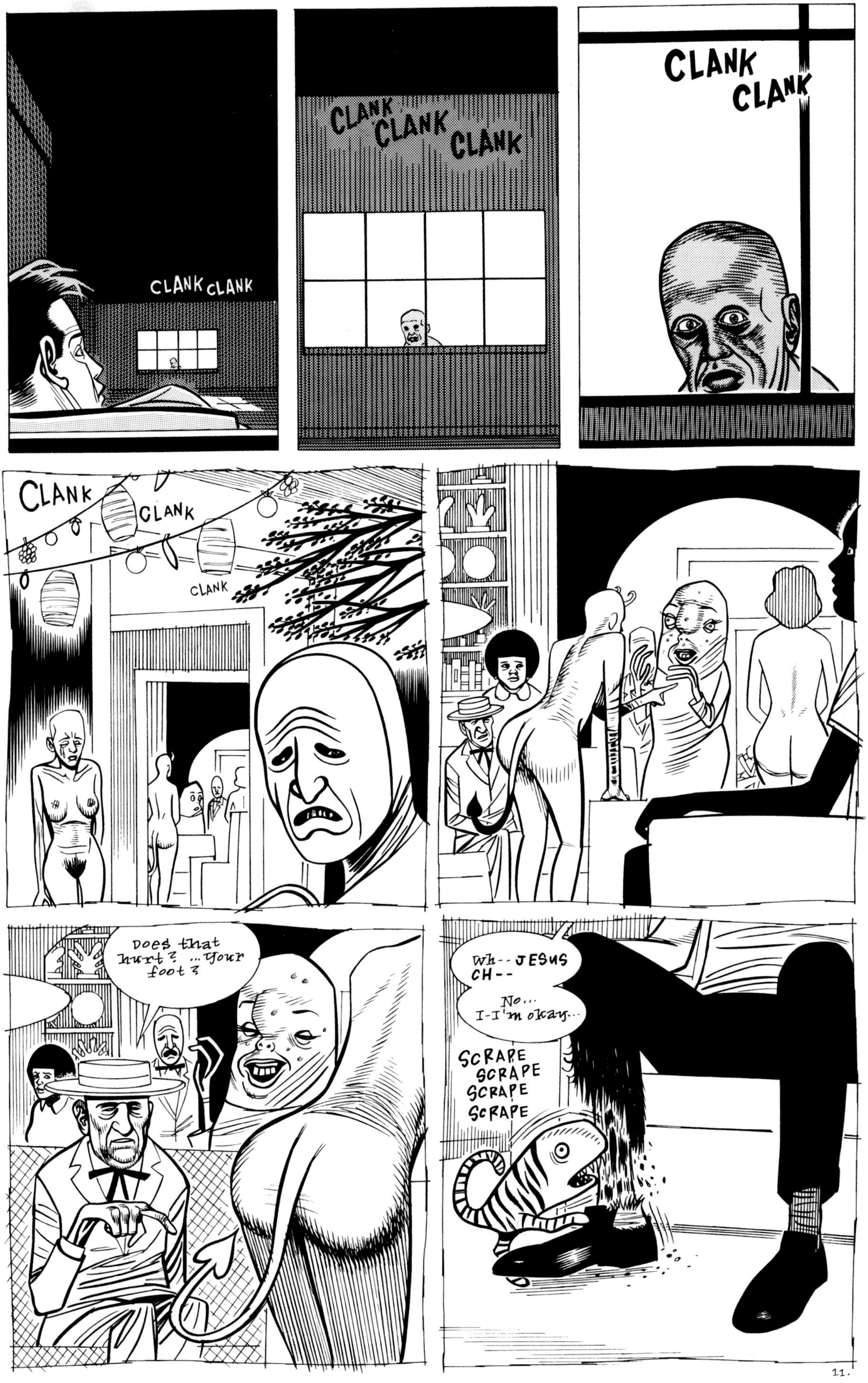
CLANK CLANK
CLANK CLANK CLANK
CLANK CLANK
CLANK CLANK CLANK
Does that hurt? ...Your foot?
Wh--JESUS CH--
No... I-I'm okay...
SCRAPE SCRAPE SCRAPE SCRAPE

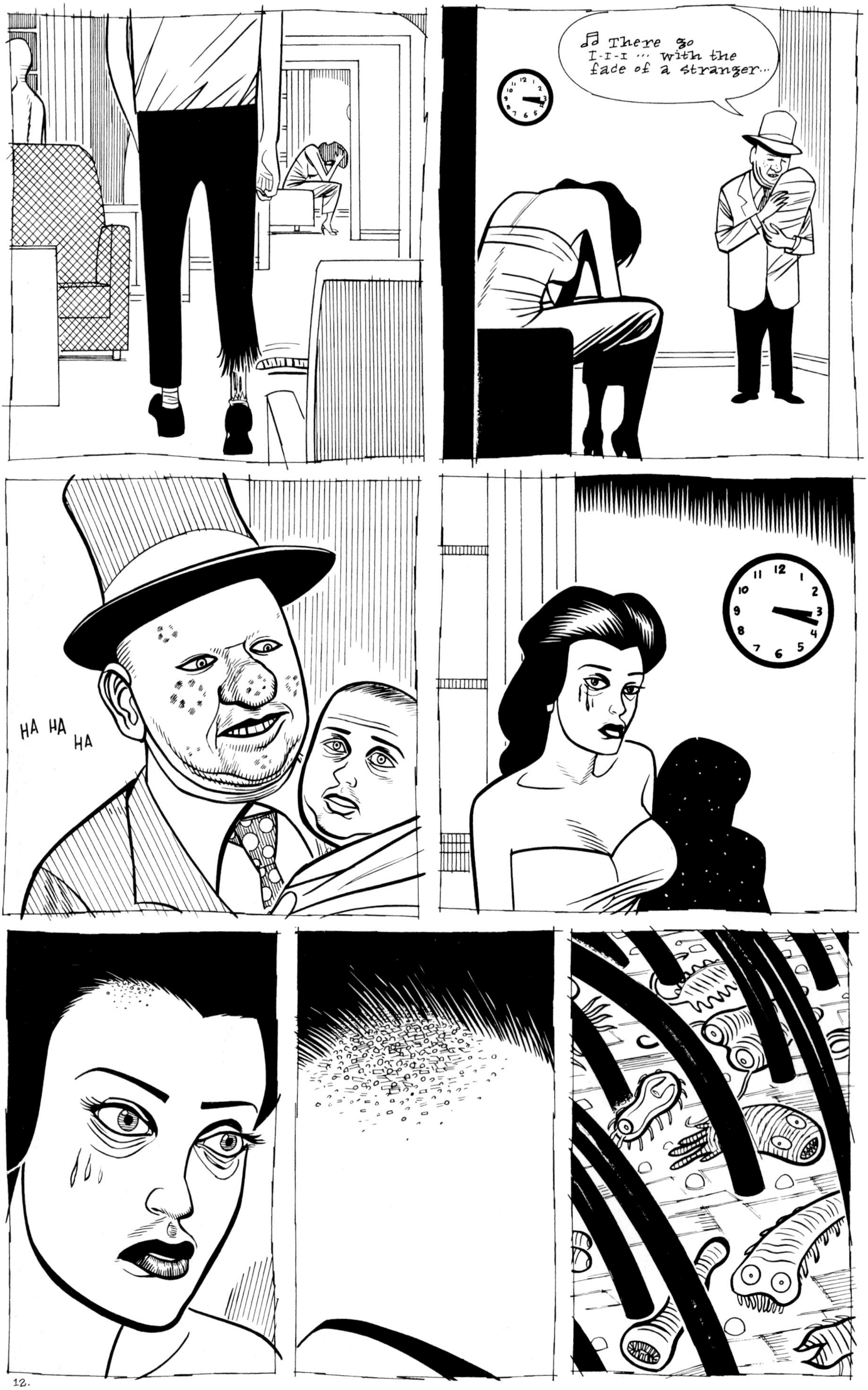
There go I-I-I ... with the face of a stranger...
HA HA HA

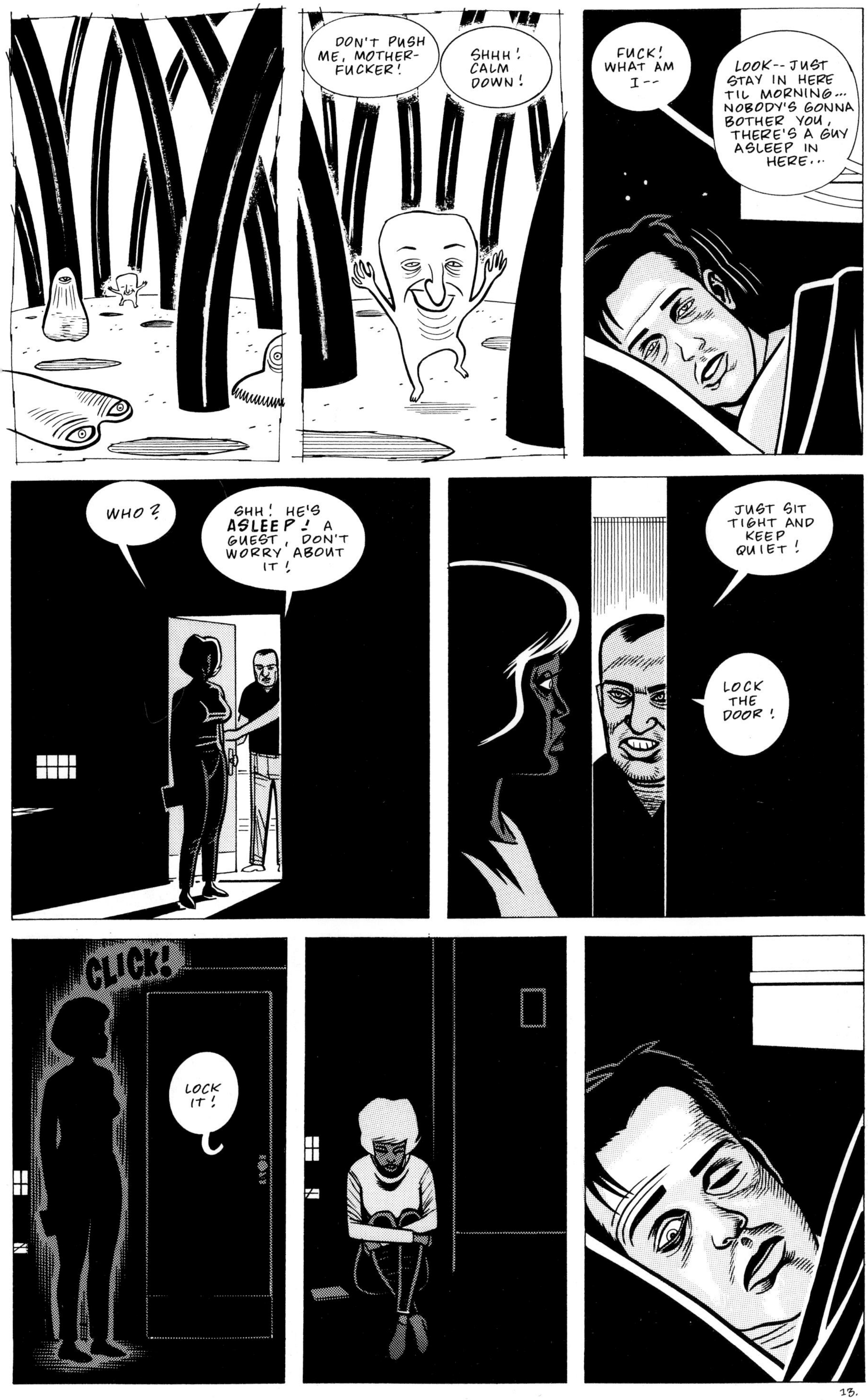
DON'T PUSH ME, MOTHER-FUCKER!
SHHH! CALM DOWN!
FUCK! WHAT AM I--
LOOK--JUST STAY IN HERE TIL MORNING... NOBODY'S GONNA BOTHER YOU, THERE'S A GUY ASLEEP IN HERE...
WHO?
SHH! HE'S ASLEEP! A GUEST, DON'T WORRY ABOUT IT!
JUST SIT TIGHT AND KEEP QUIET!
LOCK THE DOOR!
CLICK!
LOCK IT!

EEEEEK!

EEEEEK!

CLICK!

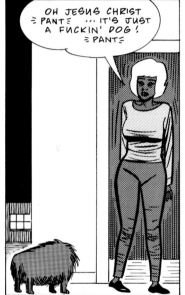

OH JESUS CHRIST ≥PANT≥ ...IT'S JUST A FUCKIN' DOG! ≥PANT≥

...I-- UH...I THINK THIS IS MY ROOM...

YEAH... HEY, DO YOU MIND IF I STAY HERE FOR A LITTLE WHILE?

I... UH... YEAH... I GUESS... IF YOU WANT...

≥COFF≥ WHAT'S THE MATTER? ARE YOU IN TROUBLE?

FUCK! HELL YES!

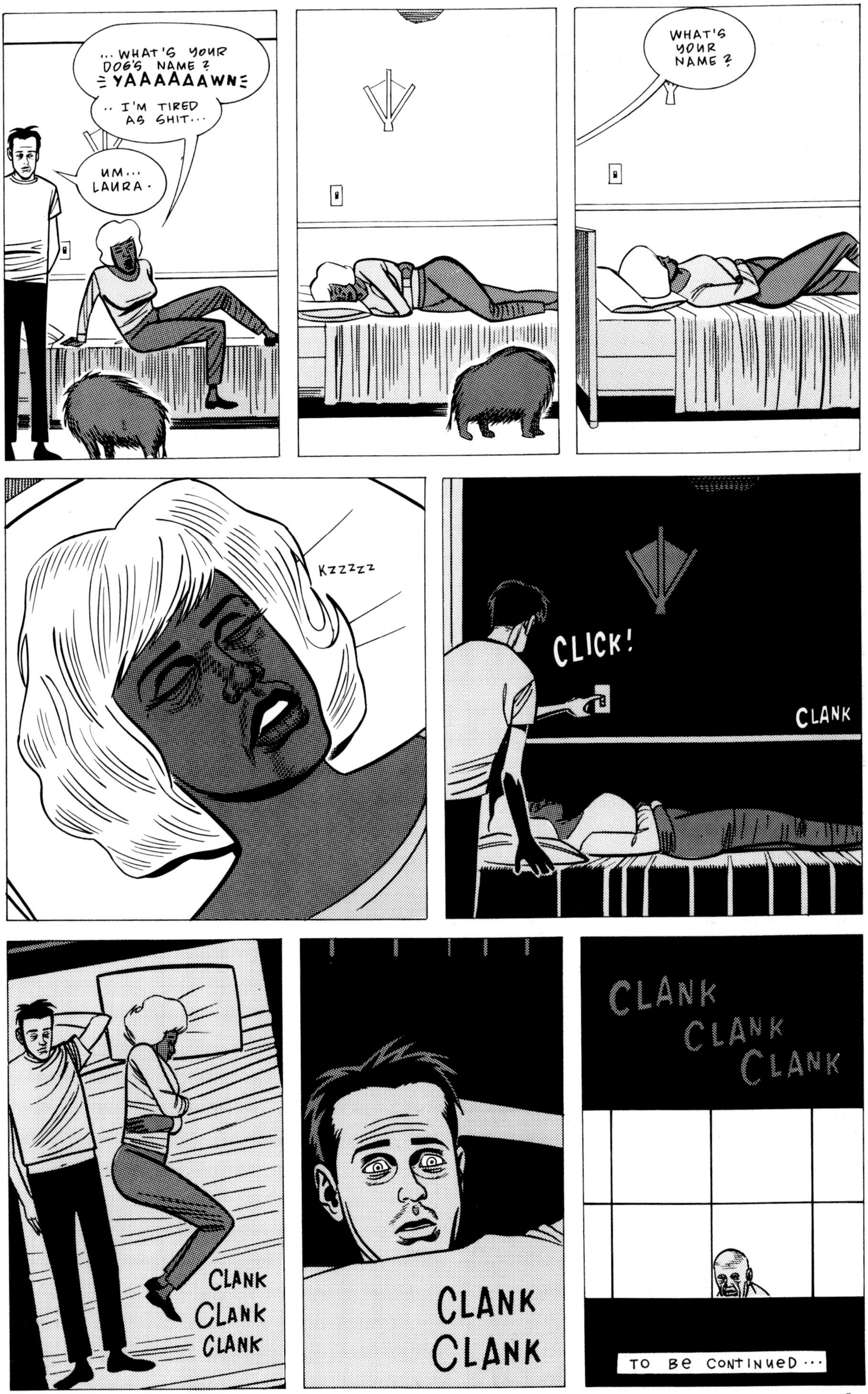
...WHAT'S YOUR DOG'S NAME ? YAAAAAAWN
.. I'M TIRED AS SHIT...
UM... LAURA.
WHAT'S YOUR NAME ?
KZZZZZ
CLICK!
CLANK
CLANK
CLANK
CLANK
CLANK
CLANK
CLANK
CLANK
CLANK
TO BE CONTINUED...

OH THOSE FUCKIN' LETTERS

Write to: EIGHTBALL
BOX 3357
CHICAGO, IL.
60654

• • • • • • • • • • • • • • •

Goddam! Eightball is a good book. Funny, provocative and anything but bland.

I wish I had something more clever to say about it but I'm too blown away.

Best to you,

Eddie Gorodetsky
New York, N.Y.

• • • • • • • • • • • • • • •

Reading Eightball is like coming down off bad acid and it's three-thirty in the morning and there's a sink full of dirty dishes and nothing on TV except Banacek reruns and you're all out of cigarettes. Beautiful!!

Keep it up,

Palmer Vreedeez
San Francisco, CA.

• • • • • • • • • • • • • • •

So, I'm at the San Diego Comic convention and the night before we started out on Guinness and worked our way up to warm, sweet, red wine and greasy, meaty pizza and the next day I wake up at about 4:30 A.M. feeling real bad and I can't get back to sleep and I feel real bad, so I start reading Eightball #4 and it's one of the best comics I've ever seen, but like I said, I feel real bad and I realize I'm gonna throw up so I carefully lay the book down on the floor next to the toilet and continue to read as I puke.

Regards,

George Parsons
Marysville, CA.

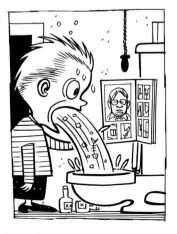

...I've read at least six reviews of Eightball and none came even close to explaining your work. Proof positive that professional critics are full o' shit!!

Yours,

Mary Fleener
Encinitas, CA.

FOR ALL YOU UNINFORMED DULLARDS IN OUR READING AUDIENCE, MS. FLEENER IS A GREAT CARTOONIST WHO KEEPS GETTING BETTER ALL THE TIME AND DESERVES YOUR ATTENTION AND RESPECT. HER SLUTBURGER STORIES IS A FOUR-STAR MYLAR-BAG CLASSIC THAT SHOULD BE ON EVERY COLLECTORS' WANT-LIST!

• • • • • • • • • • • • • • •

...At this comic shop I go to, there's this guy who looks just like [Dan Pussey] that works there who only reads infantile art. Well, people started making fun of him and began calling him 'Young Dan Pussey.' out of spite, he took all the Eightball #3's, put a red slash on 'em and put 'em on the 25¢ discount rack!

Tenderly yours,

Mike Parlette
Fair Oaks, Ca.

U.S. AMEG
CAPT. SHANK
STUMP GAL
SCROTUM LAD
AMER GHOST
WE GOT GAMING SUPP
8-BALL
HALF-PRICE BIN

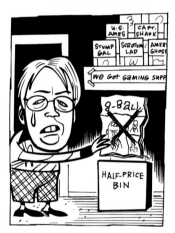

The reason you persecute us "Pussey-types" and the adult graphic fantasy sequential fiction literature that we love to draw is because you're not good enough to draw superhero comics! So study Dynamic Anatomy and stop putting down what you don't understand!

Sincerely,

Don Simpson
Pittsburgh, PA.

• • • • • • • • • • • • • • •

...Say, did you ever notice that the name Peter Bagge is almost an anagram for Bette Page?

Best,

Jay Lynch
Chicago, IL.

P.S. Eightball #4 is 'fantastic!'

STORY IDEA

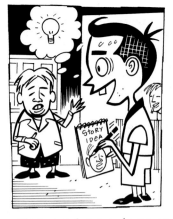

I've read a comic that made me cry, but I never read one that made me feel like an asshole until now. "Bill" (NAME CHANGED TO PROTECT INNOCENCE -- D.C.) introduced me to you in his shop a couple months ago. I thought "What a cool guy. Nice to meet the dude "Bill"s been raving about for the last two weeks". I said something really stupid like "Hey, maybe you and me could combine forces and make a story ...like you pencil and I ink..." You politely blew me off. Okay. You did it well.

So I finally read an issue of Eightball and there was a sequence patterned after our very conversation in which somebody the artist character has never met begins to suggest that the two of them should make a comic... If you wanted to make me feel like a Dan Pussey, you've done it. I hope you're happy.

By the way, I really enjoyed #'s 3 & 4. They were really funny. If you really want to be an original creator though, you might want to stop pissing people off. Every great artist is loved for his work and not his personality. You can hate everybody (as I do) without making them angry. Give it a try...

Sam Sistler
Chicago, IL.

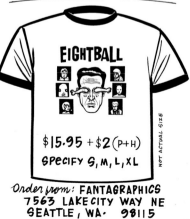

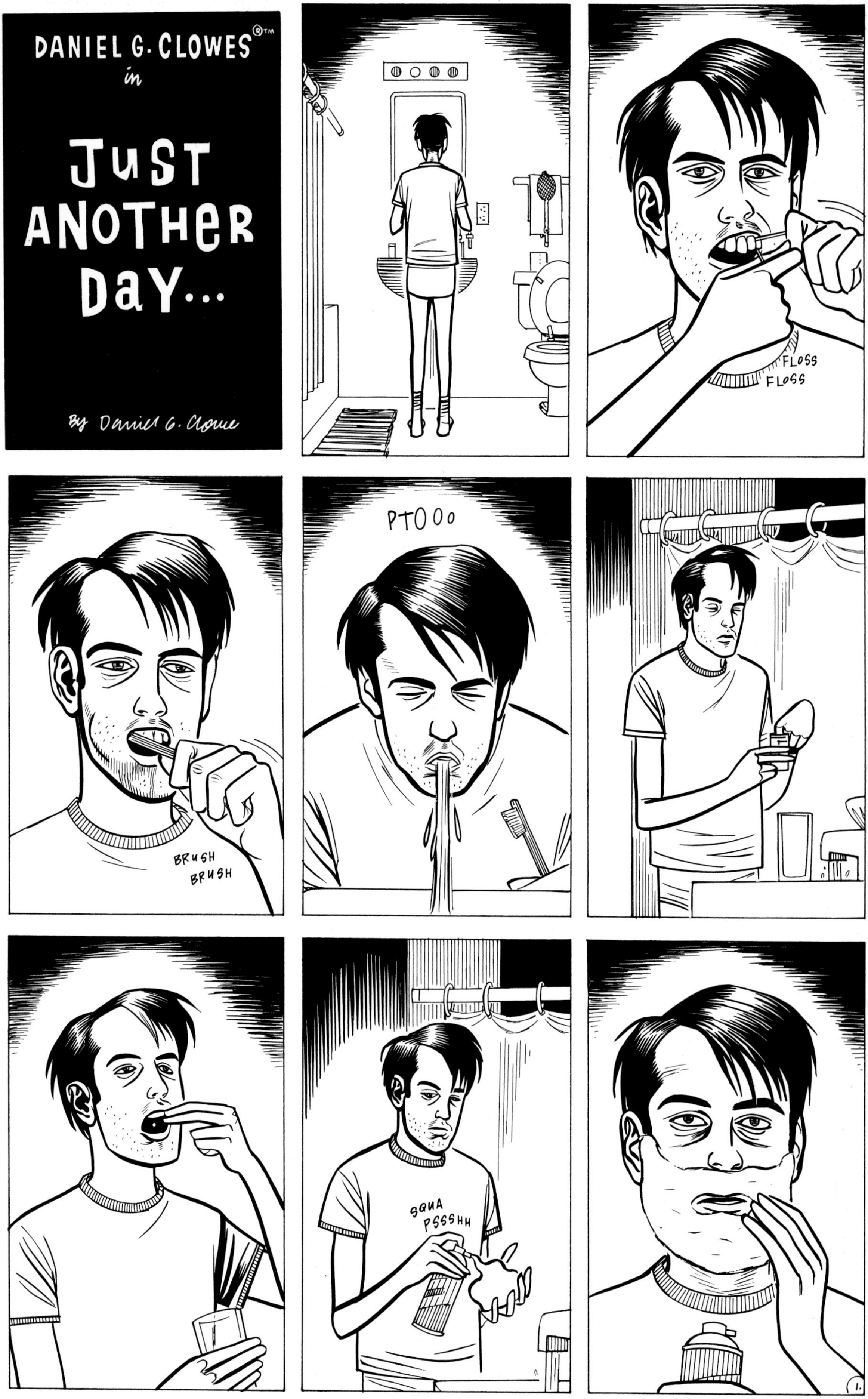
DANIEL G. CLOWES ®™
in
JUST ANOTHER DAY...
By Daniel G. Clowes
FLOSS
FLOSS
BRUSH
BRUSH
PTOOo
SQUA
PSSSHH
1.

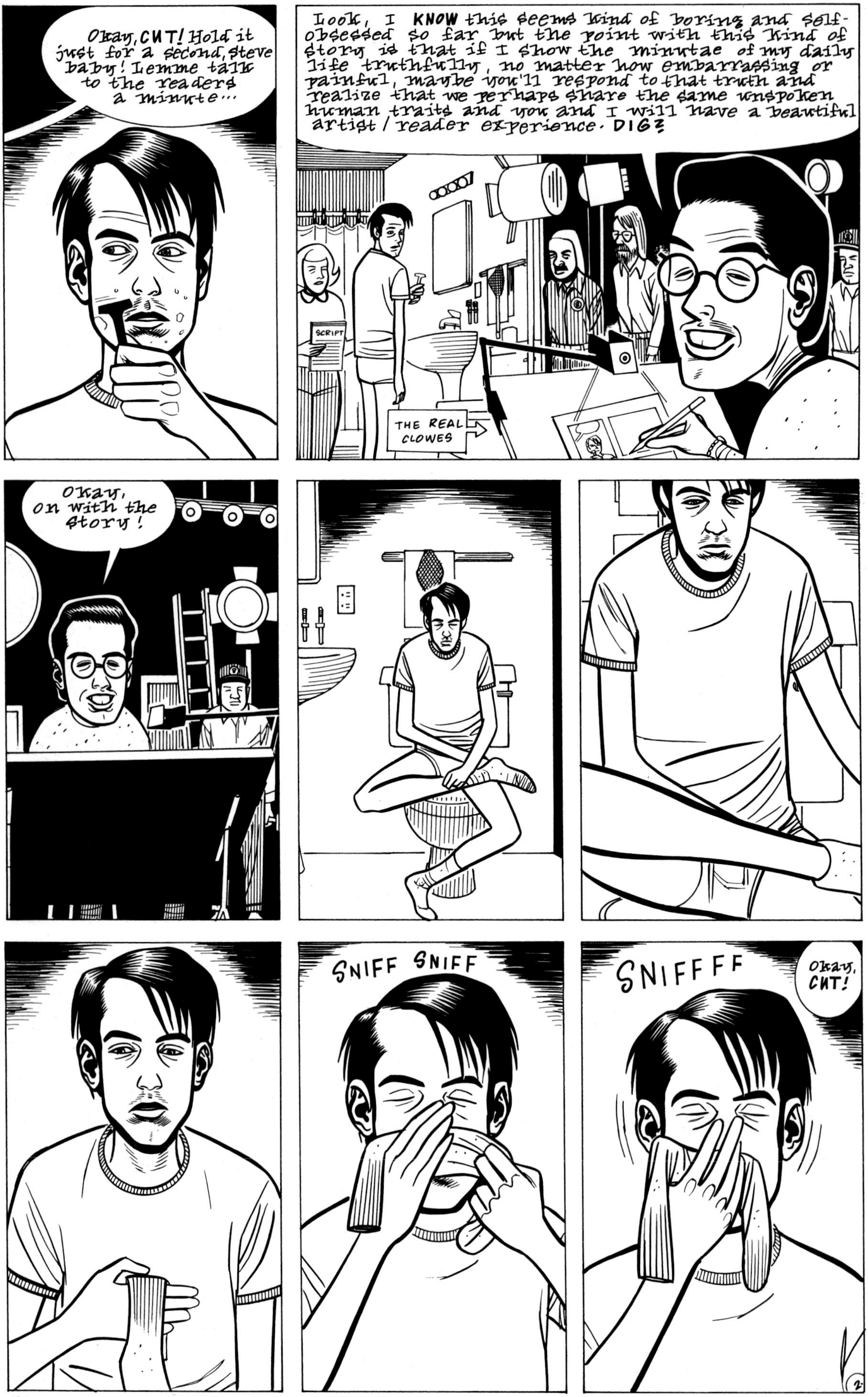
Okay, CUT! Hold it just for a second, Steve baby! Lemme talk to the readers a minute...
Look, I KNOW this seems kind of boring and self-obsessed so far but the point with this kind of story is that if I show the minutae of my daily life truthfully, no matter how embarrassing or painful, maybe you'll respond to that truth and realize that we perhaps share the same unspoken human traits and you and I will have a beautiful artist / reader experience. DIG?
SCRIPT
THE REAL CLOWES
Okay, on with the story!
SNIFF SNIFF
SNIFFFF
Okay, CUT!

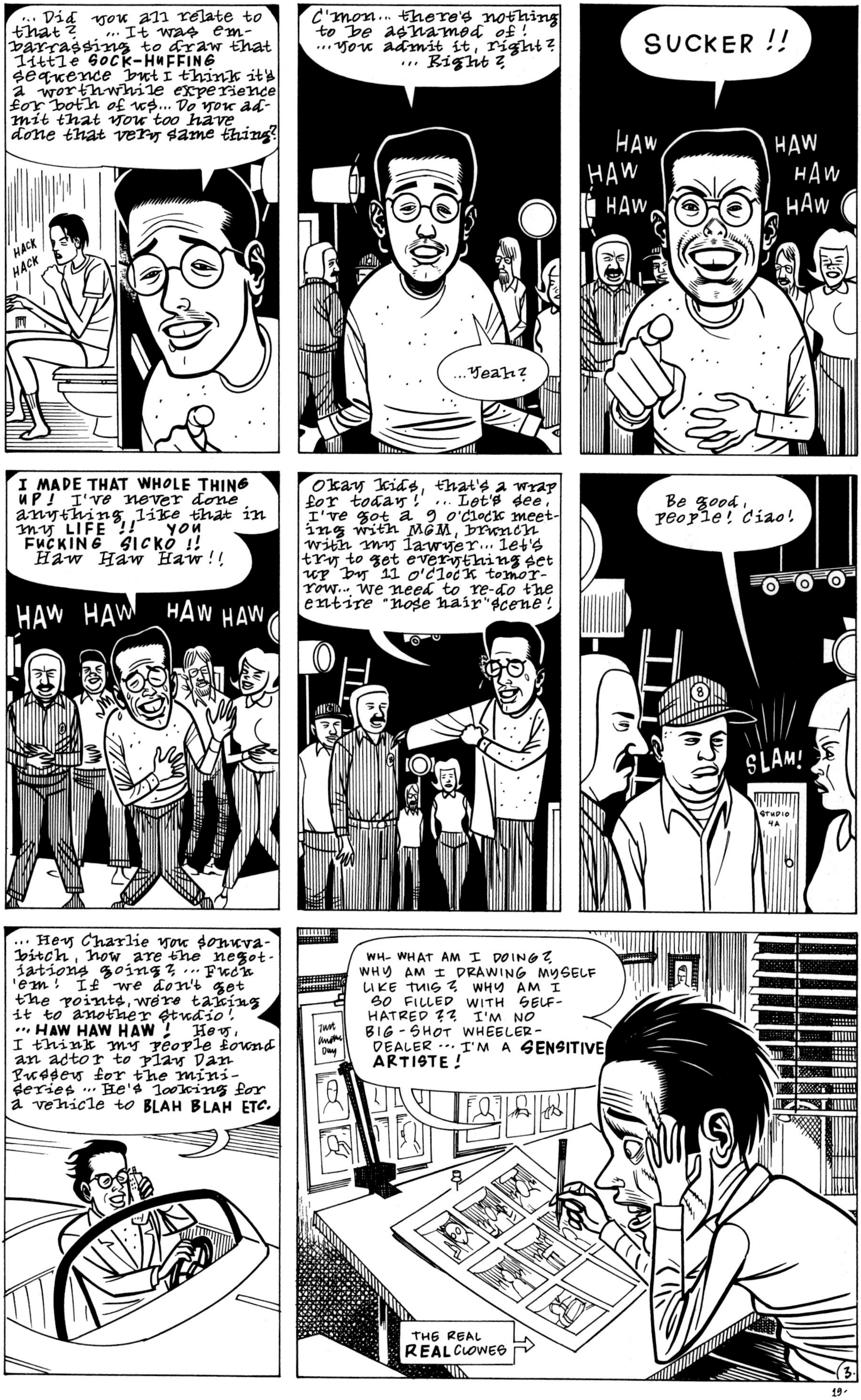
...Did you all relate to that? ...It was embarrassing to draw that little SOCK-HUFFING sequence but I think it's a worthwhile experience for both of us... Do you admit that you too have done that very same thing?
HACK HACK
C'mon... there's nothing to be ashamed of! ...You admit it, right? ...Right?
...Yeah?
SUCKER!!
HAW HAW HAW HAW HAW HAW
I MADE THAT WHOLE THING UP! I've never done anything like that in my LIFE!! YOU FUCKING SICKO!! Haw Haw Haw!!
HAW HAW HAW HAW
Okay kids, that's a wrap for today! ...Let's see, I've got a 9 o'clock meeting with MGM, brunch with my lawyer... let's try to get everything set up by 11 o'clock tomorrow... We need to re-do the entire "nose hair" scene!
Be good, people! Ciao!
SLAM!
STUDIO 4A
...Hey Charlie you sonuvabitch, how are the negotiations going? ...Fuck 'em! If we don't get the points, we're taking it to another studio! ...HAW HAW HAW! Hey, I think my people found an actor to play Dan Pussey for the mini-series... He's looking for a vehicle to BLAH BLAH ETC.
WH- WHAT AM I DOING? WHY AM I DRAWING MYSELF LIKE THIS? WHY AM I SO FILLED WITH SELF-HATRED?? I'M NO BIG-SHOT WHEELER-DEALER... I'M A SENSITIVE ARTISTE!
THE REAL REAL CLOWES
3.

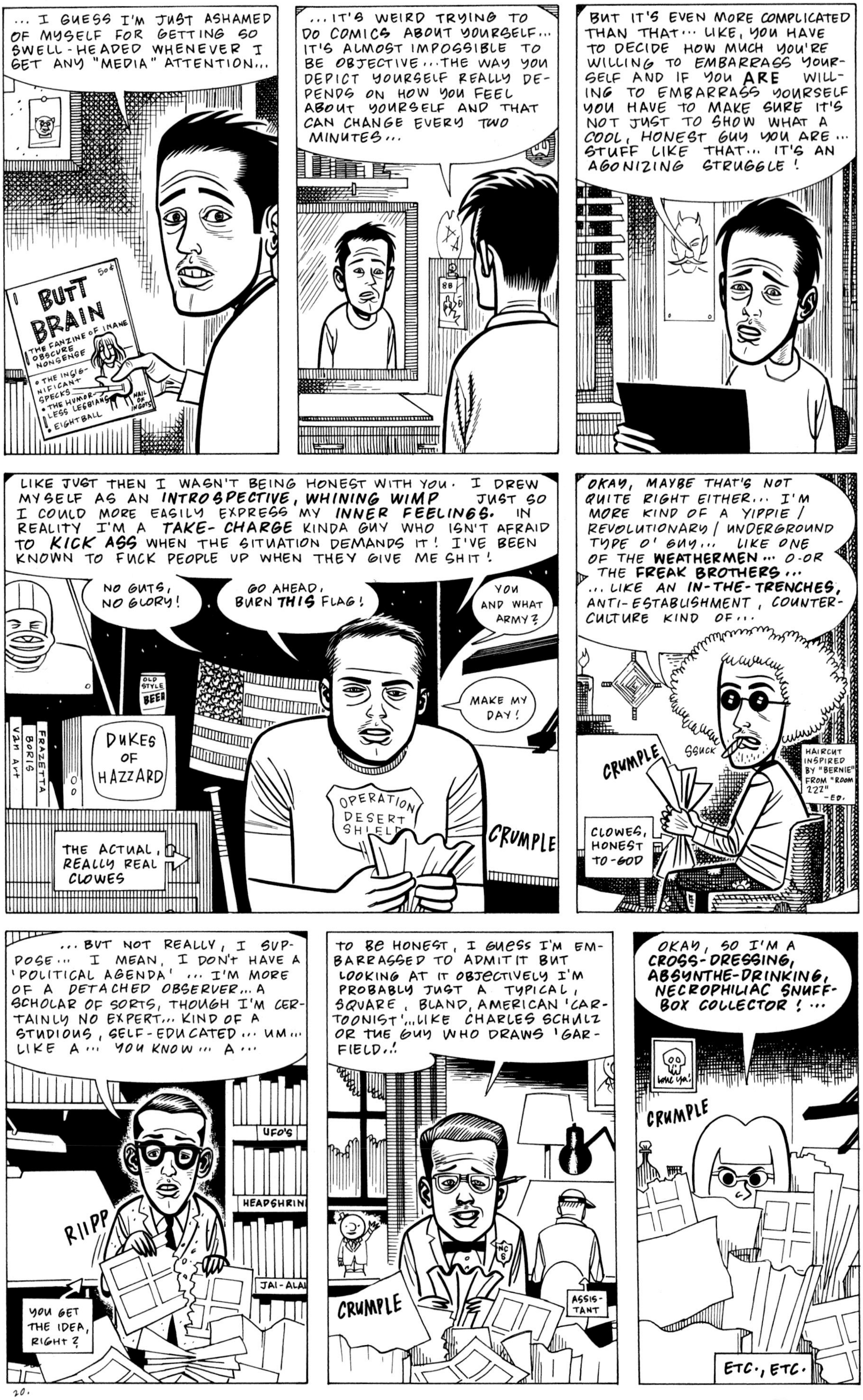
... I GUESS I'M JUST ASHAMED OF MYSELF FOR GETTING SO SWELL-HEADED WHENEVER I GET ANY "MEDIA" ATTENTION...
BUTT BRAIN
50¢
THE FANZINE OF INANE OBSCURE NONSENSE
• THE INSIG-NIFICANT SPECKS
• THE HUMOR-LESS LESBIANS
• EIGHTBALL
NAIL OF INGOTS
... IT'S WEIRD TRYING TO DO COMICS ABOUT YOURSELF... IT'S ALMOST IMPOSSIBLE TO BE OBJECTIVE... THE WAY YOU DEPICT YOURSELF REALLY DE-PENDS ON HOW YOU FEEL ABOUT YOURSELF AND THAT CAN CHANGE EVERY TWO MINUTES...
BUT IT'S EVEN MORE COMPLICATED THAN THAT... LIKE, YOU HAVE TO DECIDE HOW MUCH YOU'RE WILLING TO EMBARRASS YOUR-SELF AND IF YOU ARE WILL-ING TO EMBARRASS YOURSELF YOU HAVE TO MAKE SURE IT'S NOT JUST TO SHOW WHAT A COOL, HONEST GUY YOU ARE... STUFF LIKE THAT... IT'S AN AGONIZING STRUGGLE!
LIKE JUST THEN I WASN'T BEING HONEST WITH YOU. I DREW MYSELF AS AN INTROSPECTIVE, WHINING WIMP JUST SO I COULD MORE EASILY EXPRESS MY INNER FEELINGS. IN REALITY I'M A TAKE-CHARGE KINDA GUY WHO ISN'T AFRAID TO KICK ASS WHEN THE SITUATION DEMANDS IT! I'VE BEEN KNOWN TO FUCK PEOPLE UP WHEN THEY GIVE ME SHIT!
NO GUTS, NO GLORY!
GO AHEAD, BURN THIS FLAG!
YOU AND WHAT ARMY?
MAKE MY DAY!
OLD STYLE BEER
VAN ART
BORIS
FRAZETTA
DUKES OF HAZZARD
OPERATION DESERT SHIELD
THE ACTUAL, REALLY REAL CLOWES
CRUMPLE
OKAY, MAYBE THAT'S NOT QUITE RIGHT EITHER... I'M MORE KIND OF A YIPPIE / REVOLUTIONARY / UNDERGROUND TYPE O' GUY... LIKE ONE OF THE WEATHERMEN... O-OR THE FREAK BROTHERS...
... LIKE AN IN-THE-TRENCHES, ANTI-ESTABLISHMENT, COUNTER-CULTURE KIND OF...
SSUCK
CRUMPLE
HAIRCUT INSPIRED BY "BERNIE" FROM "ROOM 222" -ED.
CLOWES, HONEST TO-GOD
... BUT NOT REALLY, I SUP-POSE... I MEAN, I DON'T HAVE A 'POLITICAL AGENDA' ... I'M MORE OF A DETACHED OBSERVER... A SCHOLAR OF SORTS, THOUGH I'M CER-TAINLY NO EXPERT... KIND OF A STUDIOUS, SELF-EDUCATED... UM... LIKE A... YOU KNOW... A...
UFO'S
HEADSHRIN
JAI-ALAI
RIIPP
YOU GET THE IDEA, RIGHT?
TO BE HONEST, I GUESS I'M EM-BARRASSED TO ADMIT IT BUT LOOKING AT IT OBJECTIVELY I'M PROBABLY JUST A TYPICAL, SQUARE, BLAND, AMERICAN 'CAR-TOONIST'... LIKE CHARLES SCHULZ OR THE GUY WHO DRAWS 'GAR-FIELD.'
NCS
CRUMPLE
ASSIS-TANT
OKAY, SO I'M A CROSS-DRESSING, ABSYNTHE-DRINKING, NECROPHILIAC SNUFF-BOX COLLECTOR! ...
CRUMPLE
ETC., ETC.

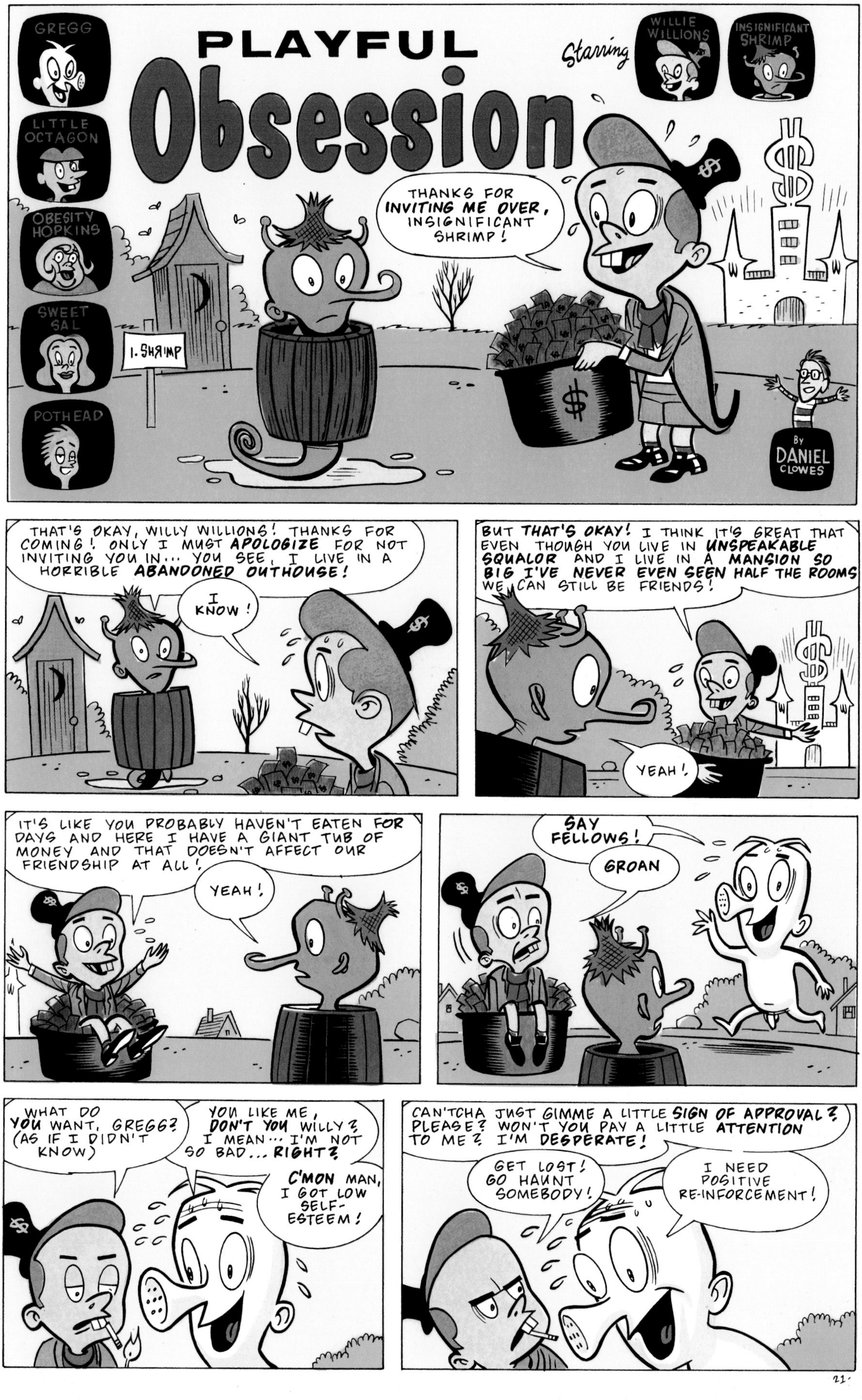
GREGG
LITTLE OCTAGON
OBESITY HOPKINS
SWEET SAL
POTHEAD
PLAYFUL Obsession
Starring
WILLIE WILLIONS
INSIGNIFICANT SHRIMP
THANKS FOR INVITING ME OVER, INSIGNIFICANT SHRIMP!
I. SHRIMP
By DANIEL CLOWES
THAT'S OKAY, WILLY WILLIONS! THANKS FOR COMING! ONLY I MUST APOLOGIZE FOR NOT INVITING YOU IN... YOU SEE, I LIVE IN A HORRIBLE ABANDONED OUTHOUSE!
I KNOW!
BUT THAT'S OKAY! I THINK IT'S GREAT THAT EVEN THOUGH YOU LIVE IN UNSPEAKABLE SQUALOR AND I LIVE IN A MANSION SO BIG I'VE NEVER EVEN SEEN HALF THE ROOMS WE CAN STILL BE FRIENDS!
YEAH!
IT'S LIKE YOU PROBABLY HAVEN'T EATEN FOR DAYS AND HERE I HAVE A GIANT TUB OF MONEY AND THAT DOESN'T AFFECT OUR FRIENDSHIP AT ALL!
YEAH!
SAY FELLOWS!
GROAN
WHAT DO YOU WANT, GREGG? (AS IF I DIDN'T KNOW)
YOU LIKE ME, DON'T YOU WILLY? I MEAN... I'M NOT SO BAD... RIGHT?
C'MON MAN, I GOT LOW SELF-ESTEEM!
CAN'TCHA JUST GIMME A LITTLE SIGN OF APPROVAL? PLEASE? WON'T YOU PAY A LITTLE ATTENTION TO ME? I'M DESPERATE!
GET LOST! GO HAUNT SOMEBODY!
I NEED POSITIVE RE-INFORCEMENT!

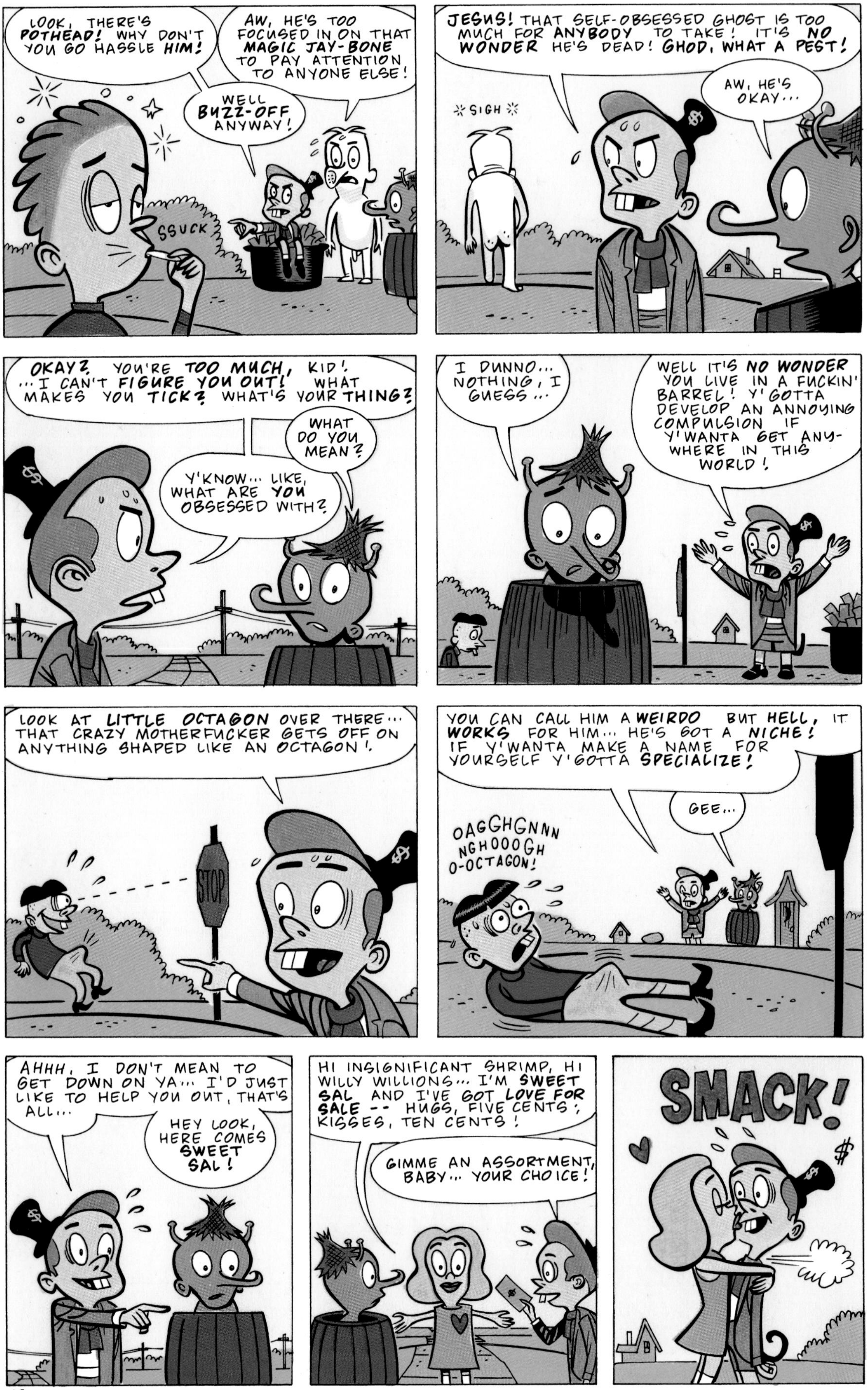
LOOK, THERE'S POTHEAD! WHY DON'T YOU GO HASSLE HIM!
AW, HE'S TOO FOCUSED IN ON THAT MAGIC JAY-BONE TO PAY ATTENTION TO ANYONE ELSE!
WELL BUZZ-OFF ANYWAY!
SSUCK
JESUS! THAT SELF-OBSESSED GHOST IS TOO MUCH FOR ANYBODY TO TAKE! IT'S NO WONDER HE'S DEAD! GHOD, WHAT A PEST!
SIGH
AW, HE'S OKAY...
OKAY? YOU'RE TOO MUCH, KID! ...I CAN'T FIGURE YOU OUT! WHAT MAKES YOU TICK? WHAT'S YOUR THING?
WHAT DO YOU MEAN?
Y'KNOW... LIKE, WHAT ARE YOU OBSESSED WITH?
I DUNNO... NOTHING, I GUESS...
WELL IT'S NO WONDER YOU LIVE IN A FUCKIN' BARREL! Y'GOTTA DEVELOP AN ANNOYING COMPULSION IF Y'WANTA GET ANYWHERE IN THIS WORLD!
LOOK AT LITTLE OCTAGON OVER THERE... THAT CRAZY MOTHERFUCKER GETS OFF ON ANYTHING SHAPED LIKE AN OCTAGON!
STOP
YOU CAN CALL HIM A WEIRDO BUT HELL, IT WORKS FOR HIM... HE'S GOT A NICHE! IF Y'WANTA MAKE A NAME FOR YOURSELF Y'GOTTA SPECIALIZE!
GEE...
OAGGHGNNN NGHOOOGH O-OCTAGON!
AHHH, I DON'T MEAN TO GET DOWN ON YA... I'D JUST LIKE TO HELP YOU OUT, THAT'S ALL...
HEY LOOK, HERE COMES SWEET SAL!
HI INSIGNIFICANT SHRIMP, HI WILLY WILLIONS... I'M SWEET SAL AND I'VE GOT LOVE FOR SALE -- HUGS, FIVE CENTS; KISSES, TEN CENTS!
GIMME AN ASSORTMENT, BABY... YOUR CHOICE!
SMACK!

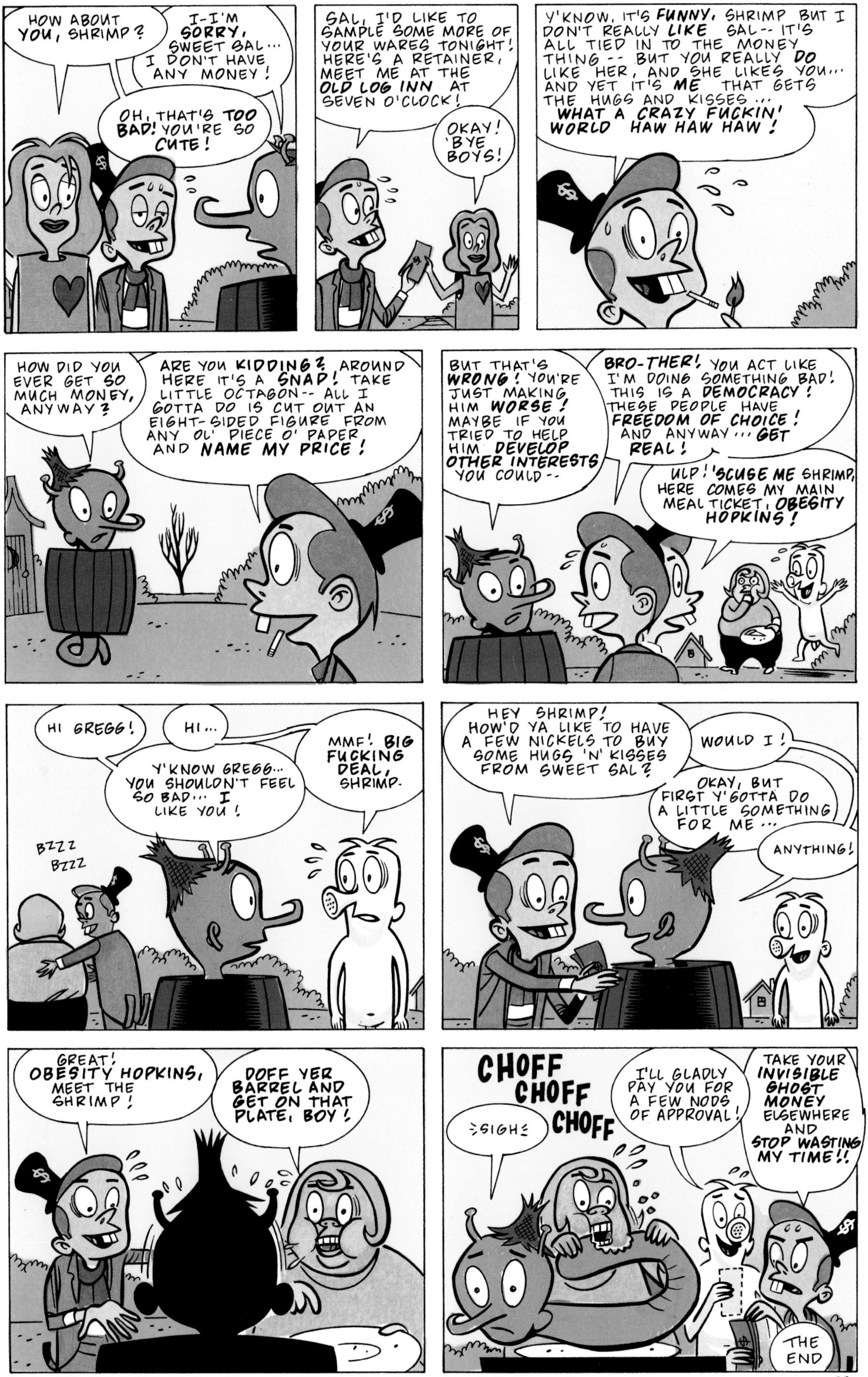

HOW ABOUT **YOU**, SHRIMP?
I-I'M **SORRY**, SWEET SAL... I DON'T HAVE ANY MONEY!
OH, THAT'S **TOO BAD!** YOU'RE SO **CUTE!**
SAL, I'D LIKE TO SAMPLE SOME MORE OF YOUR WARES TONIGHT! HERE'S A RETAINER, MEET ME AT THE **OLD LOG INN** AT SEVEN O'CLOCK!
OKAY! 'BYE BOYS!
Y'KNOW, IT'S **FUNNY**, SHRIMP BUT I DON'T REALLY **LIKE** SAL -- IT'S ALL TIED IN TO THE MONEY THING -- BUT YOU REALLY **DO** LIKE HER, AND SHE LIKES YOU... AND YET IT'S **ME** THAT GETS THE HUGS AND KISSES... **WHAT A CRAZY FUCKIN' WORLD HAW HAW HAW!**
HOW DID YOU EVER GET **SO** MUCH MONEY, ANYWAY?
ARE YOU **KIDDING?** AROUND HERE IT'S A **SNAP!** TAKE LITTLE OCTAGON -- ALL I GOTTA DO IS CUT OUT AN EIGHT-SIDED FIGURE FROM ANY OL' PIECE O' PAPER AND **NAME MY PRICE!**
BUT THAT'S **WRONG!** YOU'RE JUST MAKING HIM **WORSE!** MAYBE IF YOU TRIED TO HELP HIM **DEVELOP OTHER INTERESTS** YOU COULD --
BRO-THER! YOU ACT LIKE I'M DOING SOMETHING BAD! THIS IS A **DEMOCRACY!** THESE PEOPLE HAVE **FREEDOM OF CHOICE!** AND ANYWAY... **GET REAL!**
ULP! **'SCUSE ME** SHRIMP, HERE COMES MY MAIN MEAL TICKET, **OBESITY HOPKINS!**
HI GREGG!
HI...
Y'KNOW GREGG... YOU SHOULDN'T FEEL SO BAD... **I** LIKE YOU!
MMF! **BIG FUCKING DEAL**, SHRIMP.
BZZZ BZZZ
HEY SHRIMP! HOW'D YA LIKE TO HAVE A FEW NICKELS TO BUY SOME HUGS 'N' KISSES FROM SWEET SAL?
WOULD I!
OKAY, BUT FIRST Y'GOTTA DO A LITTLE SOMETHING FOR ME...
ANYTHING!
GREAT! **OBESITY HOPKINS**, MEET THE SHRIMP!
DOFF YER BARREL AND GET ON THAT PLATE, BOY!
CHOFF CHOFF CHOFF
SIGH
I'LL GLADLY PAY YOU FOR A FEW NODS OF APPROVAL!
TAKE YOUR **INVISIBLE GHOST MONEY** ELSEWHERE AND **STOP WASTING MY TIME!!**
THE END

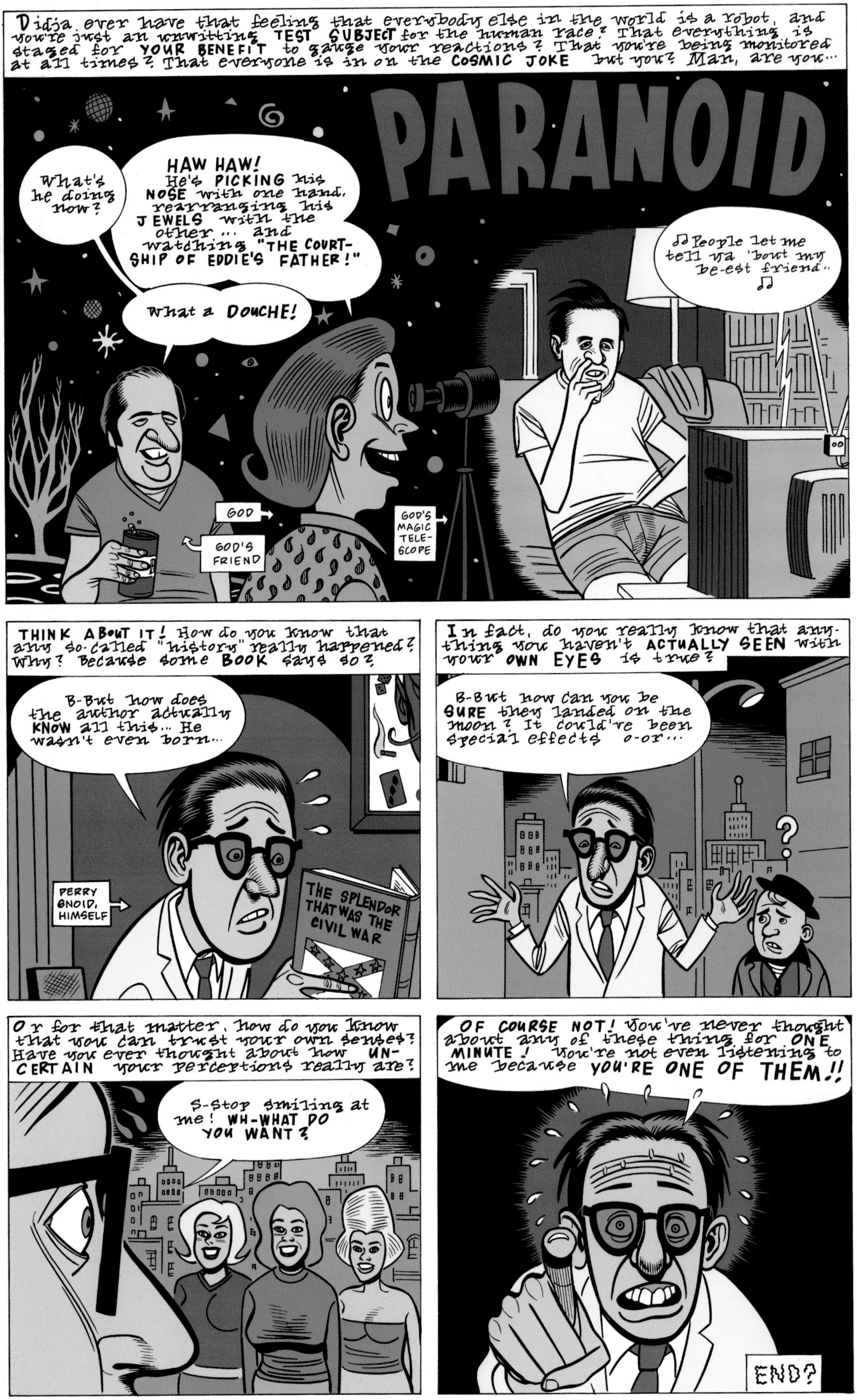

Didja ever have that feeling that everybody else in the world is a robot, and you're just an unwitting TEST SUBJECT for the human race? That everything is staged for YOUR BENEFIT to gauge your reactions? That you're being monitored at all times? That everyone is in on the COSMIC JOKE but you? Man, are you...
PARANOID
What's he doing now?
HAW HAW! He's PICKING his NOSE with one hand, rearranging his JEWELS with the other... and watching "THE COURTSHIP OF EDDIE'S FATHER!"
What a DOUCHE!
♫ People let me tell ya 'bout my be-est friend.. ♫
GOD
GOD'S FRIEND
GOD'S MAGIC TELE-SCOPE
THINK ABOUT IT! How do you know that any so-called "history" really happened? Why? Because some BOOK says so?
B-But how does the author actually KNOW all this... He wasn't even born...
PERRY ENOID, HIMSELF
THE SPLENDOR THAT WAS THE CIVIL WAR
In fact, do you really know that anything you haven't ACTUALLY SEEN with your OWN EYES is true?
B-But how can you be SURE they landed on the moon? It could've been special effects o-or...
?
Or for that matter, how do you know that you can trust your own senses? Have you ever thought about how UNCERTAIN your perceptions really are?
S-Stop smiling at me! WH-WHAT DO YOU WANT?
OF COURSE NOT! You've never thought about any of these thing for ONE MINUTE! You're not even listening to me because YOU'RE ONE OF THEM!!
END?

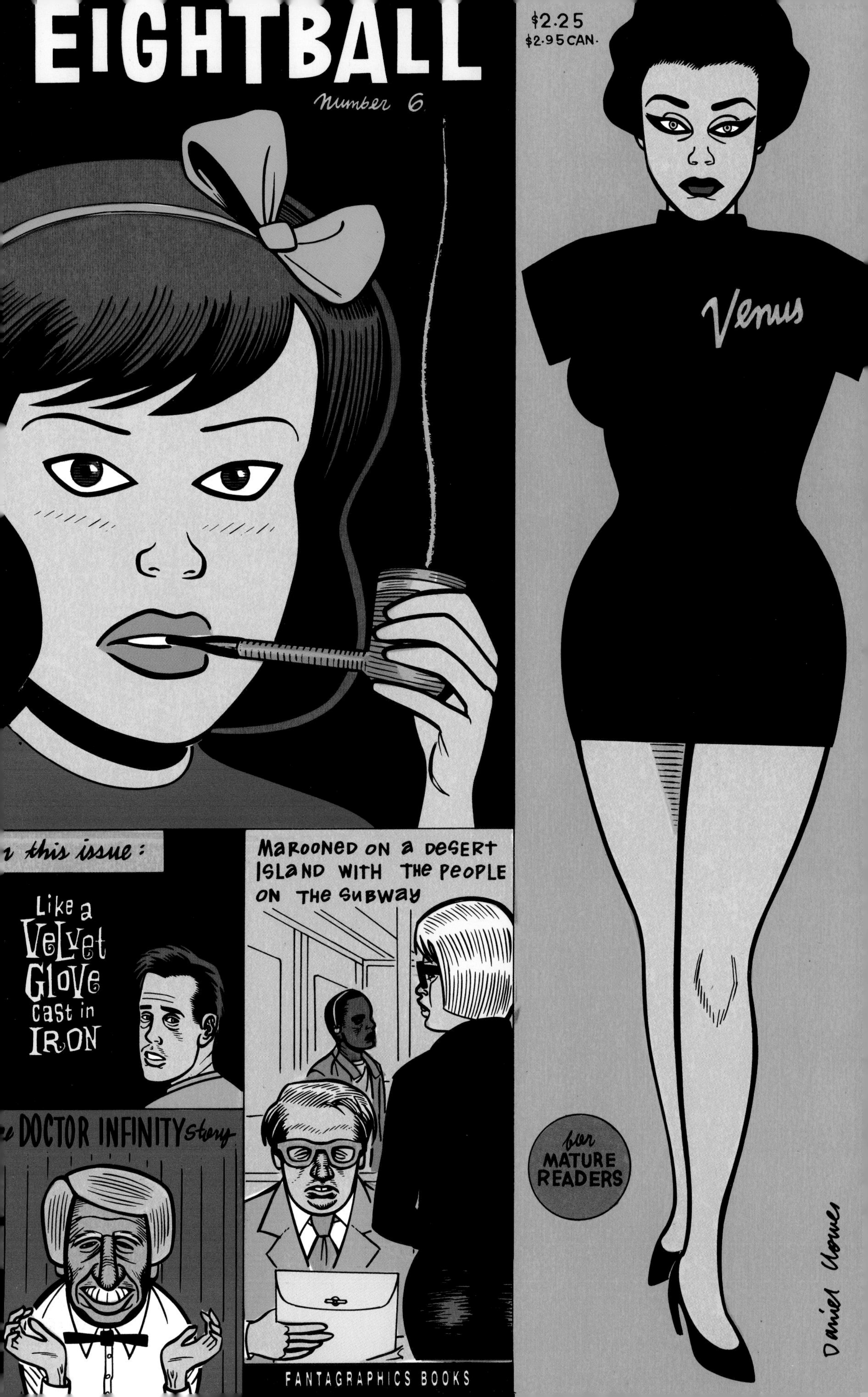
EIGHTBALL
number 6
$2.25
$2.95 CAN.
Venus
n this issue:
Like a Velvet Glove cast in IRON
MAROONED ON A DESERT ISLAND WITH THE PEOPLE ON THE SUBWAY
e DOCTOR INFINITY Story
for MATURE READERS
Daniel Clowes
FANTAGRAPHICS BOOKS

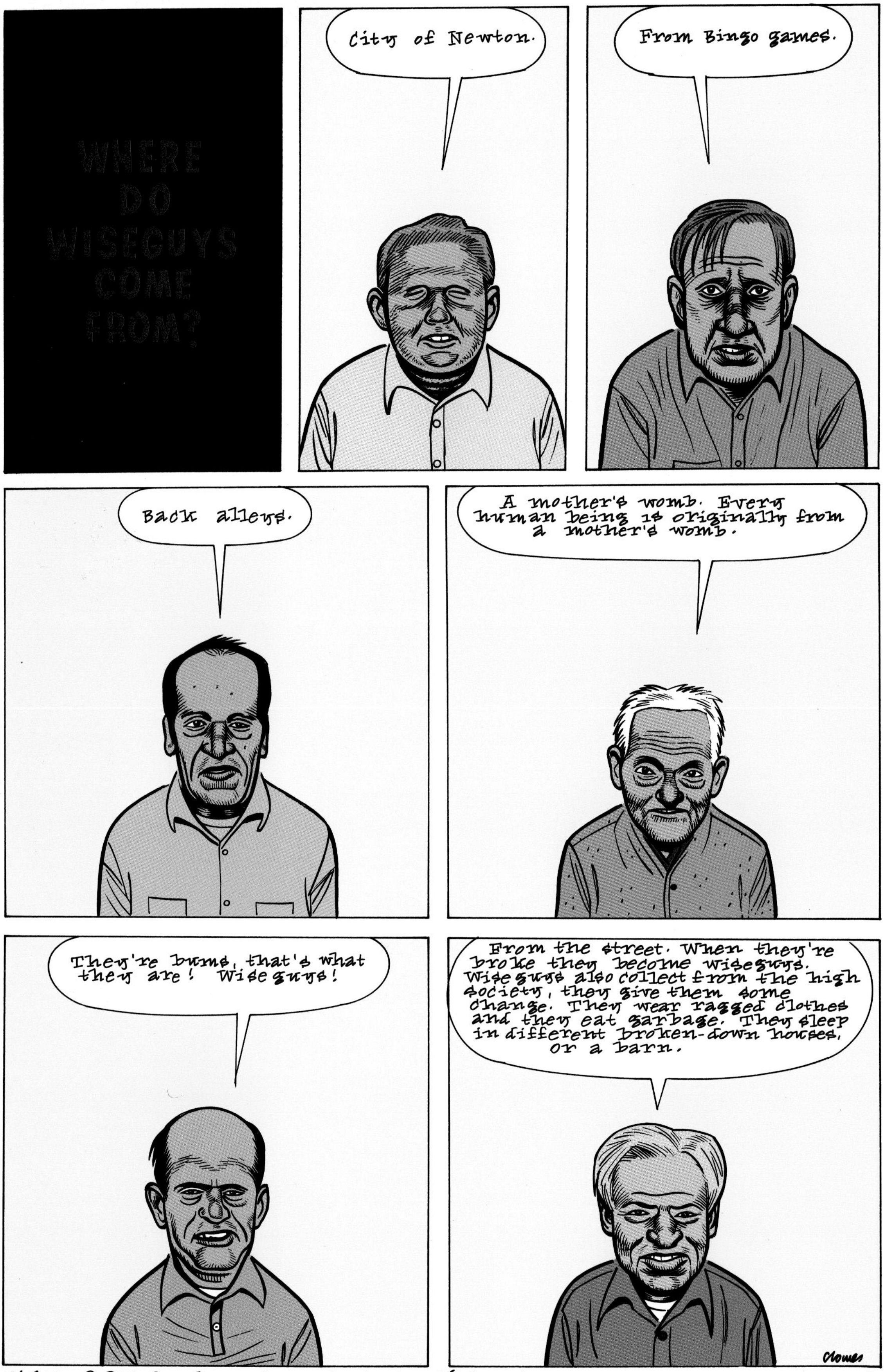

WHERE DO WISEGUYS COME FROM?
City of Newton.
From Bingo games.
Back alleys.
A mother's womb. Every human being is originally from a mother's womb.
They're bums, that's what they are! Wise guys!
From the street. When they're broke they become wiseguys. Wise guys also collect from the high society, they give them some change. They wear ragged clothes and they eat garbage. They sleep in different broken-down houses, or a barn.
Clowes

Dialogue © Dave Greenberger from DUPLEX PLANET #57 ($ubscriptions: $12 : PO BOX 1230, SARATOGA SPRINGS, NY 12866)

Eightball #6, June, 1991. *Eightball* is published thrice yearly by Fantagraphics Books, Inc., and is copyright © 1991 Fantagraphics Books, Inc. All characters, stories, and art © 1991 Daniel Clowes. No part of this magazine may be reproduced without written permission from Fantagraphics Books or Daniel Clowes. No similarity between any of the names, characters, persons, and institutions in *Eightball* and those of any living or dead persons is intended (except for satirical intent), and any such similarity that may exist is purely coincidental. Letters to *Eightball* become the property of the magazine and are assumed intended for publication in whole or in part, and may therefore be used for those purposes. First printing: April, 1991. Fantagraphics Books, 7563 Lake City Way Northeast, Seattle WA 98115. **Send for our free catalogue!**

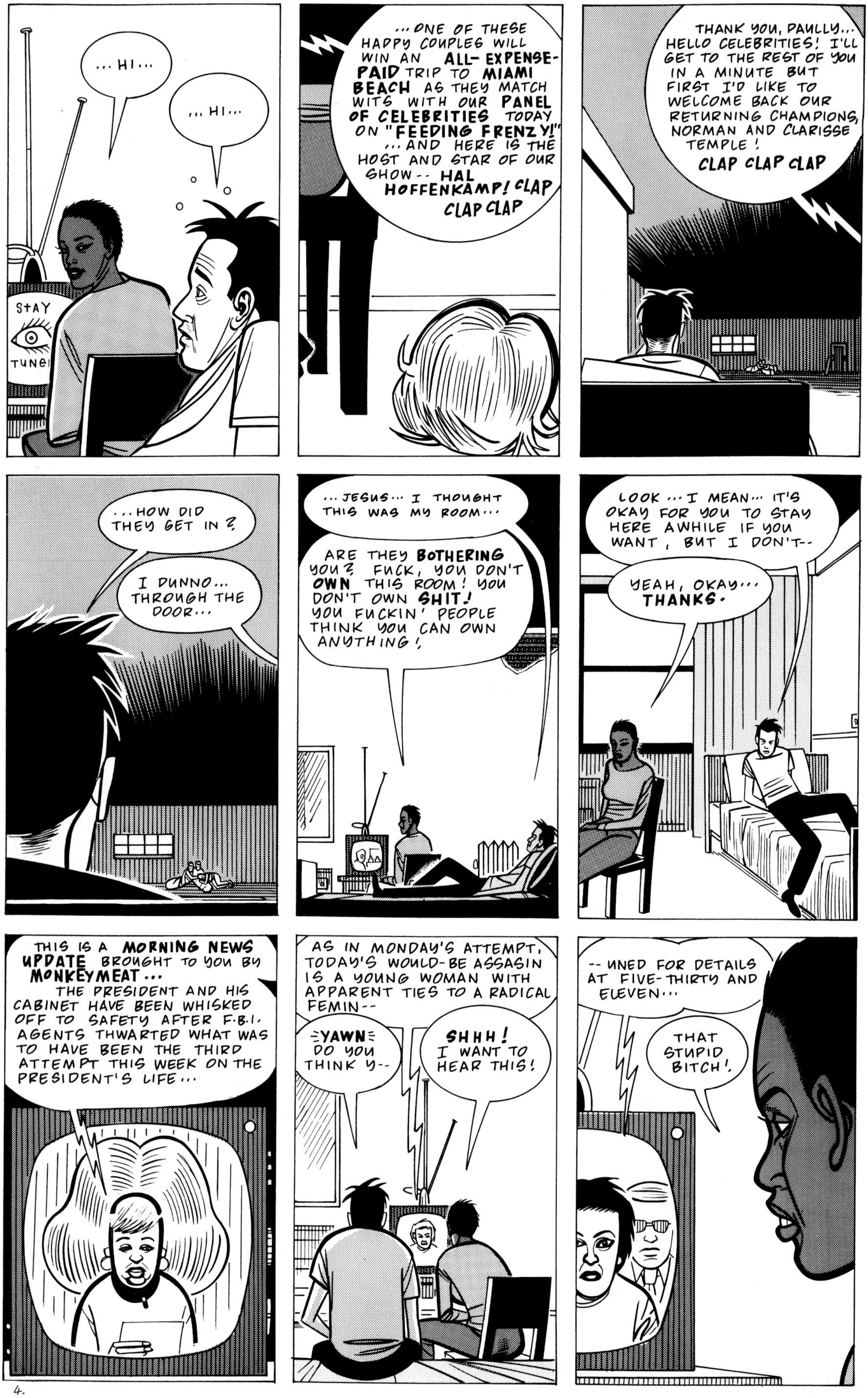
...HI...
...HI...
STAY TUNE
...ONE OF THESE HAPPY COUPLES WILL WIN AN ALL-EXPENSE-PAID TRIP TO MIAMI BEACH AS THEY MATCH WITS WITH OUR PANEL OF CELEBRITIES TODAY ON "FEEDING FRENZY!" ...AND HERE IS THE HOST AND STAR OF OUR SHOW-- HAL HOFFENKAMP! CLAP CLAP CLAP
THANK YOU, PAULLY... HELLO CELEBRITIES! I'LL GET TO THE REST OF YOU IN A MINUTE BUT FIRST I'D LIKE TO WELCOME BACK OUR RETURNING CHAMPIONS, NORMAN AND CLARISSE TEMPLE!
CLAP CLAP CLAP
...HOW DID THEY GET IN?
I DUNNO... THROUGH THE DOOR...
...JESUS... I THOUGHT THIS WAS MY ROOM...
ARE THEY BOTHERING YOU? FUCK, YOU DON'T OWN THIS ROOM! YOU DON'T OWN SHIT! YOU FUCKIN' PEOPLE THINK YOU CAN OWN ANYTHING!
LOOK... I MEAN... IT'S OKAY FOR YOU TO STAY HERE AWHILE IF YOU WANT, BUT I DON'T--
YEAH, OKAY... THANKS.
THIS IS A MORNING NEWS UPDATE BROUGHT TO YOU BY MONKEYMEAT... THE PRESIDENT AND HIS CABINET HAVE BEEN WHISKED OFF TO SAFETY AFTER F.B.I. AGENTS THWARTED WHAT WAS TO HAVE BEEN THE THIRD ATTEMPT THIS WEEK ON THE PRESIDENT'S LIFE...
AS IN MONDAY'S ATTEMPT, TODAY'S WOULD-BE ASSASIN IS A YOUNG WOMAN WITH APPARENT TIES TO A RADICAL FEMIN--
YAWN DO YOU THINK Y--
SHHH! I WANT TO HEAR THIS!
--UNED FOR DETAILS AT FIVE-THIRTY AND ELEVEN...
THAT STUPID BITCH!

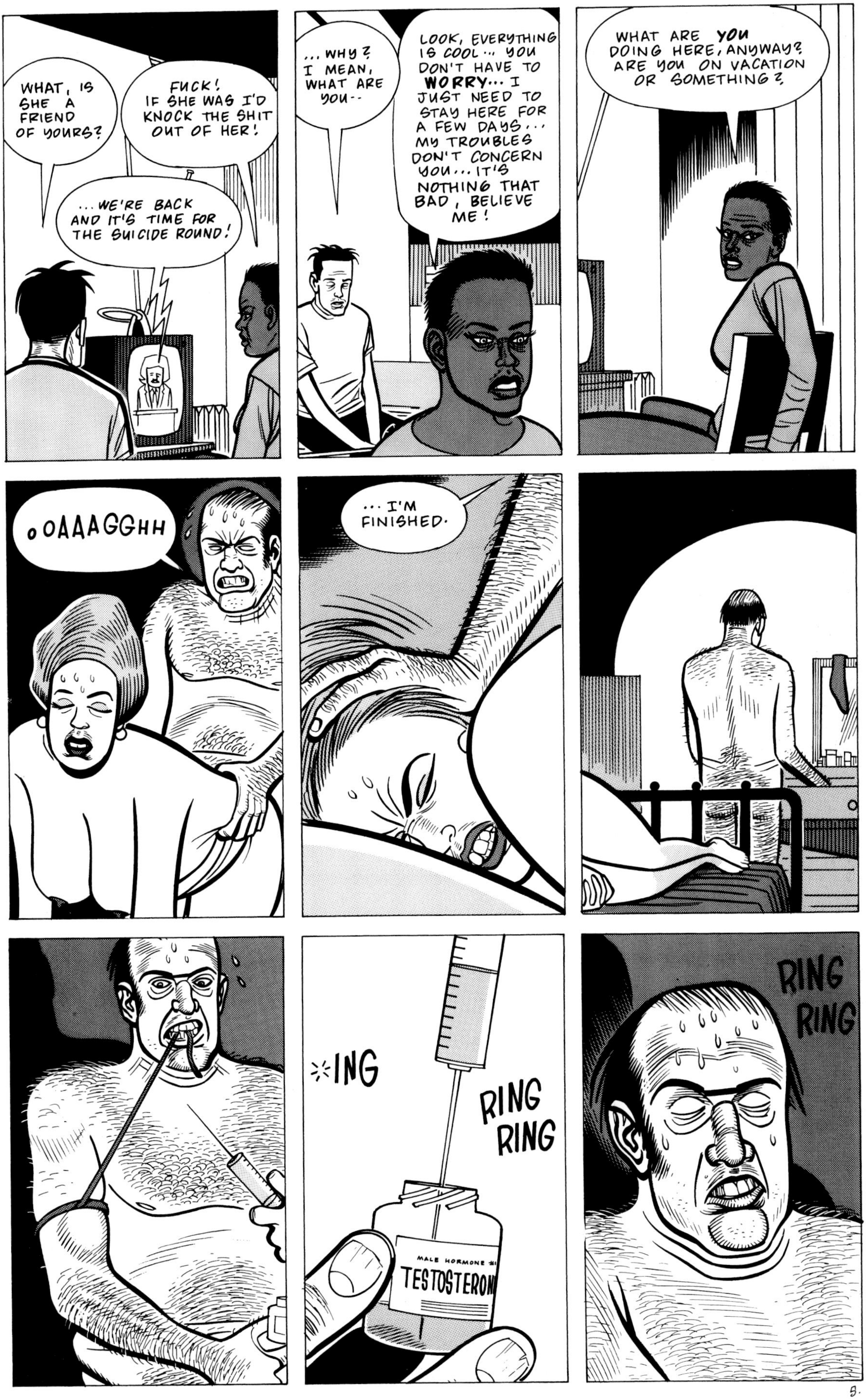
WHAT, IS SHE A FRIEND OF YOURS?
FUCK! IF SHE WAS I'D KNOCK THE SHIT OUT OF HER!
...WE'RE BACK AND IT'S TIME FOR THE SUICIDE ROUND!
...WHY? I MEAN, WHAT ARE YOU--
LOOK, EVERYTHING IS COOL... YOU DON'T HAVE TO WORRY... I JUST NEED TO STAY HERE FOR A FEW DAYS... MY TROUBLES DON'T CONCERN YOU... IT'S NOTHING THAT BAD, BELIEVE ME!
WHAT ARE YOU DOING HERE, ANYWAY? ARE YOU ON VACATION OR SOMETHING?
OOAAAAGGHH
...I'M FINISHED.
*ING
RING RING
MALE HORMONE
TESTOSTERON
RING RING

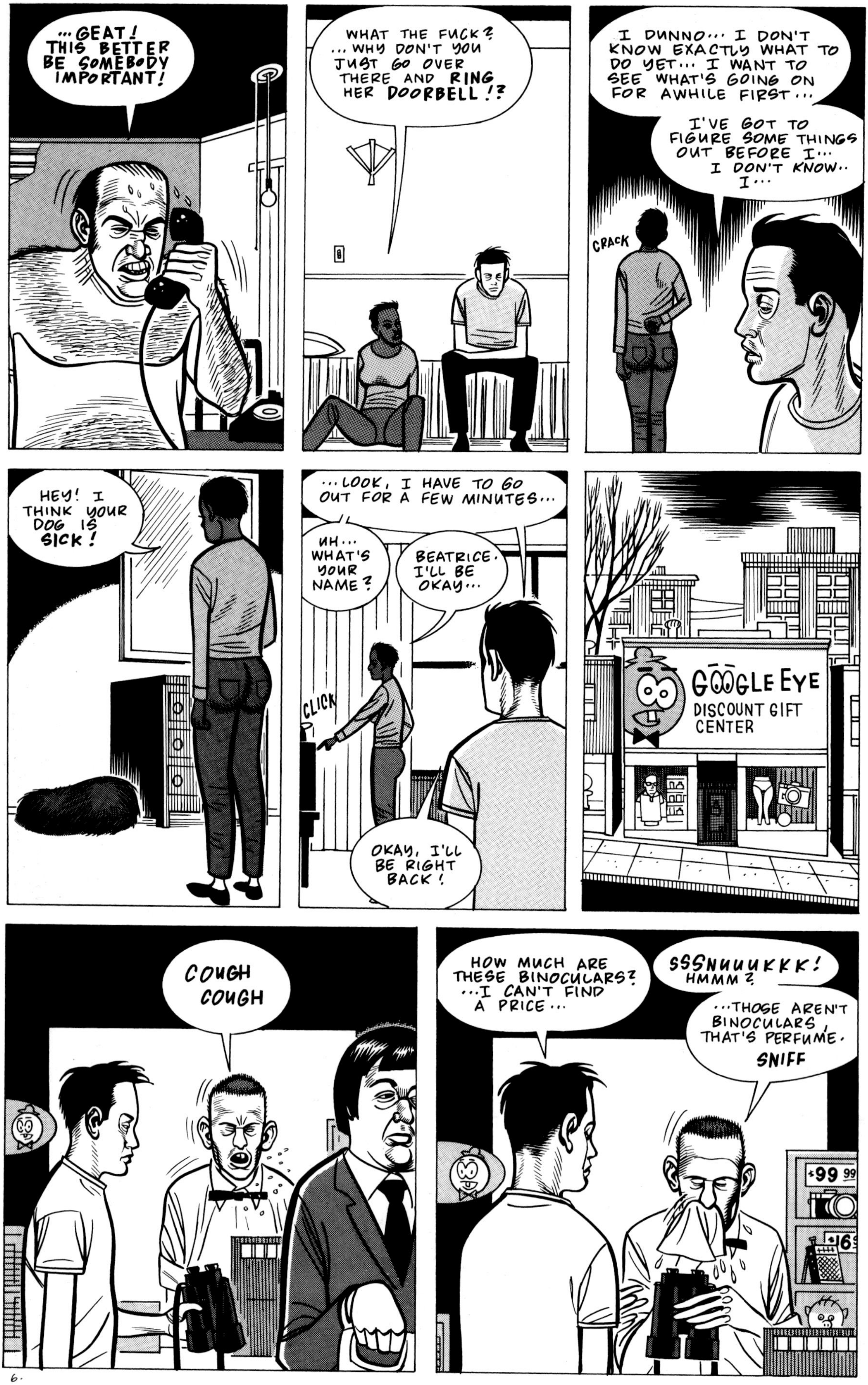
...GEAT! THIS BETTER BE SOMEBODY IMPORTANT!
WHAT THE FUCK? ...WHY DON'T YOU JUST GO OVER THERE AND RING HER DOORBELL!?
I DUNNO... I DON'T KNOW EXACTLY WHAT TO DO YET... I WANT TO SEE WHAT'S GOING ON FOR AWHILE FIRST...
I'VE GOT TO FIGURE SOME THINGS OUT BEFORE I... I DON'T KNOW.. I...
CRACK
HEY! I THINK YOUR DOG IS SICK!
...LOOK, I HAVE TO GO OUT FOR A FEW MINUTES...
UH... WHAT'S YOUR NAME?
BEATRICE. I'LL BE OKAY...
CLICK
OKAY, I'LL BE RIGHT BACK!
GOOGLE EYE
DISCOUNT GIFT CENTER
COUGH COUGH
HOW MUCH ARE THESE BINOCULARS? ...I CAN'T FIND A PRICE...
SSSNUUUKKK! HMMM?
...THOSE AREN'T BINOCULARS, THAT'S PERFUME.
SNIFF
$99 99

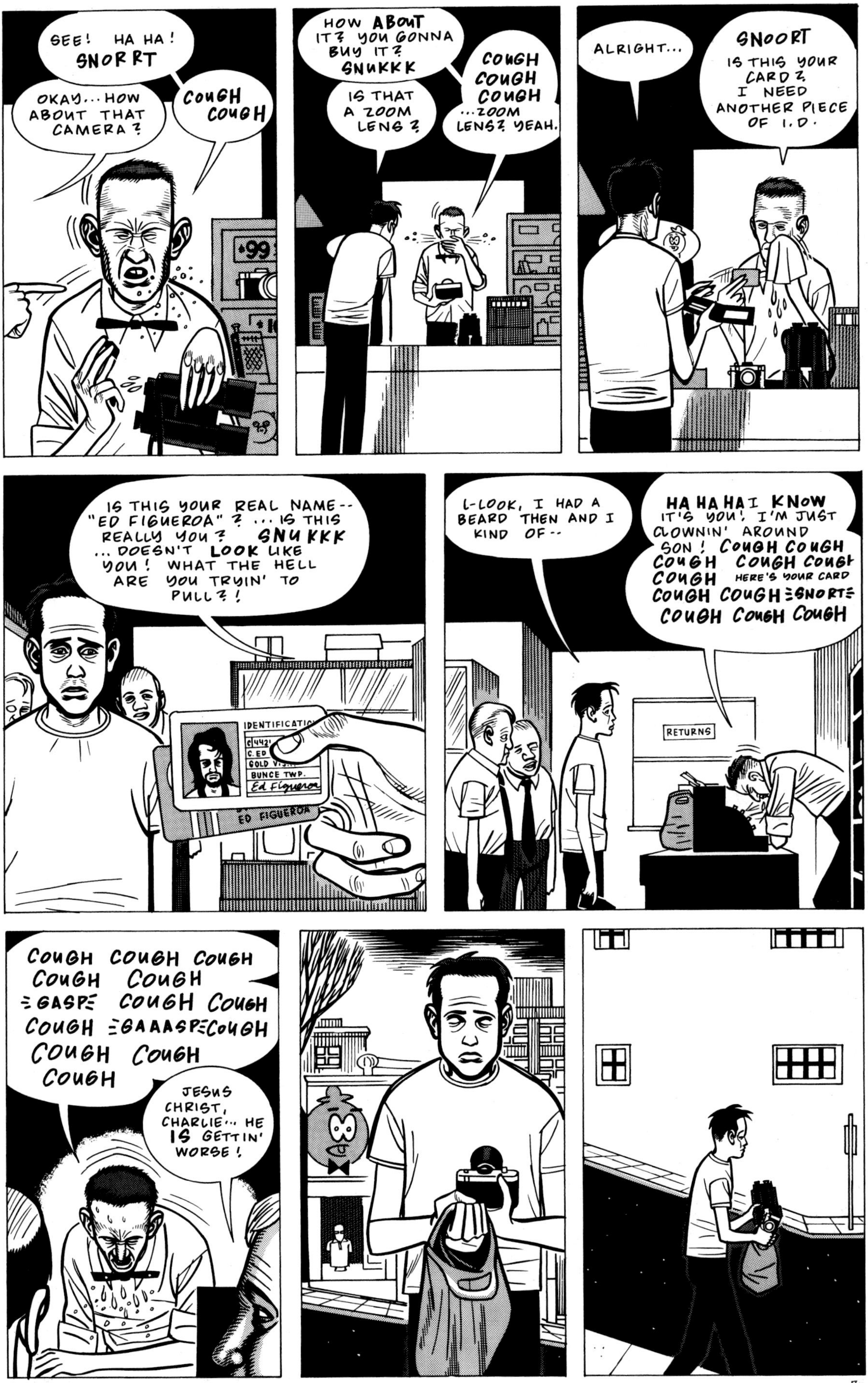
SEE! HA HA! SNORRT
OKAY... HOW ABOUT THAT CAMERA?
COUGH COUGH
.99
HOW ABOUT IT? YOU GONNA BUY IT? SNUKKK
IS THAT A ZOOM LENS?
COUGH COUGH COUGH ...ZOOM LENS? YEAH.
ALRIGHT...
SNOORT IS THIS YOUR CARD? I NEED ANOTHER PIECE OF I.D.
IS THIS YOUR REAL NAME-- "ED FIGUEROA"? ...IS THIS REALLY YOU? SNUKKK ...DOESN'T LOOK LIKE YOU! WHAT THE HELL ARE YOU TRYIN' TO PULL?!
IDENTIFICATION
BUNCE TWP.
Ed Figueroa
ED FIGUEROA
I-LOOK, I HAD A BEARD THEN AND I KIND OF--
HA HA HA I KNOW IT'S YOU! I'M JUST CLOWNIN' AROUND SON! COUGH COUGH COUGH COUGH COUGH COUGH HERE'S YOUR CARD COUGH COUGH =SNORT= COUGH COUGH COUGH
RETURNS
COUGH COUGH COUGH COUGH COUGH =GASP= COUGH COUGH COUGH =GAAASP= COUGH COUGH COUGH COUGH
JESUS CHRIST, CHARLIE... HE IS GETTIN' WORSE!

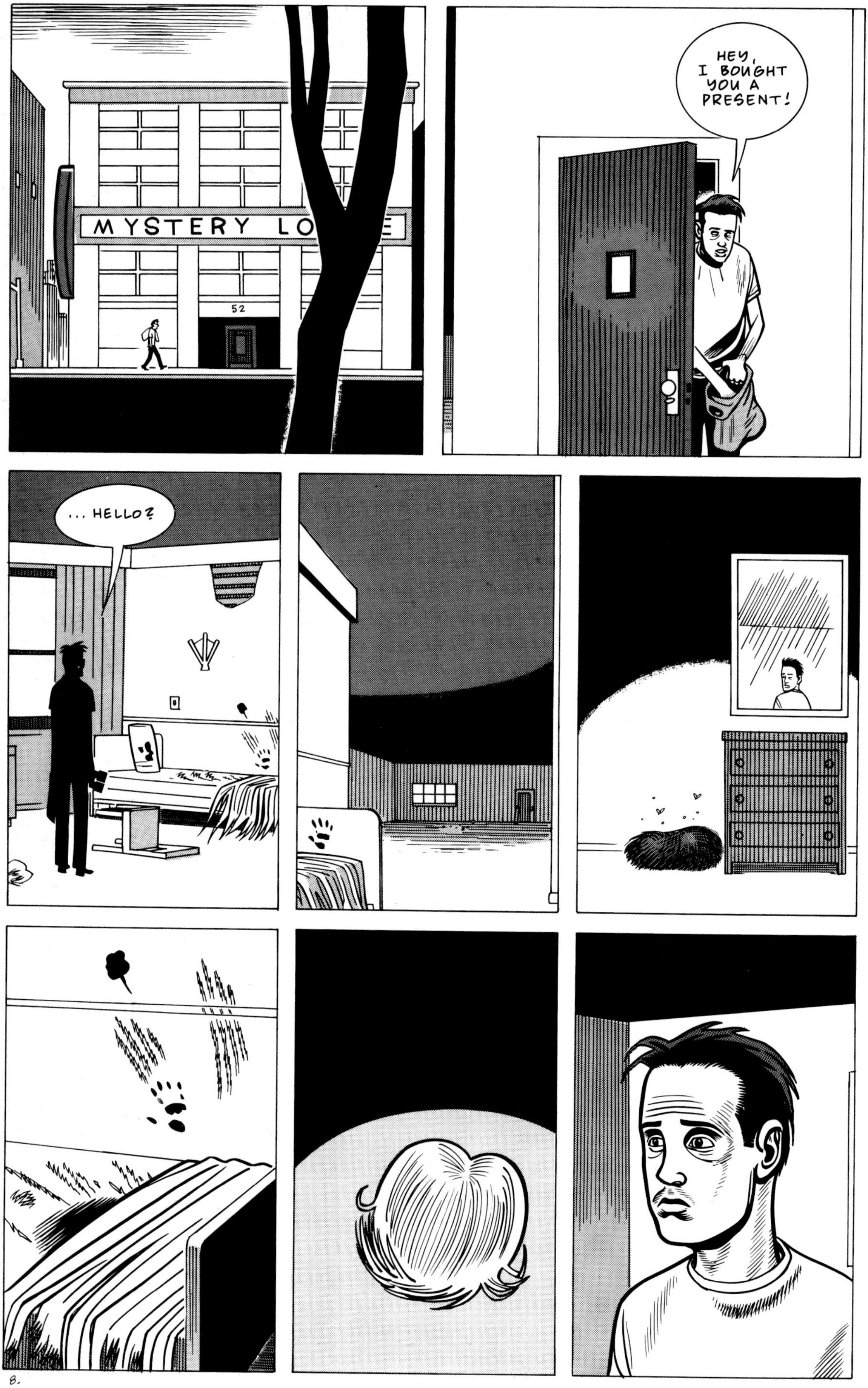
MYSTERY LO E
52
HEY, I BOUGHT YOU A PRESENT!
... HELLO?

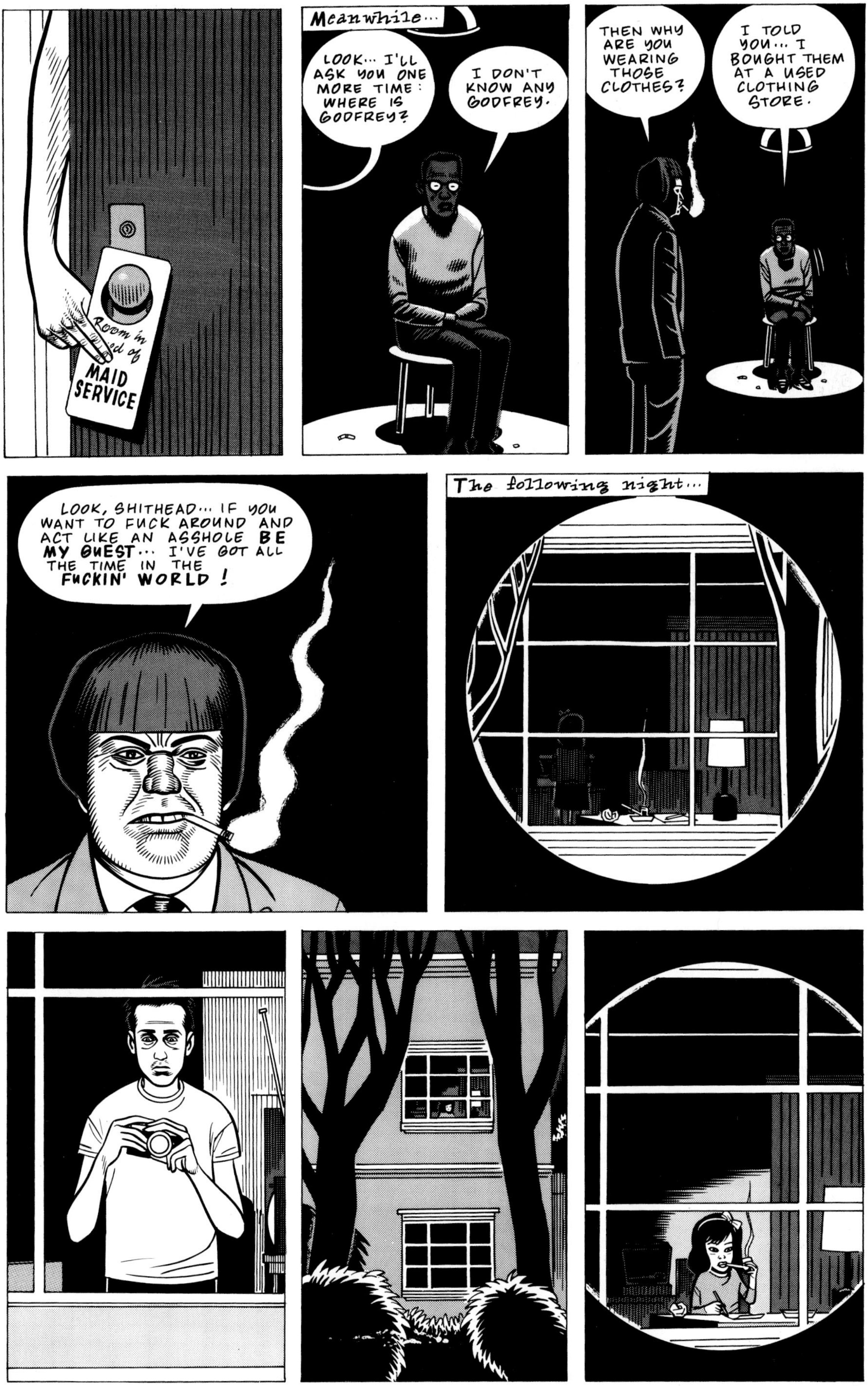
Room in need of
MAID SERVICE
Meanwhile...
LOOK... I'LL ASK YOU ONE MORE TIME: WHERE IS GODFREY?
I DON'T KNOW ANY GODFREY.
THEN WHY ARE YOU WEARING THOSE CLOTHES?
I TOLD YOU... I BOUGHT THEM AT A USED CLOTHING STORE.
LOOK, SHITHEAD... IF YOU WANT TO FUCK AROUND AND ACT LIKE AN ASSHOLE BE MY GUEST... I'VE GOT ALL THE TIME IN THE FUCKIN' WORLD!
The following night...

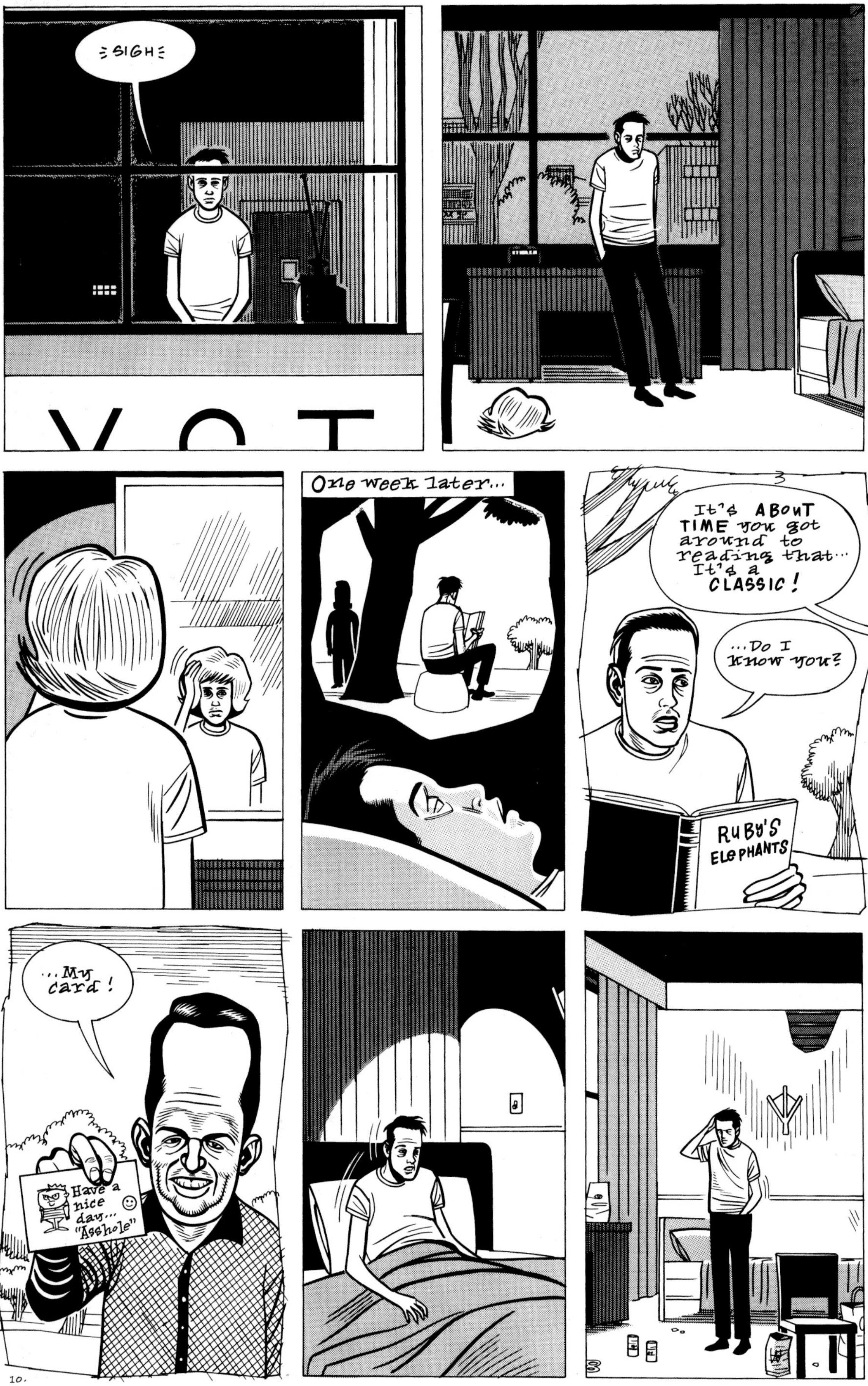

SIGH
YOT
One week later...
It's ABOUT TIME you got around to reading that... It's a CLASSIC!
...Do I know you?
RUBY'S ELEPHANTS
...My card!
Have a nice day... "Asshole"

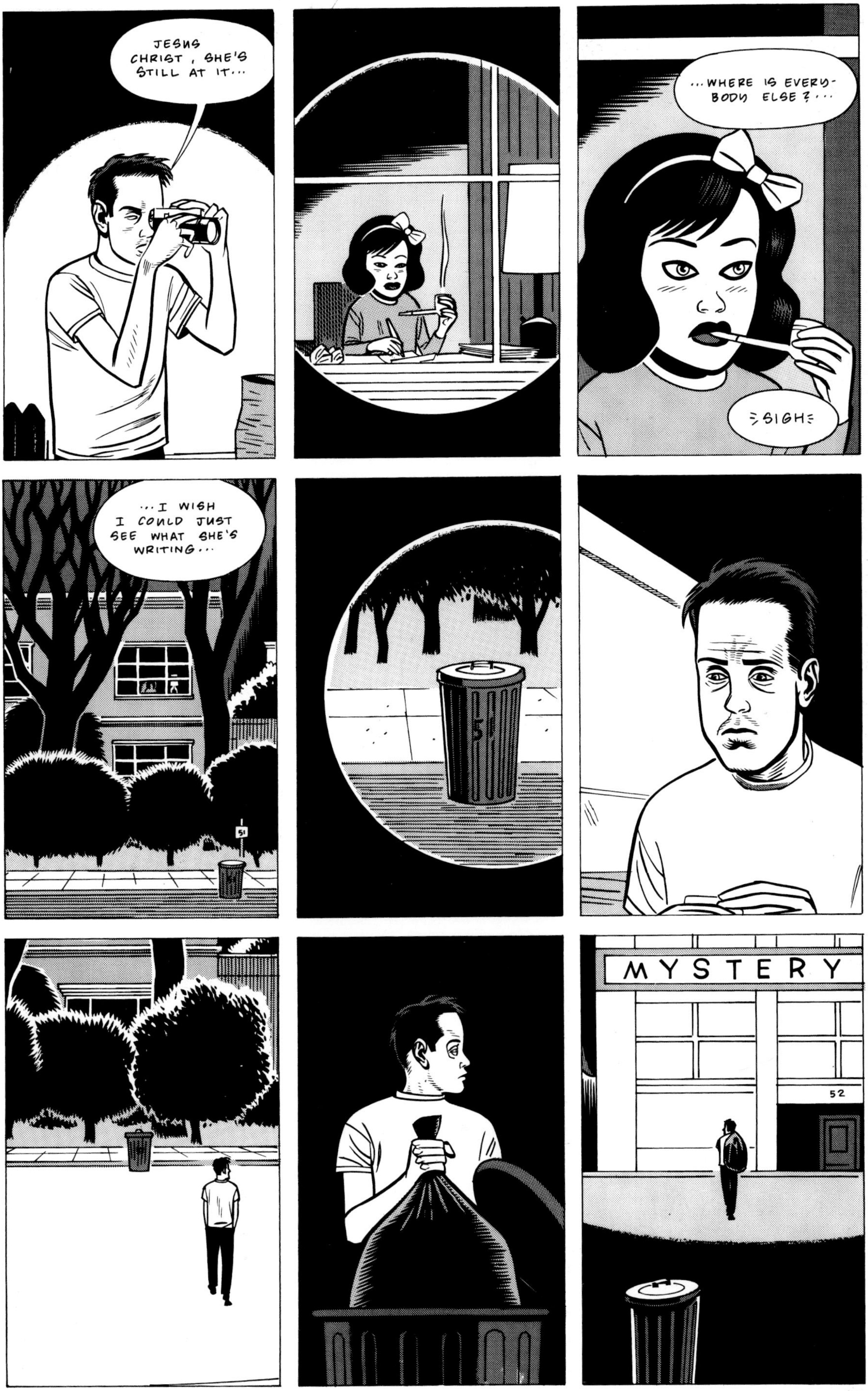
JESUS CHRIST, SHE'S STILL AT IT...
...WHERE IS EVERYBODY ELSE?...
SIGH
...I WISH I COULD JUST SEE WHAT SHE'S WRITING...
51
51
MYSTERY
52

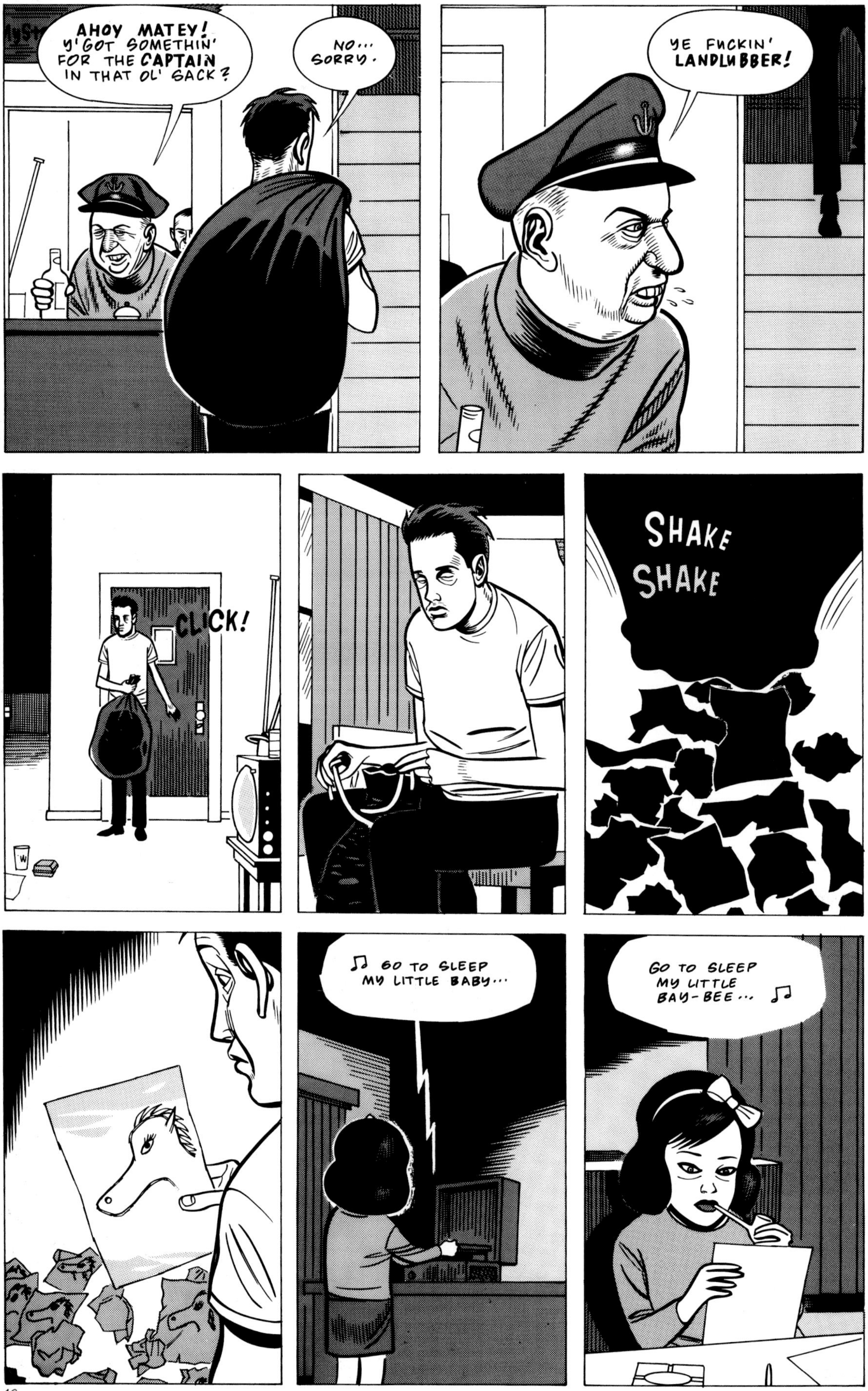
AHOY MATEY! Y'GOT SOMETHIN' FOR THE CAPTAIN IN THAT OL' SACK?
NO... SORRY.
YE FUCKIN' LANDLUBBER!
CLICK!
SHAKE
SHAKE
♫ GO TO SLEEP MY LITTLE BABY...
GO TO SLEEP MY LITTLE BAY-BEE... ♫

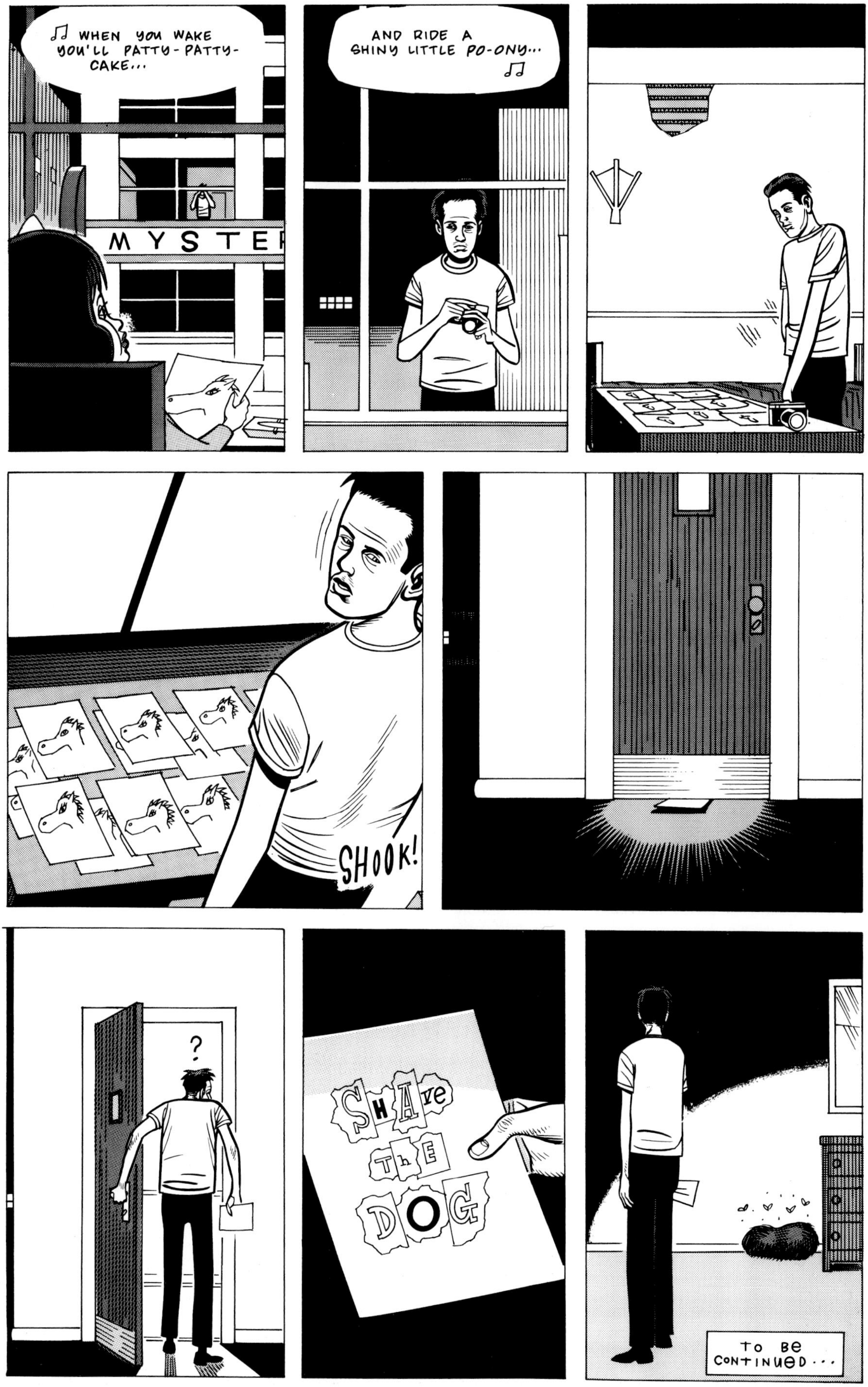
♫ WHEN YOU WAKE YOU'LL PATTY-PATTY-CAKE...
MYSTE
AND RIDE A SHINY LITTLE PO-ONY... ♫
SHOOK!
?
SHAVE THE DOG
TO BE CONTINUED...

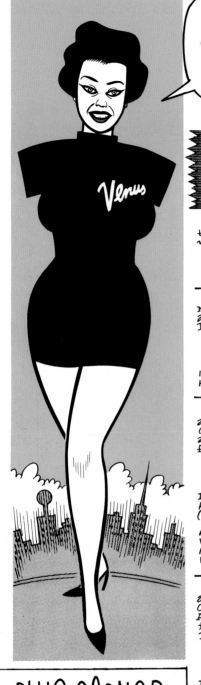

Venus
HI KIDS! WELCOME TO THE LETTERS PAGE! I'M VENUS, YOUR LOVELY HOST... THE BOSS (MY GOD-LIKE CREATOR) HAS ASKED ME TO THANK ALL OF YOU FOR YOUR KIND WORDS AND COMMENTS... WE LOVE EACH AND EVERY ONE OF YOU!

THE FLY-TRAP

WRITE TO: EIGHTBALL
BOX 3357
CHICAGO, IL.
60654

Eightball #5 is cool! And the new paper wipes clean with a moist towel!

Dave Greenberger
Saratoga Springs, NY.

8-Ball is dizzying and nervy. "The Coffee Plate" alone is worth 3 or 4 dollars.

George Meyer
The Simpsons

IS THAT ANYWHERE NEAR THE HAMPTONS?

...Say... on the cover, that ain't no octagon that Lil' Octagon is scopin'! What a swinger, he even goes for them hexagons!

Roy Tompkins
Austin, TX.

I DID THAT COVER SO FAR IN ADVANCE OF THE ISH ITSELF (FOR REASONS EVEN I DON'T UNDERSTAND) THAT "HEXAGON HENDERSON"'S NAME WAS CHANGED TO THE MORE MARKETABLE "LIL' OCTAGON" IN THE INTERIM!

...Hey, in 8-Ball a character is saying "JESUS H. CHRIST." What's the H mean? As you can see I'm practicing to swear in English, a bit...

Julie Doucet
Montreal, Que.

I THINK YOU CAN SWEAR JUST FINE, JULIE! READER: BUY DIRTY PLOTTE (JULIE'S BEE-YOO-TEE-FUL LIL' COMIC MAGAZINE) OR I WILL PERSONALLY FUCK YOU UP! (PUBLISHED BY DRAWN & QUARTERLY)

Do you ever get a boner while drawing Eightball?

Terry Moore
Toronto, Ont.

WHY DON'T YOU ASK YOUR MOTHER?

PLUG CORNER:

THE BEGUILING Toronto
BEM Pittsburgh
SEE HEAR New York
HALLEY'S COMIX Chicago

WHEN IT COMES TO SELLING "GOOD" COMICS (I.E. 8-BALL AND COMICS BY MY FRIENDS) THESE ARE FOUR OF THE FINEST RETAILERS IN NORTH AMERICA! LET'S GIVE 'EM A BIG HAND AND LOTS OF $!... IF YOU'D LIKE TO SEE YOUR STORE IN THIS SPACE: a.) SELL A LOT OF 8-BALLS. b.) WRITE AND TELL ME ABOUT IT.

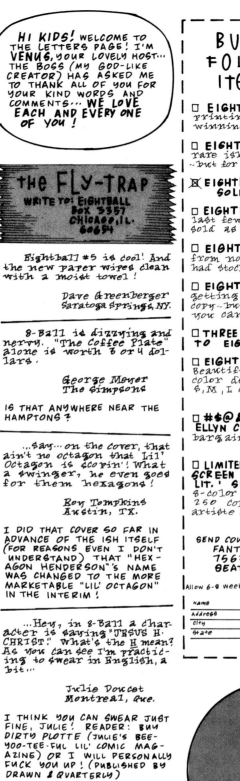

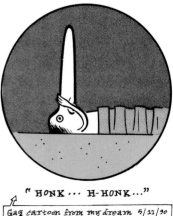

"HONK... H-HONK..."

Gag cartoon from my dream 5/11/90

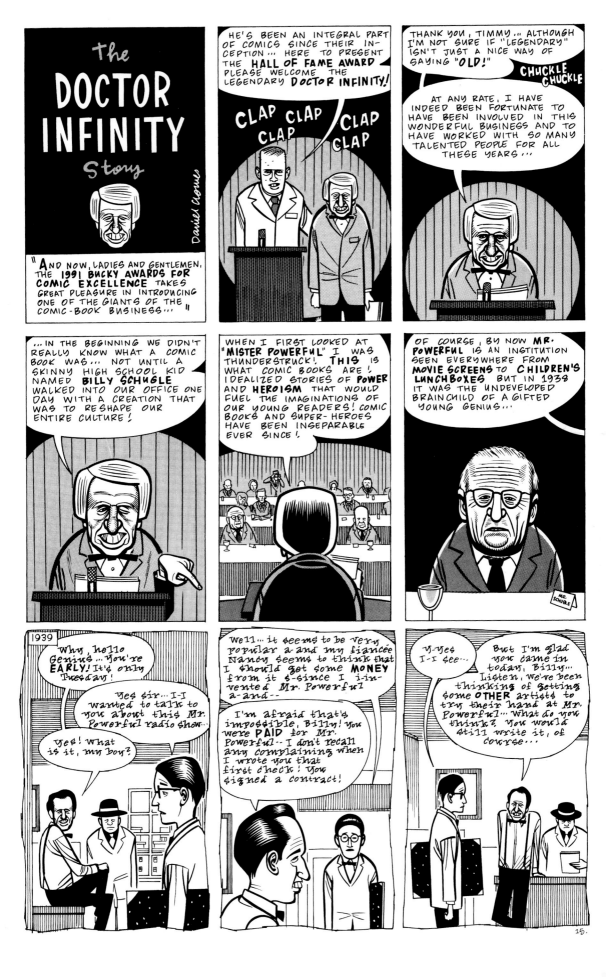

The DOCTOR INFINITY Story

Daniel Clowes

"AND NOW, LADIES AND GENTLEMEN, THE 1991 BUCKY AWARDS FOR COMIC EXCELLENCE TAKES GREAT PLEASURE IN INTRODUCING ONE OF THE GIANTS OF THE COMIC-BOOK BUSINESS..."

HE'S BEEN AN INTEGRAL PART OF COMICS SINCE THEIR INCEPTION... HERE TO PRESENT THE HALL OF FAME AWARD PLEASE WELCOME THE LEGENDARY DOCTOR INFINITY!

CLAP CLAP CLAP CLAP CLAP

THANK YOU, TIMMY... ALTHOUGH I'M NOT SURE IF "LEGENDARY" ISN'T JUST A NICE WAY OF SAYING "OLD!"

CHUCKLE CHUCKLE

AT ANY RATE, I HAVE INDEED BEEN FORTUNATE TO HAVE BEEN INVOLVED IN THIS WONDERFUL BUSINESS AND TO HAVE WORKED WITH SO MANY TALENTED PEOPLE FOR ALL THESE YEARS...

...IN THE BEGINNING WE DIDN'T REALLY KNOW WHAT A COMIC BOOK WAS... NOT UNTIL A SKINNY HIGH SCHOOL KID NAMED BILLY SCHUGLE WALKED INTO OUR OFFICE ONE DAY WITH A CREATION THAT WAS TO RESHAPE OUR ENTIRE CULTURE!

WHEN I FIRST LOOKED AT "MISTER POWERFUL" I WAS THUNDERSTRUCK! THIS IS WHAT COMIC BOOKS ARE! IDEALIZED STORIES OF POWER AND HEROISM THAT WOULD FUEL THE IMAGINATIONS OF OUR YOUNG READERS! COMIC BOOKS AND SUPER-HEROES HAVE BEEN INSEPARABLE EVER SINCE!

OF COURSE, BY NOW MR. POWERFUL IS AN INSTITUTION SEEN EVERYWHERE FROM MOVIE SCREENS TO CHILDREN'S LUNCHBOXES BUT IN 1938 IT WAS THE UNDEVELOPED BRAINCHILD OF A GIFTED YOUNG GENIUS...

MR. SCHUGLE

1939

Why, hello Genius... You're EARLY! It's only Tuesday!

Yes sir... I-I wanted to talk to you about this Mr. Powerful radio show...

Yes! What is it, my boy?

Well... it seems to be very popular a-and my fiancée Nancy seems to think that I should get some MONEY from it &-since I i-invented Mr. Powerful a-and--

I'm afraid that's impossible, Billy! You were PAID for Mr. Powerful-- I don't recall any complaining when I wrote you that first check! You signed a contract!

Y-yes I-I see...

But I'm glad you came in today, Billy... Listen, we've been thinking of getting some OTHER artists to try their hand at Mr. Powerful... What do you think? You would still write it, of course...

15.

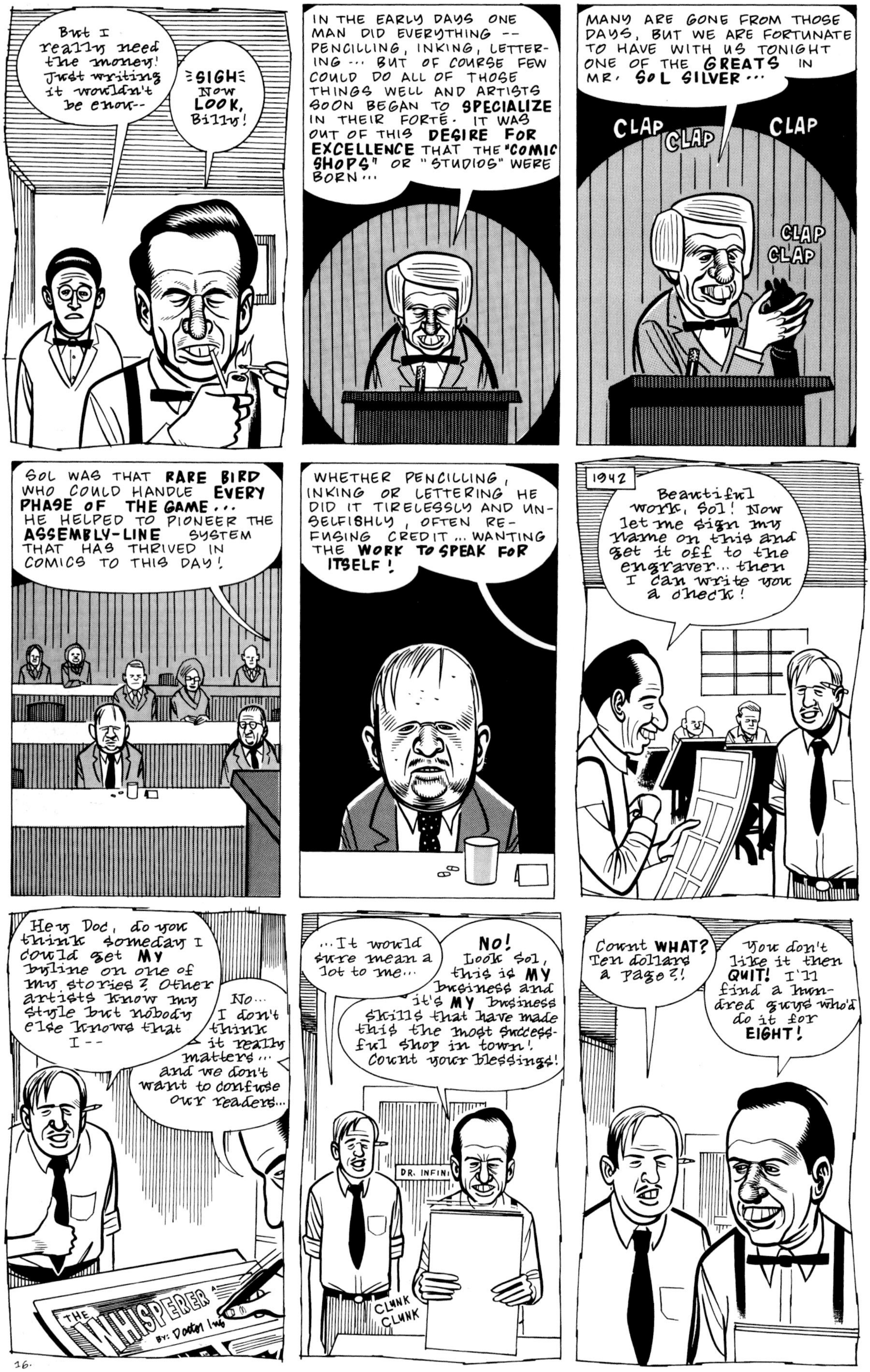
But I really need the money! Just writing it wouldn't be enou--
SIGH Now LOOK, Billy!
IN THE EARLY DAYS ONE MAN DID EVERYTHING -- PENCILLING, INKING, LETTERING ... BUT OF COURSE FEW COULD DO ALL OF THOSE THINGS WELL AND ARTISTS SOON BEGAN TO SPECIALIZE IN THEIR FORTÉ. IT WAS OUT OF THIS DESIRE FOR EXCELLENCE THAT THE "COMIC SHOPS" OR "STUDIOS" WERE BORN...
MANY ARE GONE FROM THOSE DAYS, BUT WE ARE FORTUNATE TO HAVE WITH US TONIGHT ONE OF THE GREATS IN MR. SOL SILVER...
CLAP CLAP CLAP
CLAP CLAP
SOL WAS THAT RARE BIRD WHO COULD HANDLE EVERY PHASE OF THE GAME... HE HELPED TO PIONEER THE ASSEMBLY-LINE SYSTEM THAT HAS THRIVED IN COMICS TO THIS DAY!
WHETHER PENCILLING, INKING OR LETTERING HE DID IT TIRELESSLY AND UNSELFISHLY, OFTEN REFUSING CREDIT... WANTING THE WORK TO SPEAK FOR ITSELF!
1942
Beautiful work, Sol! Now let me sign my name on this and get it off to the engraver... then I can write you a check!
Hey Doc, do you think someday I could get MY byline on one of my stories? Other artists know my style but nobody else knows that I --
No... I don't think it really matters... and we don't want to confuse our readers...
THE WHISPERER
BY: Doctor Inf
...It would sure mean a lot to me...
NO! Look Sol, this is MY business and it's MY business skills that have made this the most successful shop in town! Count your blessings!
DR. INFINI
CLUNK CLUNK
Count WHAT? Ten dollars a page?!
You don't like it then QUIT! I'll find a hundred guys who'd do it for EIGHT!

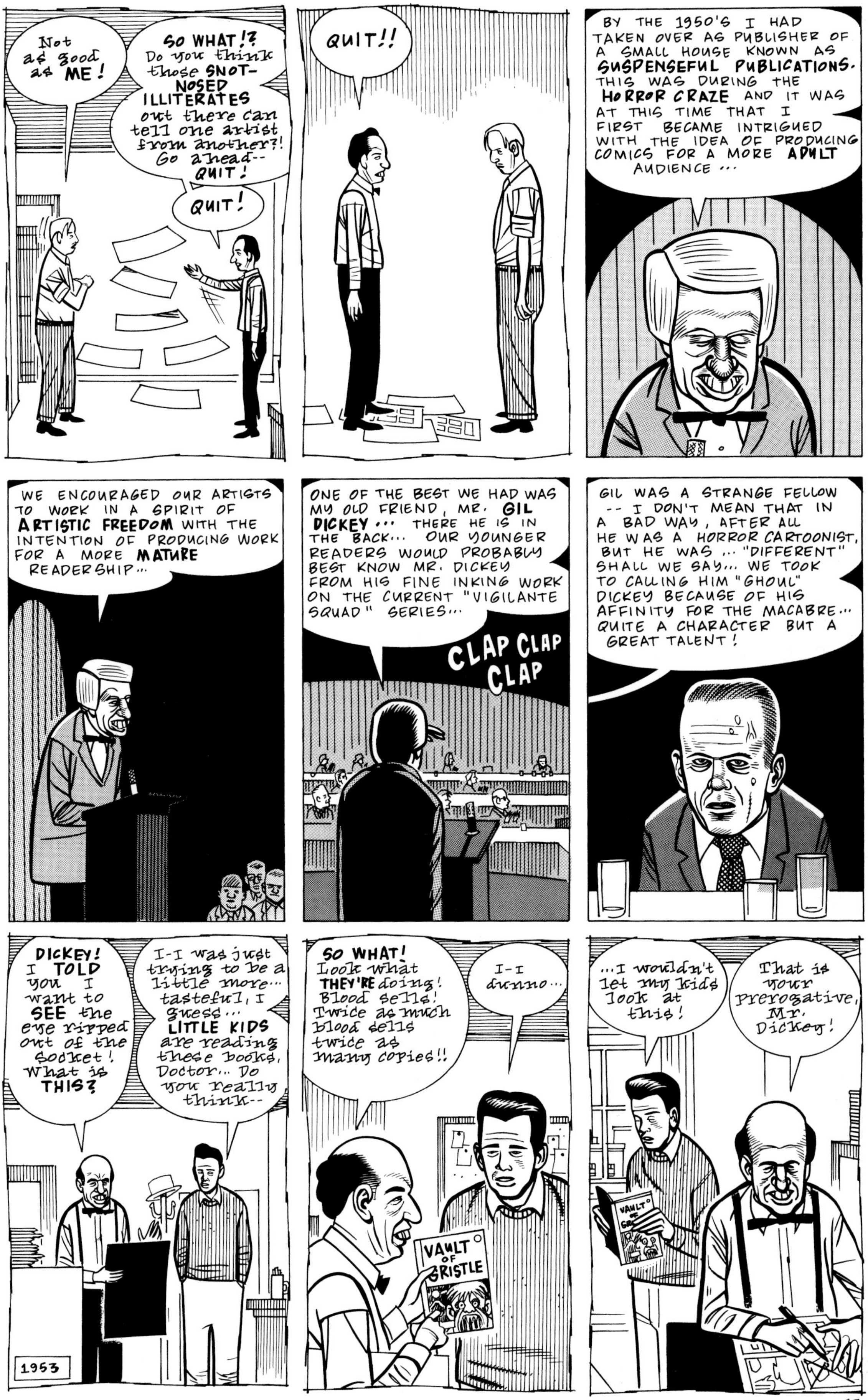
Not as good as ME!
SO WHAT!? Do you think those SNOT-NOSED ILLITERATES out there can tell one artist from another?! Go ahead-- QUIT!
QUIT!
QUIT!!
BY THE 1950'S I HAD TAKEN OVER AS PUBLISHER OF A SMALL HOUSE KNOWN AS SUSPENSEFUL PUBLICATIONS. THIS WAS DURING THE HORROR CRAZE AND IT WAS AT THIS TIME THAT I FIRST BECAME INTRIGUED WITH THE IDEA OF PRODUCING COMICS FOR A MORE ADULT AUDIENCE...
WE ENCOURAGED OUR ARTISTS TO WORK IN A SPIRIT OF ARTISTIC FREEDOM WITH THE INTENTION OF PRODUCING WORK FOR A MORE MATURE READERSHIP...
ONE OF THE BEST WE HAD WAS MY OLD FRIEND, MR. GIL DICKEY... THERE HE IS IN THE BACK... OUR YOUNGER READERS WOULD PROBABLY BEST KNOW MR. DICKEY FROM HIS FINE INKING WORK ON THE CURRENT "VIGILANTE SQUAD" SERIES...
CLAP CLAP CLAP
GIL WAS A STRANGE FELLOW -- I DON'T MEAN THAT IN A BAD WAY, AFTER ALL HE WAS A HORROR CARTOONIST, BUT HE WAS ... "DIFFERENT" SHALL WE SAY... WE TOOK TO CALLING HIM "GHOUL" DICKEY BECAUSE OF HIS AFFINITY FOR THE MACABRE... QUITE A CHARACTER BUT A GREAT TALENT!
DICKEY! I TOLD you I want to SEE the eye ripped out of the socket! What is THIS?
I-I was just trying to be a little more... tasteful, I guess... LITTLE KIDS are reading these books, Doctor... Do you really think--
1953
SO WHAT! Look what THEY'RE doing! Blood sells! Twice as much blood sells twice as many copies!!
I-I dunno...
VAULT OF GRISTLE
...I wouldn't let my kids look at this!
That is your Prerogative, Mr. Dickey!

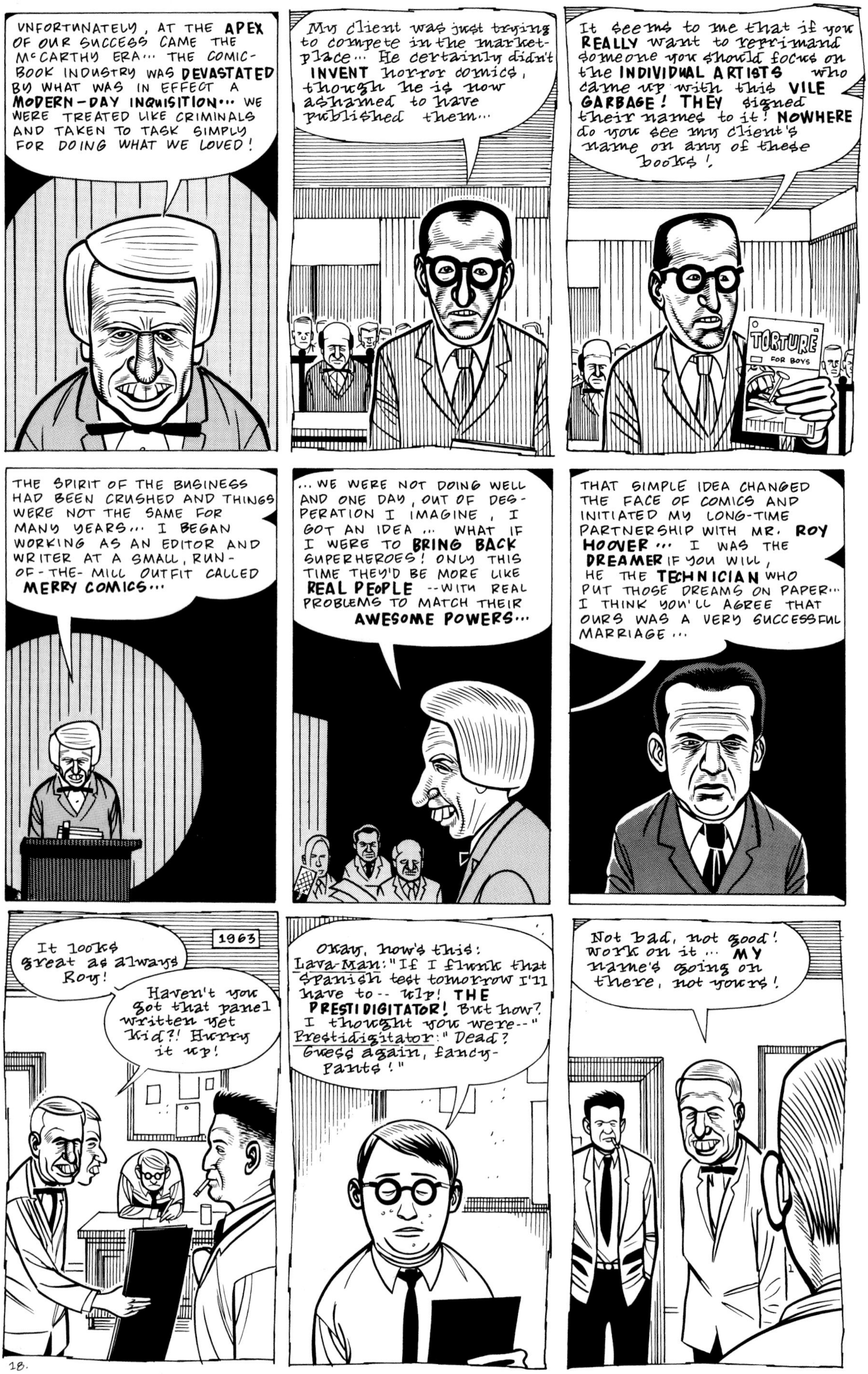
UNFORTUNATELY, AT THE APEX OF OUR SUCCESS CAME THE McCARTHY ERA... THE COMIC-BOOK INDUSTRY WAS DEVASTATED BY WHAT WAS IN EFFECT A MODERN-DAY INQUISITION... WE WERE TREATED LIKE CRIMINALS AND TAKEN TO TASK SIMPLY FOR DOING WHAT WE LOVED!
My client was just trying to compete in the market-place... He certainly didn't INVENT horror comics, though he is now ashamed to have published them...
It seems to me that if you REALLY want to reprimand someone you should focus on the INDIVIDUAL ARTISTS who came up with this VILE GARBAGE! THEY signed their names to it! NOWHERE do you see my client's name on any of these books!
TORTURE FOR BOYS
THE SPIRIT OF THE BUSINESS HAD BEEN CRUSHED AND THINGS WERE NOT THE SAME FOR MANY YEARS... I BEGAN WORKING AS AN EDITOR AND WRITER AT A SMALL, RUN-OF-THE-MILL OUTFIT CALLED MERRY COMICS...
...WE WERE NOT DOING WELL AND ONE DAY, OUT OF DES-PERATION I IMAGINE, I GOT AN IDEA... WHAT IF I WERE TO BRING BACK SUPERHEROES! ONLY THIS TIME THEY'D BE MORE LIKE REAL PEOPLE --WITH REAL PROBLEMS TO MATCH THEIR AWESOME POWERS...
THAT SIMPLE IDEA CHANGED THE FACE OF COMICS AND INITIATED MY LONG-TIME PARTNERSHIP WITH MR. ROY HOOVER... I WAS THE DREAMER IF YOU WILL, HE THE TECHNICIAN WHO PUT THOSE DREAMS ON PAPER... I THINK YOU'LL AGREE THAT OURS WAS A VERY SUCCESSFUL MARRIAGE...
1963
It looks great as always Roy!
Haven't you got that panel written yet Kid?! Hurry it up!
Okay, how's this: Lava-Man: "If I flunk that Spanish test tomorrow I'll have to-- ulp! THE PRESTIDIGITATOR! But how? I thought you were--" Prestidigitator: "Dead? Guess again, fancy-Pants!"
Not bad, not good! Work on it... MY name's going on there, not yours!

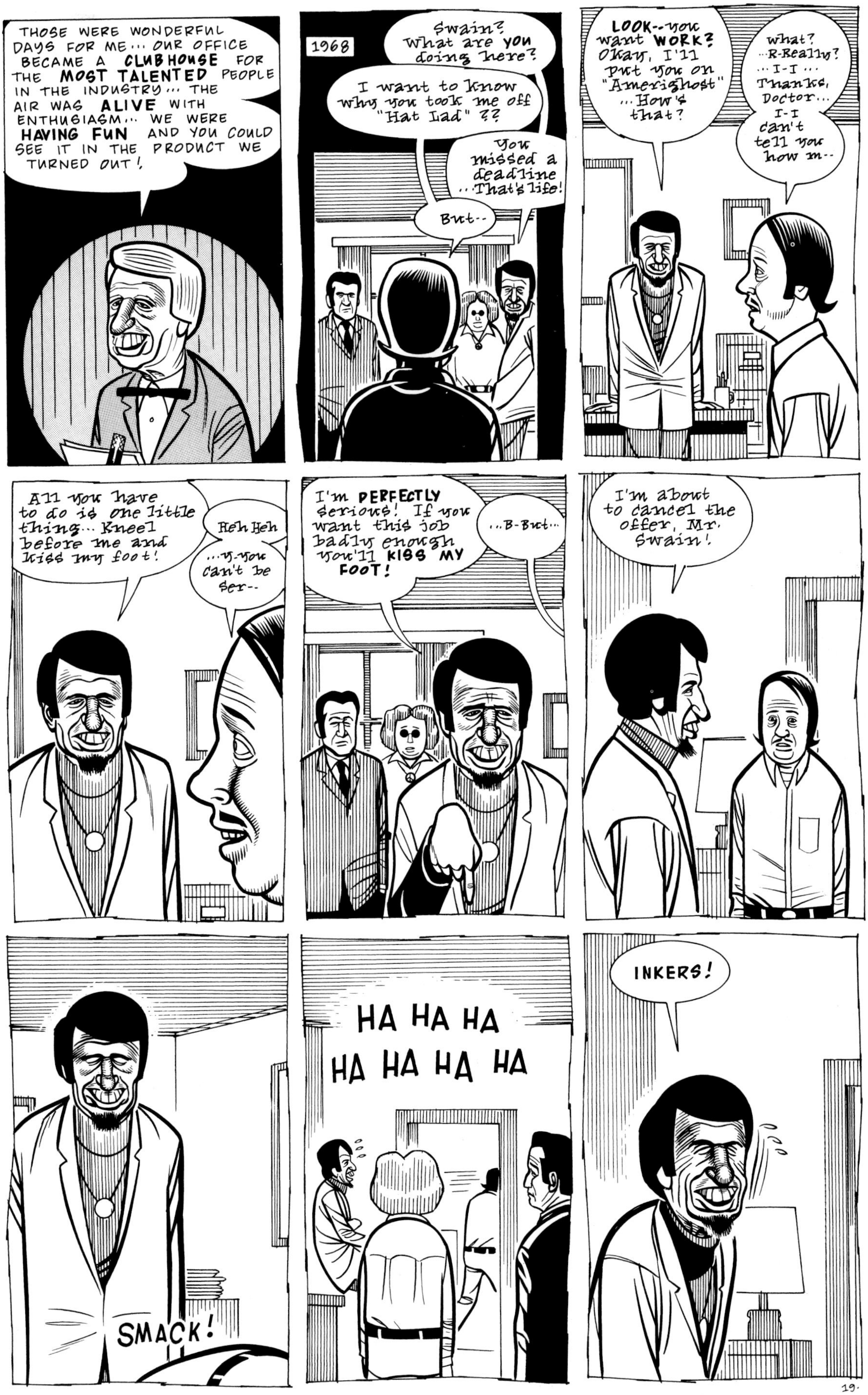
THOSE WERE WONDERFUL DAYS FOR ME... OUR OFFICE BECAME A CLUBHOUSE FOR THE MOST TALENTED PEOPLE IN THE INDUSTRY... THE AIR WAS ALIVE WITH ENTHUSIASM... WE WERE HAVING FUN AND YOU COULD SEE IT IN THE PRODUCT WE TURNED OUT!
1968
Swain? What are you doing here?
I want to know why you took me off "Hat Lad"??
You missed a deadline ...That's life!
But--
LOOK--you want WORK? Okay, I'll put you on "Amerighost" ...How's that?
What? ...R-Really? ...I-I... Thanks, Doctor...
I-I can't tell you how m--
All you have to do is one little thing... Kneel before me and kiss my foot!
Heh Heh
...Y-You can't be ser--
I'm PERFECTLY serious! If you want this job badly enough you'll KISS MY FOOT!
...B-But...
I'm about to cancel the offer, Mr. Swain!
SMACK!
HA HA HA
HA HA HA HA
INKERS!

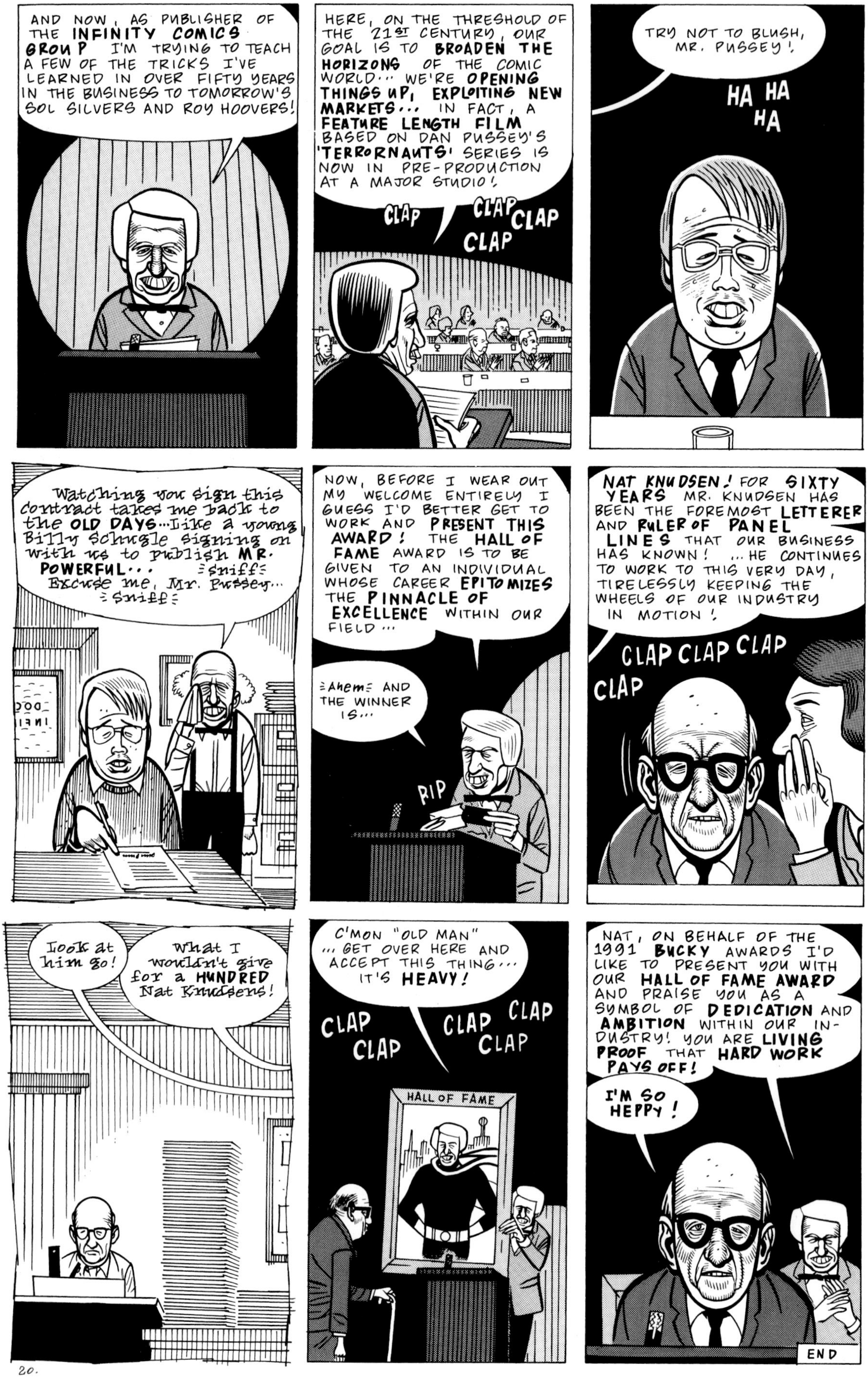
AND NOW, AS PUBLISHER OF THE INFINITY COMICS GROUP I'M TRYING TO TEACH A FEW OF THE TRICKS I'VE LEARNED IN OVER FIFTY YEARS IN THE BUSINESS TO TOMORROW'S SOL SILVERS AND ROY HOOVERS!
HERE, ON THE THRESHOLD OF THE 21ST CENTURY, OUR GOAL IS TO BROADEN THE HORIZONS OF THE COMIC WORLD... WE'RE OPENING THINGS UP, EXPLOITING NEW MARKETS... IN FACT, A FEATURE LENGTH FILM BASED ON DAN PUSSEY'S 'TERRORNAUTS' SERIES IS NOW IN PRE-PRODUCTION AT A MAJOR STUDIO!
CLAP CLAP CLAP CLAP
TRY NOT TO BLUSH, MR. PUSSEY!
HA HA HA
Watching you sign this contract takes me back to the OLD DAYS...Like a young Billy Schugle signing on with us to publish MR. POWERFUL... =sniff= Excuse me, Mr. Pussey... =sniff=
NOW, BEFORE I WEAR OUT MY WELCOME ENTIRELY I GUESS I'D BETTER GET TO WORK AND PRESENT THIS AWARD! THE HALL OF FAME AWARD IS TO BE GIVEN TO AN INDIVIDUAL WHOSE CAREER EPITOMIZES THE PINNACLE OF EXCELLENCE WITHIN OUR FIELD...
=Ahem= AND THE WINNER IS...
RIP
NAT KNUDSEN! FOR SIXTY YEARS MR. KNUDSEN HAS BEEN THE FOREMOST LETTERER AND RULER OF PANEL LINES THAT OUR BUSINESS HAS KNOWN! ...HE CONTINUES TO WORK TO THIS VERY DAY, TIRELESSLY KEEPING THE WHEELS OF OUR INDUSTRY IN MOTION!
CLAP CLAP CLAP CLAP
Look at him go!
What I wouldn't give for a HUNDRED Nat Knudsens!
C'MON "OLD MAN" ... GET OVER HERE AND ACCEPT THIS THING... IT'S HEAVY!
CLAP CLAP CLAP CLAP CLAP
HALL OF FAME
NAT, ON BEHALF OF THE 1991 BUCKY AWARDS I'D LIKE TO PRESENT YOU WITH OUR HALL OF FAME AWARD AND PRAISE YOU AS A SYMBOL OF DEDICATION AND AMBITION WITHIN OUR INDUSTRY! YOU ARE LIVING PROOF THAT HARD WORK PAYS OFF!
I'M SO HEPPY!
END

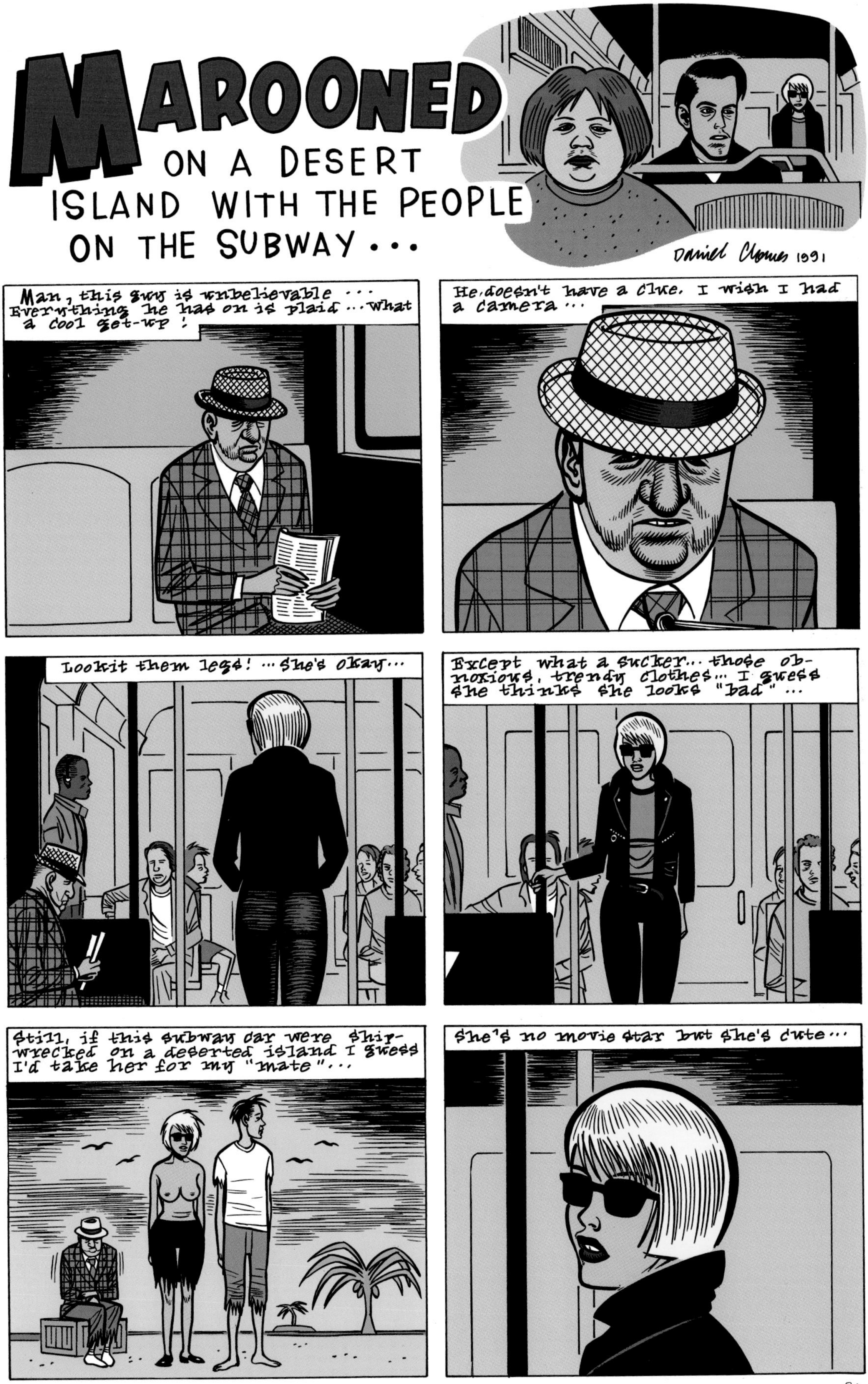
MAROONED ON A DESERT ISLAND WITH THE PEOPLE ON THE SUBWAY...
Daniel Clowes 1991
Man, this guy is unbelievable ... Everything he has on is plaid ... What a cool get-up!
He doesn't have a clue. I wish I had a camera ...
Lookit them legs! ... She's okay ...
Except what a sucker... those obnoxious, trendy clothes... I guess she thinks she looks "bad" ...
Still, if this subway car were shipwrecked on a deserted island I guess I'd take her for my "mate"...
She's no movie star but she's cute...

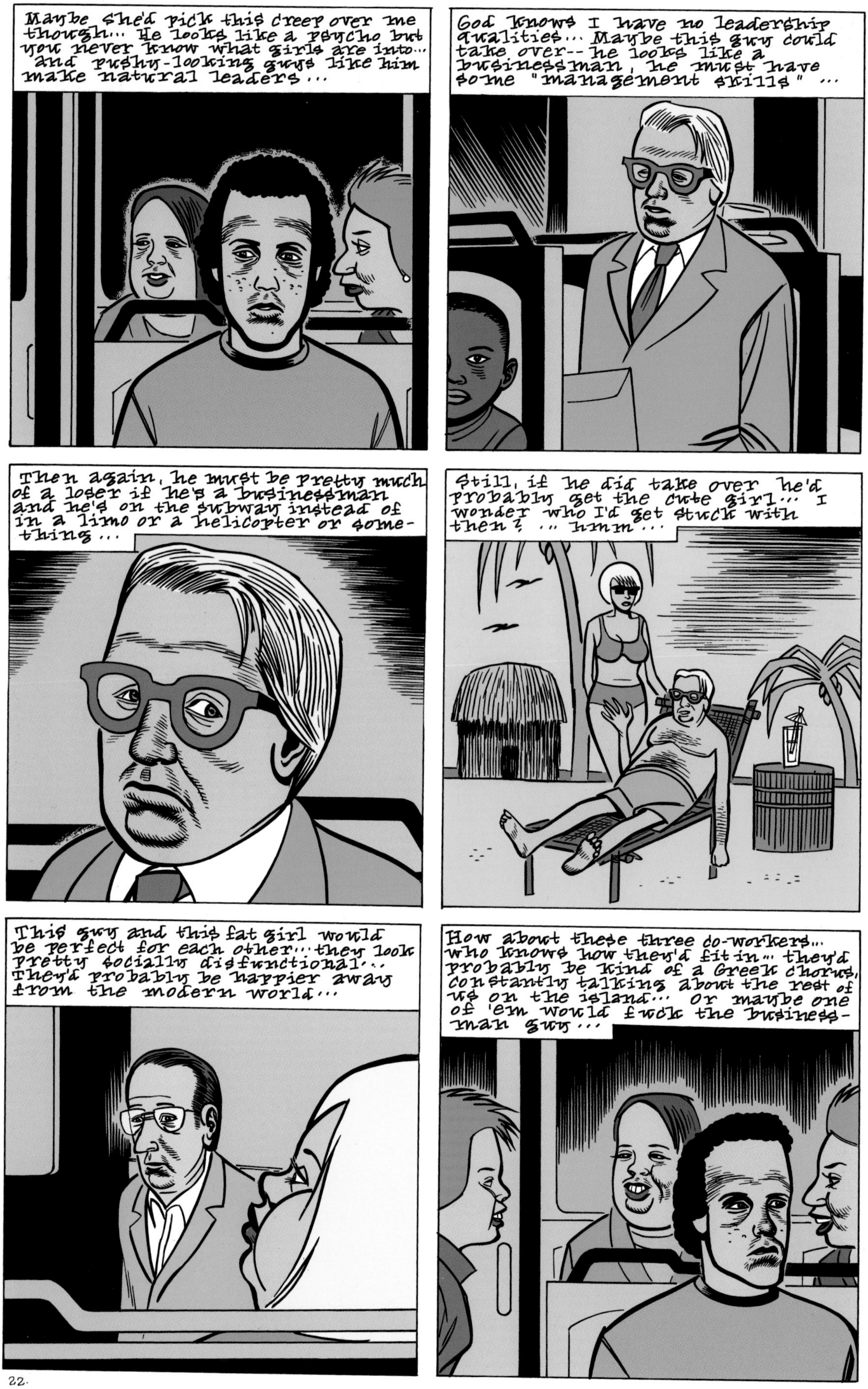
Maybe she'd pick this creep over me though... He looks like a psycho but you never know what girls are into... and pushy-looking guys like him make natural leaders...
God knows I have no leadership qualities... Maybe this guy could take over-- he looks like a businessman, he must have some "management skills"...
Then again, he must be pretty much of a loser if he's a businessman and he's on the subway instead of in a limo or a helicopter or some-thing...
Still, if he did take over he'd probably get the cute girl... I wonder who I'd get stuck with then? ... hmm...
This guy and this fat girl would be perfect for each other... they look pretty socially disfunctional... They'd probably be happier away from the modern world...
How about these three co-workers... who knows how they'd fit in... they'd probably be kind of a Greek chorus, constantly talking about the rest of us on the island... or maybe one of 'em would fuck the business-man guy...

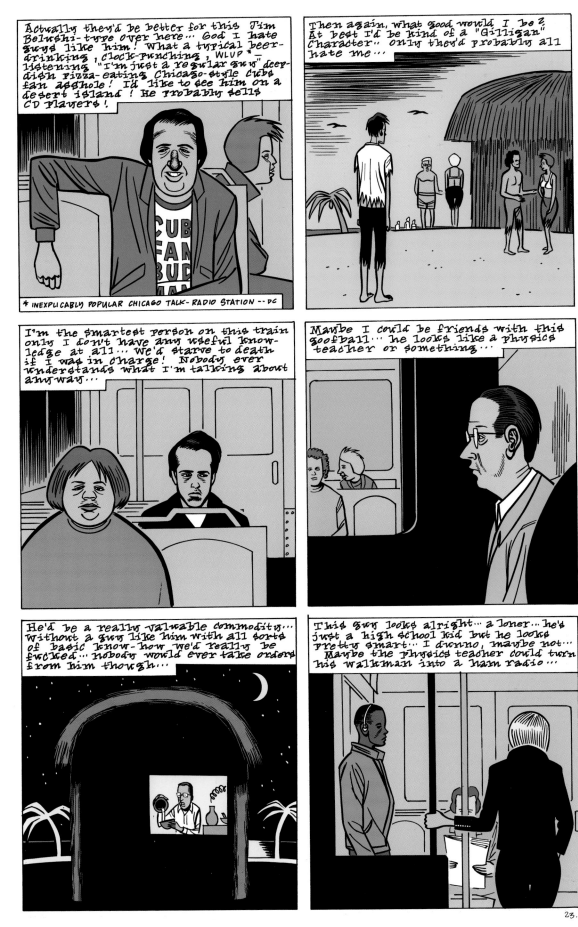

Actually they'd be better for this Jim Belushi-type over here... God I hate guys like him! What a typical beer-drinking, clock-punching, WLUP * - listening "I'm just a regular guy" deep-dish pizza-eating Chicago-style Cubs fan asshole! I'd like to see him on a desert island! He probably sells CD players!

* INEXPLICABLY POPULAR CHICAGO TALK- RADIO STATION -- DC

Then again, what good would I be? At best I'd be kind of a "Gilligan" character... only they'd probably all hate me...

I'm the smartest person on this train only I don't have any useful know-ledge at all... We'd starve to death if I was in charge! Nobody ever understands what I'm talking about anyway...

Maybe I could be friends with this goofball... he looks like a physics teacher or something...

He'd be a really valuable commodity... without a guy like him with all sorts of basic know-how we'd really be fucked... nobody would ever take orders from him though...

This guy looks alright... a loner... he's just a high school kid but he looks pretty smart... I dunno, maybe not... Maybe the physics teacher could turn his walkman into a ham radio...

23.

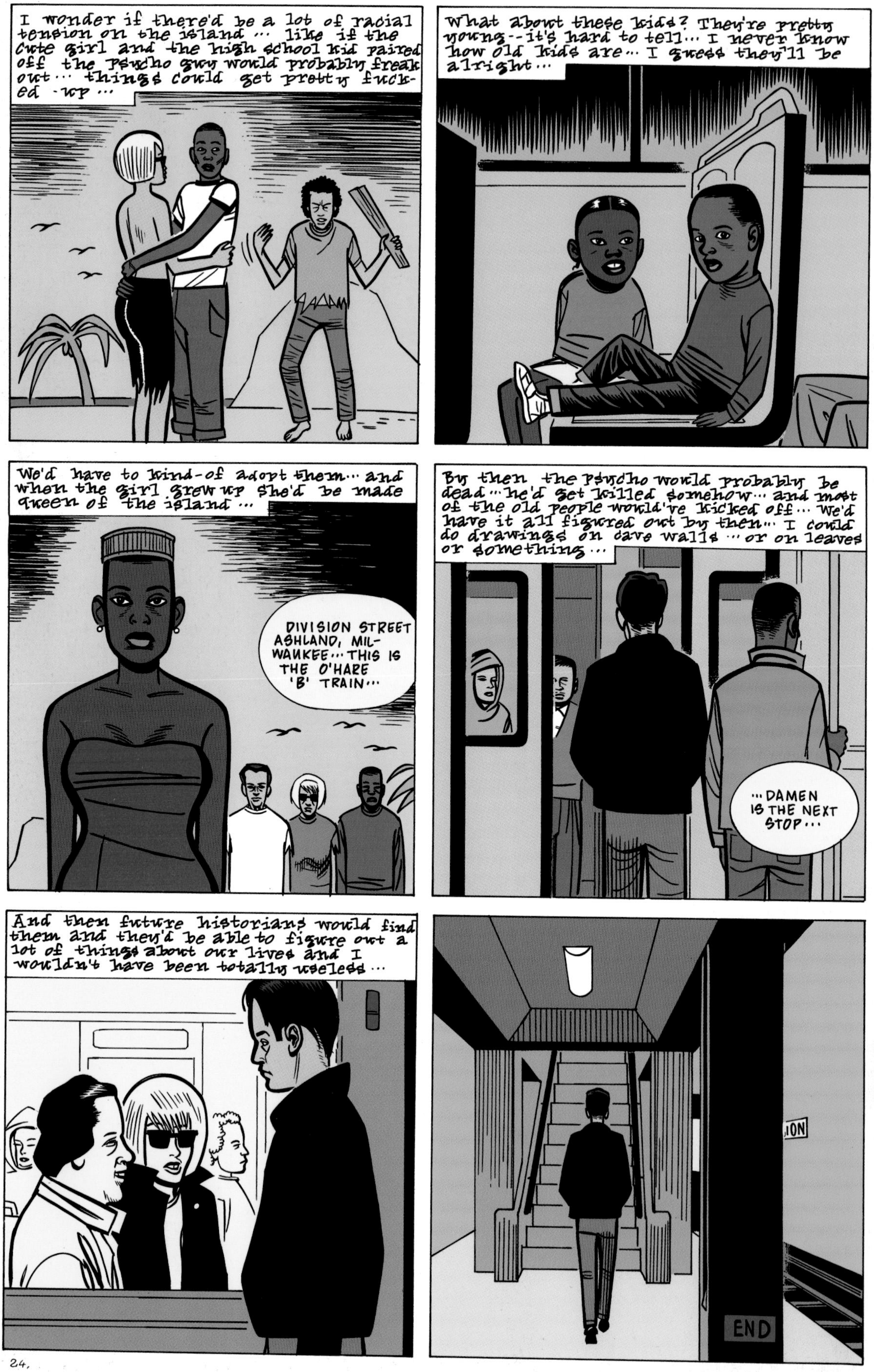
I wonder if there'd be a lot of racial tension on the island... like if the cute girl and the high school kid paired off the psycho guy would probably freak out... things could get pretty fuck-ed-up...
What about these kids? They're pretty young--it's hard to tell... I never know how old kids are... I guess they'll be alright...
We'd have to kind-of adopt them... and when the girl grew up she'd be made queen of the island...
DIVISION STREET ASHLAND, MIL-WAUKEE... THIS IS THE O'HARE 'B' TRAIN...
By then the psycho would probably be dead... he'd get killed somehow... and most of the old people would've kicked off... We'd have it all figured out by then... I could do drawings on cave walls ...or on leaves or something...
...DAMEN IS THE NEXT STOP...
And then future historians would find them and they'd be able to figure out a lot of things about our lives and I wouldn't have been totally useless...
ION
END

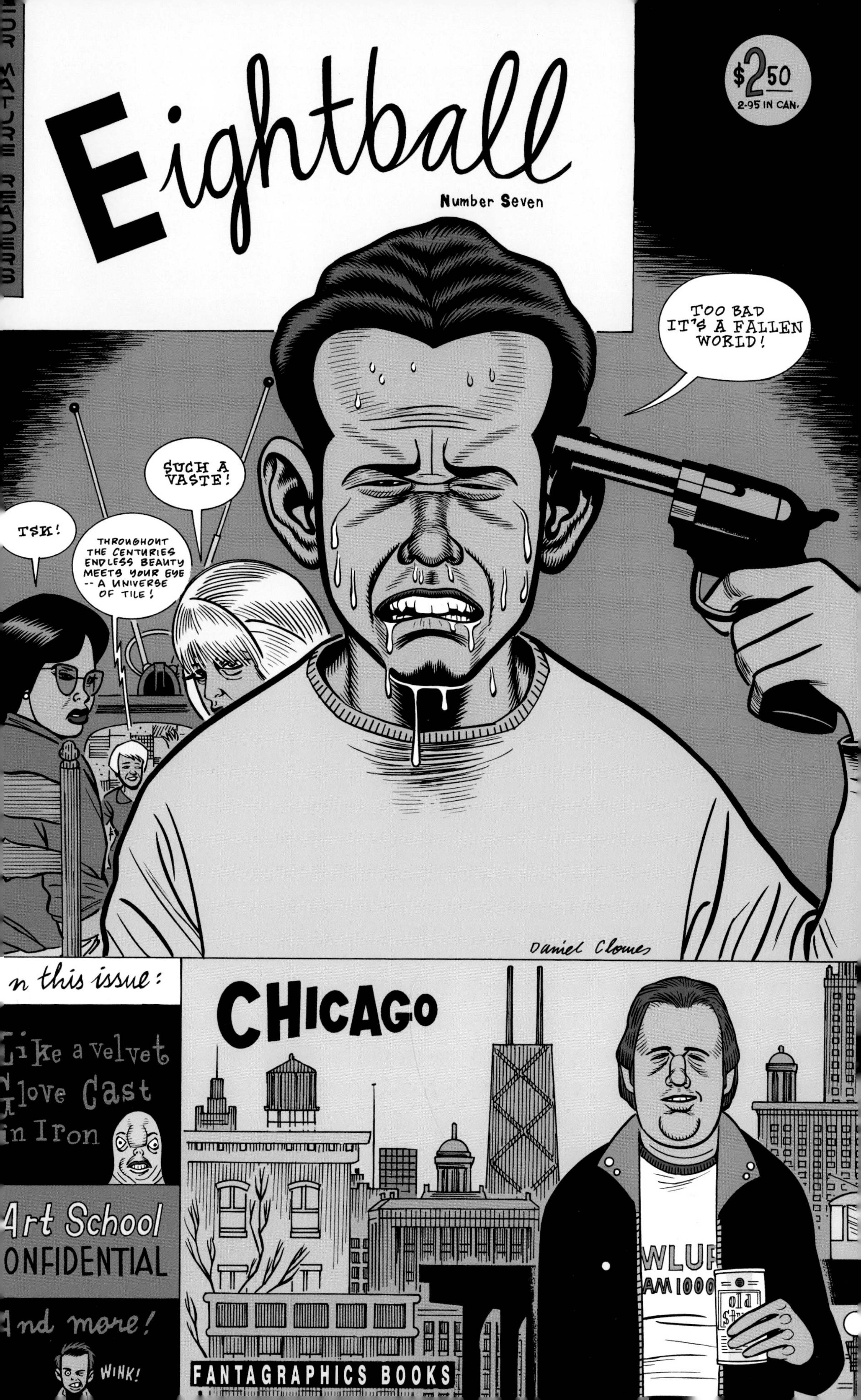
Eightball
Number Seven
$2.50
2.95 IN CAN.
TOO BAD IT'S A FALLEN WORLD!
SUCH A VASTE!
TSK!
THROUGHOUT THE CENTURIES ENDLESS BEAUTY MEETS YOUR EYE -- A UNIVERSE OF TILE!
Daniel Clowes
n this issue:
CHICAGO
ike a velvet
love Cast
in Iron
Art School
ONFIDENTIAL
nd more!
WINK!
WLUP
AM 1000
FANTAGRAPHICS BOOKS

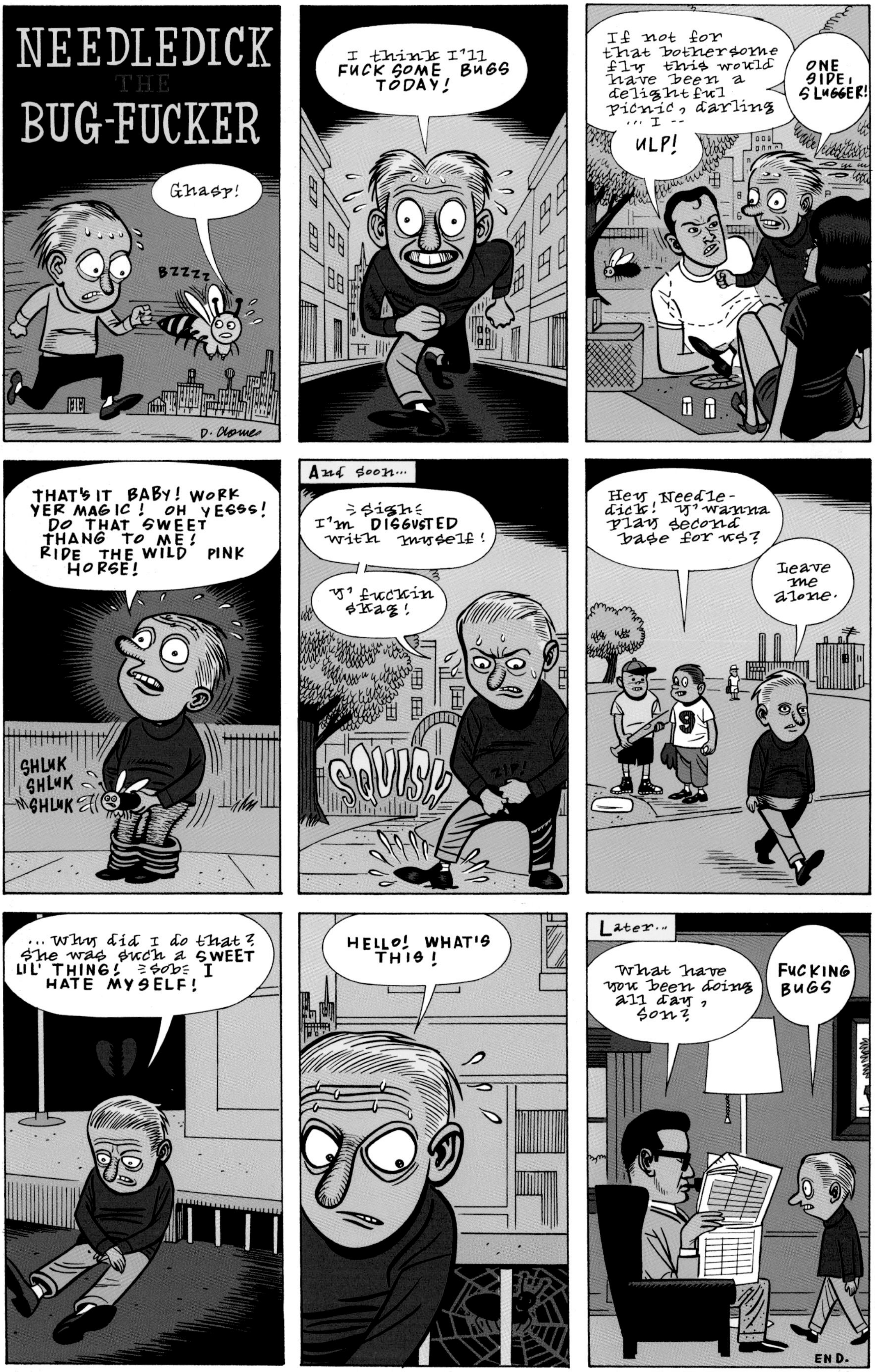
NEEDLEDICK THE BUG-FUCKER
Ghasp!
BZZZZ
D. Clowes
I think I'll FUCK SOME BUGS TODAY!
If not for that bothersome fly this would have been a delightful picnic, darling ... I --
ONE SIDE, SLUGGER!
ULP!
THAT'S IT BABY! WORK YER MAGIC! OH YESSS! DO THAT SWEET THANG TO ME! RIDE THE WILD PINK HORSE!
SHLUK SHLUK SHLUK
And soon...
≷sigh≶ I'm DISGUSTED with myself!
Y' fuckin skag!
SQUISH
ZIP!
Hey Needle-dick! Y'wanna play second base for us?
Leave me alone.
9
...Why did I do that? She was such a SWEET LIL' THING! ≷sob≶ I HATE MYSELF!
HELLO! WHAT'S THIS!
Later...
What have you been doing all day, son?
FUCKING BUGS
END.

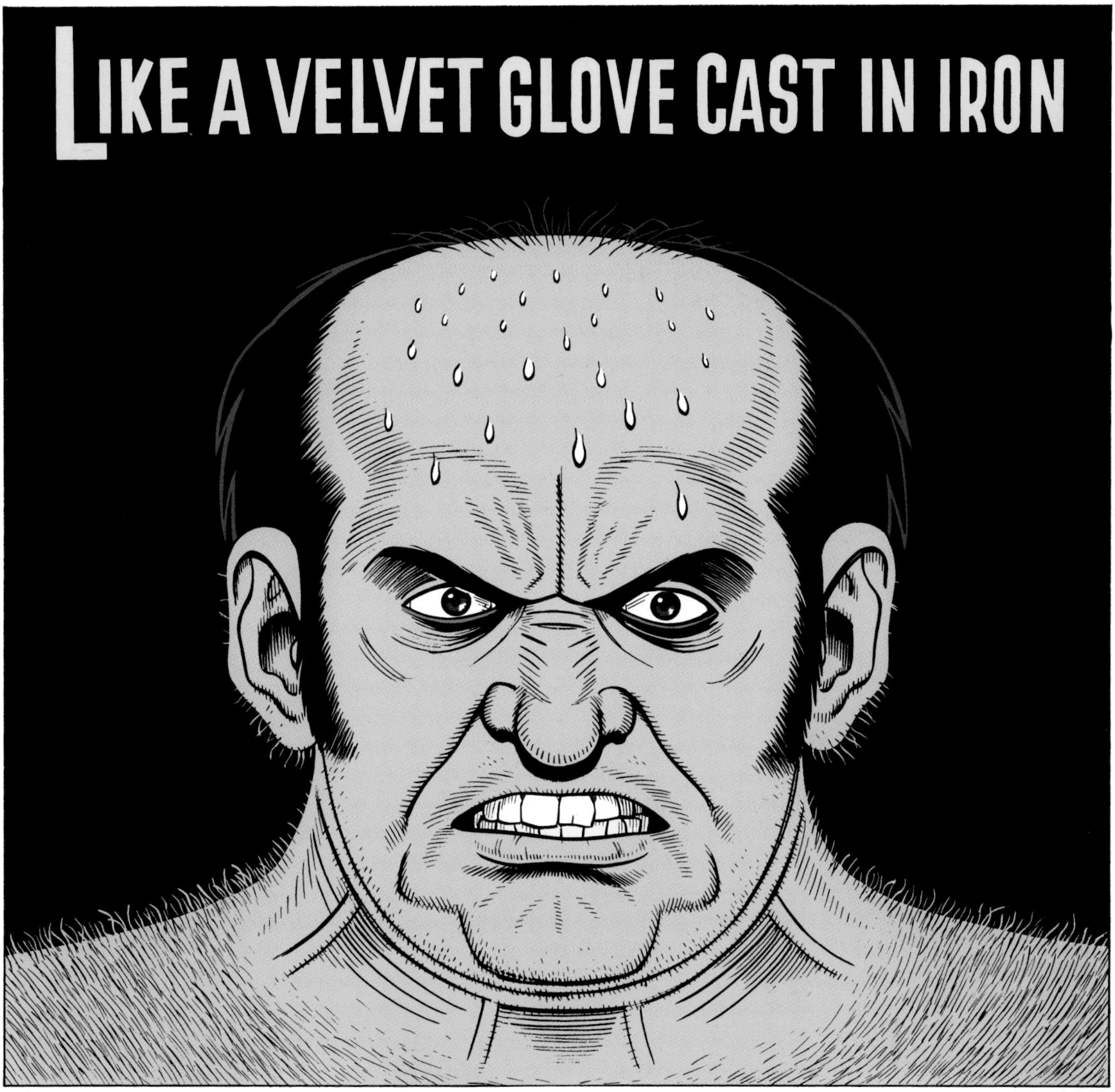
LIKE A VELVET GLOVE CAST IN IRON

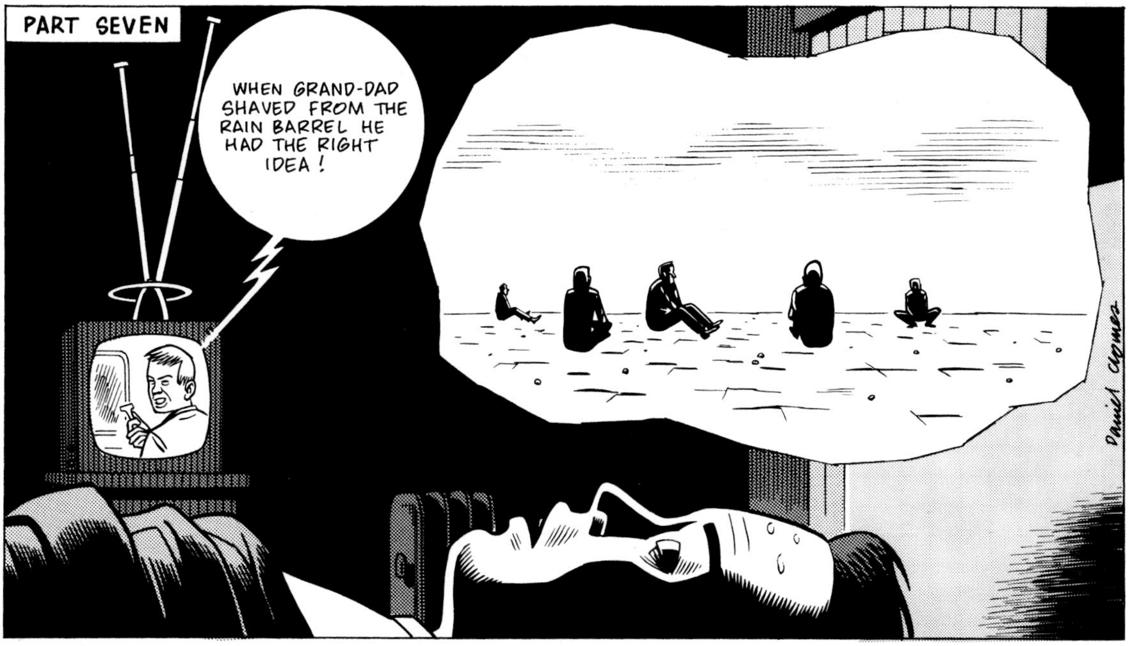
PART SEVEN
WHEN GRAND-DAD SHAVED FROM THE RAIN BARREL HE HAD THE RIGHT IDEA!
Daniel Clowes

Eightball #7, November, 1991. *Eightball* is published thrice yearly by Fantagraphics Books, Inc., and is copyright © 1991 Fantagraphics Books, Inc. All characters, stories, and art © 1991 Daniel Clowes. No part of this magazine may be reproduced without written permission from Fantagraphics Books or Daniel Clowes. No similarity between any of the names, characters, persons, and institutions in *Eightball* and those of any living or dead persons is intended (except for satirical intent), and any such similarity that may exist is purely coincidental. Letters to *Eightball* become the property of the magazine and are assumed intended for publication in whole or in part, and may therefore be used for those purposes. First printing: November, 1991. Fantagraphics Books, 7563 Lake City Way Northeast, Seattle WA 98115. PRINTED IN THE U.S.A.

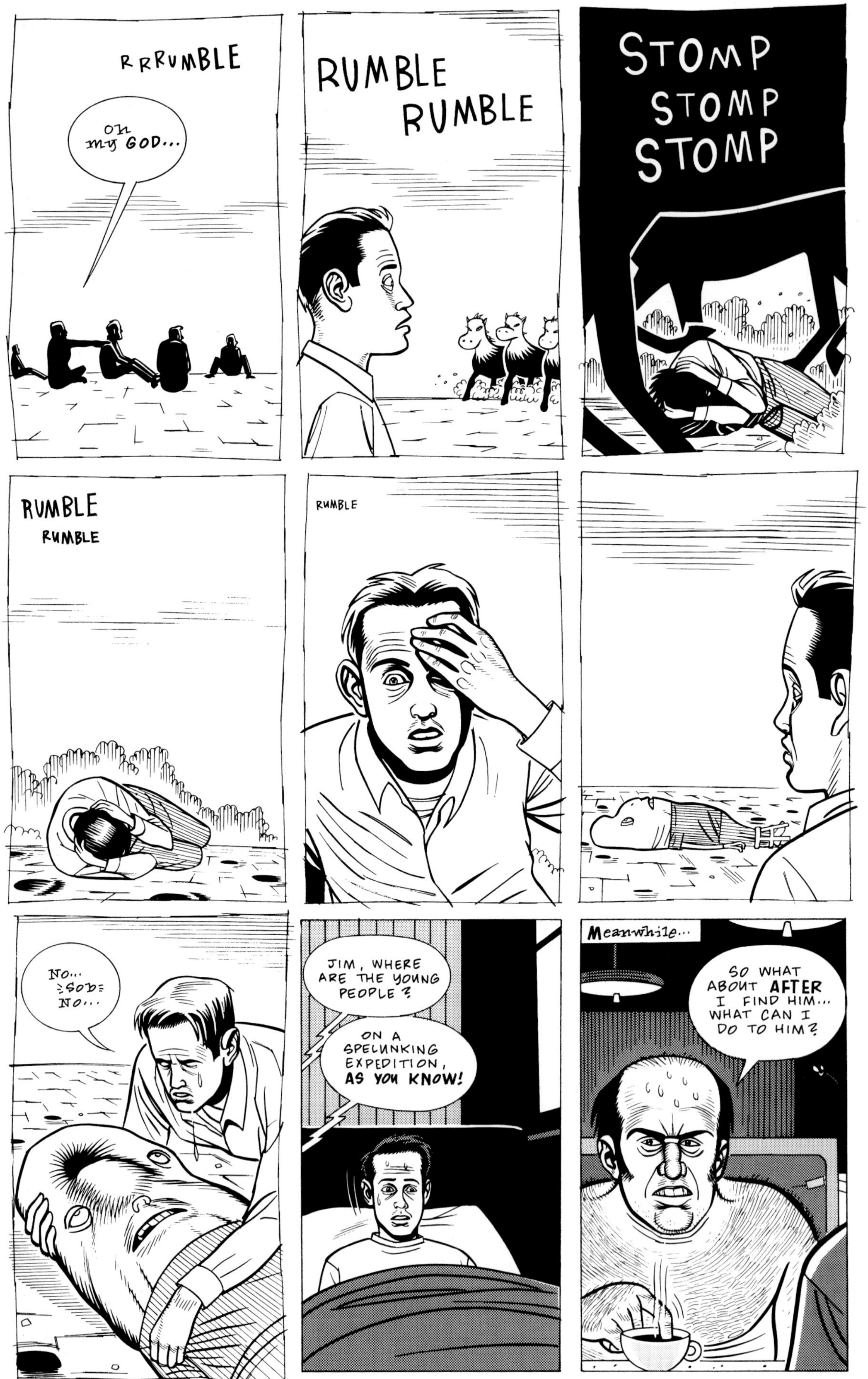
RRRUMBLE
OH MY GOD...
RUMBLE RUMBLE
STOMP STOMP STOMP
RUMBLE RUMBLE
RUMBLE
NO... SOB NO...
JIM, WHERE ARE THE YOUNG PEOPLE?
ON A SPELUNKING EXPEDITION, AS YOU KNOW!
Meanwhile...
SO WHAT ABOUT AFTER I FIND HIM... WHAT CAN I DO TO HIM?

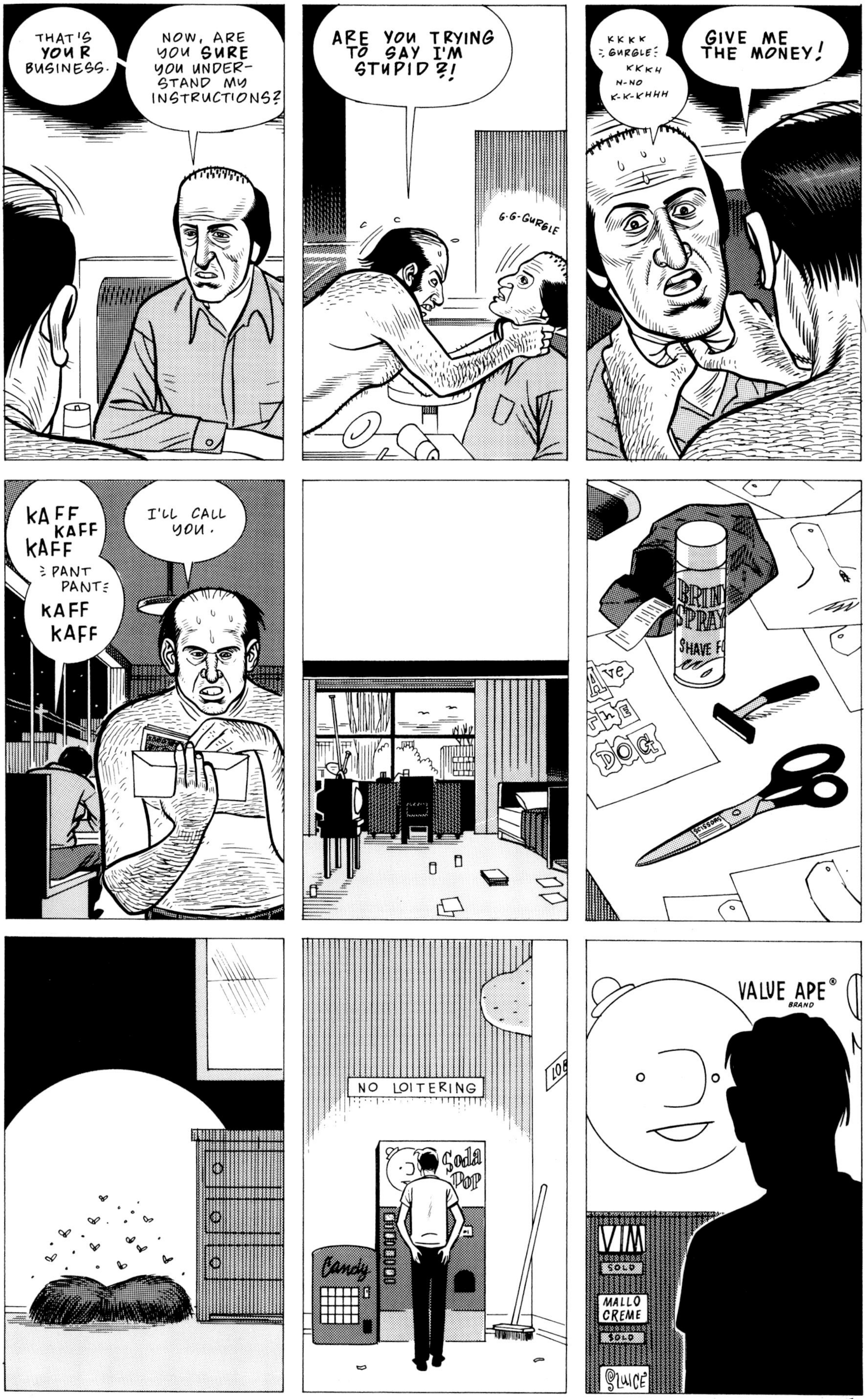
THAT'S YOUR BUSINESS.
NOW, ARE YOU SURE YOU UNDERSTAND MY INSTRUCTIONS?
ARE YOU TRYING TO SAY I'M STUPID?!
G-G-GURGLE
KKKK GURGLE KKKH N-NO K-K-KHHH
GIVE ME THE MONEY!
KAFF KAFF KAFF PANT PANT KAFF KAFF
I'LL CALL YOU.
SHAVE
THE DOG
SCISSORS
NO LOITERING
Soda Pop
Candy
VALUE APE® BRAND
VIM
SOLD
MALLO CREME
SOLD
SLUICE

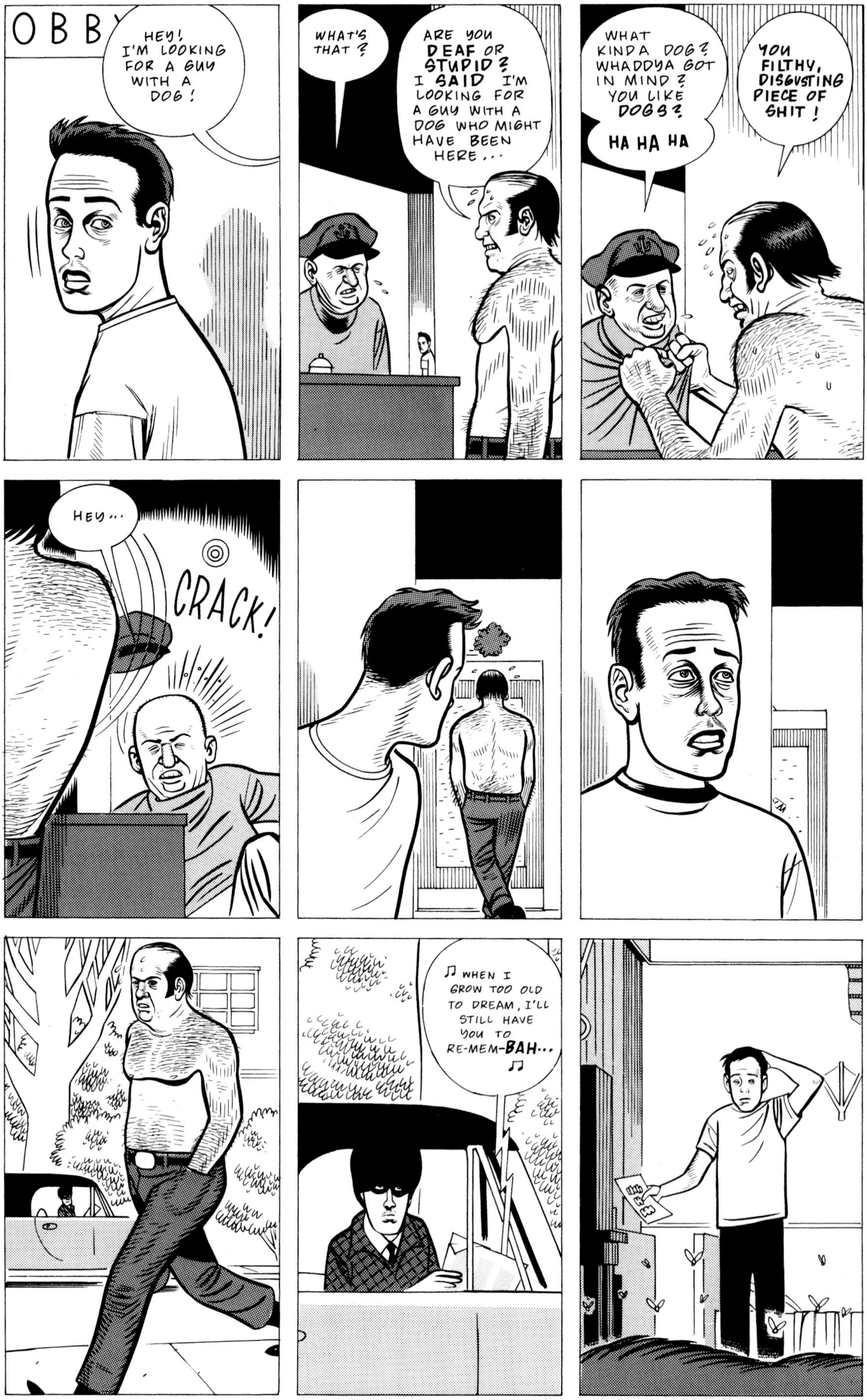
OBBY
HEY! I'M LOOKING FOR A GUY WITH A DOG!
WHAT'S THAT?
ARE YOU DEAF OR STUPID? I SAID I'M LOOKING FOR A GUY WITH A DOG WHO MIGHT HAVE BEEN HERE...
WHAT KINDA DOG? WHADDYA GOT IN MIND? YOU LIKE DOGS?
HA HA HA
YOU FILTHY, DISGUSTING PIECE OF SHIT!
HEY...
CRACK!
♫ WHEN I GROW TOO OLD TO DREAM, I'LL STILL HAVE YOU TO RE-MEM-BAH... ♫

CLLLIP!
MYST
♫ YOUAH LOVE WILL LIVE IN MY HAAAHT... ♫
1000
S
♫ GIRL OF MY DREAMS I LOVE YOU, HONEST I DO... ♫
MYS
Sometime later...
52
1000
S

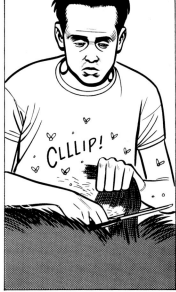

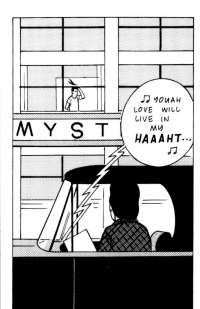

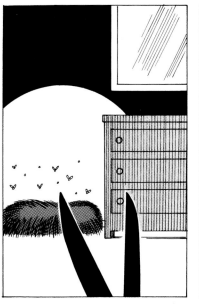

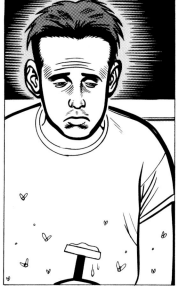

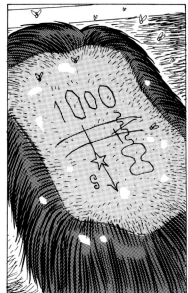

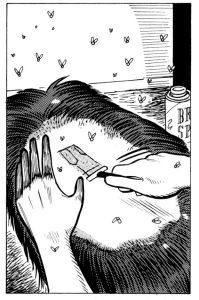

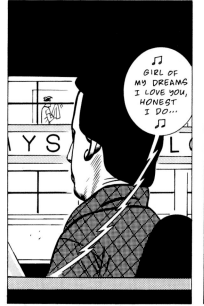

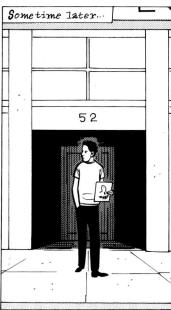

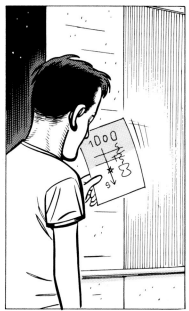

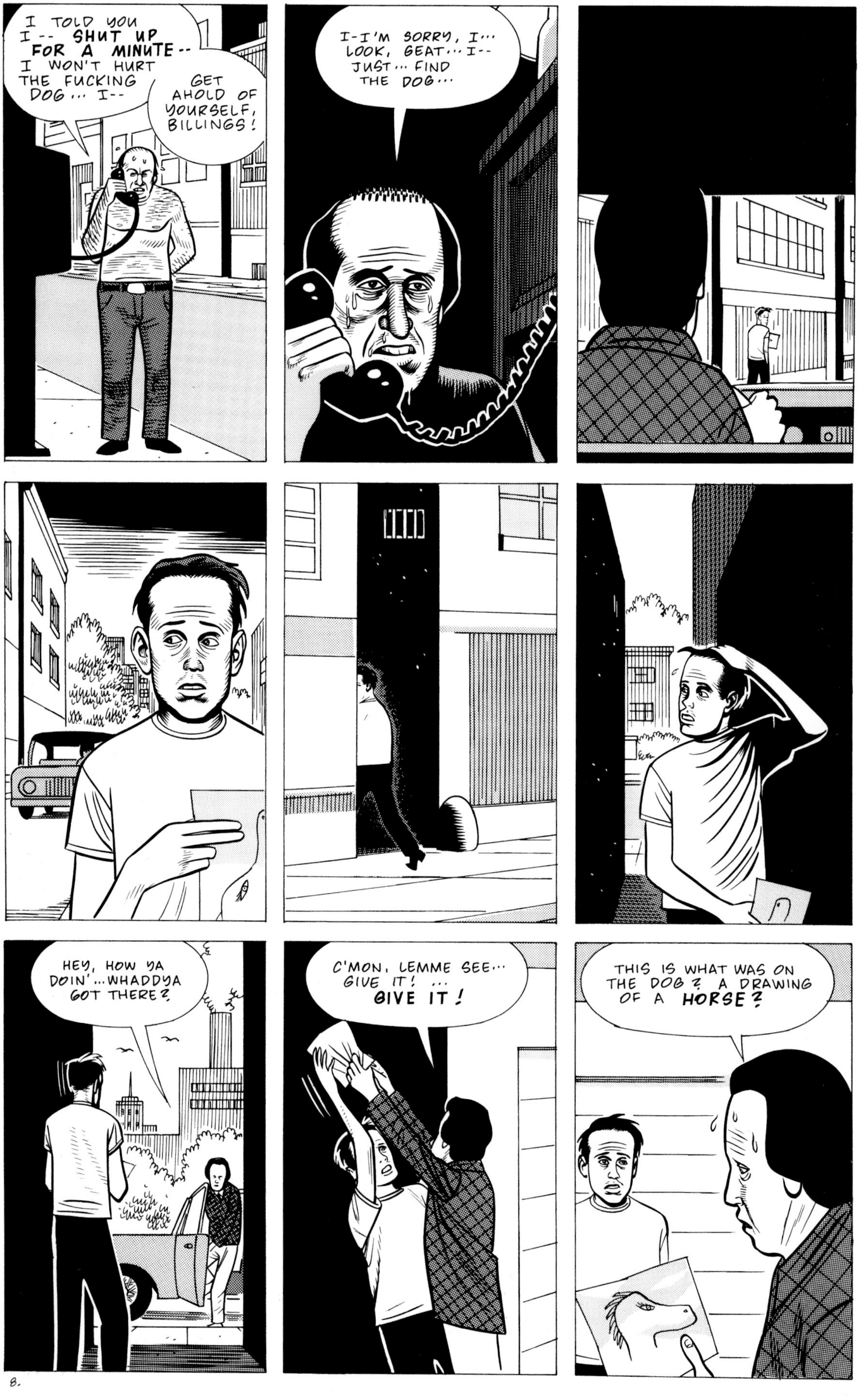
I TOLD YOU I -- SHUT UP FOR A MINUTE -- I WON'T HURT THE FUCKING DOG... I--
GET AHOLD OF YOURSELF, BILLINGS!
I-I'M SORRY, I... LOOK, GEAT... I-- JUST... FIND THE DOG...
HEY, HOW YA DOIN'...WHADDYA GOT THERE?
C'MON, LEMME SEE... GIVE IT! ... GIVE IT!
THIS IS WHAT WAS ON THE DOG? A DRAWING OF A HORSE?

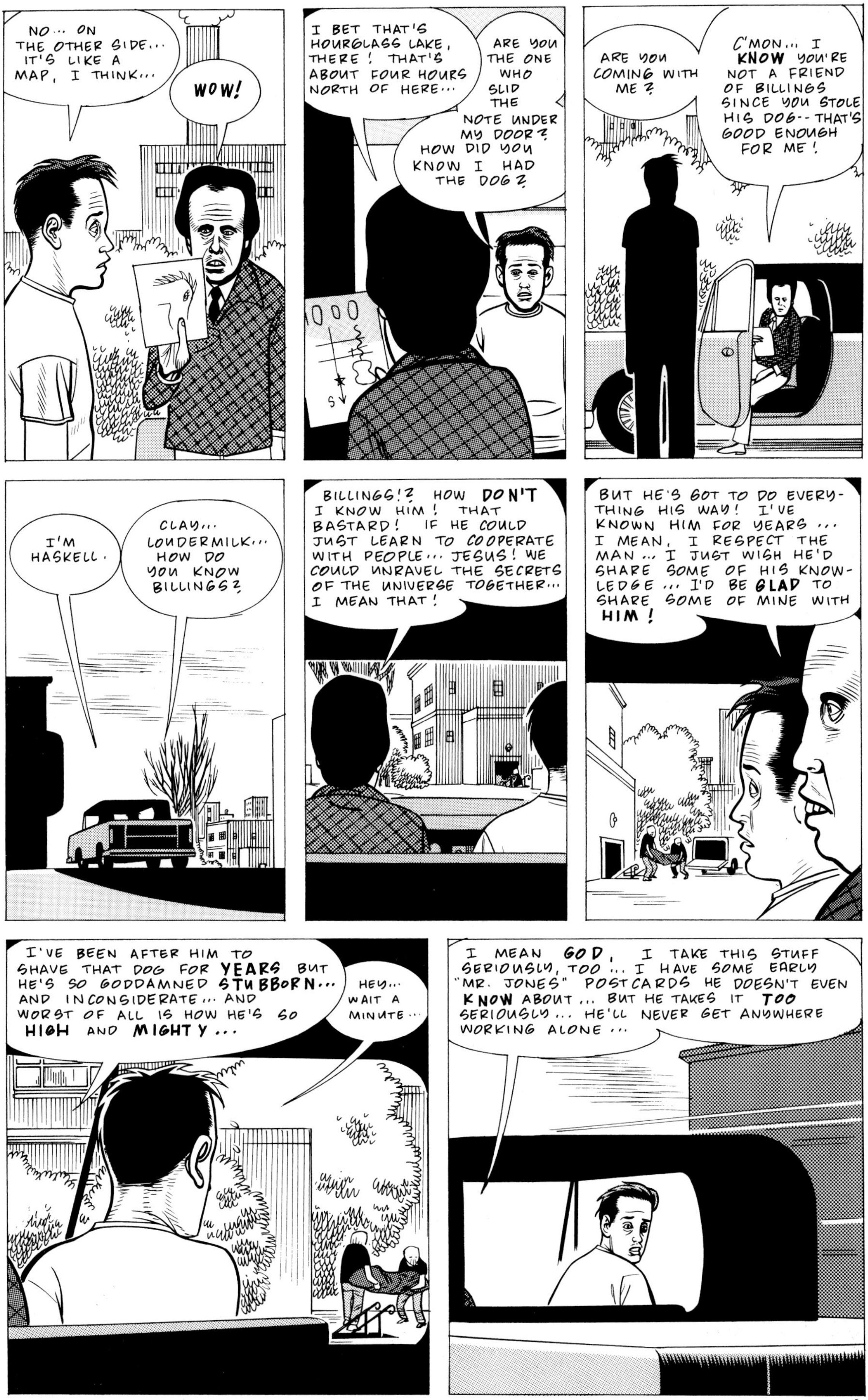
NO... ON THE OTHER SIDE... IT'S LIKE A MAP, I THINK...
WOW!
I BET THAT'S HOURGLASS LAKE, THERE! THAT'S ABOUT FOUR HOURS NORTH OF HERE...
ARE YOU THE ONE WHO SLID THE NOTE UNDER MY DOOR? HOW DID YOU KNOW I HAD THE DOG?
S
ARE YOU COMING WITH ME?
C'MON... I KNOW YOU'RE NOT A FRIEND OF BILLINGS SINCE YOU STOLE HIS DOG-- THAT'S GOOD ENOUGH FOR ME!
I'M HASKELL.
CLAY... LOUDERMILK... HOW DO YOU KNOW BILLINGS?
BILLINGS!? HOW DON'T I KNOW HIM! THAT BASTARD! IF HE COULD JUST LEARN TO COOPERATE WITH PEOPLE... JESUS! WE COULD UNRAVEL THE SECRETS OF THE UNIVERSE TOGETHER... I MEAN THAT!
BUT HE'S GOT TO DO EVERYTHING HIS WAY! I'VE KNOWN HIM FOR YEARS... I MEAN, I RESPECT THE MAN... I JUST WISH HE'D SHARE SOME OF HIS KNOWLEDGE... I'D BE GLAD TO SHARE SOME OF MINE WITH HIM!
I'VE BEEN AFTER HIM TO SHAVE THAT DOG FOR YEARS BUT HE'S SO GODDAMNED STUBBORN... AND INCONSIDERATE... AND WORST OF ALL IS HOW HE'S SO HIGH AND MIGHTY...
HEY... WAIT A MINUTE...
I MEAN GOD, I TAKE THIS STUFF SERIOUSLY, TOO... I HAVE SOME EARLY "MR. JONES" POSTCARDS HE DOESN'T EVEN KNOW ABOUT... BUT HE TAKES IT TOO SERIOUSLY... HE'LL NEVER GET ANYWHERE WORKING ALONE...

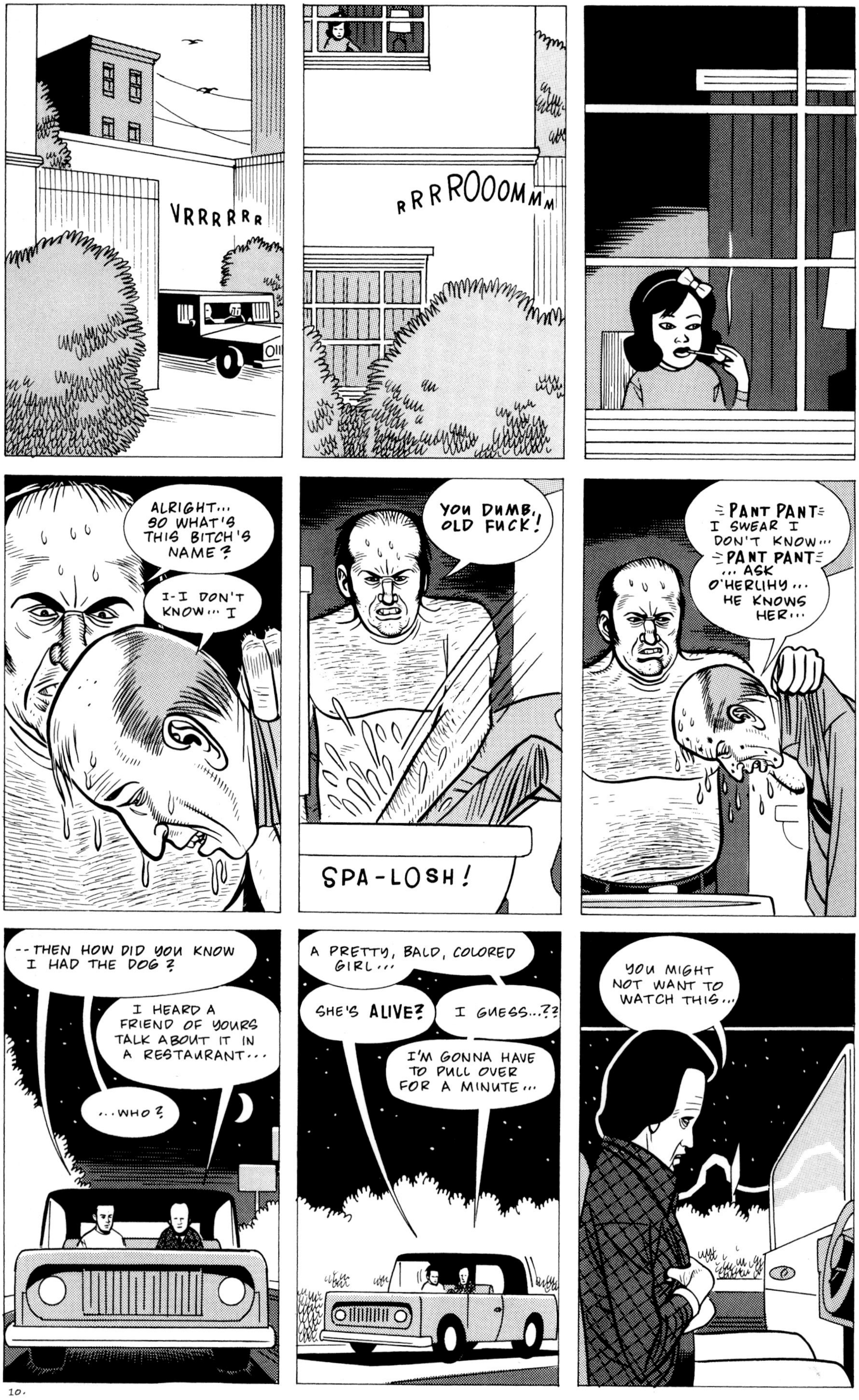
VRRRRRR
rRRROOOMMM
ALRIGHT... SO WHAT'S THIS BITCH'S NAME?
I-I DON'T KNOW... I
YOU DUMB, OLD FUCK!
SPA-LOSH!
PANT PANT I SWEAR I DON'T KNOW... PANT PANT ... ASK O'HERLIHY... HE KNOWS HER...
--THEN HOW DID YOU KNOW I HAD THE DOG?
I HEARD A FRIEND OF YOURS TALK ABOUT IT IN A RESTAURANT...
...WHO?
A PRETTY, BALD, COLORED GIRL...
SHE'S ALIVE?
I GUESS...??
I'M GONNA HAVE TO PULL OVER FOR A MINUTE...
YOU MIGHT NOT WANT TO WATCH THIS...

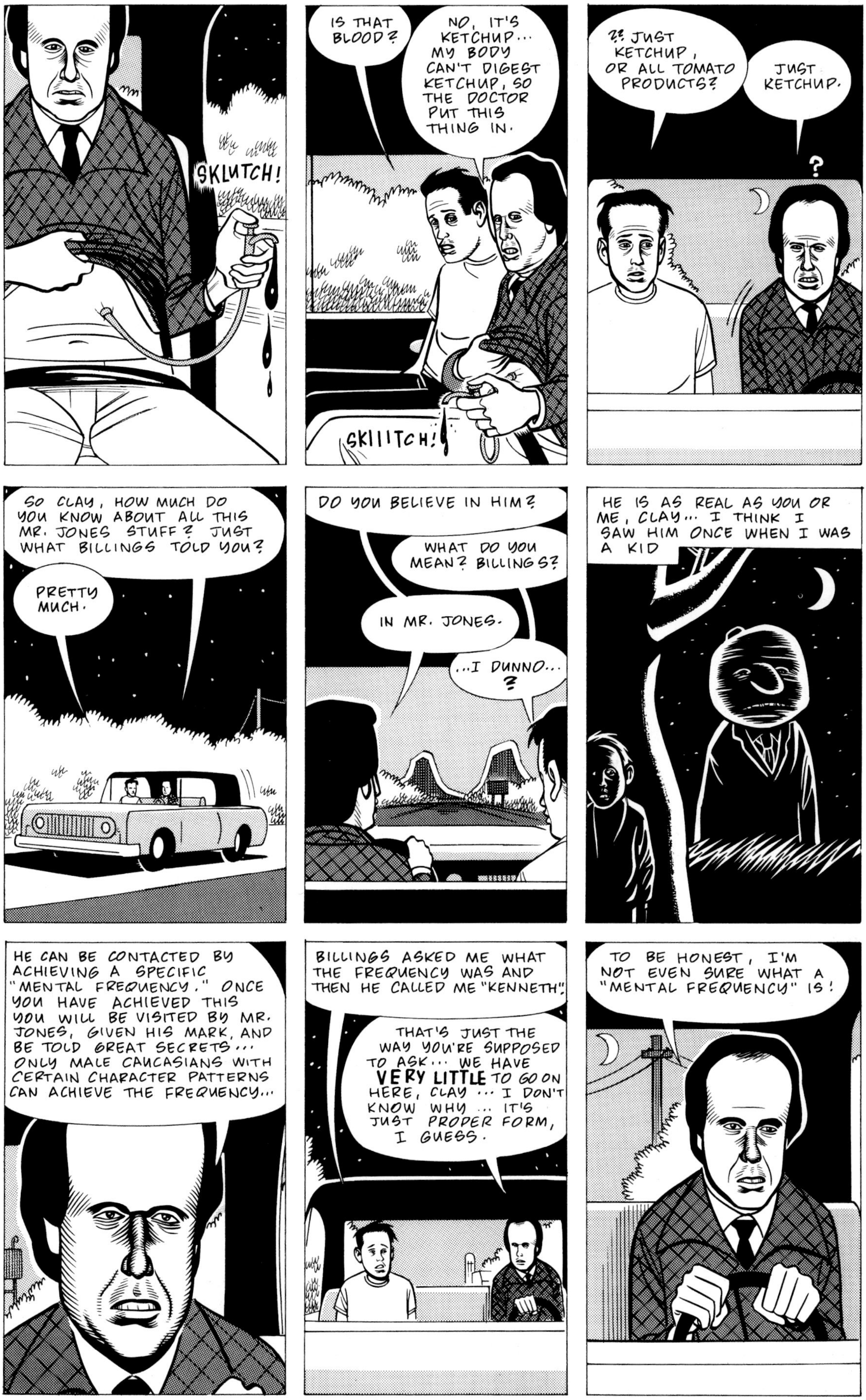
SKLUTCH!
IS THAT BLOOD?
NO, IT'S KETCHUP... MY BODY CAN'T DIGEST KETCHUP, SO THE DOCTOR PUT THIS THING IN.
SKIIITCH!
?? JUST KETCHUP, OR ALL TOMATO PRODUCTS?
JUST KETCHUP.
?
SO CLAY, HOW MUCH DO YOU KNOW ABOUT ALL THIS MR. JONES STUFF? JUST WHAT BILLINGS TOLD YOU?
PRETTY MUCH.
DO YOU BELIEVE IN HIM?
WHAT DO YOU MEAN? BILLINGS?
IN MR. JONES.
...I DUNNO...
?
HE IS AS REAL AS YOU OR ME, CLAY... I THINK I SAW HIM ONCE WHEN I WAS A KID
HE CAN BE CONTACTED BY ACHIEVING A SPECIFIC "MENTAL FREQUENCY." ONCE YOU HAVE ACHIEVED THIS YOU WILL BE VISITED BY MR. JONES, GIVEN HIS MARK, AND BE TOLD GREAT SECRETS... ONLY MALE CAUCASIANS WITH CERTAIN CHARACTER PATTERNS CAN ACHIEVE THE FREQUENCY...
BILLINGS ASKED ME WHAT THE FREQUENCY WAS AND THEN HE CALLED ME "KENNETH".
THAT'S JUST THE WAY YOU'RE SUPPOSED TO ASK... WE HAVE VERY LITTLE TO GO ON HERE, CLAY... I DON'T KNOW WHY... IT'S JUST PROPER FORM, I GUESS.
TO BE HONEST, I'M NOT EVEN SURE WHAT A "MENTAL FREQUENCY" IS!

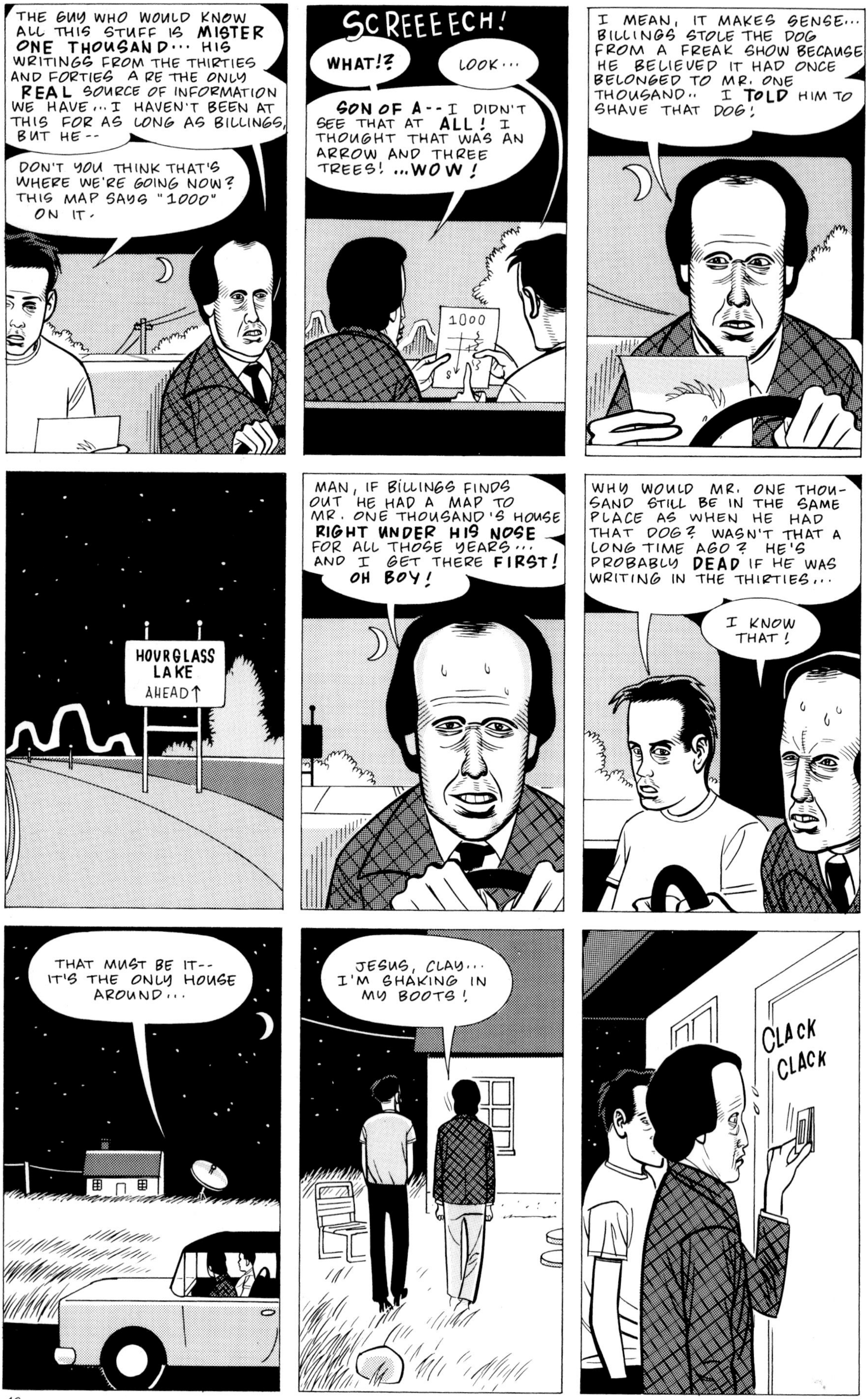
THE GUY WHO WOULD KNOW ALL THIS STUFF IS MISTER ONE THOUSAND... HIS WRITINGS FROM THE THIRTIES AND FORTIES ARE THE ONLY REAL SOURCE OF INFORMATION WE HAVE... I HAVEN'T BEEN AT THIS FOR AS LONG AS BILLINGS, BUT HE--
DON'T YOU THINK THAT'S WHERE WE'RE GOING NOW? THIS MAP SAYS "1000" ON IT.
SCREEEECH!
WHAT!?
LOOK...
SON OF A--I DIDN'T SEE THAT AT ALL! I THOUGHT THAT WAS AN ARROW AND THREE TREES! ...WOW!
1000
I MEAN, IT MAKES SENSE... BILLINGS STOLE THE DOG FROM A FREAK SHOW BECAUSE HE BELIEVED IT HAD ONCE BELONGED TO MR. ONE THOUSAND.. I TOLD HIM TO SHAVE THAT DOG!
HOURGLASS LAKE AHEAD ↑
MAN, IF BILLINGS FINDS OUT HE HAD A MAP TO MR. ONE THOUSAND'S HOUSE RIGHT UNDER HIS NOSE FOR ALL THOSE YEARS... AND I GET THERE FIRST! OH BOY!
WHY WOULD MR. ONE THOUSAND STILL BE IN THE SAME PLACE AS WHEN HE HAD THAT DOG? WASN'T THAT A LONG TIME AGO? HE'S PROBABLY DEAD IF HE WAS WRITING IN THE THIRTIES...
I KNOW THAT!
THAT MUST BE IT--IT'S THE ONLY HOUSE AROUND...
JESUS, CLAY... I'M SHAKING IN MY BOOTS!
CLACK CLACK

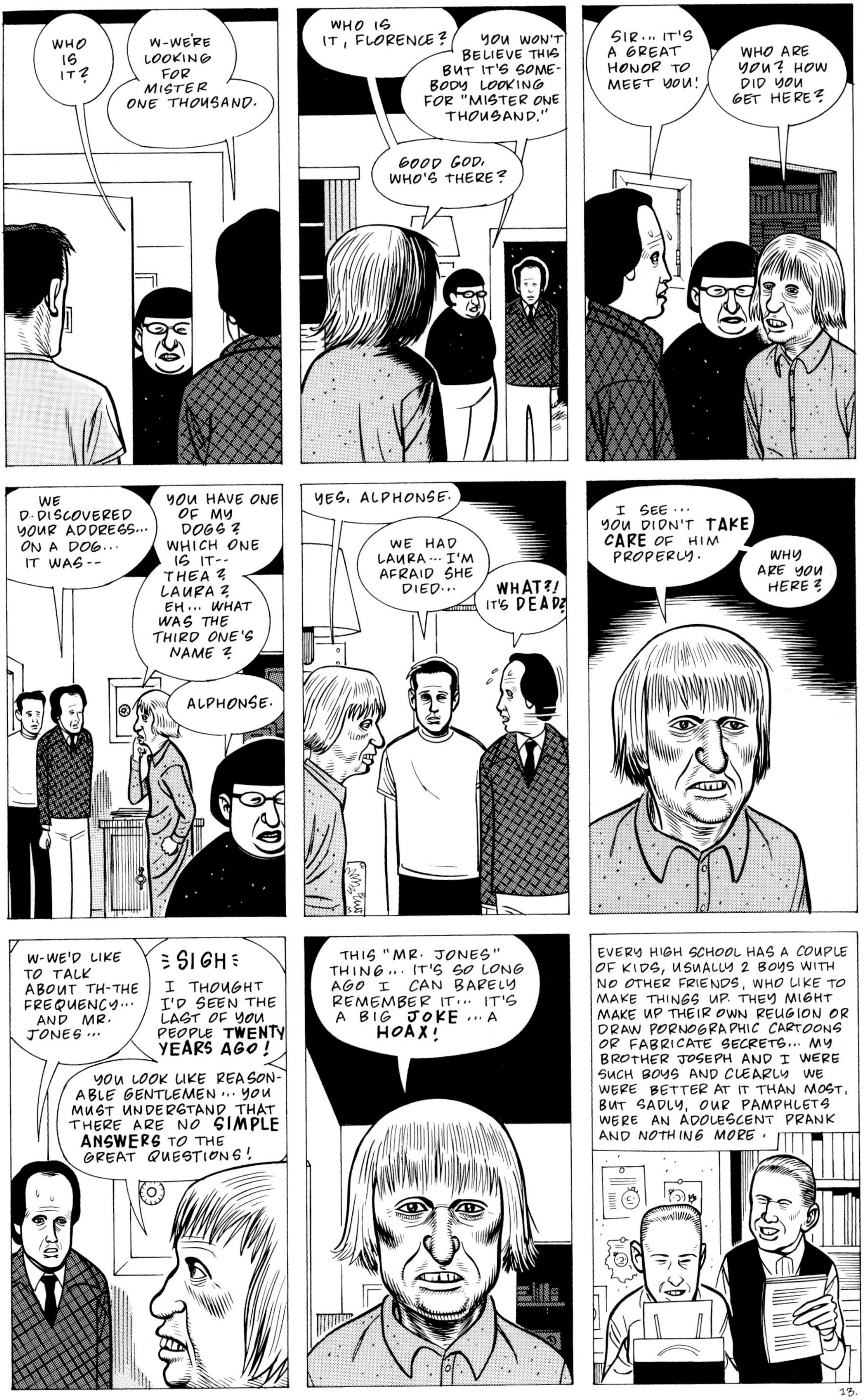
WHO IS IT?
W-WE'RE LOOKING FOR MISTER ONE THOUSAND.
WHO IS IT, FLORENCE?
YOU WON'T BELIEVE THIS BUT IT'S SOMEBODY LOOKING FOR "MISTER ONE THOUSAND."
GOOD GOD, WHO'S THERE?
SIR... IT'S A GREAT HONOR TO MEET YOU!
WHO ARE YOU? HOW DID YOU GET HERE?
WE D-DISCOVERED YOUR ADDRESS... ON A DOG... IT WAS--
YOU HAVE ONE OF MY DOGS? WHICH ONE IS IT-- THEA? LAURA? EH... WHAT WAS THE THIRD ONE'S NAME?
ALPHONSE.
YES, ALPHONSE.
WE HAD LAURA... I'M AFRAID SHE DIED...
WHAT?! IT'S DEAD?
I SEE... YOU DIDN'T TAKE CARE OF HIM PROPERLY.
WHY ARE YOU HERE?
W-WE'D LIKE TO TALK ABOUT TH-THE FREQUENCY... AND MR. JONES...
SIGH
I THOUGHT I'D SEEN THE LAST OF YOU PEOPLE TWENTY YEARS AGO!
YOU LOOK LIKE REASONABLE GENTLEMEN... YOU MUST UNDERSTAND THAT THERE ARE NO SIMPLE ANSWERS TO THE GREAT QUESTIONS!
THIS "MR. JONES" THING... IT'S SO LONG AGO I CAN BARELY REMEMBER IT... IT'S A BIG JOKE... A HOAX!
EVERY HIGH SCHOOL HAS A COUPLE OF KIDS, USUALLY 2 BOYS WITH NO OTHER FRIENDS, WHO LIKE TO MAKE THINGS UP. THEY MIGHT MAKE UP THEIR OWN RELIGION OR DRAW PORNOGRAPHIC CARTOONS OR FABRICATE SECRETS... MY BROTHER JOSEPH AND I WERE SUCH BOYS AND CLEARLY WE WERE BETTER AT IT THAN MOST. BUT SADLY, OUR PAMPHLETS WERE AN ADOLESCENT PRANK AND NOTHING MORE.

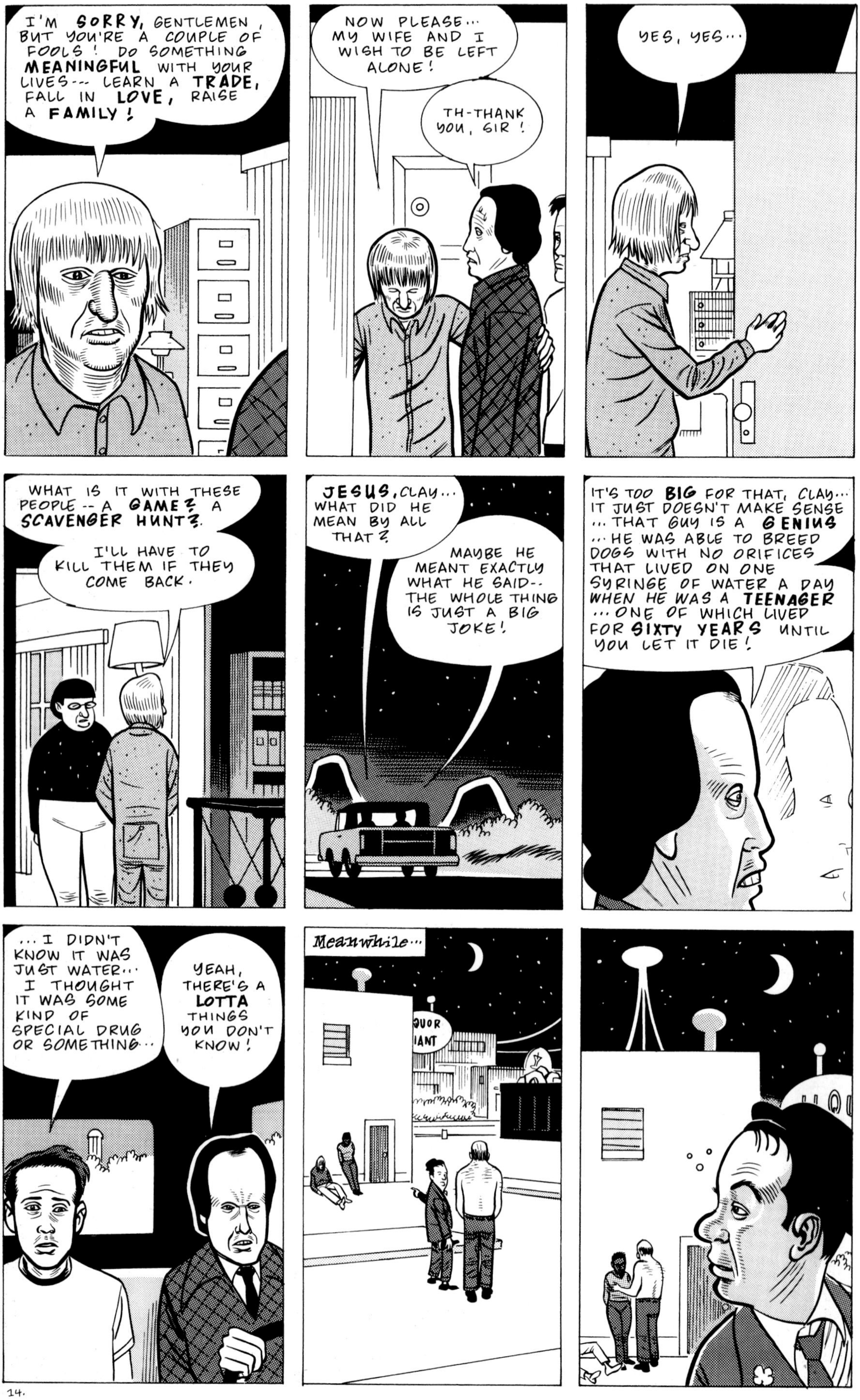

I'M SORRY, GENTLEMEN, BUT YOU'RE A COUPLE OF FOOLS! DO SOMETHING MEANINGFUL WITH YOUR LIVES--- LEARN A TRADE, FALL IN LOVE, RAISE A FAMILY!
NOW PLEASE... MY WIFE AND I WISH TO BE LEFT ALONE!
TH-THANK YOU, SIR!
YES, YES...
WHAT IS IT WITH THESE PEOPLE -- A GAME? A SCAVENGER HUNT?
I'LL HAVE TO KILL THEM IF THEY COME BACK.
JESUS, CLAY... WHAT DID HE MEAN BY ALL THAT?
MAYBE HE MEANT EXACTLY WHAT HE SAID-- THE WHOLE THING IS JUST A BIG JOKE!
IT'S TOO BIG FOR THAT, CLAY... IT JUST DOESN'T MAKE SENSE ... THAT GUY IS A GENIUS ... HE WAS ABLE TO BREED DOGS WITH NO ORIFICES THAT LIVED ON ONE SYRINGE OF WATER A DAY WHEN HE WAS A TEENAGER ... ONE OF WHICH LIVED FOR SIXTY YEARS UNTIL YOU LET IT DIE!
... I DIDN'T KNOW IT WAS JUST WATER... I THOUGHT IT WAS SOME KIND OF SPECIAL DRUG OR SOMETHING...
YEAH, THERE'S A LOTTA THINGS YOU DON'T KNOW!
Meanwhile...

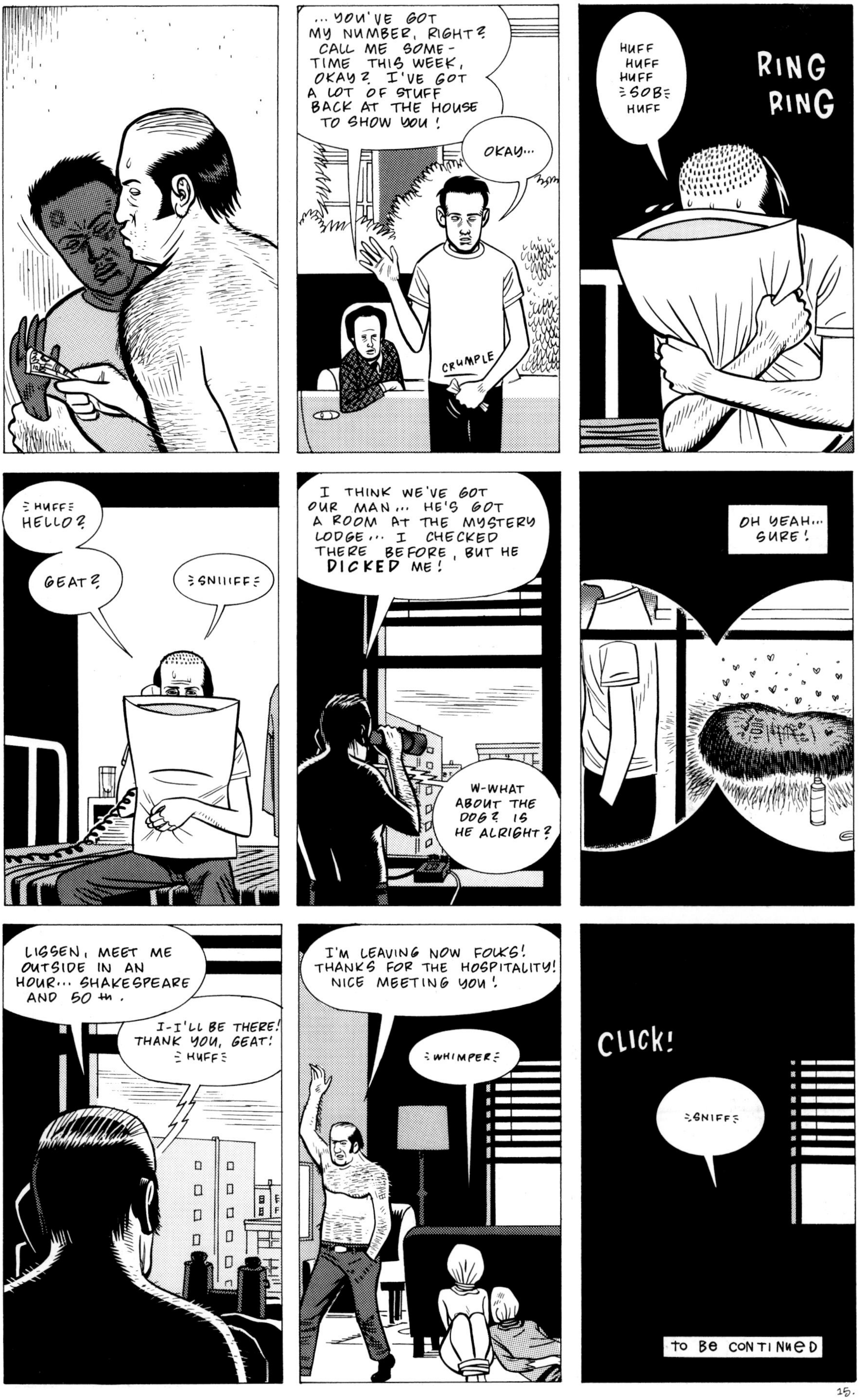
...YOU'VE GOT MY NUMBER, RIGHT? CALL ME SOME-TIME THIS WEEK, OKAY? I'VE GOT A LOT OF STUFF BACK AT THE HOUSE TO SHOW YOU!
OKAY...
CRUMPLE
HUFF HUFF HUFF =SOB= HUFF
RING RING
=HUFF= HELLO?
GEAT?
=SNIIIFF=
I THINK WE'VE GOT OUR MAN... HE'S GOT A ROOM AT THE MYSTERY LODGE... I CHECKED THERE BEFORE, BUT HE DICKED ME!
W-WHAT ABOUT THE DOG? IS HE ALRIGHT?
OH YEAH... SURE!
LISSEN, MEET ME OUTSIDE IN AN HOUR... SHAKESPEARE AND 50th.
I-I'LL BE THERE! THANK YOU, GEAT! =HUFF=
I'M LEAVING NOW FOLKS! THANKS FOR THE HOSPITALITY! NICE MEETING YOU!
=WHIMPER=
CLICK!
=SNIFF=
TO BE CONTINUED

ONE WAG TENDERS

write: EIGHTBALL
BOX 3357
CHICAGO, IL. 60654

BEFORE READING THIS LETTER COLUMN PLEASE OBSERVE ONE MINUTE OF SILENCE IN MEMORY OF THE GREAT MR. GEISEL -- Ed.

...My letter was sent back because I misread your lettering (the 5 looked like a 9). The same day I got the letter back I read in the COMICS JOURNAL that you were nominated for a Harvey award for lettering! In light of that bit you did with Nat Knudsen (8-B #6--Ed.) there's a double-irony!

Mike Parlette
Fair Oaks, Ca.

...Was wondering--is it Clowies or Close? Pussy, Peeoowsie or Poozee? ...Did I mention that you are a white male and I hate you?

Eva Schnellmeyer
Seattle, Wa.

...Your influence on the free art world is all-encompassing. Imagine my shock in discovering this German "Value Affen" advertisement...

James McNew
YO LA TENGO
Brooklyn, NY.

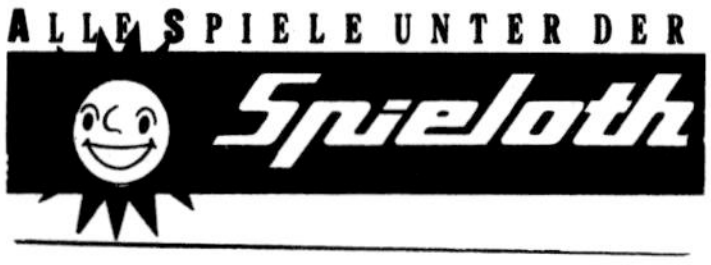

ALLE SPIELE UNTER DER
Spieloth

...Needless to say, I was quite surprised to see your work in a news mag. I certainly appreciate the effort you put into 8-BALL and I grieve that the pay isn't enough to keep your head above water but really, doing propaganda for a despot like Assad!

Joe Krois
College Pt, NY.

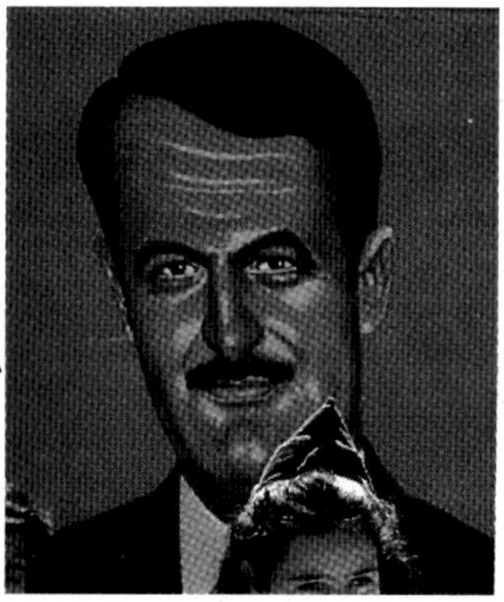

From INSIGHT magazine 8/5/91

NEW!

LOUT RAMPAGE!

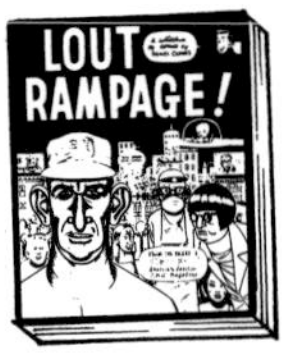

A righteous collection of Clowes comics from 8-BALL, BLAB, WEIRDO, NAT'L LAMPOON, VILLAGE VOICE, ETC.

$13.00 PPD.

EIGHTBALL #'s 1-7

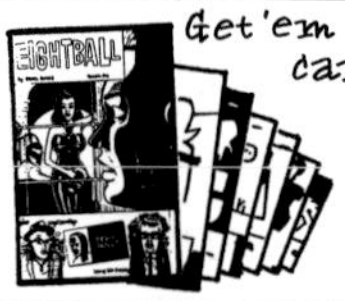

Get'em while you can or one day you'll ask "Why? Why? Oh dear God, why?"

$3.00 EA. PPD.

SUBSCRIPTION for 3 issues $7.00

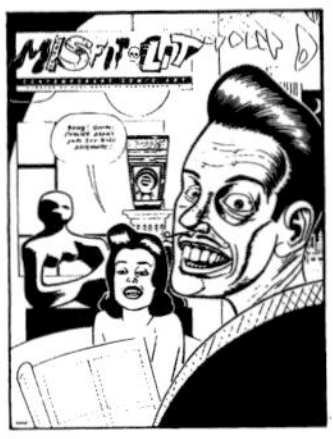

LTD. EDITION SILKSCREEN PRINT FOR

MISFIT LIT. SHOW

8-color print only 250 copies signed by the "artist"

$60.00 PPD.

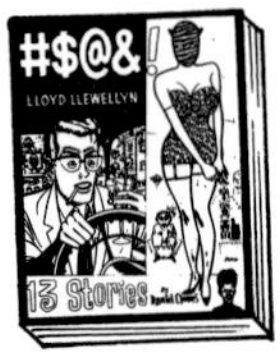

#$@&! THE LLOYD LLEWELLYN COLLECTION

contains many pages not available elsewhere so BUY IT!

$12.00 PPD.

CLOISONNÉ PIN

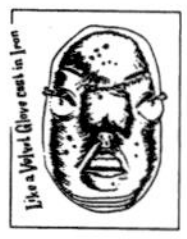

$9.00 EA. PPD.

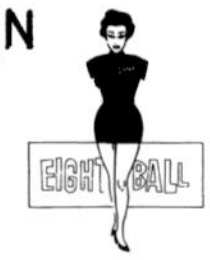

RUBBER STAMP

Are you a FRIEND or FOE of 8-BALL? Buy these items - you are my friend... otherwise, I call you FOE!

☐ Eightball #1 ☐ #2 ☐ #3 ☐ #4
☐ #5 ☐ #6 ☐ #7 ☐ Sub. to 8-Ball
☐ Lout Rampage! ☐ LLLL Collection
☐ Cloisonné Pin ☐ Rubber Stamp
☐ 8-Ball T-Shirt M L XL
☐ LLLL T-Shirt M L XL
☐ 8-Ball Mug ☐ Misfit Lit Print
☐ Velvet Glove Print

Send orders to:
FANTAGRAPHICS Books
7563 LAKE CITY WAY NE
SEATTLE, WA 98115

name ______

address ______

City ______ St. ______ Zip ______

Allow 6-8 weeks. Foreign orders add 10%. Call 1-800-657-1100

EIGHTBALL T-SHIRT

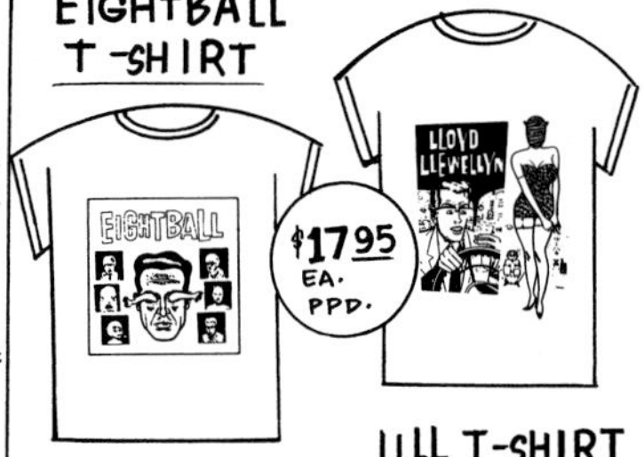

$17.95 EA. PPD.

LLLL T-SHIRT

Specify M, L or XL

EIGHTBALL MUG

You deserve to own this amazing, fully-functional item!

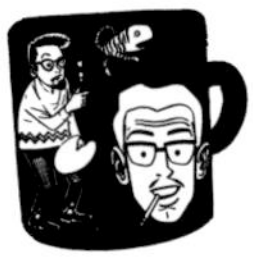

$12.00 PPD.

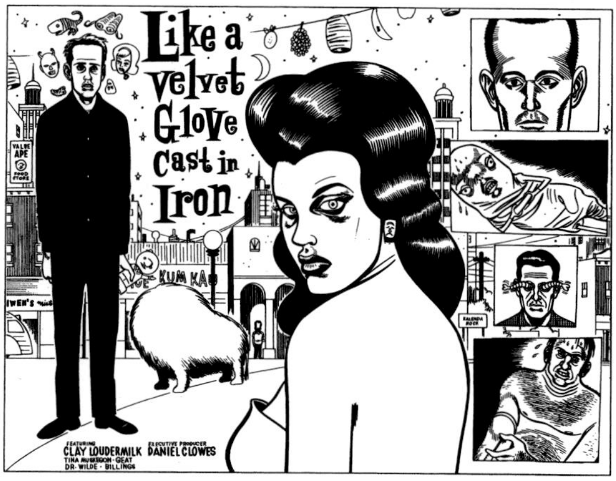

Like a Velvet Glove Cast in Iron
FEATURING CLAY LOUDERMILK TINA MUSKEGON-GEAT DR. WILDE · BILLINGS
EXECUTIVE PRODUCER DANIEL CLOWES

LIKE A VELVET GLOVE CAST IN IRON

10-color silkscreen print signed & #'d by D. Clowes

$80.00 PPD.

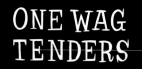

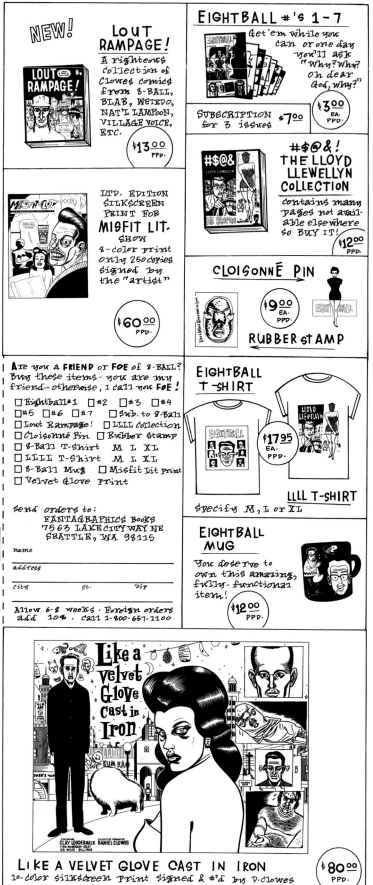

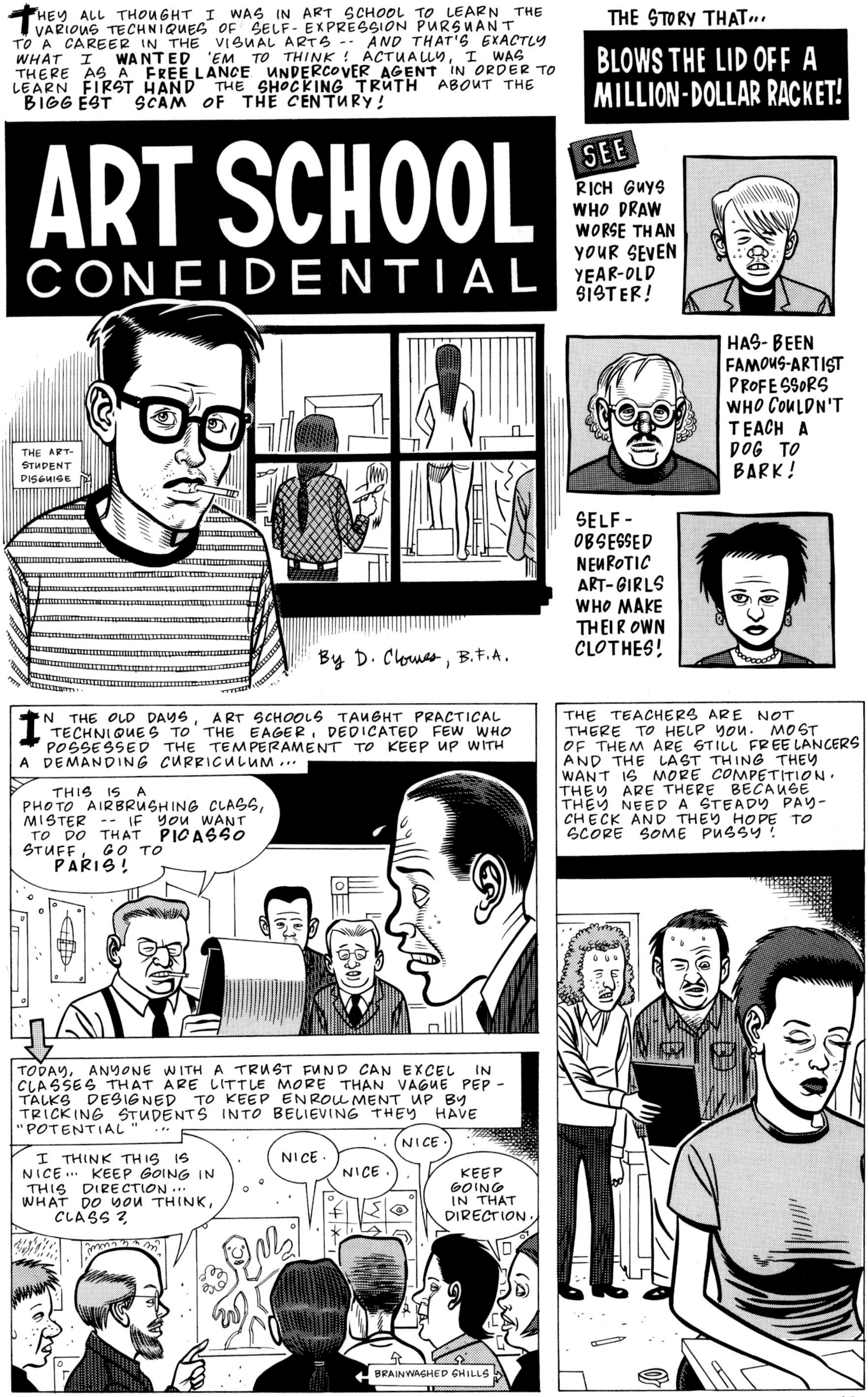

THEY ALL THOUGHT I WAS IN ART SCHOOL TO LEARN THE VARIOUS TECHNIQUES OF SELF-EXPRESSION PURSUANT TO A CAREER IN THE VISUAL ARTS -- AND THAT'S EXACTLY WHAT I WANTED 'EM TO THINK! ACTUALLY, I WAS THERE AS A FREELANCE UNDERCOVER AGENT IN ORDER TO LEARN FIRST HAND THE SHOCKING TRUTH ABOUT THE BIGGEST SCAM OF THE CENTURY!
THE STORY THAT...
BLOWS THE LID OFF A MILLION-DOLLAR RACKET!
ART SCHOOL CONFIDENTIAL
SEE
RICH GUYS WHO DRAW WORSE THAN YOUR SEVEN YEAR-OLD SISTER!
HAS-BEEN FAMOUS-ARTIST PROFESSORS WHO COULDN'T TEACH A DOG TO BARK!
SELF-OBSESSED NEUROTIC ART-GIRLS WHO MAKE THEIR OWN CLOTHES!
THE ART-STUDENT DISGUISE
By D. Clowes, B.F.A.
IN THE OLD DAYS, ART SCHOOLS TAUGHT PRACTICAL TECHNIQUES TO THE EAGER, DEDICATED FEW WHO POSSESSED THE TEMPERAMENT TO KEEP UP WITH A DEMANDING CURRICULUM...
THIS IS A PHOTO AIRBRUSHING CLASS, MISTER -- IF YOU WANT TO DO THAT PICASSO STUFF, GO TO PARIS!
TODAY, ANYONE WITH A TRUST FUND CAN EXCEL IN CLASSES THAT ARE LITTLE MORE THAN VAGUE PEP-TALKS DESIGNED TO KEEP ENROLLMENT UP BY TRICKING STUDENTS INTO BELIEVING THEY HAVE "POTENTIAL"...
I THINK THIS IS NICE... KEEP GOING IN THIS DIRECTION... WHAT DO YOU THINK, CLASS?
NICE.
NICE.
NICE.
KEEP GOING IN THAT DIRECTION.
BRAINWASHED SHILLS
THE TEACHERS ARE NOT THERE TO HELP YOU. MOST OF THEM ARE STILL FREELANCERS AND THE LAST THING THEY WANT IS MORE COMPETITION. THEY ARE THERE BECAUSE THEY NEED A STEADY PAY-CHECK AND THEY HOPE TO SCORE SOME PUSSY!

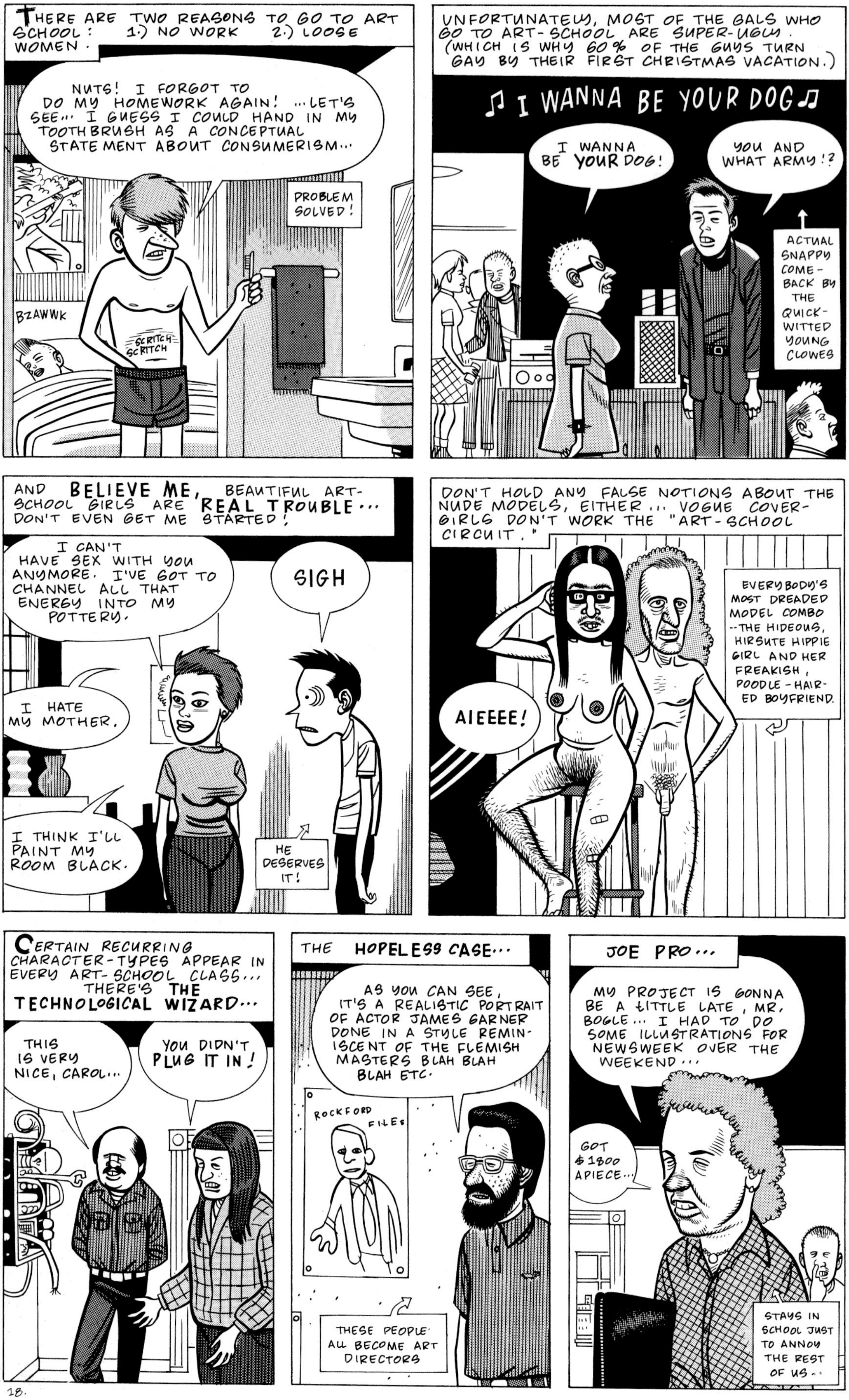
THERE ARE TWO REASONS TO GO TO ART SCHOOL: 1.) NO WORK 2.) LOOSE WOMEN.
NUTS! I FORGOT TO DO MY HOMEWORK AGAIN! ...LET'S SEE... I GUESS I COULD HAND IN MY TOOTHBRUSH AS A CONCEPTUAL STATEMENT ABOUT CONSUMERISM...
PROBLEM SOLVED!
BZAWWK
SCRITCH SCRITCH
UNFORTUNATELY, MOST OF THE GALS WHO GO TO ART-SCHOOL ARE SUPER-UGLY. (WHICH IS WHY 60% OF THE GUYS TURN GAY BY THEIR FIRST CHRISTMAS VACATION.)
♫ I WANNA BE YOUR DOG ♫
I WANNA BE YOUR DOG!
YOU AND WHAT ARMY!?
ACTUAL SNAPPY COME-BACK BY THE QUICK-WITTED YOUNG CLOWES
AND BELIEVE ME, BEAUTIFUL ART-SCHOOL GIRLS ARE REAL TROUBLE... DON'T EVEN GET ME STARTED!
I CAN'T HAVE SEX WITH YOU ANYMORE. I'VE GOT TO CHANNEL ALL THAT ENERGY INTO MY POTTERY.
SIGH
I HATE MY MOTHER.
I THINK I'LL PAINT MY ROOM BLACK.
HE DESERVES IT!
DON'T HOLD ANY FALSE NOTIONS ABOUT THE NUDE MODELS, EITHER... VOGUE COVER-GIRLS DON'T WORK THE "ART-SCHOOL CIRCUIT."
EVERYBODY'S MOST DREADED MODEL COMBO --THE HIDEOUS, HIRSUTE HIPPIE GIRL AND HER FREAKISH, POODLE-HAIRED BOYFRIEND.
AIEEEE!
CERTAIN RECURRING CHARACTER-TYPES APPEAR IN EVERY ART-SCHOOL CLASS... THERE'S THE TECHNOLOGICAL WIZARD...
THIS IS VERY NICE, CAROL...
YOU DIDN'T PLUG IT IN!
THE HOPELESS CASE...
AS YOU CAN SEE, IT'S A REALISTIC PORTRAIT OF ACTOR JAMES GARNER DONE IN A STYLE REMINISCENT OF THE FLEMISH MASTERS BLAH BLAH BLAH ETC.
ROCKFORD FILES
THESE PEOPLE ALL BECOME ART DIRECTORS
JOE PRO...
MY PROJECT IS GONNA BE A LITTLE LATE, MR. BOGLE... I HAD TO DO SOME ILLUSTRATIONS FOR NEWSWEEK OVER THE WEEKEND...
GOT $1800 APIECE...
STAYS IN SCHOOL JUST TO ANNOY THE REST OF US...

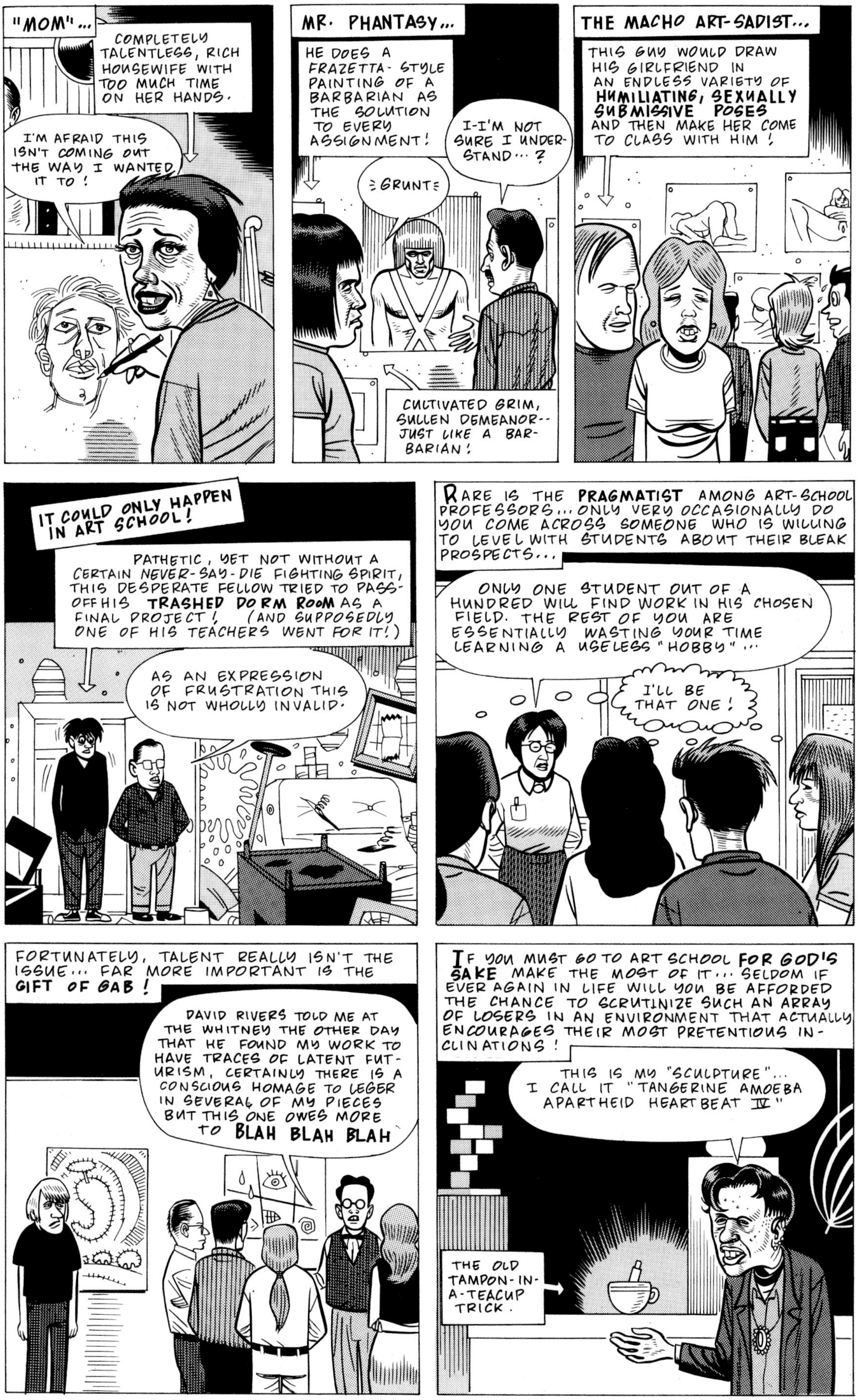
"MOM"...
COMPLETELY TALENTLESS, RICH HOUSEWIFE WITH TOO MUCH TIME ON HER HANDS.
I'M AFRAID THIS ISN'T COMING OUT THE WAY I WANTED IT TO!
MR. PHANTASY...
HE DOES A FRAZETTA-STYLE PAINTING OF A BARBARIAN AS THE SOLUTION TO EVERY ASSIGNMENT!
I-I'M NOT SURE I UNDERSTAND...?
GRUNT
CULTIVATED GRIM, SULLEN DEMEANOR-- JUST LIKE A BARBARIAN!
THE MACHO ART-SADIST...
THIS GUY WOULD DRAW HIS GIRLFRIEND IN AN ENDLESS VARIETY OF HUMILIATING, SEXUALLY SUBMISSIVE POSES AND THEN MAKE HER COME TO CLASS WITH HIM!
IT COULD ONLY HAPPEN IN ART SCHOOL!
PATHETIC, YET NOT WITHOUT A CERTAIN NEVER-SAY-DIE FIGHTING SPIRIT, THIS DESPERATE FELLOW TRIED TO PASS-OFF HIS TRASHED DORM ROOM AS A FINAL PROJECT! (AND SUPPOSEDLY ONE OF HIS TEACHERS WENT FOR IT!)
AS AN EXPRESSION OF FRUSTRATION THIS IS NOT WHOLLY INVALID.
RARE IS THE PRAGMATIST AMONG ART-SCHOOL PROFESSORS... ONLY VERY OCCASIONALLY DO YOU COME ACROSS SOMEONE WHO IS WILLING TO LEVEL WITH STUDENTS ABOUT THEIR BLEAK PROSPECTS...
ONLY ONE STUDENT OUT OF A HUNDRED WILL FIND WORK IN HIS CHOSEN FIELD. THE REST OF YOU ARE ESSENTIALLY WASTING YOUR TIME LEARNING A USELESS "HOBBY"...
I'LL BE THAT ONE!
FORTUNATELY, TALENT REALLY ISN'T THE ISSUE... FAR MORE IMPORTANT IS THE GIFT OF GAB!
DAVID RIVERS TOLD ME AT THE WHITNEY THE OTHER DAY THAT HE FOUND MY WORK TO HAVE TRACES OF LATENT FUTURISM, CERTAINLY THERE IS A CONSCIOUS HOMAGE TO LEGER IN SEVERAL OF MY PIECES BUT THIS ONE OWES MORE TO BLAH BLAH BLAH
IF YOU MUST GO TO ART SCHOOL FOR GOD'S SAKE MAKE THE MOST OF IT... SELDOM IF EVER AGAIN IN LIFE WILL YOU BE AFFORDED THE CHANCE TO SCRUTINIZE SUCH AN ARRAY OF LOSERS IN AN ENVIRONMENT THAT ACTUALLY ENCOURAGES THEIR MOST PRETENTIOUS INCLINATIONS!
THIS IS MY "SCULPTURE"... I CALL IT "TANGERINE AMOEBA APARTHEID HEARTBEAT IV"
THE OLD TAMPON-IN-A-TEACUP TRICK.

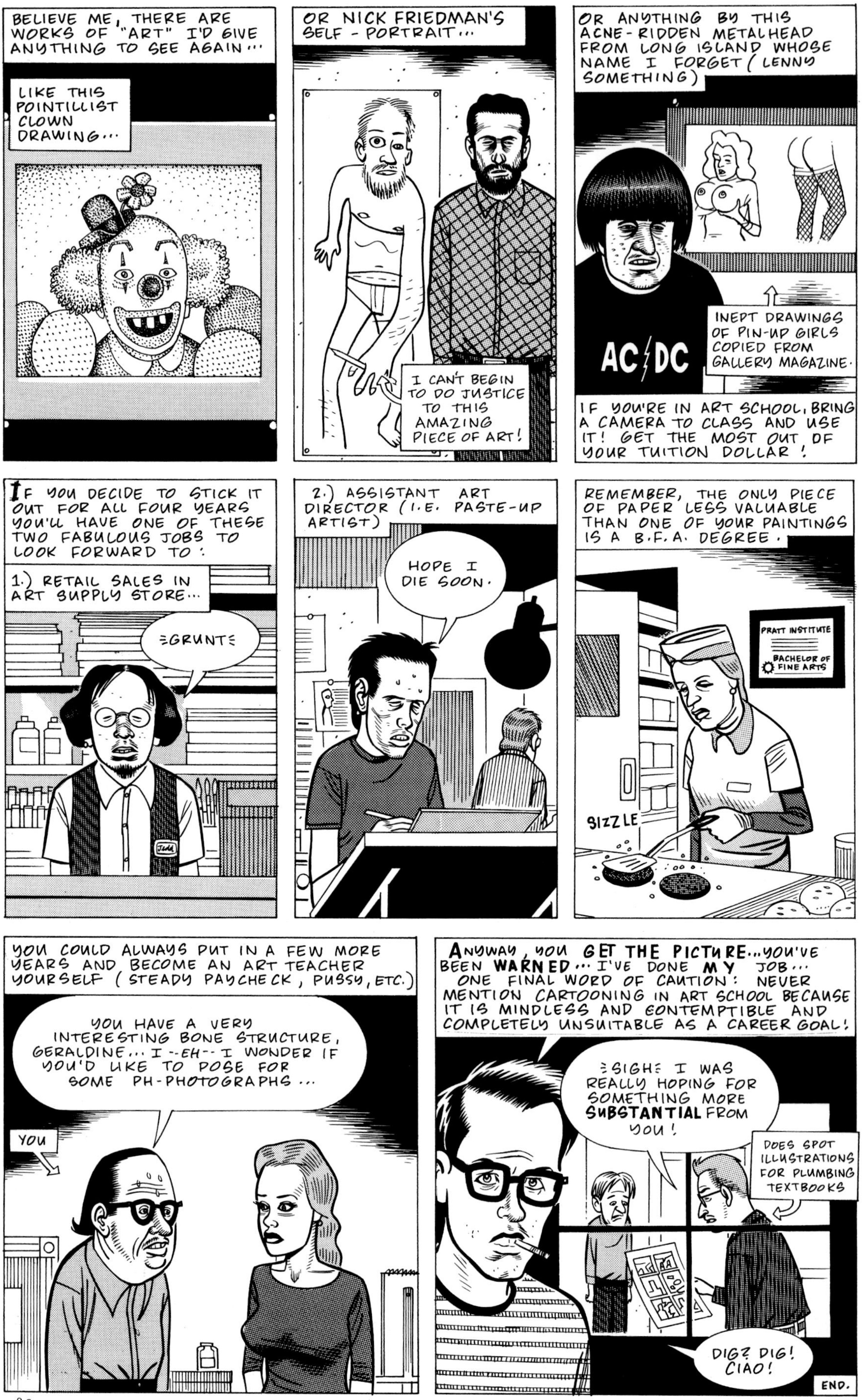

BELIEVE ME, THERE ARE WORKS OF "ART" I'D GIVE ANYTHING TO SEE AGAIN...
LIKE THIS POINTILLIST CLOWN DRAWING...
OR NICK FRIEDMAN'S SELF - PORTRAIT...
I CAN'T BEGIN TO DO JUSTICE TO THIS AMAZING PIECE OF ART!
OR ANYTHING BY THIS ACNE-RIDDEN METALHEAD FROM LONG ISLAND WHOSE NAME I FORGET (LENNY SOMETHING)
AC/DC
INEPT DRAWINGS OF PIN-UP GIRLS COPIED FROM GALLERY MAGAZINE.
IF YOU'RE IN ART SCHOOL, BRING A CAMERA TO CLASS AND USE IT! GET THE MOST OUT OF YOUR TUITION DOLLAR!
IF YOU DECIDE TO STICK IT OUT FOR ALL FOUR YEARS YOU'LL HAVE ONE OF THESE TWO FABULOUS JOBS TO LOOK FORWARD TO:
1.) RETAIL SALES IN ART SUPPLY STORE...
≡GRUNT≡
2.) ASSISTANT ART DIRECTOR (I.E. PASTE-UP ARTIST)
HOPE I DIE SOON.
REMEMBER, THE ONLY PIECE OF PAPER LESS VALUABLE THAN ONE OF YOUR PAINTINGS IS A B.F.A. DEGREE.
PRATT INSTITUTE
BACHELOR OF FINE ARTS
SIZZLE
YOU COULD ALWAYS PUT IN A FEW MORE YEARS AND BECOME AN ART TEACHER YOURSELF (STEADY PAYCHECK, PUSSY, ETC.)
YOU HAVE A VERY INTERESTING BONE STRUCTURE, GERALDINE... I --EH-- I WONDER IF YOU'D LIKE TO POSE FOR SOME PH-PHOTOGRAPHS...
YOU
ANYWAY, YOU GET THE PICTURE...YOU'VE BEEN WARNED... I'VE DONE MY JOB... ONE FINAL WORD OF CAUTION: NEVER MENTION CARTOONING IN ART SCHOOL BECAUSE IT IS MINDLESS AND CONTEMPTIBLE AND COMPLETELY UNSUITABLE AS A CAREER GOAL!
≡SIGH≡ I WAS REALLY HOPING FOR SOMETHING MORE SUBSTANTIAL FROM YOU!
DOES SPOT ILLUSTRATIONS FOR PLUMBING TEXTBOOKS
DIG? DIG! CIAO!
END.

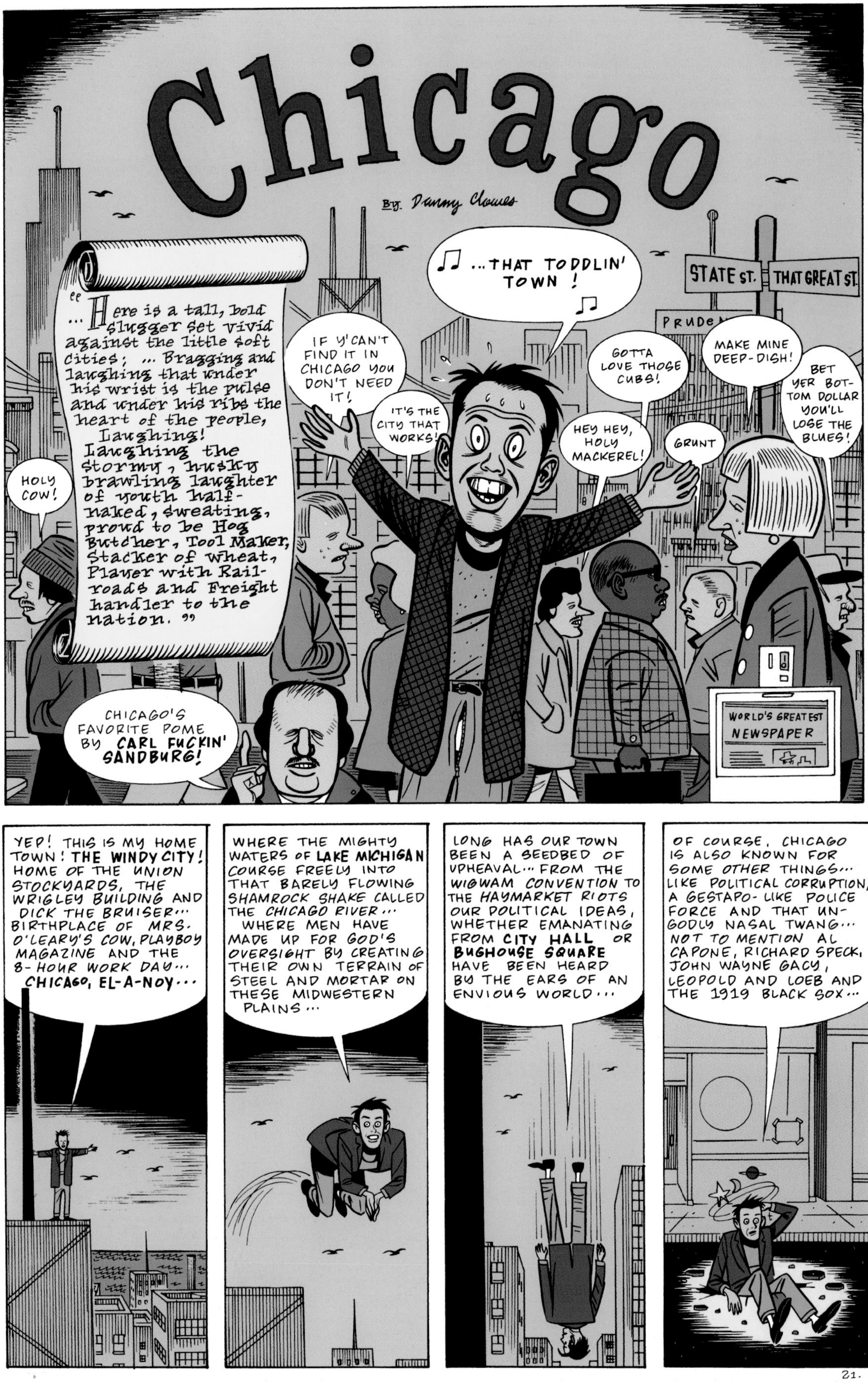
Chicago
By. Danny Clowes
"...Here is a tall, bold slugger set vivid against the little soft cities; ... Bragging and laughing that under his wrist is the pulse and under his ribs the heart of the people, Laughing! Laughing the stormy, husky brawling laughter of youth half-naked, sweating, proud to be Hog Butcher, Tool Maker, Stacker of wheat, Player with Railroads and Freight handler to the nation."
CHICAGO'S FAVORITE POME BY CARL FUCKIN' SANDBURG!
HOLY COW!
IF Y'CAN'T FIND IT IN CHICAGO YOU DON'T NEED IT!
IT'S THE CITY THAT WORKS!
♫ ...THAT TODDLIN' TOWN! ♫
STATE ST.
THAT GREAT ST.
PRUDEN
GOTTA LOVE THOSE CUBS!
HEY HEY, HOLY MACKEREL!
MAKE MINE DEEP-DISH!
GRUNT
BET YER BOTTOM DOLLAR YOU'LL LOSE THE BLUES!
WORLD'S GREATEST NEWSPAPER
YEP! THIS IS MY HOME TOWN! THE WINDY CITY! HOME OF THE UNION STOCKYARDS, THE WRIGLEY BUILDING AND DICK THE BRUISER... BIRTHPLACE OF MRS. O'LEARY'S COW, PLAYBOY MAGAZINE AND THE 8-HOUR WORK DAY... CHICAGO, EL-A-NOY...
WHERE THE MIGHTY WATERS OF LAKE MICHIGAN COURSE FREELY INTO THAT BARELY FLOWING SHAMROCK SHAKE CALLED THE CHICAGO RIVER... WHERE MEN HAVE MADE UP FOR GOD'S OVERSIGHT BY CREATING THEIR OWN TERRAIN OF STEEL AND MORTAR ON THESE MIDWESTERN PLAINS...
LONG HAS OUR TOWN BEEN A SEEDBED OF UPHEAVAL... FROM THE WIGWAM CONVENTION TO THE HAYMARKET RIOTS OUR POLITICAL IDEAS, WHETHER EMANATING FROM CITY HALL OR BUGHOUSE SQUARE HAVE BEEN HEARD BY THE EARS OF AN ENVIOUS WORLD...
OF COURSE, CHICAGO IS ALSO KNOWN FOR SOME OTHER THINGS... LIKE POLITICAL CORRUPTION, A GESTAPO-LIKE POLICE FORCE AND THAT UNGODLY NASAL TWANG... NOT TO MENTION AL CAPONE, RICHARD SPECK, JOHN WAYNE GACY, LEOPOLD AND LOEB AND THE 1919 BLACK SOX...

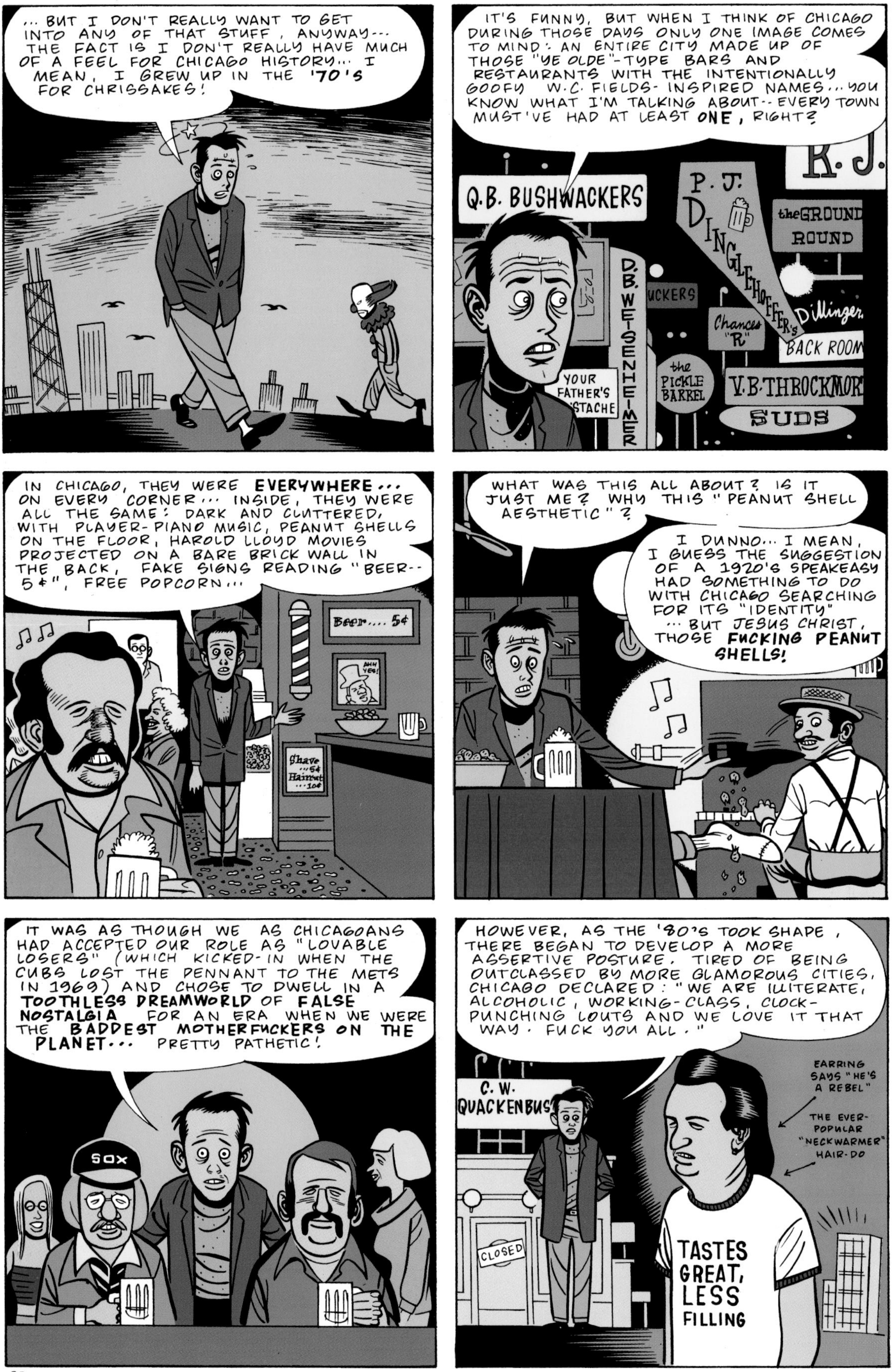
... BUT I DON'T REALLY WANT TO GET INTO ANY OF THAT STUFF, ANYWAY... THE FACT IS I DON'T REALLY HAVE MUCH OF A FEEL FOR CHICAGO HISTORY... I MEAN, I GREW UP IN THE '70'S FOR CHRISSAKES!
IT'S FUNNY, BUT WHEN I THINK OF CHICAGO DURING THOSE DAYS ONLY ONE IMAGE COMES TO MIND: AN ENTIRE CITY MADE UP OF THOSE "YE OLDE"-TYPE BARS AND RESTAURANTS WITH THE INTENTIONALLY GOOFY W.C. FIELDS-INSPIRED NAMES... YOU KNOW WHAT I'M TALKING ABOUT--EVERY TOWN MUST'VE HAD AT LEAST ONE, RIGHT?
Q.B. BUSHWACKERS
P.J. DINGLEHOFFER'S
R.J.
the GROUND ROUND
D.B. WEISENHEIMER
UCKERS
Chances "R"
Dillinger
BACK ROOM
YOUR FATHER'S STACHE
the PICKLE BARREL
V.B. THROCKMORT
SUDS
IN CHICAGO, THEY WERE EVERYWHERE... ON EVERY CORNER... INSIDE, THEY WERE ALL THE SAME: DARK AND CLUTTERED, WITH PLAYER-PIANO MUSIC, PEANUT SHELLS ON THE FLOOR, HAROLD LLOYD MOVIES PROJECTED ON A BARE BRICK WALL IN THE BACK, FAKE SIGNS READING "BEER--5¢", FREE POPCORN...
Beer.... 5¢
AHH YES!
Shave ...5¢ Haircut ...10¢
WHAT WAS THIS ALL ABOUT? IS IT JUST ME? WHY THIS "PEANUT SHELL AESTHETIC"?
I DUNNO... I MEAN, I GUESS THE SUGGESTION OF A 1920'S SPEAKEASY HAD SOMETHING TO DO WITH CHICAGO SEARCHING FOR ITS "IDENTITY" ... BUT JESUS CHRIST, THOSE FUCKING PEANUT SHELLS!
IT WAS AS THOUGH WE AS CHICAGOANS HAD ACCEPTED OUR ROLE AS "LOVABLE LOSERS" (WHICH KICKED-IN WHEN THE CUBS LOST THE PENNANT TO THE METS IN 1969) AND CHOSE TO DWELL IN A TOOTHLESS DREAMWORLD OF FALSE NOSTALGIA FOR AN ERA WHEN WE WERE THE BADDEST MOTHERFUCKERS ON THE PLANET... PRETTY PATHETIC!
SOX
HOWEVER, AS THE '80'S TOOK SHAPE, THERE BEGAN TO DEVELOP A MORE ASSERTIVE POSTURE. TIRED OF BEING OUTCLASSED BY MORE GLAMOROUS CITIES, CHICAGO DECLARED: "WE ARE ILLITERATE, ALCOHOLIC, WORKING-CLASS, CLOCK-PUNCHING LOUTS AND WE LOVE IT THAT WAY. FUCK YOU ALL."
C.W. QUACKENBUS
CLOSED
EARRING SAYS "HE'S A REBEL"
THE EVER-POPULAR "NECKWARMER" HAIR-DO
TASTES GREAT, LESS FILLING

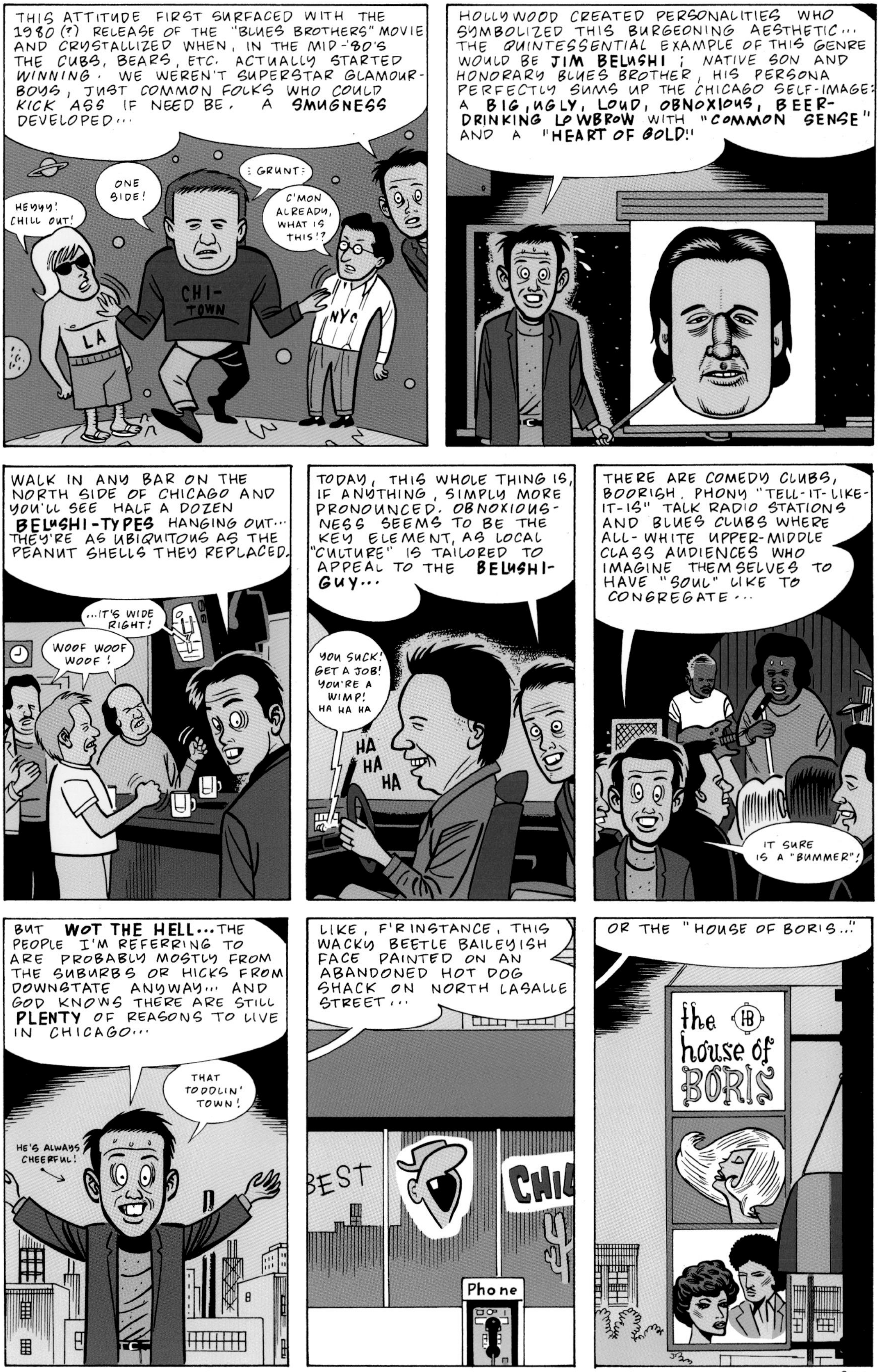

THIS ATTITUDE FIRST SURFACED WITH THE 1980 (?) RELEASE OF THE "BLUES BROTHERS" MOVIE AND CRYSTALLIZED WHEN, IN THE MID-'80'S THE CUBS, BEARS, ETC. ACTUALLY STARTED WINNING. WE WEREN'T SUPERSTAR GLAMOUR-BOYS, JUST COMMON FOLKS WHO COULD KICK ASS IF NEED BE. A SMUGNESS DEVELOPED...
HEYYY! CHILL OUT!
ONE SIDE!
GRUNT
C'MON ALREADY, WHAT IS THIS!?
LA
CHI-TOWN
NYC
HOLLYWOOD CREATED PERSONALITIES WHO SYMBOLIZED THIS BURGEONING AESTHETIC... THE QUINTESSENTIAL EXAMPLE OF THIS GENRE WOULD BE JIM BELUSHI; NATIVE SON AND HONORARY BLUES BROTHER, HIS PERSONA PERFECTLY SUMS UP THE CHICAGO SELF-IMAGE: A BIG, UGLY, LOUD, OBNOXIOUS, BEER-DRINKING LOWBROW WITH "COMMON SENSE" AND A "HEART OF GOLD!"
WALK IN ANY BAR ON THE NORTH SIDE OF CHICAGO AND YOU'LL SEE HALF A DOZEN BELUSHI-TYPES HANGING OUT... THEY'RE AS UBIQUITOUS AS THE PEANUT SHELLS THEY REPLACED.
...IT'S WIDE RIGHT!
WOOF WOOF WOOF!
TODAY, THIS WHOLE THING IS, IF ANYTHING, SIMPLY MORE PRONOUNCED. OBNOXIOUSNESS SEEMS TO BE THE KEY ELEMENT, AS LOCAL "CULTURE" IS TAILORED TO APPEAL TO THE BELUSHI-GUY...
YOU SUCK! GET A JOB! YOU'RE A WIMP! HA HA HA
HA HA HA
THERE ARE COMEDY CLUBS, BOORISH, PHONY "TELL-IT-LIKE-IT-IS" TALK RADIO STATIONS AND BLUES CLUBS WHERE ALL-WHITE UPPER-MIDDLE CLASS AUDIENCES WHO IMAGINE THEMSELVES TO HAVE "SOUL" LIKE TO CONGREGATE...
IT SURE IS A "BUMMER"!
BUT WOT THE HELL... THE PEOPLE I'M REFERRING TO ARE PROBABLY MOSTLY FROM THE SUBURBS OR HICKS FROM DOWNSTATE ANYWAY... AND GOD KNOWS THERE ARE STILL PLENTY OF REASONS TO LIVE IN CHICAGO...
THAT TODDLIN' TOWN!
HE'S ALWAYS CHEERFUL!
LIKE, F'RINSTANCE, THIS WACKY BEETLE BAILEYISH FACE PAINTED ON AN ABANDONED HOT DOG SHACK ON NORTH LASALLE STREET...
BEST
CHI
Phone
OR THE "HOUSE OF BORIS..."
the house of BORIS

Continued from inside

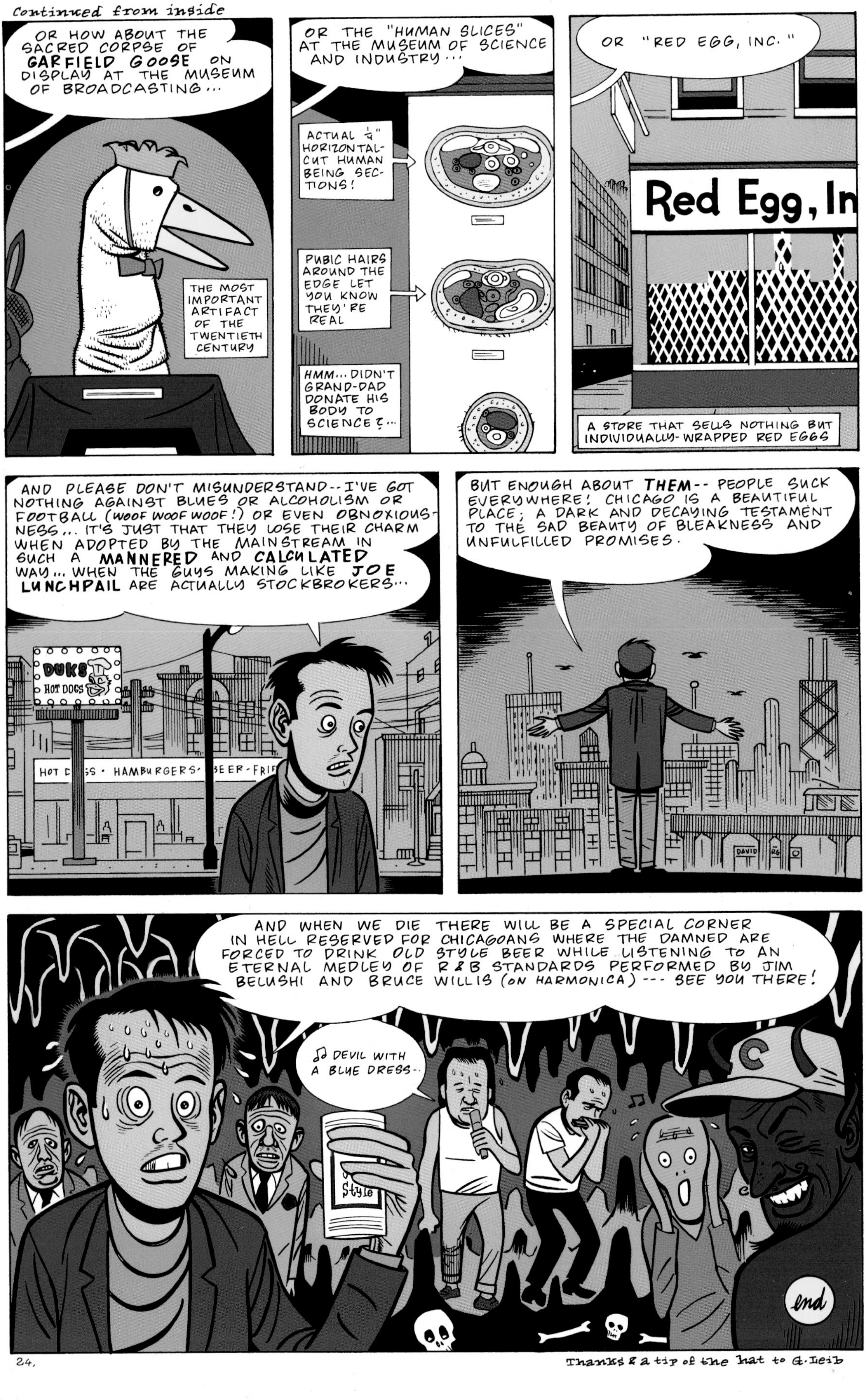
OR HOW ABOUT THE SACRED CORPSE OF GARFIELD GOOSE ON DISPLAY AT THE MUSEUM OF BROADCASTING...
THE MOST IMPORTANT ARTIFACT OF THE TWENTIETH CENTURY
OR THE "HUMAN SLICES" AT THE MUSEUM OF SCIENCE AND INDUSTRY...
ACTUAL 1/4" HORIZONTAL-CUT HUMAN BEING SECTIONS!
PUBIC HAIRS AROUND THE EDGE LET YOU KNOW THEY'RE REAL
HMM... DIDN'T GRAND-DAD DONATE HIS BODY TO SCIENCE?...
OR "RED EGG, INC."
Red Egg, In
A STORE THAT SELLS NOTHING BUT INDIVIDUALLY-WRAPPED RED EGGS
AND PLEASE DON'T MISUNDERSTAND--I'VE GOT NOTHING AGAINST BLUES OR ALCOHOLISM OR FOOTBALL (WOOF WOOF WOOF!) OR EVEN OBNOXIOUSNESS... IT'S JUST THAT THEY LOSE THEIR CHARM WHEN ADOPTED BY THE MAINSTREAM IN SUCH A MANNERED AND CALCULATED WAY... WHEN THE GUYS MAKING LIKE JOE LUNCHPAIL ARE ACTUALLY STOCKBROKERS...
DUKS HOT DOGS
HOT D GS • HAMBURGERS • BEER • FRIE
BUT ENOUGH ABOUT THEM-- PEOPLE SUCK EVERYWHERE! CHICAGO IS A BEAUTIFUL PLACE; A DARK AND DECAYING TESTAMENT TO THE SAD BEAUTY OF BLEAKNESS AND UNFULFILLED PROMISES.
DAVID
AND WHEN WE DIE THERE WILL BE A SPECIAL CORNER IN HELL RESERVED FOR CHICAGOANS WHERE THE DAMNED ARE FORCED TO DRINK OLD STYLE BEER WHILE LISTENING TO AN ETERNAL MEDLEY OF R&B STANDARDS PERFORMED BY JIM BELUSHI AND BRUCE WILLIS (ON HARMONICA) --- SEE YOU THERE!
♫ DEVIL WITH A BLUE DRESS..
Style
end

Thanks & a tip of the hat to G. Leib

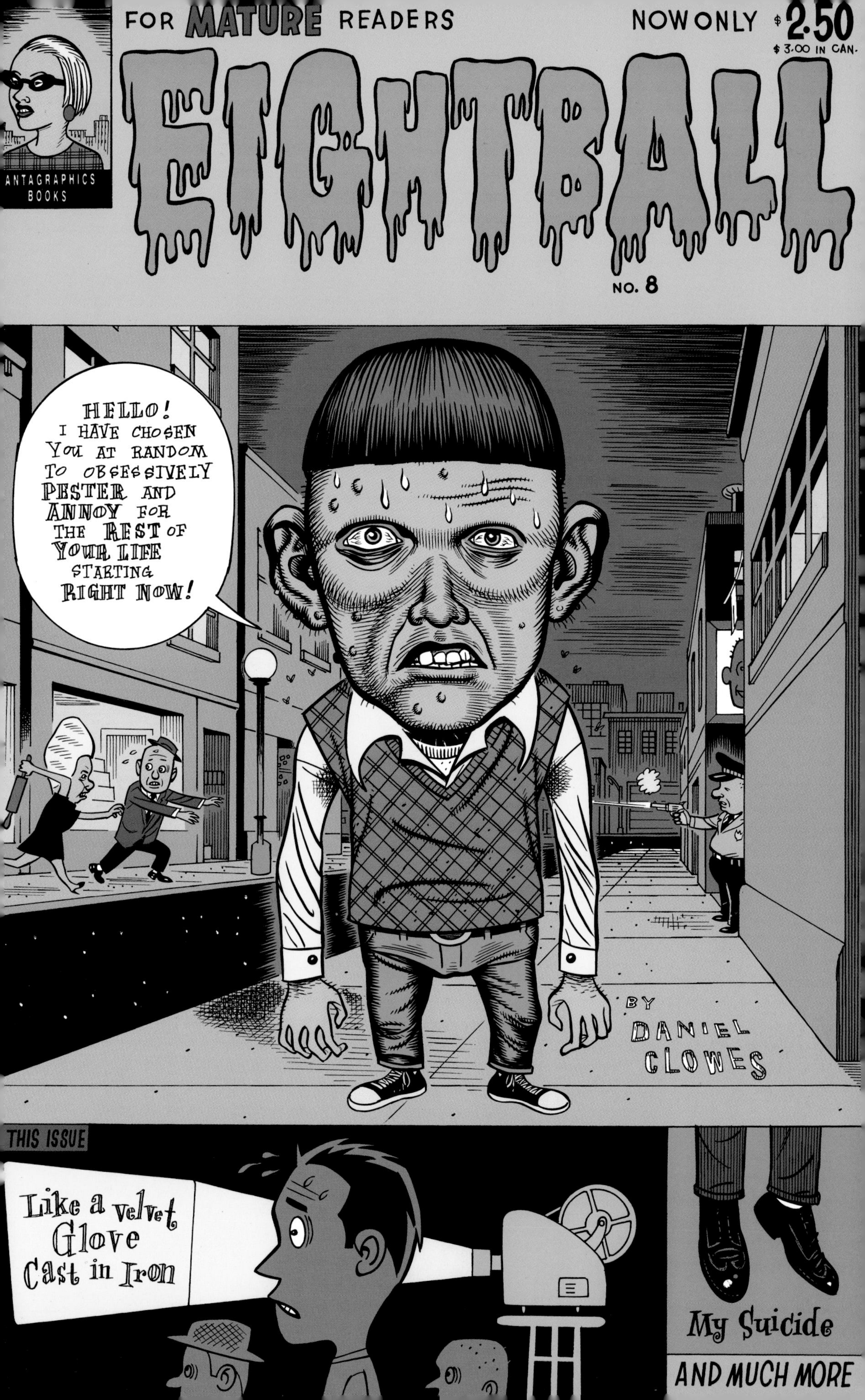
FOR MATURE READERS
NOW ONLY $2.50
$3.00 IN CAN.
ANTAGRAPHICS BOOKS
EIGHTBALL
NO. 8
HELLO! I HAVE CHOSEN YOU AT RANDOM TO OBSESSIVELY PESTER AND ANNOY FOR THE REST OF YOUR LIFE STARTING RIGHT NOW!
BY DANIEL CLOWES
THIS ISSUE
Like a Velvet Glove Cast in Iron
My Suicide
AND MUCH MORE

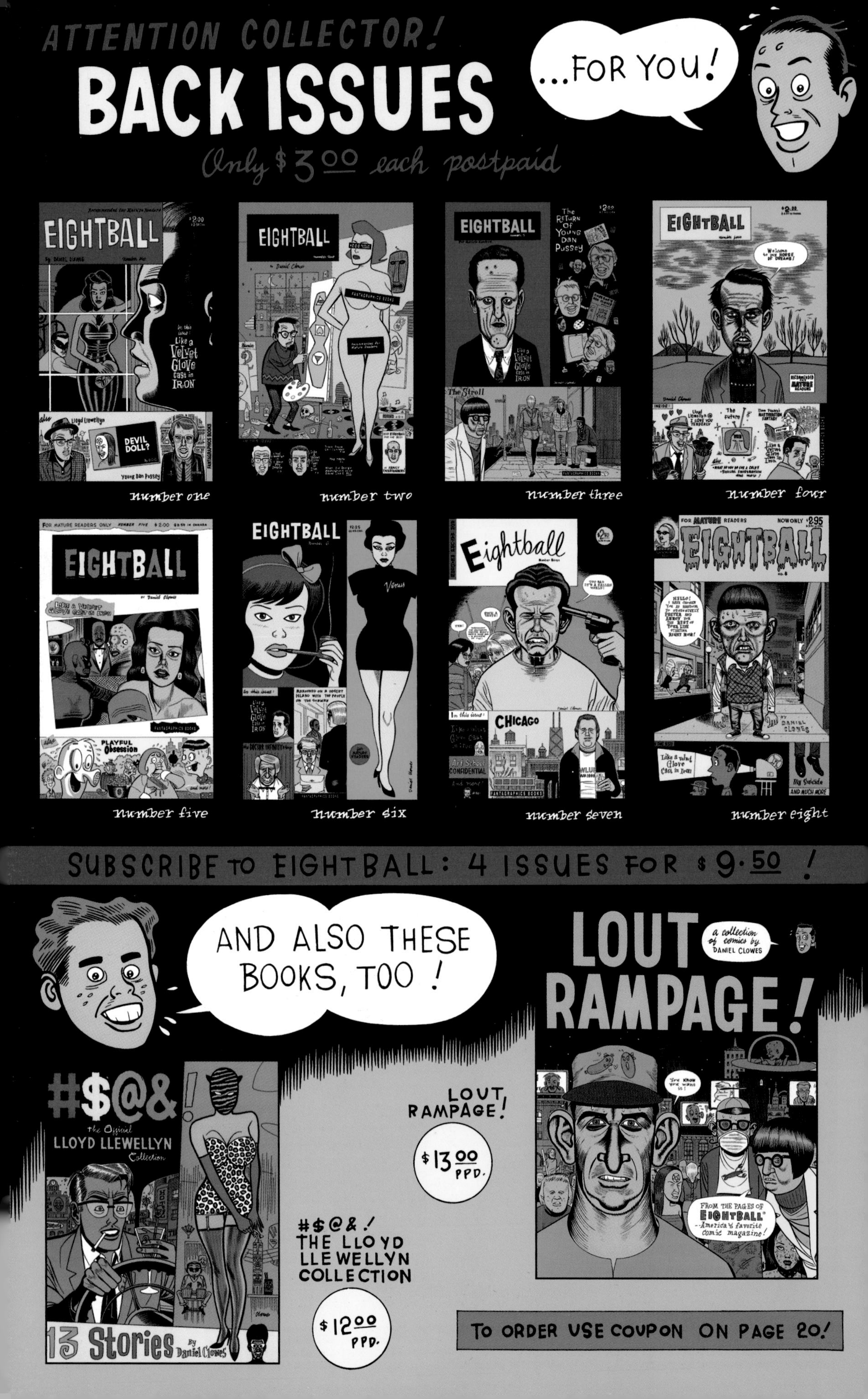
ATTENTION COLLECTOR!
BACK ISSUES
...FOR YOU!
Only $3.00 each postpaid
EIGHTBALL
number one
EIGHTBALL
number two
EIGHTBALL
The Return of Young Dan Pussey
The Stroll
number three
EIGHTBALL
Welcome to the HOUSE of DREAMS!
number four
FOR MATURE READERS ONLY NUMBER FIVE $2.00
EIGHTBALL
PLAYFUL Obsession
number five
EIGHTBALL
number six
Eightball
CHICAGO
Art School CONFIDENTIAL
number seven
FOR MATURE READERS
EIGHTBALL
HELLO! I HAVE CHOSEN YOU AT RANDOM TO PERSONALLY PESTER AND ANNOY YOU THE REST OF YOUR LIFE STARTING RIGHT NOW!
number eight
SUBSCRIBE TO EIGHTBALL: 4 ISSUES FOR $9.50 !
AND ALSO THESE BOOKS, TOO !
LOUT RAMPAGE!
a collection of comics by DANIEL CLOWES
FROM THE PAGES OF EIGHTBALL --America's favorite comic magazine!
#$@&!
the Official LLOYD LLEWELLYN Collection
13 Stories By Daniel Clowes
LOUT RAMPAGE!
$13.00 PPD.
#$@&! THE LLOYD LLEWELLYN COLLECTION
$12.00 PPD.
TO ORDER USE COUPON ON PAGE 20!

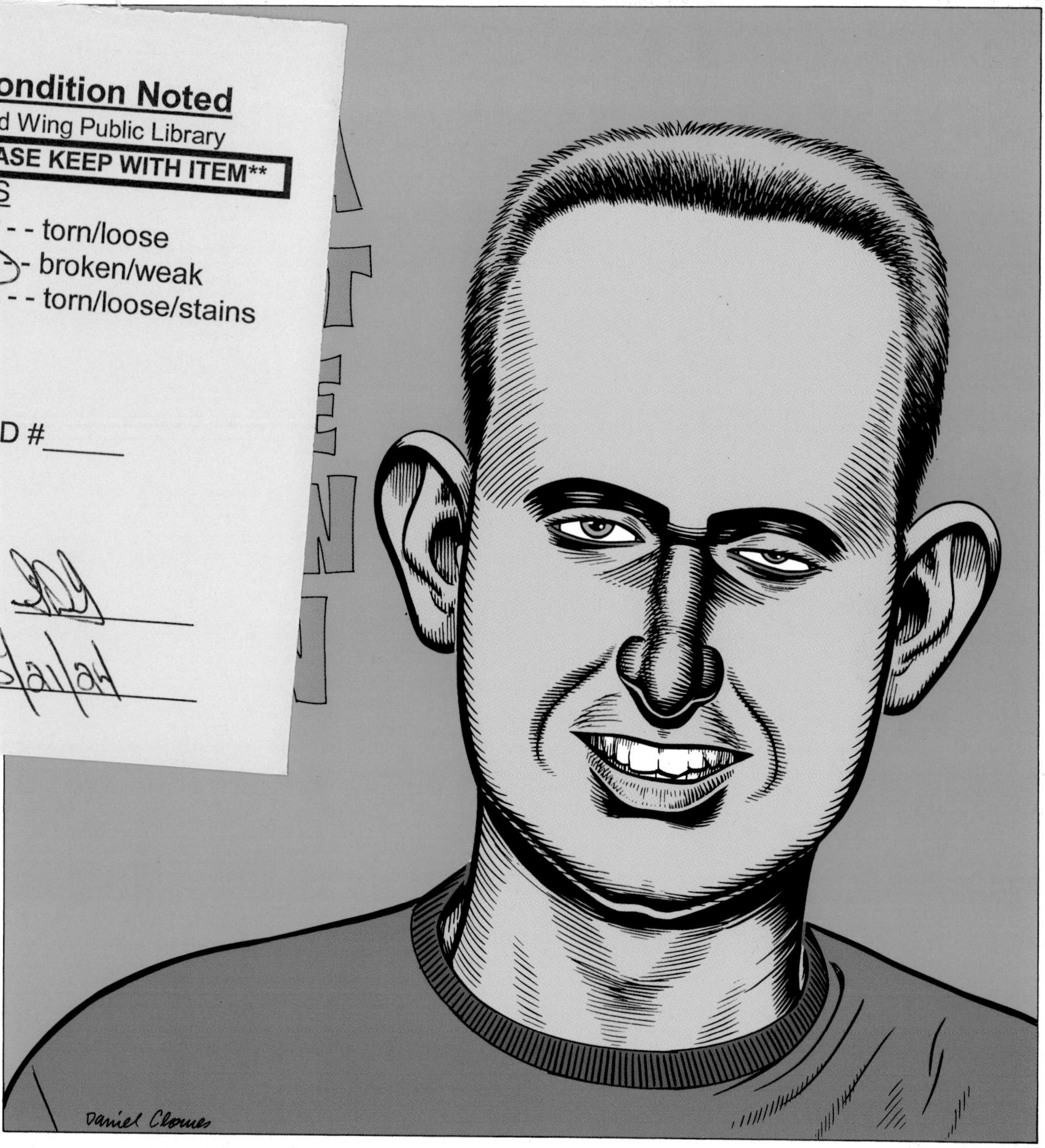
Daniel Clowes

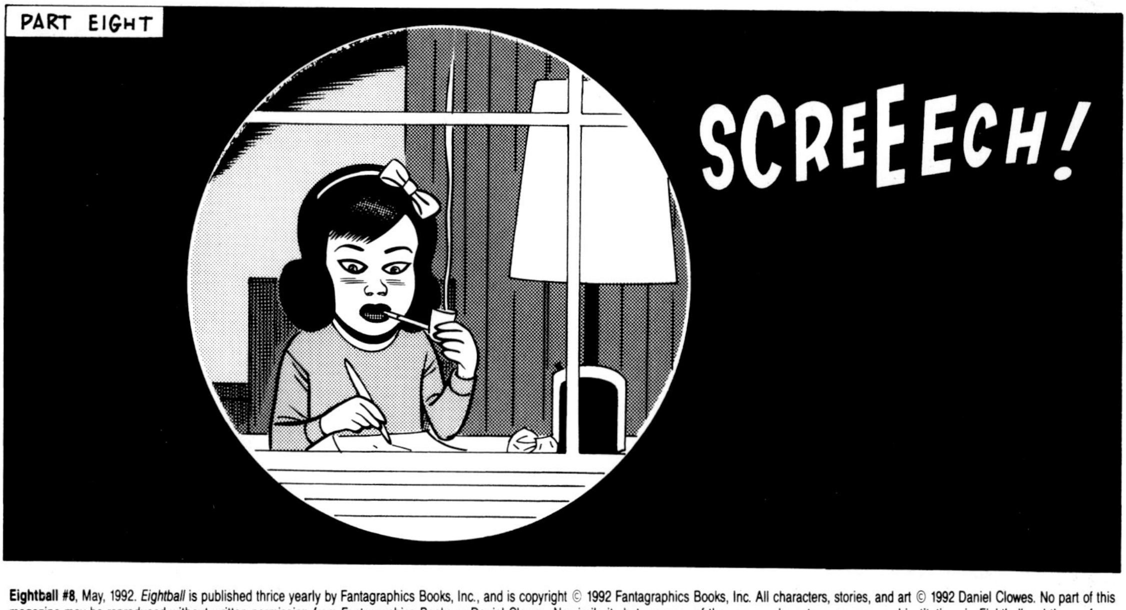
PART EIGHT
SCREEECH!

Eightball #8, May, 1992. *Eightball* is published thrice yearly by Fantagraphics Books, Inc., and is copyright © 1992 Fantagraphics Books, Inc. All characters, stories, and art © 1992 Daniel Clowes. No part of this magazine may be reproduced without written permission from Fantagraphics Books or Daniel Clowes. No similarity between any of the names, characters, persons, and institutions in *Eightball* and those of any living or dead persons is intended (except for satirical intent), and any such similarity that may exist is purely coincidental. Letters to *Eightball* become the property of the magazine and are assumed intended for publication in whole or in part, and may therefore be used for those purposes. First printing: March, 1992. Fantagraphics Books, 7563 Lake City Way Northeast, Seattle WA 98115. PRINTED IN THE U.S.A.

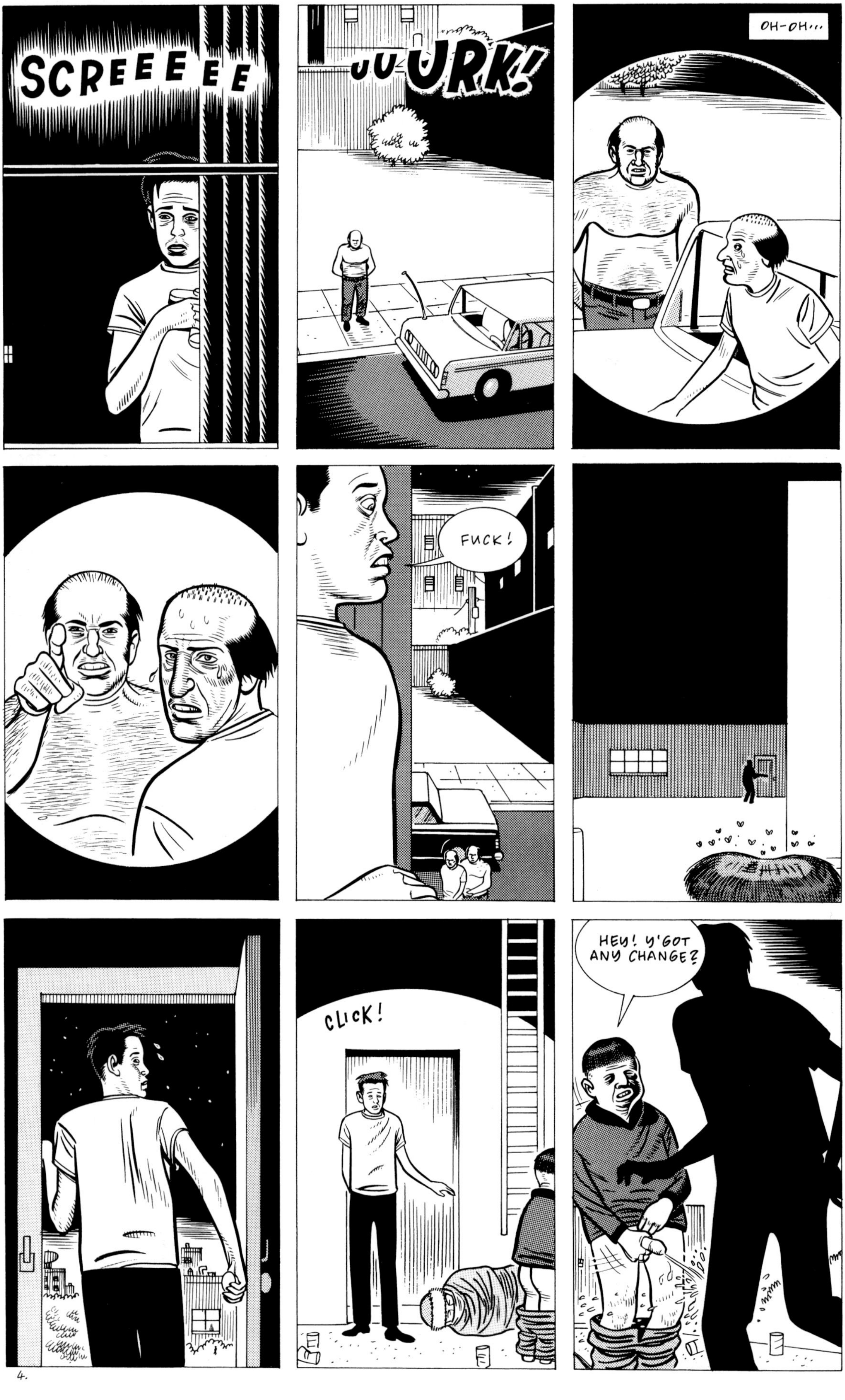
SCREEEEEE
UUURK!
OH-OH...
FUCK!
CLICK!
HEY! Y'GOT ANY CHANGE?

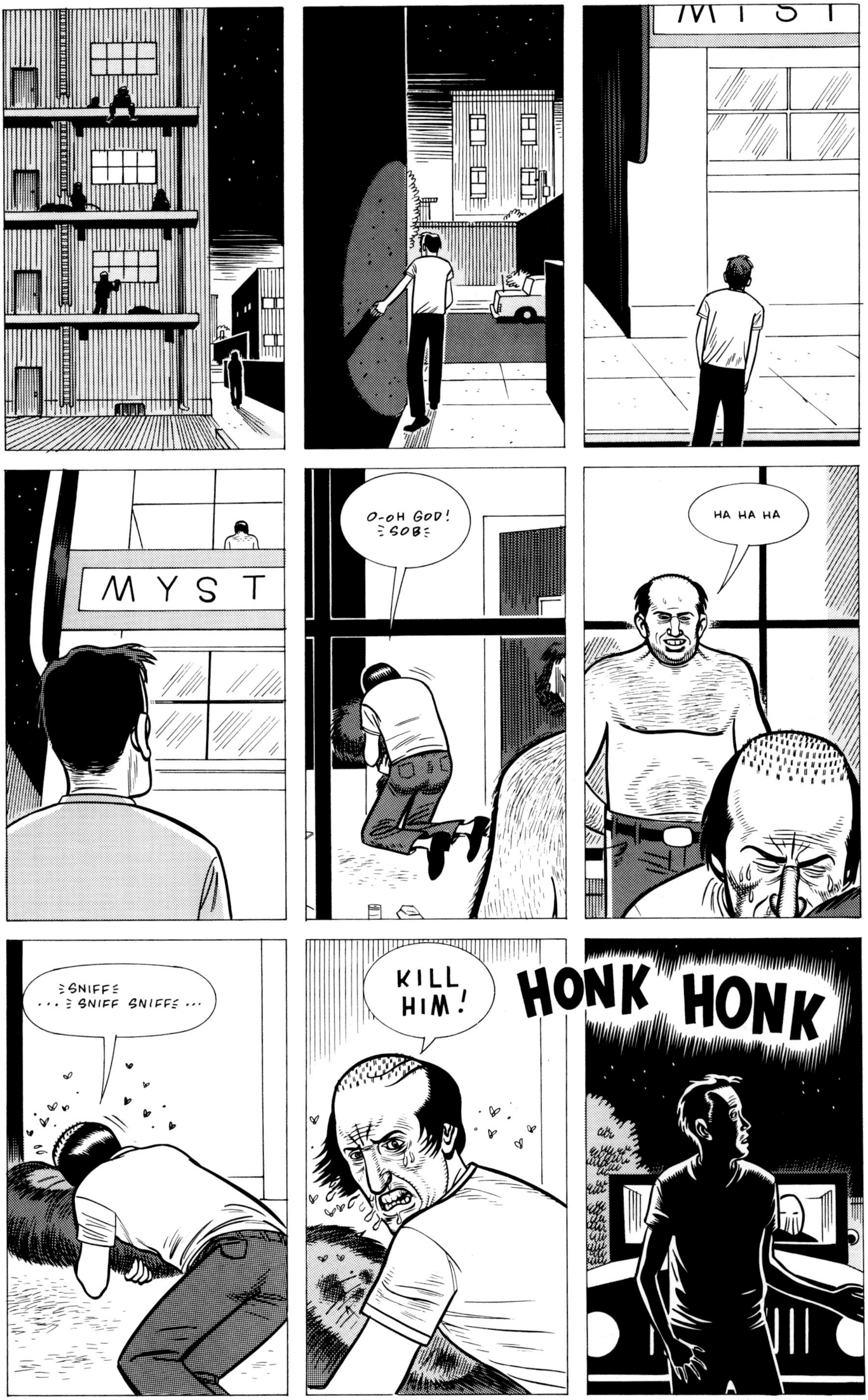
MYST
MYST
O-OH GOD! SOB
HA HA HA
SNIFF ... SNIFF SNIFF ...
KILL HIM!
HONK HONK

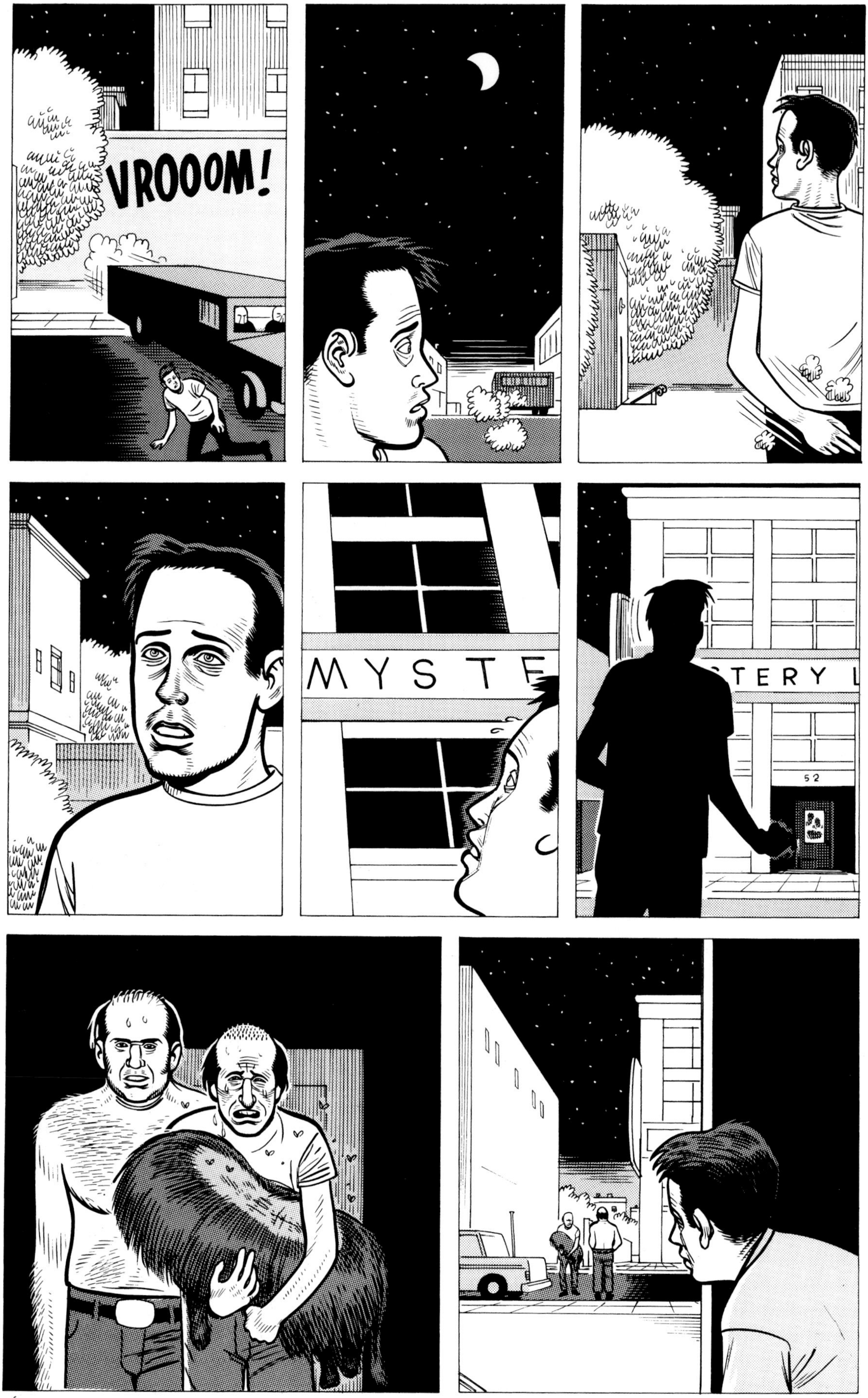
VROOOM!
MYSTE
STERY L
52

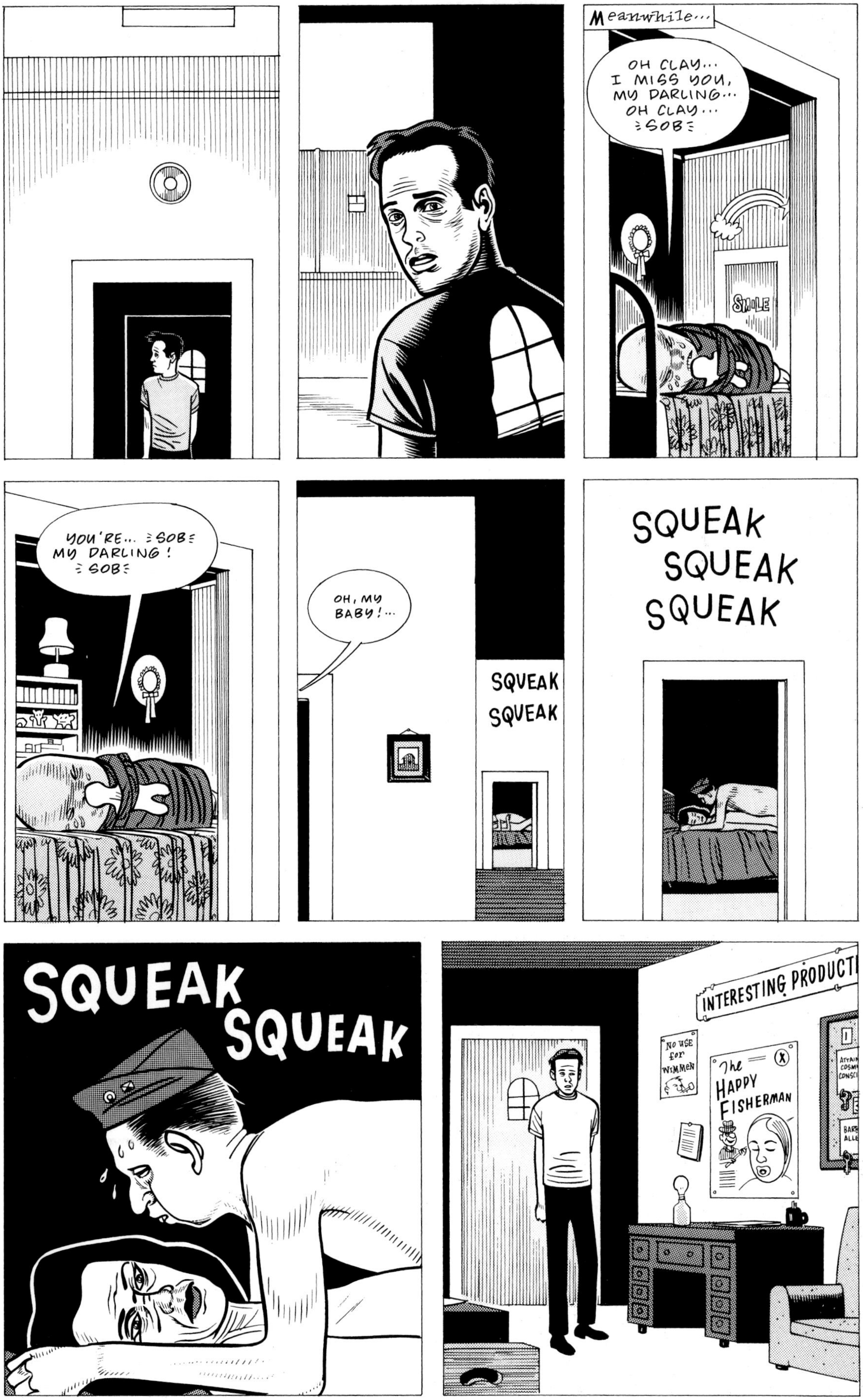
Meanwhile...
OH CLAY... I MISS YOU, MY DARLING... OH CLAY... SOB
SMILE
YOU'RE... SOB MY DARLING! SOB
OH, MY BABY!...
SQUEAK SQUEAK
SQUEAK SQUEAK SQUEAK
SQUEAK SQUEAK
INTERESTING PRODUCT
NO USE for WIMMEN
The HAPPY FISHERMAN

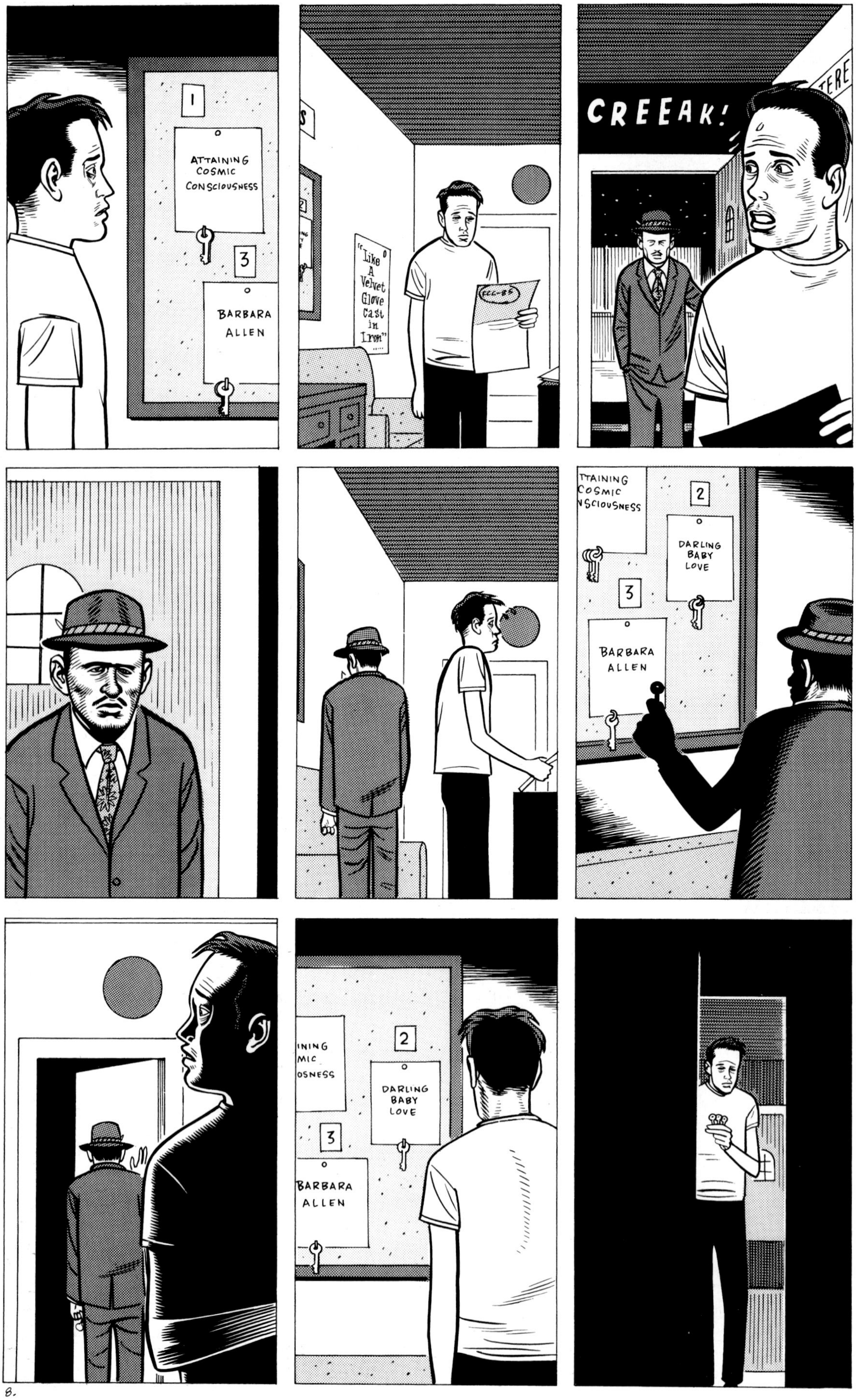
1
ATTAINING COSMIC CONSCIOUSNESS
3
BARBARA ALLEN
"Like A Velvet Glove Cast in Iron" .....
CREEAK!
TTAINING COSMIC NSCIOUSNESS
2
DARLING BABY LOVE
3
BARBARA ALLEN
INING MIC OSNESS
2
DARLING BABY LOVE
3
BARBARA ALLEN

... IMAGINE IF ONE DAY THERE WAS A HEAT WAVE THAT ONLY AFFECTED CERTAIN THINGS... THE ACTUAL WEATHER WAS WARM AND CALM, LIKE BEFORE A HURRICANE...

BUT ALL WATER, PUDDLES AND SO FORTH, WAS BLAZING HOT -- SCALDING TO THE TOUCH -- AS WERE CERTAIN METALLIC SURFACES...

A MAN COMES TOWARD YOU HOLDING SOMETHING... SUDDENLY HE THROWS IT TO THE GROUND IN EXTREME PAIN. IT'S A ROLL OF QUARTERS. YOU TRY TO PICK IT UP BUT YOUR HAND IS BURNED.

DR. WILDE

THE MAN EXPLAINS THAT ALL QUARTERS ARE BLAZING HOT AND THE BANKS ARE TRYING TO GET RID OF THEM BUT THEY'RE TOO HOT TO HOLD AND AS A RESULT, TONGS HAVE BECOME A VALU-ABLE COMMODITY.

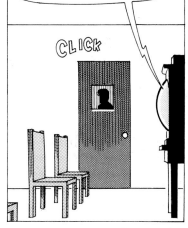
PEOPLE ARE PAYING EIGHT DOLLARS AND UP FOR A PAIR OF TONGS STRONG ENOUGH TO HOLD A ROLL OF QUARTERS. NO OTHER COINS ARE MENTIONED...

CLICK

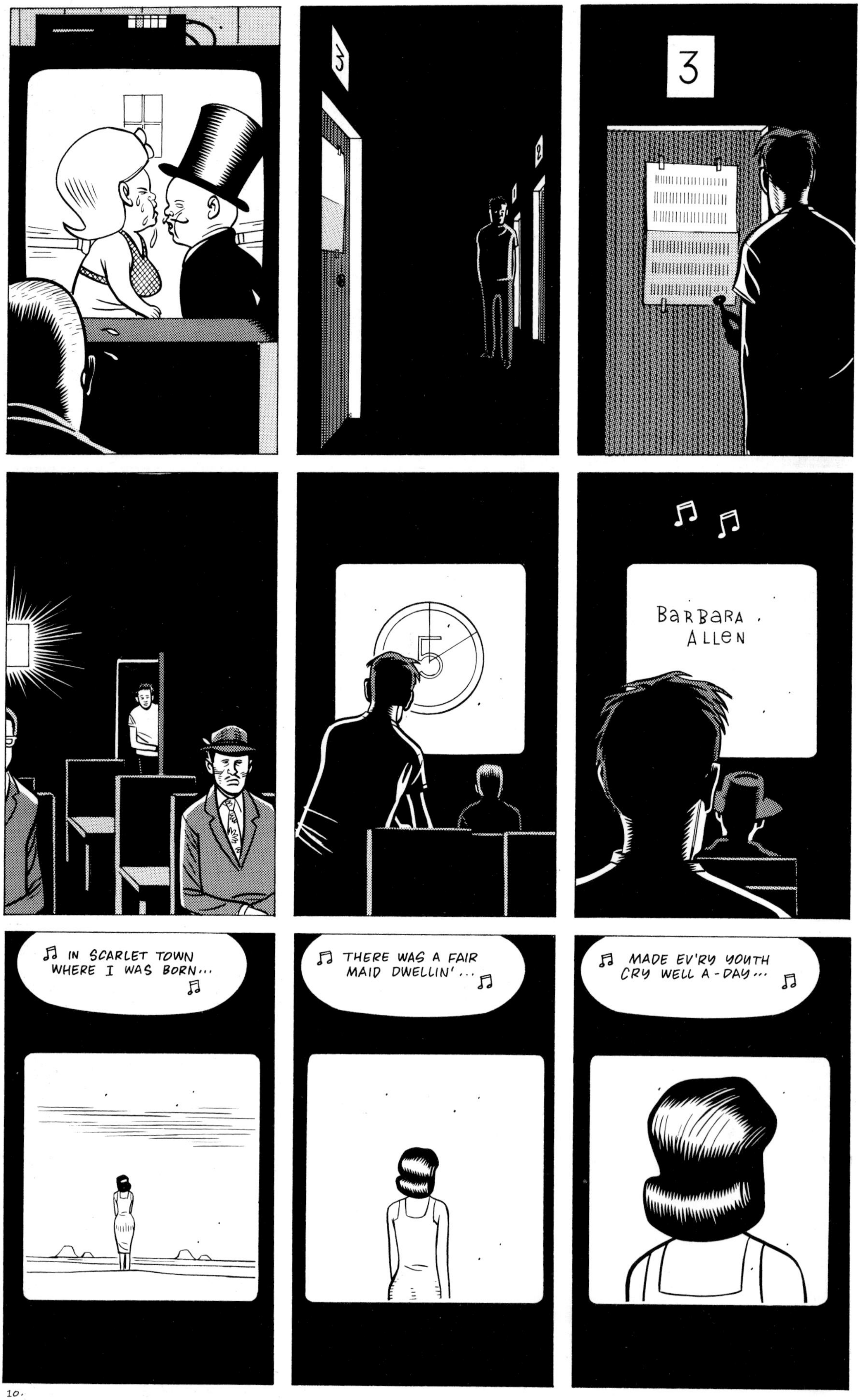

3
2
1
3
5
BARBARA ALLEN
IN SCARLET TOWN WHERE I WAS BORN...
THERE WAS A FAIR MAID DWELLIN'...
MADE EV'RY YOUTH CRY WELL A-DAY...

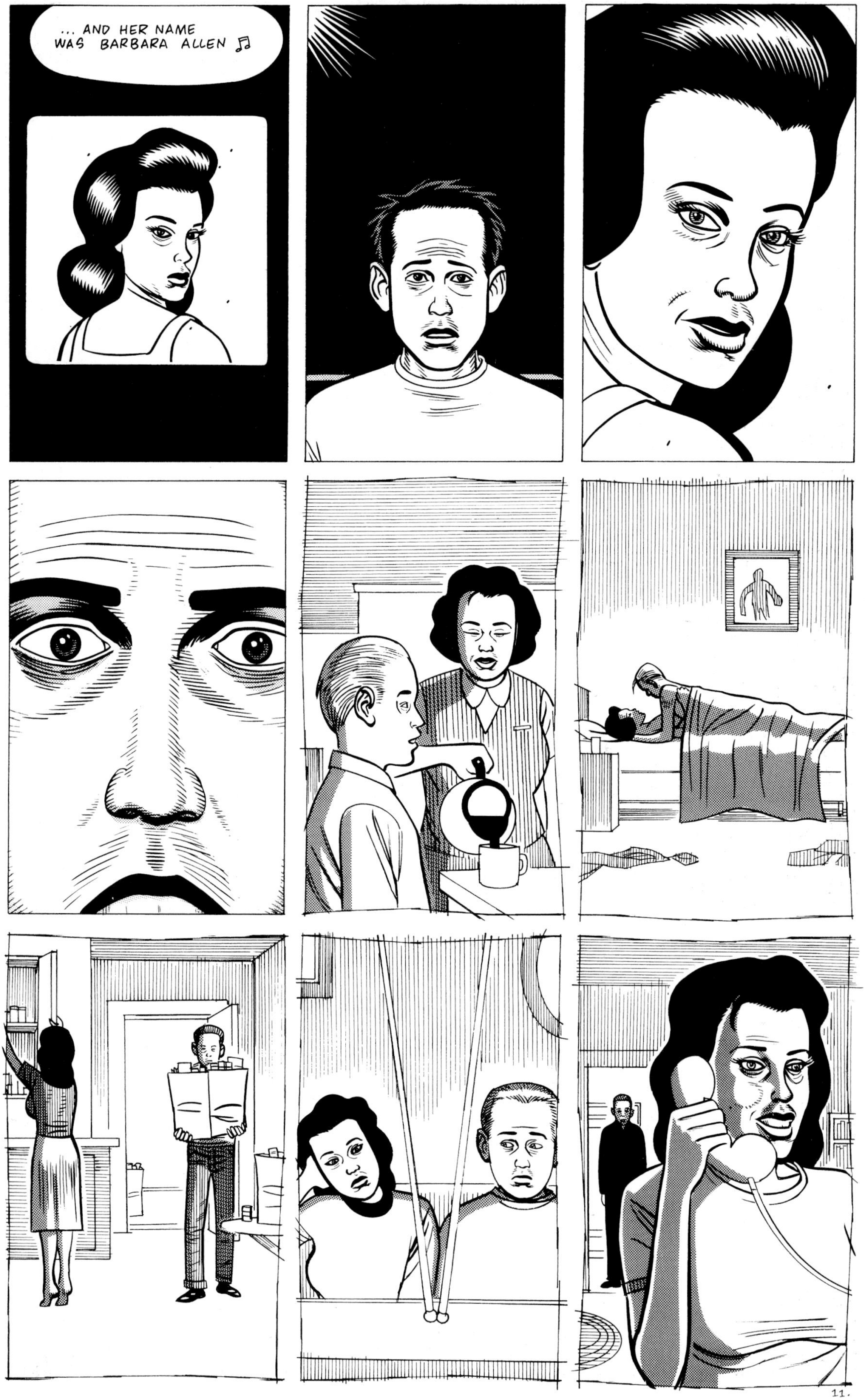
... AND HER NAME
WAS BARBARA ALLEN ♫

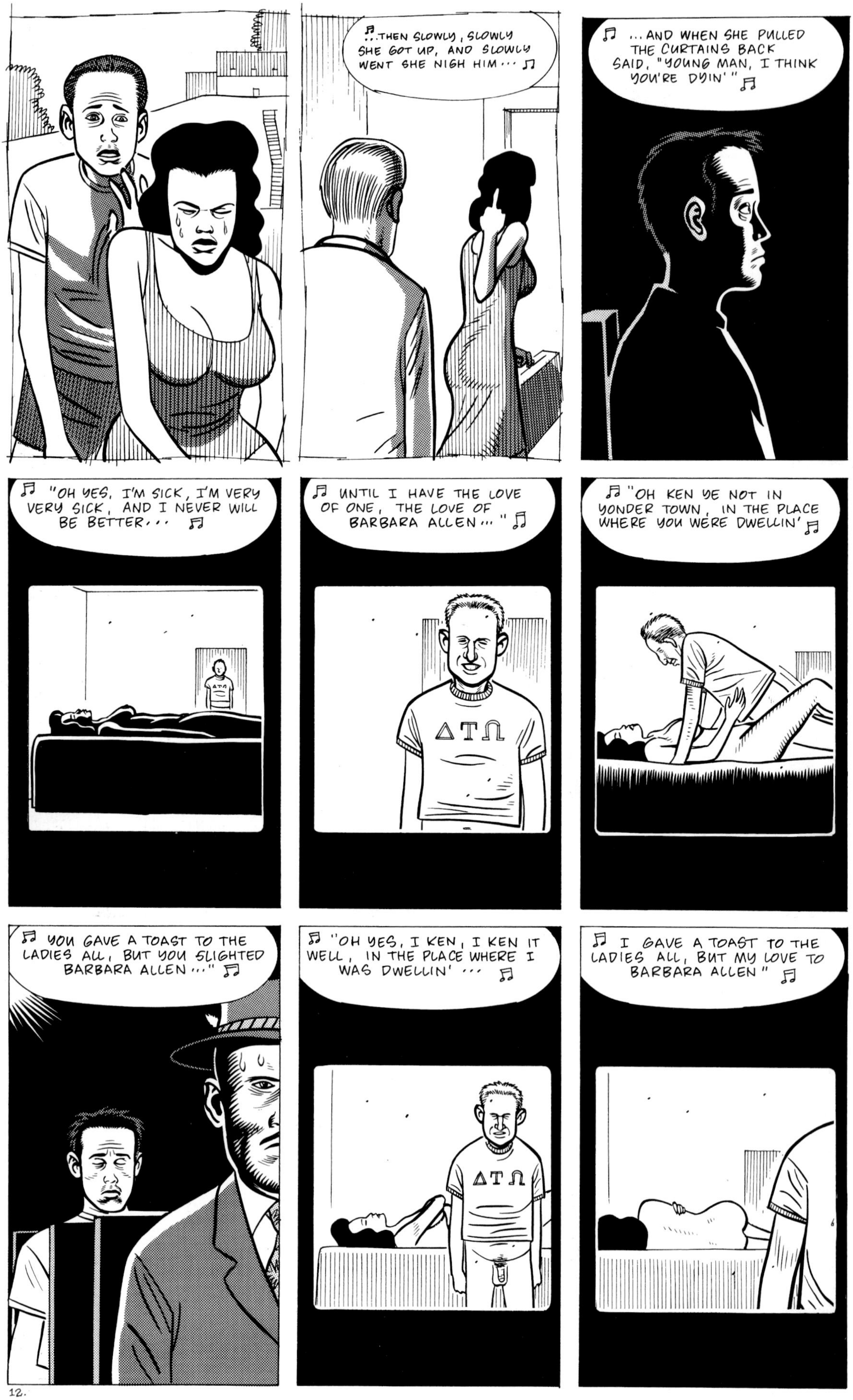
♫ ...THEN SLOWLY, SLOWLY SHE GOT UP, AND SLOWLY WENT SHE NIGH HIM... ♫
♫ ...AND WHEN SHE PULLED THE CURTAINS BACK SAID, "YOUNG MAN, I THINK YOU'RE DYIN'" ♫
♫ "OH YES, I'M SICK, I'M VERY VERY SICK, AND I NEVER WILL BE BETTER... ♫
♫ UNTIL I HAVE THE LOVE OF ONE, THE LOVE OF BARBARA ALLEN..." ♫
ΔΤΩ
♫ "OH KEN YE NOT IN YONDER TOWN, IN THE PLACE WHERE YOU WERE DWELLIN' ♫
♫ YOU GAVE A TOAST TO THE LADIES ALL, BUT YOU SLIGHTED BARBARA ALLEN..." ♫
♫ "OH YES, I KEN, I KEN IT WELL, IN THE PLACE WHERE I WAS DWELLIN'... ♫
ΔΤΩ
♫ I GAVE A TOAST TO THE LADIES ALL, BUT MY LOVE TO BARBARA ALLEN" ♫

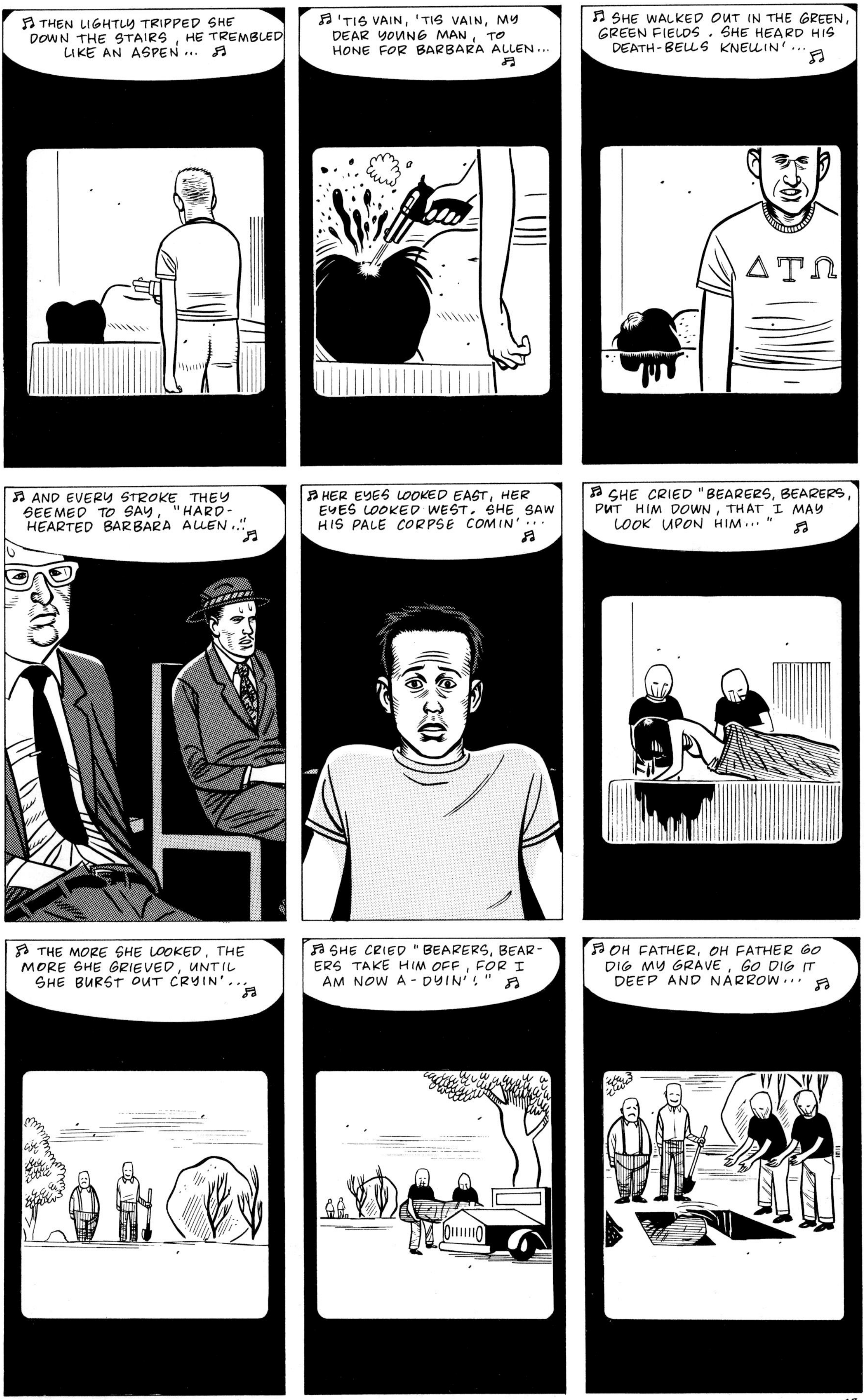
♫ THEN LIGHTLY TRIPPED SHE DOWN THE STAIRS, HE TREMBLED LIKE AN ASPEN... ♫
♫ 'TIS VAIN, 'TIS VAIN, MY DEAR YOUNG MAN, TO HONE FOR BARBARA ALLEN... ♫
♫ SHE WALKED OUT IN THE GREEN, GREEN FIELDS. SHE HEARD HIS DEATH-BELLS KNELLIN'... ♫
ΔΤΩ
♫ AND EVERY STROKE THEY SEEMED TO SAY, "HARD-HEARTED BARBARA ALLEN..." ♫
♫ HER EYES LOOKED EAST, HER EYES LOOKED WEST. SHE SAW HIS PALE CORPSE COMIN'... ♫
♫ SHE CRIED "BEARERS, BEARERS, PUT HIM DOWN, THAT I MAY LOOK UPON HIM..." ♫
♫ THE MORE SHE LOOKED, THE MORE SHE GRIEVED, UNTIL SHE BURST OUT CRYIN'... ♫
♫ SHE CRIED "BEARERS, BEARERS TAKE HIM OFF, FOR I AM NOW A-DYIN'!" ♫
♫ OH FATHER, OH FATHER GO DIG MY GRAVE, GO DIG IT DEEP AND NARROW... ♫

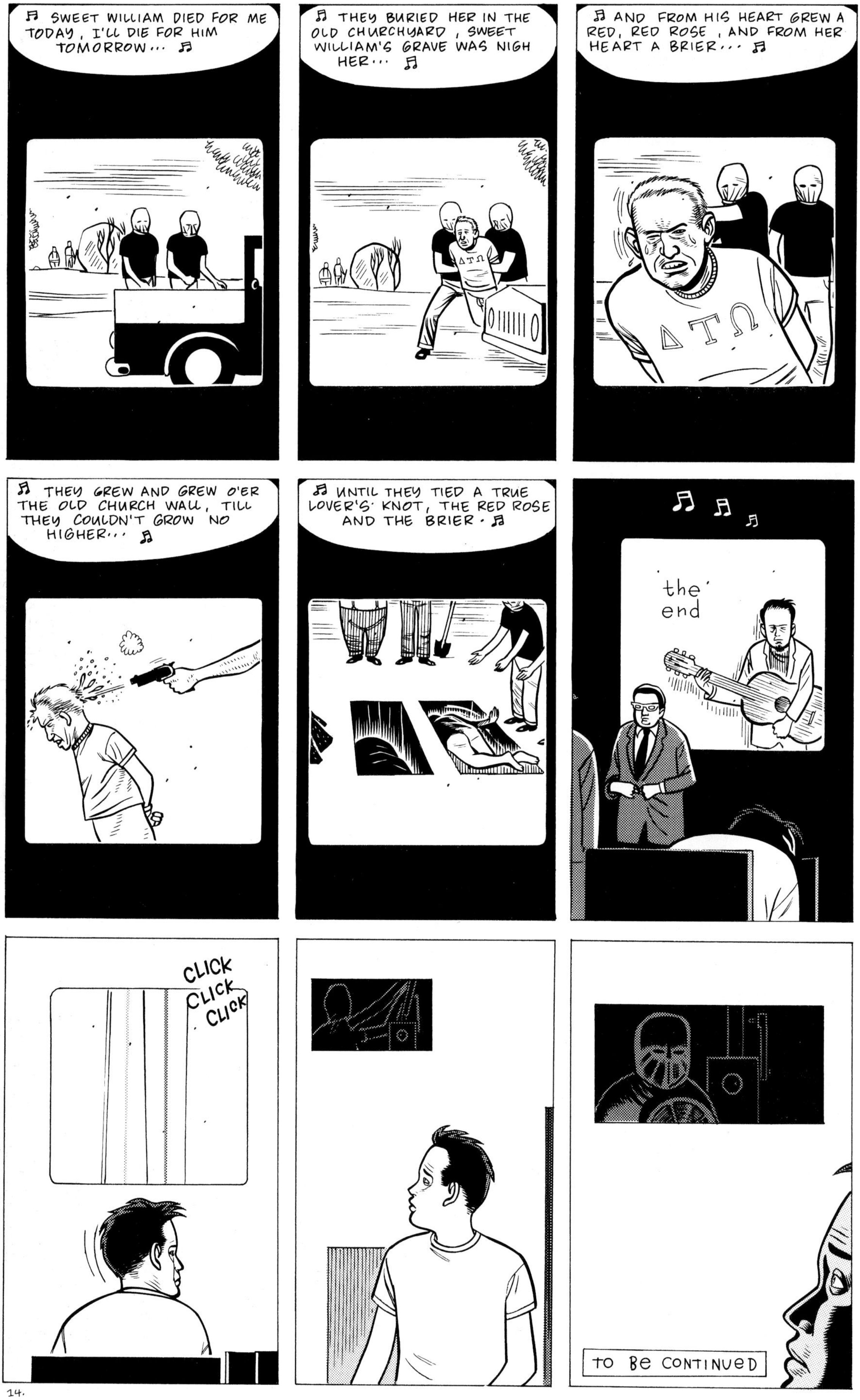
♬ SWEET WILLIAM DIED FOR ME TODAY, I'LL DIE FOR HIM TOMORROW... ♬
♬ THEY BURIED HER IN THE OLD CHURCHYARD, SWEET WILLIAM'S GRAVE WAS NIGH HER... ♬
♬ AND FROM HIS HEART GREW A RED, RED ROSE, AND FROM HER HEART A BRIER... ♬
♬ THEY GREW AND GREW O'ER THE OLD CHURCH WALL, TILL THEY COULDN'T GROW NO HIGHER... ♬
♬ UNTIL THEY TIED A TRUE LOVER'S KNOT, THE RED ROSE AND THE BRIER. ♬
the end
CLICK
CLICK
CLICK
TO BE CONTINUED

the RAGING MAIN

Write: EIGHTBALL
BOX 3357
CHICAGO, IL.
60654

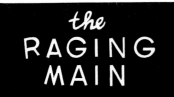

Mr. Clowes,
[Re: 8-Ball #6] I am the sole resident of Papatu, my private island off the coast of Maui. Often I have imagined being stranded on a subway with no one, save for my colorful animal companions. Moko, my trained Parrot would make a fine conductor. The iridescent tropical insects would serve well as the passengers. You can use this idea in your next comic - but I do expect some compensation - or least a "tip of the hat."

Everett Gilmore
Papatu

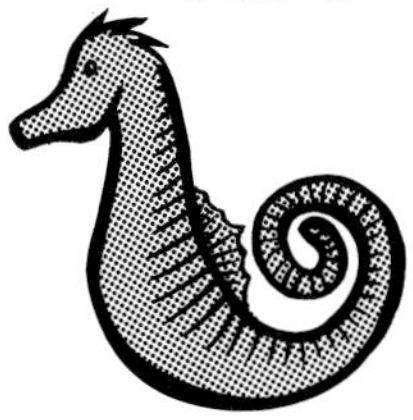

Dear Dan,
Just a note to express my appreciation for "Art School Confidential"... I've been a painter for 22 years and the most exciting thing to happen for me is a China painting class I enrolled in as a joke. It's all little old ladies who dote on me because A.) I'm the only male B.) I'm under 65. My hovel looks like a Dutch souvenir shoppe.

Charles Krafft
Seattle, Wa.

Dear Dan,
You make me sick, Clowes! You got your comic Eightball (should be Hate-ball), and all you do is piss on fanboys and art students (which you yourself once were!) Can't you think of something more positive to do with your energy, and make your work less ugly? And Jesus fucking Christ, what the fuck is going on on p.22, panel four? Those legs under the table must be six feet long! Where's your fucking sense of proportion, Clowes? And why the fuck do you draw people as midgets anyway? Face it, you're lucky to be living in America where you can get away with that horse-shit, and the commies and liberals you're in bed with too!

Don Simpson
Pittsburgh, PA

DESPITE THESE FIGHTIN' WORDS I AM STILL PROUD TO CALL YOU "FRIEND," DON! -- DC.

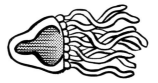

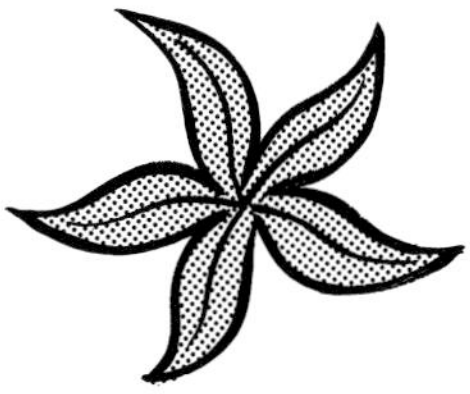

Dear Dan,
Don't hate me for this but I've never read much of your work until recently (when) I had a chance to read a huge amount of the stuff. All at a gulp! I'd read a little bit here and there before and didn't get much out of it, but now that I dig your oeuvre, man-YOWSA!
Dan Pussey is so durn funny! I love this character! I know this guy! I AM this guy! Didja notice that we hid his face on the cover of METACOPS #3? That's the "ill-conceived pop-art satire" I wrote for MONSTER COMICS.

Link Yaco
Ann Arbor, MI.

Dear Daniel Clowes,
...A few months ago I was listening to "Car Talk" and they had a puzzler: Use the following letters to spell just one word: DOENTJSOUTWR. I figured it out after a few hours. "Stowjourned" was my answer and I sent it in right away. The following week I listened to see if I'd won. The answer was "Just one word". They didn't read my name and stupid answer on the radio, but still I felt embarrassed.

Steve Lerner
Seattle, Wa.

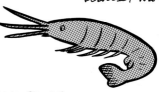

Dear Daniel,
...About "Needledick": My Vietnamese friend could relate to the boy for his small penis size but I could relate to it for another reason: When I was 15 or 16 I used to babysit for the neighbors. They had a dog named Kelly. One week they went on vacation and I was to take care of their house. I fed the dog but she was more interested in what I had in my pants. "What is it you want?" I asked, "What will you do if I give it to you?" I pulled my pants down and kneeled on the cold cement floor. Without hesitation, the dog immediately began to lick my penis. Lick! Lick! Lick! She was insatiable and I soon came. After I got off I was immediately disgusted with myself and vowed never to do such a filthy thing again!...

Name & address withheld

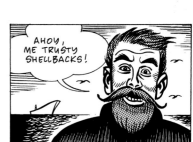

AHOY, ME TRUSTY SHELLBACKS!

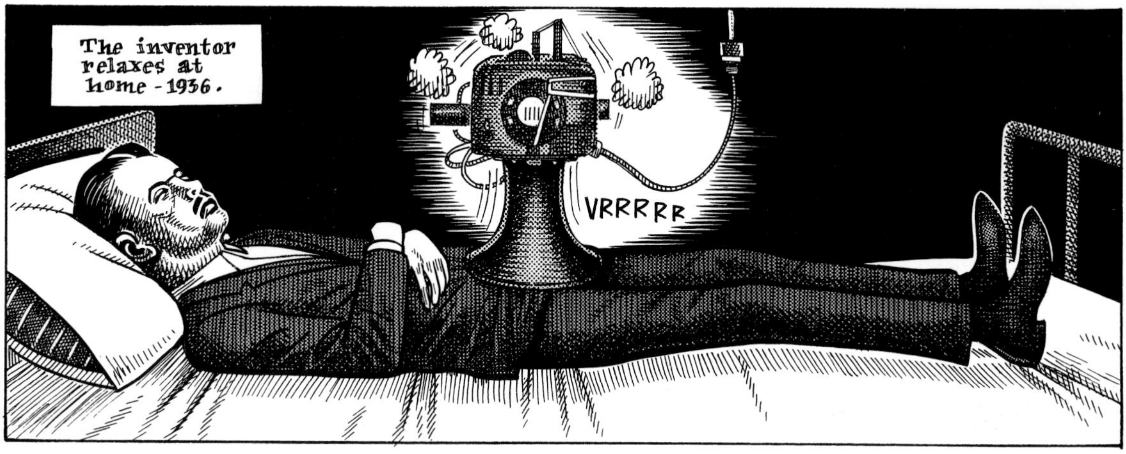

The inventor relaxes at home - 1936.
VRRRRR

PLUGSVILLE

JIM COPP / ED BROWN LPs

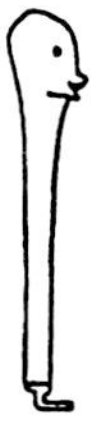

FAMED UNDERGROUND CARTOONIST WAYNO TIPPED ME OFF TO THESE GUYS A FEW YEARS AGO. THEY RECORDED 9 BRILLIANTLY WEIRD AND HILARIOUS LPs "FOR SMALL FRY AND SOPHISTICATED ADULTS" IN THE '60's WHICH IT TURNS OUT ARE (MIRACULOUSLY) STILL AVAILABLE (DIRECT FROM THE GREAT JIM COPP HIMSELF!)! IT'S LIKE FINDING OUT YOU CAN STILL ORDER *BIG FRANKIE* FROM THE BACK OF FAMOUS MONSTERS!.

SELECT FROM:

- JIM COPP TALES
- FABLE FOREST
- THIMBLE CORNER
- FIDGETY FROLIC
- EAST OF FLUMDIDDLE
- SCHOOLMATES
- GUMDROP FOLLIES
- SEA OF GLUP
- JOURNEY TO S.F. WITH THE GLUPS

LPs $7.95, CASSETTES $8.95 (+$2)
FROM: PLAYHOUSE RECORDS
BOX 36061, LA, CA. 90036

R.I.P. ZIPATONE

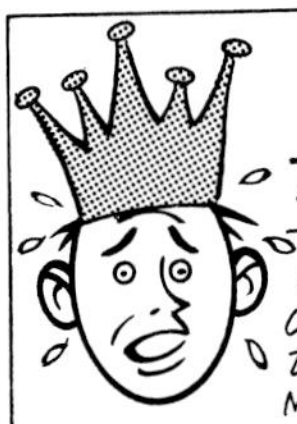

AS THE SELF-PROCLAIMED "KING OF ZIPATONE" I MUST MOURN THE PASSING OF THE ZIPATONE COMPANY. THEIR SHADING FILMS (i.e. THOSE LITTLE DOTS) WERE BY FAR THE BEST ON THE MARKET. THE COMPETITION'S SHADING FILMS ARE SO INFERIOR AS TO BE PRACTICALLY UNUSABLE. I GUESS DEMAND FOR THIS STUFF IS WAY DOWN NOW THAT YOU CAN DO EVERYTHING CHEAPER ON COMPUTERS. WOTTA WORLD! ... GOODBYE, OLD FRIEND!

more Good Stores:

COMIC RELIEF
Berkeley & S.F., Ca.

FALLOUT
Seattle, Wa.

QUIMBY'S
Chicago, Il.

GO TO THEM AND SPEND MONEY!

BEAT OF THE TRAPS

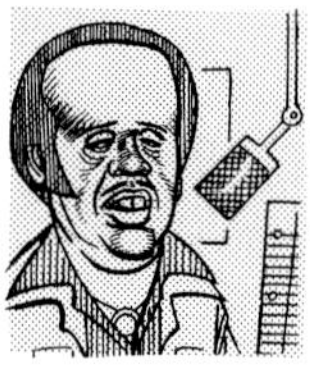

Y'KNOW THOSE ADS THAT SAY "SET YOUR POEMS TO MUSIC"? WELL THE WHOLE SCAM BEHIND THAT IS THAT YOU HAVE TO PAY TO HAVE YOUR AWKWARD, UNMARKETABLE LYRICS RECORDED BY A TIRED STUDIO BAND WHO'S NEVER SEEN YOUR WORDS UNTIL 5 MINUTES BEFORE THE SESSION. THE RESULTS ARE OFTEN PRETTY "INTENSE". THIS IS A DYNAMIC COLLECTION "GRACED" WITH A D. CLOWES COVER.

$9 PPd. FROM: (LP ONLY)
CARNAGE PRESS
BOX 627
NORTHAMPTON, MA.
01060

ALSO BUY:

LAS VEGAS GRIND, VOL. 4
STRIP RECORDS LP 004

LYRICS BY ERNEST NOYES BROOKINGS, VOL. 2 (CD)
ESD RECORDS

BECAUSE I DID THE COVERS FOR BOTH OF 'EM.

JOIN THE PUSSY HAIR CLUB!

MEMBERSHIP OPEN
Limited Time Only

Start your climb to national acclaim in the Pussy Hair Pluckers' World Book of Records by joining today!

The Pussy Hair Club membership is a Hair-Larious item ... GREAT EROTIC FUN for you or as a gift! New members receive:

- The Pubic Hair Trophy Board for mounting your favorite pluckings.
- Certified Point System and collecting techniques ... fingers, teeth, tongue, etc.!
- Membership card.
- Clear collectors box to view your collection.
- And as a special bonus—the Belly Button Fuzz Box!

Satisfaction Guaranteed

ADVERTISEMENT

DUPLEX PLANET

SUBSCRIBE NOW TO DAVID GREENBERGER'S AMAZING MAG, FEATURING AMUSING INTERVIEWS WITH LITTLE, OLD MEN. LOTSA LAFFS & COSMIC TRUTHS! $12 FOR 8 ISSUES

TO: PO BOX 1230
SARATOGA SPRINGS, NY 12866

THE MINI-COMIC EVENT OF THE CENTURY!

it's DOOFUS #1

By RICK ALTERGOTT

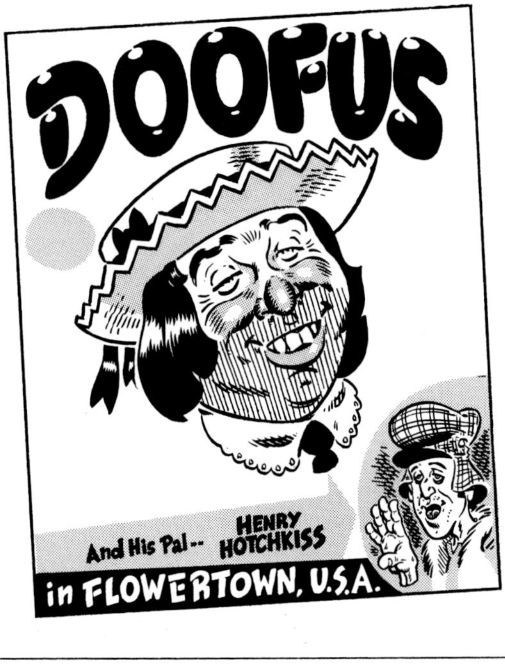
DOOFUS
And His Pal-- HENRY HOTCHKISS
in FLOWERTOWN, U.S.A.

WHO IS THE FUNNIEST CARTOONIST IN AMERICA? NOT CATHY GUISEWITE, NOT JOHNNY HART... IT'S *RICK ALTERGOTT!* WHY HAVE YOU NEVER HEARD OF HIM? MAYBE IT'S BECAUSE HIS ENTIRE CAREER CONSISTS OF TWO UNSIGNED PAGES IN WEIRDO #25! WHY? DON'T ASK! JUST BUY DOOFUS #1 AND THRILL TO THE WHOLESOME ADVENTURES OF DOOFUS AND HIS PAL, HENRY HOTCHKISS! ALSO IN THIS ISSUE: "THE DUDE" (HATEFUL, MISANTHROPIC FRATERNITY HI-JINX CO-PLOTTED BY YRS. TRULY) & "PROFESSOR EGGROD" AND MORE!

Only $2.00 POSTPAID FROM:

MAKE CHECKS PAYABLE TO D. CLOWES.

EIGHTBALL; DEPT. DOOFUS
BOX 3357, CHICAGO IL. 60654

INQUIRE ABOUT WHOLESALE RATES

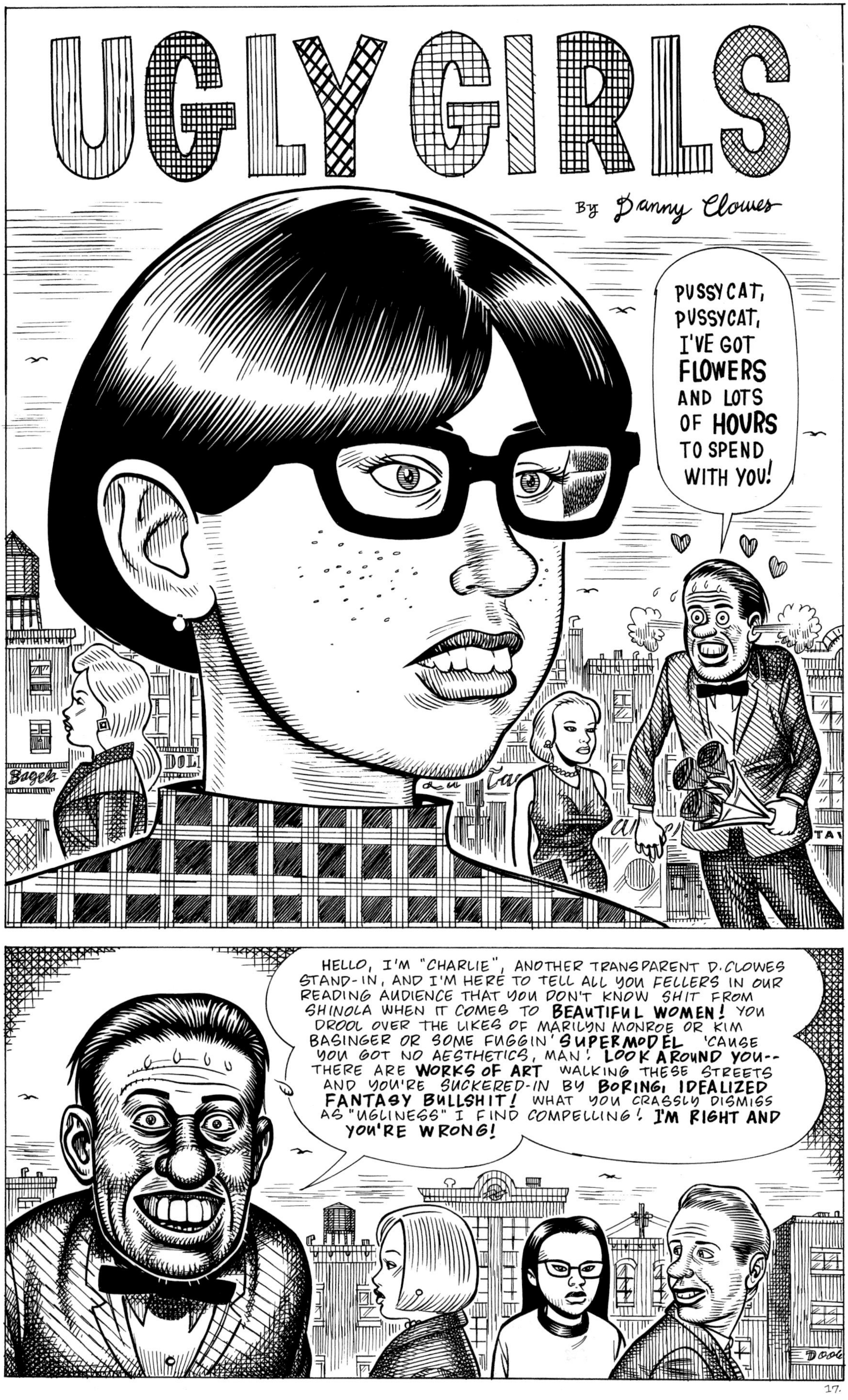
UGLY GIRLS
By Danny Clowes
PUSSYCAT, PUSSYCAT, I'VE GOT FLOWERS AND LOTS OF HOURS TO SPEND WITH YOU!
Bagels
HELLO, I'M "CHARLIE", ANOTHER TRANSPARENT D.CLOWES STAND-IN, AND I'M HERE TO TELL ALL YOU FELLERS IN OUR READING AUDIENCE THAT YOU DON'T KNOW SHIT FROM SHINOLA WHEN IT COMES TO BEAUTIFUL WOMEN! YOU DROOL OVER THE LIKES OF MARILYN MONROE OR KIM BASINGER OR SOME FUGGIN' SUPERMODEL 'CAUSE YOU GOT NO AESTHETICS, MAN! LOOK AROUND YOU-- THERE ARE WORKS OF ART WALKING THESE STREETS AND YOU'RE SUCKERED-IN BY BORING, IDEALIZED FANTASY BULLSHIT! WHAT YOU CRASSLY DISMISS AS "UGLINESS" I FIND COMPELLING! I'M RIGHT AND YOU'RE WRONG!

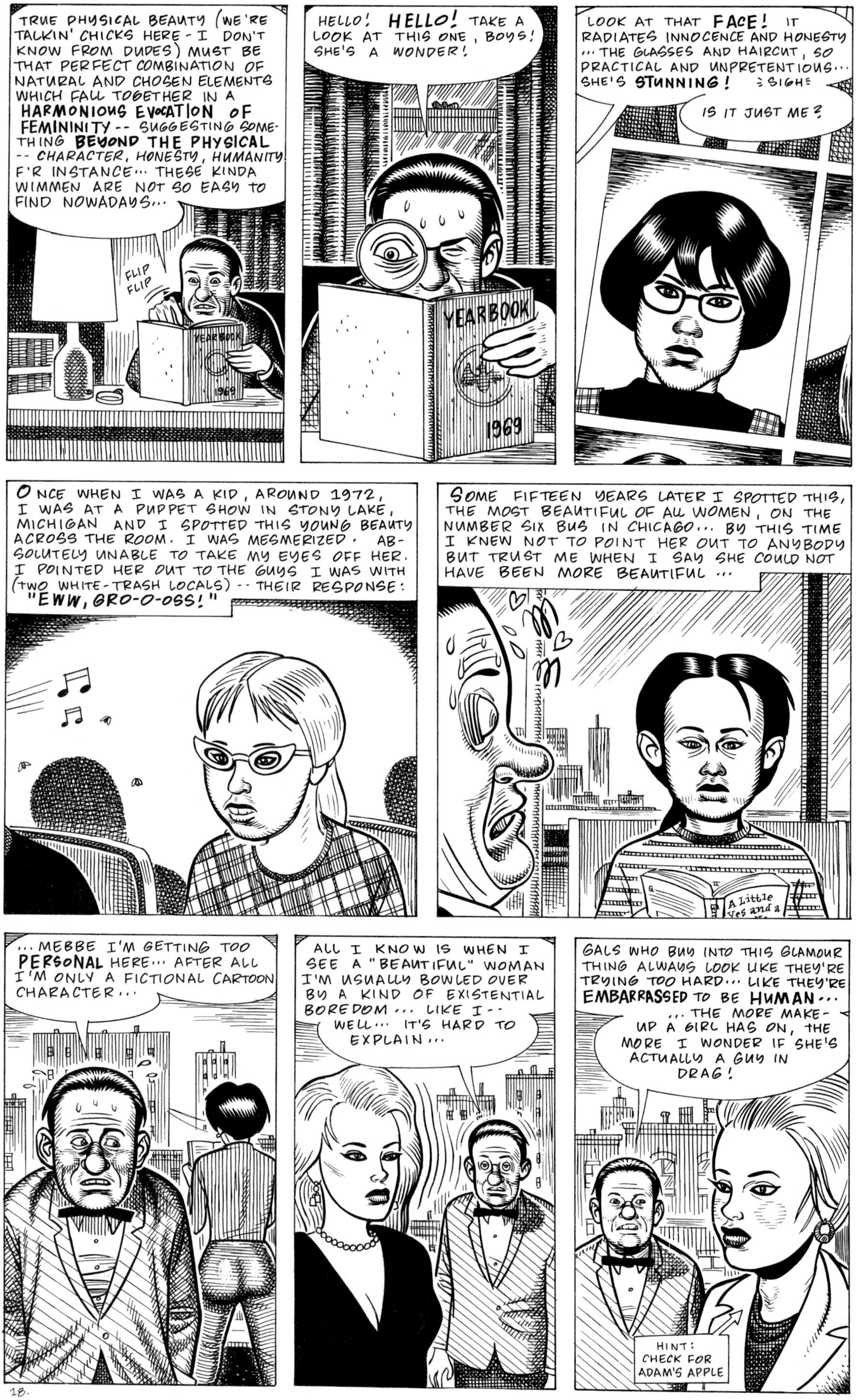
TRUE PHYSICAL BEAUTY (WE'RE TALKIN' CHICKS HERE - I DON'T KNOW FROM DUDES) MUST BE THAT PERFECT COMBINATION OF NATURAL AND CHOSEN ELEMENTS WHICH FALL TOGETHER IN A HARMONIOUS EVOCATION OF FEMININITY -- SUGGESTING SOMETHING BEYOND THE PHYSICAL -- CHARACTER, HONESTY, HUMANITY F'R INSTANCE... THESE KINDA WIMMEN ARE NOT SO EASY TO FIND NOWADAYS...
FLIP FLIP
YEARBOOK
1969
HELLO! HELLO! TAKE A LOOK AT THIS ONE, BOYS! SHE'S A WONDER!
YEARBOOK
1969
LOOK AT THAT FACE! IT RADIATES INNOCENCE AND HONESTY ... THE GLASSES AND HAIRCUT, SO PRACTICAL AND UNPRETENTIOUS... SHE'S STUNNING! ≡SIGH≡
IS IT JUST ME?
ONCE WHEN I WAS A KID, AROUND 1972, I WAS AT A PUPPET SHOW IN STONY LAKE, MICHIGAN AND I SPOTTED THIS YOUNG BEAUTY ACROSS THE ROOM. I WAS MESMERIZED. ABSOLUTELY UNABLE TO TAKE MY EYES OFF HER. I POINTED HER OUT TO THE GUYS I WAS WITH (TWO WHITE-TRASH LOCALS) -- THEIR RESPONSE: "EWW, GRO-O-OSS!"
SOME FIFTEEN YEARS LATER I SPOTTED THIS, THE MOST BEAUTIFUL OF ALL WOMEN, ON THE NUMBER SIX BUS IN CHICAGO... BY THIS TIME I KNEW NOT TO POINT HER OUT TO ANYBODY BUT TRUST ME WHEN I SAY SHE COULD NOT HAVE BEEN MORE BEAUTIFUL ...
A Little Yes and a
...MEBBE I'M GETTING TOO PERSONAL HERE... AFTER ALL I'M ONLY A FICTIONAL CARTOON CHARACTER...
ALL I KNOW IS WHEN I SEE A "BEAUTIFUL" WOMAN I'M USUALLY BOWLED OVER BY A KIND OF EXISTENTIAL BOREDOM ... LIKE I -- WELL... IT'S HARD TO EXPLAIN...
GALS WHO BUY INTO THIS GLAMOUR THING ALWAYS LOOK LIKE THEY'RE TRYING TOO HARD... LIKE THEY'RE EMBARRASSED TO BE HUMAN...
... THE MORE MAKE-UP A GIRL HAS ON, THE MORE I WONDER IF SHE'S ACTUALLY A GUY IN DRAG!
HINT: CHECK FOR ADAM'S APPLE

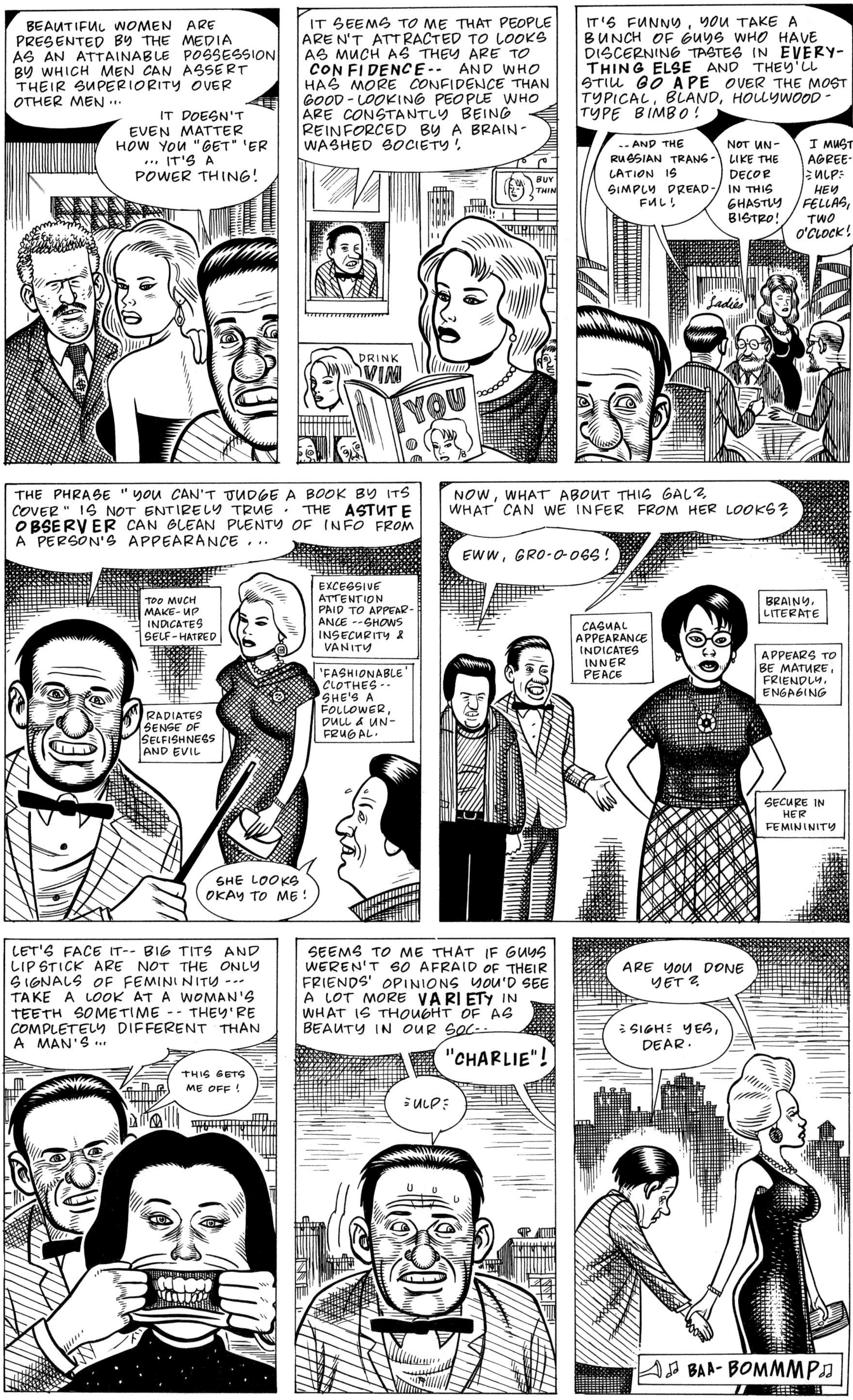
BEAUTIFUL WOMEN ARE PRESENTED BY THE MEDIA AS AN ATTAINABLE POSSESSION BY WHICH MEN CAN ASSERT THEIR SUPERIORITY OVER OTHER MEN...
IT DOESN'T EVEN MATTER HOW YOU "GET" 'ER ... IT'S A POWER THING!
IT SEEMS TO ME THAT PEOPLE AREN'T ATTRACTED TO LOOKS AS MUCH AS THEY ARE TO CONFIDENCE-- AND WHO HAS MORE CONFIDENCE THAN GOOD-LOOKING PEOPLE WHO ARE CONSTANTLY BEING REINFORCED BY A BRAIN-WASHED SOCIETY!
BUY THIN
DRINK VIM
YOU
IT'S FUNNY, YOU TAKE A BUNCH OF GUYS WHO HAVE DISCERNING TASTES IN EVERYTHING ELSE AND THEY'LL STILL GO APE OVER THE MOST TYPICAL, BLAND, HOLLYWOOD-TYPE BIMBO!
--AND THE RUSSIAN TRANSLATION IS SIMPLY DREADFUL!
NOT UNLIKE THE DECOR IN THIS GHASTLY BISTRO!
I MUST AGREE-- ÷ULP÷ HEY FELLAS, TWO O'CLOCK!
Ladies
THE PHRASE "YOU CAN'T JUDGE A BOOK BY ITS COVER" IS NOT ENTIRELY TRUE. THE ASTUTE OBSERVER CAN GLEAN PLENTY OF INFO FROM A PERSON'S APPEARANCE...
TOO MUCH MAKE-UP INDICATES SELF-HATRED
EXCESSIVE ATTENTION PAID TO APPEARANCE --SHOWS INSECURITY & VANITY
'FASHIONABLE' CLOTHES-- SHE'S A FOLLOWER, DULL & UNFRUGAL.
RADIATES SENSE OF SELFISHNESS AND EVIL
SHE LOOKS OKAY TO ME!
NOW, WHAT ABOUT THIS GAL? WHAT CAN WE INFER FROM HER LOOKS?
EWW, GRO-O-OSS!
CASUAL APPEARANCE INDICATES INNER PEACE
BRAINY, LITERATE
APPEARS TO BE MATURE, FRIENDLY, ENGAGING
SECURE IN HER FEMININITY
LET'S FACE IT-- BIG TITS AND LIPSTICK ARE NOT THE ONLY SIGNALS OF FEMININITY--- TAKE A LOOK AT A WOMAN'S TEETH SOMETIME -- THEY'RE COMPLETELY DIFFERENT THAN A MAN'S...
THIS GETS ME OFF!
SEEMS TO ME THAT IF GUYS WEREN'T SO AFRAID OF THEIR FRIENDS' OPINIONS YOU'D SEE A LOT MORE VARIETY IN WHAT IS THOUGHT OF AS BEAUTY IN OUR SOC--
"CHARLIE"!
÷ULP÷
ARE YOU DONE YET?
÷SIGH÷ YES, DEAR.
BAA-BOMMMP

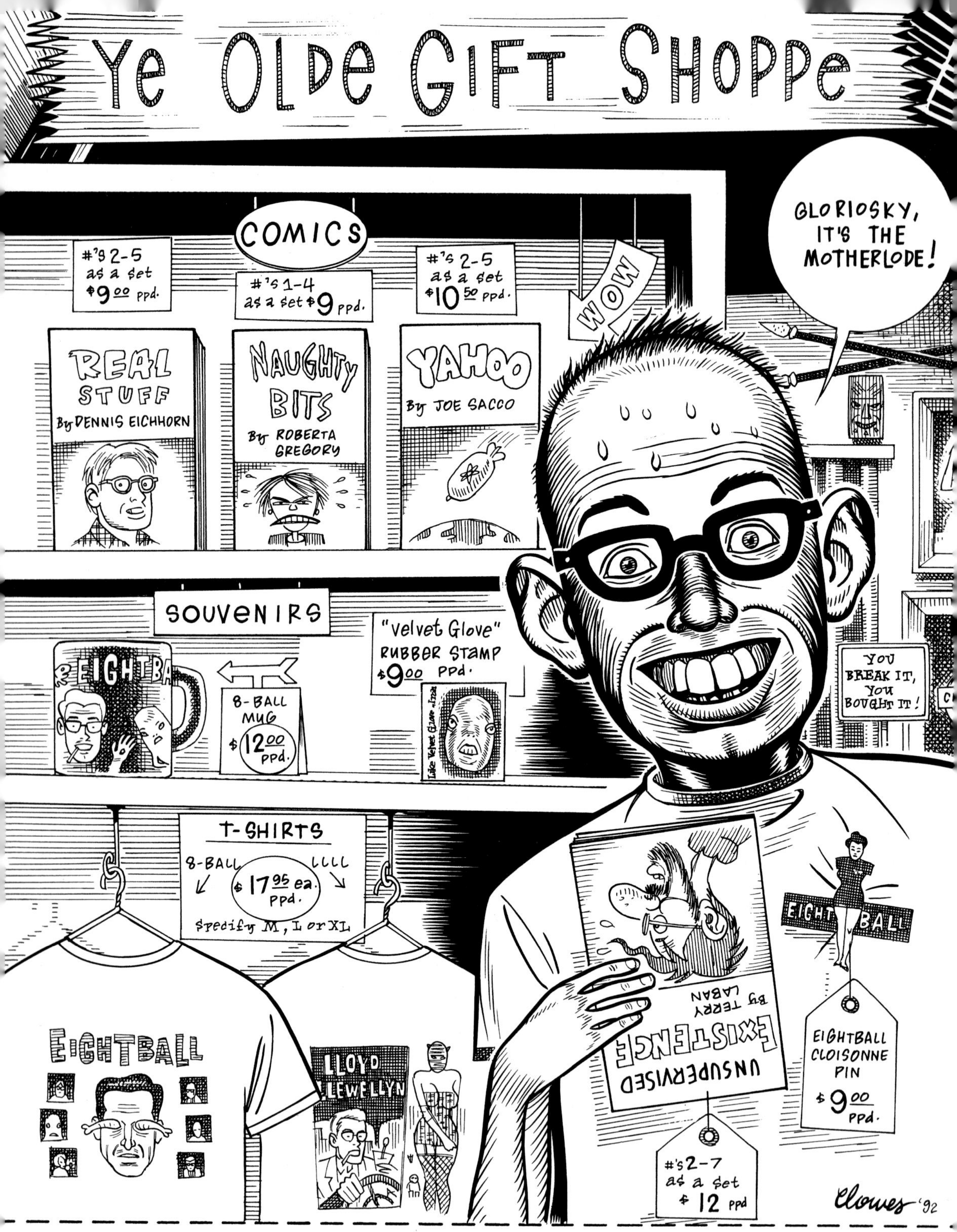
Ye Olde Gift Shoppe
COMICS
#'s 2-5 as a set $9.00 ppd.
#'s 1-4 as a set $9 ppd.
#'s 2-5 as a set $10.50 ppd.
WOW
GLORIOSKY, IT'S THE MOTHERLODE!
REAL STUFF By DENNIS EICHHORN
NAUGHTY BITS By ROBERTA GREGORY
YAHOO By JOE SACCO
SOUVENIRS
"Velvet Glove" RUBBER STAMP $9.00 ppd.
8-BALL MUG $12.00 ppd.
YOU BREAK IT, YOU BOUGHT IT!
T-SHIRTS
8-BALL LLLL $17.95 ea. ppd.
Specify M, L or XL
EIGHTBALL
LLOYD LLEWELLYN
UNSUPERVISED EXISTENCE By TERRY LABAN
#'s 2-7 as a set $12 ppd
EIGHT BALL
EIGHTBALL CLOISONNE PIN $9.00 ppd.
Clowes '92

☐ EIGHTBALL #1 ☐ #2 ☐ #3 ☐ #4 ☐ #5 ☐ #6 ☐ #7
☐ #8 $3 EA. ☐ 4-ISSUE SUB. TO 8-BALL $9.50 ☐ LLLL BOOK $12
☐ LOUT RAMPAGE! $13 ☐ REAL STUFF 2-5 (SET) $9
☐ NAUGHTY BITS 1-4 (SET) $9 ☐ UNSUPERVISED EXISTENCE 2-7 (SET) $12
☐ YAHOO 2-5 (SET) $10.50 ☐ 8-BALL CLOISONNE PIN $9
☐ 8-BALL MUG $12 ☐ 8-BALL RUBBER STAMP $9
☐ 8-BALL T-SHIRT $17.95 M L XL ☐ LL T-SHIRT $17.95 M L XL

name ______
address ______
city ______
state ______ zip ______

send orders to: FANTAGRAPHICS BOOKS
7563 LAKE CITY WAY NE
SEATTLE, WA. 98115
or call toll-free 1-800-657-1100

Allow 6-8 weeks
Foreign orders add 10%

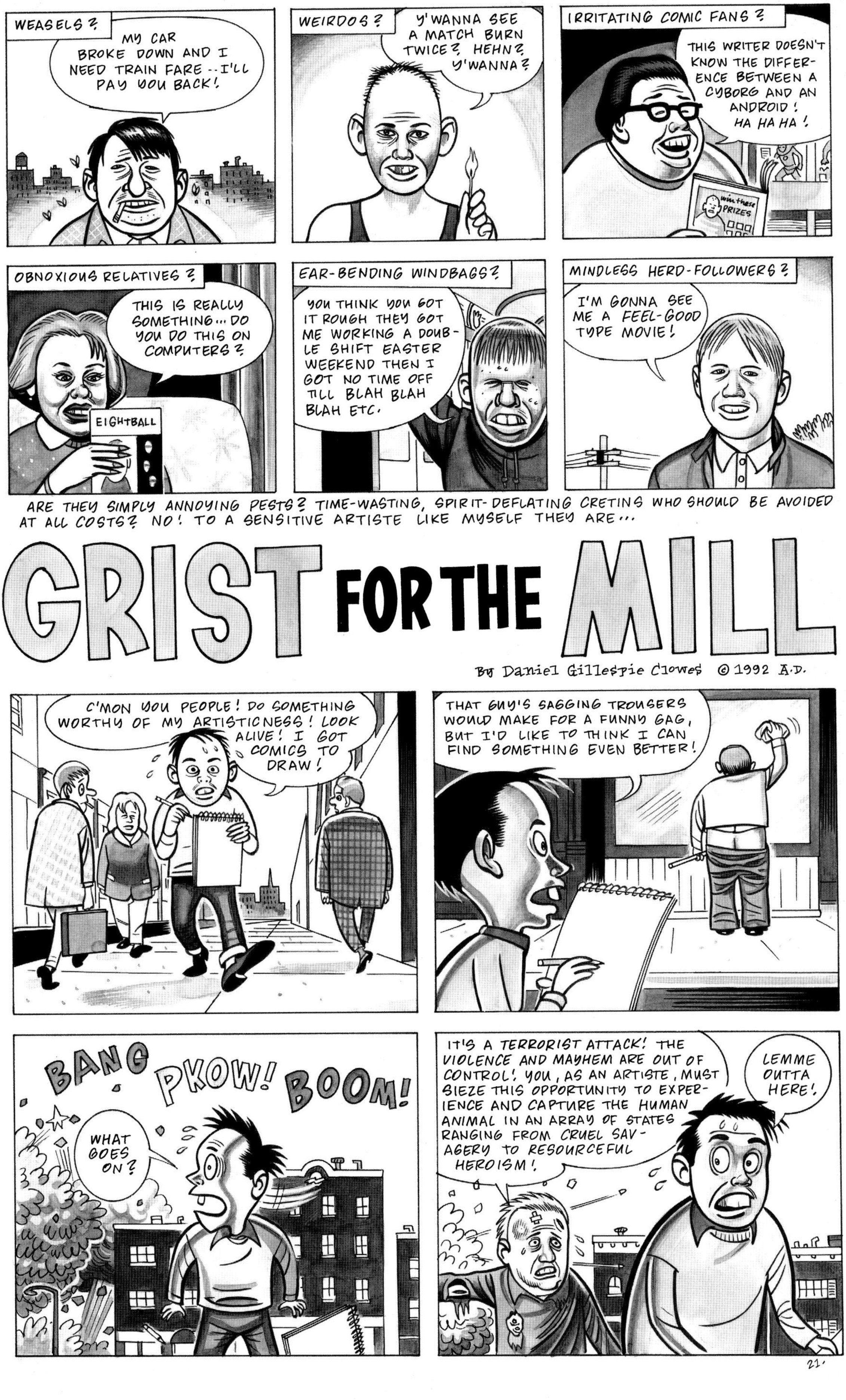
WEASELS?
MY CAR BROKE DOWN AND I NEED TRAIN FARE --I'LL PAY YOU BACK!
WEIRDOS?
Y'WANNA SEE A MATCH BURN TWICE? HEHN? Y'WANNA?
IRRITATING COMIC FANS?
THIS WRITER DOESN'T KNOW THE DIFFERENCE BETWEEN A CYBORG AND AN ANDROID! HA HA HA!
win these PRIZES
OBNOXIOUS RELATIVES?
THIS IS REALLY SOMETHING... DO YOU DO THIS ON COMPUTERS?
EIGHTBALL
EAR-BENDING WINDBAGS?
YOU THINK YOU GOT IT ROUGH THEY GOT ME WORKING A DOUBLE SHIFT EASTER WEEKEND THEN I GOT NO TIME OFF TILL BLAH BLAH BLAH ETC.
MINDLESS HERD-FOLLOWERS?
I'M GONNA SEE ME A FEEL-GOOD TYPE MOVIE!
ARE THEY SIMPLY ANNOYING PESTS? TIME-WASTING, SPIRIT-DEFLATING CRETINS WHO SHOULD BE AVOIDED AT ALL COSTS? NO! TO A SENSITIVE ARTISTE LIKE MYSELF THEY ARE...
GRIST FOR THE MILL
By Daniel Gillespie Clowes ©1992 A.D.
C'MON YOU PEOPLE! DO SOMETHING WORTHY OF MY ARTISTICNESS! LOOK ALIVE! I GOT COMICS TO DRAW!
THAT GUY'S SAGGING TROUSERS WOULD MAKE FOR A FUNNY GAG, BUT I'D LIKE TO THINK I CAN FIND SOMETHING EVEN BETTER!
BANG
PKOW!
BOOM!
WHAT GOES ON?
IT'S A TERRORIST ATTACK! THE VIOLENCE AND MAYHEM ARE OUT OF CONTROL! YOU, AS AN ARTISTE, MUST SIEZE THIS OPPORTUNITY TO EXPERIENCE AND CAPTURE THE HUMAN ANIMAL IN AN ARRAY OF STATES RANGING FROM CRUEL SAVAGERY TO RESOURCEFUL HEROISM!
LEMME OUTTA HERE!

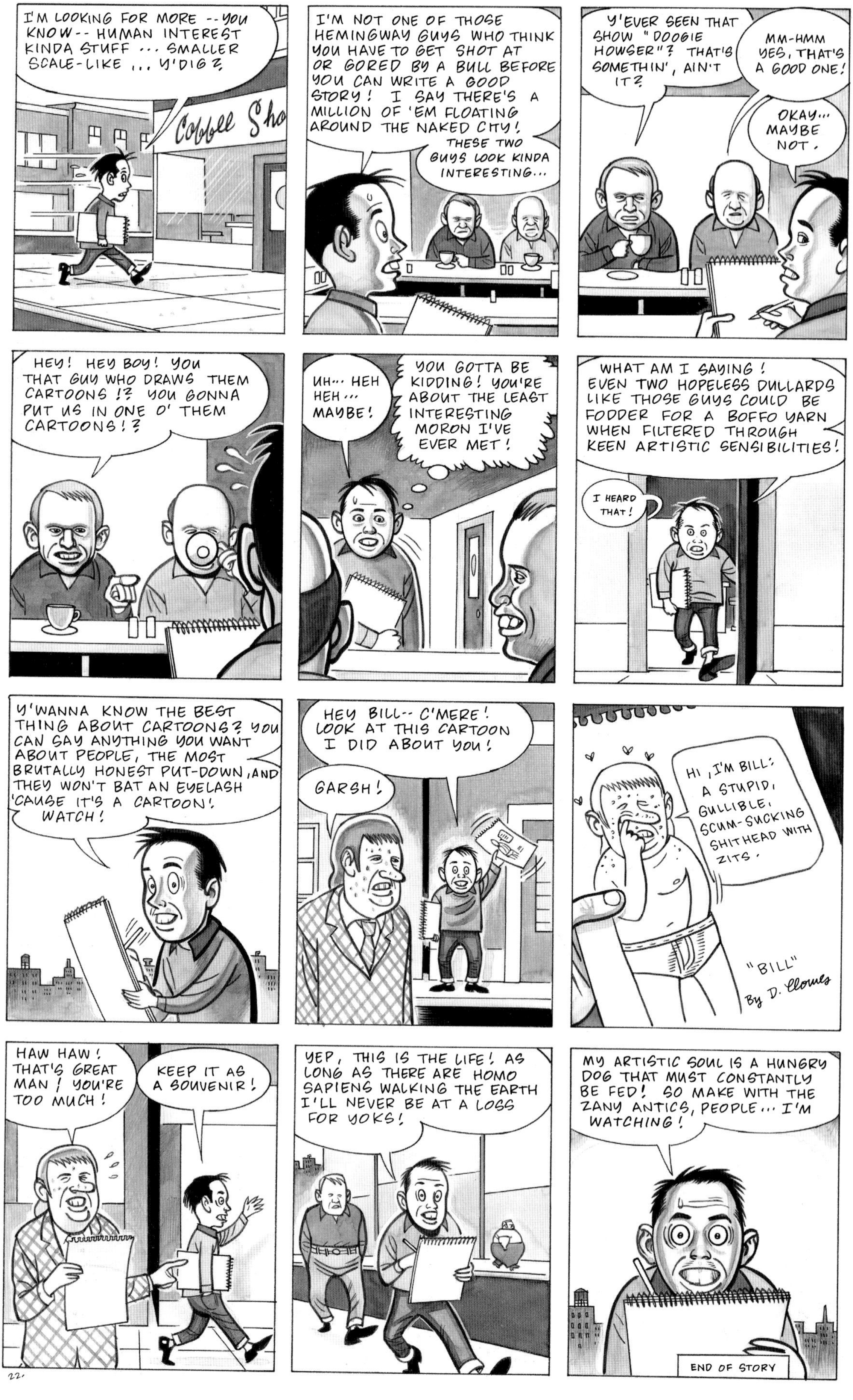
I'M LOOKING FOR MORE --YOU KNOW-- HUMAN INTEREST KINDA STUFF ... SMALLER SCALE-LIKE ... Y'DIG?
I'M NOT ONE OF THOSE HEMINGWAY GUYS WHO THINK YOU HAVE TO GET SHOT AT OR GORED BY A BULL BEFORE YOU CAN WRITE A GOOD STORY! I SAY THERE'S A MILLION OF 'EM FLOATING AROUND THE NAKED CITY!
THESE TWO GUYS LOOK KINDA INTERESTING...
Y'EVER SEEN THAT SHOW "DOOGIE HOWSER"? THAT'S SOMETHIN', AIN'T IT?
MM-HMM YES, THAT'S A GOOD ONE!
OKAY... MAYBE NOT.
HEY! HEY BOY! YOU THAT GUY WHO DRAWS THEM CARTOONS!? YOU GONNA PUT US IN ONE O' THEM CARTOONS!?
UH... HEH HEH... MAYBE!
YOU GOTTA BE KIDDING! YOU'RE ABOUT THE LEAST INTERESTING MORON I'VE EVER MET!
WHAT AM I SAYING! EVEN TWO HOPELESS DULLARDS LIKE THOSE GUYS COULD BE FODDER FOR A BOFFO YARN WHEN FILTERED THROUGH KEEN ARTISTIC SENSIBILITIES!
I HEARD THAT!
Y'WANNA KNOW THE BEST THING ABOUT CARTOONS? YOU CAN SAY ANYTHING YOU WANT ABOUT PEOPLE, THE MOST BRUTALLY HONEST PUT-DOWN, AND THEY WON'T BAT AN EYELASH 'CAUSE IT'S A CARTOON! WATCH!
HEY BILL-- C'MERE! LOOK AT THIS CARTOON I DID ABOUT YOU!
GARSH!
HI, I'M BILL: A STUPID, GULLIBLE, SCUM-SUCKING SHITHEAD WITH ZITS.
"BILL"
By D. Clowes
HAW HAW! THAT'S GREAT MAN! YOU'RE TOO MUCH!
KEEP IT AS A SOUVENIR!
YEP, THIS IS THE LIFE! AS LONG AS THERE ARE HOMO SAPIENS WALKING THE EARTH I'LL NEVER BE AT A LOSS FOR YOKS!
MY ARTISTIC SOUL IS A HUNGRY DOG THAT MUST CONSTANTLY BE FED! SO MAKE WITH THE ZANY ANTICS, PEOPLE... I'M WATCHING!
END OF STORY

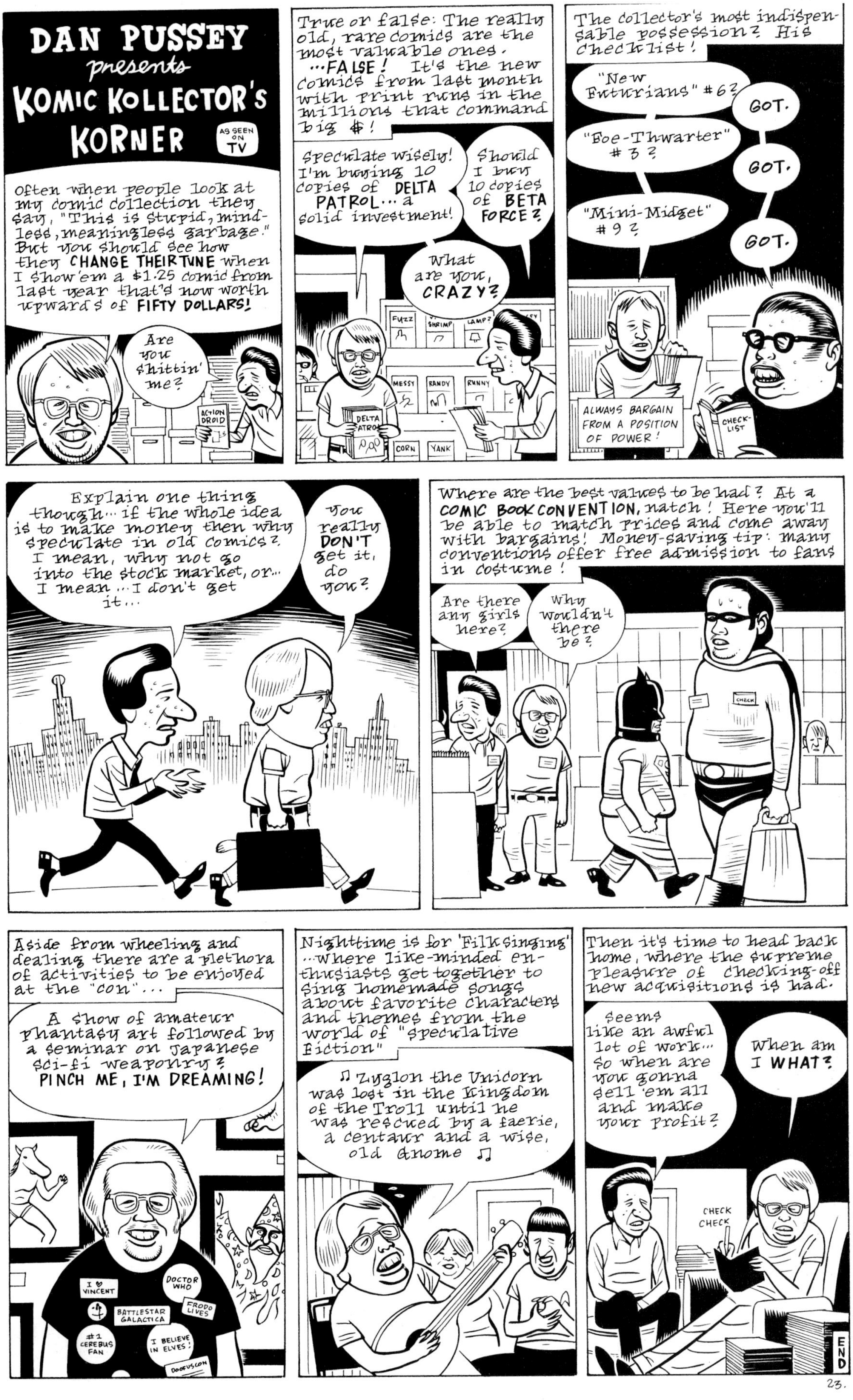
DAN PUSSEY presents KOMIC KOLLECTOR'S KORNER
AS SEEN ON TV
Often when people look at my comic collection they say, "This is stupid, mindless, meaningless garbage." But you should see how they CHANGE THEIR TUNE when I show 'em a $1.25 comic from last year that's now worth upwards of FIFTY DOLLARS!
Are you shittin' me?
ACTION DROID
True or false: The really old, rare comics are the most valuable ones. ...FALSE! It's the new comics from last month with print runs in the millions that command big $!
Speculate wisely! I'm buying 10 copies of DELTA PATROL... a solid investment!
Should I buy 10 copies of BETA FORCE?
What are you, CRAZY?
FUZZ
SHRIMP
LAMP?
MESSY
RANDY
RUNNY
CORN
YANK
The collector's most indispensable possession? His checklist!
"New Futurians" #6?
GOT.
"Foe-Thwarter" #3?
GOT.
"Mini-Midget" #9?
GOT.
ALWAYS BARGAIN FROM A POSITION OF POWER!
CHECK-LIST
Explain one thing though... if the whole idea is to make money then why speculate in old comics? I mean, why not go into the stock market, or... I mean... I don't get it...
You really DON'T get it, do you?
Where are the best values to be had? At a COMIC BOOK CONVENTION, natch! Here you'll be able to match prices and come away with bargains! Money-saving tip: many conventions offer free admission to fans in costume!
Are there any girls here?
Why wouldn't there be?
CHECK
Aside from wheeling and dealing there are a plethora of activities to be enjoyed at the "con"...
A show of amateur phantasy art followed by a seminar on Japanese sci-fi weaponry? PINCH ME, I'M DREAMING!
I ♥ VINCENT
DOCTOR WHO
BATTLESTAR GALACTICA
FRODO LIVES
#1 CEREBUS FAN
I BELIEVE IN ELVES!
DOOFUSCON
Nighttime is for 'Filksinging' ...where like-minded enthusiasts get together to sing homemade songs about favorite characters and themes from the world of "speculative fiction"
♫ Zyglon the Unicorn was lost in the Kingdom of the Troll until he was rescued by a faerie, a centaur and a wise, old gnome ♫
Then it's time to head back home, where the supreme pleasure of checking-off new acquisitions is had.
Seems like an awful lot of work... so when are you gonna sell 'em all and make your profit?
When am I WHAT?
CHECK CHECK
END

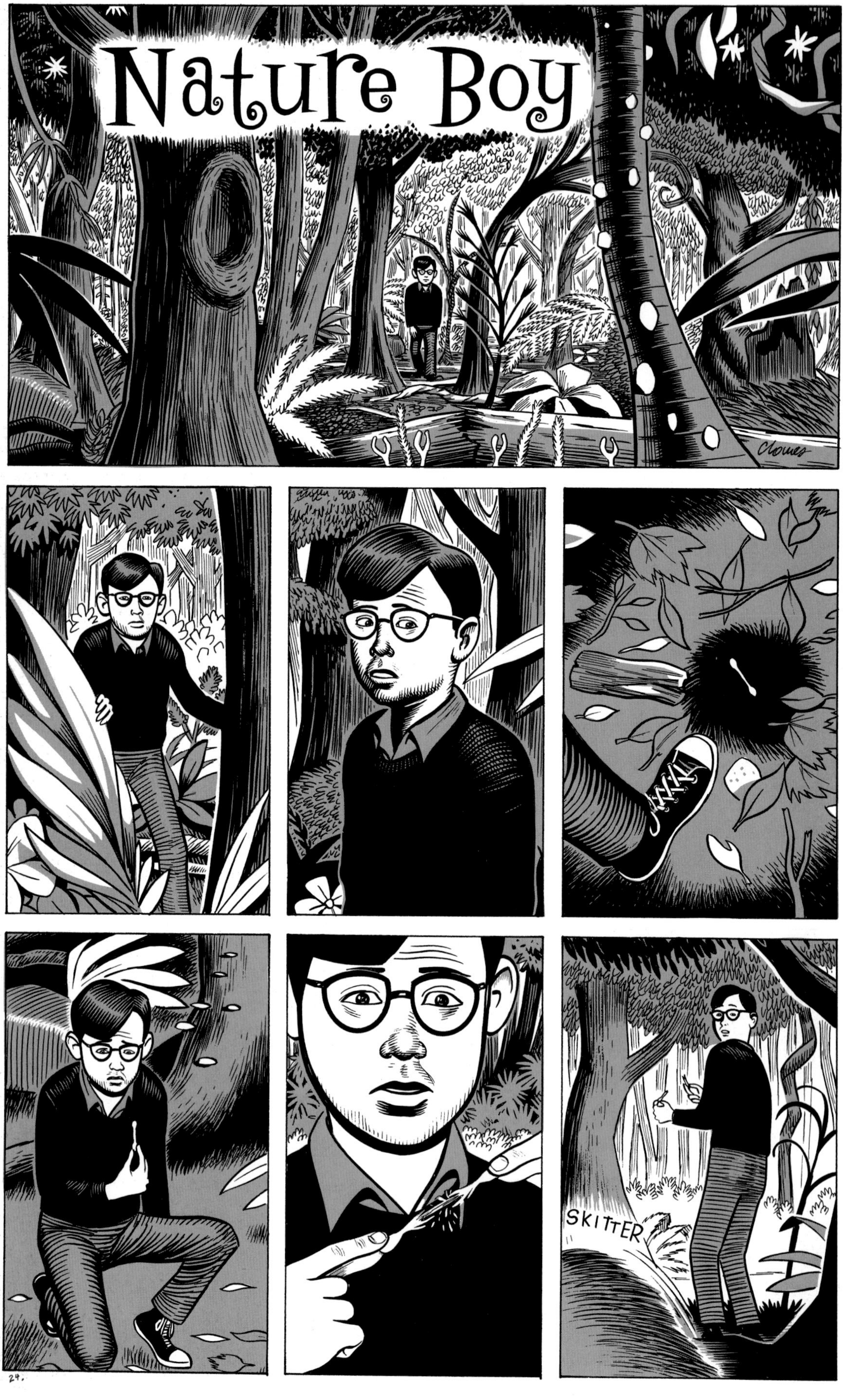
Nature Boy
Clowes
SKITTER

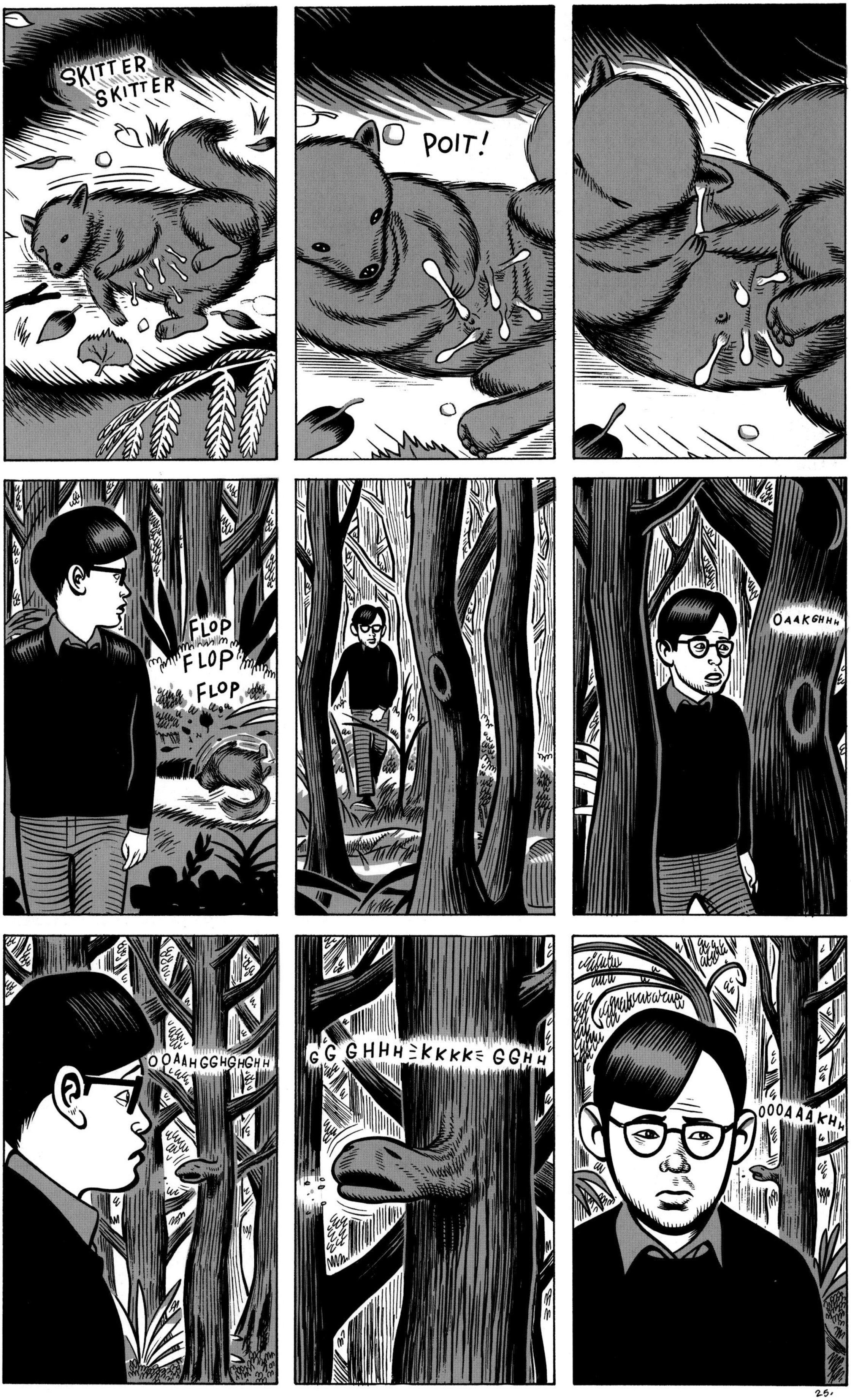
SKITTER SKITTER
POIT!
FLOP
FLOP
FLOP
OAAKGHHH
OOAAHGGHGHGHH
GG GHHH KKKK GGHH
OOOAAAKHH

BZZZZT

ZZZSSSS
FZZZZZT

KИHHH
KИHHHHH

BZZZZZK
KZZZZZT

KИHHH
KИHHH

What are you doing? You have FIVE MINUTES to get to the airport to catch your flight to Dallas! you've got to be on that plane or you'll never make your connecting flight back to here! That's a non-refundable ticket!

ZZSSSSS

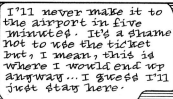

I'll never make it to the airport in five minutes. It's a shame not to use the ticket but, I mean, this is where I would end up anyway... I guess I'll just stay here.

TSSSS
BKZZT

FZZZT
KZZZZZK

END.

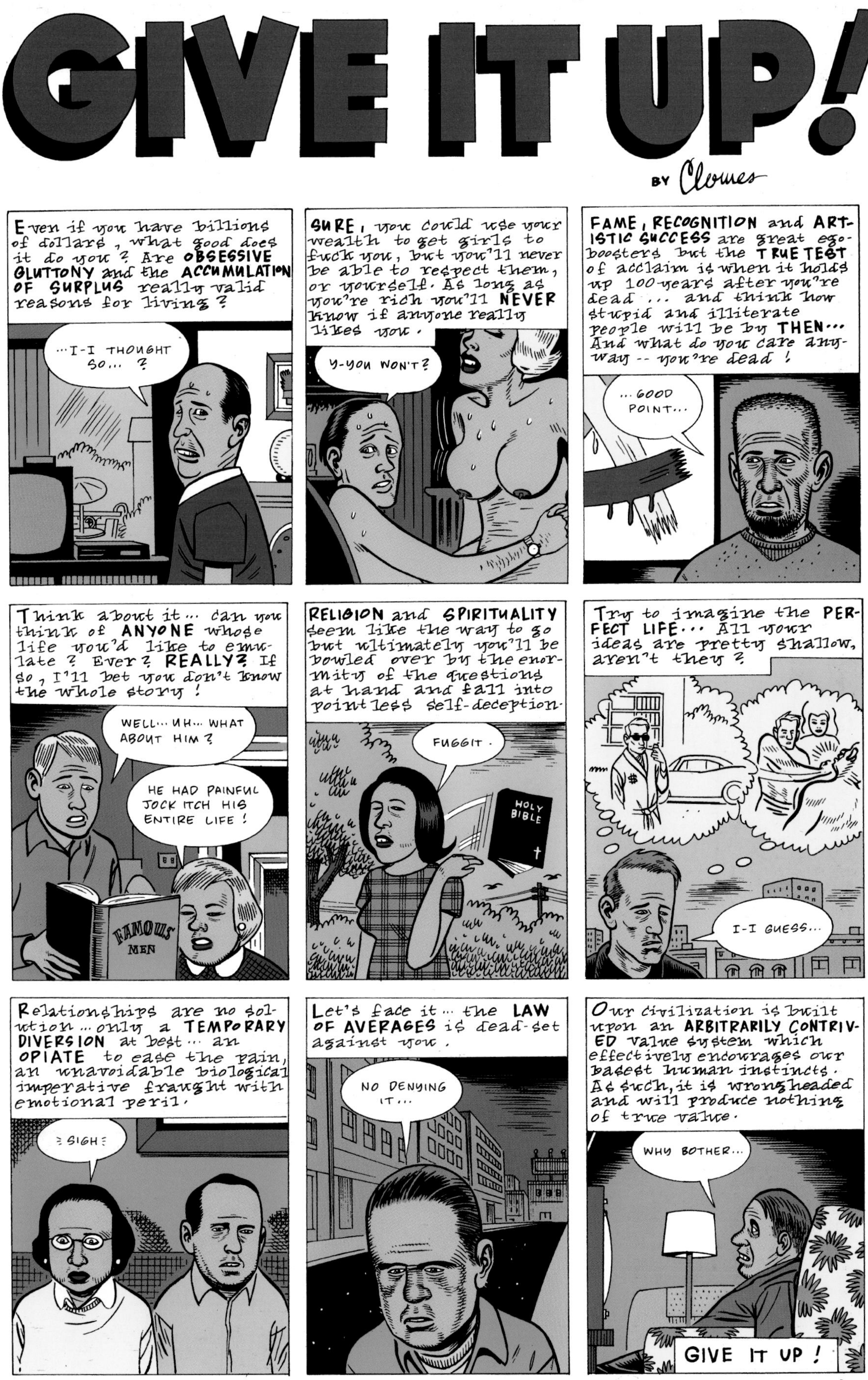
GIVE IT UP!
BY Clowes
Even if you have billions of dollars, what good does it do you? Are OBSESSIVE GLUTTONY and the ACCUMULATION OF SURPLUS really valid reasons for living?
...I-I THOUGHT SO...?
SURE, you could use your wealth to get girls to fuck you, but you'll never be able to respect them, or yourself. As long as you're rich you'll NEVER know if anyone really likes you.
Y-YOU WON'T?
FAME, RECOGNITION and ARTISTIC SUCCESS are great ego-boosters but the TRUE TEST of acclaim is when it holds up 100 years after you're dead ... and think how stupid and illiterate people will be by THEN... And what do you care anyway -- you're dead!
...GOOD POINT...
Think about it... can you think of ANYONE whose life you'd like to emulate? Ever? REALLY? If so, I'll bet you don't know the whole story!
WELL... UH... WHAT ABOUT HIM?
HE HAD PAINFUL JOCK ITCH HIS ENTIRE LIFE!
FAMOUS MEN
RELIGION and SPIRITUALITY seem like the way to go but ultimately you'll be bowled over by the enormity of the questions at hand and fall into pointless self-deception.
FUGGIT.
HOLY BIBLE
Try to imagine the PERFECT LIFE... All your ideas are pretty shallow, aren't they?
I-I GUESS...
Relationships are no solution... only a TEMPORARY DIVERSION at best... an OPIATE to ease the pain, an unavoidable biological imperative fraught with emotional peril.
SIGH
Let's face it... the LAW OF AVERAGES is dead-set against you.
NO DENYING IT...
Our civilization is built upon an ARBITRARILY CONTRIVED value system which effectively encourages our basest human instincts. As such, it is wrongheaded and will produce nothing of true value.
WHY BOTHER...
GIVE IT UP!

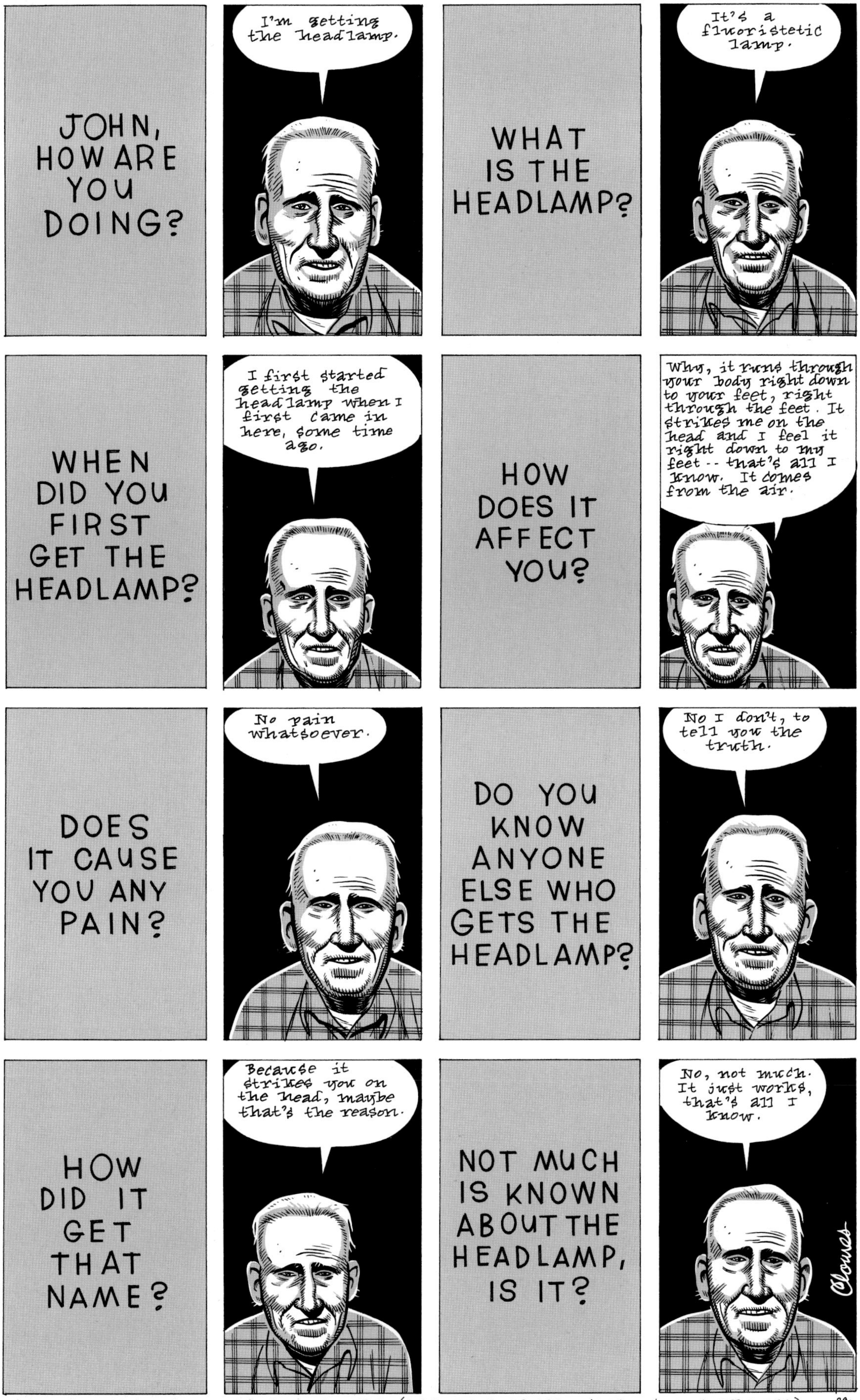

JOHN, HOW ARE YOU DOING?
I'm getting the headlamp.
WHAT IS THE HEADLAMP?
It's a fluoristetic lamp.
WHEN DID YOU FIRST GET THE HEADLAMP?
I first started getting the headlamp when I first came in here, some time ago.
HOW DOES IT AFFECT YOU?
Why, it runs through your body right down to your feet, right through the feet. It strikes me on the head and I feel it right down to my feet -- that's all I know. It comes from the air.
DOES IT CAUSE YOU ANY PAIN?
No pain whatsoever.
DO YOU KNOW ANYONE ELSE WHO GETS THE HEADLAMP?
No I don't, to tell you the truth.
HOW DID IT GET THAT NAME?
Because it strikes you on the head, maybe that's the reason.
NOT MUCH IS KNOWN ABOUT THE HEADLAMP, IS IT?
No, not much. It just works, that's all I know.
Clowes

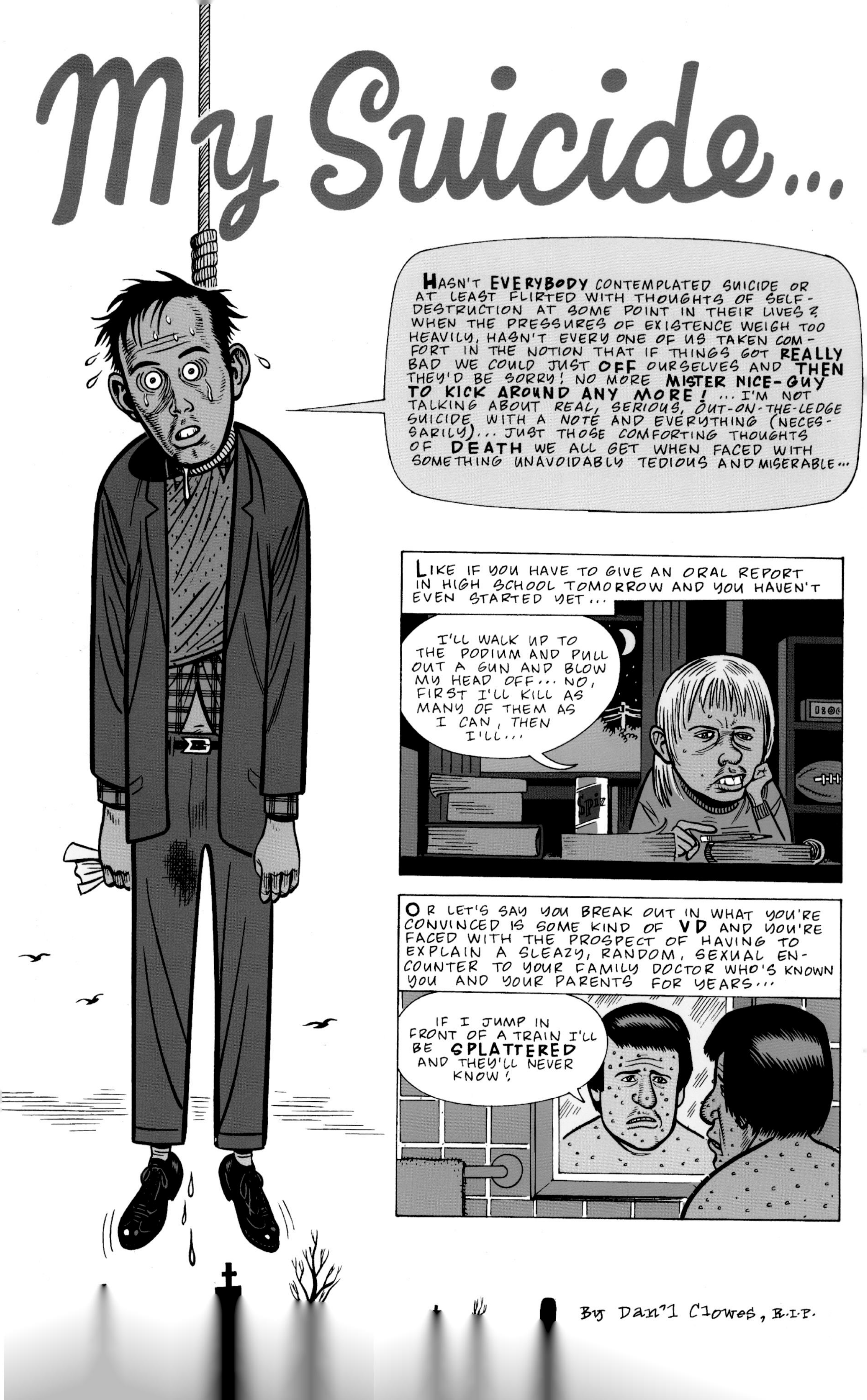
My Suicide...
HASN'T EVERYBODY CONTEMPLATED SUICIDE OR AT LEAST FLIRTED WITH THOUGHTS OF SELF-DESTRUCTION AT SOME POINT IN THEIR LIVES? WHEN THE PRESSURES OF EXISTENCE WEIGH TOO HEAVILY, HASN'T EVERY ONE OF US TAKEN COMFORT IN THE NOTION THAT IF THINGS GOT REALLY BAD WE COULD JUST OFF OURSELVES AND THEN THEY'D BE SORRY! NO MORE MISTER NICE-GUY TO KICK AROUND ANY MORE! ... I'M NOT TALKING ABOUT REAL, SERIOUS, OUT-ON-THE-LEDGE SUICIDE WITH A NOTE AND EVERYTHING (NECESSARILY)... JUST THOSE COMFORTING THOUGHTS OF DEATH WE ALL GET WHEN FACED WITH SOMETHING UNAVOIDABLY TEDIOUS AND MISERABLE...
LIKE IF YOU HAVE TO GIVE AN ORAL REPORT IN HIGH SCHOOL TOMORROW AND YOU HAVEN'T EVEN STARTED YET...
I'LL WALK UP TO THE PODIUM AND PULL OUT A GUN AND BLOW MY HEAD OFF... NO, FIRST I'LL KILL AS MANY OF THEM AS I CAN, THEN I'LL...
Spiz
OR LET'S SAY YOU BREAK OUT IN WHAT YOU'RE CONVINCED IS SOME KIND OF VD AND YOU'RE FACED WITH THE PROSPECT OF HAVING TO EXPLAIN A SLEAZY, RANDOM, SEXUAL ENCOUNTER TO YOUR FAMILY DOCTOR WHO'S KNOWN YOU AND YOUR PARENTS FOR YEARS...
IF I JUMP IN FRONT OF A TRAIN I'LL BE SPLATTERED AND THEY'LL NEVER KNOW!
By Dan'l Clowes, R.I.P.

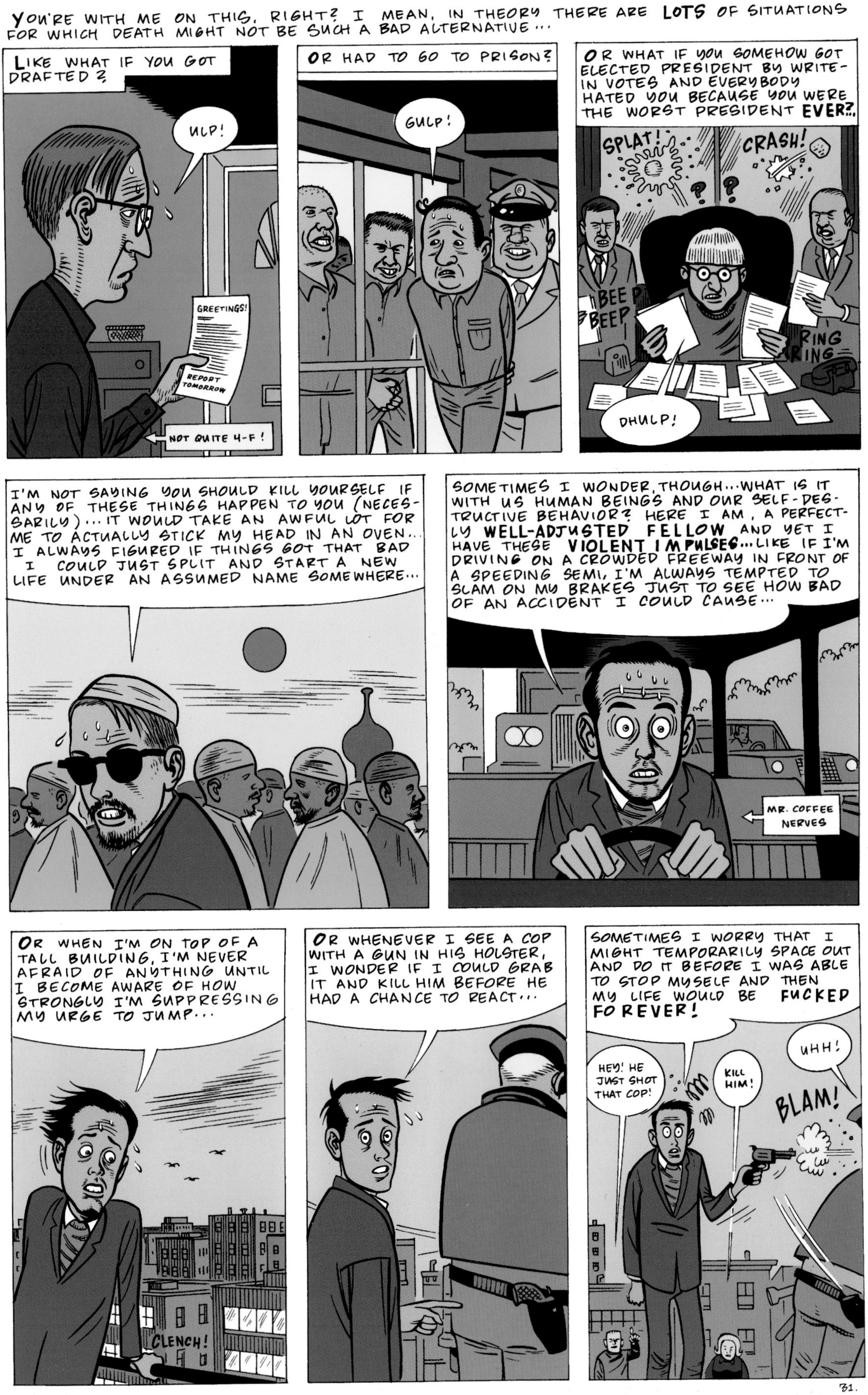
YOU'RE WITH ME ON THIS, RIGHT? I MEAN, IN THEORY THERE ARE LOTS OF SITUATIONS FOR WHICH DEATH MIGHT NOT BE SUCH A BAD ALTERNATIVE...
LIKE WHAT IF YOU GOT DRAFTED?
ULP!
GREETINGS!
REPORT TOMORROW
NOT QUITE 4-F!
OR HAD TO GO TO PRISON?
GULP!
OR WHAT IF YOU SOMEHOW GOT ELECTED PRESIDENT BY WRITE-IN VOTES AND EVERYBODY HATED YOU BECAUSE YOU WERE THE WORST PRESIDENT EVER?!
SPLAT!
CRASH!
? ?
BEEP BEEP
RING RING
DHULP!
I'M NOT SAYING YOU SHOULD KILL YOURSELF IF ANY OF THESE THINGS HAPPEN TO YOU (NECESSARILY)...IT WOULD TAKE AN AWFUL LOT FOR ME TO ACTUALLY STICK MY HEAD IN AN OVEN... I ALWAYS FIGURED IF THINGS GOT THAT BAD I COULD JUST SPLIT AND START A NEW LIFE UNDER AN ASSUMED NAME SOMEWHERE...
SOMETIMES I WONDER, THOUGH...WHAT IS IT WITH US HUMAN BEINGS AND OUR SELF-DESTRUCTIVE BEHAVIOR? HERE I AM, A PERFECTLY WELL-ADJUSTED FELLOW AND YET I HAVE THESE VIOLENT IMPULSES...LIKE IF I'M DRIVING ON A CROWDED FREEWAY IN FRONT OF A SPEEDING SEMI, I'M ALWAYS TEMPTED TO SLAM ON MY BRAKES JUST TO SEE HOW BAD OF AN ACCIDENT I COULD CAUSE...
MR. COFFEE NERVES
OR WHEN I'M ON TOP OF A TALL BUILDING, I'M NEVER AFRAID OF ANYTHING UNTIL I BECOME AWARE OF HOW STRONGLY I'M SUPPRESSING MY URGE TO JUMP...
CLENCH!
OR WHENEVER I SEE A COP WITH A GUN IN HIS HOLSTER, I WONDER IF I COULD GRAB IT AND KILL HIM BEFORE HE HAD A CHANCE TO REACT...
SOMETIMES I WORRY THAT I MIGHT TEMPORARILY SPACE OUT AND DO IT BEFORE I WAS ABLE TO STOP MYSELF AND THEN MY LIFE WOULD BE FUCKED FOREVER!
HEY! HE JUST SHOT THAT COP!
KILL HIM!
UHH!
BLAM!

Continued from inside

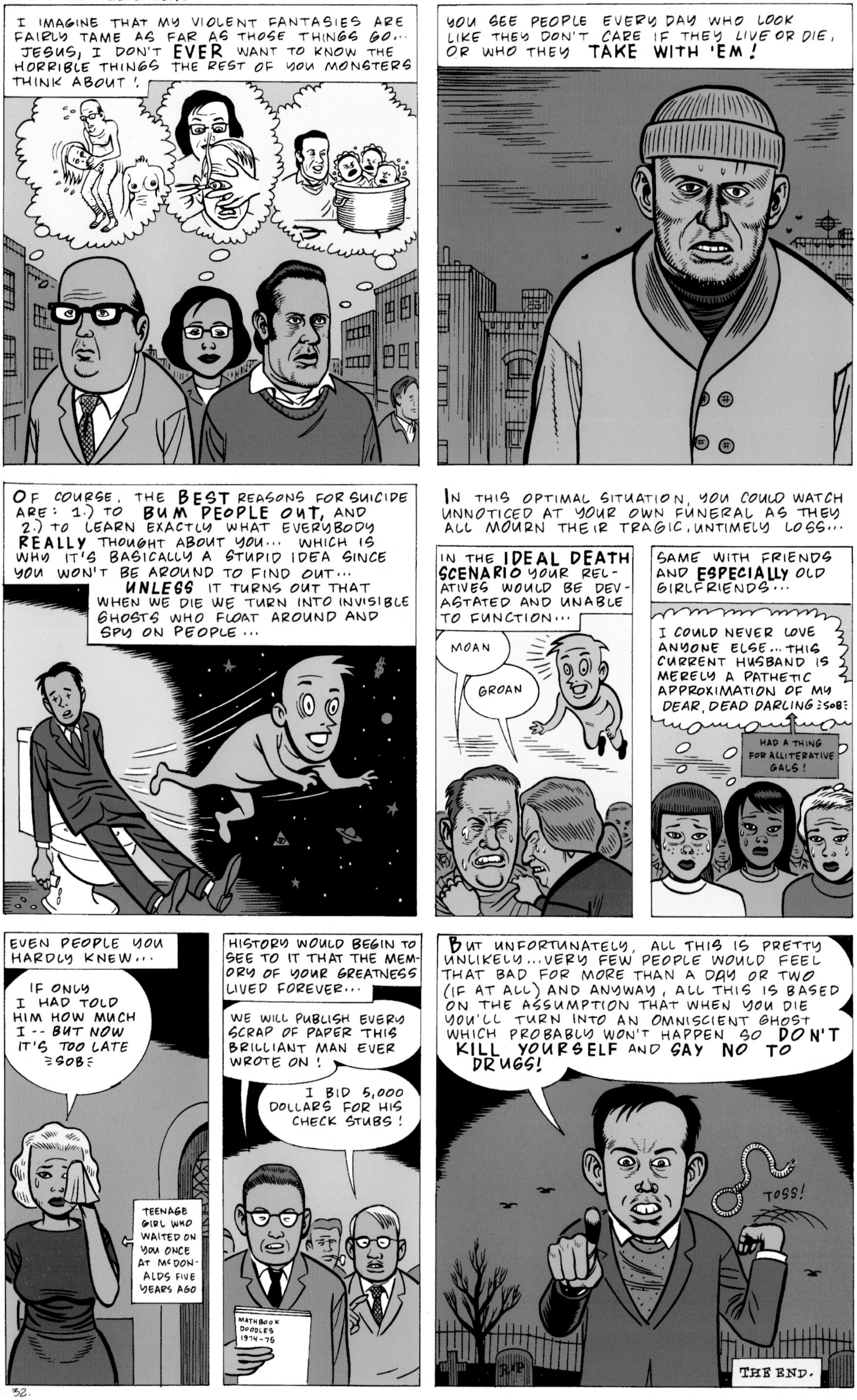
I IMAGINE THAT MY VIOLENT FANTASIES ARE FAIRLY TAME AS FAR AS THOSE THINGS GO... JESUS, I DON'T EVER WANT TO KNOW THE HORRIBLE THINGS THE REST OF YOU MONSTERS THINK ABOUT!
YOU SEE PEOPLE EVERY DAY WHO LOOK LIKE THEY DON'T CARE IF THEY LIVE OR DIE, OR WHO THEY TAKE WITH 'EM!
OF COURSE, THE BEST REASONS FOR SUICIDE ARE: 1.) TO BUM PEOPLE OUT, AND 2.) TO LEARN EXACTLY WHAT EVERYBODY REALLY THOUGHT ABOUT YOU... WHICH IS WHY IT'S BASICALLY A STUPID IDEA SINCE YOU WON'T BE AROUND TO FIND OUT...
UNLESS IT TURNS OUT THAT WHEN WE DIE WE TURN INTO INVISIBLE GHOSTS WHO FLOAT AROUND AND SPY ON PEOPLE...
IN THIS OPTIMAL SITUATION, YOU COULD WATCH UNNOTICED AT YOUR OWN FUNERAL AS THEY ALL MOURN THEIR TRAGIC, UNTIMELY LOSS...
IN THE IDEAL DEATH SCENARIO YOUR RELATIVES WOULD BE DEVASTATED AND UNABLE TO FUNCTION...
MOAN
GROAN
SAME WITH FRIENDS AND ESPECIALLY OLD GIRLFRIENDS...
I COULD NEVER LOVE ANYONE ELSE... THIS CURRENT HUSBAND IS MERELY A PATHETIC APPROXIMATION OF MY DEAR, DEAD DARLING =SOB=
HAD A THING FOR ALLITERATIVE GALS!
EVEN PEOPLE YOU HARDLY KNEW...
IF ONLY I HAD TOLD HIM HOW MUCH I -- BUT NOW IT'S TOO LATE =SOB=
TEENAGE GIRL WHO WAITED ON YOU ONCE AT McDONALDS FIVE YEARS AGO
HISTORY WOULD BEGIN TO SEE TO IT THAT THE MEMORY OF YOUR GREATNESS LIVED FOREVER...
WE WILL PUBLISH EVERY SCRAP OF PAPER THIS BRILLIANT MAN EVER WROTE ON!
I BID 5,000 DOLLARS FOR HIS CHECK STUBS!
MATHBOOK DOODLES 1974-76
BUT UNFORTUNATELY, ALL THIS IS PRETTY UNLIKELY... VERY FEW PEOPLE WOULD FEEL THAT BAD FOR MORE THAN A DAY OR TWO (IF AT ALL) AND ANYWAY, ALL THIS IS BASED ON THE ASSUMPTION THAT WHEN YOU DIE YOU'LL TURN INTO AN OMNISCIENT GHOST WHICH PROBABLY WON'T HAPPEN SO DON'T KILL YOURSELF AND SAY NO TO DRUGS!
TOSS!
RIP
THE END.

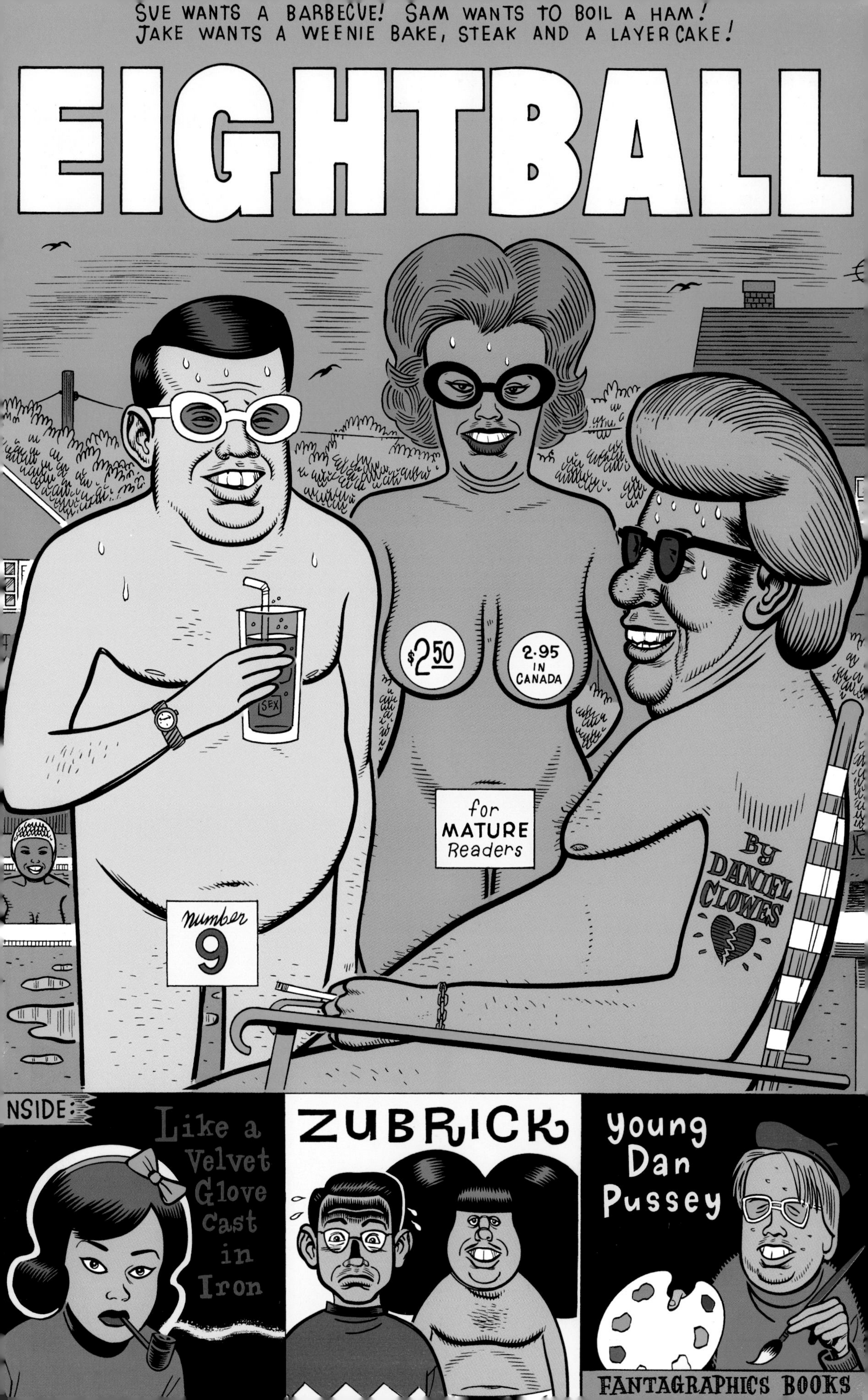
SUE WANTS A BARBECUE! SAM WANTS TO BOIL A HAM!
JAKE WANTS A WEENIE BAKE, STEAK AND A LAYER CAKE!
EIGHTBALL
$2.50
2.95 IN CANADA
SEX
for MATURE Readers
number 9
By DANIEL CLOWES
NSIDE:
Like a Velvet Glove Cast in Iron
ZUBRICK
young Dan Pussey
FANTAGRAPHICS BOOKS

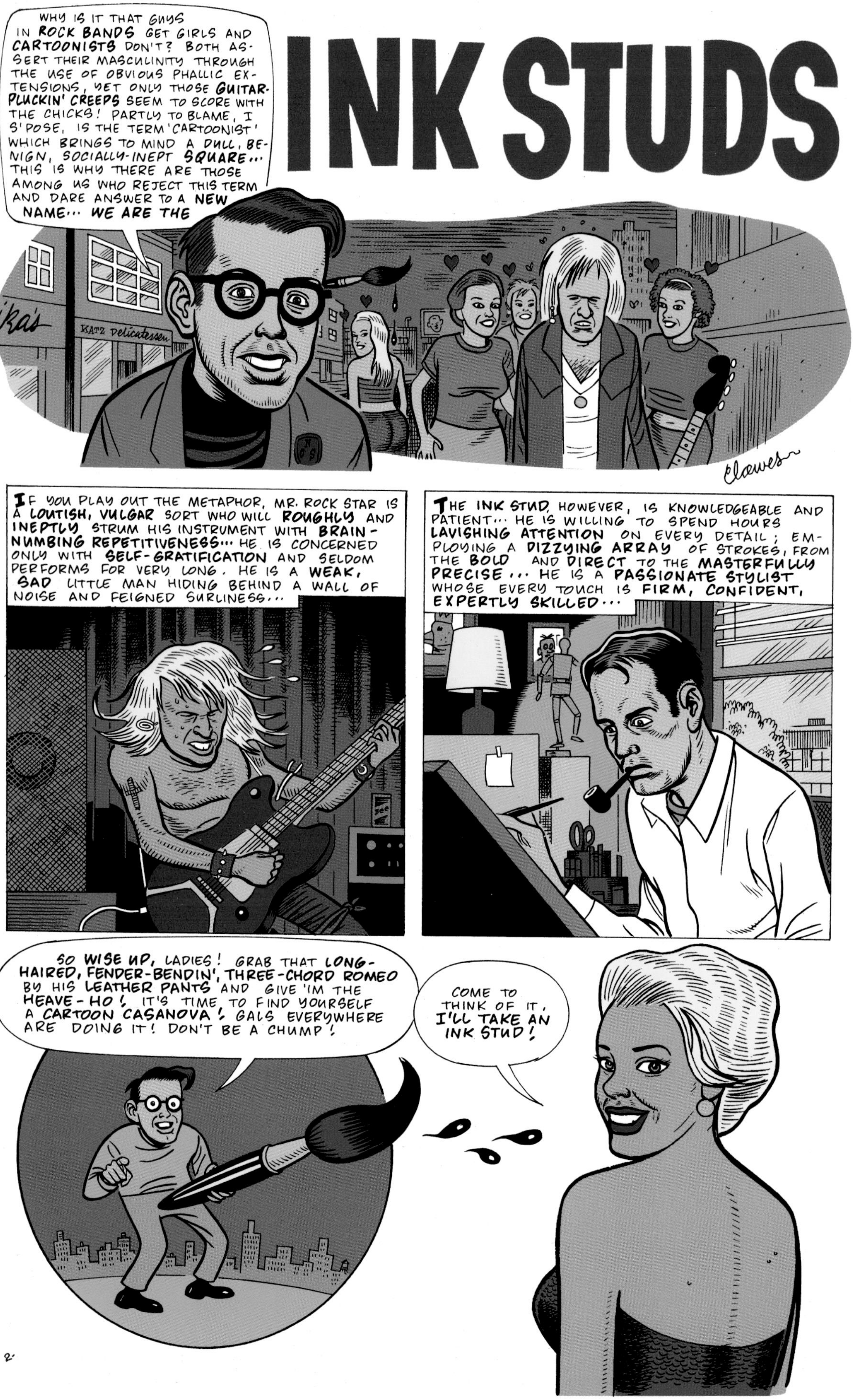
INK STUDS
WHY IS IT THAT GUYS IN ROCK BANDS GET GIRLS AND CARTOONISTS DON'T? BOTH ASSERT THEIR MASCULINITY THROUGH THE USE OF OBVIOUS PHALLIC EXTENSIONS, YET ONLY THOSE GUITAR-PLUCKIN' CREEPS SEEM TO SCORE WITH THE CHICKS! PARTLY TO BLAME, I S'POSE, IS THE TERM 'CARTOONIST' WHICH BRINGS TO MIND A DULL, BENIGN, SOCIALLY-INEPT SQUARE... THIS IS WHY THERE ARE THOSE AMONG US WHO REJECT THIS TERM AND DARE ANSWER TO A NEW NAME... WE ARE THE
KATZ Delicatessen
Clowes
IF YOU PLAY OUT THE METAPHOR, MR. ROCK STAR IS A LOUTISH, VULGAR SORT WHO WILL ROUGHLY AND INEPTLY STRUM HIS INSTRUMENT WITH BRAIN-NUMBING REPETITIVENESS... HE IS CONCERNED ONLY WITH SELF-GRATIFICATION AND SELDOM PERFORMS FOR VERY LONG. HE IS A WEAK, SAD LITTLE MAN HIDING BEHIND A WALL OF NOISE AND FEIGNED SURLINESS...
THE INK STUD, HOWEVER, IS KNOWLEDGEABLE AND PATIENT... HE IS WILLING TO SPEND HOURS LAVISHING ATTENTION ON EVERY DETAIL; EMPLOYING A DIZZYING ARRAY OF STROKES, FROM THE BOLD AND DIRECT TO THE MASTERFULLY PRECISE... HE IS A PASSIONATE STYLIST WHOSE EVERY TOUCH IS FIRM, CONFIDENT, EXPERTLY SKILLED...
SO WISE UP, LADIES! GRAB THAT LONG-HAIRED, FENDER-BENDIN', THREE-CHORD ROMEO BY HIS LEATHER PANTS AND GIVE 'IM THE HEAVE-HO! IT'S TIME TO FIND YOURSELF A CARTOON CASANOVA! GALS EVERYWHERE ARE DOING IT! DON'T BE A CHUMP!
COME TO THINK OF IT, I'LL TAKE AN INK STUD!

Like a VELVET GLOVE cast in IRON

Eightball #9, September, 1992. *Eightball* is published thrice yearly by Fantagraphics Books, Inc., and is copyright © 1992 Fantagraphics Books, Inc. All characters, stories, and art © 1992 Daniel Clowes. No part of this magazine may be reproduced without written permission from Fantagraphics Books or Daniel Clowes. No similarity between any of the names, characters, persons, and institutions in *Eightball* and those of any living or dead persons is intended (except for satirical intent), and any such similarity that may exist is purely coincidental. Letters to *Eightball* become the property of the magazine and are assumed intended for publication in whole or in part, and may therefore be used for those purposes. First printing: July, 1992. Fantagraphics Books, 7563 Lake City Way Northeast, Seattle WA 98115. **Send for our free catalogue!**

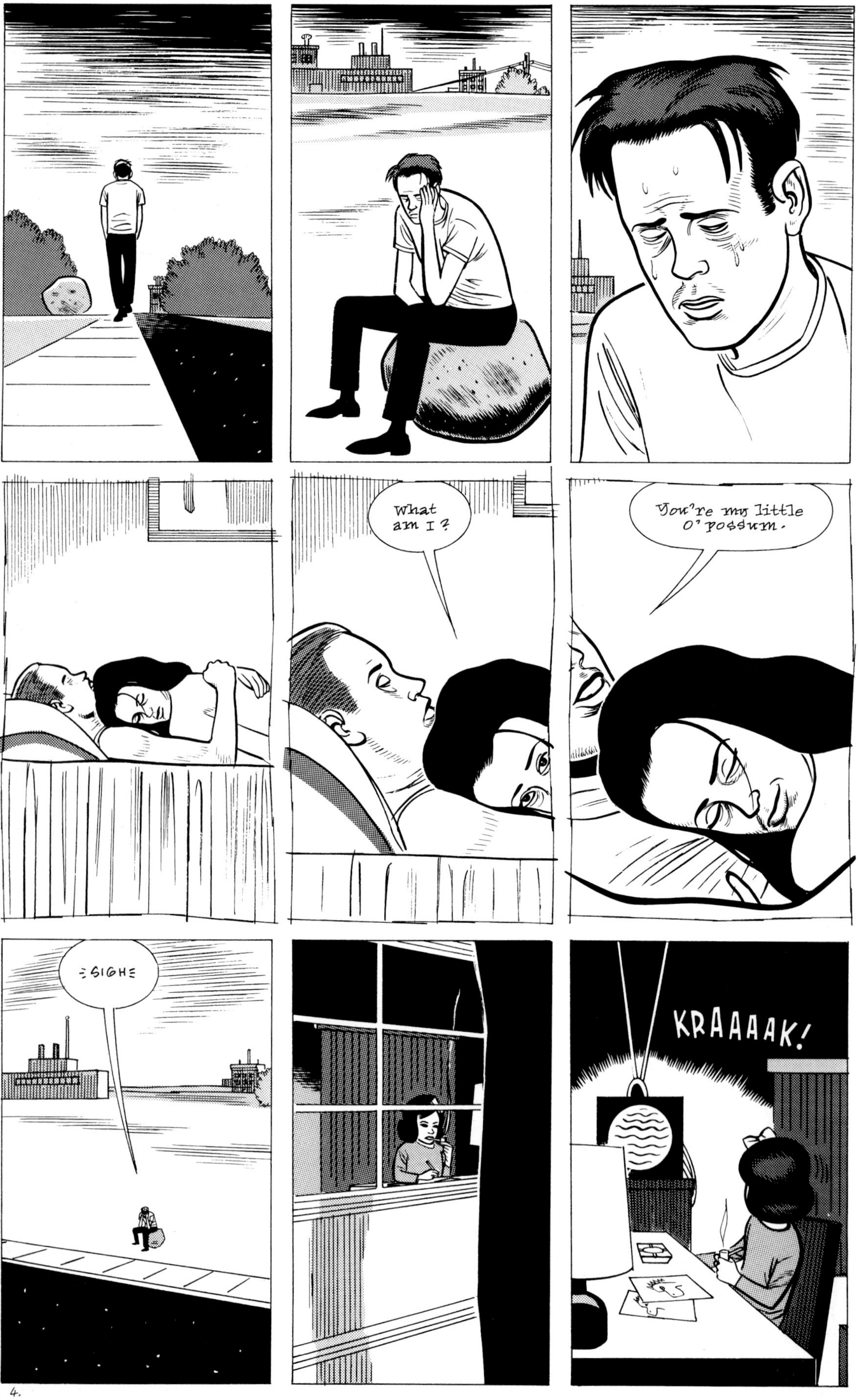
What am I?
You're my little O'possum.
SIGH
KRAAAAK!

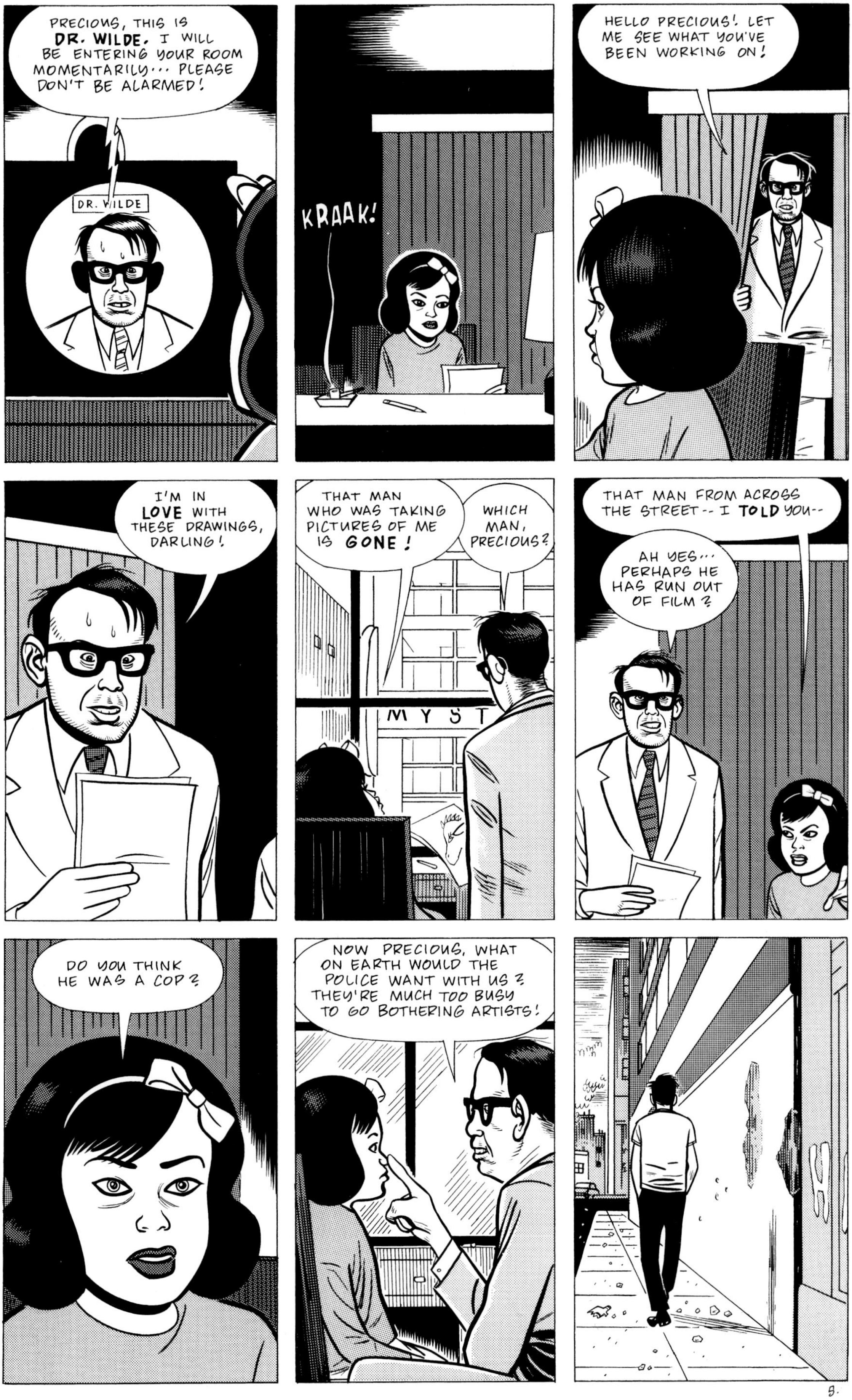
PRECIOUS, THIS IS DR. WILDE. I WILL BE ENTERING YOUR ROOM MOMENTARILY... PLEASE DON'T BE ALARMED!
DR. WILDE
KRAAK!
HELLO PRECIOUS! LET ME SEE WHAT YOU'VE BEEN WORKING ON!
I'M IN LOVE WITH THESE DRAWINGS, DARLING!
THAT MAN WHO WAS TAKING PICTURES OF ME IS GONE!
WHICH MAN, PRECIOUS?
MYST
THAT MAN FROM ACROSS THE STREET -- I TOLD YOU--
AH YES... PERHAPS HE HAS RUN OUT OF FILM?
DO YOU THINK HE WAS A COP?
NOW PRECIOUS, WHAT ON EARTH WOULD THE POLICE WANT WITH US? THEY'RE MUCH TOO BUSY TO GO BOTHERING ARTISTS!

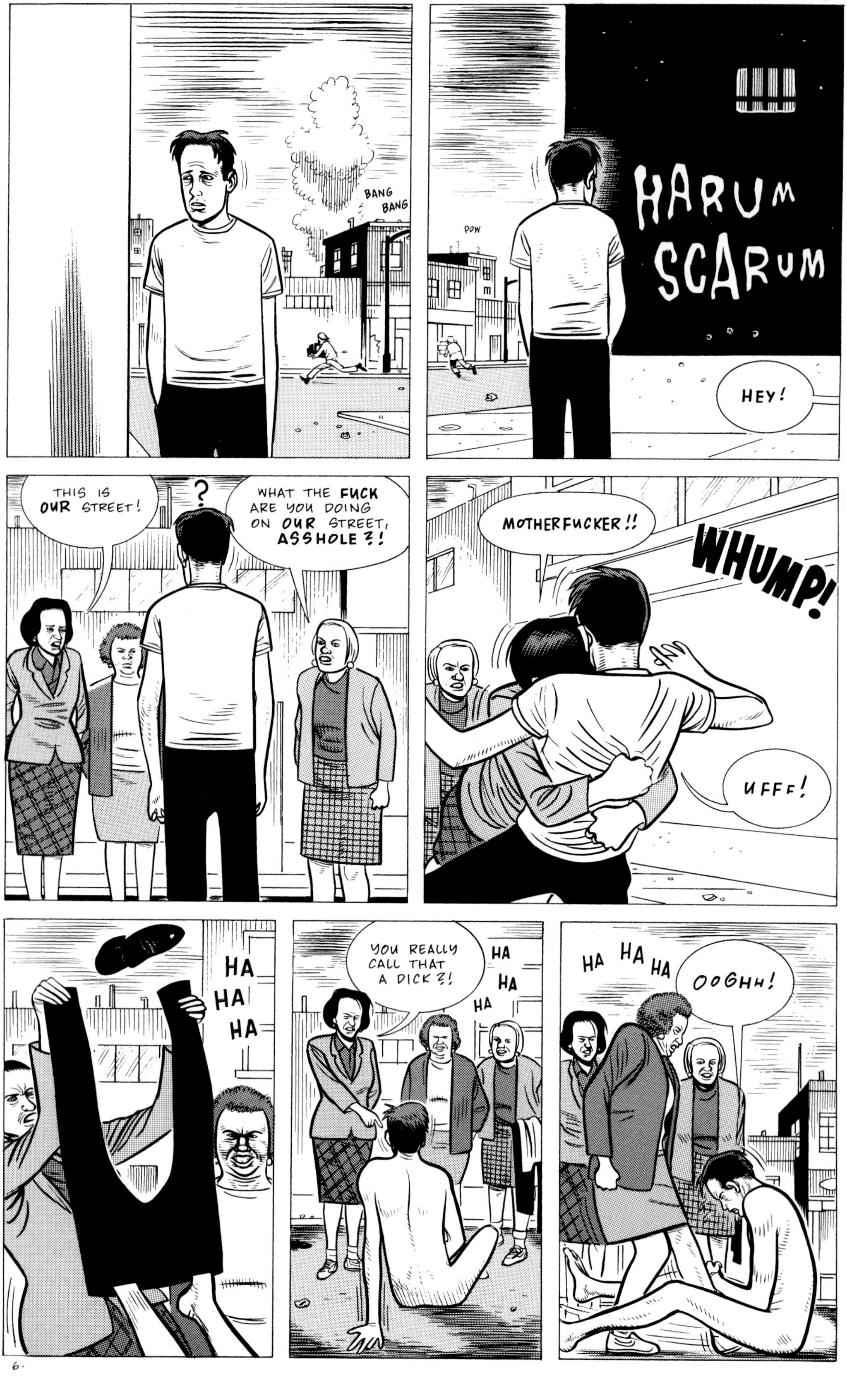
BANG
BANG
POW
HARUM SCARUM
HEY!
THIS IS OUR STREET!
?
WHAT THE FUCK ARE YOU DOING ON OUR STREET, ASSHOLE?!
MOTHERFUCKER!!
WHUMP!
UFFF!
HA
HA
HA
YOU REALLY CALL THAT A DICK?!
HA
HA
HA
HA HA HA
OOGHH!

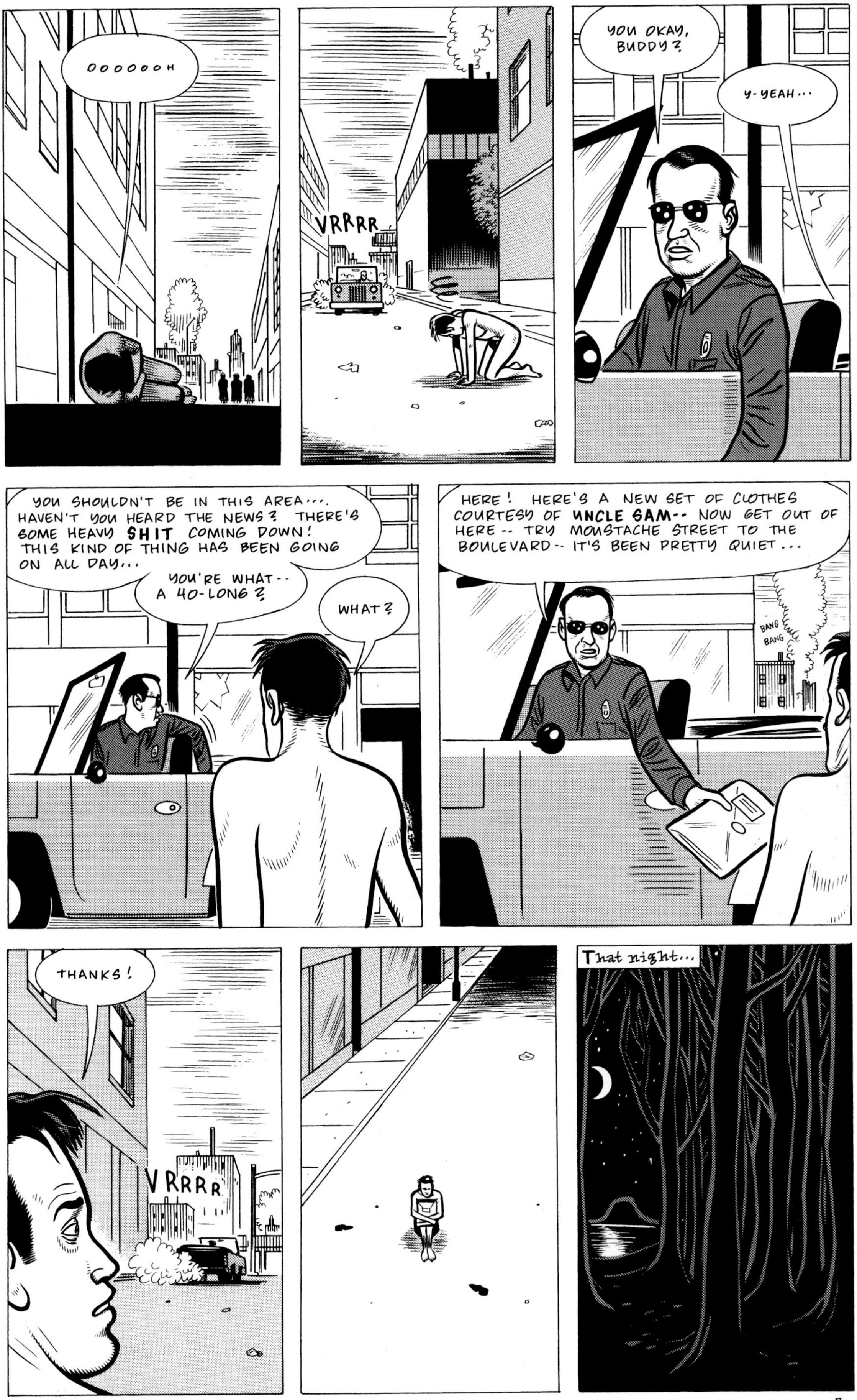
OOOOOOOH
VRRRR
YOU OKAY, BUDDY?
Y-YEAH...
YOU SHOULDN'T BE IN THIS AREA.... HAVEN'T YOU HEARD THE NEWS? THERE'S SOME HEAVY SHIT COMING DOWN! THIS KIND OF THING HAS BEEN GOING ON ALL DAY...
YOU'RE WHAT-- A 40-LONG?
WHAT?
HERE! HERE'S A NEW SET OF CLOTHES COURTESY OF UNCLE SAM-- NOW GET OUT OF HERE -- TRY MOUSTACHE STREET TO THE BOULEVARD -- IT'S BEEN PRETTY QUIET...
BANG
BANG
THANKS!
VRRRR
That night...

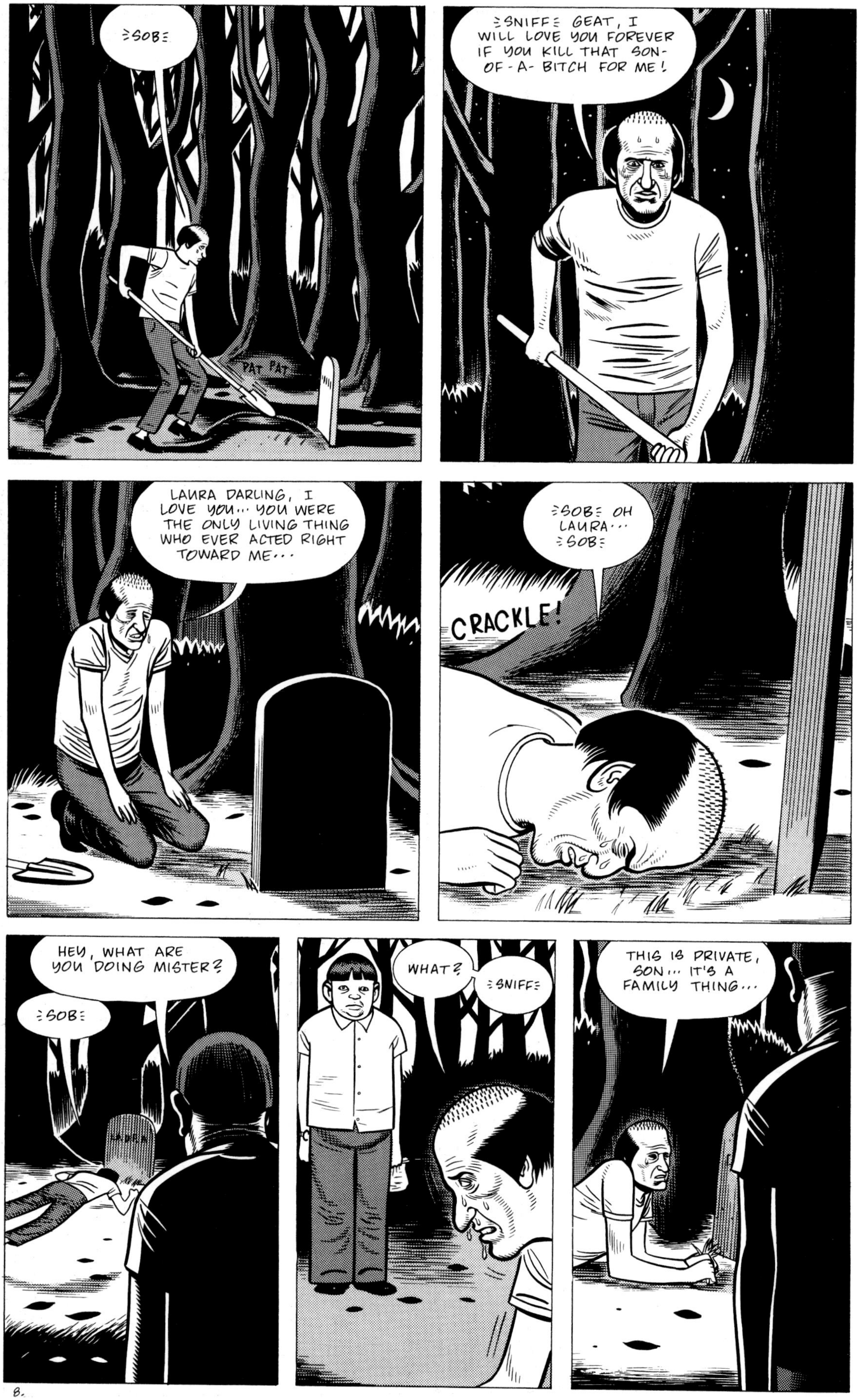
SOB
PAT PAT
SNIFF GEAT, I WILL LOVE YOU FOREVER IF YOU KILL THAT SON-OF-A-BITCH FOR ME!
LAURA DARLING, I LOVE YOU... YOU WERE THE ONLY LIVING THING WHO EVER ACTED RIGHT TOWARD ME...
SOB OH LAURA... SOB
CRACKLE!
HEY, WHAT ARE YOU DOING MISTER?
SOB
WHAT?
SNIFF
THIS IS PRIVATE, SON... IT'S A FAMILY THING...

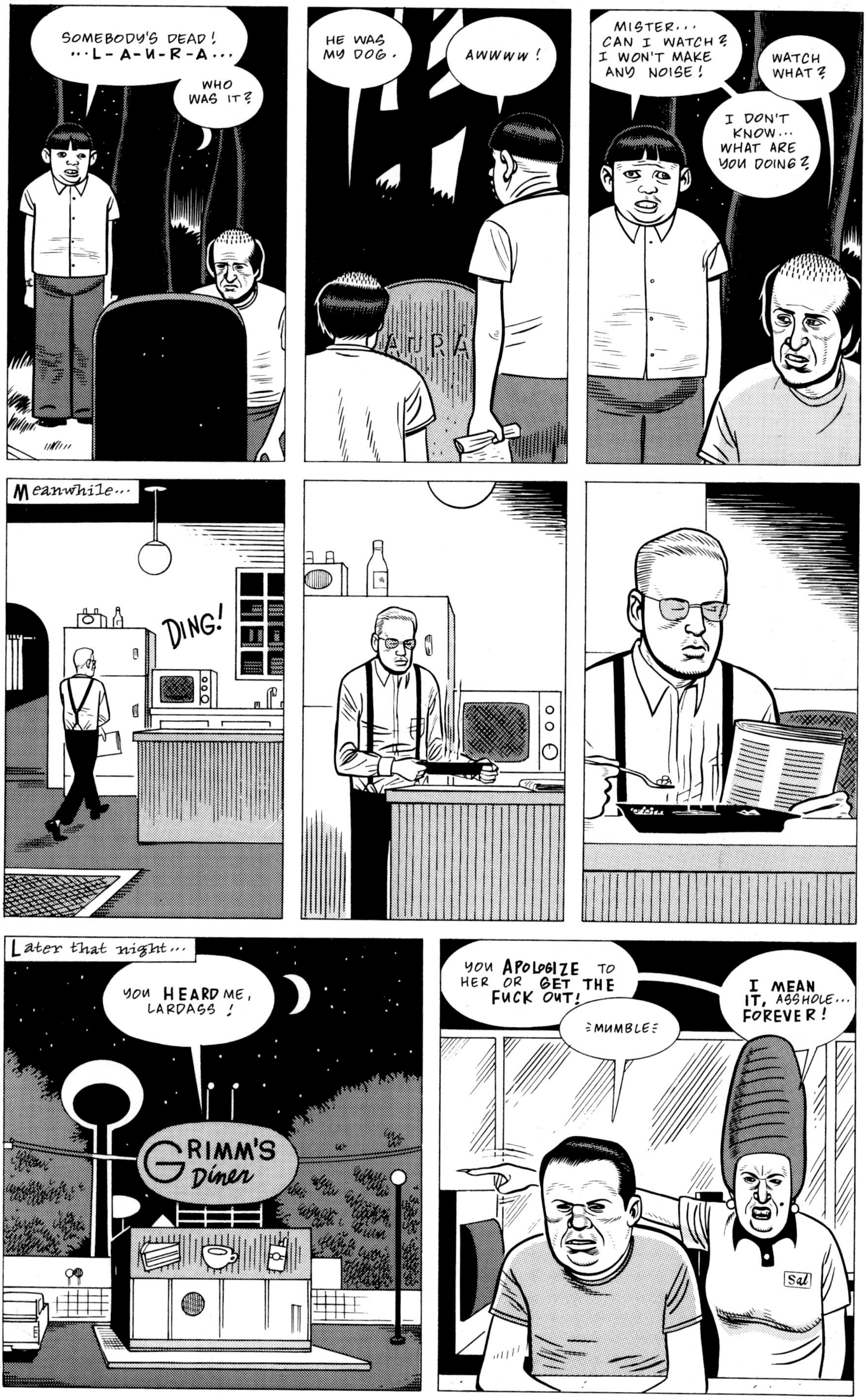
SOMEBODY'S DEAD! ...L-A-U-R-A...
WHO WAS IT?
HE WAS MY DOG.
AWWWW!
AURA
MISTER... CAN I WATCH? I WON'T MAKE ANY NOISE!
WATCH WHAT?
I DON'T KNOW... WHAT ARE YOU DOING?
Meanwhile...
DING!
Later that night...
YOU HEARD ME, LARDASS!
GRIMM'S Diner
YOU APOLOGIZE TO HER OR GET THE FUCK OUT!
I MEAN IT, ASSHOLE... FOREVER!
MUMBLE
Sal

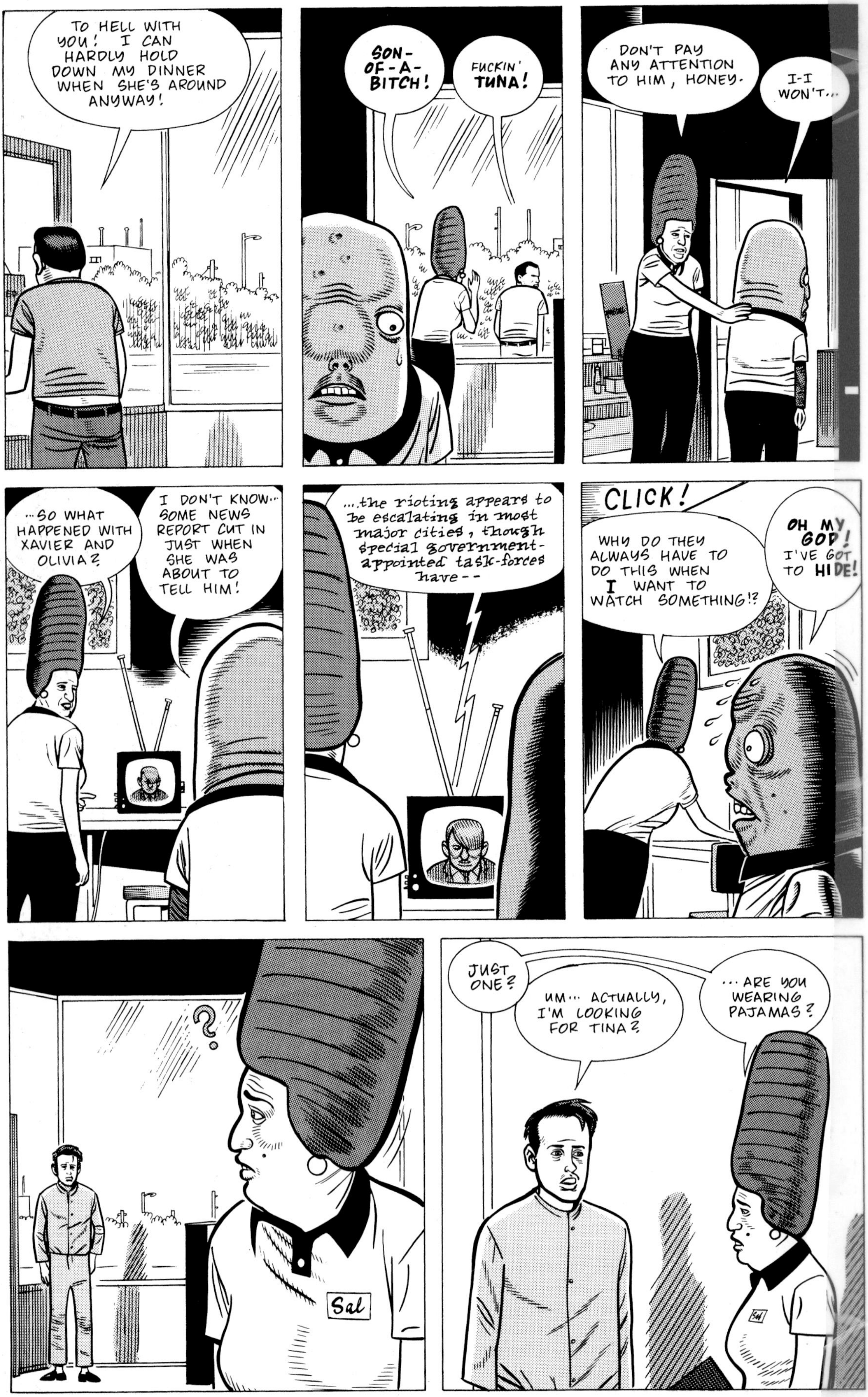

TO HELL WITH YOU! I CAN HARDLY HOLD DOWN MY DINNER WHEN SHE'S AROUND ANYWAY!
SON-OF-A-BITCH!
FUCKIN' TUNA!
DON'T PAY ANY ATTENTION TO HIM, HONEY.
I-I WON'T...
...SO WHAT HAPPENED WITH XAVIER AND OLIVIA?
I DON'T KNOW... SOME NEWS REPORT CUT IN JUST WHEN SHE WAS ABOUT TO TELL HIM!
...the rioting appears to be escalating in most major cities, though special government-appointed task-forces have--
CLICK!
WHY DO THEY ALWAYS HAVE TO DO THIS WHEN I WANT TO WATCH SOMETHING!?
OH MY GOD! I'VE GOT TO HIDE!
?
Sal
JUST ONE?
UM... ACTUALLY, I'M LOOKING FOR TINA?
...ARE YOU WEARING PAJAMAS?

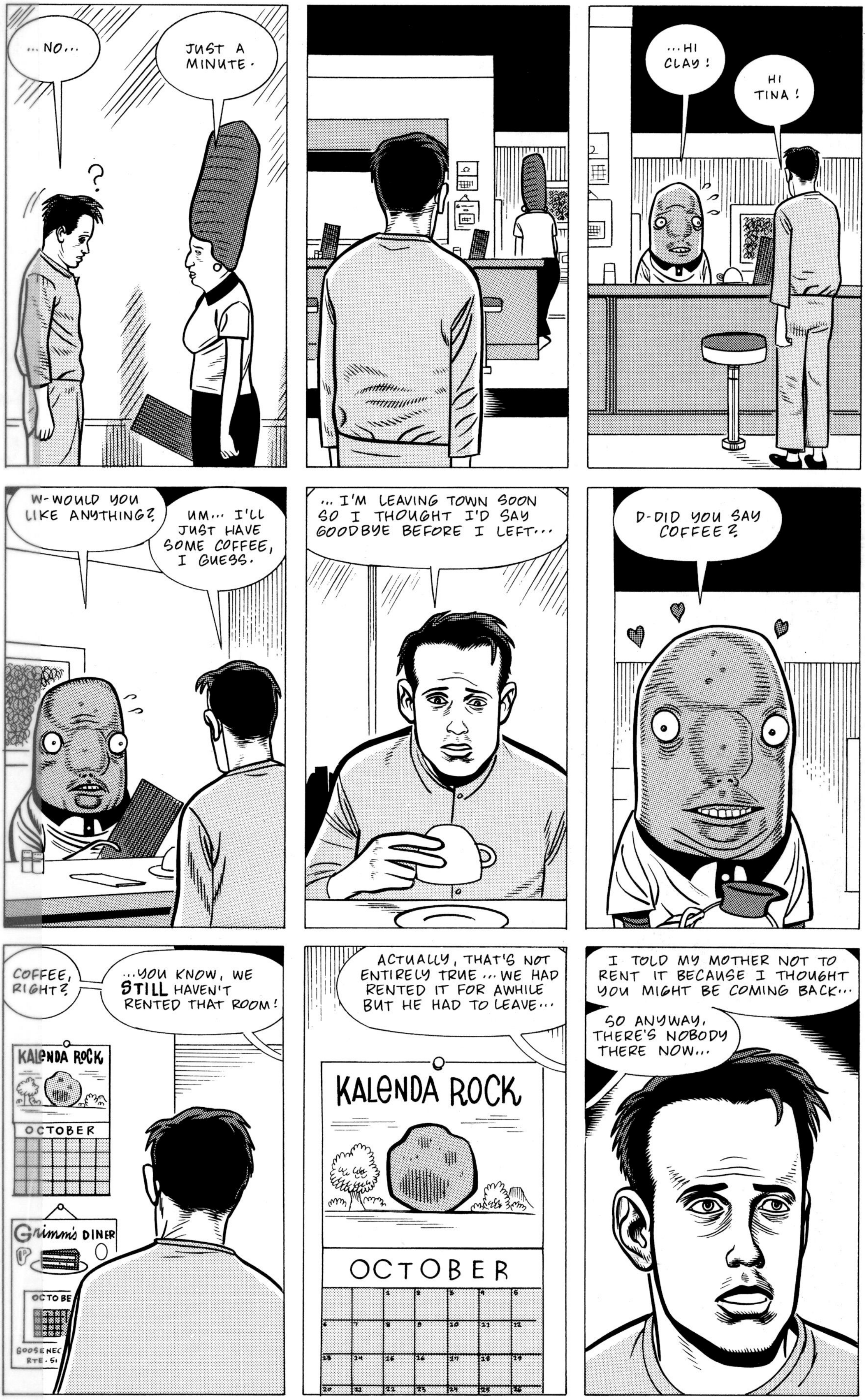

...NO...
JUST A MINUTE.
...HI CLAY!
HI TINA!
W-WOULD YOU LIKE ANYTHING?
UM... I'LL JUST HAVE SOME COFFEE, I GUESS.
... I'M LEAVING TOWN SOON SO I THOUGHT I'D SAY GOODBYE BEFORE I LEFT...
D-DID YOU SAY COFFEE?
COFFEE, RIGHT?
...YOU KNOW, WE STILL HAVEN'T RENTED THAT ROOM!
KALENDA ROCK
OCTOBER
Grimm's DINER
OCTOBE
GOOSENEC
RTE. 51
ACTUALLY, THAT'S NOT ENTIRELY TRUE ... WE HAD RENTED IT FOR AWHILE BUT HE HAD TO LEAVE...
KALENDA ROCK
OCTOBER
I TOLD MY MOTHER NOT TO RENT IT BECAUSE I THOUGHT YOU MIGHT BE COMING BACK...
SO ANYWAY, THERE'S NOBODY THERE NOW...

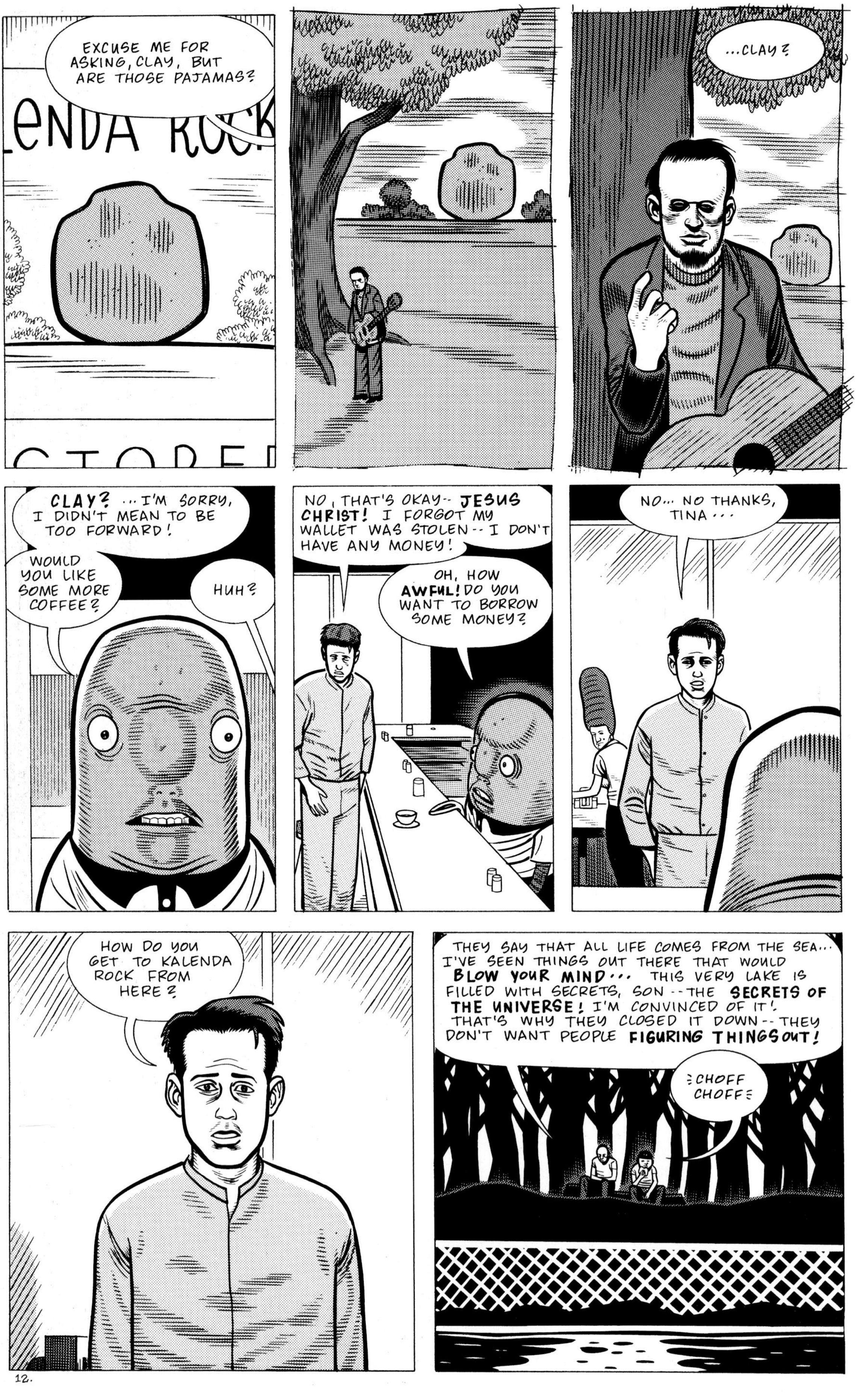
EXCUSE ME FOR ASKING, CLAY, BUT ARE THOSE PAJAMAS?
...CLAY?
CLAY? ...I'M SORRY, I DIDN'T MEAN TO BE TOO FORWARD!
WOULD YOU LIKE SOME MORE COFFEE?
HUH?
NO, THAT'S OKAY-- JESUS CHRIST! I FORGOT MY WALLET WAS STOLEN-- I DON'T HAVE ANY MONEY!
OH, HOW AWFUL! DO YOU WANT TO BORROW SOME MONEY?
NO... NO THANKS, TINA...
HOW DO YOU GET TO KALENDA ROCK FROM HERE?
THEY SAY THAT ALL LIFE COMES FROM THE SEA... I'VE SEEN THINGS OUT THERE THAT WOULD BLOW YOUR MIND... THIS VERY LAKE IS FILLED WITH SECRETS, SON -- THE SECRETS OF THE UNIVERSE! I'M CONVINCED OF IT! THAT'S WHY THEY CLOSED IT DOWN -- THEY DON'T WANT PEOPLE FIGURING THINGS OUT!
CHOFF CHOFF

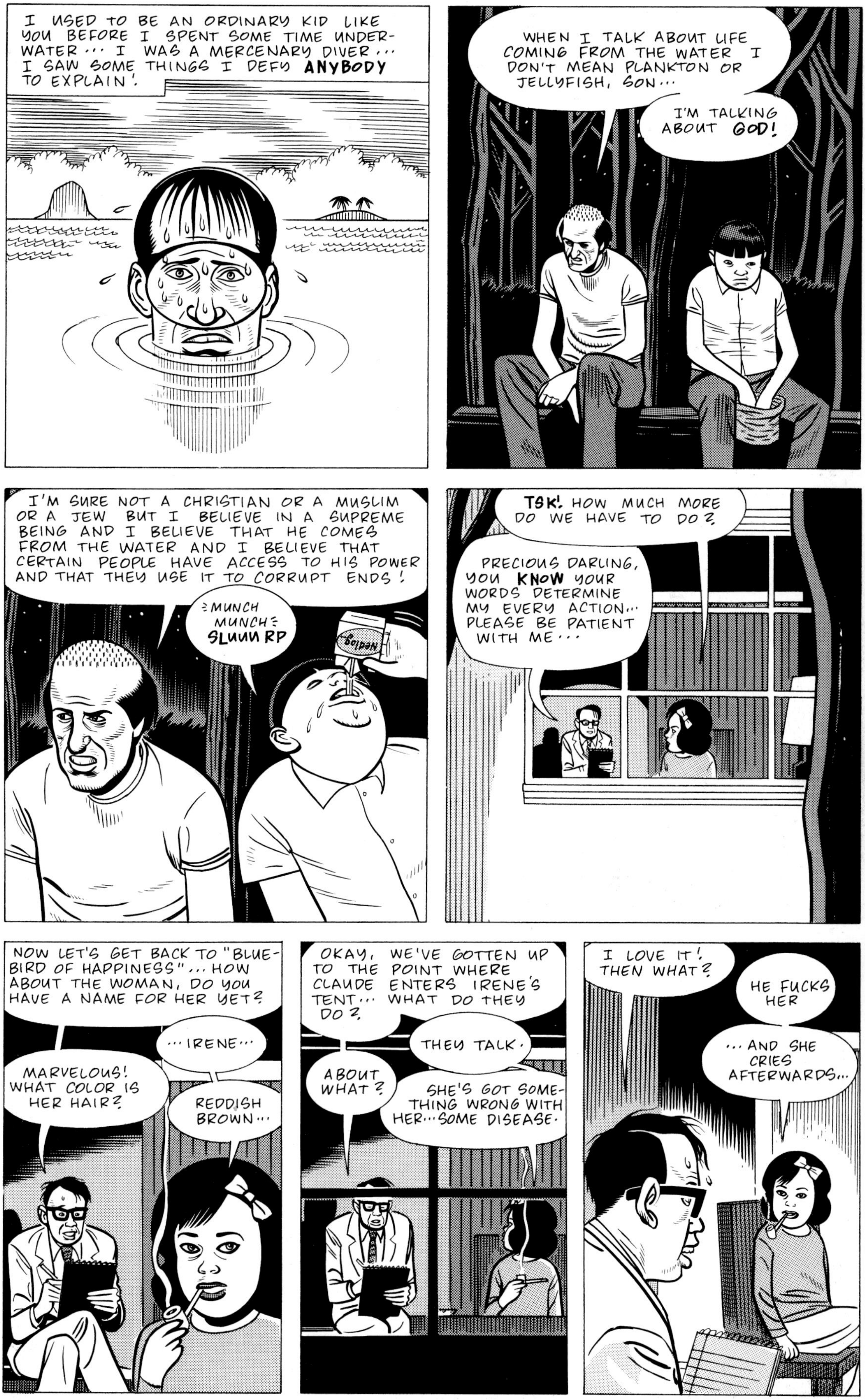

I USED TO BE AN ORDINARY KID LIKE YOU BEFORE I SPENT SOME TIME UNDERWATER... I WAS A MERCENARY DIVER... I SAW SOME THINGS I DEFY ANYBODY TO EXPLAIN!
WHEN I TALK ABOUT LIFE COMING FROM THE WATER I DON'T MEAN PLANKTON OR JELLYFISH, SON...
I'M TALKING ABOUT GOD!
I'M SURE NOT A CHRISTIAN OR A MUSLIM OR A JEW BUT I BELIEVE IN A SUPREME BEING AND I BELIEVE THAT HE COMES FROM THE WATER AND I BELIEVE THAT CERTAIN PEOPLE HAVE ACCESS TO HIS POWER AND THAT THEY USE IT TO CORRUPT ENDS!
MUNCH MUNCH SLUUURP
BOLDEN
TSK! HOW MUCH MORE DO WE HAVE TO DO?
PRECIOUS DARLING, YOU KNOW YOUR WORDS DETERMINE MY EVERY ACTION... PLEASE BE PATIENT WITH ME...
NOW LET'S GET BACK TO "BLUEBIRD OF HAPPINESS"... HOW ABOUT THE WOMAN, DO YOU HAVE A NAME FOR HER YET?
...IRENE...
MARVELOUS! WHAT COLOR IS HER HAIR?
REDDISH BROWN...
OKAY, WE'VE GOTTEN UP TO THE POINT WHERE CLAUDE ENTERS IRENE'S TENT... WHAT DO THEY DO?
THEY TALK.
ABOUT WHAT?
SHE'S GOT SOMETHING WRONG WITH HER... SOME DISEASE.
I LOVE IT! THEN WHAT?
HE FUCKS HER
...AND SHE CRIES AFTERWARDS...

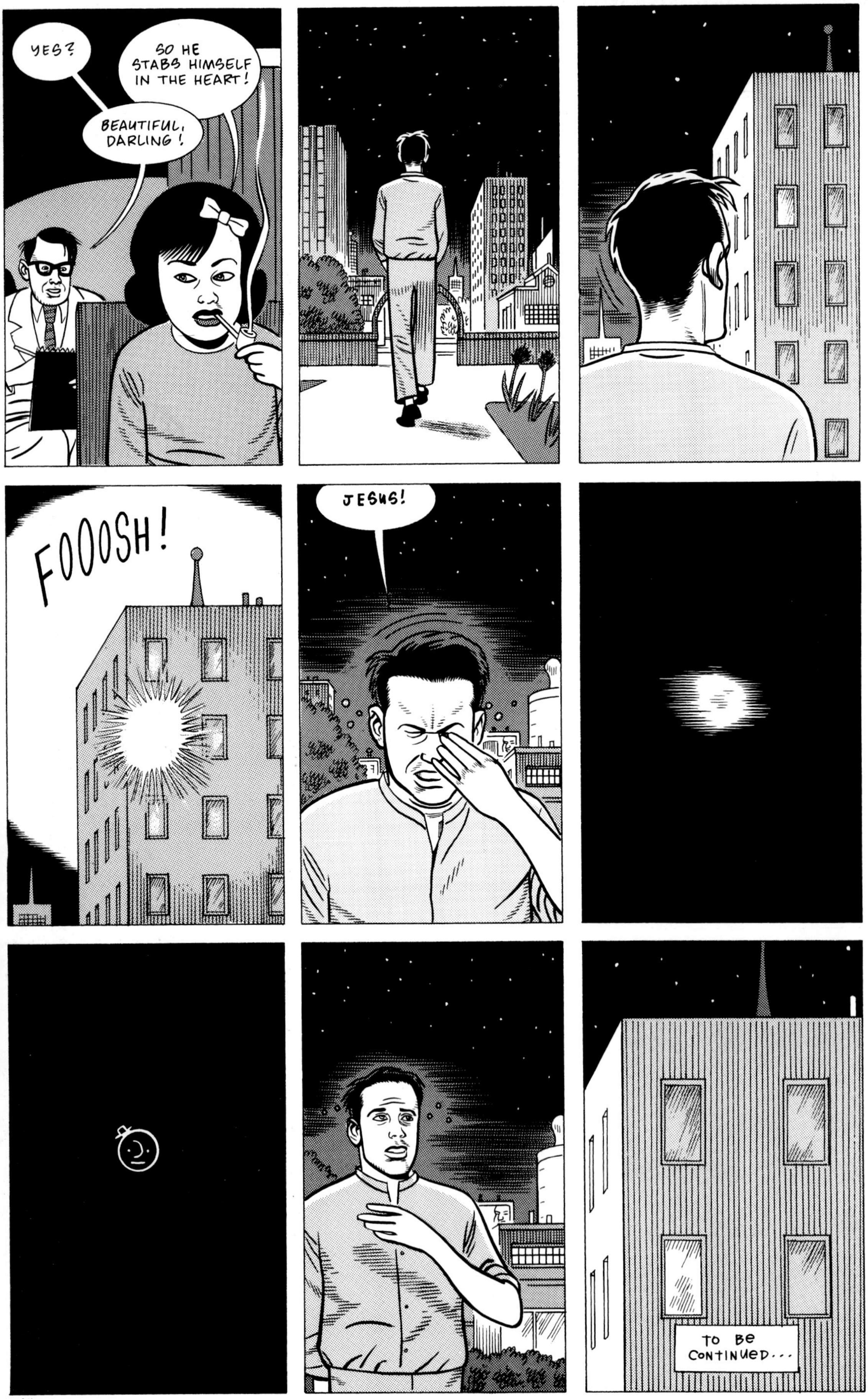
YES?
SO HE STABS HIMSELF IN THE HEART!
BEAUTIFUL, DARLING!
FOOOSH!
JESUS!
TO BE CONTINUED...

VALUE VALLEY

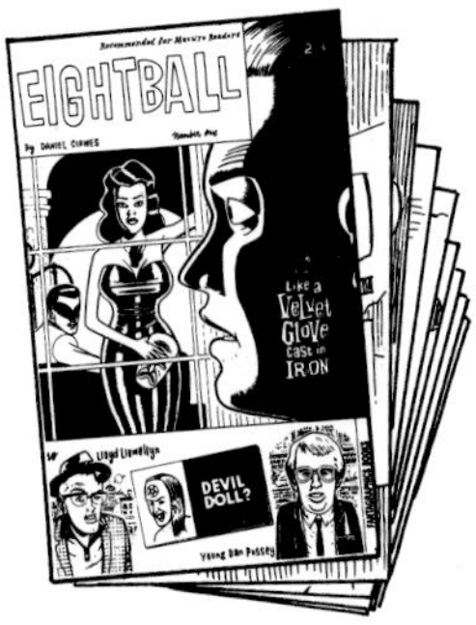
EIGHTBALL
Like a Velvet Glove Cast in Iron
DEVIL DOLL?

EIGHTBALL #'s 1-9

$3.00 ea. Ppd.

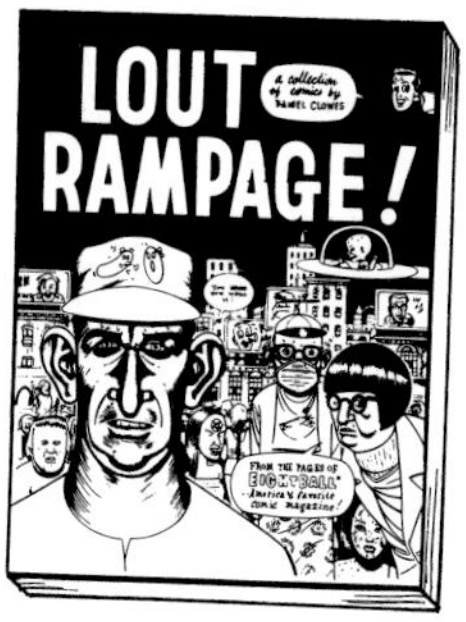
LOUT RAMPAGE!
a collection of comics by Daniel Clowes

LOUT RAMPAGE!

$13.00 Ppd.

NEW!

EIGHTBALL POSTCARDS

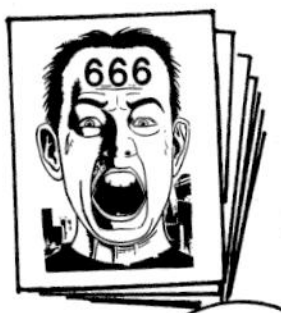
666

Set of ten! $6.00 Ppd.

EIGHTBALL MUG

$12.00 Ppd.

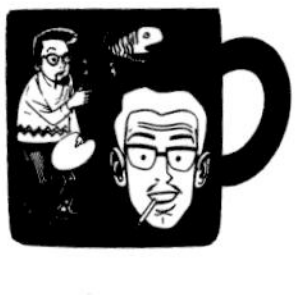

#$@&!: LLOYD LLEWELLYN COLLECTION

Very few left! $12.00 Ppd.

MISFIT LIT. SILKSCREEN

Signed + numbered! 8-color! $60.00 Ppd.

CLOISONNÉ PIN

$9.00 Ppd.

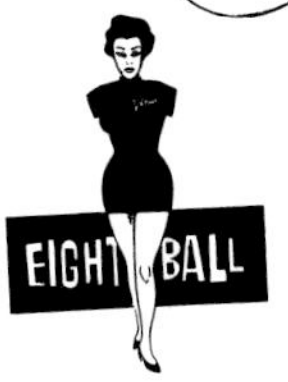
EIGHTBALL

T-SHIRTS

EIGHTBALL or LLOYD LLEWELLYN

Full-color on 100% cotton! Specify M, L or XL

$17.95 ea. Ppd.

RUBBER STAMP

$9.00 Ppd.

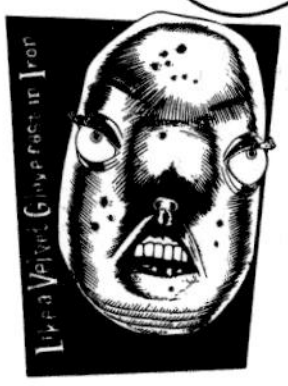
Like a Velvet Glove Cast in Iron

'VELVET GLOVE' SILKSCREEN

Signed & numbered $80.00 Ppd.

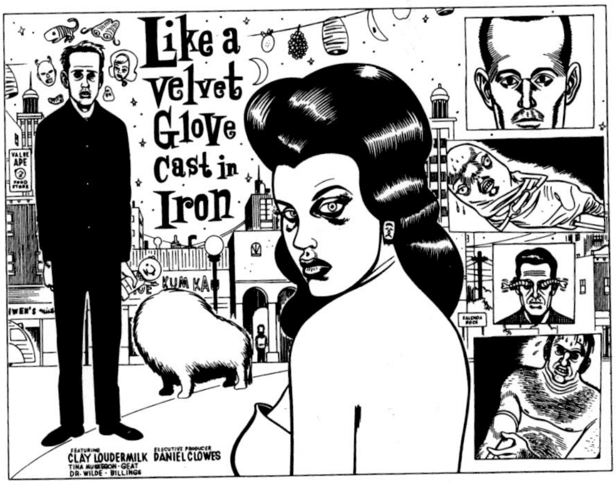
Like a Velvet Glove Cast in Iron
FEATURING CLAY LOUDERMILK
EXECUTIVE PRODUCER DANIEL CLOWES
DR. WILDE · BILLINGS

C O U P O N

○ 8-BALL #1 ○ #2 ○ #3 ○ #4 ○ #5
○ #6 ○ #7 ○ #8 ○ #9 ○ 4 ISSUE SUB. ($9.50)
○ LOUT RAMPAGE! ○ LLLL BOOK ○ POSTCARDS
○ MUG ○ CLOISONNÉ PIN ○ RUBBER STAMP
○ VELVET GLOVE SILKSCREEN ○ MISFIT LIT. SILKSCREEN
○ EIGHTBALL T-SHIRT M L XL (circle one)
○ LLLL T-SHIRT M L XL FOREIGN ORDERS ADD 10%

Send orders to: FANTAGRAPHICS BOOKS
7563 LAKE CITY WAY NE
SEATTLE, WA. 98115
Or call toll-free: 1-800-657-1100

NAME	
ADDRESS	
CITY	
STATE	ZIP

Erika Katz by D. Klowes

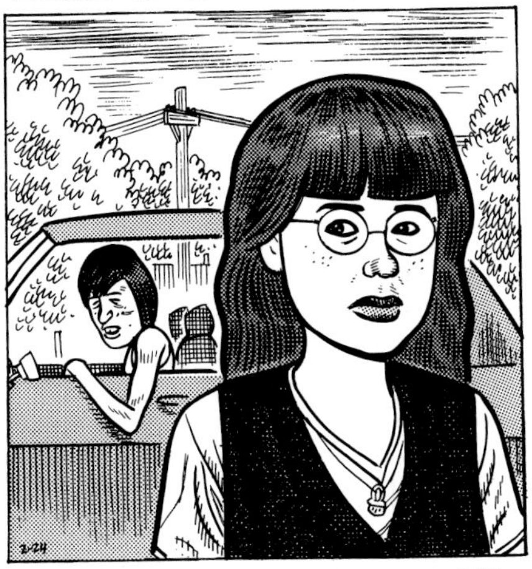

"Hey... HEY! ... Do you Party?"

PLUG CORNER

You! GET THE NEW RUBE RUBEN 45 R.P.M. RECORD!

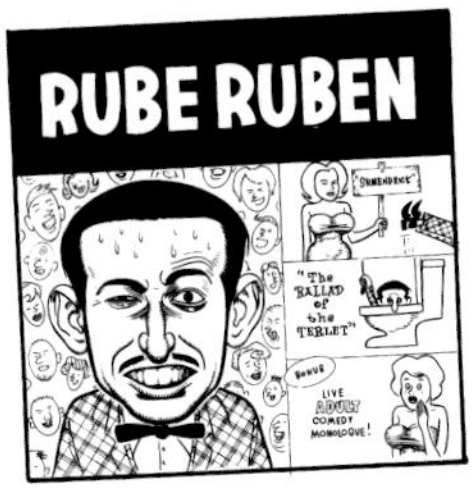
RUBE RUBEN

FEATURES 2 SONG HITS: "SHMENDRICK" AND "THE BALLAD OF THE TERLET" ALONG WITH RUBE'S LAFF-A-MINIT MONOLOGUE (THAT ADDS UP TO 3+ LAFFS!) ON THE FLIP! A MUST-HAVE FOR ALL DOUCHE-BAGS AND THEIR ILK!

Only $4.00 Ppd. Cash or M.O. only. No checks!

From: SYMPATHY FOR THE RECORD INDUSTRY
4901 VIRGINIA ST.
LONG BEACH, CA. 90805

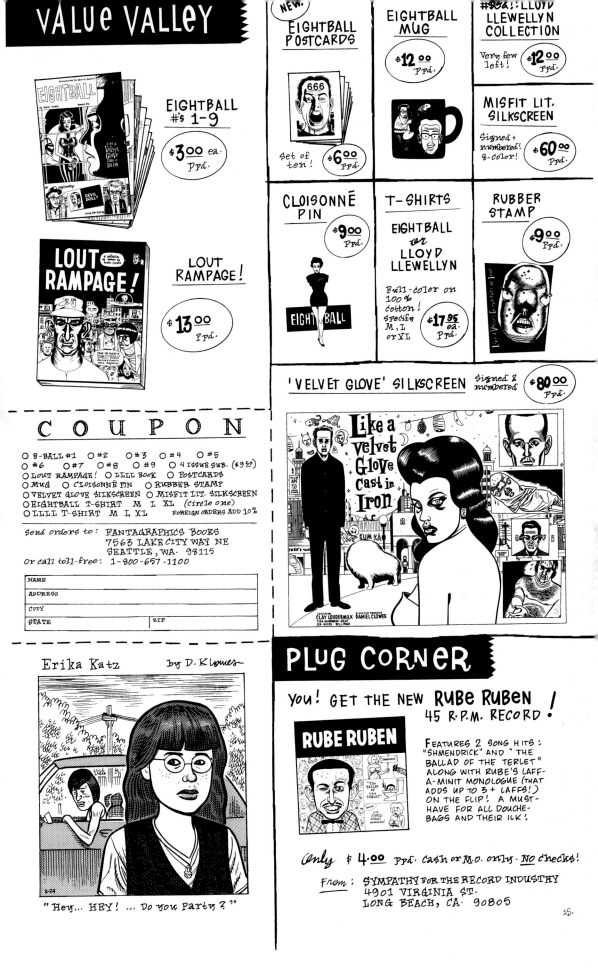

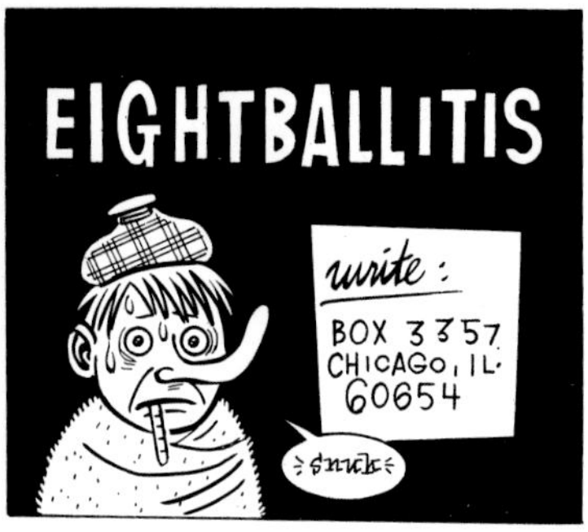
EIGHTBALLITIS
write:
BOX 3357
CHICAGO, IL.
60654
snuk

DEAR DAN,
HAVING NOW READ ALL EIGHT EXISTING ISSUES OF YOUR COMIC 'EIGHTBALL' I HAVE NOW COME TO THE HORRIFYING CONCLUSION THAT YOU ARE A VILE, BITTER, COMPASSIONLESS CYNIC WHOSE EXCESS OF CONTEMPT FOR HUMANITY ONLY GOES TO SHOW YOU HAVE NO SOUL AND NO HEART!

BOB HARTSHORN
ESSEX, ENGLAND

DAN,
HERE'S A LITTLE ANECDOTE THAT RELATES TO THE *MY SUICIDE* BIT: ONCE I WAS RIDING ON THE BACK SEAT OF A BUS WITH A GIRLFRIEND, WHEN A SECURITY COP SAT IN FRONT OF US WITH HIS GUN HANGING OUT RIGHT WITHIN INCHES OF MY HAND. SO AS A JOKE I PRETEND LIKE I'M GOING TO GRAB HIS GUN, JUST TO GET A LAUGH OUT OF THE WOMAN I WAS WITH. THERE WAS NO WAY THE SECURITY COP COULD SEE THIS GOING ON, BUT SOME KID ACROSS THE AISLE SAW ME AND YELLS, "HE'S GOIN' FOR YOUR GUN!" EVERYONE IN THE BUS TURNS AROUND AND STARES AT ME, ESPECIALLY THE 6-FOOT, 200-LB. SECURITY COP. NO ONE THOUGHT MY LITTLE JOKE WAS VERY FUNNY. WHAT A COMEDIAN.

DENNIS WORDEN
SAN JUAN CAPISTRANO, CA.

DEAR D. CLOWES:
YOU ARE A DOUBLE-ASS BITCH.

MICHAEL HASHIM
NEW YORK, NY.

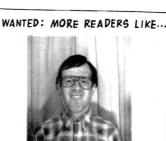

WANTED: MORE READERS LIKE...

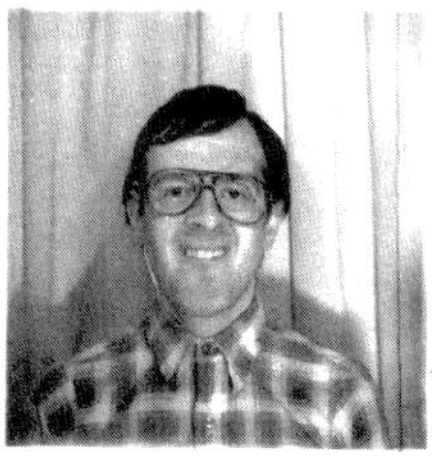

HERB LICHTENSTEIN
Chicago, IL.

DANIEL,
I THOUGHT I SHOULD WRITE. MY FIRST VENTURE OUTSIDE TODAY WAS TO GO TO THE POST OFFICE TO CHECK MY MAIL. STANDING IN FRONT OF THE HALLMARK GIFT SHOP WAS A TALL, WHITE RABBIT WEARING OVERALLS WITH BLUE AND YELLOW BALLOONS. I WONDERERED WHAT KIND OF HORRIBLE PERSON STOOD INSIDE THE COSTUME. AND AS I DREW NEARER I SUSPECTED A GAY PERSON WHEN THE KNEES DIPPED AT PASSERSBY AND SPRANG BACK HAPPILY. ON MY WAY HOME I PASSED THE RABBIT AGAIN WHICH I HAD ALMOST FORGOTTEN ABOUT WHILE I WAS IN THE P.O. THIS TIME IT SPOKE TO A CHILD. "HELLO, HOW ARE YOU?" IN AN ORIENTAL ACCENT. I WENT STRAIGHT HOME, UP THE STAIRS AND CLOSED THE DOORS. DANIEL, ARE YOU GAY? YOUR MAGAZINE IS CUTE.

TODD PRUDHOMME
NEW YORK, NY.

P.S. RE PAGE 14 OF NO. 8: WHEN A BULLET ENTERS, THERE IS NO OUTWARD SPRAY OF FRAGMENT OR LIQUID. ONLY AS THE BULLET EXITS DOES IT TAKE MATERIAL WITH IT... AND IF IT'S A HOLLOW POINT! I'M SENSITIVE TO BALLISTICS PRESENTLY BECAUSE THERE WAS AN AD FOR A CHEVY CHASE MOVIE WHERE A BULLET WAS SHOWN LEAVING HIS HEAD WITH THE SHELL STILL ON!

DAN,
I JUST PICKED UP EIGHTBALL #8 AND I'VE FINALLY REALIZED WHAT IT IS ABOUT YOUR WORK--- YOU DRAW EVERYBODY IN THE WORLD WITH WORSE TEETH THAN MINE.

BRIAN PAYNE
NORTHGLENN, CO.

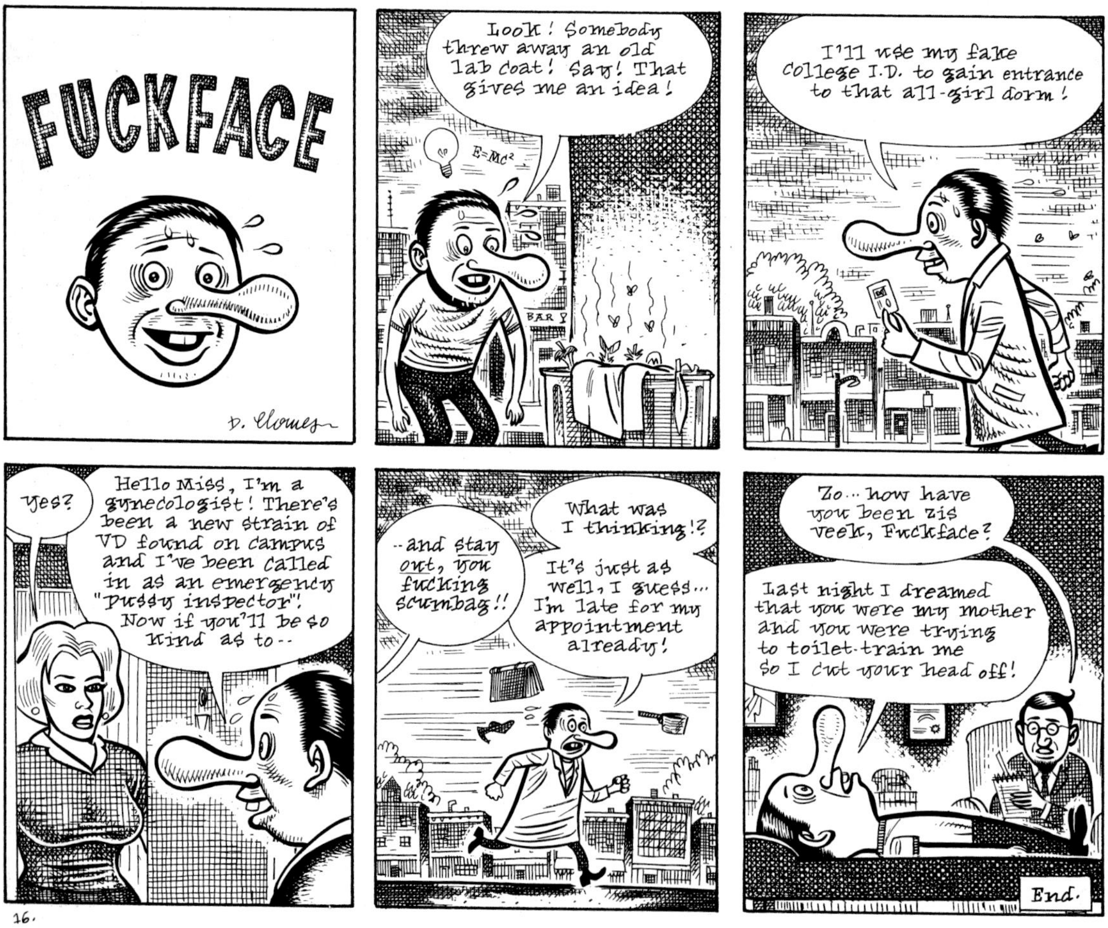
FUCKFACE
D. Clowes
Look! Somebody threw away an old lab coat! Say! That gives me an idea!
E=MC²
BAR
I'll use my fake college I.D. to gain entrance to that all-girl dorm!
Yes?
Hello Miss, I'm a gynecologist! There's been a new strain of VD found on campus and I've been called in as an emergency "pussy inspector"! Now if you'll be so kind as to--
--and stay out, you fucking scumbag!!
What was I thinking!?
It's just as well, I guess... I'm late for my appointment already!
Zo... how have you been zis veek, Fuckface?
Last night I dreamed that you were my mother and you were trying to toilet-train me so I cut your head off!
End.

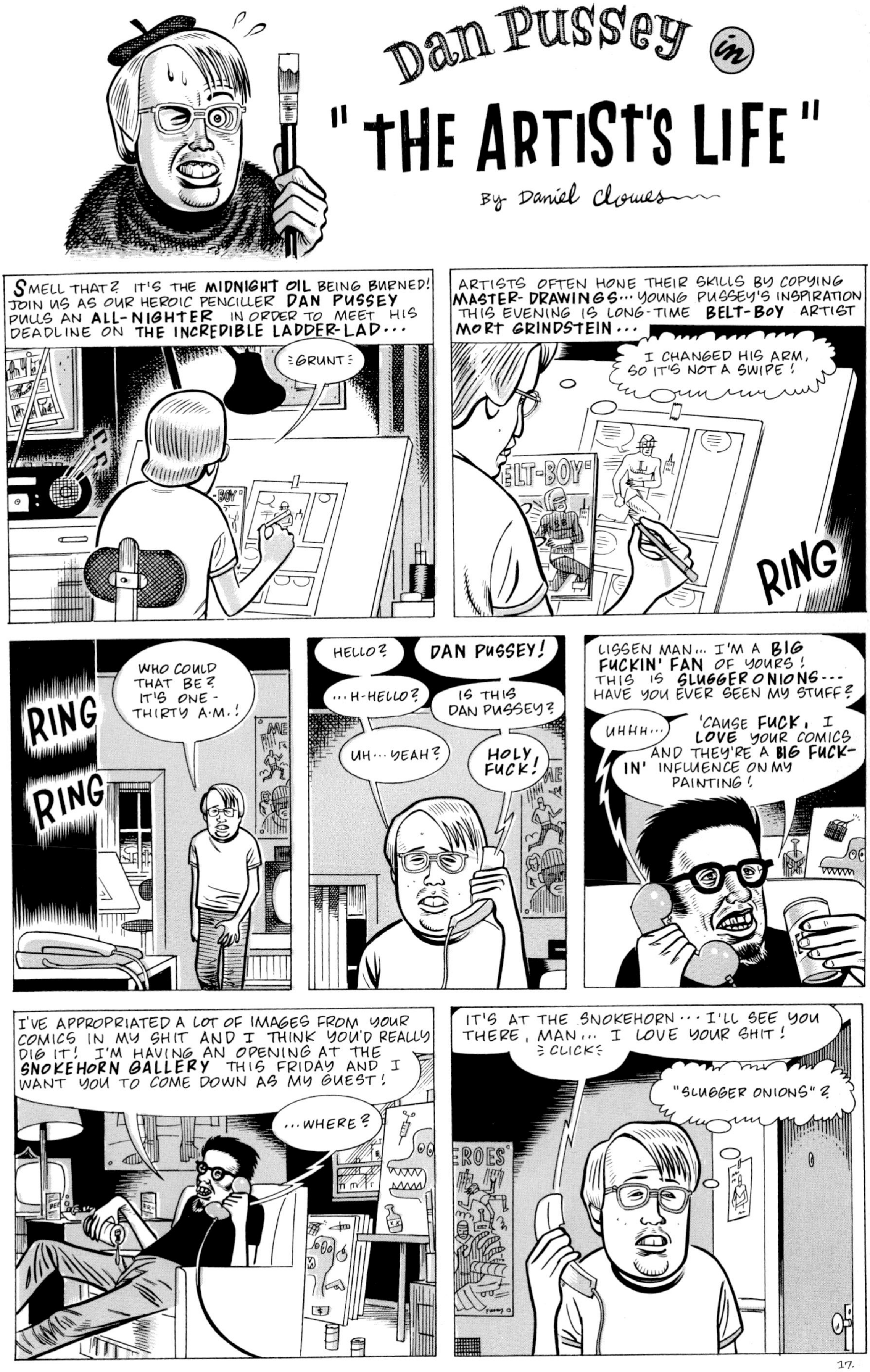
Dan Pussey in
"THE ARTIST'S LIFE"
By Daniel Clowes
SMELL THAT? IT'S THE MIDNIGHT OIL BEING BURNED! JOIN US AS OUR HEROIC PENCILLER DAN PUSSEY PULLS AN ALL-NIGHTER IN ORDER TO MEET HIS DEADLINE ON THE INCREDIBLE LADDER-LAD...
GRUNT
ARTISTS OFTEN HONE THEIR SKILLS BY COPYING MASTER-DRAWINGS... YOUNG PUSSEY'S INSPIRATION THIS EVENING IS LONG-TIME BELT-BOY ARTIST MORT GRINDSTEIN...
I CHANGED HIS ARM, SO IT'S NOT A SWIPE!
RING
RING
RING
WHO COULD THAT BE? IT'S ONE-THIRTY A.M.!
HELLO?
DAN PUSSEY!
...H-HELLO?
IS THIS DAN PUSSEY?
UH...YEAH?
HOLY FUCK!
LISSEN MAN... I'M A BIG FUCKIN' FAN OF YOURS! THIS IS SLUGGER ONIONS--- HAVE YOU EVER SEEN MY STUFF?
UHHH...
'CAUSE FUCK, I LOVE YOUR COMICS AND THEY'RE A BIG FUCKIN' INFLUENCE ON MY PAINTING!
I'VE APPROPRIATED A LOT OF IMAGES FROM YOUR COMICS IN MY SHIT AND I THINK YOU'D REALLY DIG IT! I'M HAVING AN OPENING AT THE SNOKEHORN GALLERY THIS FRIDAY AND I WANT YOU TO COME DOWN AS MY GUEST!
...WHERE?
IT'S AT THE SNOKEHORN... I'LL SEE YOU THERE, MAN... I LOVE YOUR SHIT!
CLICK
"SLUGGER ONIONS"?

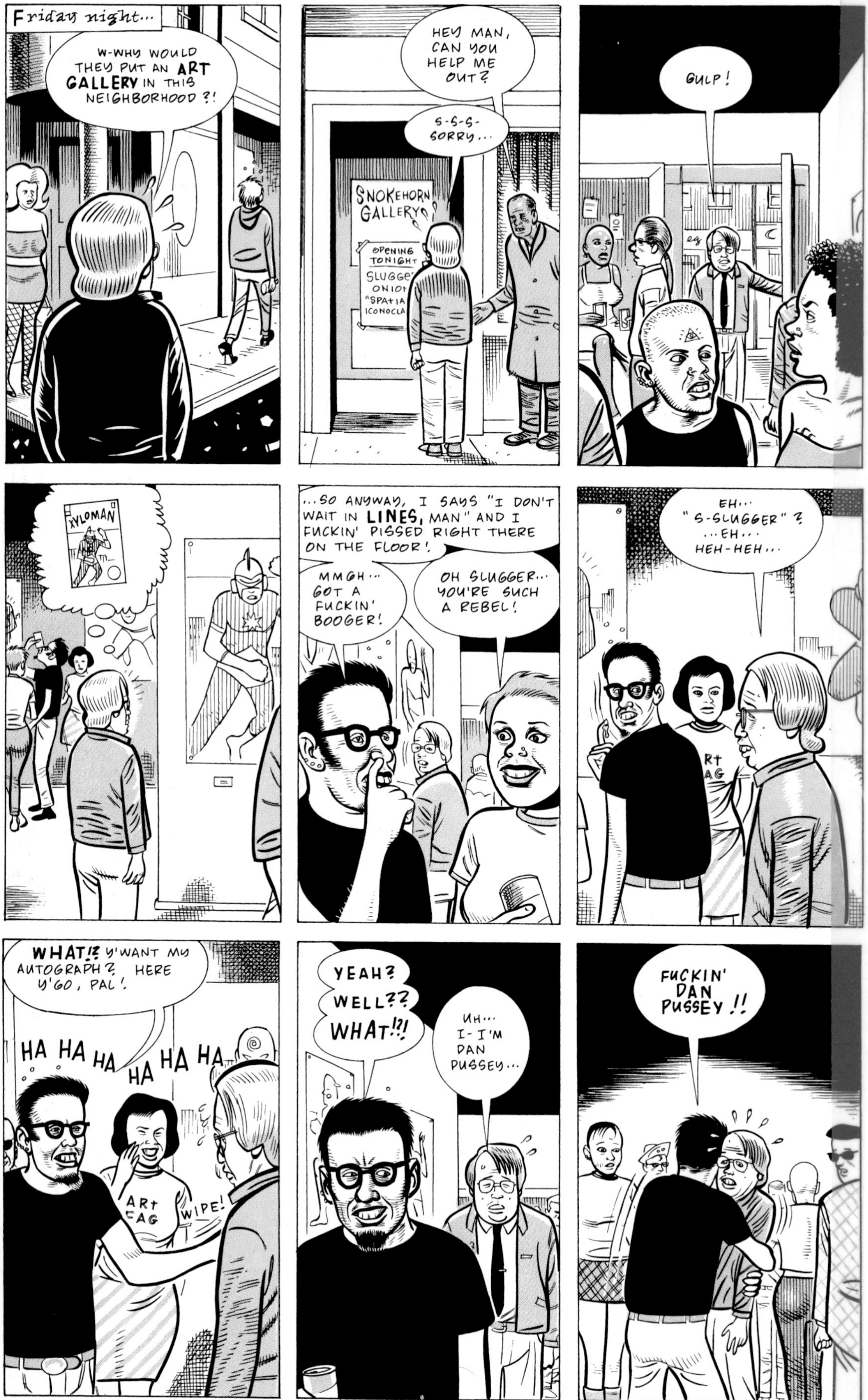
Friday night...
W-WHY WOULD THEY PUT AN ART GALLERY IN THIS NEIGHBORHOOD ?!
HEY MAN, CAN YOU HELP ME OUT?
S-S-S-SORRY...
SNOKEHORN GALLERY
OPENING TONIGHT
GULP!
XYLOMAN
...SO ANYWAY, I SAYS "I DON'T WAIT IN LINES, MAN" AND I FUCKIN' PISSED RIGHT THERE ON THE FLOOR!
MMGH... GOT A FUCKIN' BOOGER!
OH SLUGGER... YOU'RE SUCH A REBEL!
EH... "S-SLUGGER"? ...EH... HEH-HEH...
WHAT!? Y'WANT MY AUTOGRAPH? HERE Y'GO, PAL!
HA HA HA HA HA HA HA
WIPE!
YEAH? WELL?? WHAT!?!
UH... I-I'M DAN PUSSEY...
FUCKIN' DAN PUSSEY !!

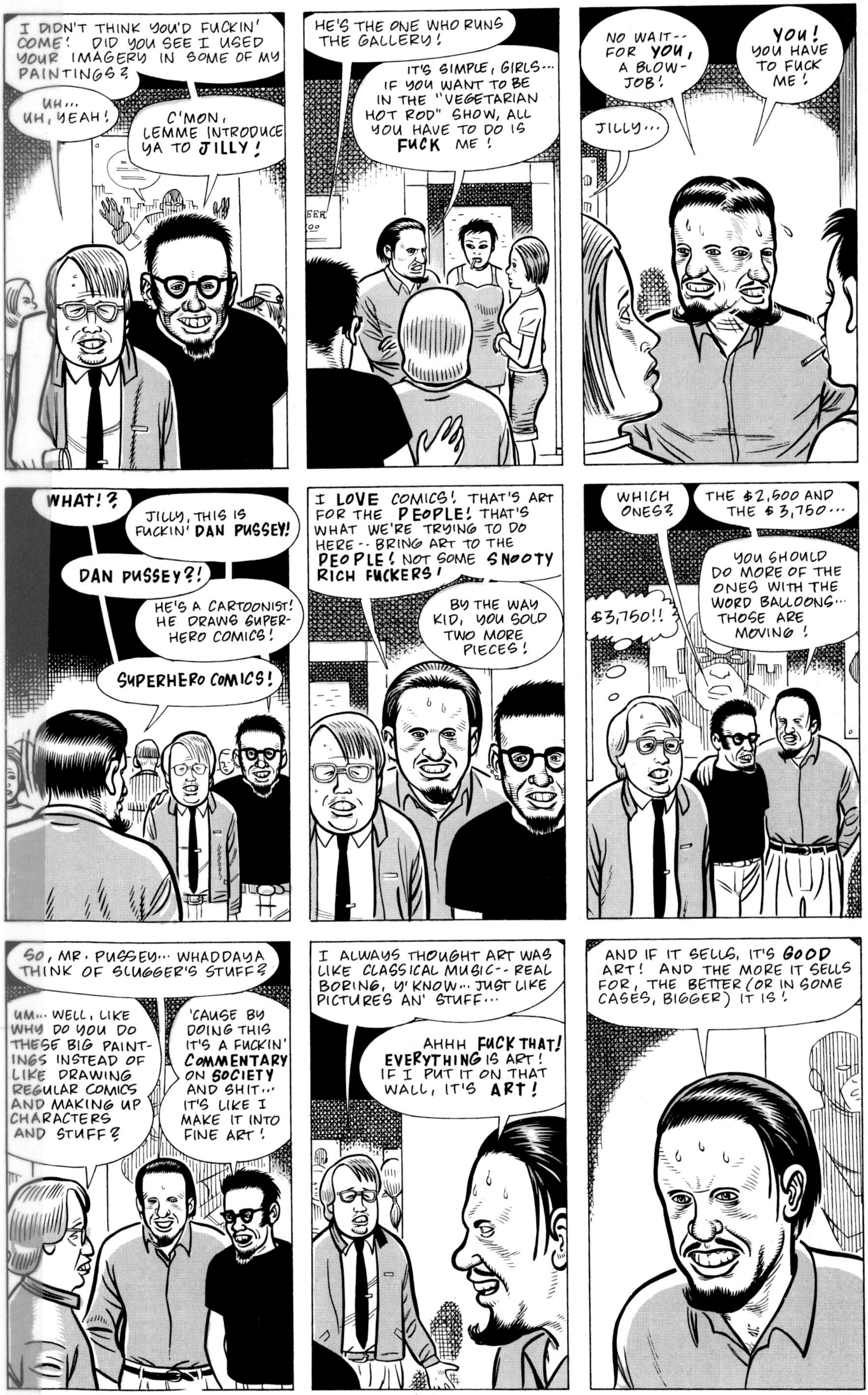
I DIDN'T THINK YOU'D FUCKIN' COME! DID YOU SEE I USED YOUR IMAGERY IN SOME OF MY PAINTINGS?
UH... UH, YEAH!
C'MON, LEMME INTRODUCE YA TO JILLY!
HE'S THE ONE WHO RUNS THE GALLERY!
IT'S SIMPLE, GIRLS... IF YOU WANT TO BE IN THE "VEGETARIAN HOT ROD" SHOW, ALL YOU HAVE TO DO IS FUCK ME!
NO WAIT-- FOR YOU, A BLOW-JOB!
YOU! YOU HAVE TO FUCK ME!
JILLY...
WHAT!?
JILLY, THIS IS FUCKIN' DAN PUSSEY!
DAN PUSSEY?!
HE'S A CARTOONIST! HE DRAWS SUPER-HERO COMICS!
SUPERHERO COMICS!
I LOVE COMICS! THAT'S ART FOR THE PEOPLE! THAT'S WHAT WE'RE TRYING TO DO HERE-- BRING ART TO THE PEOPLE! NOT SOME SNOOTY RICH FUCKERS!
BY THE WAY KID, YOU SOLD TWO MORE PIECES!
WHICH ONES?
THE $2,500 AND THE $3,750...
$3,750!!
YOU SHOULD DO MORE OF THE ONES WITH THE WORD BALLOONS... THOSE ARE MOVING!
SO, MR. PUSSEY... WHADDAYA THINK OF SLUGGER'S STUFF?
UM... WELL, LIKE WHY DO YOU DO THESE BIG PAINT-INGS INSTEAD OF LIKE DRAWING REGULAR COMICS AND MAKING UP CHARACTERS AND STUFF?
'CAUSE BY DOING THIS IT'S A FUCKIN' COMMENTARY ON SOCIETY AND SHIT... IT'S LIKE I MAKE IT INTO FINE ART!
I ALWAYS THOUGHT ART WAS LIKE CLASSICAL MUSIC-- REAL BORING, Y'KNOW... JUST LIKE PICTURES AN' STUFF...
AHHH FUCK THAT! EVERYTHING IS ART! IF I PUT IT ON THAT WALL, IT'S ART!
AND IF IT SELLS, IT'S GOOD ART! AND THE MORE IT SELLS FOR, THE BETTER (OR IN SOME CASES, BIGGER) IT IS!

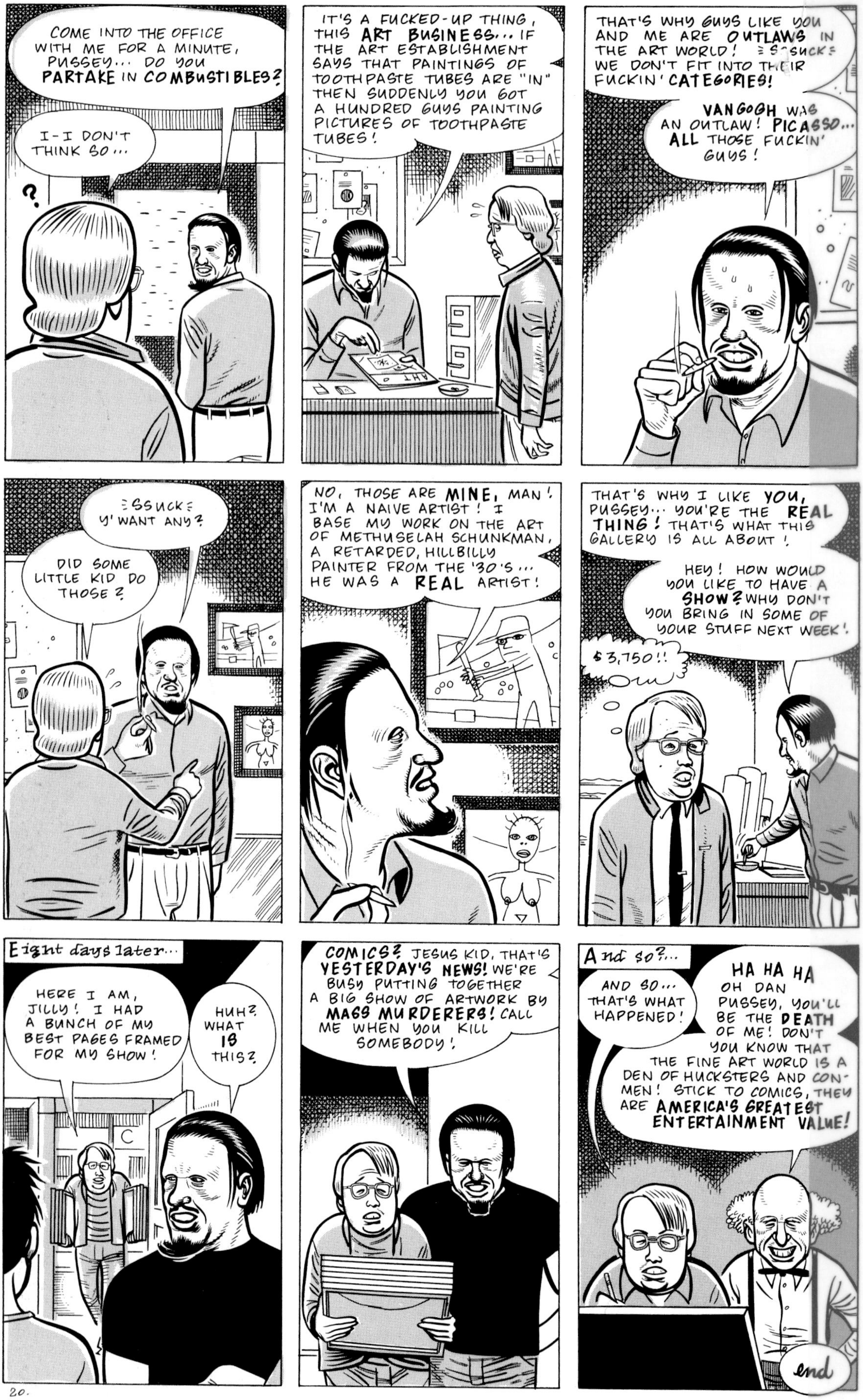
COME INTO THE OFFICE WITH ME FOR A MINUTE, PUSSEY... DO YOU PARTAKE IN COMBUSTIBLES?
I-I DON'T THINK SO...
?
IT'S A FUCKED-UP THING, THIS ART BUSINESS... IF THE ART ESTABLISHMENT SAYS THAT PAINTINGS OF TOOTHPASTE TUBES ARE "IN" THEN SUDDENLY YOU GOT A HUNDRED GUYS PAINTING PICTURES OF TOOTHPASTE TUBES!
THAT'S WHY GUYS LIKE YOU AND ME ARE OUTLAWS IN THE ART WORLD! SSSUCK WE DON'T FIT INTO THEIR FUCKIN' CATEGORIES!
VAN GOGH WAS AN OUTLAW! PICASSO... ALL THOSE FUCKIN' GUYS!
SSUCK Y' WANT ANY?
DID SOME LITTLE KID DO THOSE?
NO, THOSE ARE MINE, MAN! I'M A NAIVE ARTIST! I BASE MY WORK ON THE ART OF METHUSELAH SCHUNKMAN, A RETARDED, HILLBILLY PAINTER FROM THE '30'S... HE WAS A REAL ARTIST!
THAT'S WHY I LIKE YOU, PUSSEY... YOU'RE THE REAL THING! THAT'S WHAT THIS GALLERY IS ALL ABOUT!
HEY! HOW WOULD YOU LIKE TO HAVE A SHOW? WHY DON'T YOU BRING IN SOME OF YOUR STUFF NEXT WEEK!
$3,750!!
Eight days later...
HERE I AM, JILLY! I HAD A BUNCH OF MY BEST PAGES FRAMED FOR MY SHOW!
HUH? WHAT IS THIS?
COMICS? JESUS KID, THAT'S YESTERDAY'S NEWS! WE'RE BUSY PUTTING TOGETHER A BIG SHOW OF ARTWORK BY MASS MURDERERS! CALL ME WHEN YOU KILL SOMEBODY!
And so?...
AND SO... THAT'S WHAT HAPPENED!
HA HA HA OH DAN PUSSEY, YOU'LL BE THE DEATH OF ME! DON'T YOU KNOW THAT THE FINE ART WORLD IS A DEN OF HUCKSTERS AND CON-MEN! STICK TO COMICS, THEY ARE AMERICA'S GREATEST ENTERTAINMENT VALUE!
end

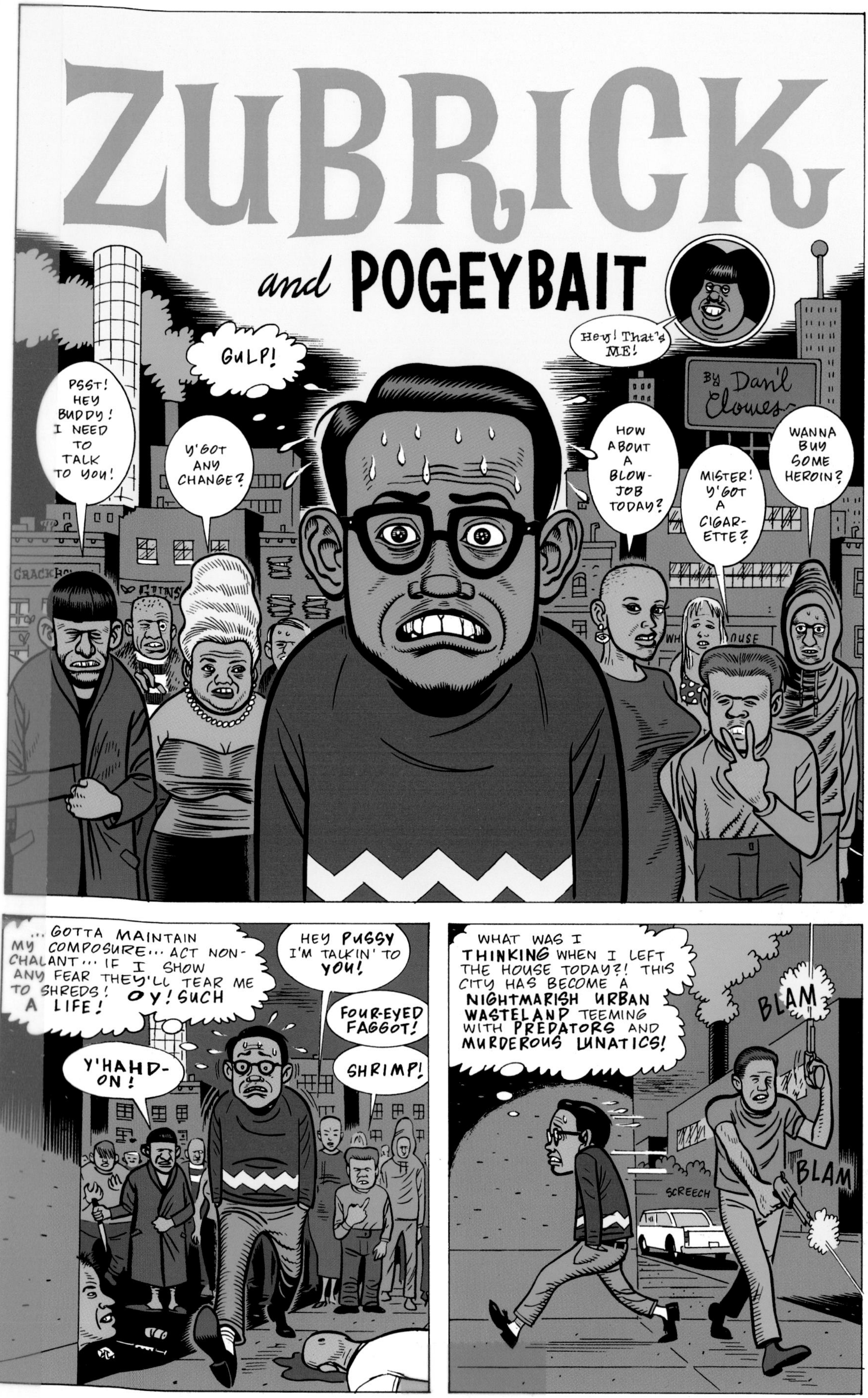
ZUBRICK
and POGEYBAIT
Hey! That's ME!
By Dan'l Clowes
GULP!
PSST! HEY BUDDY! I NEED TO TALK TO YOU!
Y'GOT ANY CHANGE?
HOW ABOUT A BLOW-JOB TODAY?
MISTER! Y'GOT A CIGAR-ETTE?
WANNA BUY SOME HEROIN?
... GOTTA MAINTAIN MY COMPOSURE... ACT NON-CHALANT... IF I SHOW ANY FEAR THEY'LL TEAR ME TO SHREDS! OY! SUCH A LIFE!
HEY PUSSY I'M TALKIN' TO YOU!
FOUR-EYED FAGGOT!
SHRIMP!
Y'HAHD-ON!
WHAT WAS I THINKING WHEN I LEFT THE HOUSE TODAY?! THIS CITY HAS BECOME A NIGHTMARISH URBAN WASTELAND TEEMING WITH PREDATORS AND MURDEROUS LUNATICS!
BLAM
BLAM
SCREECH

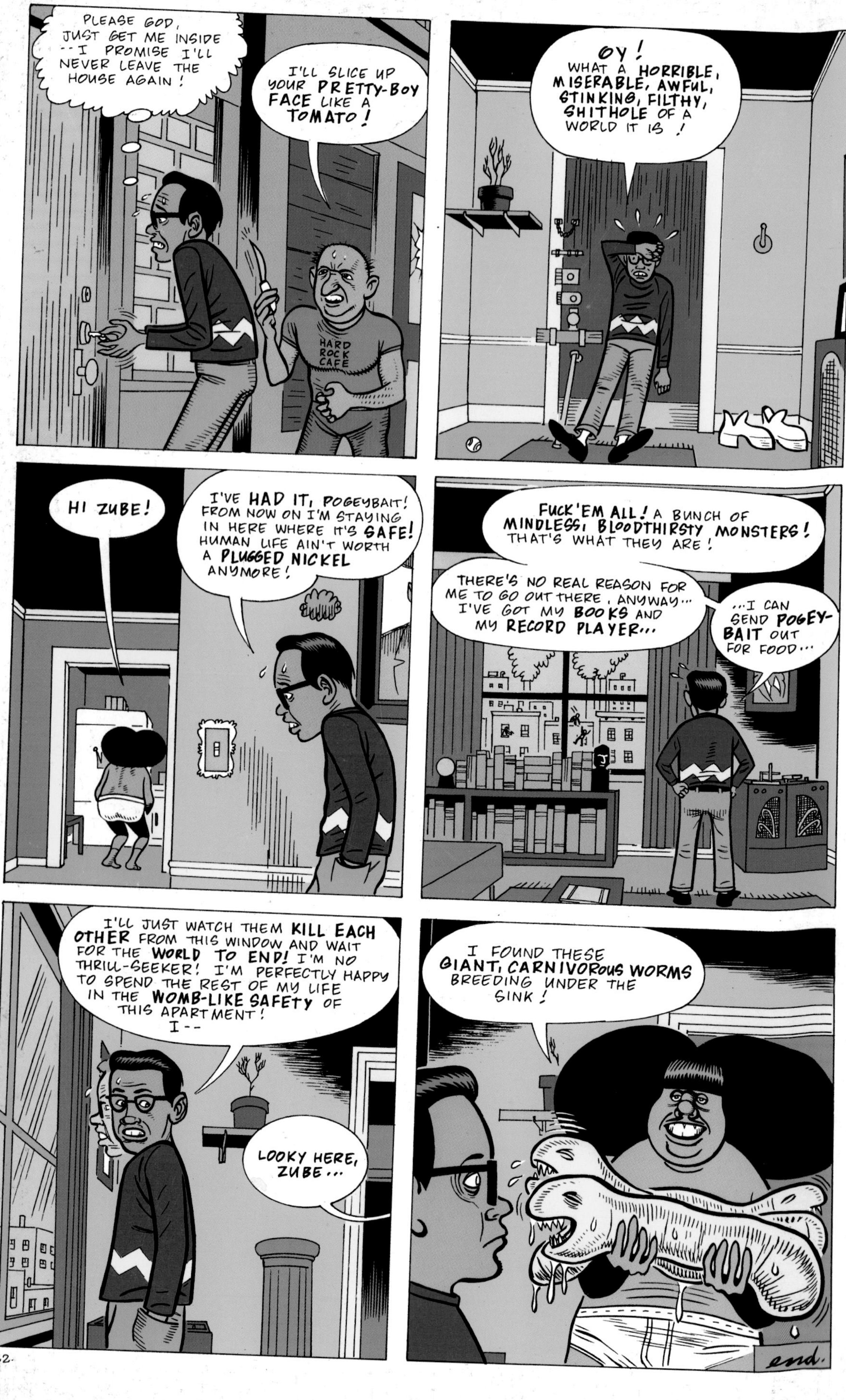
PLEASE GOD, JUST GET ME INSIDE --I PROMISE I'LL NEVER LEAVE THE HOUSE AGAIN!
I'LL SLICE UP YOUR PRETTY-BOY FACE LIKE A TOMATO!
HARD ROCK CAFE
OY! WHAT A HORRIBLE, MISERABLE, AWFUL, STINKING, FILTHY, SHITHOLE OF A WORLD IT IS!
HI ZUBE!
I'VE HAD IT, POGEYBAIT! FROM NOW ON I'M STAYING IN HERE WHERE IT'S SAFE! HUMAN LIFE AIN'T WORTH A PLUGGED NICKEL ANYMORE!
FUCK'EM ALL! A BUNCH OF MINDLESS, BLOODTHIRSTY MONSTERS! THAT'S WHAT THEY ARE!
THERE'S NO REAL REASON FOR ME TO GO OUT THERE, ANYWAY... I'VE GOT MY BOOKS AND MY RECORD PLAYER...
...I CAN SEND POGEY-BAIT OUT FOR FOOD...
I'LL JUST WATCH THEM KILL EACH OTHER FROM THIS WINDOW AND WAIT FOR THE WORLD TO END! I'M NO THRILL-SEEKER! I'M PERFECTLY HAPPY TO SPEND THE REST OF MY LIFE IN THE WOMB-LIKE SAFETY OF THIS APARTMENT! I--
LOOKY HERE, ZUBE...
I FOUND THESE GIANT, CARNIVOROUS WORMS BREEDING UNDER THE SINK!
end.

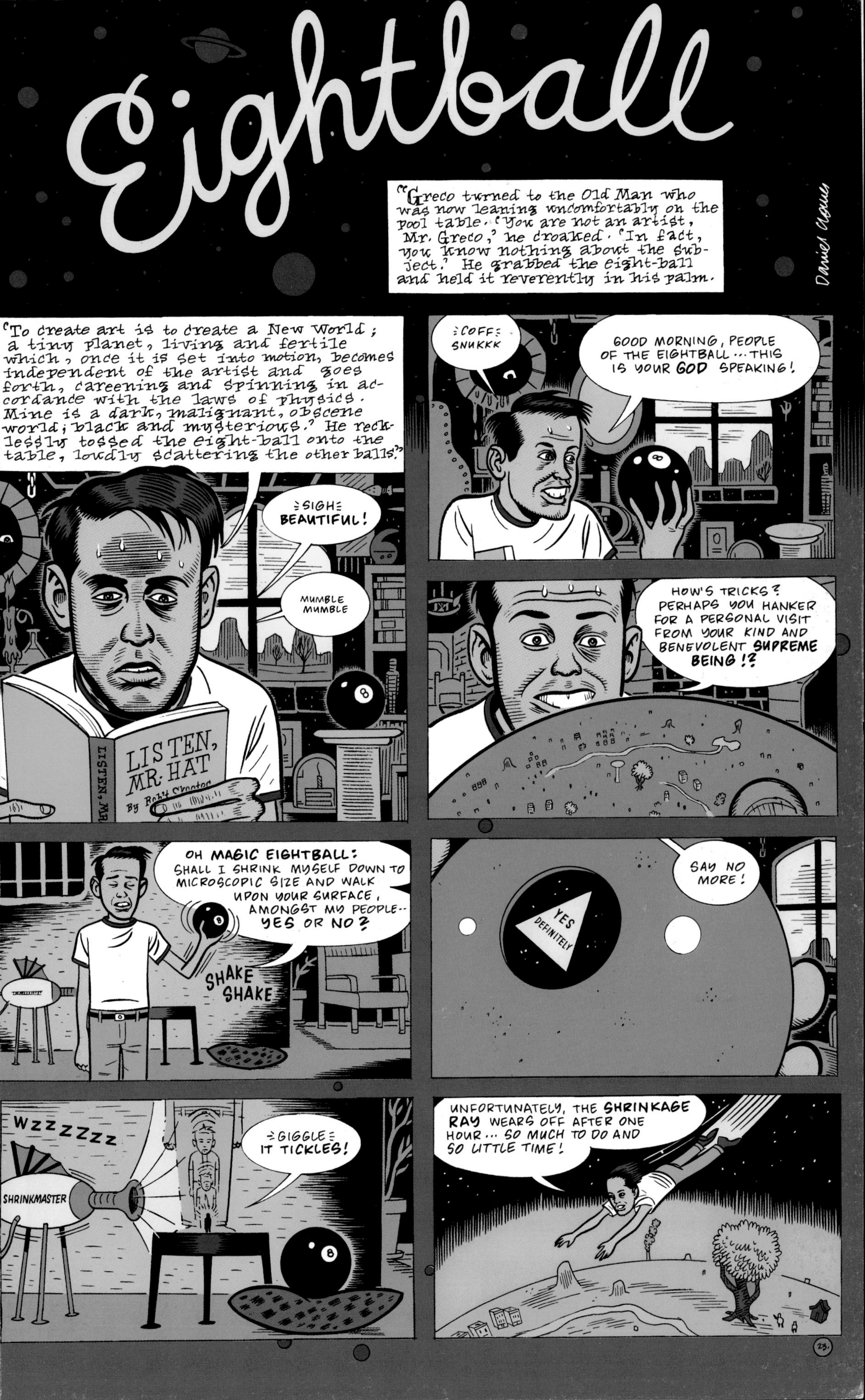
Eightball
"Greco turned to the Old Man who was now leaning uncomfortably on the pool table. 'You are not an artist, Mr. Greco,' he croaked. 'In fact, you know nothing about the subject.' He grabbed the eight-ball and held it reverently in his palm.
Daniel Clowes
'To create art is to create a New World; a tiny planet, living and fertile which, once it is set into motion, becomes independent of the artist and goes forth, careening and spinning in accordance with the laws of physics. Mine is a dark, malignant, obscene world; black and mysterious.' He recklessly tossed the eight-ball onto the table, loudly scattering the other balls."
SIGH
BEAUTIFUL!
MUMBLE MUMBLE
LISTEN, MR. HAT
COFF SNUKKK
GOOD MORNING, PEOPLE OF THE EIGHTBALL... THIS IS YOUR GOD SPEAKING!
HOW'S TRICKS? PERHAPS YOU HANKER FOR A PERSONAL VISIT FROM YOUR KIND AND BENEVOLENT SUPREME BEING!?
OH MAGIC EIGHTBALL: SHALL I SHRINK MYSELF DOWN TO MICROSCOPIC SIZE AND WALK UPON YOUR SURFACE, AMONGST MY PEOPLE-- YES OR NO?
SHAKE SHAKE
YES DEFINITELY
SAY NO MORE!
WZZZZZZ
SHRINKMASTER
GIGGLE
IT TICKLES!
UNFORTUNATELY, THE SHRINKAGE RAY WEARS OFF AFTER ONE HOUR... SO MUCH TO DO AND SO LITTLE TIME!
23.

Continued from inside

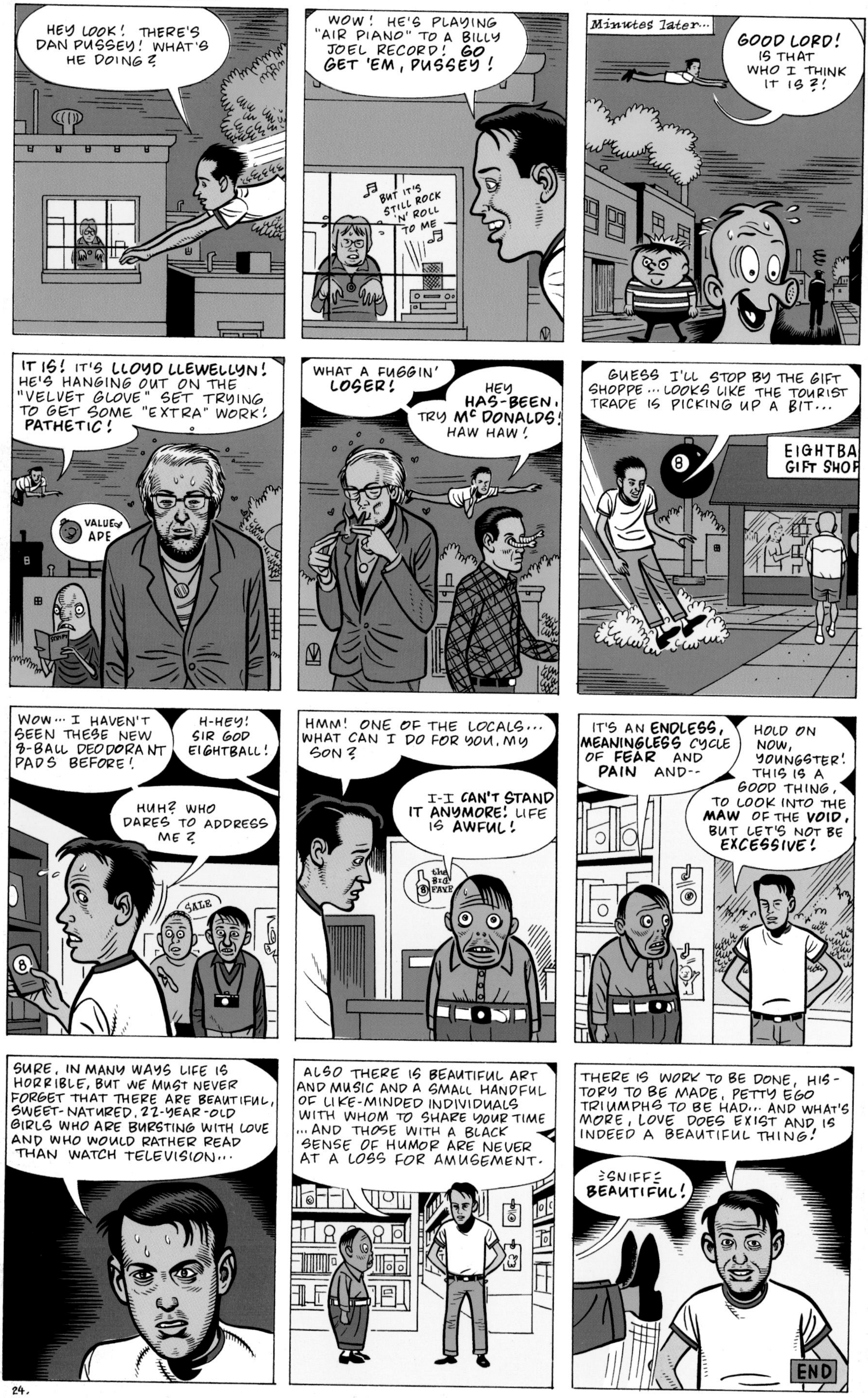
HEY LOOK! THERE'S DAN PUSSEY! WHAT'S HE DOING?
WOW! HE'S PLAYING "AIR PIANO" TO A BILLY JOEL RECORD! GO GET 'EM, PUSSEY!
BUT IT'S STILL ROCK 'N' ROLL TO ME
Minutes later...
GOOD LORD! IS THAT WHO I THINK IT IS?!
IT IS! IT'S LLOYD LLEWELLYN! HE'S HANGING OUT ON THE "VELVET GLOVE" SET TRYING TO GET SOME "EXTRA" WORK! PATHETIC!
VALUE APE
SCRIPT
WHAT A FUGGIN' LOSER!
HEY HAS-BEEN, TRY McDONALDS! HAW HAW!
GUESS I'LL STOP BY THE GIFT SHOPPE... LOOKS LIKE THE TOURIST TRADE IS PICKING UP A BIT...
EIGHTBA GIFT SHOP
WOW... I HAVEN'T SEEN THESE NEW 8-BALL DEODORANT PADS BEFORE!
H-HEY! SIR GOD EIGHTBALL!
HUH? WHO DARES TO ADDRESS ME?
SALE
HMM! ONE OF THE LOCALS... WHAT CAN I DO FOR YOU, MY SON?
I-I CAN'T STAND IT ANYMORE! LIFE IS AWFUL!
the BIG FAYE
IT'S AN ENDLESS, MEANINGLESS CYCLE OF FEAR AND PAIN AND--
HOLD ON NOW, YOUNGSTER! THIS IS A GOOD THING, TO LOOK INTO THE MAW OF THE VOID, BUT LET'S NOT BE EXCESSIVE!
SURE, IN MANY WAYS LIFE IS HORRIBLE, BUT WE MUST NEVER FORGET THAT THERE ARE BEAUTIFUL, SWEET-NATURED, 22-YEAR-OLD GIRLS WHO ARE BURSTING WITH LOVE AND WHO WOULD RATHER READ THAN WATCH TELEVISION...
ALSO THERE IS BEAUTIFUL ART AND MUSIC AND A SMALL HANDFUL OF LIKE-MINDED INDIVIDUALS WITH WHOM TO SHARE YOUR TIME ... AND THOSE WITH A BLACK SENSE OF HUMOR ARE NEVER AT A LOSS FOR AMUSEMENT.
THERE IS WORK TO BE DONE, HISTORY TO BE MADE, PETTY EGO TRIUMPHS TO BE HAD... AND WHAT'S MORE, LOVE DOES EXIST AND IS INDEED A BEAUTIFUL THING!
SNIFF BEAUTIFUL!
END

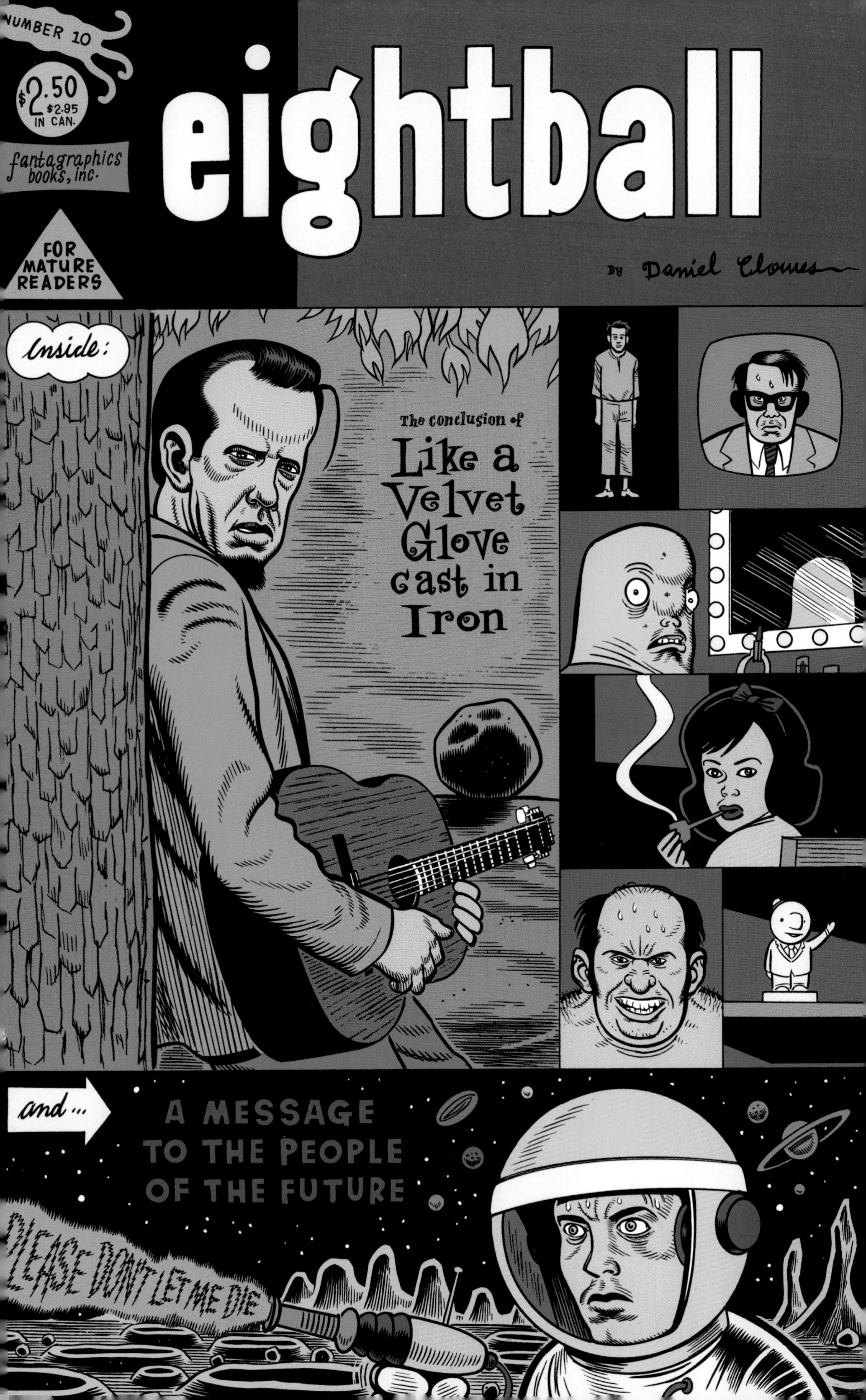

NUMBER 10
$2.50 $2.95 IN CAN.
fantagraphics books, inc.
eightball
FOR MATURE READERS
BY Daniel Clowes
inside:
The conclusion of
Like a Velvet Glove cast in Iron
and ...
A MESSAGE TO THE PEOPLE OF THE FUTURE
PLEASE DON'T LET ME DIE

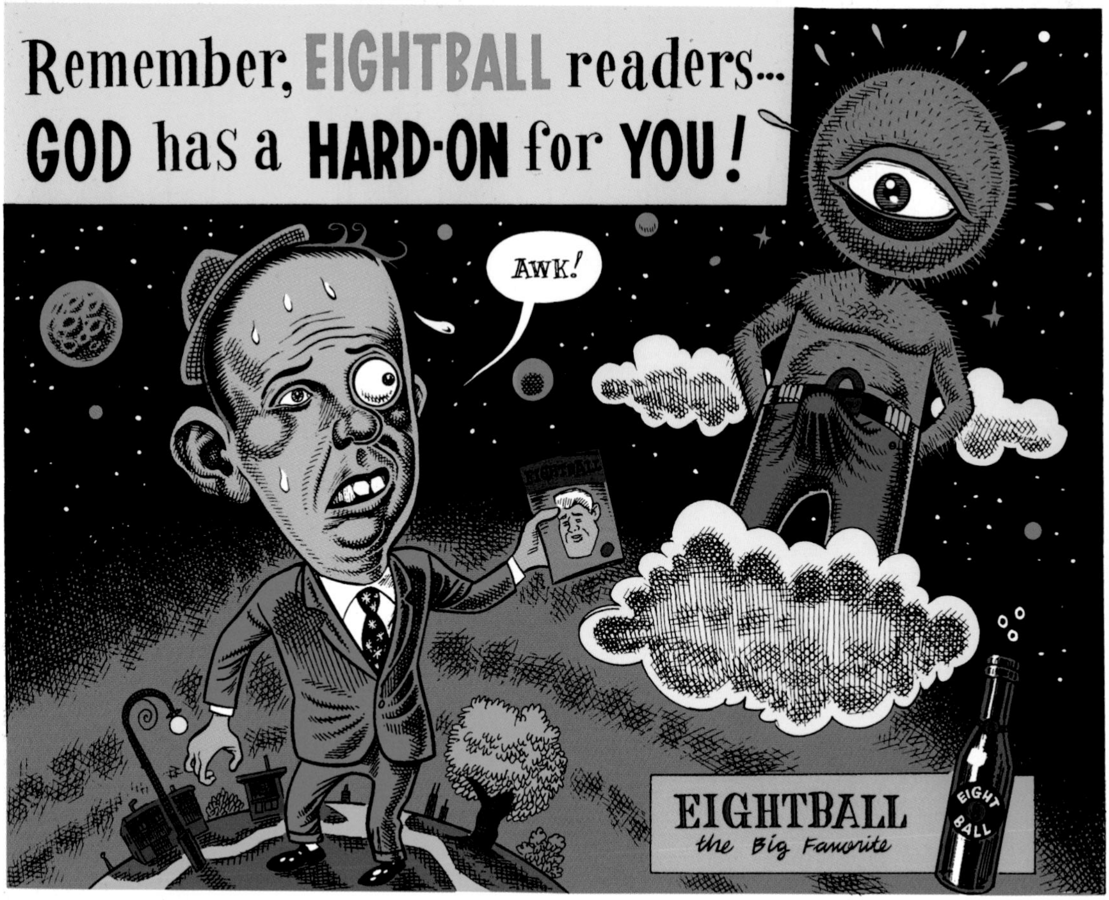

Remember, EIGHTBALL readers...
GOD has a HARD-ON for YOU!
AWK!
EIGHTBALL
EIGHTBALL the Big Favorite
EIGHT BALL

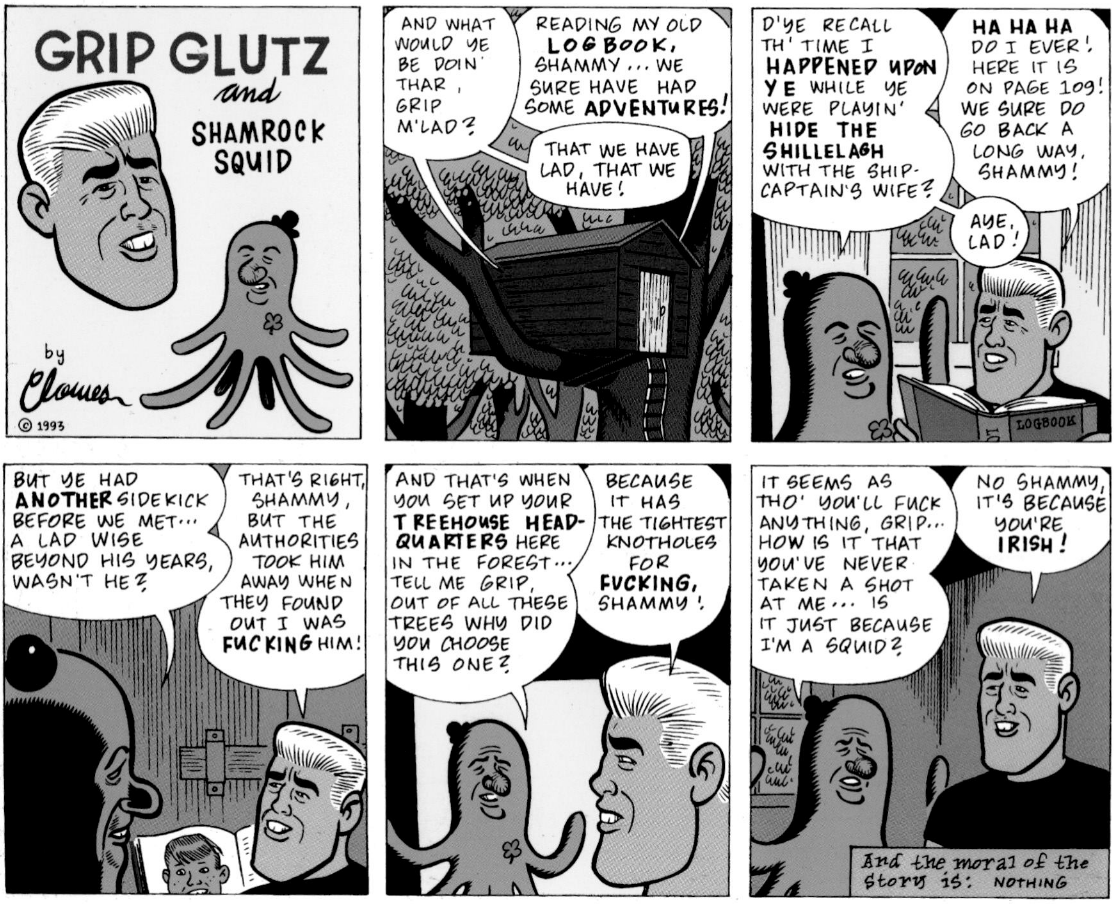

GRIP GLUTZ and SHAMROCK SQUID
by Clowes
© 1993
AND WHAT WOULD YE BE DOIN' THAR, GRIP M'LAD?
READING MY OLD LOGBOOK, SHAMMY... WE SURE HAVE HAD SOME ADVENTURES!
THAT WE HAVE LAD, THAT WE HAVE!
D'YE RECALL TH' TIME I HAPPENED UPON YE WHILE YE WERE PLAYIN' HIDE THE SHILLELAGH WITH THE SHIP-CAPTAIN'S WIFE?
HA HA HA DO I EVER! HERE IT IS ON PAGE 109! WE SURE DO GO BACK A LONG WAY, SHAMMY!
AYE, LAD!
LOGBOOK
BUT YE HAD ANOTHER SIDEKICK BEFORE WE MET... A LAD WISE BEYOND HIS YEARS, WASN'T HE?
THAT'S RIGHT, SHAMMY, BUT THE AUTHORITIES TOOK HIM AWAY WHEN THEY FOUND OUT I WAS FUCKING HIM!
AND THAT'S WHEN YOU SET UP YOUR TREEHOUSE HEAD-QUARTERS HERE IN THE FOREST... TELL ME GRIP, OUT OF ALL THESE TREES WHY DID YOU CHOOSE THIS ONE?
BECAUSE IT HAS THE TIGHTEST KNOTHOLES FOR FUCKING, SHAMMY!
IT SEEMS AS THO' YOU'LL FUCK ANYTHING, GRIP... HOW IS IT THAT YOU'VE NEVER TAKEN A SHOT AT ME... IS IT JUST BECAUSE I'M A SQUID?
NO SHAMMY, IT'S BECAUSE YOU'RE IRISH!
And the moral of the story is: NOTHING

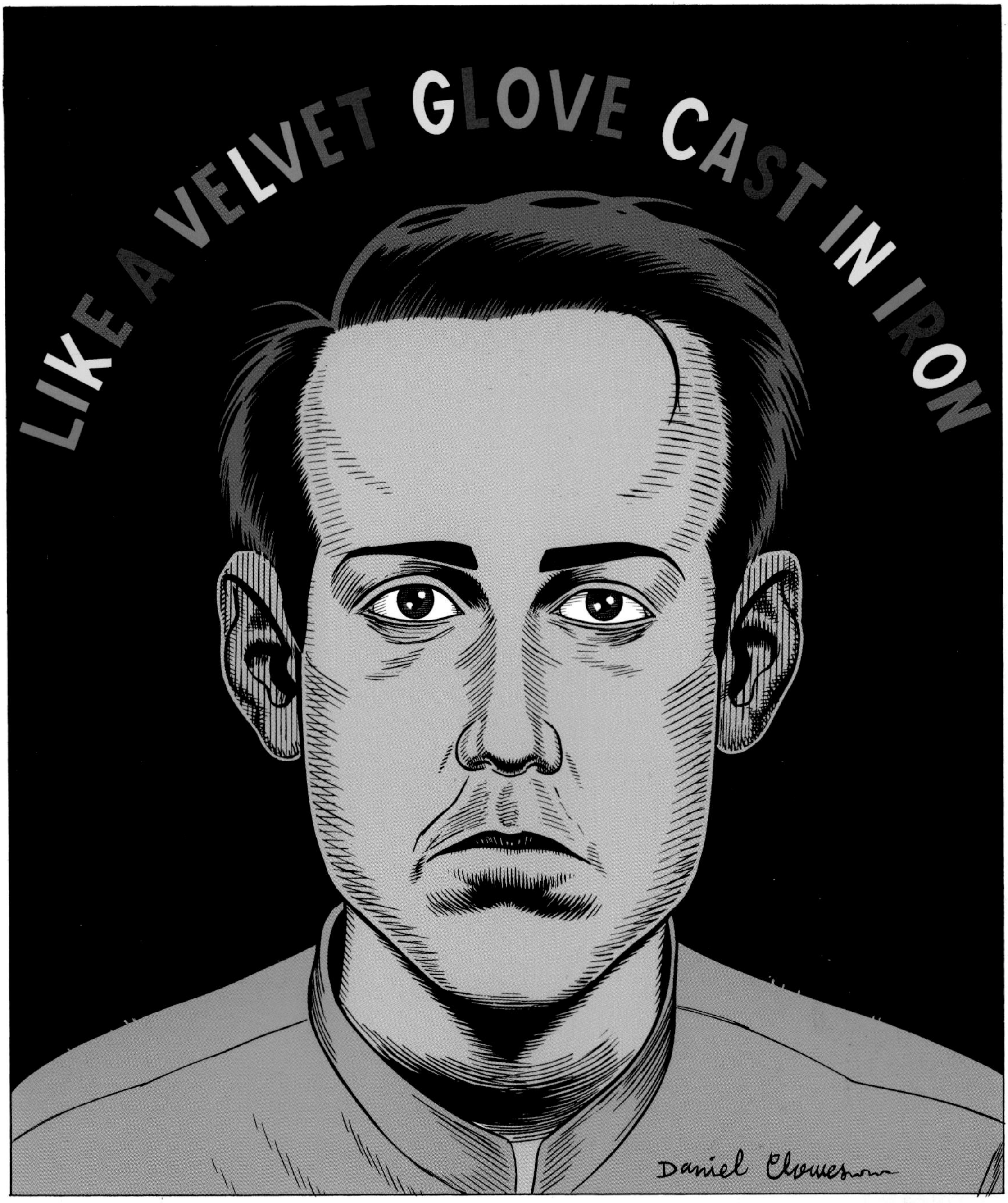
LIKE A VELVET GLOVE CAST IN IRON
Daniel Clowes

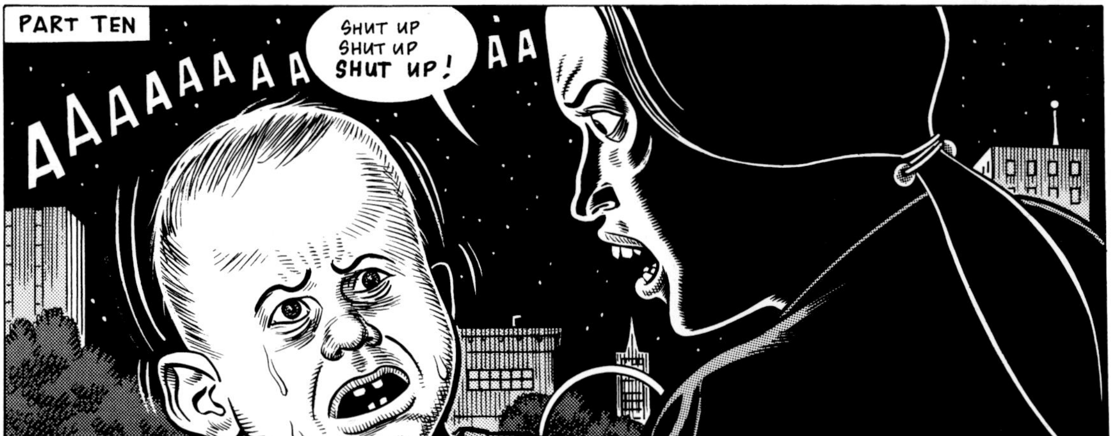
PART TEN
AAAAAAAAAA
SHUT UP
SHUT UP
SHUT UP!

Eightball #10, February, 1993. *Eightball* is published thrice yearly by Fantagraphics Books, Inc., and is copyright © 1993 Fantagraphics Books, Inc. All characters, stories, and art © 1993 Daniel Clowes. No part of this magazine may be reproduced without written permission from Fantagraphics Books or Daniel Clowes. No similarity between any of the names, characters, persons, and institutions in *Eightball* and those of any living or dead persons is intended (except for satirical intent), and any such similarity that may exist is purely coincidental. Letters to *Eightball* become the property of the magazine and are assumed intended for publication in whole or in part, and may therefore be used for those purposes. First printing: January, 1993. Fantagraphics Books, 7563 Lake City Way Northeast, Seattle WA 98115. **Send for our free catalogue**!

AAAA AAA

GOD **DAMN** IT, WON'T YOU SHUT UP!

AAAAA

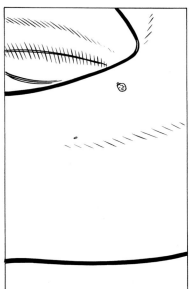

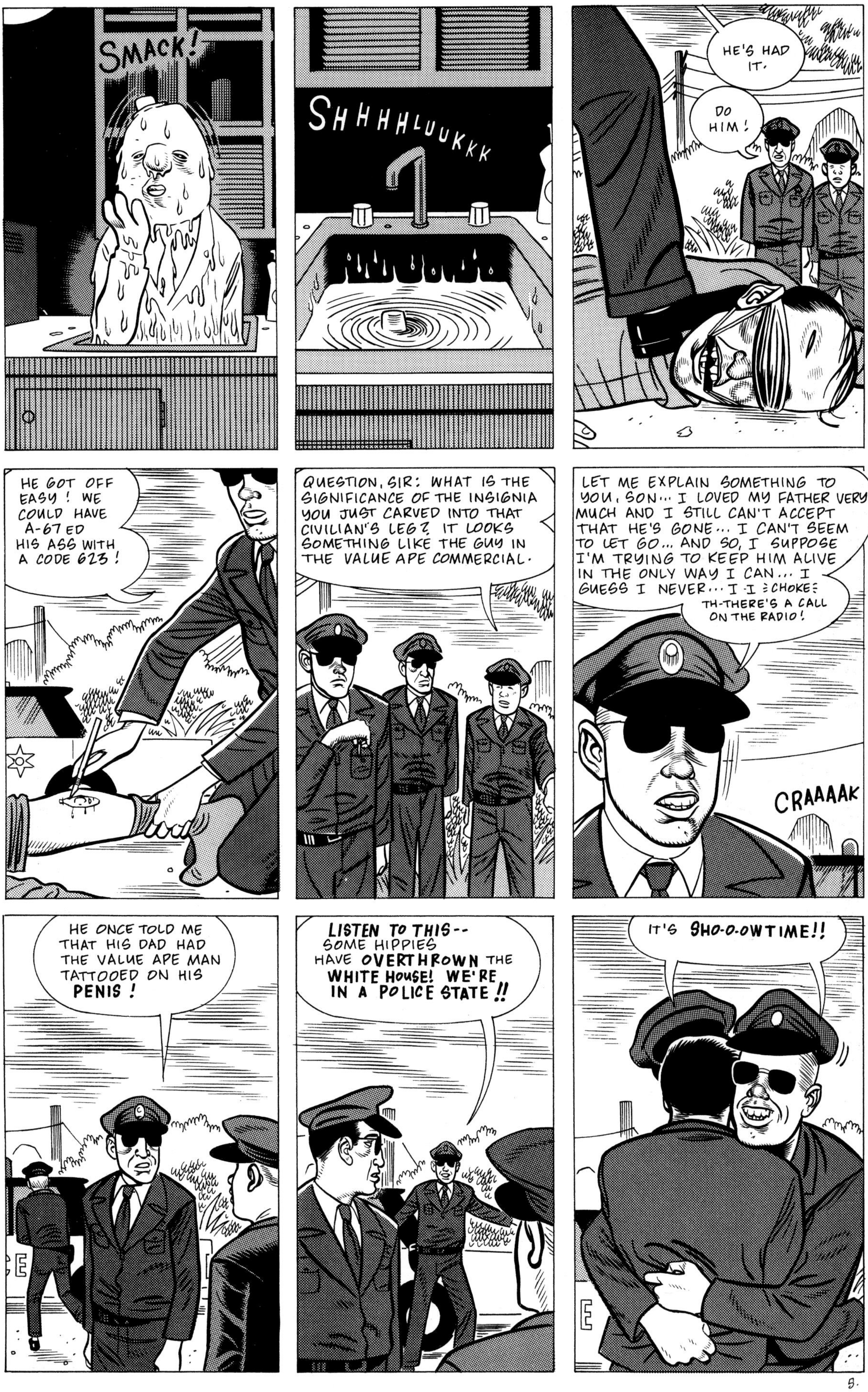
SMACK!
SHHHHLUUKKK
HE'S HAD IT.
DO HIM!
HE GOT OFF EASY! WE COULD HAVE A-67ED HIS ASS WITH A CODE 623!
QUESTION, SIR: WHAT IS THE SIGNIFICANCE OF THE INSIGNIA YOU JUST CARVED INTO THAT CIVILIAN'S LEG? IT LOOKS SOMETHING LIKE THE GUY IN THE VALUE APE COMMERCIAL.
LET ME EXPLAIN SOMETHING TO YOU, SON... I LOVED MY FATHER VERY MUCH AND I STILL CAN'T ACCEPT THAT HE'S GONE... I CAN'T SEEM TO LET GO... AND SO, I SUPPOSE I'M TRYING TO KEEP HIM ALIVE IN THE ONLY WAY I CAN... I GUESS I NEVER... I-I ≡CHOKE≡
TH-THERE'S A CALL ON THE RADIO!
CRAAAAK
HE ONCE TOLD ME THAT HIS DAD HAD THE VALUE APE MAN TATTOOED ON HIS PENIS!
LISTEN TO THIS-- SOME HIPPIES HAVE OVERTHROWN THE WHITE HOUSE! WE'RE IN A POLICE STATE!!
IT'S SHO-O-OWTIME!!

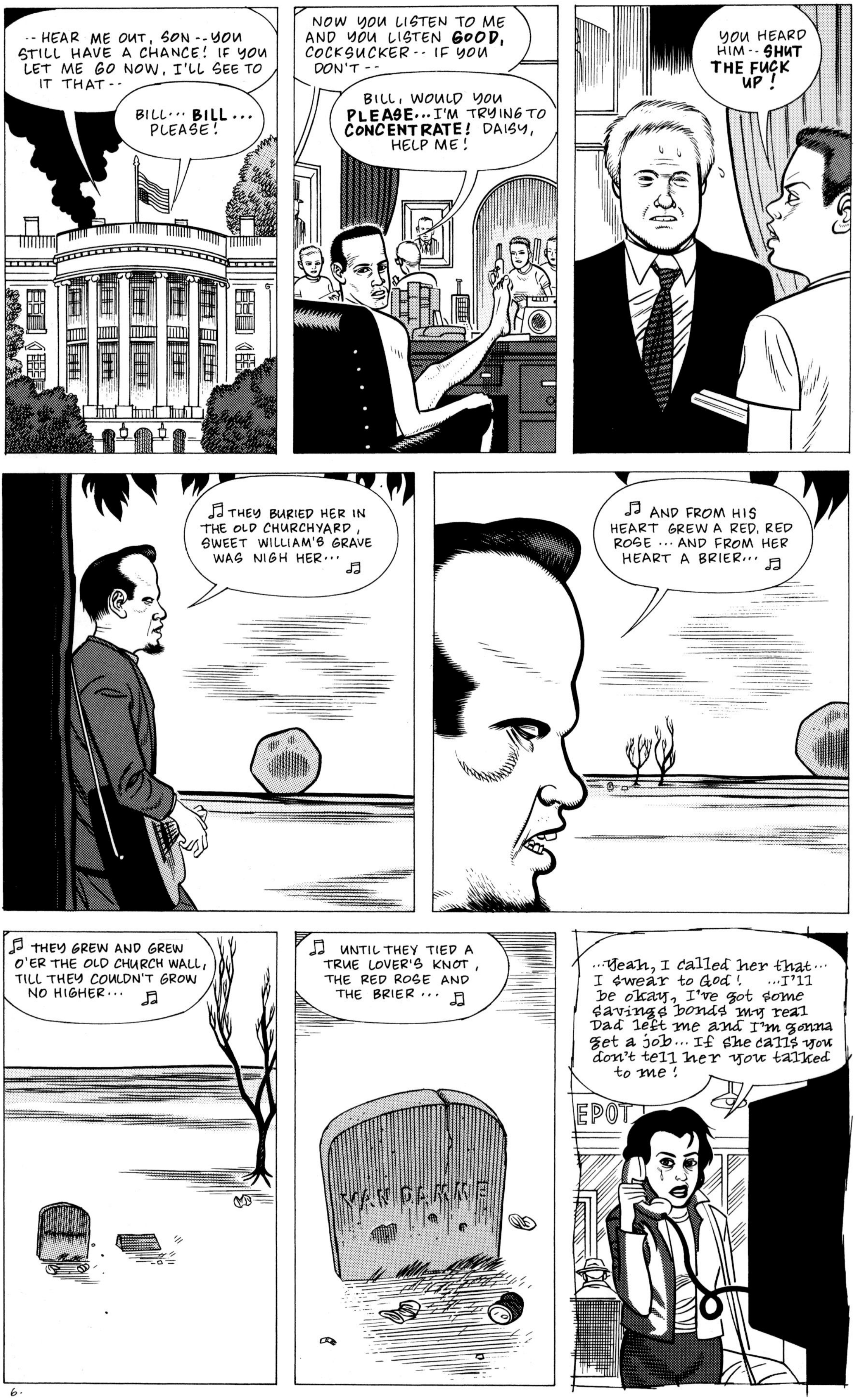
-- HEAR ME OUT, SON -- YOU STILL HAVE A CHANCE! IF YOU LET ME GO NOW, I'LL SEE TO IT THAT --
BILL... BILL... PLEASE!
NOW YOU LISTEN TO ME AND YOU LISTEN GOOD, COCKSUCKER -- IF YOU DON'T --
BILL, WOULD YOU PLEASE... I'M TRYING TO CONCENTRATE! DAISY, HELP ME!
YOU HEARD HIM -- SHUT THE FUCK UP!
♫ THEY BURIED HER IN THE OLD CHURCHYARD, SWEET WILLIAM'S GRAVE WAS NIGH HER... ♫
♫ AND FROM HIS HEART GREW A RED, RED ROSE ... AND FROM HER HEART A BRIER... ♫
♫ THEY GREW AND GREW O'ER THE OLD CHURCH WALL, TILL THEY COULDN'T GROW NO HIGHER... ♫
♫ UNTIL THEY TIED A TRUE LOVER'S KNOT, THE RED ROSE AND THE BRIER... ♫
...Yeah, I called her that... I swear to God! ...I'll be okay, I've got some savings bonds my real Dad left me and I'm gonna get a job... If she calls you don't tell her you talked to me!
EPOT

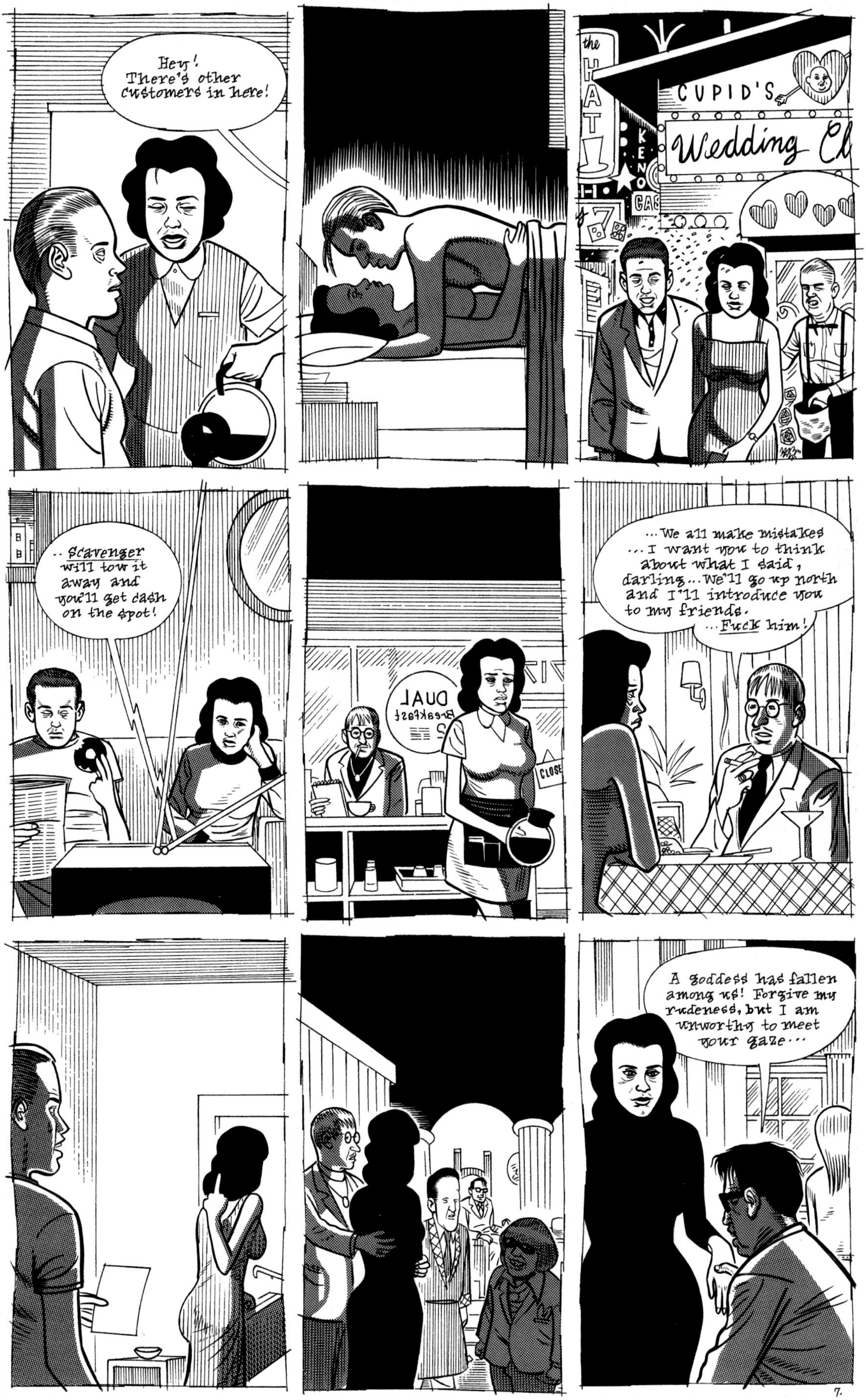
Hey! There's other customers in here!
CUPID'S
Wedding Ch
KENO
CAS
.. Scavenger will tow it away and you'll get cash on the spot!
DUAL
Breakfast
CLOSE
... We all make mistakes ... I want you to think about what I said, darling ... We'll go up north and I'll introduce you to my friends.
... Fuck him!
A goddess has fallen among us! Forgive my rudeness, but I am unworthy to meet your gaze...

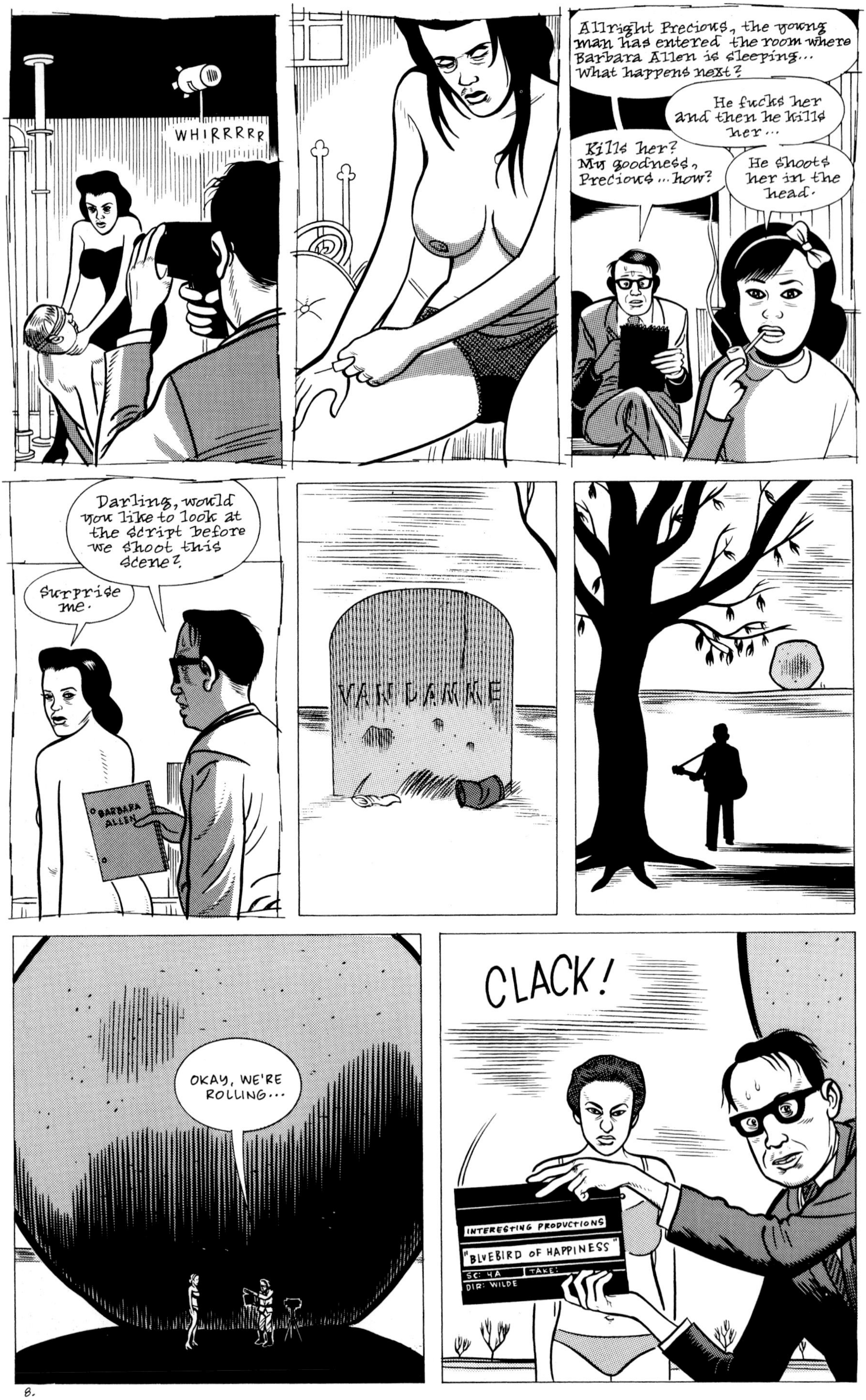

WHIRRRRR
Allright Precious, the young man has entered the room where Barbara Allen is sleeping... What happens next?
He fucks her and then he kills her...
Kills her? My goodness, Precious... how?
He shoots her in the head.
Darling, would you like to look at the script before we shoot this scene?
Surprise me.
BARBARA ALLEN
VAN DAMME
OKAY, WE'RE ROLLING...
CLACK!
INTERESTING PRODUCTIONS
"BLUEBIRD OF HAPPINESS"
SC: 4A
TAKE:
DIR: WILDE

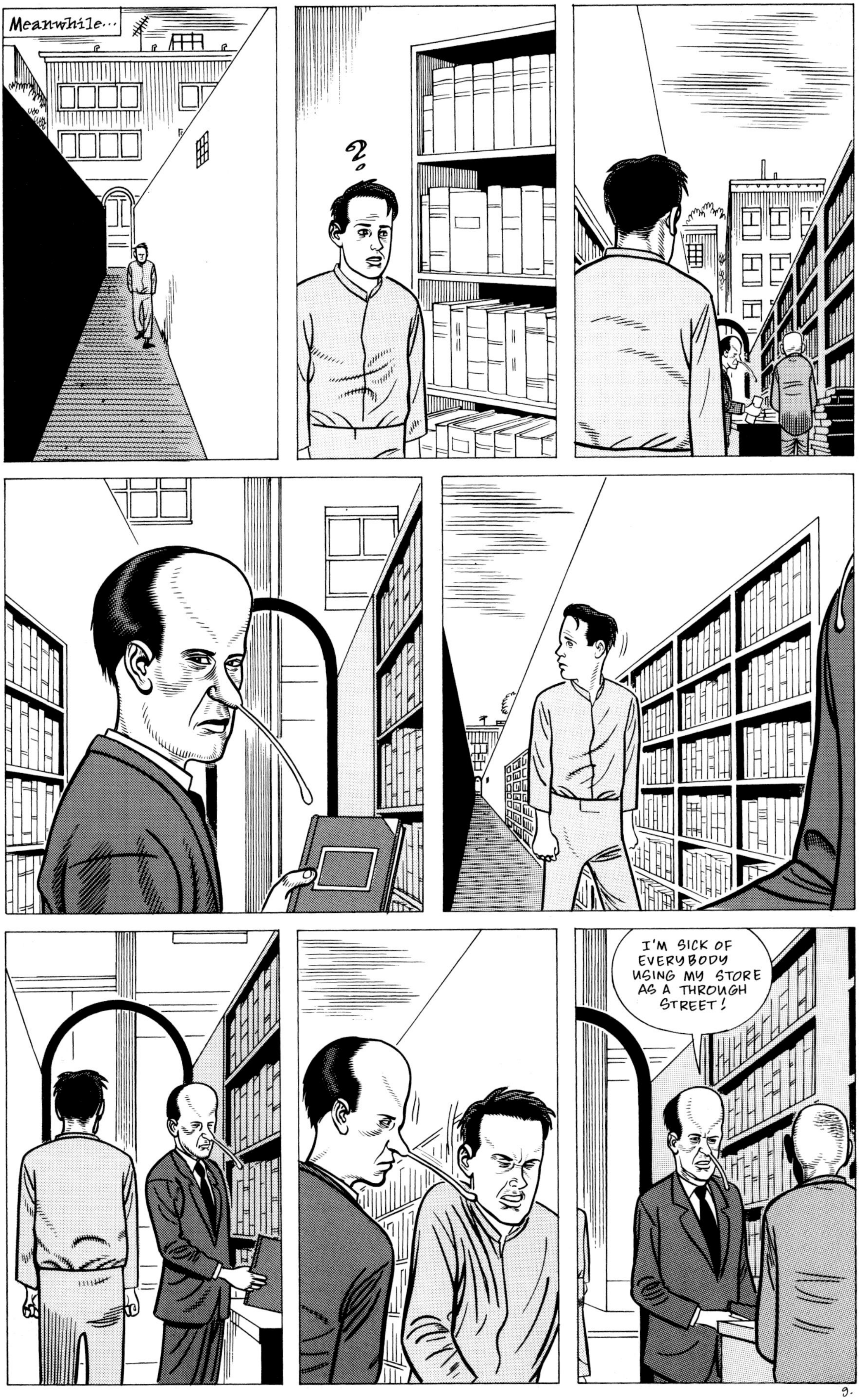
Meanwhile...
?
I'M SICK OF EVERYBODY USING MY STORE AS A THROUGH STREET!

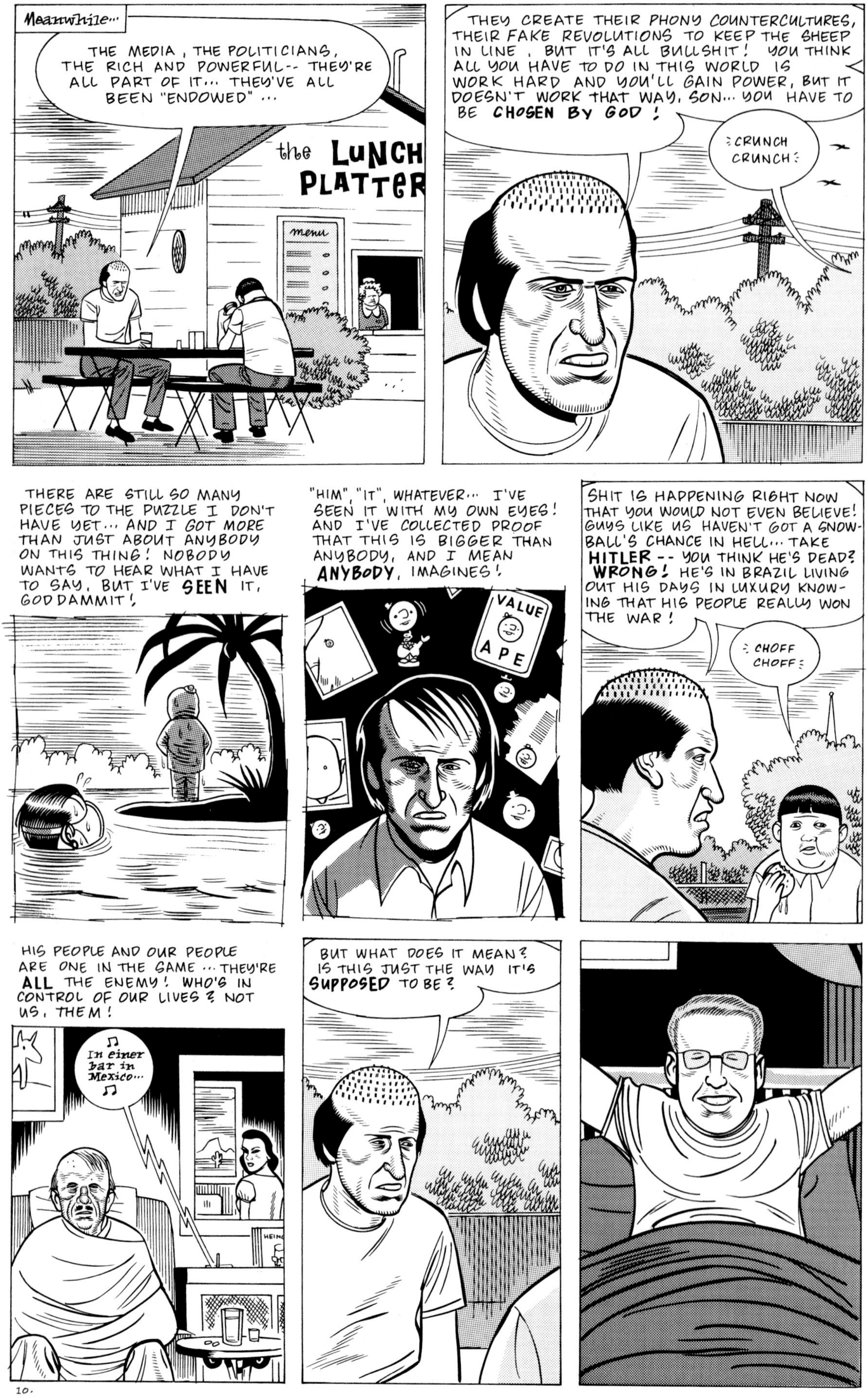
Meanwhile...
THE MEDIA, THE POLITICIANS, THE RICH AND POWERFUL-- THEY'RE ALL PART OF IT... THEY'VE ALL BEEN "ENDOWED"...
the LUNCH PLATTER
menu
THEY CREATE THEIR PHONY COUNTERCULTURES, THEIR FAKE REVOLUTIONS TO KEEP THE SHEEP IN LINE, BUT IT'S ALL BULLSHIT! YOU THINK ALL YOU HAVE TO DO IN THIS WORLD IS WORK HARD AND YOU'LL GAIN POWER, BUT IT DOESN'T WORK THAT WAY, SON... YOU HAVE TO BE CHOSEN BY GOD!
CRUNCH CRUNCH
THERE ARE STILL SO MANY PIECES TO THE PUZZLE I DON'T HAVE YET... AND I GOT MORE THAN JUST ABOUT ANYBODY ON THIS THING! NOBODY WANTS TO HEAR WHAT I HAVE TO SAY, BUT I'VE SEEN IT, GODDAMMIT!
"HIM", "IT", WHATEVER... I'VE SEEN IT WITH MY OWN EYES! AND I'VE COLLECTED PROOF THAT THIS IS BIGGER THAN ANYBODY, AND I MEAN ANYBODY, IMAGINES!
VALUE APE
SHIT IS HAPPENING RIGHT NOW THAT YOU WOULD NOT EVEN BELIEVE! GUYS LIKE US HAVEN'T GOT A SNOWBALL'S CHANCE IN HELL... TAKE HITLER -- YOU THINK HE'S DEAD? WRONG! HE'S IN BRAZIL LIVING OUT HIS DAYS IN LUXURY KNOWING THAT HIS PEOPLE REALLY WON THE WAR!
CHOFF CHOFF
HIS PEOPLE AND OUR PEOPLE ARE ONE IN THE GAME... THEY'RE ALL THE ENEMY! WHO'S IN CONTROL OF OUR LIVES? NOT US. THEM!
In einer bar in Mexico...
BUT WHAT DOES IT MEAN? IS THIS JUST THE WAY IT'S SUPPOSED TO BE?

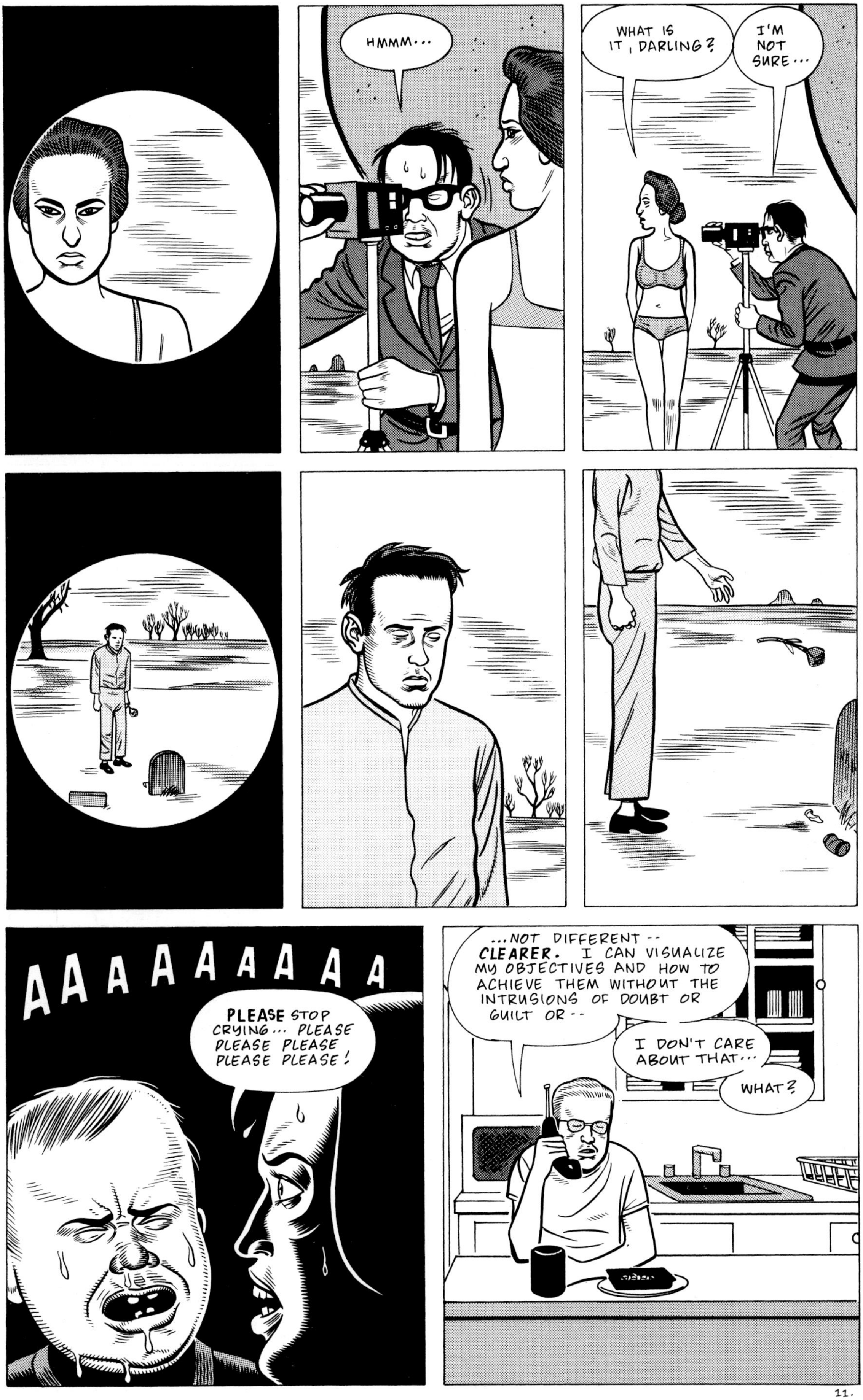
HMMM...
WHAT IS IT, DARLING?
I'M NOT SURE...
AAAAAAAAAA
PLEASE STOP CRYING... PLEASE PLEASE PLEASE PLEASE PLEASE!
...NOT DIFFERENT -- CLEARER. I CAN VISUALIZE MY OBJECTIVES AND HOW TO ACHIEVE THEM WITHOUT THE INTRUSIONS OF DOUBT OR GUILT OR --
I DON'T CARE ABOUT THAT...
WHAT?

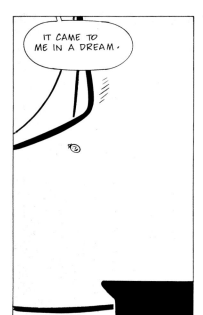

IT CAME TO ME IN A DREAM.

THE SEA ... THAT'S WHERE IT ALL COMES FROM ...ALL THE MYSTERIES OF LIFE LIE BELOW THE WATER'S SURFACE, SON...

LIFE BEGAN IN THE SEA...

IT EVOLVED AND WALKED ON TWO LEGS AND FIGURED OUT HOW TO FLY TO THE MOON BUT IT NEVER LOST SIGHT OF WHERE IT CAME FROM...

HOW DID IT ALL BEGIN? WHAT WAS THERE BEFORE? WHAT'S THE NEXT STEP? THESE ARE THE MYSTERIES OF LIFE, SON... WHATEVER I SAW OUT THERE MAY NOT HAVE THE ANSWERS BUT HE KNOWS MORE THAN WE DO...

≡SIGH≡

HEADS UP!

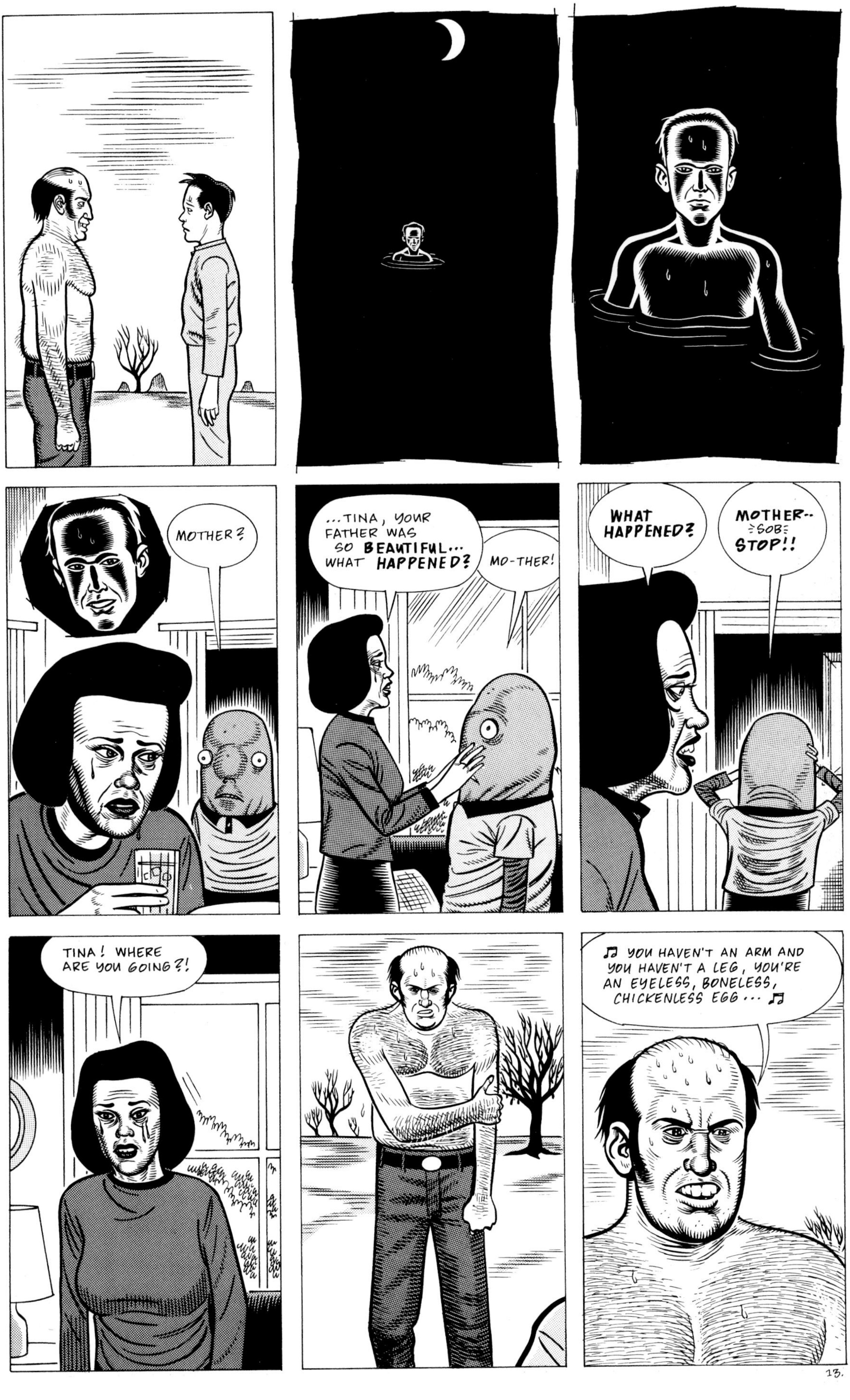
MOTHER?
...TINA, YOUR FATHER WAS SO BEAUTIFUL... WHAT HAPPENED?
MO-THER!
WHAT HAPPENED?
MOTHER-- SOB STOP!!
TINA! WHERE ARE YOU GOING?!
♫ YOU HAVEN'T AN ARM AND YOU HAVEN'T A LEG, YOU'RE AN EYELESS, BONELESS, CHICKENLESS EGG... ♫

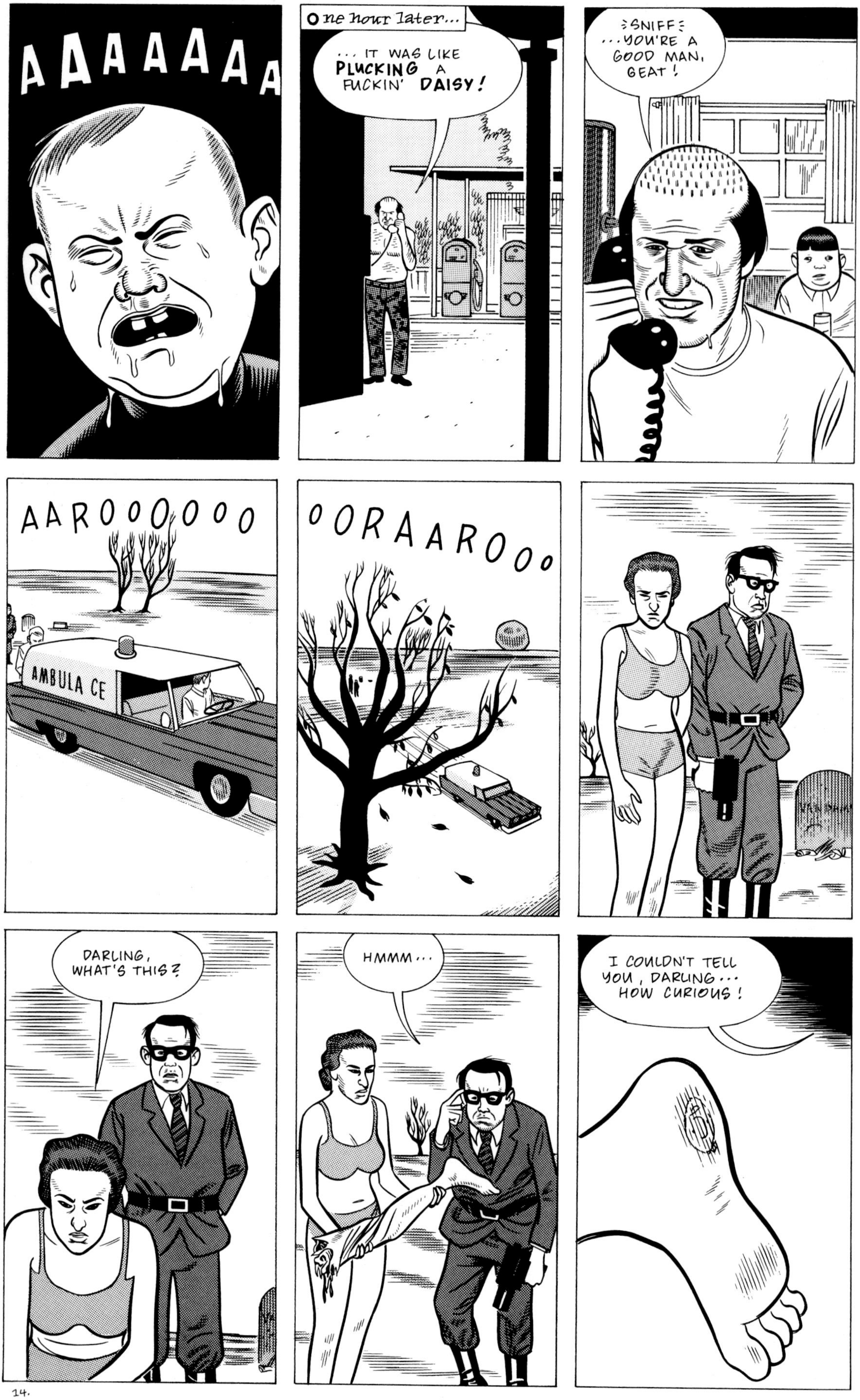

AAAAAAA
One hour later...
... IT WAS LIKE PLUCKING A FUCKIN' DAISY!
SNIFF ...YOU'RE A GOOD MAN, GEAT!
AAROOOOOOO
OORAAROOO
AMBULA CE
DARLING, WHAT'S THIS?
HMMM...
I COULDN'T TELL YOU, DARLING... HOW CURIOUS!

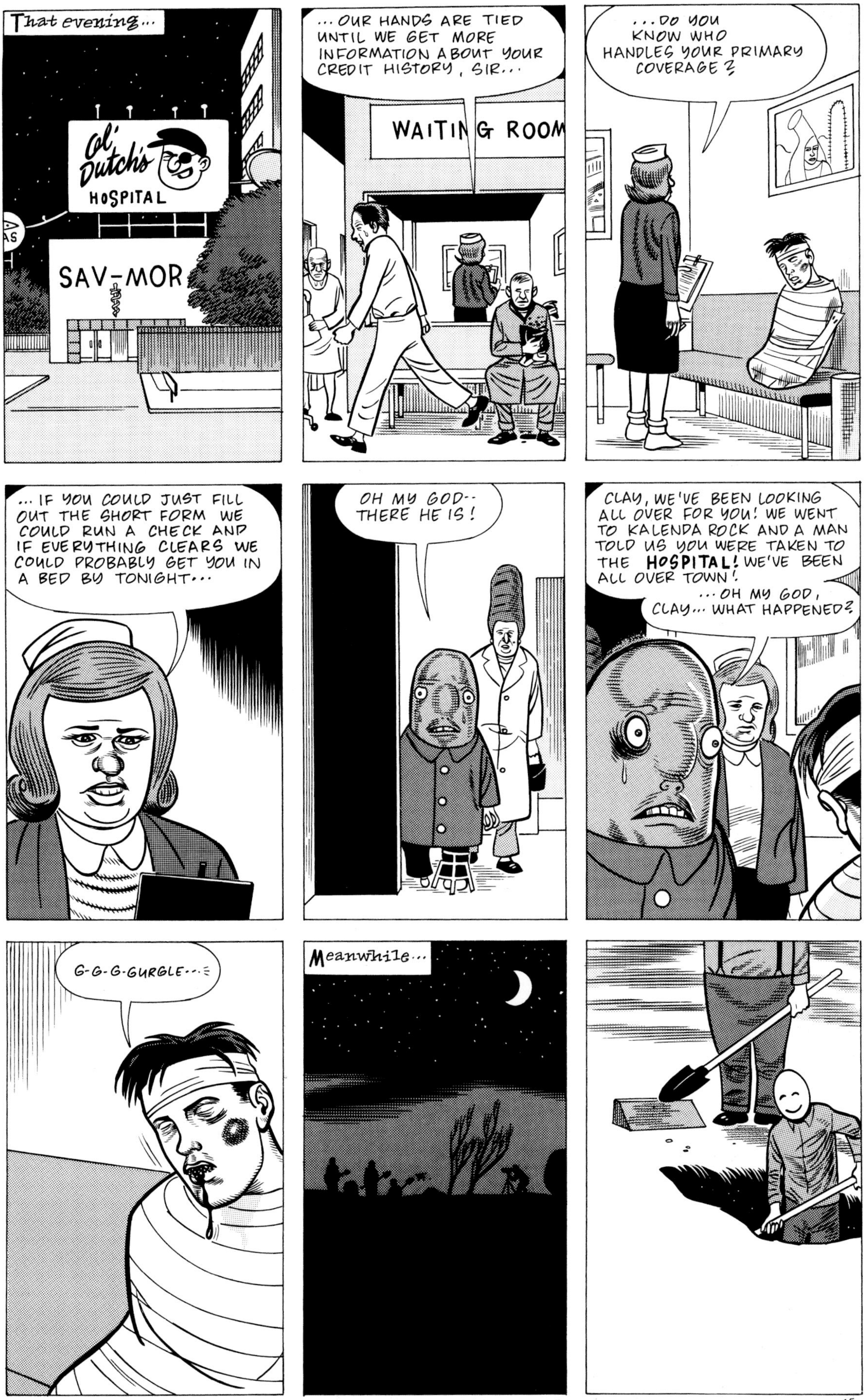
That evening...
Ol' Dutch's
HOSPITAL
SAV-MOR
...OUR HANDS ARE TIED UNTIL WE GET MORE INFORMATION ABOUT YOUR CREDIT HISTORY, SIR...
WAITING ROOM
...DO YOU KNOW WHO HANDLES YOUR PRIMARY COVERAGE?
...IF YOU COULD JUST FILL OUT THE SHORT FORM WE COULD RUN A CHECK AND IF EVERYTHING CLEARS WE COULD PROBABLY GET YOU IN A BED BY TONIGHT...
OH MY GOD-- THERE HE IS!
CLAY, WE'VE BEEN LOOKING ALL OVER FOR YOU! WE WENT TO KALENDA ROCK AND A MAN TOLD US YOU WERE TAKEN TO THE HOSPITAL! WE'VE BEEN ALL OVER TOWN!
...OH MY GOD, CLAY... WHAT HAPPENED?
G-G-G-GURGLE...
Meanwhile...

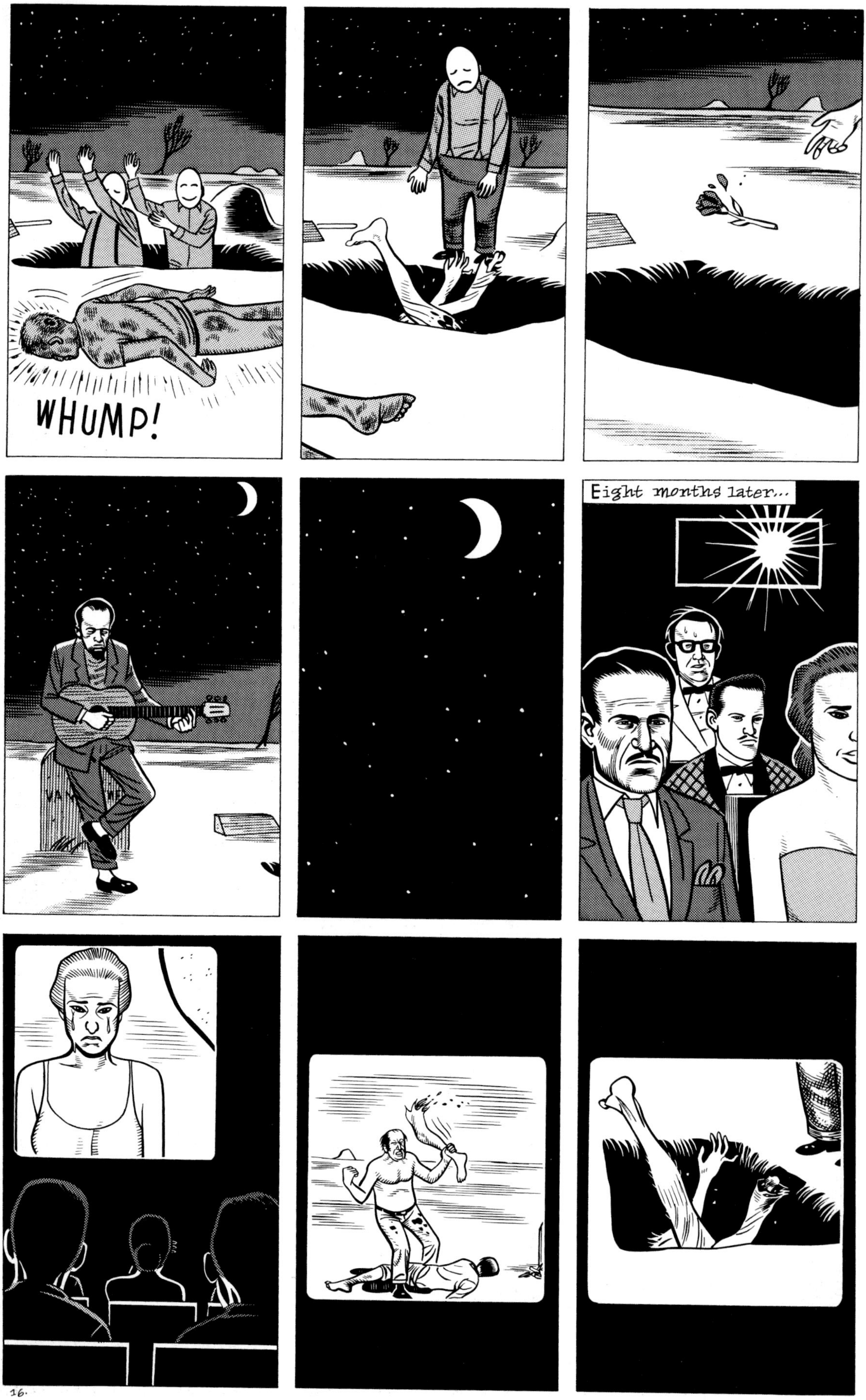
WHUMP!
Eight months later...

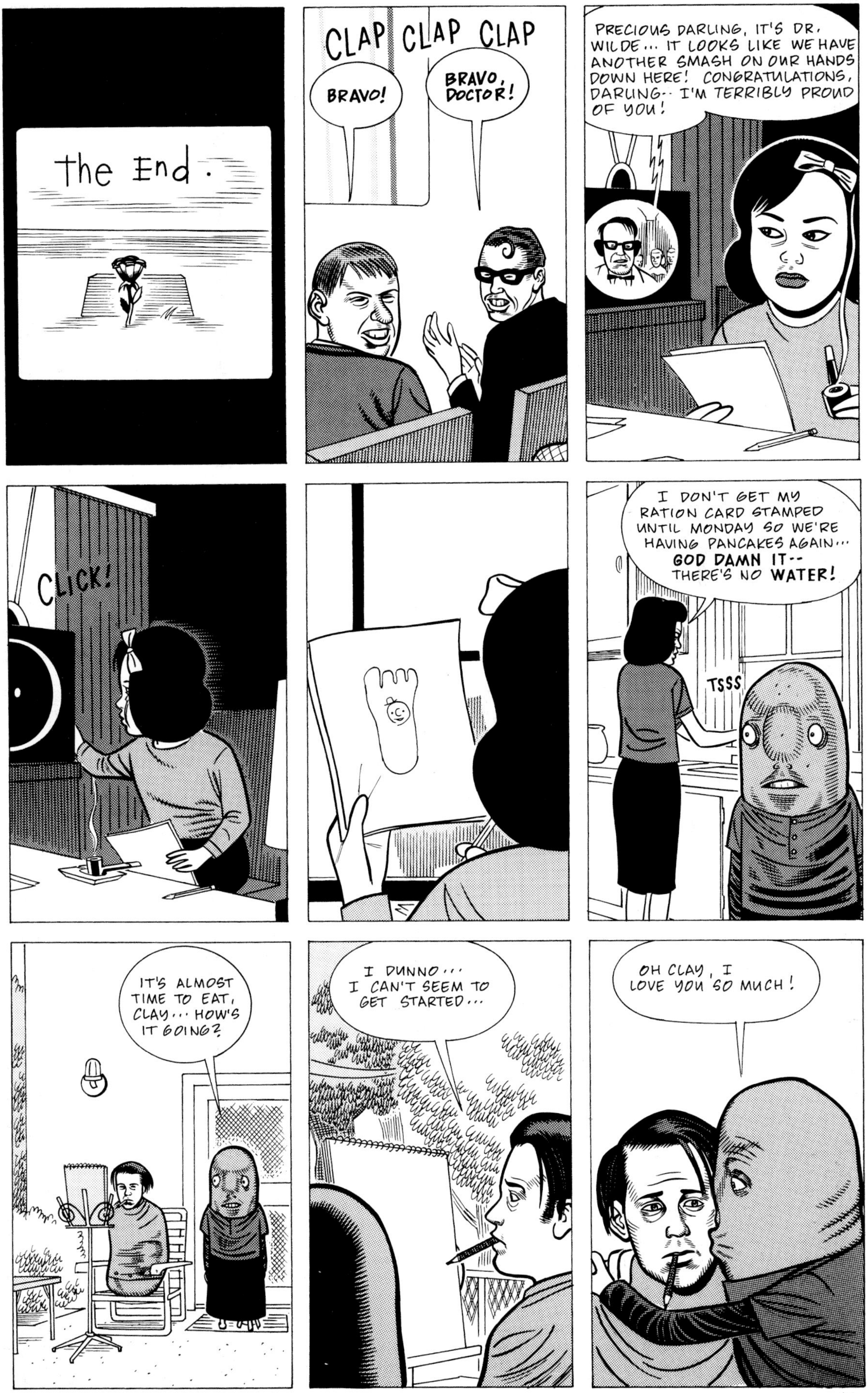
the End.
CLAP CLAP CLAP
BRAVO!
BRAVO, DOCTOR!
PRECIOUS DARLING, IT'S DR. WILDE... IT LOOKS LIKE WE HAVE ANOTHER SMASH ON OUR HANDS DOWN HERE! CONGRATULATIONS, DARLING-- I'M TERRIBLY PROUD OF YOU!
CLICK!
I DON'T GET MY RATION CARD STAMPED UNTIL MONDAY SO WE'RE HAVING PANCAKES AGAIN... **GOD DAMN IT**-- THERE'S NO **WATER**!
TSSS
IT'S ALMOST TIME TO EAT, CLAY... HOW'S IT GOING?
I DUNNO... I CAN'T SEEM TO GET STARTED...
OH CLAY, I LOVE YOU SO MUCH!

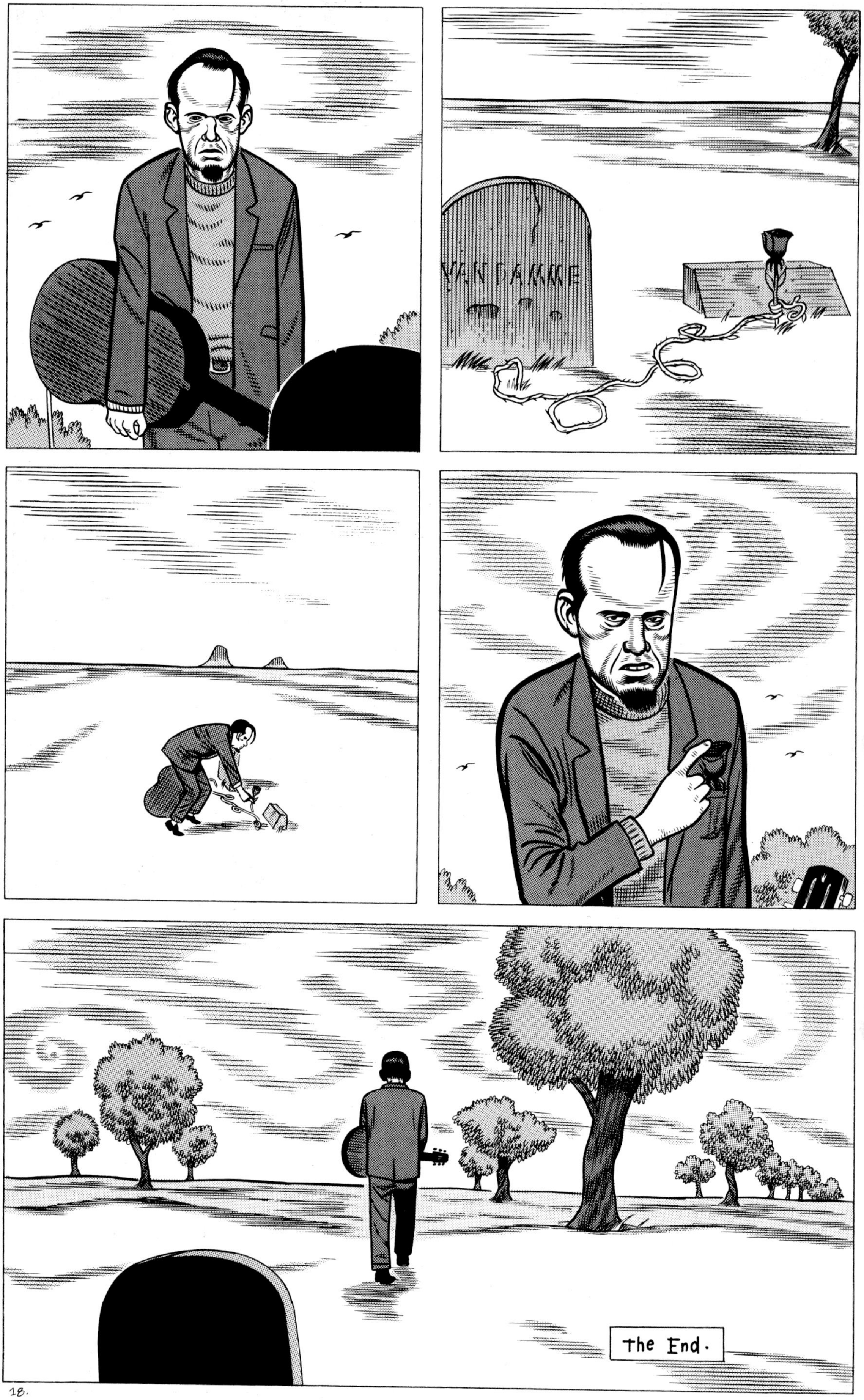
VANDAMME
the End.

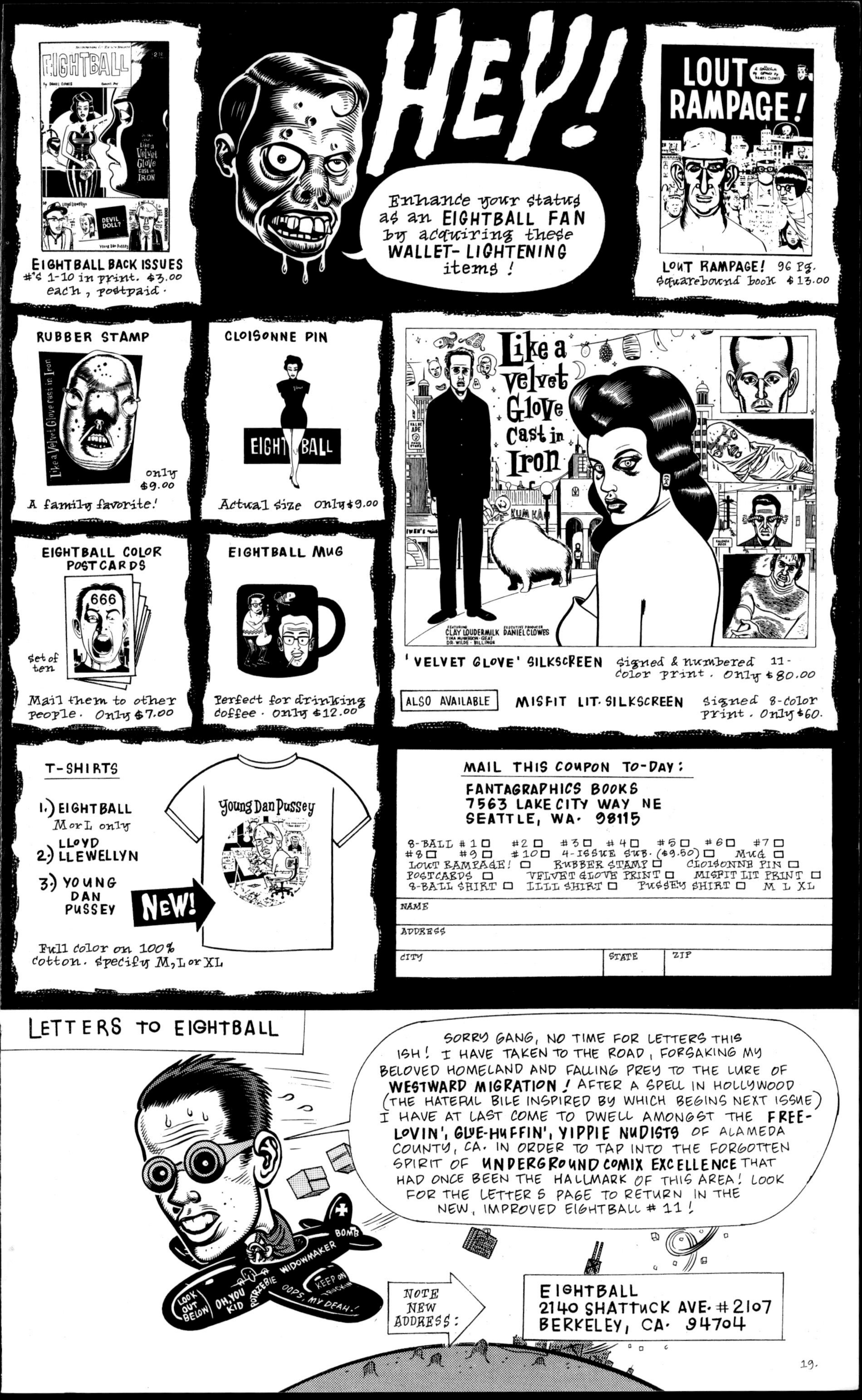
HEY!
Enhance your status as an EIGHTBALL FAN by acquiring these WALLET-LIGHTENING items!
EIGHTBALL BACK ISSUES
#'s 1-10 in print. $3.00 each, postpaid.
LOUT RAMPAGE!
LOUT RAMPAGE! 96 Pg. squarebound book $13.00
RUBBER STAMP
Like a Velvet Glove cast in Iron
only $9.00
A family favorite!
CLOISONNE PIN
EIGHTBALL
Actual size Only $9.00
Like a Velvet Glove Cast in Iron
FEATURING CLAY LOUDERMILK TINA MUSHROOM · GEAT DR. WILDE · BILLINGS
EXECUTIVE PRODUCER DANIEL CLOWES
'VELVET GLOVE' SILKSCREEN signed & numbered 11-color print. Only $80.00
ALSO AVAILABLE MISFIT LIT. SILKSCREEN signed 8-color Print. Only $60.
EIGHTBALL COLOR POSTCARDS
666
set of ten
Mail them to other people. Only $7.00
EIGHTBALL MUG
Perfect for drinking coffee. Only $12.00
T-SHIRTS
1.) EIGHTBALL M or L only
2.) LLOYD LLEWELLYN
3.) YOUNG DAN PUSSEY
NEW!
Young Dan Pussey
Full color on 100% cotton. Specify M, L or XL
MAIL THIS COUPON TO-DAY:
FANTAGRAPHICS BOOKS
7563 LAKE CITY WAY NE
SEATTLE, WA. 98115
8-BALL #1 ☐ #2 ☐ #3 ☐ #4 ☐ #5 ☐ #6 ☐ #7 ☐
#8 ☐ #9 ☐ #10 ☐ 4-ISSUE SUB. ($9.50) ☐ MUG ☐
LOUT RAMPAGE! ☐ RUBBER STAMP ☐ CLOISONNE PIN ☐
POSTCARDS ☐ VELVET GLOVE PRINT ☐ MISFIT LIT PRINT ☐
8-BALL SHIRT ☐ LLLL SHIRT ☐ PUSSEY SHIRT ☐ M L XL
NAME
ADDRESS
CITY STATE ZIP
LETTERS TO EIGHTBALL
SORRY GANG, NO TIME FOR LETTERS THIS ISH! I HAVE TAKEN TO THE ROAD, FORSAKING MY BELOVED HOMELAND AND FALLING PREY TO THE LURE OF WESTWARD MIGRATION! AFTER A SPELL IN HOLLYWOOD (THE HATEFUL BILE INSPIRED BY WHICH BEGINS NEXT ISSUE) I HAVE AT LAST COME TO DWELL AMONGST THE FREE-LOVIN', GLUE-HUFFIN', YIPPIE NUDISTS OF ALAMEDA COUNTY, CA. IN ORDER TO TAP INTO THE FORGOTTEN SPIRIT OF UNDERGROUND COMIX EXCELLENCE THAT HAD ONCE BEEN THE HALLMARK OF THIS AREA! LOOK FOR THE LETTERS PAGE TO RETURN IN THE NEW, IMPROVED EIGHTBALL #11!
BOMB
WIDOWMAKER
KEEP ON TRUCKIN
OOPS, MY DEAH!
POTRZEBIE
OH, YOU KID
LOOK OUT BELOW
NOTE NEW ADDRESS:
EIGHTBALL
2140 SHATTUCK AVE. #2107
BERKELEY, CA. 94704

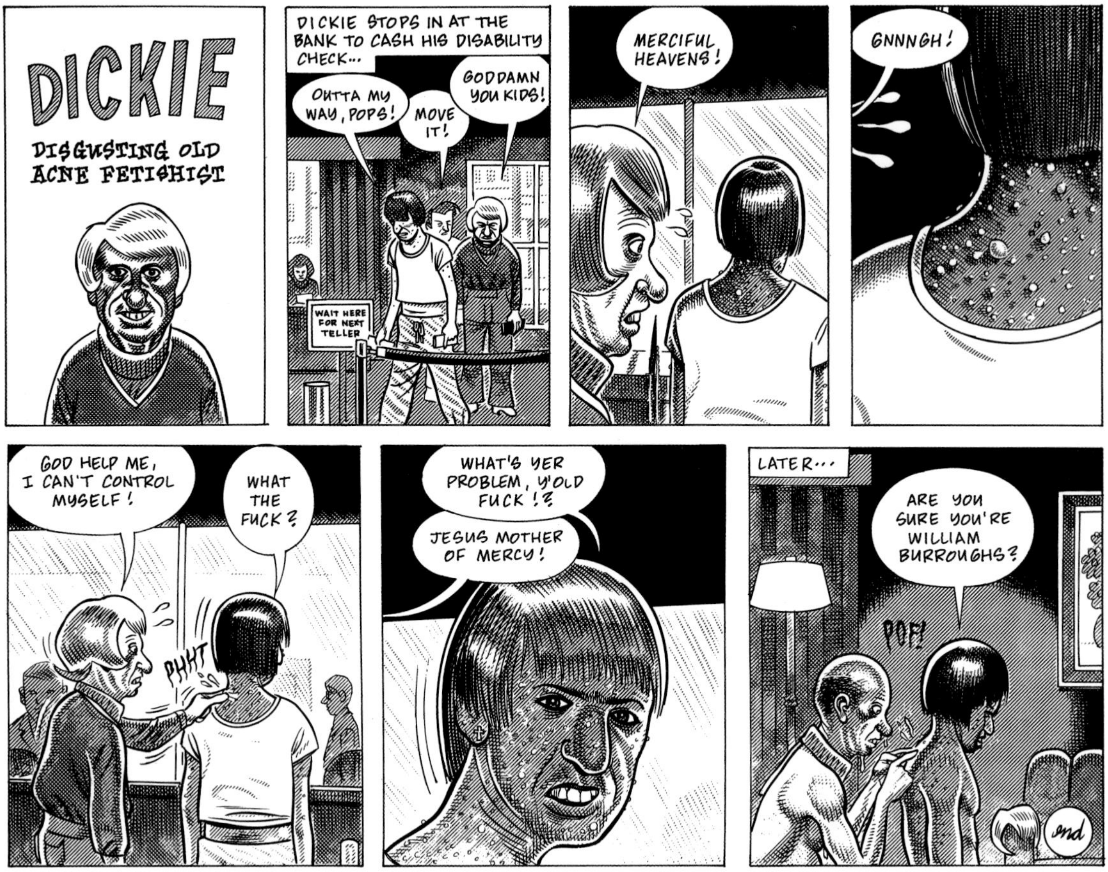
DICKIE
DISGUSTING OLD ACNE FETISHIST
DICKIE STOPS IN AT THE BANK TO CASH HIS DISABILITY CHECK...
OUTTA MY WAY, POPS!
MOVE IT!
GODDAMN YOU KIDS!
WAIT HERE FOR NEXT TELLER
MERCIFUL HEAVENS!
GNNNGH!
GOD HELP ME, I CAN'T CONTROL MYSELF!
WHAT THE FUCK?
PHHT
WHAT'S YER PROBLEM, Y'OLD FUCK!?
JESUS MOTHER OF MERCY!
LATER...
ARE YOU SURE YOU'RE WILLIAM BURROUGHS?
POF!
end

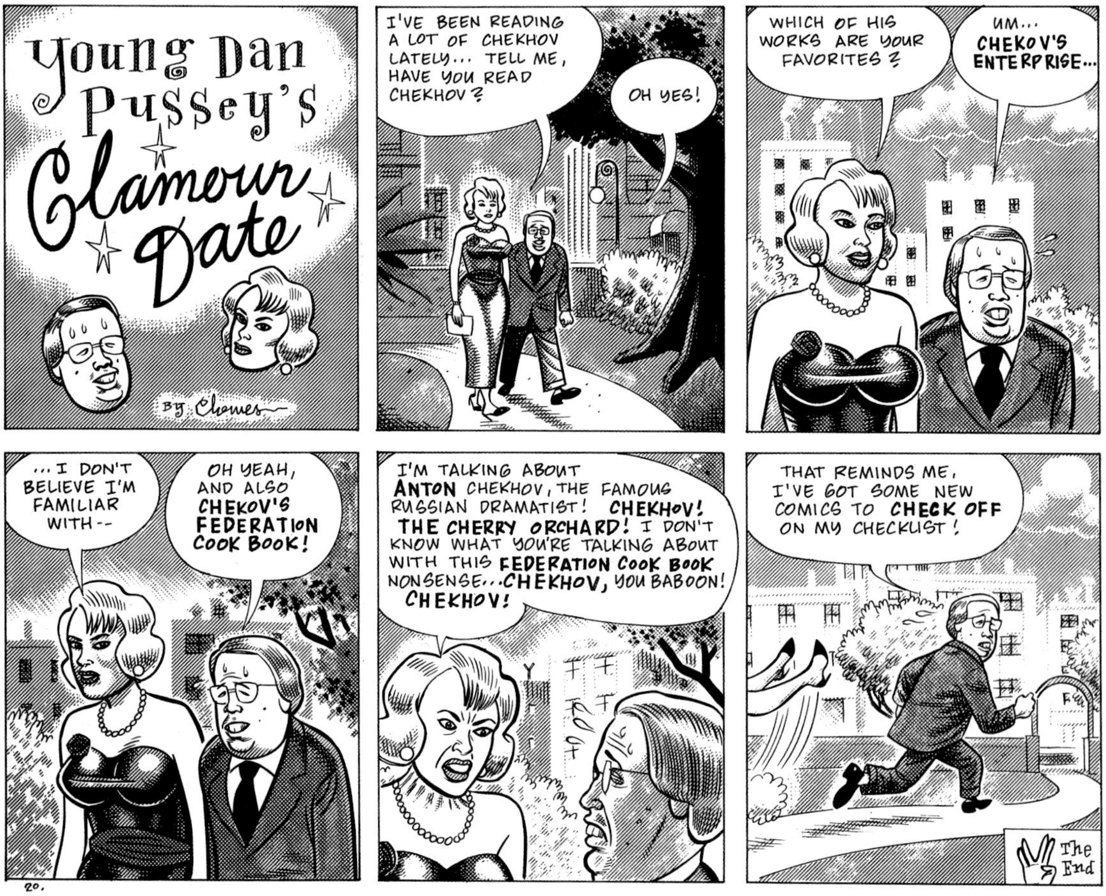
Young Dan Pussey's Glamour Date
BY Clowes
I'VE BEEN READING A LOT OF CHEKHOV LATELY... TELL ME, HAVE YOU READ CHEKHOV?
OH YES!
WHICH OF HIS WORKS ARE YOUR FAVORITES?
UM... CHEKOV'S ENTERPRISE...
...I DON'T BELIEVE I'M FAMILIAR WITH--
OH YEAH, AND ALSO CHEKOV'S FEDERATION COOK BOOK!
I'M TALKING ABOUT ANTON CHEKHOV, THE FAMOUS RUSSIAN DRAMATIST! CHEKHOV! THE CHERRY ORCHARD! I DON'T KNOW WHAT YOU'RE TALKING ABOUT WITH THIS FEDERATION COOK BOOK NONSENSE...CHEKHOV, YOU BABOON! CHEKHOV!
THAT REMINDS ME, I'VE GOT SOME NEW COMICS TO CHECK OFF ON MY CHECKLIST!
The End

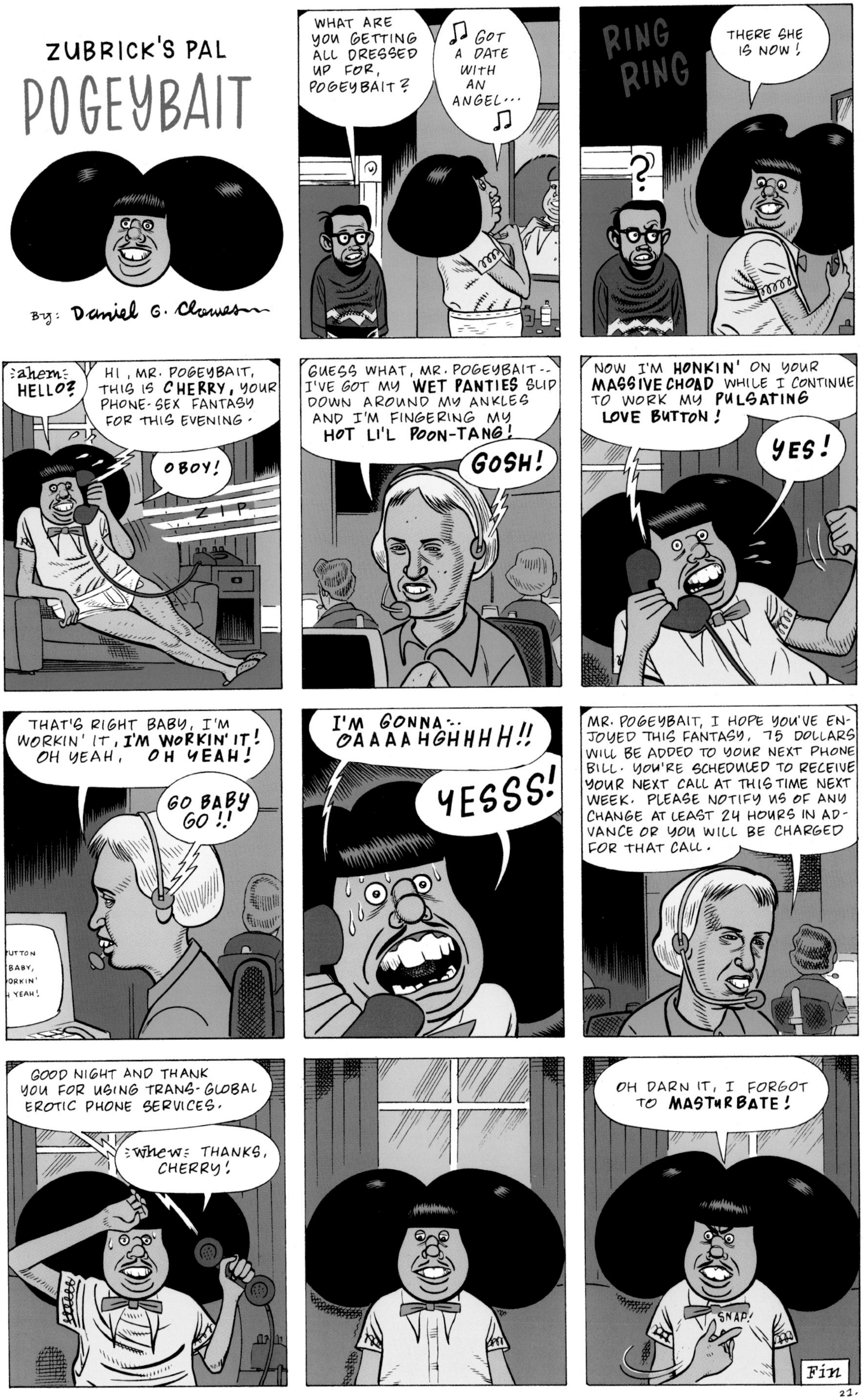
ZUBRICK'S PAL
POGEYBAIT
By: Daniel G. Clowes
WHAT ARE YOU GETTING ALL DRESSED UP FOR, POGEYBAIT?
♫ GOT A DATE WITH AN ANGEL... ♫
RING RING
THERE SHE IS NOW!
?
:ahem: HELLO?
HI, MR. POGEYBAIT, THIS IS CHERRY, YOUR PHONE-SEX FANTASY FOR THIS EVENING.
OBOY!
ZIP
GUESS WHAT, MR. POGEYBAIT -- I'VE GOT MY WET PANTIES SLID DOWN AROUND MY ANKLES AND I'M FINGERING MY HOT LI'L POON-TANG!
GOSH!
NOW I'M HONKIN' ON YOUR MASSIVE CHOAD WHILE I CONTINUE TO WORK MY PULSATING LOVE BUTTON!
YES!
THAT'S RIGHT BABY, I'M WORKIN' IT, I'M WORKIN' IT! OH YEAH, OH YEAH!
GO BABY GO!!
I'M GONNA -- OAAAAHGHHHH!!
YESSS!
MR. POGEYBAIT, I HOPE YOU'VE ENJOYED THIS FANTASY. 75 DOLLARS WILL BE ADDED TO YOUR NEXT PHONE BILL. YOU'RE SCHEDULED TO RECEIVE YOUR NEXT CALL AT THIS TIME NEXT WEEK. PLEASE NOTIFY US OF ANY CHANGE AT LEAST 24 HOURS IN ADVANCE OR YOU WILL BE CHARGED FOR THAT CALL.
GOOD NIGHT AND THANK YOU FOR USING TRANS-GLOBAL EROTIC PHONE SERVICES.
:whew: THANKS, CHERRY!
OH DARN IT, I FORGOT TO MASTURBATE!
SNAP!
Fin

Attention readers of the present day (that being the last decade of the 20th century): GO NO FURTHER. THIS IS NOT FOR YOU! This is a TIME CAPSULE. I'm here on the moon burying it to one day be dug-up and studied by your heirs in the 23rd century. The following pages contain EMBARRASSING FACTS about my personal life I don't want revealed until long after I'm dead so PLEASE, if you're still reading STOP NOW. This is...

DO NOT READ UNTIL JANUARY 2293 A.D.

A MESSAGE TO THE PEOPLE OF THE FUTURE

Clowes 1993 A.D.

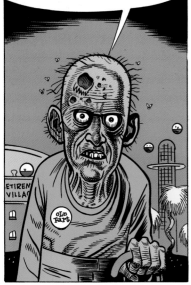

My name is Clowes. I'm an "underground cartoonist". I come from Earth. I will be over 330 years old by the time you read this.

An underground cartoonist is someone who creates pictographic scenarios, often wholly fictional, for the amusement of a small audience of marginal fringe-dwellers and drug-addicts.

OVER 18 ONLY

COFF

DOOFUS

Sometimes I'll wake up from a nap and in a moment of cosmic revelation I'll be struck by how truly strange and ludicrous this is.

W-WHY DOES ANYBODY CARE ABOUT MADE-UP PLOTLINES AND CHARACTERS WHEN THEY HAVE THEIR OWN LIVES TO LEAD??

It's not until I begin to ponder the GRIM ALTERNATIVES that I become comfortable with my own questionable existence. 95%* of all jobs are in the realm of pointless PAPER-SHUFFLING and WAGE-SLAVERY ...Beyond that, what's left?

YOU WANT I SHOULD BE A DOCTOR?

* ALL STATISTICS MADE-UP YET TRUE!

IF NOT THAT, THEN HOW ABOUT DEVOTING YOUR LIFE TO SCIENCE AND STUDYING STUFF LIKE THE ORIGIN OF THE UNIVERSE AND STUFF LIKE THAT?

YEAH SURE, OKAY... BUT WHAT DOES THAT GET YOU?

HEADACHES AND AGGRAVATION ... BESIDES, YOU DON'T GOT THE SMARTS!

YOU COULD ALWAYS TURN TO RELIGION ... BUT I SUPPOSE THAT OLD-FASHIONED STUFF JUST WOULDN'T SEEM "HIP" TO A GUY LIKE YOU...

AU CONTRAIRE, FRIEND... IN A WAY THIS WHOLE CARTOONING THING IS A RELIGIOUS ENDEAVOR!

HOW SO, OL' CHUM?

I'LL GET BACK TO IT IN A MINUTE, PAL O' MINE!

WHERE DID THEY COME FROM?

In a general sense, the only lifestyle I would endorse is a kind of 'responsible' hedonism in which the pleasures of this life are experienced fully and often. This would apply only to me and my friends -- we need other people to pave roads and deliver pizzas...

THE THREE SUNS

But seriously, if orgies are your "bag" GO GIT'EM! My personal form of hedonistic self-indulgence is to draw cartoons making fun of your excessive behavior!

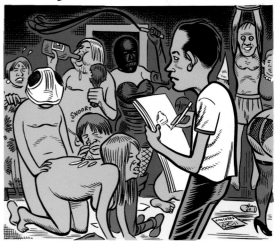

SNOORT

HEY, I THOUGHT THIS WAS SUPPOSED TO BE A "TIME CAPSULE" FOR 1993, BUT INSTEAD YOU'RE JUST GOIN' ON ABOUT MMGH

...And one thing we have plenty of here in North America during the last days of the second millennium is EXCESS! Let's have a look, shall we?

For one thing, you'll notice that there are TOO MANY PEOPLE. The place is LOUSY with 'em.... Everywhere, PEOPLE.

23.

-cont'd from inside-

And they're always BUSY! Changing things, building things, tearing down old things and replacing them with newer, cheaper, simpler things... If you detach yourself from it enough, the city begins to look like one of those sped-up films of maggots devouring a squirrel.
All that's left at the end is a SOUPY MUSH!
Things change too quickly and for no reason. Everyone is overstimulated. It's especially clear in the faces of children.
The way things are set-up, their wants can never be satisfied. They spend their days keeping busy, hoping for something less chaotic in the next world.
TRANS CORP
Many will live and die in the next 300 years. Some will spend their lives praying for eternal salvation. Others will have their heads removed and frozen.
Still others will reproduce and force their annoying peculiarities on the next generation... I have devised my own humble bid for eternity, a scheme in which YOU play a part, dear reader...
LIBRARY OF QUAINT 20th CENTURY EPHEMERA
EIGHTBALL
As long as one good citizen of the world of the future makes some attempt to read these words, I am saved.
Please don't let me die!
END.

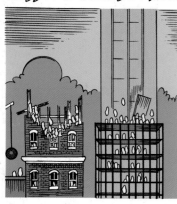

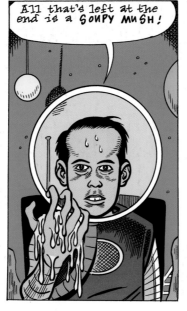

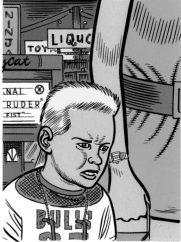

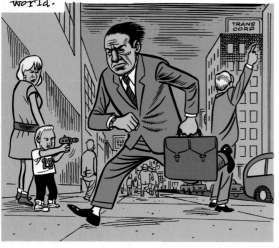

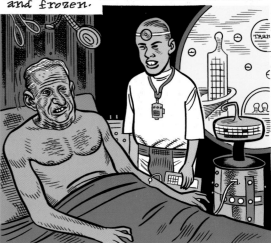

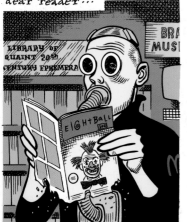

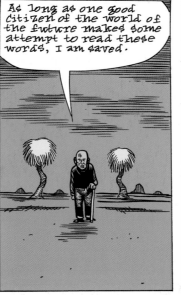

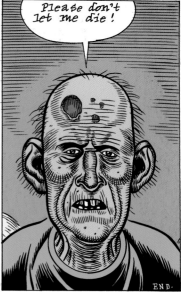

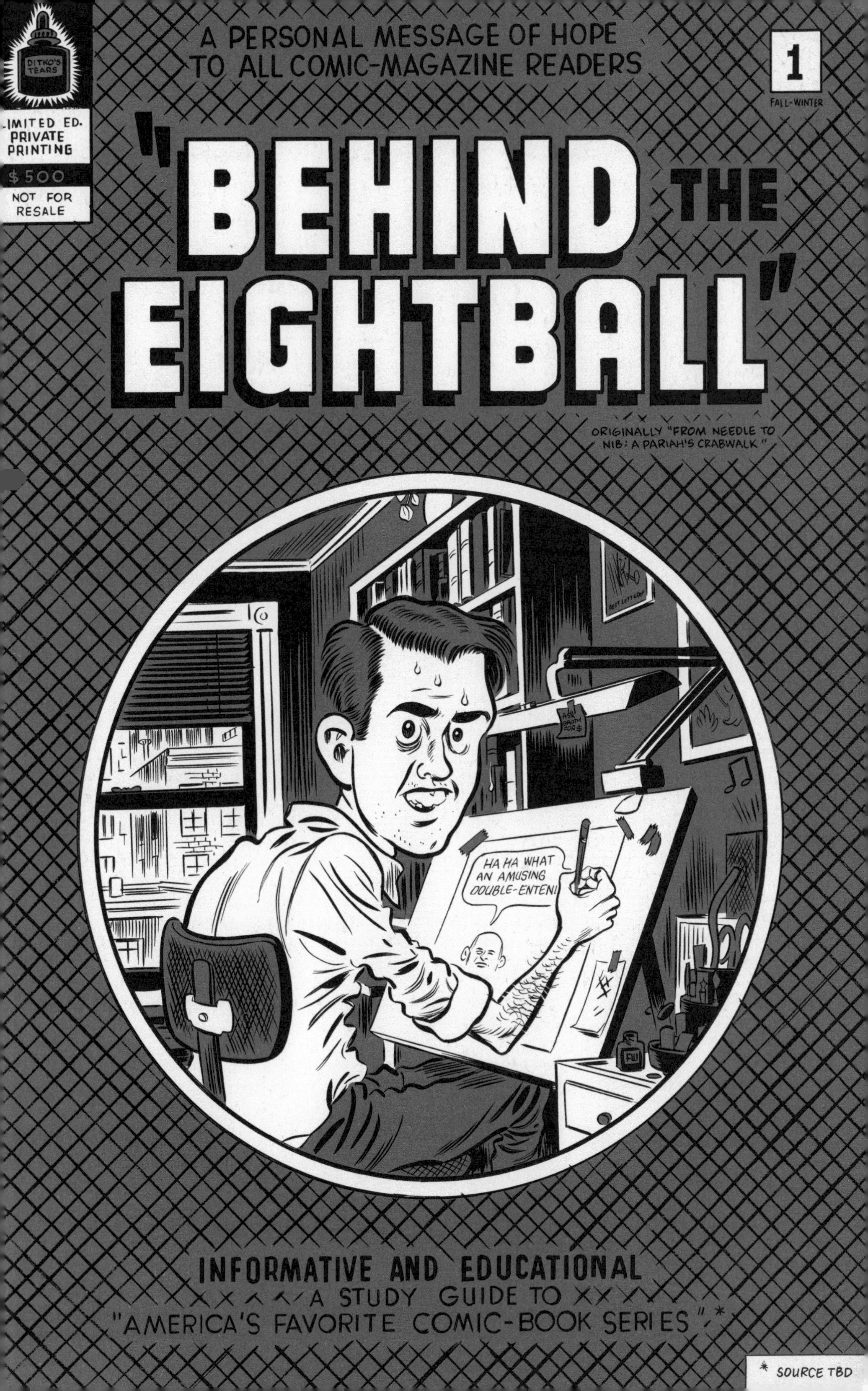

DITKO'S TEARS
LIMITED ED. PRIVATE PRINTING
$500
NOT FOR RESALE
A PERSONAL MESSAGE OF HOPE TO ALL COMIC-MAGAZINE READERS
1
FALL-WINTER
"BEHIND THE EIGHTBALL"
ORIGINALLY "FROM NEEDLE TO NIB: A PARIAH'S CRABWALK"
HA HA WHAT AN AMUSING DOUBLE-ENTENI
INFORMATIVE AND EDUCATIONAL
A STUDY GUIDE TO "AMERICA'S FAVORITE COMIC-BOOK SERIES".*
* SOURCE TBD

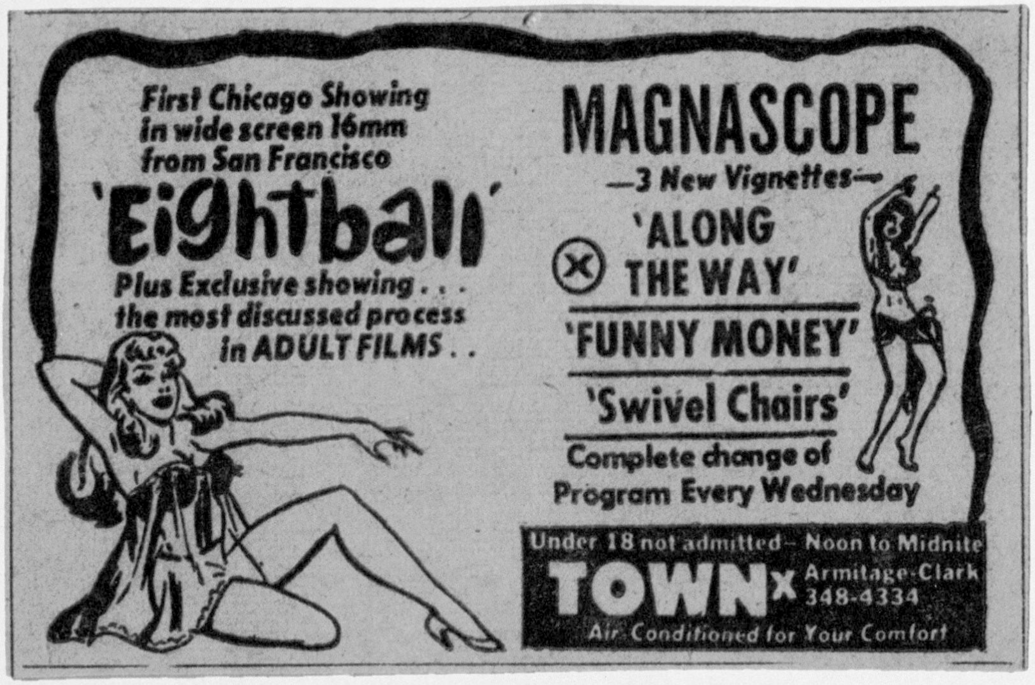
First Chicago Showing
in wide screen 16mm
from San Francisco
'Eightball'
Plus Exclusive showing...
the most discussed process
in ADULT FILMS..
MAGNASCOPE
—3 New Vignettes—
'ALONG THE WAY'
'FUNNY MONEY'
'Swivel Chairs'
Complete change of
Program Every Wednesday
Under 18 not admitted – Noon to Midnite
TOWN
Armitage-Clark
348-4334
Air Conditioned for Your Comfort

Fig. 1: *Undated Chicago newspaper clipping. Any information about the film EIGHTBALL would be very much appreciated.*

EIGHTBALL #1, OCTOBER 1989:

LIKE A VELVET GLOVE CAST IN IRON: The initial impetus for this one came from a few indelible film-going experiences at the long-departed Variety Photoplays theater in the early-'80s pre-Giuliani Union Square, which showed a random, inexhaustible series of unbilled quadruple features of no-account films (ranging from repulsive '70s porn to, very memorably, Joe Sarno's SIN IN THE SUBURBS) for an audience of sticky-footed Travis Bickles, while weathered hookers trolled the aisles and a mysterious line snaked from the men's room.

DEVIL DOLL: The result of an ill-advised decision to read sixty-plus Jack Chick tracts in one rainy afternoon after a long bus ride to a suburban Christian bookstore. At the time, a pentagram forehead tattoo was utterly unthinkable and therefore intended as over-the-top absurd in that specific Chickian way (e.g., the rock promoter in ANGELS? named "Lew Siffer") [Fig. 10], though now I probably wouldn't even look twice if a cashier at Walgreens had one, so maybe Jack was on to something about our Godless decline.

THE LAFFIN' SPITTIN' MAN: The last "real" Lloyd Llewellyn story, based on arguably the most unpleasant novelty item of all time [Fig. 3].

PUSS IN BOOTHS: There was an actual dirty bookstore in Chicago (two doors down from the comic store, natch) with this brilliant name. I never went in, much to my regret.

EIGHTBALL #2, FEBRUARY 1990:

For some reason, the indicia on this issue says 1989, but that's a lie. Nice proofreading, Kim.

Clear-eyed readers may notice not-so-subtle differences between the coloring on the covers as they flip through these two volumes. Back in those precomputer days it was very difficult to achieve the flat "process" color I was looking for, and so there were many years of pained experimentation before I blundered on to this insane process: 1) Do a black-and-white line drawing at twice the printed size. 2) Go to a place that made photostats (look it up) and get a "film positive" (line art printed on clear Mylar) of said drawing at print size. 3) At the same time, have a "blue-line" made. This was the same image printed in light (non-repro) blue on white board. 4) Color the blue-line using Pantone color film—these were flat-tone, transparent, adhesive-backed color sheets—by cutting out slightly larger shapes than needed, and trimming them on the board [Fig. 12]. 5) Line up the film positive line art over the blue-line colors, and there you are. Yeah!

p. 23: The "short hair on top, long in back" gag may seem absurdly dated at this point, but I had never seen it addressed elsewhere (the term "mullet" didn't even exist yet), and it got more response than anything else in the issue by far, both from detractors and also from defenders of what we pioneers called "the neckwarmer."

EIGHTBALL #3, JUNE 1990:

ROBERT TILTON: Back in the late '80s I got addicted to watching the nightly, tragic spectacle that was Pastor Tilton's SUCCESS-N-LIFE, shuddering as this hideous reptile preyed upon his hopeless, desperate victims in a way that was so transparently awful it seemed to single-handedly confirm (and perhaps render superfluous) all that I was hoping to say in my comics. Shortly after this one-pager appeared, he was exposed as a fraudulent, life-crushing monster (duh) and disappeared, and I stopped thinking about him, but a quick Wikipedia search tells me he's actually been back on the air for eighteen years without ever having gone to jail! Humanity is hopeless.

THE STROLL: The door in the last panel was the place I was living at the time: 1915 Division Street in Chicago. It was on the second floor, above a nonprofit for rehabilitating gang members (whose success rate I would put, anecdotally, at about 2 percent) that is now an Anthropologie. Down the block was a depressing bar that opened at 9 a.m. where I regularly saw my mailman starting the day off with a little "Dutch courage." More than once I heard gunshots and looked out the window to see a body lying in the sidewalk, where there are now European-style cafes [Fig. 11].

LETTERS PAGE: The letter from "Jane K. Lorenzen" is one of several through the years fake-written by my lifelong pal, Rick Altergott, whose influence on me, especially in these early issues, can't be overstated. I've never met anybody in my life who is even close to being as funny as Rick.

EIGHTBALL #4, OCTOBER 1990:

DAN PUSSEY'S MASTURBATION FANTASY: The idea for Dan Pussey came from a summer in 1988 spent watching reruns of the BEN CASEY show from the early '60s while sharing a studio with aforementioned chum Rick Altergott. The character Doctor Infinity was based entirely on Sam Jaffe as Dr. Zorba [Fig. 4] and the patronizing, self-satisfied vocal intonations he used when addressing young Dr. Casey. The name Infinity Comics came in part from a sub-Z-grade B&W comics publisher called Eternity Comics but also from the pretentious opening segment of BEN CASEY (YouTube it now), which featured Dr. Zorba writing on a blackboard while muttering "Man . . . Woman . . . Birth . . . Death . . . INFINITY." In fact, a scrapped opening for the first Pussey story had Dr. I saying "Marvel . . . DC . . . First . . . Eclipse . . . INFINITY." (Hard to believe, but First and Eclipse, both long-dead and mostly forgotten, were the number three and four publishers back then.)

EIGHTBALL #5, FEBRUARY 1991:

So now we have interior color, though only one eight-page signature, and glossy paper. This came about when Gary Groth sent me an envelope filled with Eros Comics (why?). Eros was a Fantagraphics imprint specializing in ridiculous porn comics for unwholesome weirdos (a few, like TIME WANKERS and KARATE GIRL, must be seen to be believed). For some reason it drove me insane that they sold well enough to warrant nice paper and color, and so I tried to guilt-trip Kim Thompson into giving me the same treatment. I was actually kind of thrown when he called my bluff and I had to go along with it.

PLAYFUL OBSESSION: When I was around fifteen I stopped reading new Marvel and DC comics and started getting into old ECs, undergrounds, NATIONAL LAMPOONS, etc. However, I'm not ashamed to admit (actually, strike that) that I still bought a stack of Harvey Comics almost every week until I was around eighteen. Looking back, I see it was more a way of dealing with crippling anxiety than anything else; nothing bathes one in calm like a splash panel of Richie Rich skiing down a slope of dollars. My addiction came to an end when I was on an airplane with my grandmother and she glanced over at the issue of HOT STUFF I was reading and asked, "Is that pornographic?" I was so ashamed of what it really was—a comic for five-year-olds—that I said "yes."

EIGHTBALL #6, JUNE 1991:

The printing on the first edition of this issue was so horrible—ambitiously detailed eye renderings turned into mockingly cartoonish black smudges—that I threw the entire box of comp copies out the window onto Division Street about two minutes after cutting it open. Later, after being told by the printer (now out of business: HA!) that we couldn't reprint until these copies were sold, I went out in the middle of the night and salvaged a few of the copies that hadn't yet been pissed on by hoboes. Many of the printing "quirks" that occurred in the original editions (see #7 and #16 for examples) I consider, for better or worse, acts of God that are now as much a part of those issues as the letters pages, but I draw the line at some of the terrible early scanning and over-inked sub-Charlton printing (inconsistent from one copy to the next), and so herein are the optimal versions (in several cases, tracked down and scanned by Mr. Buenaventura from long-ago-sold originals) of these flawed artifacts.

p. 10: I did the drawing of Clay reading the book, along with the word balloon, but I couldn't think of the right title. That night, in a dream, my childhood girlfriend gave me an oversized children's book called RUBY'S ELEPHANTS, and there it was.

EIGHTBALL #7, NOVEMBER 1991:

"Too bad it's a fallen world" came from a line in a Christian comic called "Wolf Angel" [Fig. 9] by the great John Jacobs and Ken Landgraf (FAR FRONTIER #1, Madison Comics, 1983). In the comic, WA is on an airplane looking down at the earthly landscape, commenting wistfully on the beauty below before crushing the sentiment with this cynical afterthought. The ad on the TV was ubiquitous on pre-superstation WGN in the '80s and '90s. "Endless beauty meets your eye" always struck me as a tad ambitious for a cheap-ass '80s tile store.

p. 3: This was the second issue scanned and colored digitally, and when I got my copies I was thrown by the way Geat's head looks on this splash page. I remember calling Kim and saying it looked sort of fatter than I remembered (I didn't have the original art to check it—it was still at the printer). He laughed with his familiar "you crazy artists" tone and assured me that there was no way a mere printer could actually add weight to a character. I went to bed thinking I had gone insane only to be awakened by a call from a chastened Kim telling me that the printer had in fact shrunk the art "only on the y axis" to make the indicia fit better at the bottom, something neither of us knew was possible! These were the same barbarians who had fucked up the previous issue, and I only wish there was a Failed Business graveyard so I could go there and desecrate their tombstone.

p. 14: The character in the last two panels, O'Herlihy, was added because my friend Tim Hensley had been recording a soundtrack of LIKE A VELVET GLOVE–based songs (Jenkins-Peabody Records, 1993; out of print), and among his vast backlog of (non–VELVET GLOVE) demos was a little gem called O'Herlihy. I wanted to find a way for this to get on the soundtrack, so I simply added a new character to the story, and thus it was so. Tim, aside from being a singularly gifted musician, is also, quite unfairly, a genius cartoonist (see WALLY GROPIUS, Fantagraphics, 2010, for proof) and was a big influence on the early issues of EIGHTBALL.

CHICAGO: Another good friend I must mention is Gary Leib, a fine cartoonist, printmaker, painter, and animator. This ode to my hometown was borne out of endless hours of obsessive, nostalgia-clouded discussions with Mr. Leib, over steaming platters of factory-second David Berg hot dogs, as we tried to process what had befallen the lost world of our youth [Figs. 6-8].

SEXUAL FRUSTRATION
It's EVERYWHERE! Have you noticed? I mean, just look around. Doesn't ANYBODY GET ANY PUSSY ANYMORE?
Take this guy for example, rythymically poking his ice with that straw... What's his story?
CHINK CHINK

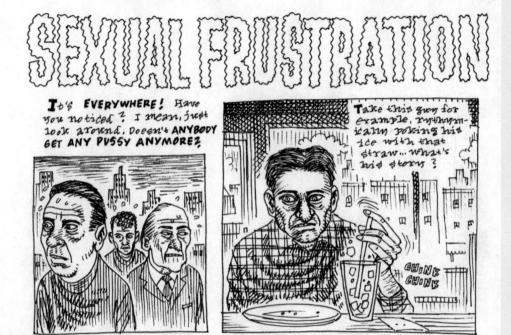

Fig. 2: *Sketchbook Drawing, 1989.*

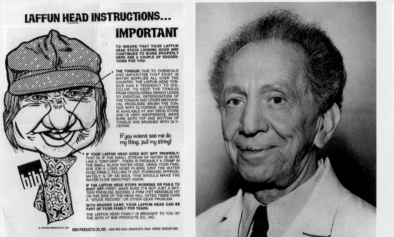

LAFFUN HEAD INSTRUCTIONS...
IMPORTANT
TO INSURE THAT YOUR LAFFUN HEAD STAYS LOOKING GOOD AND CONTINUES TO WORK PROPERLY HERE ARE A COUPLE OF SUGGESTIONS FOR YOU:
THE TONGUE: DUE TO CHEMICALS AND IMPURITIES THAT EXIST IN WATER SUPPLIES ALL OVER THE COUNTRY, THE LAFFUN HEAD TONGUE HAS A TENDENCY TO DISCOLOR. TO KEEP THE TONGUE FROM DISCOLORING (WHICH LEADS TO EVENTUAL DETERIORATION OF THE TONGUE AND OTHER MECHANICAL PROBLEMS) BRUSH THE TONGUE WITH GLYCERINE. GLYCERINE IS AVAILABLE AT ANY DRUG STORE AND IS VERY INEXPENSIVE. MAKE SURE BOTH TOP AND BOTTOM OF TONGUE ARE BRUSHED WITH GLYCERINE.
If you wanna see me do my thing, pull my string!
IF YOUR LAFFUN HEAD DOES NOT SPIT PROPERLY: THAT IS, IF THE SMALL STREAM OF WATER IS MORE LIKE A "DRIP-DRIP". THERE IS PROBABLY A CRIMP IN THE SMALL BLACK WATER HOSE. USING YOUR FINGERS (OR A LONG NOSE PLIERS) GRIP THE WATER HOSE FIRMLY, PULLING IT OUT (FORWARD) APPROXIMATELY ⅛ OF AN INCH. THIS SHOULD MAKE THE WATER FLOW SMOOTHLY AGAIN.
IF THE LAFFUN HEAD STOPS WORKING OR FAILS TO SHUT OFF: FIRST, MAKE SURE IT'S NOT JUST A BATTERY PROBLEM. SECOND, A FIRM (YET SENSIBLE) HIT ON THE SIDE OF THE HEAD WILL OFTEN TIMES CURE A "STUCK RECORD" OR OTHER GEAR PROBLEM.
WITH PROPER CARE, YOUR LAFFUN HEAD CAN BE PART OF YOUR FAMILY FOR YEARS.
THE LAFFUN HEAD FAMILY IS BROUGHT TO YOU BY THE NUTS AT BIBI PRODUCTS CO., INC.
bibi
BIBI PRODUCTS CO.,INC.

Fig. 3

Fig. 4

TODAY IS TUESDAY...
I CAN'T SEEM TO WAKE UP...
MY HEAD HURTS...
I HATE SHAKESPEARE STREET...
I DON'T KNOW WHY I CAME DOWN HERE.
THE DOUBLE-FEATURE AT THE PAVANNE IS "PUSSYCAT ROULETTE" PLUS SECOND ATTRACTION.
I CAN'T RESIST.
THE SECOND ATTRACTION I MIGHT BE SOMETHING GOOD.
I CAME DOWN HERE BECAUSE I'M JUST ANOTHER LOW-LIFE.
GOD, MY HEAD HURTS.

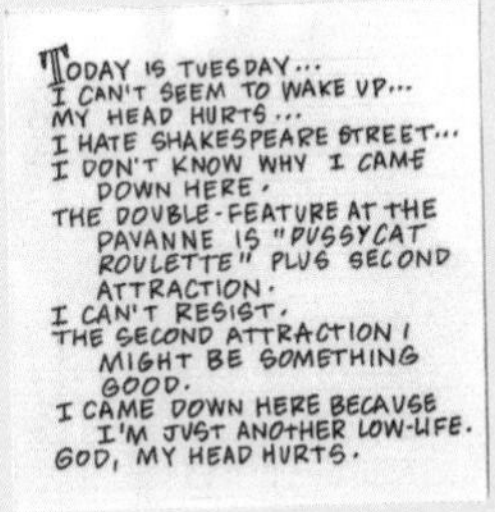

Fig. 5: *Unused narration block from the first page of LIKE A VELVET GLOVE CAST IN IRON.*

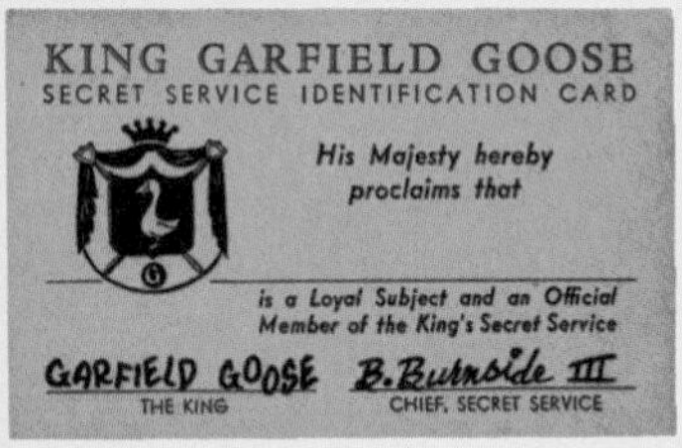
KING GARFIELD GOOSE
SECRET SERVICE IDENTIFICATION CARD
His Majesty hereby proclaims that
is a Loyal Subject and an Official Member of the King's Secret Service
GARFIELD GOOSE
THE KING
B. Burnside III
CHIEF, SECRET SERVICE

Fig. 6

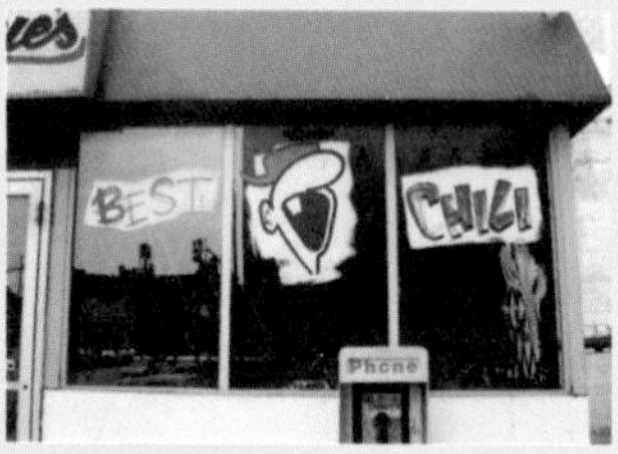
BEST
CHILI
Phone

Fig. 7

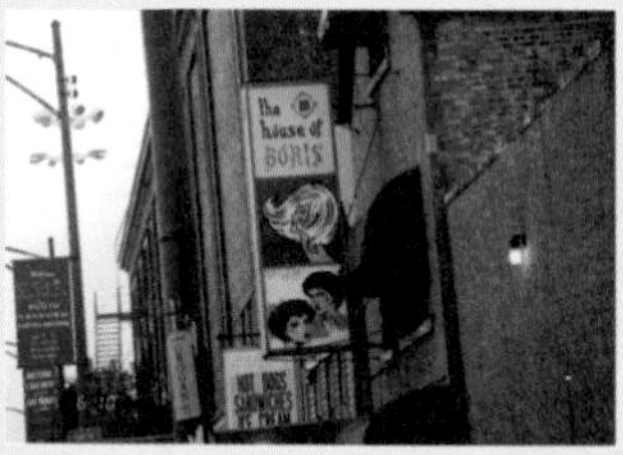
The house of BORIS

Fig. 8

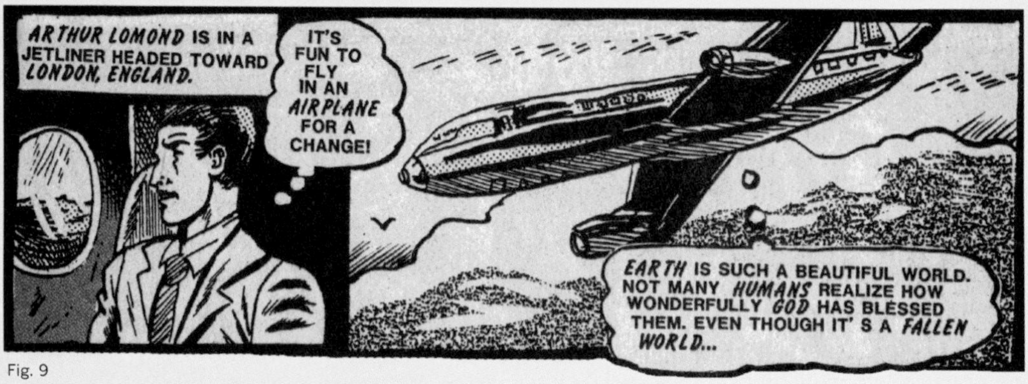
ARTHUR LOMOND IS IN A JETLINER HEADED TOWARD LONDON, ENGLAND.
IT'S FUN TO FLY IN AN AIRPLANE FOR A CHANGE!
EARTH IS SUCH A BEAUTIFUL WORLD. NOT MANY HUMANS REALIZE HOW WONDERFULLY GOD HAS BLESSED THEM. EVEN THOUGH IT' S A FALLEN WORLD...

Fig. 9

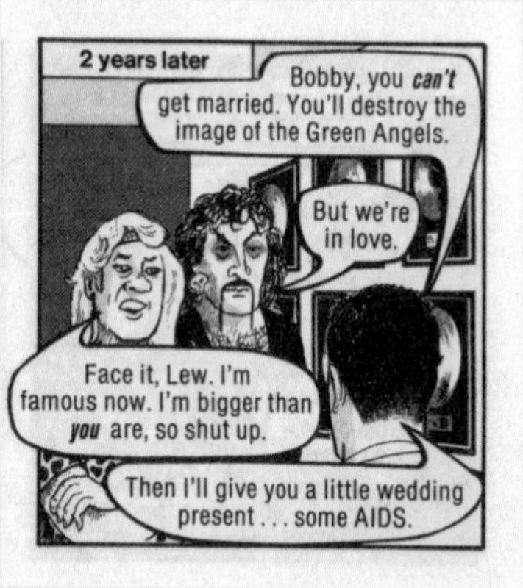
2 years later
Bobby, you can't get married. You'll destroy the image of the Green Angels.
But we're in love.
Face it, Lew. I'm famous now. I'm bigger than you are, so shut up.
Then I'll give you a little wedding present . . . some AIDS.

Fig. 10

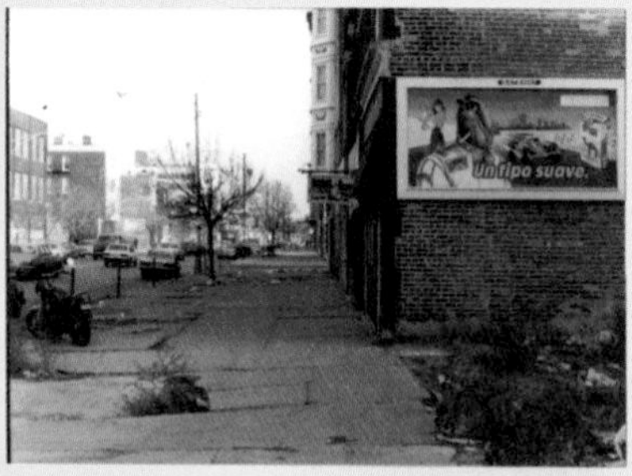
Un tipo suave.

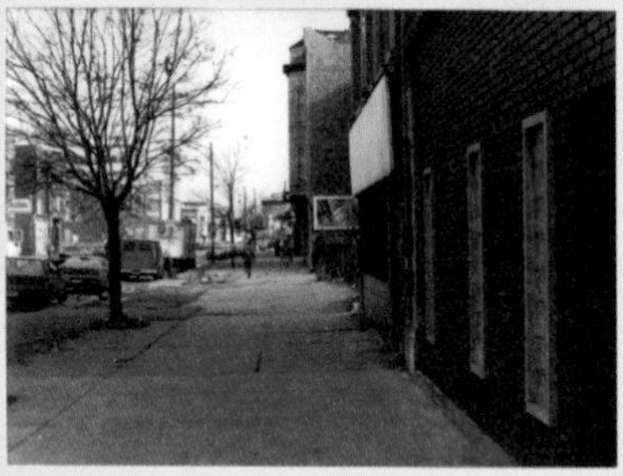

Fig. 11

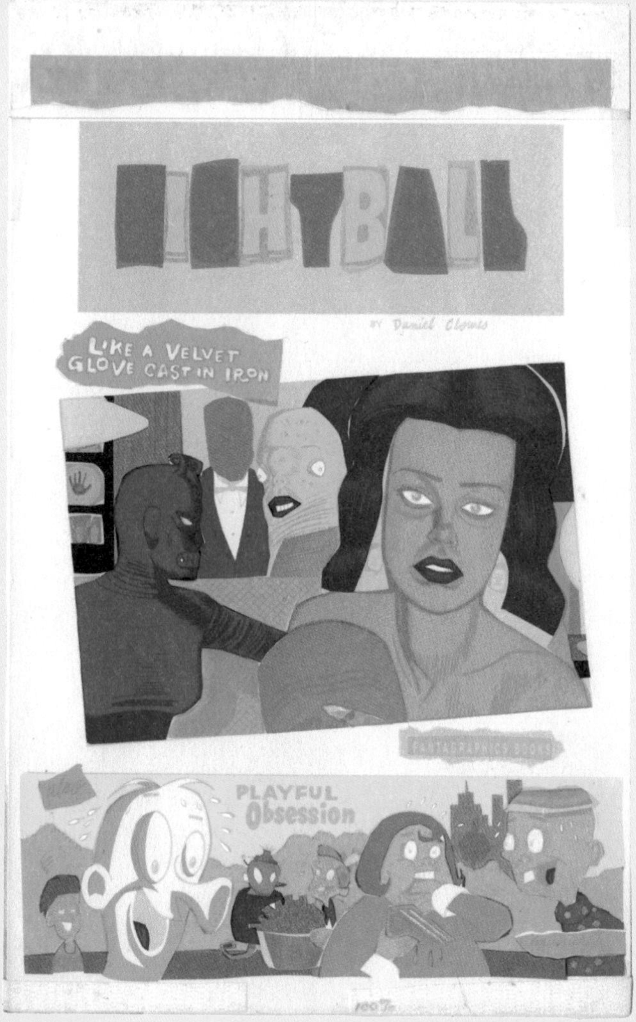
by Daniel Clowes
LIKE A VELVET GLOVE CAST IN IRON
FANTAGRAPHICS BOOKS
PLAYFUL Obsession

Fig. 12

EIGHTBALL #8, MAY 1992:

I decided I was going to try to emulate a horror comic for the cover with the notion that it would depict something truly and literally horrifying rather than an archetype-based sublimation, and this was what came to the fore. In some ways, I sort of admire this guy for his single-mindedness and dedication.

p. 16: RIP ZIP-A-TONE: The distinctive dot-pattern gray-tones used in the VELVET GLOVE story and others were achieved using a product called Zip-A-Tone, a decidedly predigital art supply from ye olden days. They came in transparent sheets with adhesive backing, and one had to cut them out carefully with an X-Acto and apply them to the artwork. They were very expensive, so the real talent lay in making the most of a sheet. I'm a sucker for anything that combines my cheapness with a challenging art project.

EIGHTBALL #9, SEPTEMBER 1992:

A lot of things happened during the making of this issue. I got divorced and went on a long road trip where I met my future wife Erika, who is depicted in a gag cartoon on page 15. My plan was to gain control of her trademark so she'd have to go through all kinds of legal hassles if she wanted to break up with me.

INK STUDS: This phrase was coined in an off-the-cuff moment by my lifelong friend Charles Schneider as a way to rebrand our glamorless ilk. At the time there was something of a "war" between cartoonists and musicians (as Peter Bagge said, "a war the rock stars don't even know about!"), and so I thought I'd use Charles's phrase to throw out the first salvo. It took on a life of its own, and I always felt guilty taking credit for my friend's work. Looking over these eighteen issues, I can see his influence throughout, and he is the prime example of a type of person I have grown to value above all others: the gentleman (or lady) scholar with deep, varied, and highly individual interests who can share them in a way that leads to a higher understanding of not just that subject, but other facets of history and culture that we'd be examining in depth ourselves if we didn't have to spend the afternoon blacking in every one of those fucking windows on that stupid building in the background.

EIGHTBALL #10, FEBRUARY 1993:

This always strikes me as an odd issue because it was drawn entirely during a four-month layover in Studio City, California where I moved entirely at random before heading north—for good, it turns out—to the eastern shore of the San Francisco Bay. It was a fun time, spending evenings with the Hernandez brothers and other friends, but I never got into a good rhythm at the board.

GRIP GLUTZ: I had assumed that everyone had grown up watching the horrific CLUTCH CARGO cartoons inflicted on innocent Chicagoans in the '60s, but apparently not. Again, YouTube immediately, especially if you want a good idea of what Grip's voice would sound like.

p. 6: This page was drawn in July 1992, a full five months before the election, and I had to decide whether to go with "Pappy" Bush, Clinton, or a surging Ross Perot. Luckily, I made the right pick, and thus the story remained current for another eight years. In a way, I wish I had gone with Perot, though.

DICKIE: This was done using another obsolete art supply—in this case justifiably so—a treated drawing paper called DuoShade board, which actually had tones imprinted on its surface that would be made visible only when a horrible-smelling developer was applied to the surface. Maybe I just got a bum batch because they all came out looking like this hideous eyesore.

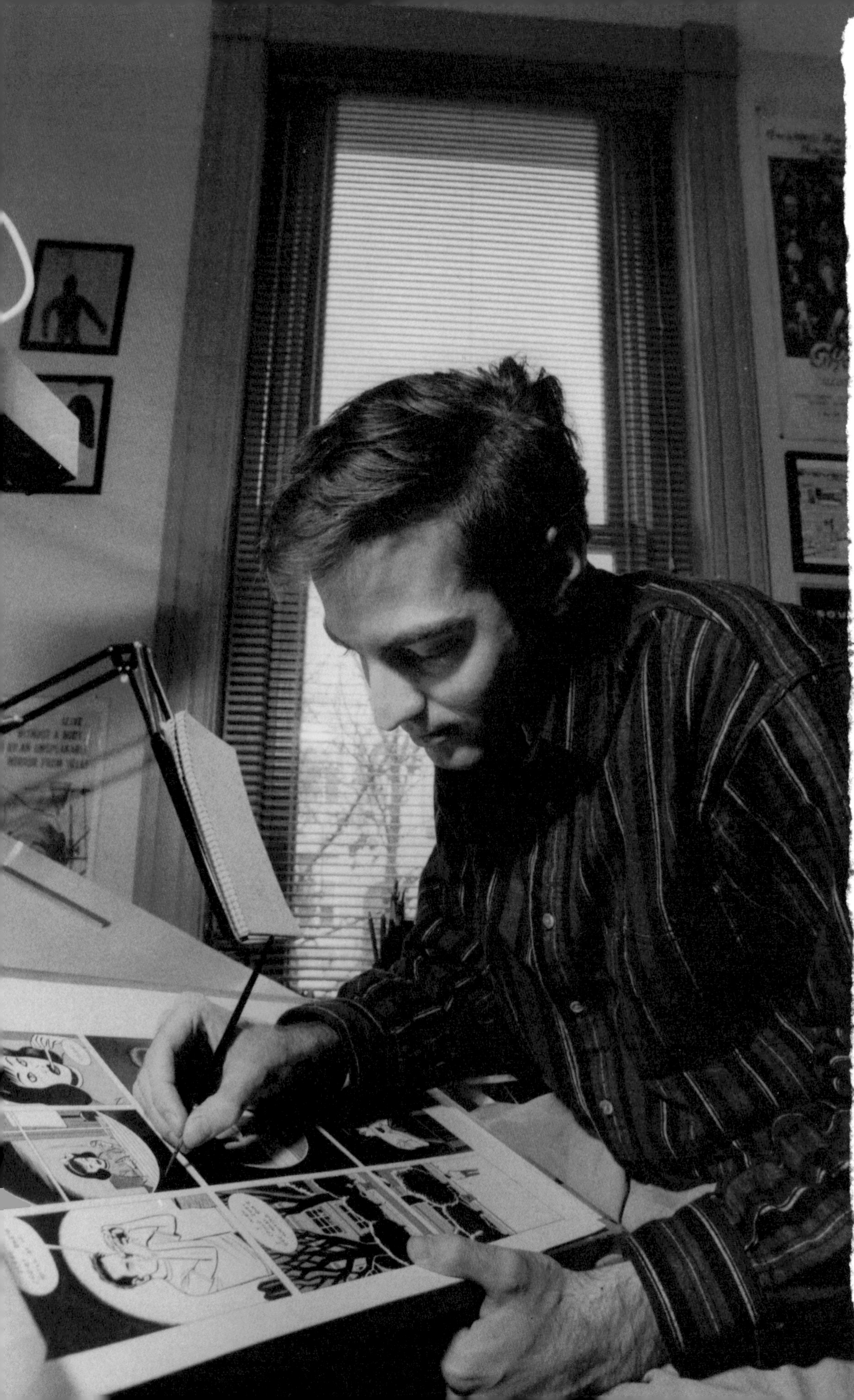

DANIEL CLOWES WISHES TO THANK:

Rick Altergott, Charles Schneider, Richard Sala, Adrian Tomine, Alvin Buenaventura, Tim Hensley, Gary Leib, Chris Ware, Susan Miller, Frances Cate, Martha Van Der Voort, Jan Portman, Harriet Clowes, George Clowes, Allison Hartman, James Clowes, Pete Friedrich, Peter Bagge, Jaime Hernandez, Gilbert Hernandez, Julie Doucet, Gilmore Tamny, Ken Parille, James Lea Cate, Chip Kidd, Francoise Mouly, Rosie and Elbert Woods, Zenner Davis, Gertrude Ogelsby, Nancy Knezevic, David Beckman, Larry Reid, Johan Kugelberg, Bob Odenkirk, Terry Laban, Patton Oswalt, Dana Gould, George Meyer, Terry Zwigoff, Lianne Halfon, Steve Buscemi, Thora Birch, Dr. David Miller, Rene DeGuzman, John Wranovics, Matthew Goldstein, Laura Ruberto, Lynne Warren, Dave Fillipi, Caitlin McGurk, Chris Oliveros, Peggy Burns, Jim Woodring, Wayno, Dennis Worden, Seth, Chester Brown, Serge Clerc, Gary Panter, Ivan Brunetti, Hillary Chute, John Kuramoto, Glenn Bray, Darryl Katz, Virginia Cartwright, Alison Colgan, Bill Wylie, Robert Crumb, Jay Lynch, Kim Deitch, Art Spiegelman, Bill Griffith, Ben Schwartz, Dan Raeburn, J. D. King, Bob Moss, Crispin Glover, Phil Milstein, Georgia Hubley, Ira Kaplan, Ed McAvoy, Steven Svymbersky, Sung Koo, Rory Root, Carson Hall, Dylan Williams, Kristine Anstine, James McNew, Jim Blanchard, Mike Dellefemine, Cliff Mott, David Greenberger, Peter Birkemoe, Devlin Thompson, Archer Prewitt, Charles Burns, Drew Friedman, Kristine McKenna, Hansje Joustra, Maki Hakui, Yasu Minegashi, Yuji Yamada, Jean-Louis Gauthey, Dirk Rehm, Doug Erb, Jules Bogdanski, Coco Shinomiya, Eddie Gorodetsky, Gaston Dominguez-Letelier, Bill Liebowitz, Mark G. Parker, Brooke Devine, Mark Frauenfelder, Jonathan Bennett, Kees Kousemaker, B. N. Duncan, Tim Warren, Ben Cooley, Todd Hignite, Paul Baresh, Erika Clowes, Charlie Clowes, Gary Groth, and Eric Reynolds.

EIGHTBALL

EIGHTBALL

Eightball

EIGHTBALL

EIGHTBALL

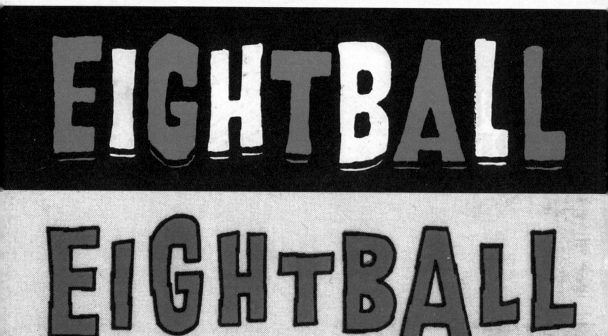